DICTIONARY OF THE
AVANT-GARDES

Other Works by Richard Kostelanetz

Books Authored

The Theatre of Mixed Means (1968); Master Minds (1969); Visual Language (1970); In the Beginning (1971); The End of Intelligent Writing (1974); I Articulations/Short Fictions (1974); Recyclings, Volume One (1974); Openings & Closings (1975); Portraits from Memory (1975); Constructs (1975); Numbers: Poems & Stories (1975); Modulations/Extrapolate/Come Here (1975); Illuminations (1977); One Night Stood (1977); Wordsand (1978); Constructs Two (1978); "The End" Appendix/"The End" Essentials (1979); Twenties in the Sixties (1979); And So Forth (1979); More Short Fictions (1980); Metamorphosis in the Arts (1980); The Old Poetries and the New (1981); Reincarnations (1981); Autobiographies (1981); Arenas/Fields/Pitches/Turfs (1982); Epiphanies (1983); American Imaginations (1983); Recyclings (1984); Autobiographien New York Berlin (1986); The Old Fictions and the New (1987); Prose Pieces/Aftertexts (1987); The Grants-Fix (1987); Conversing with Cage (1988); On Innovative Music(ian)s (1989); Unfinished Business: An Intellectual Nonhistory (1990); The New Poetries and Some Old (1991); Politics in the African-American Novel (1991); Solos, Duets, Trios, & Choruses (1991); On Innovative Art(ist)s (1992); Wordworks: Poems New & Selected (1993); Twenty-Five Years After (1993); On Innovative Performance(s) (1994)

Books Edited

On Contemporary Literature (1964, 1969); Twelve from the Sixties (1967); The Young American Writers (1967); Beyond Left & Right: Radical Thought for Our Times (1968); Possibilities of Poetry (1970); Imaged Words & Worded Images (1970); Moholy-Nagy (1970, 1991); John Cage (1970, 1991); Social Speculations (1971); Human Alternatives (1971); Future's Fictions (1971); Seeing Through Shuck (1972); In Youth (1972); Breakthrough Fictioneers (1973); The Edge of Adaptation (1973); Essaying Essays (1975); Language & Structure (1975); Younger Critics in North America (1976); Esthetics Contemporary (1978, 1989); Assembling Assembling (1978); Visual Literature Criticism (1979); Text-Sound Texts (1980); The Yale Gertrude Stein (1980); Scenarios (1980); Aural Literature Criticism (1981); The Literature of SoHo (1981); American Writing Today (1981, 1991); The Avant-Garde Tradition in Literature (1982); Gertrude Stein Advanced (1989); Merce Cunningham: Dancing in Space and Time (1992); John Cage: Writer (1993); Writings About John Cage (1993)

Books Coauthored & Edited

The New American Arts (1965)

Books Cocompiled & Introduced

Assembling (Twelve volumes, 1970–1981)

Performance Scripts

Epiphanies (1980); Seductions (1986); Lovings (1991)

Limited Editions: Books & Prints

Numbers One (1974); Word Prints (1975); Tabula Rasa (1978); Inexistences (1978); Constructs Three (1991); Intermix (1991); Constructs Four (1991); Fifty Untitled Constructivst Fictions (1991); Constructs Five (1991); Flipping (1991); Constructs Six (1991); Two Intervals (1991); Parallel Intervals (1991)

Audiotapes

Experimental Prose (1976); Openings & Closings (1976); Foreshortenings & Other Stories (1977); Praying to the Lord (1977, 1981); Asdescent/Anacatabasis (1978); Invocations (1981); Seductions (1981); The Gospels/Die Evangelien (1982); Relationships (1983); The Eight Nights of Hanukah (1983); Two German Horspiel (1983); New York City (1984); A Special Time (1985); Le Bateau Ivre/The Drunken Boat (1986); Resume (1988); Onomatopoeia (1988); Carnival of the Animals (1988); Americas' Game (1988); Kaddish (1990); Ululation (1992); Epiphanies (1982–); More or Less (1988–)

Extended Radio Features

Audio Art (1978); Text-Sound in North America (1981); Hörspiel USA: Radio Comedy (1983); Glenn Gould as a Radio Artist (1983); Audio Writing (1984); Audio Comedy Made in America Today (1986); New York City Radio (1987); Orson Welles as an Audio Artist (1988); Norman Corwin: Pioniere der US-Radiokunst (1991)

Videotapes

Three Prose Pieces (1975); Openings & Closings (1975); Declaration of Independence (1979); Epiphanies (1980); Partitions (1986); Video Writing (1987); Home Movies Reconsidered (1987); Two Erotic Videotapes (1988); Americas' Game (1988); Invocations (1988); The Gospels Abridged (1988); Kinetic Writing (1989); Video Strings (1989); Onomatopoeia (1990); String Two (1990); Kaddish (1990)

Films Produced & Directed

Epiphanies (in German, 1983; in English, 1981–)

Films Coproduced & Directed

Constructivist Fictions (1978); Ein Verlorenes Berlin (1983); Ett Forlorat Berlin (1984); A Berlin Lost (1985); Berlin Perdu (1986); El Berlin Perdido (1987); Berlin Sche-Einena Jother (1988)

Holograms

On Holography (1978); Antitheses (1985); Hidden Meanings (1989)

Retrospective Exhibitions

Wordsand (1978)

DICTIONARY OF THE

AVANT-GARDES

Richard Kostelanetz

with contributions by Richard Carlin, Geof Huth, Gerald Janecek,
Katy Matheson, H.R. Brittain, John Robert Colombo,
Ulrike Michal Dorda, Charles Doria, and Robert Haller

a cappella books

Library of Congress Cataloging-in-Publication Data

Kostelanetz, Richard
    The dictionary of the avant-gardes / Richard Kostelanetz with
assistance from H.R. Brittain . . . [et. al.].
        p. cm.
    Includes bibliographical references.
    ISBN 1-55652-202-9 : $16.95
    1. Arts, Modern—20th century—Dictionaries.   2. Avant-garde
(Aesthetics)—History—20th century—Dictionaries.   3. Artists—
Biography—Dictionaries.   I. Brittain, H.R.   II. Title.
NX456.K67 1993
700'.9'04—dc20   93-17793
                                                                 CIP

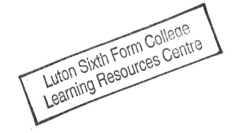
a cappella books
an imprint of
Chicago Review Press, Incorporated

Editorial offices:
P.O. Box 380
Pennington, NJ 08534

Business/sales offices:
814 N. Franklin St.
Chicago, IL 60610

For Nicolas Slonimsky
Cher maître

The avant-garde was something constituted from moment to moment by artists—a relative few in each moment—going toward what seemed the improbable. It was only after the avant-garde, as we now recognize it, had been under way for some fifty years that the notion of it seemed to begin to correspond to a fixed entity with stable attributes.
—Clement Greenberg, "Counter-Avant-Garde" (1971)

In the case of Duchamp, the antagonism he arouses is an element of his role, and even, if one wishes, of his greatness and profundity.
—Harold Rosenberg, Art on the Edge (1975)

For a very long time everybody refuses and then almost without a pause almost everybody accepts. In the history of the refused in the arts and literature the rapidity of the change is always startling. When the acceptance comes, by that acceptance the thing created becomes a classic. It is a natural phenomena, a rather extraordinary natural phenomena that a thing accepted becomes a classic. And what is the characteristic quality of a classic? The characteristic quality of a classic is that it is beautiful. . . . Of course it is beautiful but first all beauty in it is denied and then all the beauty of it is accepted. If every one were not so indolent they would realize that beauty is beauty even when it is irritating and stimulating not only when it is accepted and classic.
—Gertrude Stein, "Composition as Explanation" (1926)

The situation of [Arnold] Schoenberg is typical—he was never in fashion and now he's become old-fashioned.
—Milton Babbitt, Words about Music (1987)

The viability of a genre like the viability of a family is based on survival, and the indispensable property of a surviving family is a continuing ability to take in new members who bring fresh genetic material into the old reservoir. So the viability of a genre may depend fairly heavily on an avant-garde activity that has often been seen as threatening its very existence, but is more accurately seen as opening its present to its past and to its future.
—David Antin, "The Stranger at the Door" (1988)

To write a history of the avant-garde is already to contain it: obviously within a narrative structure and thus inevitably within a certain ideological regime, a certain formation of (pre)judgments. Every history is to some extent an attempt to determine (to comprehend and to control) the avant-garde's currency, its demise, or its survival today.
—Paul Mann, The Theory-Death of the Avant-Garde (1991)

PREFACE

It takes approximately twenty years to make an artistic curiosity out of a modernistic monstrosity, and another twenty to elevate it to a masterpiece.
—Nicolas Slonimsky, Lexicon of Musical Invective *(1953)*

My principal reason for doing a book of this title would be to defend the continuing relevance of the epithet "avant-garde," which frequently appears in my own critical writing. A second reason is that I enjoy reading dictionaries myself and own a goodly number of them; but as my library lacks a dictionary of avant-gardes, the first reader for any book of that title would be myself. A third reason is that I've come to think there is only one art, called Art, and thus that dance, literature, etc., are merely academic categories, designed to make the history and the material of Art more accessible to beginners.

My basic measures of avant-garde work are esthetic innovation and initial unacceptability. Add to this my own taste for art that is extreme, unique, distinct, coherent, witty, technological, and esthetically resonant. (An artist's courage in the choice of subject, such as scatology, say, or child abuse, is not avant-garde if the artist's esthetic is traditional. Nor is the first play by a three-handed dwarf avant-garde by virtue of the peculiarities of its author.) It follows that the most consequential artists, in any medium, are those who make genuine discoveries about the possibilities of art.

Though one often hears about "the death of the avant-garde," usually from publicists with cemeteries to defend, it is not the purpose of this book to engage in an argument I take to be Talmudic at best.

Though most entries feature contemporary avant-garde activities, major historical figures, some of whom worked two centuries ago, are acknowledged as well. Though the epithet "avant-garde" is applicable to other cultural domains, they are not covered here.

Proclaiming the avant-garde's death is no less disreputable than the claim, from another corner, of one or another group to represent "*the* avant-garde" to the exclusion of all others. In this book are entries on individuals representing opposed positions, if not contrary esthetics, both avant-garde.

Trained in cultural history, I think I can discern the future from the past; and because I don't often read newsprint, I can claim an ignorance of, if not resistance to, fashions of many kinds. One principle behind my writing about the avant-garde in one art is an authority gained from familiarity with avant-garde work in other arts.

This book is admittedly biased, not only in judgments but in selections, because it is impossible to write about the avant-gardes, with any integrity and excellence, without seeming opinionated. (If you don't like opinions, well, you're welcome to read the telephone directory.) Because this book was written not just to be consulted but to be read from beginning to end, it eschews abbreviations that interrupt attention. I would have liked to do more entries on avant-garde artists new to the 1980s and 1990s, those born after 1950, who are true heroes at a time when the idea of an esthetic vanguard has been subjected to all sorts of Philistine attack, and apologize now to those individuals, whoever you are, whose names will be featured in future editions.

Most of this book was written in several months, drawing mostly upon my memory and sometimes upon earlier reviews and notes that were generally made when I first experienced something. In writing critically about art (or in editing anthologies), I have learned to trust my memory to separate the strongest work from everything else. One reason for so much faith in memory is that it does not lie to me, which is to say that no matter my personal feelings toward the artist, no matter what reviews of his or her work I might have read, no matter what other factors might try to influence me, if I cannot remember an artist's work distinctly, it probably was not strong enough. It follows that only art that has lodged in my head will survive in my critical writing. (One of my favorite ways of testing the true quality in any well-known artist's work is to ask myself, as well as others, whether any specific work[s] can be identified.) Quite simply, what my memory chose to remember for me became the basis for this *Dictionary*. In my mind was the image of the great Erich Auerbach, a German scholar living in Istambul during World War II, writing his grandly conceived *Mimesis* (1946) mostly from memory, without footnotes, because useful libraries were far away.

Because I resist doing anything professional, even a dictionary entry, that anyone else can do better, I recruited colleagues to write as many entries as possible (giving them, if the truth be known, pro-rata portions of the advance, on a per-page basis), adding a bibliography proportionate to the length of their entry. These colleagues' names appear after the entries (which are otherwise mine); it is not for nothing that their names accompany mine on the title page. (The order of multiple bibliographical entries, I should explain, is based not upon the alphabet or chronology but upon esthetic judgments.) Names and terms followed by an asterisk (*) receive fuller treatment in an alphabetically placed entry.

My model arts lexicographer, who deserves the dedication of this book, is Nicolas Slonimsky, who, incidentally, prefers the epithet "lectionary" to "dictionary" because the first term refers to reading, the second to speaking. (May this book appear before his centenary, 28 April 1994.) My model for the writing of concise remarks is Ambrose Bierce, an American author too opinionated to be "great," but whose best writing (see the entry on him) nonetheless survives changes in fashion.

I would be disingenuous if I did not thank previous compilers of basic arts information—all of them—without whom, to be frank, the following pages would have been inconceivable. Another source frequently used, must I confess, was earlier writings by myself. I am also grateful to Andrew Benker, Richard Carlin, Daryl Chin, Marc Dachy, Geof Huth, Larry Qualls, Thomas Wiloch, and especially Chris Potash for their considerate line-editing of the manuscript, and for proofreading Ann Blair Davis, Markus Heide, and John Rocco.

A book with so much detail about contemporary figures will surely contain misspellings and other minor errors of fact, as well as unintentional omissions. Sometimes I left question marks in lieu of such shortcuts as making educated guesses (as in, say, death-dates that could not be confirmed, particularly of individuals not yet customarily included in such compendia) or of dropping a reference entirely. If only to prepare for a second edition, the author welcomes corrections and suggestions, by mail please if they are to go into a single file, to P.O. Box 444, Prince St., New York, New York 10012-0008. To be helpful, I have tried, whenever possible, to add addresses of smaller publishers and record companies hoping that they survive for the life of this book. If anyone has disappeared, please let me know. No kidding.

Thanks is extended to Richard Carlin for this opportunity to encapsulate a lifetime of enthusiasms.

Richard Kostelanetz, New York, New York, 14 May 1993

INTRODUCTION

The avant-garde consists of those who feel sufficiently at ease with the past not to have to compete with it or duplicate it.
—Dick Higgins, "Does Avant-Garde Mean Anything?" (1970)

The avant-garde cannot easily become the academy, because avant-garde artists usually sustain the quality which made them avant-garde artists in the first place. The styles they develop will become academic in other hands.
—Darby Bannard, "Sensibility of the Sixties" (1967)

The term "avant-garde" refers to those out front, forging a path that others will take. Initially coined to characterize the shock troops of an army, the epithet passed over into art. Used precisely, avant-garde should refer, first, to rare work that satisfies three discriminatory criteria: it transcends current esthetic conventions in crucial respects, establishing discernible distance between itself and the mass of current practices; it will necessarily take considerable time to find its maximum audience; and it will probably inspire future, comparably advanced endeavors. Only a small minority can ever be avant-garde; for once the majority has caught up to something new, whether as creators or as an audience, what is genuinely avant-garde will, by definition, be someplace else. Problems notwithstanding, it remains a critically useful category.

As a temporal term, avant-garde characterizes art that is "ahead of its time"—that is beginning something—while "decadent" art, by contrast, stands at the end of a prosperous development. "Academic" refers to art that is conceived according to rules that are learned in a classroom; it is temporally post-decadent. Whereas decadent art is created in expectation of an immediate sale, academic artists expect approval from their social superiors, whether they be teachers or higher-ranking colleagues. Both academic art and decadent art are essentially opportunistic, created to realize immediate success, even at the cost of surely disappearing from that corpus of art that survives merely by being remembered. One fact shared by both decadent art and academic art is that they realize their maximal audience upon initial publication.

One secondary characteristic of avant-garde art is that, in the course of entering new terrain, it violates entrenched rules—it seems to descend from "false premises" or "heretical assumptions"; it makes current "esthetics" seem irrelevant. For instance, Suzanne Langer's theory of Symbolism, so prominent in the forties and even the fifties, is hardly relevant to the new art of the past three decades. It offers little insight into, say, the music of John Cage (*) or Milton Babbitt (*), the choreography of Merce Cunningham (*), or the poetry of John Ashbery (*), where what you see or hear is generally most, if not all, of what there is. This sense of irrelevance is less a criticism of Langer's theories, which five decades ago seemed so persuasively encompassing, than a measure of drastic difference.

One reason why avant-garde works should be initially hard to comprehend is not that they are intrinsically inscrutable or hermetic but that they defy, or challenge as they defy, the perceptual procedures of artistically educated people. They forbid easy access or easy acceptance, as an audience perceives them as inexplicably different, if not forbiddingly revolutionary. In order to begin to comprehend them, people must work and think in unfamiliar ways. Nonetheless, if an audience learns to accept innovative work, it will stretch their perceptual capabilities, affording them kinds of esthetic experience previously unknown. Edgard Varèse's (*) revolutionary *Ionisation* (1931), for instance, taught a generation of listeners about the possible coherence and beauty in what they had previously perceived as noise.

It follows that avant-garde art usually offends people, especially serious artists, before it persuades; and it offends them not in terms of content, but in terms of Art. They assert that Varèse's noise (or Cage's, or Babbitt's) is unacceptable as music. That explains why avant-garde art strikes most of us as esthetically "wrong" before we acknowledge it as possibly "right"; it "fails" before we recognize that it *works*. (Art that offends by its content challenges only as journalism or gossip, rather than as Art, and is thus as likely to disappear as quickly as journalism or gossip.)

Those most antagonized by the avant-garde are not the general populace, which does not care, but the guardians of culture, who do, whether they be cultural bureaucrats, established artists, or their epigones, because *they* feel, as they sometimes admit, "threatened."

Though vanguard activity may dominate discussion among sophisticated professionals, it never dominates the general making of art. Most work created in any time, in every art, honors long-passed models. Even today, in the United States, most of the fiction written and published and reviewed has, in form, scarcely progressed beyond early 20th-century standards; most poetry today is similarly decadent.

The past that the avant-garde aims to surpass is not the tradition of art but the currently decadent fashions; for in Harold Rosenberg's (*) words, "Avant-garde art is haunted by fashion." Because avant-gardes in art are customarily portrayed as succeeding one another, the art world is equated with the world of fashion, in which styles also succeed each other. However, in both origins and function, fashion and art are quite different. *Fashion* relates to the sociology of lucrative taste; *avant-garde*, to the history of art. In practice, avant-garde activity has a dialectical relationship with fashion, for the emerging remunerative fashions can usually be characterized as a synthesis of advanced art (whose purposes are antithetical to those of fashion) with more familiar stuff. When fashion appears to echo advanced art, a closer look reveals the governing model as art actually of a period recently past.

The term "avant-garde" can also refer to individuals creating such path-forging art; but even by this criterion, the work itself, rather than the artist's intentions, is the ultimate measure of the epithet's applicability to an individual. Thus, an artist or writer is avant-garde only at certain crucial points in his or her creative career, and only those few works that were innovative at their debut comprise the history of modern avant-garde art. The phrase may also refer to artistic groups, if and only if most of its members are (or were) crucially contributing to authentically exploratory activity.

The term is sometimes equated with cultural antagonism, for it is assumed that the avant-garde leads artists in their perennial war against the Philistines. However, this Philistine antagonism is a secondary characteristic, as artists' social position and attitudes descend from the fate of their creative efforts, rather than the reverse. Any artist who sets out just to mock the Philistines is not likely to do anything additional.

Certain conservative critics have recently asserted that "the avant-garde no longer exists," because, as they see it, the suburban public laps up all new art. However, it is critically both false and ignorant to use a secondary characteristic in lieu of a primary definition. *Avant-garde* is an art-historical term, not a sociological category. The conservative charge is factually wrong as well, as nearly all avant-gardes in art are ignored by the middle-class public (and its agents in the culture industries) precisely because innovative work is commonly perceived as peculiar, if not unacceptable, not only by the mass public but by those producers who make a business of selling "art" in large quantities. Indeed, the pervasiveness of those perceptions is, of course, a patent measure of a work's being art-historically ahead of its time. Those who deny the persistence of the avant-garde are comparable to those who deny the persistence of poverty, each by its fakery implicitly rationalizing retrograde attitudes and perhaps the retention of tenuous privileges.

Because the avant-garde claims to be prophetic, the ultimate judge of current claims can only be a future cultural public. For now, future-sensitive critics should proceed under the assumption that they might, just might, be wrong.

Kirby, Michael. *The Art of Time*. NY: Dutton, 1969.

Kostelanetz, Richard, ed. *Esthetics Contemporary*. 2nd ed. Buffalo, NY: Prometheus, 1979.

Krantz, Stewart. *Science and Technology in the Arts*. NY: Van Nostrand Reinhold, 1974.

Mann, Paul. *The Theory-Death of the Avant-Garde*. Bloomington, IN: Indiana University, 1991.

McLuhan, Marshall. *Understanding Media*. NY: McGraw-Hill, 1964.

Moholy-Nagy, L. *Vision in Motion*. Chicago, IL: Paul Theobald, 1947.

Motherwell, Robert, ed. *The Dada Painters and Poets*. NY: Wittenborn, 1951.

Myers, George, Jr. *An Introduction to Modern Times*. Detroit, MI: Lunchroom, 1982.

Peckham, Morse. *Man's Rage for Chaos*. Philadelphia, PA: Chilton, 1965.

ABISH, Walter (1931). Born in Vienna, raised in Shanghai's Jewish community during World War II, Abish worked in city planning before he began publishing. The mark of his novel *Alphabetical Africa* (1974) is its severe compositional discipline. The first chapter has only words beginning with the letter *A* ("Ages ago, Alex, Allen and Alva arrived at Antibes," etc.). For the second chapter, he additionally uses words beginning with the letter *B*. Only by the *Z* chapter, which is in the middle of the book, does the full alphabet become available, then to contract again to a conclusion composed exclusively of words beginning with the letter *A*. As Jerome Klinkowitz (*) has sensitively written, "Like breathing in and then breathing out, the reader has experienced the expansion and contraction, the life and death of a work of fiction." The next two Abish books are collections of stories, some of them more experimental than others. Each pair of paragraphs in "In So Many Words" is preceded by a numeral announcing how many words are in the following paragraph; while the second paragraph in each pair, set in roman type, tells a dry story, the first paragraph contains all of its successor's words set in italics in alphabetical order. In short, Abish displays a fascination with numbers reminiscent of Raymond Queneau (*), though lacking the latter's extravagant wit and audacity. It was Abish's good fortune, or misfortune, to write *How German Is It* (1980), a far more accessible novel that won him a Guggenheim fellowship, a CAPS grant, and later a lush MacArthur fellowship, in addition to a contract from a slick publisher not known for publishing the kinds of writers acknowledged in this book. In spite of all this support from benefactors not otherwise known to be responsive to the mute, withdrawal strategies of Marcel Duchamp (*), the only thing Abish has published since, with a small press (*), is a book of experimental prose derived entirely from "found" texts.

Abish, Walter. *Alphabetical Africa*. NY: New Directions, 1974.

———. *In the Future Perfect*. NY: New Directions, 1977.

ABSTRACT EXPRESSIONISM (c. 1958). If only because it emphasizes esthetic qualities, this term has come to be the most acceptable epithet for the innovative painting that became prominent in New York in the late 1940s (and was thus sometimes called the "New York School" [*]). Drawing not only from Surrealism (*) but from jazz-based (*) ideas of improvisatory gestural expression, these artists laid paint on the canvas in ways that reflected physical attack, whether in the extended dripped lines of Jackson Pollock (*) or in the broad strokes of Franz Kline (*). "Action painting," another epithet once popular for this style of painting, was coined by the critic Harold Rosenberg (*), whose theory was that these abstractions represented the artist's mental state at the moment(s) of composition. One esthetic characteristic of such painting was "all-over" composition, which is to say that the activity was just as strong near the edges of the canvas as in the center, purportedly in contrast to the more hierarchical focusing typical of traditional art. Willem de Kooning's (*) work is customarily placed within this term, even though his best paintings acknowledge figuration and focusing; so are Barnett Newman (*) and Ad Reinhardt (*), perhaps because they were roughly the same age as the others (and thus belonged to the "New York School"), even though their art proceeds from nonexpressionist premises.

Rosenberg, Harold. "The American Action Painters." In *The Tradition of the New*. NY: Horizon, 1959.

Sandler, Irving. *The Triumph of American Painting*. NY: Praeger, 1970.

ABSTRACTION (c. 5000 B.C.). This term defines artwork, whether visual, aural, or verbal, that neither represents nor symbolizes anything in the mundane world; but, because pure abstraction is primarily an ideal, it also refers to work that at least approaches the absence of identifiable representation. Although some commentators make a case for abstraction as a new development in the history of visual art, such a generalization necessarily depends upon ignorance of Islamic art that obeys the proscription against graven images. (Those arguing for the uniqueness of modern abstraction dismiss such Islamic art as "decorative.") Within modern Abstract Art are two divergent traditions, one emphasizing structure and the other favoring expression; examples of both of these traditions appear not only in painting and sculpture but music and literature. One reason for the piety that "painting is more advanced than poetry" is that abstraction became more acceptable among visual artists than among poets in our century.

Seuphor, Michel. *A Dictionary of Abstract Painting: Preceded by a History of Abstract Painting.* NY: Paris Book Centre, 1957.

ACTION PAINTING. See ABSTRACT EXPRESSIONISM

ABSURD, THEATRE OF THE. The term comes from Martin Esslin's brilliant 1961 book of the same title. In the plays of Samuel Beckett (∗) and Eugène Ionesco (∗), and to a lesser extent others, Esslin found nonsensical and ridiculous events that have sufficient metaphysical resonance to suggest the ultimate absurdity, or meaninglessness, of human existence. The innovation was to *demonstrate* the theme of absurdity, in contrast to an earlier theater, identified with Jean-Paul Sartre (1905–1980) and Albert Camus (1913–1960), where characters debate it. At the end of Ionesco's *The Chairs*, a particularly neat model of the convention, a hired lecturer addresses a nonexistent audience in an indecipherable tongue. This is the absurd surface. Because the lecturer's message is supposed to represent the final wisdom of a ninety-five-year-old couple, the meaningless message becomes an effective symbol for metaphysical void. In a more familiar example, two men wait for a mysterious Godot who obviously is not coming. On the strictly theatrical influence of absurd theater, the *Cambridge Guide to Literature in English* (1988) says: "The carrying of logic *ad absurdum*, the dissolution of language, the bizarre relationship of stage properties to dramatic situation, the diminution of sense by repetition or unexplained intensification, the rejection of narrative continuity, and the refusal to allow character or even scenery to be self-defining have become acceptable stage conventions." (Thanks for the summary.) A quarter-century ago, I found a similar absurdist style in certain early-1960s American fiction by John Barth (∗), Joseph Heller (1922), and Thomas Pynchon (∗), among others.

Esslin, Martin. *The Theatre of the Absurd* (1961). Rev. ed. Garden City, NY: Doubleday Anchor, 1969.

Kostelanetz, Richard. "The American Absurd Novel" (1965). In *The Old Fictions and the New.* Jefferson, NC: McFarland, 1987.

ACADEMIC CRITICS. When professors discuss avant-garde art, particularly literature, they tend to focus upon the more conservative, more accessible dimensions of an artist's work, in part to make their criticism more digestible to the ignorant (e.g., students and colleagues), rather than pursuing radical implications to their critical extremes. Thus, it becomes opportune for even an advocate of the more experimental Gertrude Stein (∗) to confine discussion to *Three Lives* (drafted around 1904) and/or *The Autobiography of Alice B. Toklas* (1933); an academic discussion of Merce Cunningham (∗), say, will feature his connections to ballet rather than his departures from it; Velimir Khlebnikov (∗) will be portrayed as the epitome of Russian Futurism (∗) rather than the more radical Aleksei Kruchonykh (∗). Academics tend as well to reveal incomplete familiarity with new developments (especially if they would be unknown to their fellow professors).

The now-forgotten books that Wallace Fowlie published twenty to thirty years ago epitomize such deficiencies; J.H. Matthews wrote comparable books two decades ago; Marjorie Perloff, among others, has published similar volumes more recently. One rule evident in these books is simply: When a professor writes three words about an avant-garde subject, one of them is likely to be superficial and a second to reveal ignorance, even if the writing comes accompanied, as it usually is, by encomia from other academics. (If you think about the time and effort spent to get these blurbs, you begin to understand why such books disappoint.)

Among the full-time academics who have written intelligent books on avant-garde art at one time or another count Sally Banes on dance, Gerald Janecek (∗) on Russian literature, Roger Shattuck (only in *The Banquet Years*, 1958), Michael Kirby (∗) in *The Art of Time* (1969), Mark Ensign Cory on German radio, Jack Burnham on sculpture, Hugh Kenner (∗) on Buckminster Fuller (∗), L. Moholy-Nagy (∗) (though he actually worked as an art-college administrator while writing *Vision in Motion*), Jo-Anna Isaak in *The Ruin of Representation* (1986), and the classicist Donald Sutherland writing in 1951 on Gertrude Stein. It is lamentable, alas, that there are not many more professors remaining academic, while genuinely innovative art measures itself as avant-garde by a healthy distance from the academy.

Banes, Sally. *Terpsichore in Sneakers* (1980). 2nd ed. Middletown, CT: Wesleyan University, 1987.

———. *Democracy's Body: The Judson Dance Theater, 1962–64.* (1983). Durham, NC: Duke University, 1993.

Burnham, Jack. *Beyond Modern Sculpture*. NY: Braziller, 1968.

———. *The Great Western Salt Works*. NY: Braziller, 1974.

Cory, Mark Ensign. *The Emergence of an Acoustical Art Form*. Lincoln, NE: University of Nebraska Studies, 1974.

Shattuck, Roger. *The Banquet Years*. NY: Harper, 1958.

ACCONCI, Vito (1939). He began as a poet and translator; and though Acconci subsequently had a distinguished career as a visual artist, mounting exhibitions and producing videotapes as well as presenting live performances, his poetry remains his most innovative work. One 350-line poem was distributed one line per page over 350 separate sheets of paper, which were then bound into 350 copies of Acconci's otherwise uniform magazine, *0 to 9*. His definitive work is *Book Four* (1968), which he self-published in photocopies. As literature on the cusp of conceptual art (∗), it contains a series of self-reflexive texts, beginning with a page that reads at its upper left: "(It stopped back.   )," and then at its lower right: "(This page is not part/of the four books/and is at the top)," with the page entirely blank in between. *Book Four* concludes with a Gertrude Steinian (∗) text in which separate sentences, in sum suggesting a narrative, are each preceded by the numeral "1." Of Acconci's performance pieces, I remember best one in which he invited you into a kind of confessional booth and told you an authentic secret; another in which he sat at the bottom of a stairwell, blindfolded, with a metal pipe in his hand, defending the space in front of him with a genuine violence; a third, *Seedbed* (1972), in which he purportedly masturbated under a sloping wood floor, letting spectators hear the sound of his effort. Remembering that Acconci attended New York City's toughest Jesuit high school, I think he has been making a Catholic art concerned with abnegation and spiritual athleticism.

Kirshner, Judith Russi. *Vito Acconci*. Chicago, IL: Museum of Contemporary Art, 1980.

Diacono, Mario. *Vito Acconci* (in Italian, with illustrations in English and a bibliography). NY: Out of London, 1975.

ACTION PAINTING. See ABSTRACT EXPRESSIONISM; ROSENBERG, Harold

AGAM, Yacov (1928; b. Jacob Gipstein). An Israeli who moved to Paris as a very young man, Agam has created the epitome of Jewish rationalist art that, thanks to his artistry, realizes irrational ends. Respecting the commandment proscribing graven images, Agam works with simple geometric illusions, such as an undulated surface whose imagery changes as the viewer moves from side to side. Even though nothing physical changes, this movement creates the illusion of kinetic (∗) art. Agam has also made transformable sculptures composed of modular elements that can be varied by spectators—that exist, indeed, only through audience interaction. The French historian Frank Popper speaks of "inventions, ranging from the single print to the holograph by way of multigraphs, polymorph graphics, interspaceographs, environmental graphics, primographics, and video graphics. Agam's other achievements include constructions with artificial light, water-fire sculptures, monumental mixed media works such as the fountain at the Défence complex near Paris."

Popper, Frank. *Origins and Development of Kinetic Art*. Greenwich, CT: New York Graphic Society, 1968.

Yacov Agam. Neuchâtel, Switzerland: Griffon, 1966.

ALBERS, Josef (1888–1976). A student and then an instructor at the Bauhaus (∗), Albers emigrated to America soon after that school was closed by the Nazi authorities, teaching at Black Mountain College (∗) until 1949 and then at Yale University until his retirement. Intentionally confining his imagery to rectangles within rectangles, which he considered scrupulously neutral shapes, he created paintings and drawings based primarily upon the relationships of shapes and of colors. His series "Homage to the Square" reportedly includes hundreds of paintings that are not only distinctly his, but they also suggest alternative directions, as only the best teacher's art can. The fact that little need be said about his art should not diminish any estimate of his achievement.

Albers, Josef. *The Interaction of Color.* 2 vols. New Haven, CT: Yale University, 1963.

ALBERT-BIROT, Pierre (1876–1967). An inventive writer, Albert-Birot produced poems, plays, and fictions that were experimental in all sorts of ways. He edited the magazine *SIC* (1916–1919), its title an acronym for *Sons Idées Couleurs* (Sounds Ideas Colors). In its pages appeared figures associated with Italian Futurism (*), Surrealism (*), and Dada (*), along with chapters of his novel *Grabinoulor* (1919). Barbara Wright, who specializes in translating avant-garde French texts into English, describes Albert-Birot's principal activities as "poems of every conceivable kind: sound poems, typographical poems, simultaneous poems, poster-poems, square, rectangular, chess-board poems. And even straightforward poems. Plays. Novels." Albert-Birot should be remembered, if for nothing else, for his classic aphorism "If anything can be said in prose, then poetry should be saved for saying nothing." That's a liberating idea; too bad nobody known to me had thought of it before and few have observed it since.

Albert-Birot, Pierre. *The First Book of Grabinoulor.* Trans. Barbara Wright. Elmwood Park, IL: Dalkey Archive, 1987.

ALLEN, Roberta (1945). Whereas many avant-garde writers were influenced by conceptual art (*), Allen actually did it, before she began publishing. She exhibited pieces concerned with the ambiguity of direction, position, and placement, particularly favoring arrows that pointed in contrary directions, so "that the meaning of a sign is not inherent in the sign," as she once told me. Her prose writings are spare, almost minimal, held together by the thoughts of a female narrator adrift in the world. In *The Daughter* (1992), episodes from childhood alternate with recollections of traveling in Latin America.

Allen, Roberta. *Everything in the World There Is to Know.* Aachen, Germany: Ottenhausen, 1981.

———. *The Daughter.* Brooklyn, NY: Semiotext(e), 1992.

AMERICAN ACADEMY OF ARTS AND LETTERS (1904)/NATIONAL INSTITUTE OF ARTS AND LETTERS (1898–1993). These are self-replicating clubs of artists, composers, and writers that, notwithstanding their names, include among their members remarkably few of the Americans mentioned in this book. (The former was until 1993 an inner circle of fifty drawn from the latter.) Its literature department can be characterized as less advanced than its music division, while that devoted to visual arts is, by common consent, the most backward of all. When I first observed its membership, around 1965, I thought that every major writer born before 1910 (and thus fifty-five at the time) belonged; now, a quarter-century later, that qualitative generalization covers only authors born before 1911 (Bern Porter [*] being the oldest flagrant omission). What AAAL represents culturally is a European model for collecting retrograde (and thus fundamentally un-American) kinds of talents. What it displays provincially is a weakness for middling writers appearing frequently in *The New Yorker*. The distinguished Harvard professor Harry Levin (1912), himself a member of the NIAL, called it, in a memorable phrase, "one of those professional societies which exist primarily for mutual admiration." Because this is the United States, rather than Europe, the conservative Academy's influence on the development and even the direction of native culture is, thankfully, negligible. That last fact perhaps accounts for why no book-length history of it exists.

Levin, Harry. *Memories of the Moderns.* NY: New Directions, 1980.

AMIRKHANIAN, Charles (1945). A pioneering American sound poet, educated in music as well as literature, Amirkhanian began his compositional career in the wake of Steve Reich's (*) *It's Gonna Rain* (1965) by using looped audiotape and several tape recorders to create *If In Is* (1971), which he characterizes as "an eleven-minute tape based on strong rhythmic patterns created through the repetition of three words ('mini,' 'bullpup,' 'banjo')." In *Seatbelt, Seatbelt* (1973), his strongest work in this form (and, in my judgment, one of the best American text-sound [*] pieces), the title word is repeated in various ways, by an increasing number of voices, until the chorus suddenly switches to "chung chung quack quack bone" in unison, and then to "cryptic cryptic quack quack" before dividing into two groups, one pair saying the first sequence, the second pair the second sequence. The remainder of this fifteen-minute piece has other propulsive variations within a severely limited verbal palette. Amirkhanian has since produced other kinds of audio art, which I have heard but scarcely remember—indicating to me that it is not as strong as his earlier work. A native Californian, whose critical taste is prejudicially disposed to West Coast culture, he has long been an executive at the Pacifica radio station in Berkeley.

Amirkhanian, Charles. *Seatbelt, Seatbelt* (1973). On *Lexical Music*. Berkeley, CA: 1750 Arch Street S-1779, 1979.

———. *Mental Radio*. NY: Composers Recordings SD 523, 1985.

ANALOG-TO-DIGITAL CONVERSION. Whereas film records the image of an object, standard audiotape and videotape record continuous wave forms as magnetic impulses that, when played back through a transducer (or audio/video player), reproduces the original recorded sound or image. The epithet "digital" (*) refers to the conversion of analog impulses into a binary form that can be stored *digitally* in a computer or on a computer disc. The only way to turn such digital information into sound or image would be through an opposite process—digital-to-analog conversion. By this last method it becomes possible for codes created wholly within a computer to be understood as sound.

Holmes, Thomas B. *Electronic and Experimental Music*. NY: Scribner's, 1985.

ANDERSON, Beth (1950). Although scarcely a prolific speech composer, Anderson has created some masterpieces in that special vein. Drawing upon her Kentucky upbringing, she introduced tobacco auctioneering rhythm to the simple phrase, "If I were a poet, what would I say," to produce audio art that transcends both the phrase and any recall of that folk model. As a music composer, Anderson has worked with instruments and tape, for pieces both short and long, including *The Fat Opera* (1991). After collaborating on the publication of *Ear* (intermittently in San Francisco, 1973), she came to New York. There she founded and for many years published the new music magazine, *Ear-New York* (1975–1991), although that fact was not acknowledged in later issues of that journal.

Anderson, Beth. "If I Were a Poet." In *Text-Sound Texts*, ed. Richard Kostelanetz. NY: Morrow, 1980.

ANDERSON, Laurie (1947). Laurie Anderson was briefly popular in the early '80s, following the surprise hit of her eight-minute audio montage "O Superman." Working in New York since 1973, Anderson had been exposed to the musical experiments of Brian Eno (*) and Philip Glass (*) in evolving her stage shows that included spoken word (often electronically distorted), tape loops, synthesized sounds, mime, film, and light shows. Her best-known work in this mode was the seven-hour production *The United States* (1984), the audio portion of which was released as a five-volume set by rock label Warner Brothers in the wake of her pop hit. By the mid-'80s, however, she had disappeared from the pop scene as well as from more progressive venues.

Anderson's work fails to meet the claims made for it, whether as visual art, music, writing, or performance; for it has from its beginnings been invariably more slick than avant-garde and more acceptable than challenging. It follows that Anderson herself fakes, speaking in a reprinted interview about the American writer-vagrant Joe Gould (c. 1889–1957): "He wrote an autobiography, extremely excessive and beautiful. He left out nothing." What makes this anecdote dubious is that the Gould "autobiography," on which he claimed to be working for decades, never appeared in print; indeed, no manuscript was found at his death. (Thus does a fake invoke a fake.) Anderson told another interviewer about seeing "an Oscar (sic) Schlemmer revival of some Bauhaus dance work," which is a feat that would belong in another sort of compendium, because Oskar Schlemmer (*) died four years before Anderson was born.

Anderson, Laurie. *The United States*. NY: Warner Brothers 25192-1, 1984.

White, Robin. "Laurie Anderson" (1980). In *Art Talk in the Early 80s* (1988), ed. Jeanne Siegel. NY: Da Capo, n.d.

Summer, Melody, ed. *The Guests Go into Supper*. San Francisco, CA: Burning Books, 1986.

ANDRE, Carl (1935). Andre, more than anyone else, persuasively established the idea of a situational sculpture in which materials, sometimes purchased or found (rather than fabricated), are imported into a particular space (usually where "art" is the currency of admission). Because

Carl Andre, "Lever," 1966. *Courtesy National Gallery of Canada, Ottawa.*

these sculptures exist only in that situation, only for the duration of their display there, the parts can be separated and retrieved at the exhibition's end, if not later organized into a totally different work—what Andre calls "clastic" art. As these works may be taken apart (or gathered up) and recomposed, they look intentionally unfinished and impermanent (thus denying the classic piety that "sculptural art" must necessarily be a finished product); they also look as though someone else could easily duplicate them with commonly available materials. Therefore his sculpture *Lever* (1966) assumes an untraditional horizontal form, consisting of 137 pieces of separate but visibly identical (and thus interchangeable) firebricks laid side to side in a single line thirty feet across the floor. An adept aphorist ("Art is what we do; culture is what is done to us"), Andre has also written comparably innovative, nonsyntactical literary texts that, although they are exhibited from time to time (and even reprinted in the catalogues accompanying exhibitions), have yet to be collected into a book.

Waldman, Diane. *Carl Andre.* NY: Guggenheim Museum, 1970.

Carl Andre. The Hague, The Netherlands: Haags Gemeentemuseum, 1969.

ANGER, Kenneth (1932). A child of the Los Angeles film world, Anger began precociously with a trilogy of Surrealistic (∗) and disjointed films that were juvenile in both content and, seemingly, inspiration, the antithesis of slick Hollywood films: *Fireworks* (1947), *Eaux d'Artifice* (1953), and *Inauguration of the Pleasure Dome* (1954, recut 1966). Only with *Scorpio Rising* (1964) did Anger emerge as a successful filmmaker. The subject is motorcyclists, and this film emphasizes their insane love of their machines, their attempts to imitate film heroes such as James Dean, and their rowdy, implicitly homoerotic parties. In the third section of the film, against the motorcyclists are juxtaposed some blue-tinted scenes from a black-and-white version of the Christ story. This last contrast is reinforced by the shrewd use on the soundtrack of rock 'n' roll music that has the distinct virtue of being both resonant and ironic at once. As Anger's cutting from one kind of scene to another becomes quicker, the movie becomes hysterically funny. The film somewhat resembles Pop (∗) painting in its use of quotations, as well as its author's ambivalent attitude toward popular materials. Anger also wrote the classic exposés of individual turpitude (as distinct from corporate sin) in Hollywood, *Hollywood Babylon* (1965) and *Hollywood Babylon II* (1984).

Anger, Kenneth. *Hollywood Babylon.* Phoenix, AZ: Associated Professional Services, 1965.

———. *Hollywood Babylon II.* NY: Dutton, 1984.

ANTHEIL, George (1900–1959). Residing in Europe in the middle 1920s, Antheil became the epitome of the outrageous avant-garde American composer, producing piano pieces with such aggressive titles as *Sonata sauvage, Mechanisms,* and *Airplane Sonata.* Returning to America for a one-person Carnegie Hall concert in 1927, he composed a *Ballet mécanique* (having already produced a score for a Ferdinand Léger film of the same title) with airplane propellers, several pianos, and many drums. (In a 1989 complete recreation of this concert, I thought it by far the strongest work on the program.) Lionized by the literati, Antheil helped Ezra Pound (∗) to complete his opera *Le Testament de Villon* (1926), and in return became the subject of Ezra Pound's booklet *Antheil and the Treatise on Harmony* (1927). Back in America in the early 1930s,

Antheil produced less distinguished operas before moving to Hollywood, where he wrote undistinguished film music and a syndicated newspaper column offering advice to the romantically distraught. No longer an avant-garde composer by his forties, he published a memoir with the audacious title *Bad Boy of Music* (1945).

Antheil, George. *Bad Boy of Music* (1945). Los Angeles, CA: Samuel French, 1990.

Ford, Hugh. "George Antheil." In *Four Lives in Paris*. San Francisco, CA: North Point, 1987.

Pound, Ezra. *Le Testament de Villon* (1926). Conducted by Reinbert de Leeuw. Breukelen, Holland: Philips 9500 927, 1980.

ANTIN, David (1932). Beginning as an independent New York poet and art critic, Antin became a Southern Californian and state-university academic. A handful of his essays are illuminating and persuasive—especially one on the unprecedented character of video and another on American poetry between the wars; others are unintelligible in ways more typical of, and available to, professors than lay writers. His early poems, collected in the marvelously titled *Code of Flag Behavior* (1968), reveal an arbitrary Expressionism (*) that becomes more pronounced in the "talk poems" he developed in the 1970s. Essentially improvisations that exploit his intimidating facility with complex sentences (in the tradition of the art historian Meyer Schapiro, who declaimed them more gracefully), these solo gabfests customarily begin as philosophical investigations before sinking invariably into anecdotes that have only tenuous connections to the initial concerns. Antin's works are sometimes transcribed to appear in print, their eccentric spacing and lack of punctuation purportedly reflective of his speech.

Antin, David. *Tuning*. NY: New Directions, 1984.

——. *What It Means to Be Avant-Garde*. NY: New Directions, 1993.

ANTIN, Eleanor (1935). Initially more modest than her husband David (*), Antin mailed to selected correspondents in the early 1970s, one every fortnight, a series of black-and-white photographic postcards showing fifty pairs of tall black boots in various settings. Especially in sequence, the herd of boots assumes a life of its own, the photographs becoming an epistolary

Eleanor Antin, "100 Boots on the Job." Signal Hill, California, Feb. 15, 1972, 12:15 p.m. (Mailed Sept. 11, 1972.) *Courtesy Ronald Feldman Fine Arts, New York.*

narrative that, as a measure of Antin's esthetic integrity, never became a book. She also made videotapes, installations, and even a book based upon her assuming the persona of a Russian ballerina several decades ago. For a brief while, such stunts were called "post-conceptual art," the prefix "post" being no more substantial here than it is for "postmodernism" (*), perhaps because, in both cases, the prefix functions to rationalize decline.

Antin, Eleanor. *100 Boots*. San Diego, CA: Privately published, 1970.

APOLLINAIRE, Guillaume (1880–1918; b. Guillelmus Apollinaris de Kostrowitzky). Born of a Polish mother who brought her fatherless sons to Monaco, where they received a French education, Kostrowitzky, known even in his adult years as "Kostro," took a French name for a mercurial literary career that included art criticism, plays, fiction, pornography, and poetry. His first avant-garde contribution was the *poème simultané*, "Zone" (in *Alcools*, 1913), in which events in several places are portrayed in adjacent lines, as though the writer were a bird rapidly moving from place to place. To foster perceptions that are not linear but spatial, Apollinaire adopted the simple innovation of eschewing punctuation. His second innovation, presaging literary Minimalism (*), is the one-line poem, "Chantre" (or "Singer"), which William Meredith (1919) translates as "And the single string of the trumpets marine." Apollinaire's third major innovation was visual poems (✻) that he called "calligrammes," in which words are typeset or handwritten to make expressive shapes, which he dubbed "visual lyricism." For "Il pleut" (or "It rains"), the letters stream down the page, in appropriately uneven lines; "The Little Car" has several shapes reflective of automotive travel; "Mandolin Carnation and Bamboo" incorporates three roughly representational forms onto the same page. Some of these handwritten poems have lines extending at various angles, words with letters in various sizes, musical staves, or diagonal typesetting, all to the end of enhancing language. Not only do such poems display a freedom in the use of materials, but Apollinaire apparently made it a point of principle not to repeat any image. Another, perhaps lesser, innovation he called "conversation poems" ("Les Fenêtres" and "Lundi Rue Christine"), because they were assembled from morsels overheard (and in their spatial leaping resemble "Zone").

Apollinaire's best-remembered play, *Les Mamelles de Tirèsias* (*The Breasts of Tiresias*, 1918, but written many years before), is a satire on sex and genius that Martin Esslin rates as a distinguished precursor to the Theatre of the Absurd (✻). Apollinaire's strongest piece of criticism is the essay "L'Esprit nouveau et les poètes" ("The New Spirit and the Poets," 1918), which is no less valid today than it was then, because of its avant-garde emphasis upon surprise as an esthetic value. It should not be forgotten that, in the cultural milieus of Paris at the beginning of the century, Apollinaire performed invaluable service in bringing together advanced artists and writers and helping them understand one another. As Roger Shattuck elegantly put it, "He wrote on all subjects, in all forms, and for all purposes. For him there was no separation of art and action; they were identical."

Apollinaire, Guillaume. *Calligrammes* (1918). Trans. Anne Hyde Greet. Berkeley, CA: University of California, 1980.

———. *Alcools* (1913). Trans. William Meredith, intro. and notes Francis Steegmuller. Garden City, NY: Doubleday, 1964.

Shattuck, Roger, ed. *Apollinaire*. NY: New Directions, 1949.

Themerson, Stefan. *Apollinaire's Lyrical Ideograms*. London, England: Gabberbocchus, 1968.

ARAKAWA (1936; b. Shusaku A.). It is easier to describe Arakawa's paintings than say what they mean. His paintings tend to be large, usually containing sketchily rendered images, devoid of colors other than black-gray-white. There are letters produced with large stencils, as well as handwriting with roman letters. The simple names for these paintings are customarily devoid of symbolic suggestion. The parts are sufficiently distant from one another, as well as from the painting's title, to suggest mysteries that are not easily penetrated, and indeed they aren't. Arakawa has also collaborated with his wife, Madeline Gins (✻), in producing a visual-verbal book, *The Mechanism of Meaning*, that has gone through three radically different editions (1971, 1979, 1988). It is no less penetrable than his visual art, finally posing the question, rarely raised, of how much unintelligibility is acceptable in contemporary art. It is not for nothing that few articles about Arakawa's work are long and that even shorter appreciations come to drastically different conclusions.

Arakawa, and Madeline H. Gins. *The Mechanism of Meaning*. 3rd ed. NY: Abbeville, 1988.

ARDITTI QUARTET (1974). In nearly every instrumental genre are individuals who make a specialty of performing avant-garde works that no one else can do. What David Tudor (✻) was to the traditional piano, Paul Zukofsky (1943) was to the solo violin, Loretta Goldberg (1945) has become to electric keyboards, and Margaret Leng Tan (1944) is becoming to the grand piano, Irvine Arditti's string quartet has become to its literature. His group's typical feat is to perform the complete string quartets of Elliott Carter (✻), Mauricio Kagel (✻), or György Ligeti (✻) in a single evening or on a single set of discs. They did so well with John Cage's (✻) early quartets that he wrote some new ones for them. In their taste for high modernist music, the London-based Ardittis, as they are commonly called, contrast with the San Francisco–based Kronos Quartet, who have made a specialty of adapting pop songs to their instruments and of playing flashier, more accessible music.

Arditti Quartet. *Complete String Quartets of John Cage*. 2 vols. NY: Mode 17, 27, 1989, 1992.

Goldberg, Loretta. *Soundbridge*. N.p.: Opus One CD 152, n.d. (c. 1991).

ARIAS-MISSON, Alain (1936). A truly "mid-Atlantic" literary artist, a Harvard-educated classicist who was for many years a simultaneous interpreter at the United Nations, Arias-Misson has published literature and produced performances in both America and Europe. His first novel, *Confessions of a Murderer, Rapist, Fascist, Bomber, Thief* (1974), engages contemporary history in an imaginative way, as a series of fictionalized glosses on reproduced newspaper clippings, becoming, in sum, a coherent portrait of the gratuitous violence in our time. What is stylistically special about the novel is the exploitation of both the language and photographs of journalism. Arias-Misson has also produced, more in Europe than here, "public poems," which are language-based provocative performances, the words customarily appearing as signs rather than speech.

Arias-Misson, Alain. *The Public Poem Book.* Calaone-Baone, Italy: Factotumbook, 1978.

ARMAJANI, Siah (1939). An Iranian who emigrated to America in the 1960s, Armajani moved from creating eccentric sculpture to elegant and highly original pedestrian bridges. Beginning with models that were included in museum sculptural exhibitions, he was eventually invited to execute commissions. Perhaps the most successful, the 375-foot Irene Hixon Whitney Bridge (1988), arches over several lanes of highway, connecting the sculpture garden of the Walker Art Center to central Minneapolis. A slim structure with a

Siah Armajani, "Ilene Hixon Whitney Bridge," 1988. *Courtesy the Walker Art Center.*

curved arc that becomes inverted in the middle, the bridge incorporates words from American writers as various as Herman Melville and John Ashbery (∗) and colors reflective of American intellectual history. ("The yellow is from Monticello," Armajani once told an interviewer. "Jefferson called it the color of wheat, of the harvest.") These bridges rank as architecture to some, but not to others.

Crowe, Ann Glen. "Siah Armajani." In *Contemporary Masterworks*, ed. Colin Naylor. Chicago, IL: St. James, 1991.

ARMAN (1928; b. Armand Fernandez). As one of the self-proclaimed "New Realists" in Paris at the beginning of the 1960s, Arman used authentic objects, generally in abundance—no, overwhelming abundance. Simple though the idea of making a sculpture of only one kind of thing was, he produced, with audacity and witty style, accumulations of, for example, dollar bills, bullets, musical instruments, old cameras, watch parts, and kitchen utensils. Sometimes these accumulations are welded together; other times they lie free in a glass case. If metacollage consists of elements with something in common, these would be meta-assemblages. "He is always bending the object to his entirely personal and purely arbitrary will," writes the critic Henry Martin (1942), "as though to tell us that will is what we are most truly made of." Though the process of making his assemblages reflects mad and messy inspiration, the results are always neat and picturesque.

Martin, Henry. *Arman.* NY: Abrams, 1973.

ARMITAGE, Merle (1893–1975). By most measures the most distinctive book designer of his generation, Armitage used, in Dick Higgins's summary, "color and printed end leaves in most books, few rules or 'spinich' (characteristic of Bauhaus and Art Deco design), large page folios, minimalist title spreads with very large type size, unusual mixtures of type faces, and, in his later books, recurring visual motifs, such as a Navaho rug in a book on Stravinsky." Armitage also authored and edited many volumes about modern art and modern dance, in addition to working as a promoter, publicist, and presenter of concerts, for which he customarily designed memorable brochures. Among his numerous books were anthologies of criticism about Igor Stravinsky (∗), Martha Graham (∗), Arnold Schoenberg (∗), and George Gershwin (1898–1937). Though many of these volumes were reissued in their times, few are in print now. In 1957, the UCLA Library mounted an exhibition of his books. He worked briefly as an art director of slick magazines and in titling design for Hollywood studios. Armitage reportedly declared, "I write in order to have something to design." *Accent on Life* (1965) is Armitage's autobiography.

Armitage, Merle. *Martha Graham: The Early Years* (1937). NY: Da Capo, 1978.

ARMORY SHOW (1913). Officially called "The International Exhibition of Modern Art" and installed at the 69th Regiment Armory in New York from 17 February to 15 March 1913, this was the single most influential exhibition of avant-garde painting ever in America. With over 1,600 objects, it was really two exhibitions within a single space. The American section, which contained roughly three-quarters of the items, was an unbiased comprehensive survey of current American activity. In the European section, however, were canvases by Impressionists,

Marcel Duchamp, "Nude Descending a Staircase, No. 2," 1913. *Courtesy the Philadelphia Museum of Art: The Louise and Walter Arensberg Collection.*

Georges Seurat, the Symbolists Odilon Redon and Puvis de Chavannes, Paul Cézanne, Vincent Van Gogh (eighteen items), Pierre Gauguin, Henri Matisse (forty items), while Pablo Picasso (∗) and Georges Braque, for two, were slighted. The edge of new European art was represented by Francis Picabia (∗) and Marcel Duchamp (∗), whose "Nude Descending a Staircase, No. 2" (1913) inspired outraged reviews in the press (a newspaper critic dubbed it "Explosion in a Shingle Factory"). The lack of sophistication of the American public notwithstanding, nearly a half million people saw the show in New York and at its later venues in Chicago and Boston, many of them remembering it for years afterwards.

Brown, Milton W. *The Story of the Armory Show.* NY: Abbeville, 1988.

Schapiro, Meyer. "The Armory Show." In *Modern Art.* NY: Braziller, 1978.

ARMSTRONG, Sara Garden (1943). In a series called *Airplayers*, begun in 1982, Armstrong has made a series of progressively more complex kinetic (∗) sculptures that depend upon mechanically blown air for their movements. Notwithstanding surfaces reminiscent of Eva Hesse (∗), these become in their breathing somewhat anthropomorphic, especially when several are exhibited in a single space, and their shadows create landscapes on the surrounding walls. The sounds initially come from the blowers switching on and off. By *Airplayer XIII* (1991), Armstrong had added two computers to control both variously and randomly the emission of lights and sounds. Armstrong also produced extremely inventive book-art, likewise titled *Airplayers* (1990), that is filled with page-turning surprises, including, in addition to illustrations of her sculptures, such unusual materials as transparent sheets, silkscreened plastic vinyl, sandblasted lenses, and an LCD (liquid-crystal display).

Armstrong, Sara Garden. *Airplayers.* NY: Willis, Locker, & Owens, 1990.

ARP, Jean (1887–1966; b. Hans A.). Born a German citizen in Strasbourg, Arp moved easily between France and Germany (and between two first names), between the French and German languages, and between visual art and poetry. In the first respect, he made abstract reliefs dependent upon cutouts and highly distinctive sculptures utilizing curvilinear shapes. He worked with automatic composition, chance, and collaborations. He appropriated the epithet "concrète art," even though his biomorphic forms were quite different from the geometries of Theo van Doesburg (∗), who originated the term, and Max Bill (∗), who popularized it. Arp spoke of wanting "to attain the transcendent, the eternal which lies above and beyond the human." *Papiers déchirés* he composed by tearing up paper whose pieces fell randomly onto the floor in an analogue to the "automatic writing" of Surrealism (∗). One quality peculiar to Arp's work is the integration of contraries, which is to say that his art seems to belong to Surrealism as well as Dada (∗), to Constructivism (∗) as well as Expressionism (∗). His poems are commonly praised for their "lyrical innocence," especially by more conservative critics; those preferring a sharper edge decry a recurring silliness. Arp also published criticism that included *Die Kunstismen* (Isms of Art, 1925), written in collaboration with El Lissitzky (∗), in which the two participants correctly identified all the avant-garde movements dating back to 1914. Oddly, this percipient text is not reprinted in the standard English-language anthology of Arp's writings. Not unlike other Dadaists, he evaded conscription into World War I with a certain theatrical style. As Matthew Josephson tells it, the German consul in Zurich gave Arp "a form to fill in, listing about thirty questions starting with his birth. He wrote down the day, month, and year—1889 [sic]—on the first line, repeated this for all the rest of the questions, then drew a line at the bottom of the page, and added it all up to the grand total of something like 56,610!"

Jean, Marcel, ed. *Arp on Arp: Poems, Essays, Memories.* NY: Viking, 1972.

Read, Herbert. *The Art of Jean Arp.* NY: Abrams, 1968.

ARTAUD, Antonin (1896–1948). Artaud is the author of a theoretical book so extraordinary, *Le Théâtre et son double* (1938; *The Theatre and Its Double,* 1958), that it lends authority to everything else he ever did: books of plays, his movie appearances, even his persistent madness. Influenced particularly by Balinese dancers he saw in Paris in the early 1930s, Artaud imagined a Western theater that would neglect realism and narrative for kinetic images, rituals, and even magic. Such theater could surround the audience, even enticing it to participate. Thus, under the banner of "theatre of cruelty," he forecast not only Peter Brook's (1925) more radical performances and the Living Theater (∗), but Happenings (∗) and subsequent performance art (∗). Though Artaud aspired to create consequential avant-garde art, it is as a theorist that he is mostly remembered.

Artaud, Antonin. *The Theatre and Its Double* (1938). Trans. M.C. Richards. NY: Grove, 1958.

ARTE POVERA, L'ART CONTEMPORAIN, ART INFORMEL, ART BRUT, ART AUTRE, SUPERREALISM, NEW ESTHETIC, ART OF THE REAL, TRANSAVANTGARDE, NEO-GEO, UNEXPRESSIONISM, etc. These terms are grouped together because they were used at one time or another to merchandise a new group of artists; and although some of the individual artists promoted under these banners might have survived, the terms did not, mostly because they (and others with a similarly short life span) were coined out of the intelligence of advertising and promotion rather than art criticism and art history. (What is surprising is that most of the critics adopting such opportunistic epithets survived their decline and disappearance, perhaps indicating how the business of criticism differs from the life of art.)

To list one or another book over many others makes unnecessarily invidious comparisons.

ARTIST'S BOOKS. This term arose in the 1970s to encapsulate anything bookish made by individuals established in the visual-arts world or who had gone to art school. Like most art terms based on biography, rather than the intrinsic properties of the art, it was a marketing device, designed to sell works to an audience respectful of "artists"; and because of the biographical base, the term forbade qualitative distinctions, "better" artists not necessarily producing superior books. Artistically considered, alternative book forms should be called *book-art*; the produce, *book-art books* (to further distinguish them from "art books," which are illustrated books, customarily in a large format, about visual art). Some of us have favored this esthetic definition over the autobiographical, without success so far. Among the major practitioners of book-art are Sol LeWitt (*), Tom Phillips (*), Dieter Rot (*), Paul Zelevansky (*), and Sara Garden Armstrong (*).

Lyons, Joan, ed. *Artists' Books*. Layton, UT: Peregrine Smith, 1985.

ASHBERY, John (1927). Because Ashbery has by the 1990s become the epitome of the "Major American Poet," it is easy to forget that he began as a fairly experimental writer. His long poem "Europe" (1960) is a classic of acoherent diffuseness, which is to say that the poet drew words from a variety of sources, barely connecting them. (Acoherence in literature is comparable to atonality in music.) When this poem appeared in Ashbery's second book, *The Tennis Court Oath* (1962), the critic John Simon (1925), a sure barometer of conservative prejudices, wrote, "It never deviates into—nothing so square as sense!—sensibility, sensuality, or sentences." None of Ashbery's later poems equal "Europe" for esthetic deviance. Ashbery also coedited two moderately avant-garde English-language literary journals published in France, *Locus Solus* (1960–1962, named after a book by Raymond Roussell [*], on whom Ashbery wrote his M.A. thesis) and *Art and Literature* (1964–1968).

Ashbery, John. *The Tennis Court Oath*. Middletown, CT: Wesleyan University, 1962.

ASHLEY, Robert (1930). Ashley's specialty has been a theatrical music that draws upon speech that he customarily performs in oddly flat and barely intelligible ways, as though he were talking to himself. For subjects, Ashley usually draws upon American myth. In *Perfect Lives* (1983), he both scored and wrote a seven-part opera designed for the scale of television; versions also exist on two audiocassettes and three compact discs (and parts were adapted for live performance). Ashley's book of that same title is also radically different from any other book about an opera, lacking any photographs or musical scores. (Only the video of *Perfect Lives* was, at last report, unavailable.) *Atalanta* (1985) is a more conventional opera that, given its middle American content, sounds odd in Italian.

Ashley, Robert. *Perfect Lives*. NY: Lovely Music 4913 & 4947, 1983; 4917.3, 1991; New York–San Francisco: Archer Fields–Burning Books, 1991.

ASSEMBLAGE. This term was purportedly coined in the early 1950s by the French artist Jean Dubuffet (1901–1985) initially for lithographs made from paper collages (*) and then for small sculptures made from papier-mâché, scraps of wood, sponge, and other debris. The word was popularized by a 1961 exhibition at New York's Museum of Modern Art, whose catalog spoke of works that "are predominantly *assembled* rather than painted, drawn, modeled, or carved." On display were by-then classic collages along with sculptures by Louise Nevelson (*), Richard Stankiewicz (1922–1983), Joseph Cornell (*), and Edward Kienholz (*), whose contribution was really a tableau (which differs from sculpture in having a theatrical frontside, forbidding close access). By now, the epithet "assemblage" functions best as a definition for three-dimensional collage.

Seitz, William C. *The Art of Assemblage*. NY: Museum of Modern Art, 1961.

ATTIE, Dotty (1938). Taking the comic-book form of sequential panels, Attie has made an unusually allusive art that echoes classical painting, particularly Ingres (1780–1867), and Victorian literature, particularly Anthony Trollope (1815–1882). Her square, bordered panels tend to have either picture or text, in either case propelling a narrative; and beneath the innocuous surface are hints of menace and nightmare. The pictures are usually drawn from details in masterpiece paintings (thus making her work comparable to music compositions that draw phrases from the classics). "Often as not," writes the curator Howard Fox, "her stories involve the nobility of another century, usually in polite company at formal social occasions. This innocent facade seems to mask an underlying corruption."

Dottie Attie: Paintings and Drawings. Pittsburgh, PA: Pittsburgh Center for the Arts, 1989.

AUDIO ART. This term arose in the 1980s to define esthetic experience based on sound, as distinct from music on one side and language on the other. It can exist in live performance, whether on radio or on stage, as well as on audiotape. Typical pieces of audio art are about the sound of something—say, the sound of seduction, the sound of the language of prayer, the sound of particular cities, or sounds of nature. Among the major practitioners are John Cage (*) (particularly in his early *Williams Mix*, 1953), Sorrel (Doris) Hays (*) (especially in her *Southern Voices*, 1981), Jackson Mac Low (*), Makoto Shinohara (1931, especially in *City Visit* [1971]), Frits Wieland (especially in *Orient Express*), and Noah Creshevsky (*).

Lander, Dan, and Micah Lexier, eds. *Audio by Artists*. Toronto, Canada: Art Metropole, 1990.

AUSTIN, Larry (1930). A professor who founded the extravagantly designed periodical *Source: Music of the Avant-Garde* (1967–1974), which printed variously alternative scores and interviews, as well as including ten-inch records of previously suppressed music. Austin has worked adventurously with Electronic Music (*), live-electronic performance, and theatrical conceptions. I remember best *The Magicians* (1968), which was performed on Halloween on a stage bathed in black light, with two screens that apparently swiveled with the breeze. The performers included several children performing elementary tasks, singing songs that resounded through an amplification system that treated soft high notes gently. Austin spoke of this piece as a "time object. I wanted to take music out of the context of a dramatic flow of consequential events and to lose, as much as possible, the sense of time." More recently, Austin has used computers not only to make music but to create interactive situations for live ensembles.

Austin, Larry, ed. *Source: Music of the Avant-Garde* (13 vols.). Davis, CA: Composer/Performer Federal, 1967–1974.

AVERY, Tex (1908 [or 1907]–1980; b. Frederick B.A.). After directing "Oswald the Rabbit" cartoons, he became a principal creator of Bugs Bunny (1936), the most anarchistic hero in all American film (but, needless to say, a descendant of preternaturally wise rabbits in American folklore and literature). What distinguished an Avery cartoon from a Walt Disney, say, are such qualities as quicker pace, a sharper edge, continuous detailed movement, greater violence (though no injury is permanent), and unsupervised activities (typically devoid of parents, say). Avery also nurtured the talents of Chuck Jones (1912), I.M. Freleng (1900, aka Friz), and other Warner Bros. animators. Among Avery's other creations

were Chilly Willy the penguin, Droopy the dog, and Lucky Ducky. Avery's Bugs Bunny cartoons are widely available on videotape.

Adamson, Joe. *Tex Avery: King of Cartoons* (1975). NY: Da Capo, 1985.

AYLER, Albert (1936–1970). More than any other, Ayler realized the highly abrasive, Expressionistic (*) music that seemed to become the avant-garde edge for the younger jazz cognoscenti in the 1960s. He performed on the tenor saxophone, often in collaboration with his brother Donald, a trumpeter; among the records that epitomize his style is *Bells* (ESP, 1965), which captures a live concert at New York's Town Hall of 1 May 1965. I have played this single-sided record for people who think themselves enthusiasts for everything "way out," only to watch them wince. Ayler's body was found in New York's East River, but the cause of his death has never been explained.

Albert Ayler (with "Bells," recorded in 1965). Therwil, Switzerland: Hat Hut CD 6039, 1990

Albert Ayler Trio. *Spiritual Unity*. New York: ESP-Disk 1002, 1965.

BAADER, Johannes (1885–1955). An architect by training, Baader became the ironic *Oberdada* in the brief life of Berlin Dada (*), proclaiming himself "President of the League of Intertelluric Superdadaist Nations." As a dense collagist, he filched posters off the streets and mixed fragments of them with newspaper articles and miscellaneous numbers and letters. In 1919 and 1920, he exhibited two different versions of his *Handbuch des Oberdadaismus* (Manual of Superdadaism, abbreviated to HADO), which presages later book-art created mostly for gallery exhibitions. In the center of the 1919 Dada Fair, Baader constructed an early assemblage (*), the *Plasto-Dio-Dada-Drama*, which, in a departure, included "instructions for gazing at it": "Monumental Dadaist architecture on five floors with three gardens, a tunnel, two lifts, and a door shaped like a top hat. The ground floor or level is the fate predetermined before birth and has nothing to do with the story. Description of the floor: 1) The Preparation of the Oberdada. 2) The Metaphysical Ordeal. 3) Initiation. 4) The World War. 5) The World Revolution." Baader also exhibited a plan for a zoo without bars that was actually realized in a different form.

Dachy, Marc. *The Dada Movement*. NY: Rizzoli, 1990.

BABBITT, Milton (1916). Credit Arnold Schoenberg (1874–1951) with inventing an entirely new language for music—a revolutionary reordering of tonal possibilities; but credit Milton Babbitt with extending the serial (*) idea to musical dimensions other than pitch—duration (including rhythm), register, dynamics (attack), and timbre. The result of this logical extension of Schoenberg's ideas was a twelve-tone music of unprecedented structural complexity, in which every note contributed to several kinds of serial relationships. From this principle of simultaneous development, Babbitt developed a revolutionary esthetic that equated excellence with "the multiplicity of function of every event" (the variety of serial relationships each note developed). "I want a piece of music to be literally as much as possible," he once said; and his favorite words of praise are "profoundly organized" and "structurally intricate." Recorded examples of this phase of Babbitt's career include *Du* (1951), a song cycle, and *Composition for Four Instruments* (1948).

Because his music was too difficult for nearly all musicians, he began in the mid-1950s to use an early music synthesizer (*) that was constructed, with Babbitt as a consultant, by RCA. It offered the twofold possibility of achieving precisely all of the complicated effects he desired and of fixing on audiotape a "performance" for all time. From this encounter came such serial compositions as *Ensembles for Synthesizer* (1964) and *Philomel* (1964) in which even the listener unfamiliar with serial music theory can hear a complexity of articulation and an absence of repetition. It is fair to say that success came to Babbitt in the 1960s, in his late forties, when he became a chaired professor of music at Princeton University. Of the numerous commissions he has subsequently received, I would particularly recommend *Phonemena* (1974, from "phonemes," not "phenomena"), which typically exists in two versions—one for soprano and tape, the second for soprano and piano. He is probably one of few individuals mentioned in this book to receive a MacArthur "genius" grant. Perhaps this success reflects his talents as a stand-up speaker who is at once witty and provocative, brilliant and engaging.

Babbitt, Milton. "The Composer as Specialist." In *Esthetics Contemporary* (1978), ed. Richard Kostelanetz. 2nd ed. Buffalo, NY: Prometheus, 1989.

Babbitt, Milton. *Phonemena* (1974), *Reflections* (1975), *Post-Partitions* (1966). NY: New World Records 209, 1977.

Dembski, Stephen, and Joseph N. Straus, eds. *Milton Babbitt: Words about Music*. Madison, WI: University of Wisconsin, 1987.

BACH, P.D.Q. (1959). This entry belongs under P.D.Q. Bach (1807–1742?), because this "dummy" produces far more innovative music than his ventriloquist, Peter Schickele (1935). Perhaps the greatest and most fertile comic composer in musical history, P.D.Q. Bach excels at mixing cultural periods, beginning with his titles: *Concerto for Horn and Hardart* (referring to a chain of automats in New York City), *Iphigenia in Brooklyn, Hansel and Gretel and Ted and Alice*, and *The Safe Sextette*. P.D.Q. does not quote classical compositions as much as write melodies of similar structure and texture but with a contemporary sense of harmony and musical literacy. The innovation is pseudo-classical music that reflects the influence of modernists such as Stravinsky (*) and incidentally resembles conceptually certain fictions by Jorge Luis Borges (*). Especially in concert tours, P.D.Q. Bach's work is customarily introduced by a disheveled figure called "*Professor* Peter Schickele" who claims scholarly expertise on P.D.Q. Because P.D.Q.'s subjects-for-disruption have included not only the Bach family but Mozart, Copland, and Schickele's Juilliard classmate Philip Glass (*), it could be said that P.D.Q. has produced a kind of Dada (*) music funnier than that of, say, Satie (*) and Slonimsky (*).

Schickele, Peter. *The Definitive Biography of P.D.Q. Bach*. NY: Random House, 1976.

Kostelanetz, Richard. "Peter Schickele (1989)." In *On Innovative Music(ian)s*. NY: Limelight, 1989.

BALL, Hugo (1886–1927). A co-founder of Dada (*) who ended his short life as a Catholic writer, the mercurial Ball, born in Switzerland, began by rejecting German Expressionism (*) as fundamentally violent. He reportedly coined the term "Dada," which he picked randomly from the dictionary, meaning "hobby horse," among other definitions. Ball is best remembered for early sound poetry, which he called "Klanggedicht (1916)," that made equal sense in every language. One poem begins: "gadji beri bimba/ glandridi laula lonni cadori/ gadjama bim geri glassala," which sounds just as fresh today as it did then.

Ball, Hugo. *Flight Out of Time*. Ed. John Elderfield. NY: Viking, 1974.

BARLOW, Clarence (1945; aka Klarenz B.). Though born and educated in Calcutta, where he took his first degrees in science, Barlow has become one of the major avant-garde composers in the German-speaking world, residing for many years in Cologne. His fortes are the use of computers in composition (since 1971), tonality and metricism based on number theory, pastiches that draw upon his musical literacy, and language creations that depend upon his personal fluency in various tongues. The cofounder of GIMIK (Initiative Music and Informatics Cologne), he produced an acoustic portrait of his birthplace for the "Metropolis" series of Westdeutscher Rundfunk. He is currently the artistic director of the Institut voor Sonologie (1967) in The Hague, The Netherlands.

Barlow, Klarenz. *Çoğluotobüsişletmesi*. Mainz, Germany: Wergo 60098, 1982.

BARNES, Djuna (1892–1982). Though she did other things in her life, including journalism, illustration, short fiction, poetry, and a play, Barnes is best remembered for *Nightwood* (1936), a novel that T.S. Eliot (*) testified, in his preface to the first edition, had "a quality of doom and horror very nearly related to that of Elizabethan tragedy." Barnes's style combines Elizabethan English with turn-of-the-century avant-garde prose, giving *Nightwood* the quality of elegant nightmare.

Barnes, Djuna. *Nightwood*. London, England: Faber, 1936.

———. *Ryder*. Elmwood Park, IL: Dalkey Archive, 1990.

BARNETT, Peter H. (1945). A philosophy professor married to an art curator, Barnett also produces conceptually original and profound book-art. His interest is visually portraying philosophical questions. The first and most accessible of his books consists of unanswerable questions, all handwritten in capital letters: "Can critical activity take place where there is not yet theory?" Four statements of this sort appear in the four quadrants of square pages; but to complicate the reading experience, Barnett has cut away outside quadrants from many pages, so that a question in the lower right-hand corner becomes a continuous counterpoint to the questions on previous pages from which the lower right-hand corner has been cut away.

The structure of *Time Trap* (1980) depends upon a string that runs through the middle of all the book's pages, its ends tied to make a loose circle. I own a handmade dummy copy of his third book, *Reciprocal Encoding-Decoding Construction*, which measures 14-inches square, bound on both sides, with die-cut pages that must be turned if the book is to be understood (which means, as one measure of its mediumistic integrity, that it cannot be conveniently exhibited in an art gallery). Unlike Barnett's two previous books, this work can be reproduced only by hand. Because each of these three books is far more complicated than its predecessor (much in the tradition of James Joyce [*]), it is not surprising that the fourth, *Thinking Without Surfaces* (1987), was done on and for a computer disc.

Barnett, Peter H. *Time Trap*. Brooklyn: Assembling (P.O. Box 444, Prince St., New York, NY 10012-0008), 1980.

BARRON, Susan (1947). After premedical studies, Barron began working as a photographer specializing in supremely fine-textured small-scale prints, mostly of fields, trees, and lakes. These were collected in *Another Song* (1981), a book produced in an edition of only fifty-three copies, each with thirty-nine original prints. Her magnum opus is *Labyrinth of Time* (1987), a one-of-a-kind eleven-volume book that updates the tradition of the unique illuminated manuscript. In its large pages filled with photographs, drawings, etchings, collages (many of which involve words, in several languages; some of which are music), Nicolas Barker, the Keeper of Rare Books and Manuscripts at the British Museum, finds "a true labyrinth, a passage that leads you on, . . . something to wander through, astounded by an illusion here, captivated by a message there, like one of the dioramas that so delighted our forefathers. The change from one medium to another, the differences in scale (large to small letters, vast and minute pictures) all engage and lure mind and eye into the maze."

Barron, Susan. *Another Song*. NY: Callaway Editions, 1981.

Cage, John. "Another Song." In *X*. Middletown, CT: Wesleyan University, 1982.

BARTH, John (1930). Through the late 1960s, in his own late thirties, John Barth was testing the extremes of literature. "Frame Tale," the opening story in his 1968 collection *Lost in the Funhouse*, appears in the form of a Möbius strip that, when read appropriately, must be cut out of the book and its ends pasted together with a single twist, so that it will forever read: ". . . once upon a time there was a story that began. . . ." Another story, "Menelaiad," adds interior quotations until several sets appear around every new quotation. My anthology *Breakthrough Fictioneers* (1973) includes a marvelous visual fiction, subtitled "A stereophonic narrative for authorial voice," which is *not* reprinted in any of his books. Around this time I saw Barth give a literary recital in which, standing between two loudspeakers, he spoke live in a trio between two prerecorded tapes of his own voice. This performance invigorated the otherwise decadent art of the literary recital. In both practice and later theory, Professor Barth retreated from advanced positions for more opportune and acceptable kinds of fiction and literary performance.

Barth, John. *Lost in the Funhouse*. Garden City, NY: Doubleday, 1968.

BARZUN, Henri-Martin (1881–1972). In an essay on "The Aesthetics of Dramatic Poetry" (1912–1914), published in his own periodical *Poème et Drame*, Barzun presented his theory of "*simultanèisme*," which the historian Marc Dachy describes as "a program for adapting the musical technique of polyphony to literary creation. He composed odes that later took the form of 'dramas' consisting of poems (dramatism) and songs alternating three groups of four voices each. As the attempt to express reality under all its aspects, not in succession but simultaneously, it can be seen as an extension of the Cubist rendering of objects and figures from several angles at once." The idea was not for Barzun

alone, as Dachy reprints a collaborative simultaneous poem ("The Admiral's in Search of a House to Rent," [1916] composed by "R. Huelsenbeck [*], Tr. Tzara [*], M. Janco [*].") In 1967, Barzun, by then long a resident of America, sent me an inscribed copy of *Orpheus: Choric Education*, which was subtitled "A Record of Labors and Achievements 1920–1945" and filled with reminiscences and encomia, as well as manifestos and sample texts. An informative article on him in English was written by his son Jacques (1907), a noted American cultural historian.

Barzun, Jacques. "Some Notes on Créteil and French Poetry." *New Directions* 9 (1946).

Dachy, Marc. *The Dada Movement, 1915–1923*. NY: Rizzoli, 1990.

BAUDELAIRE, Charles (1821–1867). French poet and critic, is commonly credited with initiating literary modernism. The poems collected in *Les Fleurs du mal* (*Flowers of Evil,* 1857) include "Correspondences" in which Baudelaire expresses the theory, basic to Symbolism (*), that the different sensations of sound, color, and perfume become associated with one another, creating images that, instead of being descriptive, are evocative or suggestive, thereby enabling the poet to portray deeper levels of psychological experience. As a person of letters, Baudelaire also produced translations of Edgar Allan Poe (giving the American decadent more influence in France than he had at the time at home), and brilliant art criticism, collected in two volumes.

Baudelaire, Charles. *Mirror on Art*. Trans. Jonathan Mayne. Garden City, NY: Doubleday Anchor, 1956.

BAUDRILLARD, Jean (1929). This confession no doubt reflects serious defects in my otherwise elaborate education and literacy, but my Anglo-American head has trouble reading Frogthink written like an inadequate translation from the French that supposedly gains profundity from the inadequacy of the translation and/or the text's initial opacity. So I find Baudrillard no more edifying than Roland Barthes, Louis Althusser, Luce Irigary, and Jacques Derrida (*), and other French thinkers customarily characterized (and merchandised) as progressive, even though their rhetorical strategies stink of old-fashioned, class-aggrandizing elitism. What can be understood in Baudrillard seems no more than familiar radical platitudes about evil capitalism—the sort of remarks that can be profound only to people who have not encountered them before, which is to say undergraduates and undereducated post-undergraduates. My skepticism of adult English-speakers who revere these guys equals that reserved for those who claim they "understand" the IRS guidelines. If you don't believe me, read (or try to read) them yourselves, and don't be surprised if your mind wanders or you fall asleep.

Baudrillard, Jean. *For a Critique of the Political Economy of the Sign.* St. Louis, MO: Telos, 1981.

BAUHAUS (1919–1933). In its short lifetime, the Bauhaus was the most advanced school for architecture and applied arts. Not surprisingly, it became more influential after its premature death by Nazi decree, if not the epitome of avant-garde esthetics well into the 1950s. Its teachers included Walter Gropius (1883–1969), Ludwig Mies van der Rohe (*), Oskar Schlemmer (*), Herbert Bayer (1900), and L. Moholy-Nagy (*), who disseminated its ideas in subsequent teaching and writings. Among the central Bauhaus ideas were the adaptation of technology to artistic uses, the refusal to distinguish between fine and applied art, and the teaching of all the arts collectively on the persuasive assumption that literacy in only one form or only one communications medium signifies functional illiteracy before the diversity of contemporary information. The Bauhaus's so-called foundation course became a general introduction to materials, from which the individual student could then ideally concentrate on the medium of his or her choice. This last purpose accounts for why the original Bauhaus in Weimar (1919–1925) had no course officially in architecture; that was added, purportedly for practical reasons, after its move to Dessau (1925). The Bauhaus books, edited and designed by Moholy-Nagy, became the first series of extended illustrated essays on high modernism.

Though Bauhaus ideas encouraged solid and economical construction over esthetic excellence, the result of Bauhaus influence has been new kinds of formalism: in design, artificial streamlining; in architecture, the slick glass-walled boxes that have become depressingly abundant on the American urban landscape. Similarly, an initially anti-academic educational program, emphasizing individual enthusiasm and choice over particular results, generated its own academic pieties of stylistic correctness (geometric patterns in textiles, say, rather than representational images). In both architecture and design-education, then, a limited interpretation of the Bauhaus esthetic placed an emphasis upon certain end products, rather than upon educational processes that might produce entirely different results.

Wingler, Hans Maria. *The Bauhaus* (1962, 1968). Cambridge, MA: M.I.T., 1969.

BAUSCH, Pina (1940). Born in Germany, Bausch trained at the (Kurt Jooss [1901–1979]) Folkwang School in Essen before studying at the Juilliard School of Dance in New York, where she worked with, among others, the Expressionistic (*) ballet choreographer Anthony Tudor (1908–1987). Becoming director of the city-subsidized Wuppertal Dance Theater company in 1973, Bausch evolved a *Tanz Theater* ("dance theater") that is a rich and complex amalgam of movement, text, music, and stunning visual effects. In *Nelken* (*Carnations*, 1982), the stage is filled with flowers; for *Arien* (*Arias*, 1979) it is a pool of water. Although her performers are trained dancers, their movements rarely display virtuosic skills, instead reflecting dance techniques in their stylized interactions, mimed incidents, and gestural repetitions.—Katy Matheson

Servos, Norbert. *Pina Bausch—Wuppertal Dance Theater.* Cologne, Germany: Ballett-Bühnen-Verlag, 1984.

BEBOP (c. 1945). Perhaps the first musical form named after its characteristic sound, Bebop was the brainchild of a group of second-generation jazz (*) musicians who disliked the brash commercialism and easy accessibility of big-band jazz. Saxophonist Charlie Parker (*) and trumpeter Dizzy Gillespie (1917–1993) evolved a technique for improvising over standard chord progressions to create entirely new and unexpected melodies. In this manner they produced "new" compositions out of old standards, allowing the rhythm instruments (piano, bass, and drums) to play their old parts. Working in smaller ensembles, these Bebop musicians invented a new kind of "chamber jazz" that became popular in the 1950s. They demonstrated a free interplay among ensemble members, with a generally lighter and more subtle approach to rhythm than was heard in big-band or raucous Dixieland groups. Finally, Bebop musicians displayed a greater intellectualism than their jazz predecessors, believing that jazz was a true art form, and not merely a popular fad.—Richard Carlin

Goldberg, Joe. *Jazz Masters of the '50s.* NY: Da Capo, 1979.

BECK, Stephen (1950). In 1976, I saw extraordinary video works that were so unfashionable that I did not see, or even hear of, them again for fifteen years. One Beck piece *Video Weavings* (1974), has hypnotic, metamorphosing geometric shapes that changed color rapidly. The syntax of change consisted mostly of pulsations, in and out, but the speeds of change are quick and the colors are ethereal. Beck had synthesized imagery directly onto videotape, in live time (rather than distorting images previously recorded with a camera), thanks to a Direct (i.e., cameraless) Video Synthesizer that he, as a B.S. in Electrical Engineering and Computer Science (EECS), had invented in 1969.

"I had developed various styles—geometrics, metamorphosis, soft edge, etc.," he wrote in the mid-1970s. "It was very much an invention spawned by inner necessity, as Kandinsky put it." (Beck was also early in putting color bars at the beginning of the tape, asking viewers to "tune" their monitors before playing the tape, much as musicians tune their instruments before performing a score.) In 1972, for *Illuminated Music,* Beck also synthesized imagery in live time over a San Francisco TV station—a feat rarely, if ever, repeated in this age of pretaped transmission. In addition to making live concerts with his video synthesizer, Beck collaborated with the filmmaker Jordan Belson (1926) on one of the first film/video collaborations, *Cycles* (1974), which was available in both media.

If only because Beck's tapes were made without a camera (and all the nuisances that accompany the shooting of videotape, not to mention film), they suggest the possibility of producing video much as one writes books—mostly by oneself. Beck has recently been involved with creating and designing electronic toys and games, as well as varieties of computer-assisted "virtual reality," which he thinks (as do I) may or may not be an artistic medium.

Beck, Stephen. *Illuminated Music.* Berkeley, CA: Electronic Video Creations (c/o Lapis, 1100 Marina Village Pkwy., Alameda, CA, 94501), 1984.

———. "Image Processing and Video Synthesis." In *Eigenwelt der Apparatewelt/Pioneers of Electronic Art.* Linz, Austria, and Sante Fe, NM: Ars Electronica and the Vasulkas (Rt. 6, Box 100, 87501), 1992.

BECKETT, Samuel (1906–1989). Working against the grain of his upbringing, Beckett was an Irishman whose first successful works were written in French. A disciple of James Joyce (∗), whose sucession of books came to increasingly epitomize esthetic abundance, Beckett instead explored lessness or, to be precise, lessness as moreness, or, to be more precise, the possibilities of moreness with lessness; for Beckett's fundamental effort has been language so spare it would render silence resonant. His quiet in such early plays as *Waiting for Godot* is by now universally familiar, but his later plays are yet more spare, often consisting of monologues punctuated by silences so uniquely resonant we call them Beckettian.

There has been a parallel, if less familiar, evolution in his fiction—away from the repetitious, limited vocabulary (which now curiously seems more Steinian than Joycean) through *L'Innommable* (1955, translated as *The Unnamable* [1958]), which many regard as his greatest novel, to such nonsyntactic flows as this from *Comment c'est* (1961): "in me that were without when the panting stops scraps of an ancient voice in me not mine." With images of pointless activities, personal discomfort, and historical meaninglessness, this passage illustrates the Beckettian knacks of being at once abstract and very concrete, at once lightly comic and deadly serious.

Beckett transcended being a one-note author by using various ways to realize his themes—extended prose, short prose, live theater, radio plays, and ballets—appearing with sufficient time between them to make each work a cultural event. It should not be forgotten that back in 1929 Beckett wrote an essay about *Finnegans Wake* (∗) that ranks among the classics of genuinely avant-garde criticism. Not unlike Joyce, Beckett is perhaps best read in parts, rather than as a whole. He has translated all his works into English, at times with collaborators.

Beckett, Samuel. *I Can't Go On, I'll Go On: A Selection from Samuel Beckett's Work*. Ed. and intro. Richard W. Seaver. NY: Grove, 1976. (This single volume contains not only *Waiting for Godot* and the first part of *Comment c'est* but also his essay "Dante. . . Bruno. Vico. . .Joyce." [1929].)

BELGUM, Erik (1961). Among the best of the younger writers of fiction, let alone experimental fiction, Belgum draws upon a background in avant-garde music and a familiarity with advanced word processors to produce highly innovative texts that in their original form exploit laser-printer typography to enhance their style. Such books should be reproduced directly from typescript, just as typewriter literature (*) was. I find in his fugitive texts a recurring interest in aberrant speech. Belgum, who lives in Minneapolis, also produces audio art (*), for which there is presently as much of a future in the U.S. as for, say, the best contemporary geometric painting.

Belgum, Erik. *The Man Who Could Talk*. Minneapolis, MN: Privately published (2620 Fremont Ave. S., # 103, 55408), 1991.

BELL, Larry (1939). A decade younger than Robert Irwin (*), whose ideas were particularly influential in Southern California, Bell has specialized in glass and plastic sculptures that unusually affect light. After making framed cubes containing mirrored and coated glass, he used new technological processes to make panels that were at different times transparent, translucent, and even opaque. These were sometimes placed on a transparent base to allow light to pass through all parts of the work. Especially when exhibited together, these panels could be a strong presence in museum exhibitions such as "Spaces" at the Museum of Modern Art in 1970.

Larry Bell: Works from New Mexico. Lyon, France: Musée d'Art Contemporain, 1989.

BENCHLEY, Robert (1889–1945). Beginning as a Harvard boy who worked for slick magazines and newspapers, Benchley became the epitome of the cultivated essayist, first as the drama editor of the original *Life* and then as a theater critic for *The New Yorker*. Improbable though it seems now, he was invited to make several cheaply produced short films in which, standing before a camera that he addresses as he would a friend, he

ineptly lectures on banal subjects he obviously knows nothing about: *The Sex Life of the Polyp* (1928), *The Trouble with Husbands* (1940), *How to Take a Vacation* (1941), and *How to Sleep* (1935, which won an Academy of Award for best short comedy, wonder of wonders). The result is subtle irony, camp of a sort not often seen today, even on television. His example, along with those of The Three Stooges (1934–1959) films and Bugs Bunny cartoons, reminds us that, after the advent of sound, much of the most advanced Hollywood-produced work appeared in low-budget short films that are rarely acknowledged by film historians. Once Hollywood ceased producing shorts, independent filmmakers had a near total monopoly on innovative cinema.

Maltin, Leonard. *Selected Short Subjects* (1972). NY: Da Capo, n.d.

BENJAMIN, Walter (1892–1940). A brilliantly insightful German literary critic, Benjamin became, well after his premature death, a hero to radical intellectuals around the world. He figures in this book by authoring "The Work of Art in the Age of Mechanical Reproduction" (1936), which remains one of the most insightful essays on the modernist difference. "For the first time in world history, mechanical reproduction emancipates the work of art from its parasitical dependence upon ritual. To an ever greater degree the work of art reproduced becomes the work of art designed for reproducibility," he wrote. "But the instant the criterion of authenticity ceases to be applicable to artistic production, the total function of art is reversed. Instead of being based on ritual, it begins to be based on another practice—politics." Most students of high modernism (*), including me, would give their eyeteeth to have written sentences like these.

Benjamin, Walter. "The Work of Art in the Age of Mechanical Reproduction" (1936). In *Illuminations*. NY: Schocken, 1969.

BENNETT, John M. (1942). While working as a university librarian specializing in Latin Americana, Bennett has produced a variety of experimental poems. Many of these reflect the arbitrariness of Surrealism (*); some are done in absentee collaboration with others. Most of these have been scattered in many chapbooks that, while each may have its point, diffuse Bennett's impact. Among their titles, in sum perhaps reflective of his particular imagination, are *Lice, Jerks, Burning Dog, Parts, Nose Death, Nips Poems, Milk, Fenestration, Meat Watch, Meat Dip,* and *Tempid.* Under the banner of Luna Bisonte (Moon Bison) Prods, Bennett has also issued printed labels and audiotapes of his own authorship, in addition to publishing *Lost and Found Times* (1975–), which has probably been the most persistently experimental literary magazine to survive for more than a decade in America. This longevity reflects, along with his collaborations with many colleagues, Bennett's genuine professional generosity. *Johnee's Box* is a cased retrospective of his "visual and sound-text poetry." Do not confuse him with John Bennett (1938), no middle initial, who is a provocative small-press writer living in the state of Washington.

Bennett, John M. *Johnee's Box.* Cincinnati, OH: Volatile (P.O. Box 32740, 45201), 1991.

Trawick, Leonard M. "John Bennett's Poetry of Beauty and Disgust." *The Gamut* 16 (Fall 1985).

BERIO, Luciano (1925). An Italian composer working in various media with various materials, Berio often combines spoken texts, sung texts, acoustic and electronic instruments, taped sounds, lighting effects, and theatrical movements including dance. He regards all types of sound—from speech to noise to so-called "musical" sound—as forming a single continuum and himself as not so much a "composer" of works but an assembler, putting together different elements to create a total esthetic experience. The division between musical concert, spoken word, and theatrical event is an artificial one, he believes, and in his compositions he has worked toward synthesizing these elements, citing as his principal predecessor not a musician but the author James Joyce (*), who also tried to combine language and music. Some of his strongest early pieces, such as *In Circles* (1960, to a text by E.E. Cummings [*]), were composed for his wife at that time, the American singer Cathy Berberian (1925–1983), who was regarded among the supreme interpreters of avant-garde music. Berio's best-known work is his *Sinfonia,* composed for the New York Philharmonic's 125th anniversary in 1968 and revised in 1969.—with Richard Carlin

Berio, Luciano. *Sinfonia for Eight Voices and Orchestra.* Italy: Ades 14.122-2 (c. 1990).

———, and E.E. Cummings. *In Circles* (1960). NY: Time 58003, n.d. (c. 1962).

BERNARD, Kenneth (1930). An ultimate fringe writer, Bernard's work might have remained unknown, were his plays not picked up in the late 1960s by John Vaccaro's Play-House of the Ridiculous, which developed apart from Charles Ludlam's (*) theater with a similar name. Remembering the Ridiculous's commitment to extremes of language and content, Bernard writes this about himself: "His decimation of plot and character, his mixture of dictions, his addiction to both low and high cultures, his palimpsest reference and quotation, all combined with large and deadly themes obviously appealed to the apocalyptic, parodic mania-despair of the Play-House." One additional departure, apparently too strong for Vaccaro, who refused to produce it, is *How We Danced While We Burned* (1973), requiring that the theater itself be made into a cabaret that resembles a German beer hall. It becomes clear that the emcee is the commandant of a death camp and that the performers are inmates. When they step off the interior stage, the audience's attention is drawn to a sign above a heavy metal door reading, ominously, "EXIT." The suggestion, almost too much to bear, is that each actor has made his or her last performance. As Bernard's plays were less frequently produced in the 1980s, he turned to fictions, most of them very short, that have what he calls "first-person narrations that contain inward-spiraling ironies."

Bernard, Kenneth. *Night Club and Other Plays.* NY: Winter House, 1971.

———. *Two Plays: How We Danced While We Burned; La Justice or The Cock That Crew.* Santa Maria, CA: Asylum Arts (P.O. Box 6203, 93465), 1990.

———. *From the Distinct File.* Boulder, CO and Normal, IL: Fiction Collective, 1992.

BERNE, Stanley (1923), and Arlene ZEKOWSKI (1922). Berne and Zekowski are tied together not only because they have been married for forty years but also because they customarily publish their books in tandem and reflect a common esthetic, which holds that the conventional sentence is esthetically outmoded. Usually classified as "fiction," their books are typically difficult, in the tradition of Gertrude Stein (∗) at her most opaque. They are innovative stylists remembered not for their "content" but for their original ways of structuring language. They aptly characterize themselves as "pure researchers in literature." Their original banner was "neonarrative," which advocates transcending, according to the critic Welsh Everman, "the traditional literary elements of character, theme, plot, chronology, even storiness and grammar, in favor of a flow of language." Like Stein before them, they have experimented with not one alternative style but several; and their individual works, though different, are complementary. While Zekowski sometimes favors severely truncated sentences, Berne's sentences are often long and elegant. Dick Higgins (∗) thinks Berne "is more romantic and less inclined to linguistic experiment, while [Zekowski] is less focused on grammar and has a more classical thrust." Their names are rarely mentioned in literary histories and they are not listed in *Contemporary Novelists*, even though they have been publishing for decades. Now that their principal publisher has disappeared, their special books are available only from themselves (P.O. Box 4595, Santa Fe, NM 87502-4595).

Berne, Stanley. *Future Language*. NY: Horizon, 1976.

Zekowski, Arlene. *Breaking Images*. NY: Horizon, 1976.

BERNSTEIN, Charles (1950). The most conspicuous of the language-centered poets (∗) who gained a precarious prominence in the 1980s, Bernstein is initially a personable publicist, very much in the tradition of F.T. Marinetti (∗), whom Bernstein resembles in his modes of operation and general impact. Trained at Harvard in philosophy and thus rhetorically skilled, Bernstein's writing is derived from early Clark Coolidge (∗) and middle Gertrude Stein (∗). Though his experiments in poetry are various, there is not enough consistent character, even in the kinds of experimental intelligence, for many (if any) poems published under his name to be immediately recognizable as his, which is to say that they lack signature. The second, perhaps related problem is that few, if any, are individually memorable. Ask even his admirers which poems they like best, and you will find them unable to identify

anything. Thus, Bernstein's career raises the radical question of whether a purportedly major experimental poet can be someone whose *poems*, apart from his or her theories, lack signature and are not remembered. (You can understand why he and his supporters might want to argue "yes.") Nearly all the essays in his book *Content's Dream* (1986) are about himself and his close colleagues. If only to mock the historicism of T.S. Eliot (∗) and Ezra Pound (∗), say, Bernstein discusses no poet earlier than W.C. Williams (∗), analyzing his work only in relation to the group gathered around his inventively titled, photocopied magazine *L=A=N=G=U=A=G=E*. The fact that Bernstein was selected to replace Robert Creeley (1926, whose historical memory is likewise short) in the poetry chair at SUNY-Buffalo perhaps reflects a revolution less less in poetry than in academic standards for poets' acceptability.

Bernstein, Charles. *Content's Dream*. Los Angeles, CA: Sun & Moon, 1986.

BEUYS, Joseph (1921–1986). Beuys was a German sculptor and art-college professor who customarily made his sculptures out of found material, such as bricks or bits of felt. Often, his "sculptures" were assembled and disassembled on the spot, as part of the work itself, by the viewers; thus his art had some of the qualities of a theatrical event. He also exhibited his drawings, which the *Oxford Companion to 20th Century Art* succinctly say "do not for the most part invite assessment by current or traditional standards." The most extraordinary innovation of Beuys's career was getting his image, usually wearing a broad-brimmed hat in a frontal photo, to be far more memorable than his work. "Dressed like an old-fashioned rural worker, his gaze beaming intently from under the brim of his fedora," the American art critic Carter Ratcliff wrote, "Beuys personified a Europe that advances optimistically while maintaining contact with a myth of its pastoral origins." Beuys became much like a car salesman or some other huckster who puts his face in his promotions in lieu of any ostensible product, in Beuys's case art of dubious worth (or else the seductive face wouldn't have been necessary, natch). Some people were impressed by this radical transvaluation of esthetic merchandising; others, including me, were not.

Nonetheless, Beuys got a lot of publicity for his claims of experiencing a miracle in World War II, as though that would give a saintly authority to his subsequent work; but all that was affected, as far as any larger public was concerned, was distribution of pictures of his face.

Ratcliff, Carter. "Ways to Be." In *Breakthroughs*. NY: Rizzoli, 1991.

Tisdall, Caroline. *Joseph Beuys*. NY: Guggenheim Museum, 1979.

BIEDERMAN, Charles (1906). Initially a geometric painter who also made abstract reliefs, in the early 1940s Biederman assimilated Alfred Korzybski's theories about the general structure of language. Moving to Red Wing, Minnesota, he produced a series of self-published books, beginning with his masterwork *Art as the Evolution of Visual Knowledge* (1948), that rank among the most ambitious writing projects ever undertaken by an American artist. His themes were that representational art hampers human invention (especially after the development of the camera) and that his kind of Constructivism (*), which he called Constructionism, should avoid all illusion, including virtual space. Not wishing to deny the possibility of three dimensions, Biederman favored reliefs that are commonly regarded as "bridging" painting and sculpture. One charm of his writings is the assurance with which he proceeds.

Biederman, Charles. *Art as the Evolution of Visual Knowledge*. Red Wing, MN: Charles Biederman, 1948.

BIERCE, Ambrose (1842–1914?). A courageous independent author, of an adventurous character more possible in the United States than in Europe, Bierce belongs to the avant-garde tradition less for his fiction, which was no less conventional when it was written than it is today, than for his aphorisms, which are distinctly original precisely for their dictionary-like form and their cynicism. Indeed, this tart inversion of both the lexicographical and aphoristic tradition gives his concise paragraphs a distinctly modernist signature. Only a 20th-century aphorist could have written: "Faith, n. Belief without evidence in what is told by one who speaks without knowledge, of things without parallel"; or "Politics is the conduct of public affairs for private advantage." To sense how unacceptable Bierce the

American aphorist has been, consider that the W.H. Auden–Louis Kronenberger edited *Book of Aphorisms* (1962) has only one line from Bierce, compared to over thirty-five from Sir Francis Bacon and forty-nine from George Santayana; and that there is nothing by Bierce in *The Concise Oxford Dictionary of Quotations* (1964). Begun in a weekly newspaper in 1881, his "The Cynic's Word Book," as it was originally called, finally appeared under a less appropriate, if more fanciful, name. He disappeared in Mexico in 1913.

Bierce, Ambrose. *The Devil's Dictionary* (1906). NY: Dover, 1958.

BILL, Max (1908). One of the few Swiss artists with an international avant-garde reputation, Bill is a severe geometricist predisposed to mathematical formulas, in his words, "arisen by virtue of their original means and laws—without external support from natural appearances." In 1936, he adopted the term "Concrete Art," which had been coined by Theo van Doesburg (*) only a few years before, as superior to Abstract Art (*), and this epithet was subsequently adopted by other Swiss artists such as Richard Lohse (1902) and Karl Gerstner (1930). As a painter, Bill favored complicated geometries; as a sculptor, austere materials with smooth surfaces, which are sometimes large enough to become monuments. Bill also organized major exhibitions of Abstract Art, beginning with that of his hero Georges Vantongerloo (*). Long a teacher, in the early 1950s Bill was appointed chief of the Hochschule für Gestaltung in Ulm, which became the European center for his kind of Constructivism (*).

Max Bill. Zürich, Switzerland: Gimpel & Hanover, 1963.

BILLINGS, William (1746–1800). A tanner by trade, Billings compensated for a lack of formal education by closely studying the music manuals popular in his time until he could create compositions scarcely less eccentric now than they were then. His song "Jargon," which is filled with dissonances perhaps humorous, is prefaced by a "manifesto" to the Goddess of Discord. He invented a "fuging piece" composed of independent vocal lines that enter one after another and sometimes echo one another. His sometimes humorous pieces ended in a different key from that used at the beginning. Even today, it is hard to believe that such music was composed in 18th-century America. Though some of his hymns became popular ("Chester," "The Rose of Sharon"), Billings died poor, America being no more supportive of its avant-garde then than now; yet his music is continually being "rediscovered." I include Billings here partly to deflect the false academic question of "When did the avant-garde start?" If an 18th-century composer of such initially unacceptable originality is denied the honorific "avant-garde," then consider the silly epithet "proto-avant-garde."

Billings, William. *The Continental Harmony* (1794). Ed. Hans Nathan. Cambridge, MA: Harvard University, 1961.

BIRKHOFF, George D. (1884–1944). While a Harvard professor (and the only tenured one included in this book, so different was Harvard then from now), he proposed in his *Aesthetic Measure* (1933) the formula $M = O/C$, where, "within each class of aesthetic objects," M equals esthetic measure, O is order, and C is complexity. However, one problem with this "quantitative index of [art objects'] comparative aesthetic effectiveness" is that it offers no empirical methods for specifying exact degrees of each factor in the equation. A second problem is its predisposition to measuring unity in variety, which is at best only one of several dimensions of artistic value. Such deductive theorizing, in contrast to the inductive generalizations more appropriate to science, prompted Thomas Munro (✳), a sympathetic observer, to comment in 1946 that quantitative esthetics so far "has dealt less with works of art than with preferences for various arbitrary, simplified linear shapes, color combinations, and tone-combinations." Wait until the next century, maybe.

Birkhoff, George D. *Aesthetic Measure*. Cambridge, MA: Harvard University, 1933.

Eysenck, H.J. *Sense and Nonsense in Psychology*. Baltimore, MD: Penguin, 1958.

BISSETT, Bill (1939). A Canadian poet, Bissett resembles W. Bliem Kern (✳) and Norman Henry Pritchard II (✳) in his eccentric orthography and in performing visually idiosyncratic texts that often depend upon repeating a single phrase,

such as "Awake in th Red Desert," which is also the title of a 1968 collection. However, whereas a repeated phrase becomes something else in Kern and Pritchard, in Bissett it remains audibly the same. In opening one of his chapbooks he accurately outlines his way of working:

Spelling—mainly phonetic
Syntax—mainly expressive or musical rather than grammatic
Visual form—apprehension of th spirit shape of the pome rather than stanzaic nd rectangular
Major theme—search fr harmony
Characteristic stylistic device—elipse
General source—there is nly one. . . i don't feel th I, i e ME writes but that I transcribe indications of flow mused spheres sound

Regarding his orthography, Caroline Bayard has written: "*You* invariably becomes *yu*; most terminal endings in *le*, such as *single*, become *ul*(*singul*); *ought* is transcribed as *ot*; *thought* and *brought* as *thot* and *brot*. All past participles are contracted into *d*'s, such as *sd* for *said* or *movd* for *moved*. Long diphthongs such as the [i:] of *beautiful* are recorded as *beeutiful*. Phonetic representation is obviously what Bissett is striving for."

Self-educated, extremely prolific and self-indulgent, Bissett is an iconoclastic, free spirit. Someday, someone other than himself will collect the gems from a mountain of distinctive work. Not unlike other visual poets, he has also exhibited paintings.

Bissett, Bill. *Selected Poems: Beyond Even Faithful Legends*. Vancouver, Canada: Talonbooks, 1980.

Bayard, Caroline. *The New Poetics in Canada and Quebec*. Toronto, Canada: University of Toronto, 1989.

BLACK MOUNTAIN COLLEGE (1933–1957). Even though it never had more than 100 students at any time in its regular sessions, it was, by the measure of producing avant-garde professionals, the most successful art school ever in America—an American Bauhaus (✳), although unlike the original Bauhaus it did not produce any major styles identifiable with it. One way in which Black Mountain College transcended its prototype was in incorporating music into the curriculum. Among its distinguished alumni are the painters Robert Rauschenberg (✳) and Kenneth Noland (1924), the poets Robert Creeley

(1926) and Jonathan Williams (∗), the filmmakers Arthur Penn (1922) and Stan VanDerBeek (∗), and the sculptors John Chamberlain (∗) and Kenneth Snelson (∗). The reasons for its success appear to have been that the teachers were active professionals (including at various times John Cage [∗], Merce Cunningham [∗], Buckminster Fuller [∗], Josef Albers [∗], Paul Goodman [1911–1972], Franz Kline [∗], and Alfred Kazin [1914]), it taught all the arts (rather than just visual art or just music), and the school was small in size. Though American arts educators are forever trying and even claiming to recreate Black Mountain, the mold must have been broken.

Harris, Mary Emma. *The Arts at Black Mountain College*. Cambridge, MA: M.I.T., 1986.

BLAKE, William (1757–1827). Blake was by many measures the most original British poet, who not only self-published his major illuminated books, but drew upon his training as an engraver to print and hand-color them. He had to self-publish, because no one else could have reproduced his mixtures of picture and script with any fidelity. The next time you hear a wise guy say that only "loser poets" self-publish or self-print (which becomes more possible in this age of photocopying), always cite the counterexample of Blake. It is hard for us to understand now how unacceptable Blake once was. S. Foster Damon (1893–1971), who was my great teacher at college, told me that when he was a graduate student at Harvard after World War I, students typically responded to the mention of Blake's name with "Oh, he was crazy," swiftly terminating all discussion of his work. In response, Damon wrote the first major book on Blake's work in America (in 1924), showing its ultimate consistencies by a systematic study of Blake's idiosyncratic mythology.

More than 150 years after his death (and a half-century after Damon's first Blake book), this British artist's work remains incompletely observed. In his preface to *The Illuminated Blake* (1974), David V. Erdman writes that even after years of lecturing on Blake's "pictorial language," he was shocked to make further discoveries: "that there were numerous animal and human forms of punctuation that I had not noticed at all! Nor was their presence or absence unimportant in the drama of the work, not to mention the choreography." Precisely because Blake's handwritten words and pictures were physically separate (and he neither found shape in words alone nor considered fragmenting language), he is not a progenitor of visual poetry (∗), Pattern Poetry (∗), or Concrete Poetry (∗), as they are understood here. Rather, successors to his example include Kenneth Patchen (∗) and, curiously, photographers such as Duane Michals (∗), among many others, who handwrite highly personal captions to their work. Don't be surprised by Blake's influence on photographers, most of whom are, of necessity, likewise self-printers, at least in beginning the distribution of their work.

Erdman, David V. *The Illuminated Blake*. Garden City, NY: Doubleday Anchor, 1974.

Damon, S. Foster. *The Blake Dictionary*. Providence, RI: Brown University, 1965.

BLANC, Mel (1908–1989; b. Melvin Jerome Blank). Beginning as a musician, Blanc became in the heyday of American radio comedy "the man of a thousand voices," because he could do imitations, at once credible and ironic, of nearly anything that made a distinctive sound. He could do animals; he could do innumerable national accents; for *The Jack Benny Show* he mimicked the sound of a sputtering car—a stunt for which I know no precedent. For cartoons such as Tex Avery's (∗) Bugs Bunny series, Blanc made animals speak English with nuances that reflected their animal nature. In many cartoons, he spoke all the voices, giving each character a sound unique to him, her, or it. Perhaps the surest measure of his extraordinary talents is that, even after his death, there has been no one quite like him, though many opportunities remain for anyone with such verbal dexterity to display his or her stuff.

Blanc, Mel, and Philip Bashe. *That's Not All Folks!* NY: Warner, 1988.

BLANCO, Juan (1920). By common consent the most distinguished Cuban composer of his generation, Blanco is best respected for music that is channeled to many loudspeakers distributed over a space. Little about him appears in English print. Visiting Puerto Rico in 1990, I heard of a tape work designed to be played through speakers distributed throughout a hospital, among other radical departures in the presentation of contemporary music. John Vinton's _Dictionary of Contemporary Music_ describes these works by Blanco: "_Contrapunto espacial I_ for organ with 3 wind groups, 4 percussion groups distributed throughout the space to make triangular and rhomboidal floor patterns (1965–1966); _Poema espacial No. 3,_ 'Viet-Nam,' sound-light composition for 4 tape tracks distributed live to 37 loudspeakers (c. 1968–); _Contrapunto espacial II,_ 'Erotofonías,' for 60 strings divided into 20 groups, 5 percussion groups, guitar, alto saxophone, 3 tape tracks derived from recitations of the Song of Solomon (1968); _Contrapunto espacial IV,_ 'Boomerang,' for 10 actors, 5 instrumental groups, tape (1970);" and so on. My attempts to get more recent information from Cuban cultural agencies here were not successful.

"Juan Blanco." In _Dictionary of Contemporary Music,_ ed. John Vinton. NY: Dutton, 1974.

BLAST (1914–1915). Edited by Wyndham Lewis (*), this was commonly regarded as the most advanced English-language magazine of its time. When its two issues were republished in America in 1981, _Blast_ still looked advanced, if only for typographical deviance greater than that developed, say, at the Bauhaus in the 1920s. Marshall McLuhan (*) paid homage to both the spirit and design of _Blast_ with his _Counterblast_ (1969, designed by Harley Parker), a manifesto about Canadian cultural independence. With its large page size (twelve inches by nine and one-half inches), "bright puce colour" cover, crudely uneven large typefaces, and extra space between paragraphs and graphic "designs," as they were called in the table of contents, _Blast_ represented British Vorticism (*) in both form and content. Never before had so much abstract visual art been presented in a British magazine. Among the contributors to the second number were Gaudier-Brzeska (*), T.S. Eliot (*, with his first British publication), Ezra Pound (*), Ford Madox Ford (1873–1939, under the name F.M. Hueffer), and the editor, who also contributed illustrations. The principal criticism made in retrospect is that Lewis's contributions made everyone else seem less radical, as perhaps they were. Lewis later edited another magazine that had three numbers, _The Enemy_ (1927–1929).

Lewis, Wyndham. _Blast 1_ (1915). Santa Barbara, CA: Black Sparrow, 1981.

———. _Blast 2_ (1915). Santa Barbara, CA: Black Sparrow, 1981.

Hanna, Susan J., "Blast." In _British Literary Magazines: The Modern Age, 1914–1984,_ ed. Alvin Sullivan. Westport, CT: Greenwood, 1986.

BLUM, Eberhard (1940). An accomplished flutist specializing in contemporary music, Blum has also become a great performing speaker of infamously difficult modern texts, such as Kurt Schwitters's (*) _The Ursonate,_ Ernst Jandl's German translation of John Cage's (*) _45' for Speaker,_ and Richard Kostelanetz's (*) _Stringsieben_ (1981), among others. It is not just a matter of other performers not approaching his level; few can even begin to recite these pieces.

Blum, Eberhard. _62 Mesostics re Merce Cunningham._ Therwil, Switzerland: Hat Hut CD 6095, 1991.

———. _Kurt Schwitters Ursonate._ Therwil, Switzerland: Hat Hut CD 6109, 1992.

BODIN, Lars-Gunnar (1935). As a Swede atuned to the international avant-garde from his professional beginnings, Bodin wrote experimental poetry, produced mixed-means theater (*), and interviewed John Cage (*) at length before focusing upon electro-acoustic composition. His tapes have appeared on radio, discs, and in mixed-media presentations that include song, dance, and even visual art. I find in some of his recent works a narrative quality that suggests acoustic fiction, which is to say a story composed entirely of a sequence of sounds. For many years the chief of EMS, the Stockholm Institute of Electro-Acoustic Music, he recently received a state stipend that will keep him an independent artist for the rest of his life.

Bodin, Lars-Gunnar. _Clouds._ Stockholm, Sweden: Fylkingen FLYP 1020, n.d.

BONSET, I.K. See VAN DOESBURG, Theo

BONTECOU, Lee (1931). In his richly insightful essay on "The Aesthetics of the Avant-Garde" (1969), Michael Kirby notes, "It should not be surprising that even the artists who are involved with the avant-garde do not agree among themselves about the artistic worth of particular pieces. (I can think of only two artists whose work as a whole has achieved an even approximately unanimous acceptance, for however brief a time, among my many friends and acquaintances who are artists.)" Though he did not identify them, it was clear to me, reading that essay at the time, that one example was Claes Oldenburg (*) around 1966; the other, he had to tell me, was Lee Bontecou around 1960. Bontecou had made fairly large wall-mounted sculptures, with cloth swatches leading from the bottom edges to a large dark hole in the middle. The image echoed jet-engine exhausts, with an added hint of soft female sexuality; it was radically original for sculpture. What else she has done, or what she has done since, I do not know, because it is rarely seen. She remains an example of an artist whose work was avant-garde for a brief moment in the time of modernist art.

Kirby, Michael. "The Aesthetics of the Avant-Garde." In *Esthetics Contemporary*, ed. Richard Kostelanetz. 2nd ed. Buffalo, NY: Prometheus, 1989.

Ratcliff, Carter. *Lee Bontecou*. Chicago, IL: Museum of Contemorary Art, 1972.

BOOK-ART. See ARTIST'S BOOKS

BORETZ, Benjamin. See RANDALL, J.K.

BORGES, Jorge Luis (1899–1986). A prolific Argentinian writer who was at turns both decidedly avant-garde and self-consciously conventional, Borges was educated in Europe (and buried in Geneva) and always read English in the original. He is best treasured for a group of short stories that he called *Ficciones* (1944; rev. 1961). Written in forms typical of expositions (e.g., a critical article, a librarian's report, a footnoted scholarly essay, a writer's obituary), these fictions portray as they exemplify the primacy of the imagination. One is about a man who discovers in his edition of an encyclopedia an imaginary country previously unknown to him or anyone else. The classic Borges is "Pierre Menard, Author of Don Quixote," which appears to be a sober, straightforward obituary of a writer whose "admirable ambition was to produce [out of his

own head] pages which would coincide—word for word and line for line—with those of Miguel de Cervantes." In one of the shrewdest passages, the narrator shows how the same words that might have been obscure in the 16th century become in the 20th century a meditation on William James. What begins as a complicated joke raises critical questions about authenticity, professional integrity, interpretation, and much else. Like the book it resembles, *Pale Fire* (1962) by his exact contemporary Vladimir Nabokov (*), *Ficciones* broaches subtleties that many readers miss.

Borges, Jorge Luis. *A Reader*. Eds. Emir Rodriguez Monegal and Alastair Reid. NY: Knopf, 1981.

BORY, Jean-François (1938). By the late 1960s, Bory had established himself as the master of visual fiction, which is to say images—in his case customarily including words—that suggest narrative through the transitions from page to page. He made the rectangular page, rather than the sentence or the paragraph, the basic unit of fictional exposition. In "Spot" (1967), for instance, the same image of miscellaneous letters is progressively magnified over seven right-hand pages until the page is all but entirely blackened by just a portion of the middle letter. This inundating image becomes an ironic inversion of the otherwise progressive process of magnification (in a form similar to Eugène Ionesco's [*] ironically linear *The New Tenant*, in which the room fills up with so many objects that the new occupant is smothered). "Spot," like later Bory visual fictions, is neat and clean (and thus graphic) rather than handmade (or painterly).

In his classic collection, *Post-Scriptum* (1970), is a longer visual fiction, a novella if you will, "Saga," in which the phrase *On y va*, or "One Gets By," is superimposed over background photographs. Its twenty-eight pages portray a descent into a mysterious realm, where images are forbidding and unclear, and vaguely perceptible letters are scrambled. The reader then encounters surreal maps where places are renamed as parts of speech, only to emerge at the conclusion with an image identical to that at the beginning. When I first read "Saga," I wrote, "Within less than thirty pages, in sum, is all the material and linear experience of a silent movie or, perhaps, a novel." Two decades later, I am no less impressed. Bory also coedited with the French poet Julien Blane (1942) the seminal periodical *Approches* (1966–1969). More recently, he has exhibited word-based objects.

Bory, Jean-François. *Post-Scriptum*. Paris, France: Eric Losfeld, 1970.

———, ed. *Once Again*. NY: New Directions, 1968.

BOULEZ, Pierre (1925). Why is he here? As a composer, Boulez incorporated avant-garde developments into more familiar structures, always rationalizing what might otherwise be perceived as steps backward with claims to independence and individuality, pretending that his conservative opportunism should be regarded as avant-garde. Nicolas Slonimsky (∗) writes, "He specifically disassociated himself from any particular modern school of music." As a musical director, beginning with *Domaine Musical* in Paris in 1953 and later with the New York Philharmonic (1971–1978) and the BBC Symphony Orchestra, Boulez tends to include avant-garde works without favoring them. That perhaps accounts for why his interpretations of them tend to be neither excellent nor eccentric. In 1974, the French government appointed him chief of the Institut de Recherche & Coordination Acoustique/Musique, called IRCAM (commonly pronounced "ear-com"), which purportedly does something incomparably futuristic, although no one would ever know it from those results publicly released. Boulez's unending assumption of seats of power forces dependent colleagues to be respectful; but once he is deposed, don't be surprised to see his reputation fall and his work forgotten.

Boulez, Pierre. *Notes of an Apprenticeship*. Trans. Herbert Weinstock. NY: Knopf, 1968.

BRANCUSI, Constantin (1876–1957). Apprenticed to a cabinetmaker, Brancusi studied art first in Bucharest and then in Munich, finally reaching Paris in 1904. Though his initial work reflected first the influence of Auguste Rodin (1840–1917), and he then created faces resembling those in Amadeo Modigliani's (1884–1920) work, Brancusi finally concentrated on abstract sculpture, which he thought captured the "essence" of things beneath surface characteristics. After 1910, he made it a point of principle to carve everything himself, rather than employing craftsmen, and to work without prior clay models. A proto-Minimalist (∗), Brancusi favored simple abstract shapes, one barely different from another, sometimes duplicating in polished bronze what he had previously done in wood, or vice versa. He thought of his sculptures as beings—his thin verticals, for instance, as birds, thicker horizontals as fishes. "I live in a desert," he once declared, "alone with my animals." His most ambitious image was the *Endless Column*, whose first version, 23 feet high, was carved in wood in 1920; in Rumania in 1937, he made a cast iron *Endless Column* nearly 100 feet tall. He struck his contemporaries as being in touch with spiritual currents not available to normal people. In spite of his penchant for replicating his work, his work and career have come to represent a standard of integrity.

Geist, Sidney. *Brancusi: A Study of the Sculpture*. NY: Grossman, 1968.

Giedion-Welcker, Carola. *Constantin Brancusi*. NY: Braziller, 1959.

THE BREAD AND PUPPET THEATER (1962–1974). Formed by Peter Schumann (1934), a German refugee then living in lower Manhattan, the company took its name from the dark homemade bread that they shared with audiences after each performance and from the use of stick puppets. The spectacle-styled pieces are usually

Bread and Puppet Theater demonstrating in Greenwich Village against the Vietnam War, 15 March 1965. *Photo © 1993, Fred W. McDarrah.*

narrated by someone who controls the sound, while the puppets, usually quite large, often require several people to manipulate them. I have seen them work in churches as well as outdoors, with and for both adults and children, often recruiting performers on the spot during its tours. The historian Theodore Shank reports that by 1981 Schumann "had created well over a hundred productions." Many of the works are political parables that incorporate mythical figures and biblical images. Typical titles include *The Twelve Stations of the Cross* (1972), *Christmas Story* (1967, 1974), and *A Monument for Ishi—An Anti-Bicentennial Pageant* (1975). After the core group disbanded in 1974, several Bread and Puppet alumni have formed similar companies.

Brecht, Stefan. *The Bread and Puppet Theater.* 2 vols. NY: Methuen, 1988.

Shank, Theodore. *American Alternative Theatre.* NY: Grove, 1982.

BRECHT, George (1926).

Trained in science, he worked initially as a quality-control supervisor and research chemist before becoming an artist. Having studied with John Cage (*) at the New School in 1958 and 1959, he participated in Fluxus (*) activities organized by George Maciunas (*). Brecht's first innovation was a particular kind of minimal text, some of which were headlined "events." Examples read in their entirety: "INSTRUCTION * Turn on a radio./ At the first sound, turn it off." "THREE DANCES: 1. Saliva//2. Pause./ Urination./ Pause.//3. Perspiration." *The Book of the Tumbler in Fire* (1978) is a self-retrospective of works from 1962. Brecht also coedited an unprecedented anthology wholly of paradoxes. The critic Henry Martin (1942) writes: "The internal logic of George Brecht's work is entirely impossible to describe, since his problem as an artist is always and only to work towards an intuitive grasp of the problems of knowledge and awareness that are central to his own individual being in the universe."

Brecht, George. *The Book of the Tumbler in Fire.* Intro. by Henry Martin. Milan, Italy: Multiplitha, 1978.

Hughes, Patrick, and George Brecht, eds. *Vicious Circles and Infinity.* Garden City, NY: Doubleday, 1975.

BRETON, André (1896–1966).

Initially part of Paris Dada (*), Breton broke with Tristan Tzara (*) and became the founder and self-styled "pope" of Surrealism (*). Primarily a novelist and theoretical critic, he was a physically imposing figure whose specialty was manifestos that formulated and reformulated the Surrealist esthetic. As a literary radical, he preached the virtues of "automatic writing" and of the "exquisite corpse," which was his term for collaboration; he edited collections that are still useful, including *Anthologie de l'humour noir* (1940), which finds Surrealist precursors in Jonathan Swift, G.C. Lichtenberg, Charles Fourier, Thomas de Quincey, Edgar Allan Poe, and Lewis Carroll (*), among others, creating the image of an underground tradition dating back several centuries. Authoritarian in temper, Breton convened his followers daily at certain Parisian cafés. Exiled in the U.S. during World War II, he refused to learn English and, after the War ended, returned to France. His negative example perhaps accounts for why the notion of a self-conscious artists' group has never had much currency in the U.S. in general and New York in particular. Breton's creative writings, once so prominent, are now forgotten, his novels no less than his poetry.

Breton, André. *What Is Surrealism?* Ed. Franklin Rosemont. NY: Monad, 1978.

Balakian, Anna. *André Breton.* NY: Oxford, 1971.

BROWN, Bob (1886–1959; b. Robert Carlton B.).

Brown is another one of those early 20th-century avant-garde writers whose reputations were lost in the insufficient assimilation of extreme modernism. (Whenever you hear anyone say that "all avant-garde art has been accepted," point to individuals like Brown, among too many others.) After a peripatetic career as a stock-market speculator, a magazine publisher in South America, and the inventor of a proto-microfilm reader (according to Hugh Ford's *Four Lives in Paris* [1987]), Brown became both a "straight" poet and a visual poet. Perhaps because his work in the former vein resembles the informal poetry popularized by the "New York School" in the late 1960s, I would think that anyone reading it today would find the later work fresher. In addition to publishing his own poetry, he edited *Readies for Bob Brown's Machine* (1931), an anthology that included the more experimental works of many of his contemporaries.

Brown, Bob. *1450/1950.* NY: Jargon-Corinth, 1959.

BROWN, Earle (1926). Echoing both John Cage (*) and Alexander Calder (*), Brown developed in the early 1950s graphic notation that encouraged both aleatory and improvisatory techniques. *Folio* (1952–1953) is actually six compositions in which the performer is instructed to vary the duration, pitch, and rhythm. *25 Pages* (1953) is designed to be played by as many as twenty-five pianists, reading the music pages in any desired order and playing the notes upside down or right-side up. His *Available Forms I* (1961) and *Available Forms II* (1962), respectively for chamber ensemble and full orchestra, contain pages of eccentric (but fixed) notation, or "available forms," which may be sounded in any order, repeated, and combined in varying tempi, all at the spontaneous discretion of the performers. Nicolas Slonimsky (*) finds Brown's music representing "a mobile assembly of plastic elements in open-ended or closed forms. As a result, his usages range from astute asceticism and constrained constructivism to soaring sonorism and lush lyricism." Perhaps because he favors conventional modernist musical instrumentation, Brown's music sometimes sounds serial (*), notwithstanding differences in compositional philosophies.

Brown, Earle. *Times Five* (1963), *Octet I* (1953), *December 1952.* NY: CRI SD 330, 1974.

BROWN, Trisha (1936). One of several distinguished dancers associated with the Judson Dance Theater (*), Brown has made the wit and intelligence of her inquiries the core of her esthetic. Her early works included "equipment pieces" that explored the possibilities of body movements with a variety of supports, such as ropes enabling dancers to "walk" up a vertical wall. For her "accumulation pieces," Brown developed various strategies for gathering movement material. She frequently incorporates improvisational structures in her works. In recent years, her work has depended more upon virtuoso

dance technique, rather than ordinary movements. She has collaborated with Robert Rauschenberg (*) and Donald Judd (*), among others.— Katy Matheson

"Trisha Brown." In *Contemporary Dance*, ed. Anne Livet. NY: Abbeville, 1978.

BRUCE, Neely (1944). Bruce was one of seven harpsichordists in the original performance of John Cage's (*) *HPSCHD* (*) and the sole pianist on William Duckworth's (*) *The Time Curved Preludes.* He has also composed dozens of songs (some of them to texts of the more experimental American poets), a four-act opera about the American Revolution, and an eccentrically eclectic oratorio, *The Plague* (1983), which incorporates a variety of familiar musical styles both high and low, classical and contemporary, in a way that might be classified as "postmodernist" were not the final result, at least in the British group Electric Phoenix's recording, so peculiar. With typical wit, Bruce speaks of his "eclecticism which is occasionally so extreme as to be virtually incomprehensible."

Bruce, Neely. *The Plague* (1983), performed by Electric Phoenix. NY: Mode 20, 1991.

BRYANT, Allan (1931). I include him here not because I know his music but because I don't and should. A Princeton-educated American who has worked mostly in Europe, at times in collaboration with MEV (*), he also made, according to Slonimsky, "*Quadruple Play* for Amplified Rubber Bands utilizing Contact microphones and coordinated with an Audio-controlled Lighting System (1966); *Impulses* for a Variety of Percussion, Concussion, and Discussion Sounds (1967); *X-es Sex*, an intersexual happening with Boots and Balloons (1967); also political works, e.g., *Liberate Isang Yun* (1967), for a Multimilliondecibel Electronic Sound calculated to reach the ears of the South Korean abductors of the dissident Korean Composer," all of which I would have loved to have seen and heard. Such compositional ideas deserve inclusion here if only for their conceptual quality.

Bryant, Allan C. *Space Guitar.* NY: CRI 366, 1977.

BRYARS, Gavin (1943). Bryars has been a mysterious figure, a Briton known only for a few compositions, most of which depend upon the possibilities for repetition offered by audiotape. *Jesus Blood Never Failed Me Yet* (1971) draws upon a London tramp's a cappella singing of an old English hymn, which is looped to repeat itself and then gradually accompanied by strings and other instruments. Because the only recording of it has long been out of print, it has become a favorite of American radio stations that like to surprise their audiences and avant-garde music buffs who like to shock their friends. *The Sinking of the Titanic* (1969) repeats in slightly different ways, for well over an hour, tunes reportedly played by the ship's drowning orchestra. *Media* (1982) is an opera produced in collaboration with the theater artist Robert Wilson (∗). Bryars also founded the Portsmouth Sinfonia whose sublimely comic recordings were produced by Brian Eno (∗).

Bryars, Gavin. *Three Viennese Dances*, performed by the Arditti Quartet (∗). NY: ECM 829484-1, n.d. (c. 1990).

———, et al. *Portsmouth Sinfonia*. NY: Columbia KC 33049, 1974.

BUCKLEY, Lord (1906–1960; b. Richard Myrle B.). Though Buckley's monologues are known to me only from recordings made in the 1950s, I'm prepared to rank him the strongest and most original practitioner of that great American standup art. He becomes, therefore, the precursor of, among others, Lenny Bruce (1925–1966), Richard Pryor (1940), George Carlin (1938), and Joan Rivers (1937), who are all good and sophisticated in different ways. Buckley was a Caucasian of unknown American origins who feigned British manners and yet specialized in rendering a familiar story in the jive (African-American) lingo of his time. Take, for instance, this passage from "The Naz," which retells the life story of the man from Nazareth:

> But, I'm gonna' put a Cat on you, who was the Sweetest, Grooviest, Strongest, Wailiness, Swinginest, Jumpinest, most far out Cat that ever Stomped on this Sweet Freen Sphere, and they called this here Cat, THE NAZ, that was the Cat's name.
>
> He was a carpenter kitty. Now the Naz was the kind of a Cat that came on so cool and so wild and so groovy and so WITH IT, that when he laid it *down WHAM!*. It stayed there! Naturally, all the rest of the Cats say:

"Dig what this Cat is puttin' down! Man! Look at that Cat Blow!"

Because Buckley introduced slang that has since become more familiar, his monologues sound contemporary to a degree that those of, say, Will Rogers (1879–1935) do not. Even today, long after his death, not much is known, or believed, about Buckley's life.

Buckley, Lord. *Hiparama of the Classics*. San Francisco, CA: City Lights, 1980.

———. *His Royal Hipness*. Santa Monica, CA: Discovery 71001, 1992.

BUÑUEL, Luis (1900–1983). Filmmaker who successfully translated Surrealistic (∗) imagery onto the screen. Working originally in conjunction with the artist Salvador Dali (∗), Buñuel created the classic *Un Chien andalou* (*The Andalusian Dog*, 1928) incorporating Freudian imagery such as the putting out of an eye (from the Oedipal myth) and ants crawling out of the center of a hand. In his later career, Buñuel achieved fame as a social critic in his biting satires of middle-class life, such as *The Discrete Charm of the Bourgeoise* (1972) and *The Phantom of Liberty* (1974). In these later films, he continued to use dreamlike narratives, discontinuous story lines, and "shocking" imagery, making him the only practitioner on a large scale of a Surrealist cinema.

Buñuel, Luis. *My Last Sigh*. NY: Knopf, 1983.

BURDEN, Chris (1946). In the early 1970s, Burden commanded respectful attention for a series of one-person performance pieces that customarily involved genuine personal risk: He imprisoned himself in a university locker for five days; he crawled on broken glass; he stuck pins into his stomach; he asked a friend to shoot him in the arm; he lay under a tarpaulin on a Los Angeles street; he had himself chained to the floor between bare electrical wires and buckets of water that, if knocked over, might have electrocuted him; and so on. For *Transfixed* (1974), Burden had himself "crucified" on the back end of a Volkswagen with nails driven through his hands. He subsequently created fuel-efficient, one-person land transports and sculptural pieces with many parts, some of which incorporated political thrusts unpopular in the art world, such as *The Reason for the Neutron Bomb* (1979), in which 50,000 nickels, each with a match on top, symbolize the number of Soviet tanks on Eastern European borders.

Chris Burden: A Twenty-year Survey. Newport Beach, CA: Newport Harbor Art Museum, 1988.

BURGESS, Gelett (1866–1951). Burgess suffered from the most heinous effects of Andy Warhol's (∗) fifteen minutes of fame; he is remembered more for a single four-line verse, "The Purple Cow," written in 1895 ("I never saw a purple cow . . .") than for anything else he ever did. Burgess left his mark on the lexicon of English with such coinages as "blurb," "bromide," and "goup." He even developed a little book of 100 such coinages, and his use of them represents the next step after Lewis Carroll's (∗) "Jabberwocky" toward a fully realized language for new creative expression: "No more tintiddling slubs, like fidgelticks,/ Rizgidgeting your speech, shall lallify;/ But your jujasm, like vorgid gollohix,/ Shall all your woxy meem golobrify!" Early in his career, Burgess edited a few literary magazines, including *Le Petit Journal de Refusées*, printed on discontinued samples of wallpaper. Although primarily a writer, Burgess also enjoyed building things, including nonsense machines. When in 1910 he showed thirty of his watercolors under the title "Experiments in Symbolistic Psychology," critics debated (to no apparent resolution) whether the works were serious art or satirical deflations. The truth of the matter should not be important to us.—Geof Huth

Burgess, Gelett. *Burgess Unabridged: A New Dictionary of Words You Have Always Needed* (1914). Hamden, CT: Archon, 1986.

BURKE, Kenneth (1897). A protean figure, still working in his mid-nineties, Burke long ago produced theoretical treatises that were so "ahead of their time" that they are still in print, continually rediscovered by each new self-conscious group of American critics. He is now as much a hero to Marxists as he was to the text-oriented "New Critics" so prominent in the 1940s and 1950s, and what Burke had to say is not lost on "Deconstructionists" either. The persistence of his influence is amazing, given how thick and digressive, and often abstruse and abstract, his books are. Burke is also a fiction writer and, to no surprise, an experimental poet whose more unusual works include visual poems (∗), called "Flowerishes," and a conceptual poem, "Project for a Poem on [F.D.] Roosevelt," which is really a suggestive prose outline that succeeds, poetically, on its own terms. Though I have read Burke many times and written on him more than once, I'm sure that a subsequent commentator on avant-garde literature will find innovation(s) I've missed.

Burke, Kenneth. *Collected Poems.* Berkeley, CA: University of California, 1968.

Kostelanetz, Richard. "Kenneth Burke at 92." In *The New Poetries and Some Old.* Carbondale, IL: Southern Illinois, 1991.

BURROUGHS, William S. (1914). An American original, the Harvard-educated scion of a family memorialized on a brand of adding machines, Burroughs came late to literature, beginning with an undistinguished memoir, *Junkie* (1953, published under the pseudonym of William Lee). Inspired by his friendship with Allen Ginsberg (∗), he dabbled in formal experiments, some of them done in collaboration with others, including the mixing of passages drawn from different sources, not only in adjacent paragraphs but in the horizontal lines of the page. Some of this experimentation dominates shorter pieces, collected in several books, beginning with *The Exterminator* (1960, with Brion Gysin [∗]); it informs *Naked Lunch* (1959) as well, which remains his masterpiece. Most of Burroughs's other books are indubitably prosaic in style and structure. Some readers admire his rendering of narcotic experiences, including withdrawal; others his dark vision; yet others his homosexual fantasies; all of which have little to do with what makes some of his writing avant-garde.

Burroughs, William. *Naked Lunch* (1959). NY: Grove, n.d.

BURY, Pol (1922). Whereas most kinetic sculptures incorporate quick movements, this Belgian sculptor makes work that moves slowly, very slowly. *The Staircase* (1965) has several circular slanted platforms on a vertical core over six feet high. On each of these platforms are several tiny balls that slowly, ever so slowly, roll down the

Pol Bury, "The Staircase (L'Escalier)," 1965. *Photo: Robert E. Mates © The Solomon R. Guggenheim Foundation, New York.*

inclines; but instead of falling off, they roll back up. The French critic Frank Popper describes earlier work by Bury as being "mobile planes" made of masonite. In contrast to those kinetic sculptors who expose their work's mechanisms, Bury hides his, thus becoming a magician whose tricks remain unknown to even the most inquisitive spectator.

Popper, Frank. *Origins and Development of Kinetic Art.* London, England: Studio Vista, 1968.

BUTE, Mary Ellen (1904–1983). Originally a painter from Texas, Bute assisted the pioneering light artist Thomas Wilfred (*) and collaborated with Leon Theremin (*) on the possibility of sound-light synchronization; she also worked with the musicologist-mathematician Joseph Schillinger (*), all before making her own animated abstract films. Her earliest works, based upon mathematical formulas, display, in Lewis

Jacobs's words, "ever-changing lights and shadows, growing lines and forms, deepening colors and tones, the tumbling, racing impressions evoked by the musical accompaniment." Her later animations were created to music, some of them by filming an oscilloscope screen. She also made a feature-length version of James Joyce's *Finnegans Wake* (1965). None of Bute's films were at last report publicly available.

Bute, Mary Ellen. "Abstronics." In Russett, Robert, and Cecile Starr. *Experimental Animation.* NY: Van Nostrand Reinhold, 1976.

BUTOH (1959). Though this Japanese dance-theater originated in 1959, cofounded by Tatsumi Hijikata (*) and Kazuo Ohno (*), only in the 1980s did Western audiences become familiar with it. Although the term "Butoh" incorporates different approaches, a typical performance might include nearly nude, grimacing dancers in white body paint who are striking grotesque poses or contorting in slow motion, summoning up images of nature, crisis, and ancestral spirits. Some, but not all, of the Butoh performances incorporate improvisation. The stark, dangerous aspect of Butoh was evident in Sankai Juku's *Jomon Sho* (*Hommage to Pre-History*, 1982), in which several performers, nearly nude and covered with white powder, hung upside down at perilous heights. (The risk was real; in 1985, in Seattle, one performer fell to his death.)

Sankai Juku in "Kinkan Shonen," 1984. *Photo © 1993, Jack Vartoogian.*

Although drastically different from such reigning forms as traditional Japanese dance and mainstream Euro-American modern dance, Butoh reflects some of their influence (e.g., the slow-motion esthetic of the Japanese stage and the angst of German Expressonistic [*] dance). Other performers and companies central to the development of Butoh include Yoko Ashikawa (1947) and the company Hakutobo (founded in 1974), Akaji Maro and the company Dai Rakuda Kan (founded in 1972), Ushio Amagatsu and the company Sankai Juku (founded in 1975), Natsu Nakajima (1943) and the company Muteki-sha (founded in 1969), and Min Tinaka (1945).—Katy Matheson

Viala, Jean, and Nourit Masson-Sekine. *Butoh: Shades of Darkness*. Tokyo, Japan: Shufonotomu, 1988.

Butoh: Dance of the Dark Soul. NY: Aperture, 1987.

The Drama Review, T110 (Summer 1986).

Blackwood, Michael. *Butoh: Body on the Edge of Crisis*. NY: Michael Blackwood Productions, 1990.

BUTOR, Michel (1926). First connected to the "nouveau roman" (*) school that emerged in France in the late 1950s, Butor has remained the most experimental of that bunch, working in various innovative ways, including extended criticism. Beginning in the 1960s, after securing a modest fame, he explored alternative structures and typographical possibilities, particularly in *Mobile* (1963), a detailed but elliptical portrait of America as seen not from the road but from the air, as though the author were a helicopter landing here and there. Advancing the art of travel writing, Butor composed a mosaic of impressions along with quotations from historic memoirs (especially François René de Chateaubriand's 18th-century *America*). Later works exemplifying his historical-geographic imagination include *6 810 000 litres d'eau par second (étude stéréophonique)* (1965; *Niagara: A Stereophonic Novel* [1969]) and *Boomerang* (1978; *Letters from the Antipodes* [n.d.]). As a literary artist, Butor has tried to replace two-dimensional linear history with a three-dimensional spatial one.

Butor, Michel. *Mobile*. Trans. Richard Howard. NY: Simon & Schuster, 1964.

BYRUM, John (1952). An experimental poet and publisher, Byrum works with nonsyntactic streams of unrelated words and, more successfully, with visual poems (*) that have one word in larger type, its letters distributed over the page, juxtaposed against other words, mostly in smaller type. "They exist as matrices rather than as linear constructions," he writes about this last innovation. "Each is a multiplex of con- and divergent apparitions, a polyvocality at play in the languaged fields." Byrum also likes rectangular arrays whose letters spell one set of words horizontally, another set vertically—in the tradition of "magic squares." The most illuminating criticism of Byrum's poetry comes from Bob Grumman (*), naturally.

Byrum, John. *Meant*. [Mentor, OH:] 1 2 3 4 5 6 7 8 9, 1987.

CAGE, John (1912–1992). He was one of the few individuals of whom it can be said, without dispute, that had he not existed, the development of more than one art would have been different. A true polyartist (*), Cage produced

John Cage preparing a piano, c. 1960s. *Photo: Ross Welser, courtesy Artservices/Lovely Music.*

distinguished work in music, theater, literature, and visual art. As a de facto esthetician, he had a discernible influence upon the creation of music, theater, the visual arts, and, to a lesser extent, literature and social thought. His principal theme, applicable to all arts, was the denial of false authority by expanding the range of acceptable and thus employable materials, beginning with non-pitched "noises," which he thought should be heard as music "whether we're in or out of the concert hall."

Though some consider Cage an apostle of "chance," I think of him as an extremely fecund inventor who, once he transcended previous conventions, was able to realize a wealth of indubitably original constraints. The famous "prepared piano" (∗), which prevented the emergence of familiar keyboard sounds, was merely the beginning of a career that included scrupulously alternative kinds of musical scoring, idiosyncratically structured theatrical events, and unique literary forms. Perhaps because Cage never doubled back, never dismissing his earlier works as unacceptable, his art remained challenging and generally unacceptable to the end. In the last months of his life, he completed a ninety-minute film whose visual content was a white screen violated by various shades and shapes of gray.

When I first began following Cage's activities, three decades ago, no one, but no one, received so many persistently negative comments, not just in print but in collegial conversations. When invited to give the 1988–1989 Charles Eliot Norton lectures at Harvard, perhaps the most prestigious appointment of its kind, he delivered statements so barely connected that few professors returned after Cage's initial lecture! As an anarchist from his professional beginnings, he worked, as much through example as assertion, to eliminate authority and hierarchy, even in his life, never accepting a position that might give him cultural power (as distinct from influence), never composing any work that requires an authoritarian conductor or even a lead instrumentalist who stands before a backup group. When Cage accepted the Norton position that gave him a title elevating him above the rest of us humans, I asked him what it was like being a Harvard professor. "Not much different from not being a Harvard professor," he replied, true to his politics.

Not unlike other avant-garde artists, Cage made works, in his case in various media, that are much more or much less than art used to be. Though the Minimal (∗) pieces should not be slighted, in my considered opinion the greatest Cage works are his Maximal (∗) compositions: *Sonatas and Interludes for Prepared Piano* (1946–1948) is his longest and most exhaustive exploration of his first musical invention. *Williams Mix* (1953) is a tape collage composed of thousands of bits, intricately fused onto six tapes that should be played simultaneously, so that the result is an abundance of sounds within only several minutes. In *HPSCHD* (∗) (1969), Cage filled a 15,000-seat basketball arena with a multitude of sounds and sights, and *Europera* (∗) (1987) draws upon 19th-century European opera for musical parts, costumes, and scenarios that are then distributed at random to performers in a professional opera company. Given my bias toward abundance, my favorite Cage visual art is the sequence of Plexiglas plates that became *Not Wanting to Say Anything About Marcel* (1969); my favorite Cage text, the Harvard lectures that became the long poem *I–VI* (1990).

In his notorious silent piece, the superficially much, much less 4'33" (1952), he became an avatar of conceptual art (∗). By having the distinguished pianist David Tudor (∗) make no sound in a concert otherwise devoted to contemporary piano music, Cage framed four minutes and thirty-three seconds of a pianist's silence to suggest that the inadvertent sounds within the auditorium constitute the "musical" experience and, by extension, that all sounds, whether intentional or not, can be considered music. (One strain of conceptual art consists of demonstrations or statements that convey radical esthetic implications.)

Cage has also revolutionized musical scoring (eventually collecting an anthology of *Notations* [1969] that mostly reflects his influence), introducing graphic notations and prose instructions in place of horizontal musical staves. The most extraordinary of his own scores is the two-volume *Song Books (Solos for Voice, 3–92)* (1970), which contains, in part through length and number, an incomparable wealth of alternative performance instructions. He was also among the rare artists whose statements about his own work were more true and insightful than his critics' writings.

Cage, John. *Silence*. Middletown, CT: Wesleyan University, 1961.

———. *I–VI*. Cambridge, MA: Harvard University, 1989.

Kostelanetz, Richard. *Conversing with Cage*. NY: Limelight, 1988.

———. "The Keystone of the Cagean Canon (1989)"; "*HPSCHD*: Environmental Abundance (1969)"; "John Cage, 75, Writes First, 'Great American' Opera (1988)"; and others. In *On Innovative Music(ian)s*. NY: Limelight, 1989.

———. "Two Ways of Polyartistry (1990)." In *On Innovative Art(ist)s*. Jefferson, NC: McFarland, 1992.

———, ed. *John Cage* (1970). 2nd ed. NY: Da Capo, 1991.

———, ed. *John Cage: Writer*. NY: Limelight, 1993.

———, ed. *Writings About John Cage*. Ann Arbor, MI: University of Michigan, 1993.

CALDER, Alexander (1899–1976). The son and grandson of sculptors, but also an alumnus of the Stevens Institute of Technology, Calder was a great inventor who saw that the early modern avant-garde idea of kinetic art (∗) could be realized without motors. Calder is most closely associated with art that moved through the balancing and counterbalancing of weight within the piece itself, which he called mobiles. Initially Calder used simple wooden shapes, most of them painted, which are delicately suspended from wooden dowels. In lieu of physical space typical of previous sculpture, a mobile creates virtual space, which is to say that it assumes a lot more space than it physically takes up. Of all of Calder's many enthusiasts, none is more curious, or perceptive, than the French writer Jean-Paul Sartre, who wrote: "A mobile does not suggest anything; it captures genuine living movements and shapes them. Mobiles have no meaning, make you think of nothing but themselves. They are, that is all; they are absolutes. There is more of the unpredictable about them than in any other human creation." These Calder sculptures can be divided into those that hang from supports and those that rest on the ground. Having become known for "mobiles," he had to give another name to his stationary sculptures, "stabiles," which seems an ironic joke on himself.

Calder, Alexander. *An Autobiography with Pictures*. NY: Pantheon, 1966.

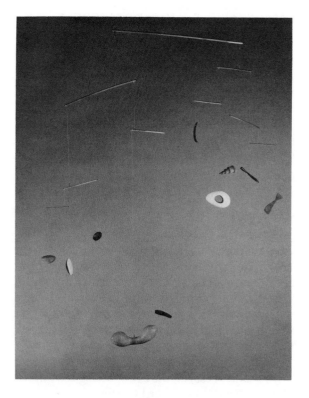

Alexander Calder, "Mobile," c. 1943–1946. *Photo: David Heald © The Solomon R. Guggenheim Foundation, New York.*

Marder, Joan M. *Alexander Calder*. NY: Cambridge University, 1992.

CALDIERO, A.F. (1949). Sicilian-born, New York-reared, Caldiero has created distinguished sound poetry and performance, as well as visual art, most of it as elaborate expositions of spiritual themes that draw upon his European background. "The sacred and the secular have been at the very core of my formative years," he writes. "For me this twin presence is a pivot between sideshow and temple, between entertainer or jester and priest. In the process of making and presenting a work, this precarious position is the opening by which I can hope to glimpse the Real." He moved to Utah around 1980 and has since been exhibiting and performing mostly in and around Salt Lake City.

McEntire, Frank. *Dreams and Shields: Spiritual Dimensions in Contemporary Art*. Salt Lake City, UT: Salt Lake Art Center, 1992.

CALLAHAN, Michael. See USCO

CAMINI, Aldo. See VAN DOESBURG, Theo

CANADA COUNCIL (1958). A culturally superior counterpart to our own National Endowment for the Arts (∗), this makes the NEA look amateur perhaps because of the Canadian recognition that the best work must be supported if culture is to survive. Should you not believe me, just compare its publicly available annual reports to those of the NEA.

Canada Council, P.O.Box/Case postale 1047, Ottawa, Canada K1P 5V8

CAPTAIN BEEFHEART (1941, b. Don Van Vliet). The personally mysterious Beefheart and his ever-changing backup Magic Band were favorites of '60s rock critics even as they achieved only marginal commercial success. Befriended by Frank Zappa (∗), Beefheart resembled him in his bizarre sense of humor, unusual subject matter for pop music, and anarchistic noisy "accompaniments." Beefheart also forecast later pop stars who often assumed alter egos (e.g., David Bowie, among others) and presaged the ear-splitting assaults of "heavy metal."—Richard Carlin

Captain Beefheart. *Trout Mask Replica*. Burbank, CA: Straight 1053, 1969.

CARDEW, Cornelius (1936–1981). In that vacuum that is avant-garde culture in Great Britain, Cardew filled a big balloon, less for his own originality than for his association with advanced developments elsewhere in the world. The son of a noted potter, he sang in the chorus at Canterbury Cathedral from 1943 to 1950 and studied, from 1953 to 1957, at London's Royal Academy of Music (granting a lifetime imprimateur unknown elsewhere), before assisting Karlheinz Stockhausen (∗) and writing music, mostly for piano, in the serial (∗) tradition. Coming under the contrary influence of John Cage (∗) in the 1960s, Cardew then practiced and preached graphic scores and indeterminacy, cofounding AMM, an improvisatory group that resembled the Americans in MEV (∗). By the 1970s, he was writing, mostly for nonmusicians, several compositions that acknowledged the influence of Mao Zedong, incidentally renouncing his bourgeois past and, need we say, the influence of Stockhausen, but still winning attention as a former R.A.M. golden boy.

Cardew, Cornelius. *Scratch Music*. London: Latimer, 1972.

CARLOS, Wendy (1939, b. Walter C.). Educated first in physics and then in music composition, Carlos released *Switched-on Bach* in 1968, which was the first album of "Electronic Music" (∗) to sell a million copies. Working with an early monophonic Moog (∗) synthesizer, Carlos laid individual lines of notes on a multi-track (∗) tape recorder. He then adjusted the levels of the various tracks (or lines) in creating (literally mixing them down onto) a two-track, stereophonic tape. It was painstaking and pioneering work, unlike anything anyone had done (or thought about doing) in Electronic Music before; but one result, especially in comparing Carlos's interpretation of J.S. Bach's *Brandenburg* concerti to traditional instrumental recordings, was revealing contrapuntal lines that were previously muffled. Carlos subsequently produced other albums, some likewise original interpretations of classical warhorses, others of his own music (e.g., the soundtrack to Stanley Kubrick's *A Clockwork Orange* [CBS PC-31480]), none of which were quite so innovative or successful. Born Walter Carlos, he became Wendy in the early seventies, discussing this gender reassignment at length in a *Playboy* interview (May 1979).

Carlos, Walter. *Switched-on Bach*. NY: Columbia MK-7194, 1968.

Darter, Tom, compiler. *The Art of Electronic Music*. NY: Morrow, 1984.

CARROLL, Lewis (1832–1898; b. Charles Lutwidge Dodgson). A university lecturer in mathematics who was also an ordained minister, Carroll wrote *Alice's Adventures in Wonderland* (1865), the first children's book to have enough cultural resonance to interest sophisticated adult readers as well. Martin Gardner (∗), among others, has interpreted the book as portraying more than three dimensions and similarly sophisticated themes. *Through the Looking-Glass and What Alice Found There* (1872) continues the story, with a greater sense of what adults might appreciate. *The Hunting of the Snark* (1876) is a highly metrical nonsense poem, written well before similar efforts by Kenneth

Koch (∗), among others. After you've read Carroll, whose complete literary works fit into a single volume, check out the editions intelligently annotated by Martin Gardner.

Carroll, Lewis. *The Works*. London: Paul Hamlyn, 1965.

CARTER, Elliott (1908). Educated in English literature before he turned to music composition, Carter was, until his forties, one of many Americans working in "neoclassicism," which was in the 1930s and 1940s an encompassing term for tonal music that acknowledged traditional forms (purportedly in reaction to 19th-century romantic Expressionism [∗]). With his first *Piano Sonata*, he began to explore overtones (sounds inadvertently produced by notes in combination) and also the ways in which these overtones create their own semblance of melodies. Carter's *Sonata for Cello and Piano* (1948) incorporates a musical idea that he would subsequently develop: the individuality of each instrument that keeps them from blending together completely. This idea was developed in a series of string quartets that rank among the strongest in contemporary music (1952, 1959, 1971). These abolish key signatures and introduce the innovative technique since called "metrical modulation," which depends upon continual changes of speed. That is to say, his rhythms are neither regular nor syncopated but continually rearticulated until the sense of perpetual rhythmic rearticulation becomes itself a major theme of the piece. Such music realizes a textual intensity that reflects the complexity of serial music (∗) without following Schoenbergian rules. Indeed, precisely because Carter's best music must be reheard even to begin to be understood, it could be said that he composes not for the live concert hall but for reproductive media, at first records and then cassette tapes and now compact discs, which enable listeners to hear an initially inscrutable work as often as they wish.

Edwards, Allen. *Flawed Words and Stubborn Sounds: A Conversation with Elliott Carter*. NY: Norton, 1971.

Kostelanetz, Richard. "Elliott Carter (1968)." In *On Innovative Music(ian)s*. NY: Limelight, 1989.

CASTILLEJO, José Luis (c. 1930). Among the most extreme books ever to come my way are *The Book of Eighteen Letters* (1972), *El Libro de las Dieciocho Letras* (1972), and *The Book of*

i's (1969), all of them well-produced hardbacks. The first and the second are essentially similar, differing only in their title and dedication pages, which are in English in the first and in Spanish in the second. Both are dedicated to Walter Marchetti, a principal of the Spanish group Zaj (∗). Each page consists of fifteen lines of type that runs continuously from margin to margin, with thirty letters in each line. The lines on each page are composed of only two letters, mixed so that no letter appears more than twice in succession. Therefore, the book's closing line reads: "k g k g k g k g k k g k g k g k g g k g k g k g k g g k g k."

Accompanying the book is a separate sheet with Castillejo's English-language manifesto entitled "Modern Writing," which declares, not unreasonably, that "words, syllables, stories, sounds, psychology, music, etc. are no longer needed in writing; advanced writing can do without intermediary elements," which certainly don't appear in *Eighteen Letters*. "The freedom achieved by writing (as a 'medium') may perhaps become," he continues, "an inspiration (a 'metaphor') of what could be achieved elsewhere (in the 'reality'), independently and without imitation." This statement gives a political dimension to books authored by a man who was at the time working in Bonn (Germany) for Generalissimo Franco's embassy.

The Book of i's likewise has pages almost nine inches high and five and three-quarter inches wide. On most of them, centered, is a lowercase "i," in sum five-eighths inches high, its dot very visible. Many of the book's pages, sometimes five in succession, are completely blank. On the verso of the title page appears "Copyright 1969." In this book was enclosed another separately printed manifesto, likewise in clear English, that opens: "My books are to mark the beginning of a true writing." Together, these volumes constitute such an impressive avant-garde debut that I regret to report that nothing further from Castillejo has come my way, not even any news, for two decades now. I don't even know where he is.

Castillejo, José Luis. *The Book of i's*. N.p.: n.p., 1969.

CELENDER, Don (1930). Celender's characteristic exhibitions have been horizontal eye-level mountings of the responses to cunning questionnaires that he has sent to circumscribed groups of people. Sometimes these responses are also bound into eight and one-half inch by eleven inch books published by his New York gallery. To get serious answers, he depends upon the pseudoauthority of academic stationery to inform recipients that he is indeed a chaired professor with a Ph.D. The most successful is still *Museum Piece* (1975), for which museums around the world were asked to send, for "a research project dealing with museum architecture" a photograph of "your loading dock, or receiving area." The request was open and yet unprecedented enough to prompt officials of each museum to respond in a revealing manner. One wrote that it has no "loading dock" because its collection is permanent; another asks Celender for funds to hire someone to photograph its dock. (No fool he, Celender wanted only their letter.) The reply from the National Museum of Korea might seem tasteless if Celender had not reproduced the accompanying letterhead and signature as well: "We removed new building in 1972. But this museum has not any receiving area. The loading dock is imperfection. Anyway inveloped photos are loading dock from outside to inside. Dock is basement."

Celender constructs shrewd response-devices that encourage people (and institutions) to display themselves merely by providing answers that they think are "normal" to them; but by assembling their separate responses into a single context, he not only makes found art (*) that is uniquely identifiable with his name, but he allows his respondents to contrast and augment one another in a burgeoning irony that is marvelously funny, a rare quality in the visual-arts world.

Celender, Don. *Museum Piece*. NY: O.K. Harris (383 West Broadway, 10012), 1975.

CÉLINE, Louis-Ferdinand (1894–1961; b. L.-F. Auguste Destouches). He was a notable French writer and, by all reports, a humane doctor, in spite of his disagreeable Fascist politics and bursts of despicable anti-Semitism. Seriously wounded in the head during World War I, he suffered for the rest of his life from vertigo, chronic migraine, partial paralysis of his right arm, and a constant buzz in his ears. Out of this deranged mentality, he concocted a literary style of unprecedented

splenetic frustration and despair, whose truest subject is not society but his damaged head:

> My great rival is music, it sticks in the bottom of my ears and rots . . . it never stops scolding. . . it dazes me with blasts of the trombone, it keeps on day and night. I've got every noise in nature, from the flute to Niagara Falls . . . Wherever I go, I've got drums with me and an avalanche of trombones . . . for weeks on end I play the triangle . . . On the bugle I can't be beat. I still have my own private birdhouse complete with three thousand five hundred and seven birds that will never calm down. I am the organs of the Universe.

As his translator Ralph Manheim (1907–1992) points out, the slight innovation of three dots, "which so infuriated academic critics at the time, . . . mark the incompleteness, the abruptness, the sudden shifts of direction characteristic of everyday speech." Those who can read his Parisian slang, itself new to literature, testify that Céline's prose is even more extraordinary in the original.

Céline, Louis-Ferdinand. *Death on the Installment Plan* (1933). Trans. Ralph Manheim. NY: New Directions, 1966.

CENDRARS, Blaise (1887–1961; b. Frédéric-Louis Sauser). Born in Switzerland of a Scottish mother, Cendrars wrote in French and lived a mercurial cosmopolitan life. Creating the persona of himself as a man of action, he concocted a propulsive, rhythmically abrupt literary style that informed both his poetry and his prose. To put it differently, self-possessed and up-to-date, he made much, in style as well as content, of the mania of being so self-possessed and up-to-date. "I have deciphered all the confused texts of the wheels and I have assembled the scattered elements of a most violent beauty/That I control/And which compels me," he writes in *La Prose du Transsibérien*.

Cendrars, Blaise. *Selected Writings*. Ed. Walter Albert. NY: New Directions, 1966.

CHAIKIN, Joseph (1935). See OPEN THEATER

CHAMBERLAIN, John (1927). Taking from David Smith (*) a taste for industrial materials and a competence in welding, Chamberlain made sculptures composed initially of iron pipes and then of

crushed automobile parts, usually preserving their original industrial colors. Even with materials as resonant as cars, he finds formal qualities rather than social comment, the compositional syntax of his sculpture reflecting de Kooning's (∗) interpretation of Cubism (∗). Though he later worked with other materials, including urethane and fiber glass, and then galvanized steel and aluminum, nothing else Chamberlain ever did was quite as stunning and innovative as his "junk sculpture."

Waldman, Diane. *John Chamberlain*. NY: Guggenheim Museum, 1971.

CHAMPION, Charles L. (1972). A poet-publisher residing in Tucson, AZ, Champion is mentioned here to illustrate my belief that the idea of the avant-garde survives, even among artist/writers born in the 1970s. Champion has published his visual poems and asyntactical poems, as well as chapbooks by others, under the imprint "eXpeRimeNtaL pReSs" and in a periodical called *eXpeRimeNtal (basEmeNt)* (1991– ; 3740 N. Romano Rd., A-191, Tucson, AZ 85705). Long may he thrive.

CHATHAM, Rhys (1953). His characteristic compositions group many of the same instruments together, producing a sea of sounds reflecting the texture and sonorities of each instrument. With some humor, Chatham claims that music from a brace of electric guitars should be classified as "rock," that from a gang of saxophonists as "jazz," and that from strings as "classical." In part because the resulting sounds depend upon seeing their origins, Chatham's music is invariably more successful in live concerts than on discs. A New Yorker by birth, he has recently been living in France.

Chatham, Rhys. *Die Donnergötter*. Berlin, Germany: Dossier ST 7538 (Koloniestr. 25A, D-1000/65), 1987.

CHICHERIN, Aleksei Nikolaevich (1889–1960). Initially Futurist (∗) in his orientation, Chicherin became the founder and theoretician of Russian Literary Constructivism in the early 1920s, attempting to apply the principles of Constructivism (∗) (practical application of avant-garde achievements in the visual arts to design and architecture) within the literary sphere. The main

principle was "maximal concentration of function on units of the construction" ("We Know," 1922). His most significant works are *Fluks* (1922), in which he introduced a system of phonetic transcription and diacritical marks to convey the precise features of idiolect, and his contributions to the important Constructivist collection *Change of All* (1924). His works in *Change of All* initially employ a transcription like those in *Fluks*, which are designed to ensure the accurate performance of a compact text, but step by step the recitational cues become more elaborate, resembling musical notation, while the text becomes briefer. In the final stages of this development, verbal elements give way entirely to geometric figures that can be interpreted symbolically. His booklet *Kan-Fun* (1926) elaborates on his theories of Constructivist functionalism. However, a split developed between Chicherin and his less radical, more practical colleagues in Literary Constructivism, who expelled him from their association in 1924. He spent the latter part of his life quietly working as a book designer.—Gerald Janecek

Janecek, Gerald. "A. N. Chicherin, Constructivist Poet." *Russian Literature* XXV (1989).

CHILDS, Lucinda (1940). Noted throughout her career for her cool but dramatic performing presence, Childs contributed to the innovative spirit of the Judson Dance Theater (∗). In *Carnation* (1964), she made surprising use of props such as a colander that she placed on her head like a weird hat and foam hair curlers and sponges that she both stuffed into her mouth and attached to her colander-hat. Her later choreography reflects Minimalism (∗). In the evening-length *Dance* (1979, in collaboration with music by Philip Glass [∗] and film and decor by Sol LeWitt [∗]), eight dancers seem to be in perpetual motion as they sweep through the space. In technically based but minimally ranged movements that seem highly repetitious but are full of subtle changes, their carriage is elegant, their legs extend and point (but do not lift high), and they move buoyantly (but close to the ground, eschewing, say, spectacular leaps).—Katy Matheson

Kreemer, Connie. "Lucinda Childs." In *Further Steps: Fifteen Choreographers on Modern Dance*. NY: Harper & Row, 1987.

CHOPIN, Henri (1922). A Frenchman who emigrated to England in 1968, this Chopin published the periodical *Ou*, which included a record, of mostly text-sound (∗), along with printed texts. His own compositions display hysterical articulations and overlapping speech-sounds, thanks to elementary multi-tracking (∗); they are, by common consent, unforgettable. His 1979 book-length history of sound poetry suffers from an egocentrism that makes it no more reliable as criticism than as history (see Claudia Reeder's review in my anthology *Aural Literature Criticism* [1981]), although the book comes with two audiocassettes containing works by Michel Seuphor (∗), François Dufrêne (∗), Brion Gysin (∗), Sten Hanson (∗), and Bernard Heidsieck (∗), among others, whose audio realizations are unavailable elsewhere.

Chopin, Henri. *Poésie sonore internationale*. Paris, France: Jean-Michel Place, 1979.

CHRISTO (1935; b. C. Jarachev). Born in Bulgaria, Christo emigrated first to Paris, where he took a wife whose enterprise other artists and their wives envy, and then to New York. His original sculptural idea, in the late 1950s, involved wrapping familiar objects in cloth, initially, I suppose, to give them esthetic value by destroying their original identity. Instead of moving on to other ideas, he has expanded wrapping to monumental and, at times, comic proportions, including at various times wrapping an exhibition space in Berne, Switzerland, a section of

Christo and his wife, Jeanne Claude, in their Crosby Street Loft in front of a wrapped sofa, 29 December 1976. *Photo © 1993, Fred W. McDarrah.*

Australian coast, islands in Miami's Biscayne Bay, and the Museum of Contemporary Art in Chicago. He also built a fence running twenty-four miles long in California in 1976. Christo's installation of hundreds of oversize umbrellas in Southern California and Japan (1991) became notorious, particularly after several umbrellas toppled during storms, endangering local populations. Though some of his projects are unrealized, including one long in progress for the Berlin Reichstag and another for New York City's Central Park, Christo's proposals, presented in drawings, benefit from arriving in the wake of conceptual art (∗).

Bourdon, David. *Christo*. NY: Abrams, 1971.

CHRYSSA (1933; b. C. Vardea Mavromichali). Born in Athens, Chryssa studied in Paris and San Francisco before embarking in 1956 on a precocious exhibition career with works using letter forms for their design possibilities rather than any specific communication. Initially preceding Andy Warhol (∗) in the repetitive use of popular imagery, she turned to dark Plexiglas boxes filled with neon lamps programmed to turn themselves on and off. Inspired by New York's Times Square, whose vulgarity she found poetic, she made *Times Square Sky* (1962) and *Gates to Times Square* (1964–1966). The latter work is ten feet tall, built of steel, aluminum, and Plexiglas, in the shape of a three-dimensional triangle, supporting stacked rows of metal letters amid flowing curves of neon script, likewise enclosed in gray Plexiglas boxes. In works she calls "luminates" she reflects her birthplace, which to my recollection has more neon light than any other city.

Restany, Pierre. *Chryssa*. NY: Abrams, 1977.

CINEMASCOPE (c. 1925). Invented by the French physicist Dr. Henri Chrétien (1879–1956), this is the name for a film projection system that produces a far wider image than that of conventional film. Thirty-five-millimeter film is shot with an anamorphic lens that squeezes the wider image into the standard film ratios, and then, to be seen properly, this compressed image must be projected through a compensating lens that extends it horizontally. CinemaScope was first used commercially for *The Robe* (1953) and contributes, in my opinion, to the excellence and character of such films as David Lean's *Lawrence of Arabia* (1962) and Stanley Kubrick's *2001* (*). When shown on television or videotapes, such films generally are visually compromised unless reproduced in the so-called "letterbox" format with their tops and bottoms blackened.

Lean, David. *Lawrence of Arabia* (1962). Revised print, letterbox format. Burbank, CA: RCA/Columbia Pictures Home Video, 1989.

CINERAMA (c. 1938). Invented by Fred Waller (1886–1954), this is the name for a three-screen projection system whose images are recorded by three synchronized cameras. The synchronized films were then projected with their seams aligned onto a curvilinear screen that filled the audience's horizontal vision. *This Is Cinerama* (1952) was one of the great moviegoing experiences of my youth, establishing my taste for physically expanded film. The success of that film prompted the use of CinemaScope (*), which offered the economic advantage of requiring only one projector at the esthetic expense of a flatter, less extended image; but every time I remember any multiple projection, I wish that I could see *This Is Cinerama* again. It is unfortunate that it is no longer available, some of its esthetic terrain superseded by more recent developments such as IMAX (*).

Belton, John. *Widescreen Cinema*. Cambridge, MA: Harvard University, 1992.

ČIURLIONIS, Mikalojus (1875–1911). A trained Lithuanian composer who worked in Warsaw as a choral conductor from 1902 to 1909 and whose Symbolist music resembles that of his contemporary Alexander Scriabin (*), he developed theories of "tonal ground formation" that presaged serial (*) music. A proto-polyartist (*), Čiurlionis later became a painter of cosmic, Symbolist landscapes, often in series, with such musical titles as *Sonata of the Stars* and *Prelude and Fugue*. *Sea Sonata* (1908–1909), for instance, has panels with titles such as "Allegro," "Andante," and "Finale." The third number (1914) of the St. Petersburg magazine *Apollon*, as well as a 1961 issue of the Brooklyn journal *Lituanus* (Vol. 7,

no. 2), were entirely devoted to the composer-painter who, like Kandinsky (*), explored analogies between the two arts. One principal scholar on Čiurlionis has been Vytautas Landsbergis (1932), who, after editing his letters, writing monographs, and introducing his visual art, became president of Lithuania in 1990. Čiurloinis died young of tuberculosis.

Landsbergis, Vytautas. *Pasaulio sutv°erimas* [Creation of the World, with text in several languages]. Vilnius, Lithuania: Vaga, 1971.

———. *Sonatos ir fugos* [Sonatas & Fugues, with text in several languages]. Vilnius, Lithuania: Vaga, 1971.

CLOSE, Chuck (1940). Continuing the most familiar tradition of human portraiture, Close has created innovative paintings that depend upon making faces large, say nine by seven feet, and thus capturing a wealth of facial detail. Initially working in black and white before turning to color, he nonetheless kept his method of subjecting a photograph to a grid of varying light and dark areas that were then transferred to canvas. Especially in prints, watercolors, and pastels,

Chuck Close, "Self Portrait," oil on canvas, 1991. *Photo: Bill Jacobson, courtesy The Pace Gallery.*

Close customarily reveals his alternative processes by leaving the grid visible. Sometimes his blurred images resemble computer printout, increasing the impression of impersonality. Though working with sizes conducive to heroic sentiment, Close still presents individuals objectively. Severely crippled by a spinal-artery collapse in his late forties, he has recently been making grid-portraits with brighter colors and with less realistic images.

Lyons, Lisa, and Robert Storr. *Chuck Close*. NY: Rizzoli, 1987.

COBBING, Bob (1920). A sometime civil servant, farmer, teacher, and manager of a London literary bookshop, Cobbing has for many years been the principal mover and shaker in British experimental literature, first as a prolific poet, then as a strong performer especially of his sound poems, but also as the founder of the chapbook-publishing Writers Forum (since 1963) and coeditor of the occasional periodical *Kroklok* (1971), which was at its beginnings among the most avant-garde literary magazines in England. If only for his organizational work with the Poetry Society, the National Poetry Centre, and the Association of Little Presses, Cobbing has been a model literary citizen.

Not unlike other strong poets who survive apart from career-managing publishers/agents, he has published scores of books, in addition to audiotapes. His texts-for-print include linear poems, sound poems, self-obliterating texts, classic Concrete Poetry (*), pseudo-alphabets, pseudo-words, and much, much else. Perhaps the best one-volume introduction to his work is *bill jubobe* (1976), which the poet selected in collaboration with a colleague. Cobbing has also performed improvisations with other sound poets and instrumentalists. To gauge the scope of his work, consider this statement from 1975: "At present I am working on single-voice poems; multi-voiced poems; poems based on words; poems not using words or even letters; poems for electronic treatment on tape; poems for 'voice as instrument and instruments as speaking voices'; poems as scores for dance or drama, invitations to act out an event in space, sound, and choreography." In his prolific eclecticism, Cobbing very much resembles his American contemporary Jackson Mac Low (*).

Cobbing, Bob. *bill jubobe*. Toronto, Canada: Coach House, 1976.

Mayer, Peter, ed. *Bob Cobbing & Writers Forum*. Sunderland, England: Ceolfrith Press, 1974.

COCTEAU, Jean (1889–1963). Cocteau was one of those figures who flirt with the avant-garde without ever joining it, perhaps because he was too self-conscious of his early celebrity to be courageously radical, mostly because he simply lacked originality. He once told Francis Picabia (*), "You are the extreme left, I am the extreme right." As a slick polyartist (*), Cocteau wrote plays and directed films, in addition to exhibiting drawings that, in Lucy R. Lippard's (*) phrases, "remained firmly Picassoid, dry, coquettish, over-refined, and elegant." In his pretentious compromises, as well as his position in French culture, Cocteau very much resembles the composer Pierre Boulez (*).

Brown, Frederick. *An Impersonation of Angels*. NY: Viking, 1968.

Steegmuller, Francis. *Cocteau: A Biography*. Boston, MA: Atlantic Monthly, 1970.

COINTET, Guy de (1940?–1983). After working as a visual artist's assistant, Cointet exhibited, usually in a Los Angeles gallery, drawings whose imagery consists only of sans-serif capital letters and numbers. Many of these drawings of superficially disconnected signs were actually codes that, though he was French, could be "translated" into English. When collecting some of them into books, Cointet usually incorporated a semantically clear English sentence into a text that was otherwise unintelligible. For instance, one page in *A Few Drawings* (1975) opens: "IN A FRENZY OF CURIOSITY THE HAPPY MOTHER TRIES HARD TO SEE: 107 325/ 290 344 58726 956 325/ 418 932 69408 571 823. . . ." One of his earlier books has, even for its title, just signs resembling parentheses, tilted at various angles to become an uncompromised pseudo-language, punctuated only by occasional staves of music. Sometimes he would hire professional actors to perform his texts. Though a skeptic might say such work "is easy to do," I've not seen anyone do anything similar since. Cointet died young of a mysterious illness.

Cointet, Guy de. *TSNX C24VA7ME: A PLAY BY DR HUN*. Venice, CA: Sure Co (76 Market Street), 1974.

———. *Espahor ledet ko uluner!*. N.p. (Los Angeles?): n. p. (self?), n.d. (c. 1976).

COLEMAN, Ornette (1930). Born in Texas, self-taught as a musician, Coleman around 1960 caused a stir in the world of jazz (*) music comparable to that of Igor Stravinsky (*) in classical music decades before him. His innovation was instrumental independence, which is to say that the soloist performs independently of any pre-assigned harmonic scheme, and that everyone in his group performs with scant acknowledgment of the percussionist's beat. Called "free jazz" (*), Coleman's improvisations gained a strong following in the sixties.

Coleman, Ornette. *The Shape of Jazz to Come*. NY: Atlantic SD 1317, 1959.

COLLAGE. The earliest fine-art examples of collage depended upon the incorporation of real objects, such as bits of newspaper or other mass-produced images, into the picture's field, the objects at once contributing to the image and yet suggesting another dimension of experience. Initiated by Cubists (*), the principle was extended by Futurists (*), Dadaists (*), and Surrealists (*), always in ways typical of each. Collage was, by many measures, the most popular innovation of early 20th-century art. Later collages depended upon using separate images for ironic juxtapositions; others functioned to expand the imagery available to art. The collage principle influenced work in other arts, including sculpture, where assemblage (*) is three-dimensional collage; photomontage (*); music, where the post–World War II development of audiotape facilitated the mixing of dissimilar sounds; and video (*), even though that art did not begin until the late 1960s. Max Ernst's *La femme 100 têtes* (1932) is a book-length narrative composed of collages. The Czech artist Jiří Kolář (*) (whose last name is pronounced to sound like "collage") has extended the principle, often in ironic ways, to

works he calls "crumplage," "rollage," "inter-collage," "prollage," "chiasmage," and "anti-collage." Another innovation in this tradition is the composer Mauricio Kagel's (*) "Metacollage," where all the materials for his mix come from a single source (e.g., Beethoven's music, for example, or 19th-century German culture). I believe that collage, as an easily adopted innovation, had become dead by the 1960s, which is to say that, although collages continue to appear, none of them, especially in visual art, are strikingly original or excellent.

Janis, Harriet, and Rudi Blesh. *Collage*. Philadelphia, PA: Chilton, 1967.

COLOMBO, John Robert (1936). Very much an odd man out in Canadian poetry, a prolific writer and editor whose achievements are so numerous they are foolishly taken for granted, Colombo has worked with a variety of unusual poetic strategies. His first books were found poetry (*), each dependent upon making art from esoteric texts found in his unusually wide reading; his term at the time was "redeemed prose." The Canadian critic Douglas Barbour writes that Colombo's *The Great Cities of Antiquity* (1979) "is a collection of found poems in a dizzying variety of modes, based on entries in the famous Eleventh Edition of the *Encyclopedia Britannica*. Written in 1969, it is possibly Colombo's most extreme collage, a veritable textbook on the many formal experiments of modern and post-modern poetry." Of the poems written out of his own head, consider "Secret Wants" in *Neo Poems* (1971). A full-time bookmaker, writing and editing volumes for publishers both large and small (no false snob he), Colombo has also edited several anthologies of poetry and of science fiction, including *New Direction in Canadian Poetry* (1970, perhaps the only English-language anthology of avant-garde poetries aimed at high-school students), in addition to compiling such pioneering compendia as *Colombo's Canadian References* (1976), *Colombo's Book of Canada* (1978), and *The Dictionary of Canadian Quotations* (1991), which all have the distinction of being books that nobody else could do, even if they tried.

Colombo, John Robert. *Neo Poems*. Vancouver, Canada: Sono Nis, 1970.

————. *Selected Poems*. Windsor, Canada: Black Moss, 1982.

————. *Off-Earth*. Toronto, Canada: Hounslow, 1987.

COLOR-FIELD PAINTING (c. 1950). The idea is to use color apart from drawing, apart from shape, and apart from shading, until it acquires a purely visual status. However, in contrast to monochromic painting, most color-field work involves at least two colors, which prompt surprising retinal responses, such as ambiguous figure-ground reversals, usually along the sharply delineated border between the colors. The last fact prompted the epithet "hard-edge abstraction," which is also used to describe this style of painting. One master is Ellsworth Kelly (1923), who was also among the first to paint on non-rectangular canvases. In my living room is a Suzan Frecon (1941) painting, in which a deeply repainted black rectangle sits in the center of a very white larger canvas. Stand at least fourteen feet away from this work and stare at it intently, and you will observe that the black rectangle starts to shimmer. (And the shimmering won't stop!)

Ellsworth Kelly. NY: Whitney Museum of American Art, 1982.

COMBINE. See RAUSCHENBERG, Robert

COMPUTER (c. 1945). Information is entered, by one of many possible channels, into a machine that converts it into digital impulses that can then be manipulated in a variety of ways. Such information may be words, as many of us do with word processors; it may also be pictures or sounds. In music, computers now enable composers to create on their cathode-ray tubes works that can be transformed, thanks to digital-to-analog conversion, into audiotape that may be played back through conveniently available transducers. In literary composition, computers had less influence until the 1980s, with the development first of the affordable "personal computer" that could sit on your desk next to, or in place of, the typewriter, and then of multi-path hypertexts (*) that are best "read" not in print but on a cathode-ray tube.

In visual art, the influence of the computer has been more problematic, in part because it works so much better with abstraction than representation. Look at the catalogue of the first institutional computer-art exhibition, *Cybernetic Serendipity*, organized in 1968 by Jasia Reichardt for the Institute of Contemporary Arts in London, and you'll be struck by the lack of interesting art. This exhibition partially accounts for the anonymous author of the entry on computer art in *The Oxford Companion to Twentieth-Century Art* (1981) declaring, partly out of ignorance, "By the mid 1970s no visual art of significant quality had been produced with the aid of computers." By the 1980s, exhibitions were filled with computer graphics different in content but lacking individual style, all in contrast to the distinguished computer-assisted art of Manfred Mohr (*). My own opinion, evident occasionally in this book, is that computers have been most successful in film (particularly by Stan VanDerBeek [*]) and then video animation, but the latter happens to be the artistic use to which I put them.

Goodman, Cynthia. *Digital Visions: Computers and Art.* NY: Abrams, 1987.

Reichardt, Jasia, ed. *Cybernetic Serendipity*. London, England: Studio International, 1968.

CONCEPTUAL ARCHITECTURE (forever). This is my coinage for architectural proposals that were never realized, and were in some cases never intended to be realized, but have sufficient clarity and originality to be exhibited. The classic modernist example is Vladimir Tatlin's (*) *Monument to the Third International* (1920), which had considerable influence on subsequent architecture, even though it was never realized. A more recent example was Buckminster Fuller's (*) proposal to put a geodesic dome over an entire city. Alison Sky and Michelle Stone compiled a marvelous anthology of comparable plans drawn from American history.

The critical question posed by the exhibition or publication of such work is whether the proposal can have an esthetic status comparable to its realization and thus whether a comprehensive critical appraisal of, say, an architect's work should include those images that were never realized along with those that were. If, like myself, you affirm the former position, then you must consider extending the principle to other cultural areas. If only to raise the possibility of doing so, I self-published a 140-page book *Unfinished Business* (1991), collecting grant applications, anthology outlines, and proposals for both books and media compositions, all of which went unrealized for reasons beyond my control, raising the question whether such "unfinished business" belongs to my intellectual record.

Sky, Alison, and Michelle Stone. *Unbuilt America*. NY: McGraw-Hill, 1976.

Vostell, Wolf, and Dick Higgins, eds. *Fantastic Architecture*. NY: Something Else, 1970.

Kostelanetz, Richard. *Unfinished Business: An Intellectual Nonhistory*. NY: Archae Editions, 1991.

CONCEPTUAL ART (c. 1960). The radical idea is that a statement, which need not be in words, can generate an esthetic experience, if properly interpreted. The classic forerunner, conceived nearly a decade before the epithet was coined, is John Cage's (*) oft-called "silent" (actually noise) piece, *4'33"* (1952), in which, in a concert situation, pianist David Tudor (*) plays no notes for the required duration of four minutes and thirty-three seconds. By framing the performance situation, Cage suggested that all the miscellaneous noises heard in that space during that duration constitute "music." It logically follows that any unintended noise, even apart from the *4'33"* enclosure, could provide esthetic experience.

Much depends upon context. A later, charming example was Claes Oldenburg's (*) "inverted monument" for New York City, for which he hired professional grave diggers to excavate and then fill in a large rectangular hole behind New York's Metropolitan Museum (rather than, say, a garbage dump, which would be contextually less resonant).

Self-conscious conceptual art, which arrived in the late 1960s, customarily took such forms as written instructions, esthetically undistinguished photographs, scale models, maps, or documentary videotapes, all of which are theoretically intended to suggest esthetic experiences that could not be evoked in any other way. The sometime economist Henry Flynt (1940) is commonly credited with originating the radical notion in his 1961 essay "Concept Art," which he defined as "first of all an art of which the material is concepts, as the material of e.g. music is sound."

Among the pioneering practitioners were Douglas Huebler (1924), Joseph Kosuth (1944), Lawrence Weiner (1940), John Baldessari (1931), the German-American Hans Haacke (*), and Frenchman Daniel Buren (1938). In Sol LeWitt's (*) classic phrase, "In conceptual art, the ideas, or concept, is the most important aspect of the work."

Flynt, Henry. *Blueprint for a Higher Civilization*. Milan, Italy: Multhipla, 1975.

Vries, Gerd de, ed. *Über kunst/On Art*. Cologne, Germany: DuMont, 1974.

CONCRETE POETRY. Concrete Poetry aims to reduce language to its concrete essentials, free not only of semantic but syntactical necessities. It is often confused with sound poetry (*) and visual poetry (*) (which are, respectively, the enhancement of language primarily in terms of acoustic qualities and the enhancement of language primarily through image), but is really something else. The true Concrete Poem is simply letters or disconnected words scattered abstractly across the page or a succession of aurally nonrepresentational (and linguistically incomprehensible) sounds. In his or her use of language, the poet is generally reductive; the choice of methods for enhancing language could be expansive. Unfortunately, the earliest anthologies of Concrete Poetry did more to obscure than clarify the issue of its differences. Among its truest practitioners are Ian Hamilton Finlay (*), Dom Sylvester Houédard (*), Haroldo and Augusto de Campos (1929, 1931), Décio Pignatari (1927), Max Bense (1910), Pierre Garnier (1928), Mary Ellen Solt (*), Paul de Vree (1909–1984), Heinz Gappmayr (1925), and Eugen Gomringer (*). What had first seemed puzzling to readers, not to mention critics, has recently inspired a growing scholarly literature.

Solt, Mary Ellen, ed. *Concrete Poetry: A World View*. Bloomington, IN: Indiana University, 1970.

Williams, Emmett, ed. *An Anthology of Concrete Poetry*. NY: Something Else, 1967.

McCullough, Kathleen. *Concrete Poetry: An Annotated International Bibliography*. Troy, NY: Whitston, 1989.

CONCRETISM. See FOUND ART

CONRAD, Tony (1940). His film *The Flicker* (1966) has such classic simplicity you wonder why no one thought of doing it before—a film consisting entirely of black frames and white frames, alternating in various patterns and frequencies, causing the eye to see nonexistent colors and even images. The structure appears to be that black frames, comparatively sparse at the beginning, become more frequent in the middle only to become sparse again. The sometime critic Sheldon Renan speaks of "forty-seven different patterns of black and white combinations." As the experience of continuous sharp reversals produces peculiar effects on the viewer's sensibility, the implicit point is that even the most minimal abstract film can be very moving, if not emotionally then at least viscerally. Meanwhile, the soundtrack's buzzing noise that resembles an airplane motor becomes faster and faster while fluctuating slightly in volume throughout. No summary can duplicate that experience of actually seeing *The Flicker*.

Renan, Sheldon. *An Introduction to the American Underground Film.* NY: Dutton, 1967.

CONSTRUCTIVISM (c. 1920s). In the decade after World War I, this term was, like Futurism (*), adopted by two groups, one in Russia, the other in Western Europe, whose aims were sufficiently different to distinguish between them. Coming in the wake of the Bolshevik Revolution, most Soviet Constructivists were Abstract (*) artists participating in social change with applied projects that nonetheless reflected their esthetic heritage. Thus, the historical exhibition *Art Into Life* (1990) included large-scale graphics, environments, photomontage, stage designs, and architectural proposals along with paintings and sculptures. The key figure in this exhibition was Aleksandr Rodchenko (*), whose environmental *The Workers Club* (1925) included unusual chairs and reading tables. Also in this exhibition was Vladimir Tatlin's (*) *Letatlin* (1932), which is the model for a flying machine; El Lissitzky (*); and various works by Gustav Klucis (*), a Latvian slighted in previous surveys. (This exhibition did not include Antoine Pevsner [1886–1962] and Naum Gabo [*], brothers who objected to utilitarian art, or the mercurial Kazimir Malevich [*], who was strictly speaking not a Constructivist.) Once cultural policy

tightened in Russia, culminating in the purges of the 1930s, Russian Constructivism disintegrated. Klucis died in a World War II concentration camp and Tatlin died a decade after of food poisoning, in relative obscurity.

European Constructivism, sometimes called International Constructivism, favored conscious and deliberate compositions that were supposedly reflective of recently discovered universal and objective esthetic principles. Thus, its artists made scrupulously nonrepresentational Abstract constructions that differed from the other avant-gardes of the earlier 20th century in favoring simplicity, clarity, and precision. Among the principal participants at the beginning were Theo van Doesburg (*), Piet Mondrian (*), and Hans Richter (*); the principal magazines were *De Stijl* (*) and Richter's *G*. Among the later International Constructivists were Michel Seuphor (*), Georges Vantongerloo (*), Joaquin Torres-García (*), Charles Biederman (*), and Moholy-Nagy (*). The last artist introduced Constructivist ideas to the Bauhaus (*), where he taught from 1923 to 1928; and as the publisher of the pioneering Bauhaus books, Moholy-Nagy issued a collection of Mondrian's essays in 1925 and Malevich's *The Non-Objective World* in 1927. When Naum Gabo moved to England, he collaborated with the painter Ben Nicholson (1894–1982) and the young architect J.L. Martin in editing *Circle* (1937), an impressive anthology subtitled *International Survey of Constructive Art*. Constructivism came to America with art-school teachers such as Moholy-Nagy and Josef Albers (*), the former in Chicago after 1938, the latter first at Black Mountain College (*) from the middle 1930s to the late 1940s and then at Yale. Constructivism survives in certain kinds of Minimal geometric sculpture; in the mobiles of George Rickey (*), who incidentally wrote an excellent history of the movement; in certain strains of color-field (*) painting; in the Constructivist fictions of Richard Kostelanetz (*); and in the magazine *The Structurist* (1958), which the American-Canadian artist Eli Bornstein (1922) edits out of the University of Saskatchewan.

Andrews, Richard, and Milena Kalinova, eds. *Art Into Life*. NY: Rizzoli, 1990.

Rickey, George. *Constructivism: Origins and Evolution.* NY: Braziller, 1967.

COOLIDGE, Clark (1939). Very much a progenitor of "language-centered" poetry (∗), Coolidge began, in *Flag Flutter & U.S. Electric* (1966), with forays into post-Ashberyian (∗) poetic structuring in which he attempted to realize semblances of literary coherence without using such traditional organizing devices as meter, metaphor, exposition, symbolism, consistent allusion, or declarative statements. His most avant-garde work appears in *Space* (1970), including an untitled poem beginning "by an I" that contains individually isolated words no more than two letters long, scattered across the space of the page (which then appeared to be Coolidge's primary compositional unit). These words are nonetheless related to one another—not only in terms of diction and corresponding length (both visually and verbally) but also in spatial proximity. *Suite V* (1972), published as a chapbook, is yet more outrageously spare, containing only pairs of three-letter words in their plural forms, with one four-letter word at the top of the page and the other at the bottom of otherwise blank pages.

Coolidge has published many other books in the past two decades, all of them with smaller presses (as one measure of his continuing integrity), but none of them is quite as avant-garde or as consequential as his opening moves. One of the thicker collections, *Solution Passage: Poems 1978–81* (1986), contains elaborations of Noam Chomsky's "colorless green ideas sleep furiously," which is to say phrases that seem syntactically acceptable without making semantic sense. In the late 1960s, Coolidge also worked as the drummer for Serpent Power, one of the more culturally sophisticated rock groups, which was headed by the San Francisco poet David Meltzer (1937).

Coolidge, Clark. *Space*. NY: Harper & Row, 1970.

———. *Suite V*. NY: Adventures in Poetry, 1972.

———. *Solution Passage: Poems 1978–81*. Los Angeles, CA: Sun & Moon, 1986.

COPY CULTURE (c. 1980s). One important aspect of our culture is the numerous technological opportunities, chiefly xerography (∗), that allow *individuals* to produce and reproduce "publications" cheaply. Because xerography allows the quick and simple reproduction of images, it encourages distribution to others. The most important concept in copy culture is that an individual, without the prerequisite of massive amounts of capital, can copy and distribute art, literature, or political ranting without resorting to a "publisher" as an intermediary. The advantages of this system of personal dissemination are present not only in xerography, but also in audiotape, videotape, computer disks and, to a lesser degree, microfiche. Precisely because such methods of reproduction are more accessible to the individual, they make possible the unfettered distribution of even the most avant-garde, or culturally unacceptable, arts.—Geof Huth

CORNELL, Joseph (1907–1973). An American original, without formal art education, Cornell made small boxes with cutaway fronts—a form closer to reliefs and a theatrical proscenium than sculpture in demanding a view from the frontal perpendicular perspective—and meticulously filled these boxes with many objects not usually

Joseph Cornell, "Untitled (The Pharmacy)," c. 1942. *Photo: Carmelo Guadagno and David Heald © The Solomon R. Guggenheim Foundation, New York.*

found together in either art or life. "Their imagery includes mementos of the theater and the dance, the world of nature and that of the heavens," writes the historian Matthew Baigell. "Cornell's boxes also often contain 19th century memorabilia (especially those made during the 1940s, of ballerinas)." Miniaturized tableaus, rather than true sculptures, these boxes combine the dreaminess of Surrealism (∗) with the formal austerity of Constructivism (∗) and the free use of materials typical of Dada (∗). Each enclosure seems, not unlike a Jackson Pollock (∗) painting, to represent in objective form a particular state of mind in a moment of time, as well as an immense but circumscribed world of theatrical activity. Cornell often produced works in series, exploring themes through variations. Though others have made excellent tableaus, no one else ever did boxed sculpture so well.

Ashton, Dore. *A Joseph Cornell Album* (1974). NY: Da Capo, n.d.

CORRIGAN, Donald (1943). One of the most audacious conceptual artists (∗), for professional courage the equal of Elaine Sturtevant (∗), Corrigan exhibited charts of power in the art world, particularly in his hometown. In his *Tree of Modern Art in Washington, DC* (1972), a detailed drawing measuring twenty-three by eighteen inches, Corrigan graphs relationships and sympathies among the commercial galleries on one side and the nonprofit institutions on the other in a brilliant and accurate way, adding art critics, art schools, and constellations of avowedly independent individuals, by his documentation making the invisible visible, which is what visual art has always done. Rarely permitted to exhibit, Corrigan gave up visual art by the 1980s; he was recently working, like Herman Melville and Clement Greenberg (∗) before him, for the U.S. Customs Service.

Kostelanetz, Richard, ed. *Essaying Essays* (1975). NY: Archae, 1981.

CORTÁZAR, Julio (1914–1984). An Argentine who lived mostly in Paris, whose books were initially published everywhere besides his two home countries, Cortázar made formal alternatives a recurring subject. He prefaces *Rayuela*

(1963; *Hopscotch*, 1966) with the advice that it "consists of many books, but two books above all. The first can be read in a normal fashion, and it ends with Chapter 56." He then suggests an alternative route beginning with chapter 73 and continuing with "1-2-116-3-84-4-71-5-81-74. . ." that not only includes certain chapters twice but directs the reader as far as chapter 155. The American edition did surprisingly well, perhaps because the cover of its 1967 paperback edition promised "life/love/sex." Although other books of his have appeared in English, I've yet to find any translations of the more experimental short pieces in *La vuelta al día en ochenta mundos* (1967) and *Ultimo Round* (1969), both of which were published in Mexico.

Cortázar, Julio. *Hopscotch*. Trans. Gregory Rabassa. NY: Pantheon, 1966.

COWELL, Henry (1897–1965). If Aaron Copland (1900–1990) was the great mainstream arts politician of his time, distributing patronage to a wide variety of composers who would remain personally indebted to him, Cowell was the great radical mover and shaker, helping establish the reputations of a large number of American composers, beginning with Charles Ives (∗).

As a teenager, Cowell wrote and performed piano pieces that incorporated what he called tone-clusters, which are produced by striking groups of adjoining notes simultaneously, customarily not with one's fingers but a fist, a palm, or even a whole forearm. Within the composition, the clusters became huge blocks of sound moving up and down the keyboard, sometimes becoming atonal clouds that complemented the melodic lines. In the early 1920s, while still in his own mid-twenties, Cowell directly attacked the strings of a grand piano—plucking, striking, sweeping, and dampening them as though they were on a harp; sometimes stroking them with a china darning egg. His classic *Aeolian Harp* required that one hand works the piano keyboard, holding down keys, while the other "plays" the strings until the sound of the depressed keys decays. In the 1930s, he collaborated with Leon Theremin (∗) in constructing a keyboard percussion instrument that he called the "rhythmicon," a precursor of modern drum machines, to create music with overlapping rhythmic patterns.

As a prolific composer, Cowell worked with a variety of ideas, some of them more radical than others, beginning with alternative ways of striking the piano. Some pieces from the 1930s have parts of varying lengths that he said the performers may assemble to their tastes, even excluding or repeating sections. Others permitted improvisation in certain sections. Later pieces drew upon Americana and modal folk tunes. Late in his career, Cowell discovered Asian musics and their instruments, less for quotations than for sonorities and rhythms unavailable in the West. Typical pieces from this period combine an Asian soloist with a Western orchestra. Some mellifluous works composed just before his death reflect Persian music.

As a musical theorist, Cowell wrote between 1916–1919 *New Musical Resources* (not published until 1930), whose theme was expanding the musical palette. He edited and partially authored *American Composers on American Music: A Symposium* (1933), which was the first survey of native achievement. With his wife Sidney Robertson Cowell (1903), he published the first book on *Charles Ives and His Music* (1955), which remains a model of its introductory kind. Cowell was often the first to write extended articles on emerging American composers; so that nearly every composer's bibliography, from Carl Ruggles (1876–1971) to John Cage (∗), includes a reference to Cowell. As an advocate of American composers, he founded New Music not only to publish their works but to record them. Among the composers issued under the New Music imprint were Ives, Ruggles, and Virgil Thomson (1896–1989); it even included distinguished Europeans such as Arnold Schoenberg (1874–1951) and Anton Webern (∗).

As a generous teacher, Cowell directed musical activities intermittently at New York's New School from 1928 to 1963 and also taught at Columbia from 1951 to 1965; he gave private lessons to John Cage, Lou Harrison (1917), and George Gershwin (1898–1937). Sent to San Quentin prison on a trumped-up sex charge in 1937, he spent four years giving music lessons to his fellow inmates and organizing a band. As both a teacher and as a publicist, he preceded current opinion in insisting that Americans pay greater attention to "music of the world's peoples," as he called it, directing the recording of world music for Folkways in the early 1950s.

Cowell, Henry. *New Musical Resources* (1930). NY: Something Else, 1969.

———, ed. *American Composers on American Music: A Symposium* (1933). NY: Ungar, 1962.

Mead, Rita. *Henry Cowell's New Music 1925–1936.* Ann Arbor, MI: UMI Research, 1981.

Hays, Sorrel. "The Legacy of Henry Cowell." In *The Piano Music of Henry Cowell.* Washington, D.C.: Smithsonian/Folkways SF 40801, 1992.

CRAWFORD [SEEGER], Ruth (1901–1953). The wife of noted musicologist Charles Seeger, the mother of the folksingers Peggy S. (1935) and Mike S. (1933) and stepmother to Pete S. (1919), she composed several advanced chamber works of a quality that has become more appreciated over time. The most famous is her *String Quartet* (1931), whose slow movement, according to Nicolas Slonimsky (∗), "anticipates the 'static' harmonies and 'phase shifts' prominent in minimal music." The pianist-composer Sorrel Hays (∗) praises Crawford's 1920s piano preludes for "structural spareness divorced from nineteenth-century harmonies and climactic structures." After her family's move to Washington, D.C., in 1935, Crawford's music succumbed to the political fashions of the time and her family's folkloristic interests. She reportedly transcribed several thousand American folk songs from recordings at the Library of Congress and made exquisite piano accompaniments for hundreds of them. Some of the latter appear in two childrens' songbooks that are still in print.

Crawford, Ruth. *String Quartet*, recorded by the Arditti String Quartet (∗). NY: Grammavision R21S-79440, n.d.

CRESHEVSKY, Noah (1945). Trained in music composition at the Eastman School of Music and Juilliard, Creshevsky became by the 1980s an audiotape artist using familiar devices of processing and editing in distinguished ways. *In Other Words* (1976) enhances the distinctive voice of John Cage (∗). His *Highway* (1978), which is *musique concrète* (∗) of and about familiar Americana, becomes an acoustic trip through the aural equivalent of Pop Art (∗). His ten-minute *Strategic Defense Initiative* (1986), its title alluding to President Reagan's "Star Wars" proposal, draws upon the soundtrack of Bruce Lee movies to satirize sadism. Another Creshevsky departure involves giving instrumentalists a score composed not of traditional musical notes but only of words.

Creshevsky, Noah. *Man and Superman.* NY: Centaur 2126 (8867 Highland Rd, #206, Baton Rouge, LA 70808), 1992.

CROSBY, Harry (1898–1929). Commonly regarded as the epitome of the self-destructive 1920s poet (and vulgarly exploited for that myth in a Geoffrey Wolff biography), Crosby also wrote some "mad" inspired prose, and at least one great visual poem (∗) that will ensure his literary immortality, which Jerome Rothenberg reprints in *Revolution of the Word* as "Photoheliograph (for Lady A.)."

Crosby, Harry. *Shadows of the Sun: The Diaries.* Ed. Edward Germain. Santa Barbara, CA: Black Sparrow, 1977.

CROWDER, Al (1904–1981). Crowder was a radio personality who invented the imaginary company Orville K. Snav and Associates and its line of BunaBs. Each BunaB was actually an example of primitive conceptual art (∗). Conceived as a form of humor (which is the most conceptual art can hope for), these BunaBs were generally small pieces of machinery that Crowder-Snav distributed with arcane and ridiculous instructions and warranties. The most famous BunaB (produced in an edition of 40,000) was two pieces of wire taped together and stored in an empty clarinet reed case. The customer who returned its registration card would be greeted with a long, rambling letter explaining the difficulties of Orville K. Snav's life at that particular time. Two other BunaBs were interesting examples of praecisio: # 3, "The Man's Between Shave Lotion," which was an empty plastic bottle whose contents were to be reconstituted by adding water; and # 5, a completely blank record, designed to be listened to while watching television.—Geof Huth

Dickson, Paul. *Family Words: The Dictionary for People Who Don't Know a Frone from a Brinkle.* Reading, MA: Addison-Wesley, 1988.

CUBISM (c. 1907–1921). Cubism was the creation of the painters Georges Braque (1882–1963) and Pablo Picasso (∗), working separately in Paris around 1907. Art historians customarily divide its development into two periods: Analytic Cubism (1907–1912) and Synthetic Cubism (1912–1921). The signature of Cubism is the rendering of solid objects—whether they be musical instruments, household objects, or human forms—as overlapping "cubes" or planes, giving the illusion of portraying simultaneously several different perspectives and, by extension, different moments in time. Regarding its radical implications, the art historian Robert Rosenblum (1927) wrote:

> For the traditional distinction between solid form and the space around it, Cubism substituted a radically new fusion of mass and void. In place of earlier perspective systems that determined the precise location of discrete objects in illusory depth, Cubism offered an unstable structure of dismembered planes in indeterminate spatial positions. Instead of assuming that the work of art was an illusion of a reality that lay behind it, Cubism proposed that the work of art was itself a reality that represented the very process by which nature is transformed into art. In the new world of Cubism, no fact of vision remained absolute.

The rigorous Analytic phase represented Cubism at its most austere or pure, as painters eschewed traditional subject matter and a full palette in the course of dissecting light, line, and plane, incidentally draining emotional content from painting. Thus, a typical Cubist still life from this period might consist of several intersecting planes portrayed in various neutral, nearly monochromic tones (often different shades of brown). Synthetic Cubism, by contrast, introduced objects found in the real world, such as newspaper clippings, wallpaper, ticket stubs, or matchbooks, which were attached to the canvas. Rosenblum comments, "Perhaps the greatest heresy introduced in this collage concerns Western painting's convention that the artist achieve his illusion of reality with paint or pencil alone." Cubist painters introduced an additional visual irony by simulating these objects, thus introducing trompe l'oeil effects by creating false woodgrains or wallpaper patterns, making it appear as if fragments of these objects were part of the canvas. A fuller palette and more sensuous texture were other hallmarks of Synthetic Cubism.

The Cubist movement was perhaps as important as an intellectual revolt against "pretty" art as for its actual products. Many Cubist paintings inspired heated debate not only among art critics but among the general public as well. The most famous single example was Marcel Duchamp's (∗) *Nude Descending a Staircase, No. 2* (1912), which was the star of the New York Armory Show (∗), although it could be said that Duchamp departed from Cubism as quickly as he entered it. The power of Cubism is evident not only in such immediate successors as Futurism (∗) and Vorticism (∗), especially in Wyndham Lewis's (∗) illustrations for Shakespeare's *Timon of Athens* (1913 or 1914), but also in the careers of such older artists as Piet Mondrian (∗) and Kazimir Malevich (∗), and then, more than a generation later, in the best work of Willem de Kooning (∗), among other major painters.—with Richard Carlin

Rosenblum, Robert. *Cubism and Twentieth-Century Art* (1961). NY: Abrams, 1977.

CUBO-FUTURISM (c. 1909). This term arose in Russia to distinguish native work from European Cubism (∗). Whereas the work of Natalia Goncharova (1882–1962) and Mikhail Larionov (1882–1964) favored a post-Picasso (∗) modernist primitivism based upon Russian peasant art, the brothers Burliuk (Vladimir [1886–1916] and David [1882–1967]) preferred more urban subjects. The innately mercurial Kazimir Malevich (∗) used this epithet for works he submitted to exhibitions in 1912 and 1913. Vladimir Markov's *Russian Futurism* (1968) devotes an entire chapter to Cubo-Futurism in poetry.

Gray, Camilla. *The Russian Experiment in Art.* London, England: Thames & Hudson, 1962.

Markov, Vladimir. *Russian Futurism.* Berkeley, CA: University of California, 1968.

CUMMINGS, E.E. (1894–1962). The avant-garde Cummings is not the author of lyrics reprinted in nearly every anthology of American verse or of a name entirely in lowercase letters, but of several more inventive, less familiar poems. Appreciation of this alternative Cummings should begin with such poetic wit as "Gay-Pay-Oo" for the Soviet secret police (G.P.U); his use of prefixes and suffixes to modify a root word in various subtle ways (so that "unalive" is not synonymous with dead); his evocative typography (as in a familiar poem about grasshoppers, or "t,a,p,s," or "SpRiN,K,LiNG"); and his integration of the erotic with the experimental. He wrote poems that cohere more in terms of sound than syntax or semantics: "bingbongwhom chewchoo /laugh dingle nails personally /bing loamhome picpac /obviously scratches tomorrowlobs." He wrote abstract poetry long before most of the language-centered (∗) gang were born, the opening poem of *1 X 1* (1944) beginning: "nonsum blob a / cold to /skylessness /sticking fire //my are you / are birds our all/ and one gone/ away the they." "No Thanks" (1935) is an extraordinary poem beginning "brIght" that contains only eleven discrete words, all six letters or less in length; they are successfully broken apart and nonsyntactically combined to form fifteen lines of forty-four words—all three-letter words appearing thrice, all four-letter words four times, etc. With such rigorous structures Cummings presaged several major developments in contemporary avant-garde poetry. Though some of these innovations were not included in earlier selections and collections of Cummings's poetry, thankfully they all appear in the latest edition of his *Collected Poems* (1991), which incidentally demonstrates that these more experimental poems were done throughout his career, rather than, say, being bunched within a short period. No appreciation of the avant-garde Cummings would be complete without acknowledging his *Eimi* (1933, long out-of-print), a memoir of his disillusioning 1931 trip to the Soviet Union, as audacious in style as it is in content; and his visual art, which has never been fully exhibited (even though his oeuvre reportedly includes over 2,000 paintings and over 10,000 sheets of drawings).

Cummings, E.E. *The Collected Poems, 1904–62*. NY: Norton, 1991.

———. *Eimi*. 2nd ed. NY: Grove, 1958.

Kostelanetz, Richard. "E.E. Cummings" (1980). In *The Old Poetries and the New*. Ann Arbor, MI: University of Michigan, 1981.

CUNNINGHAM, Merce (c. 1919). After years off the edge of American dance, Cunningham became, beginning in the late 1960s, the principal figure in advanced American choreography, remaining, even today, the most influential individual, as much by example as by becoming a monument whose activity still intimidates his successors. Originally part of Martha Graham's (*) dance company, he presented in 1944, in collaboration with John Cage (*), his first New York recital of self-composed solos. Rejected by dance aficionados who were devoted to prior masters, Cunningham earned his initial following among professionals in other arts.

The initial reason for the dance world's neglect was that Cunningham had drastically reworked every dimension of dance-making: not only the articulation of time, but the use of space; not only the movements of dancers' bodies, but their relationship to one another on the stage. If most ballet and even modern dance had a front and a back, Cunningham's works are designed to be

Merce Cunningham in "Changeling," 1957. *Photo: Richard Rutledge, courtesy The Cunningham Dance Foundation.*

Carolyn Brown, Valda Setterfield, Meg Harper, Gus Solomons jr, and Merce Cunningham in "Walkaround Time," 1968. *Photo: Oscar Bailey, courtesy The Cunningham Dance Foundation.*

seen from all sides; and though theatrical custom has forced him to mount most of his performances on a proscenium stage (one that has a front and a back), his pieces have also been successfully performed in gymnasiums and museums.

Time in Cunningham's work is nonclimactic, which means that a piece begins not with a fanfare but a movement, and it ends not with a flourish but simply when the performers stop. Because he eschews the traditional structure of theme and variation, the dominant events within a work seem to proceed at an irregular, unpredictable pace; their temporal form is, metaphorically, lumpy. "It's human time," he explains, "which can't be too slow or too fast, but includes various time possibilities. I like to change tempos."

His dances generally lack a specific subject or story, even though interpretation-hungry spectators sometimes identify particular subjects and/or the semblance of narrative (and more than one Cunningham dancer has suspected the existence of secret stories). It follows that his dancers eschew dramatic characterizations for nonparticularized roles, which is to say that Cunningham dancers always play themselves and no one else. Just as he defied tradition by allowing parts of a dancer's body to function disjunctively and nonsynchronously, so his staging lacks a center; important events occur all over the performing area—even in the corners. The result is organized disorganization, so to speak, that seems chaotic only if strict forms of ordering are expected.

The titles of his works tend to be abstract (*Aeon* [1961], *Winterbranch* [1964]), or situational (*RainForest* [1968], *Summerspace* [1958], *Place* [1966]), or formally descriptive (*Story* [1963], *Scramble* [1967], *Walkaround Time* [1968]). As his dancers' gestures have been ends in themselves, rather than vehicles of emotional representation or narrative progression, Cunningham freed himself to explore the possibilities of human movement. In this respect, he has been incomparably inventive and remarkably prolific. To put it differently, once he decided that the old rules need not be followed, he was free to produce many dances filled with unfamiliar moves and innovative choreographic relationships.

Because Cunningham's activities are not symbolic of human activities or emotions, they are meant to be appreciated as ends in themselves. His dance thus demands not empathy from the spectator but, as Cage once explained, "your faculty of kinesthetic sympathy. It is this faculty we employ when, seeing the flight of birds, we ourselves, by identification, fly up, glide and soar." What seems at first inscrutable about Cunningham's choreography is quite comprehensible, providing one does not strive too hard to find underlying "significances." What you see is most of what there is.

Another departure comes with his use of music. Whereas most choreographers draw their inspirations from particular scores, Cunningham composes all but a few of his pieces without music; his dancers count to themselves for their cues. What music is heard in his work is customarily composed apart from the dance, as is the decor and costumes, and thus not mixed with the dance until the final rehearsals. The music tends to be harshly atonal and rhythmically irrelevant, as Cunningham has for his accompaniments long favored John Cage and those composers gathered around him.

Cunningham's choreographies are generally many-sided, nonlinear, nonexpressionistic, spatially noncentered, temporally nonclimactic, and compositionally assembled. The decor and sound are supplementary, rather than complementary; and the dancers are highly individualized. Though his art is avant-garde, his sensibility is classical, which is to say precise, Constructivist (∗), and severe. He reveals the enormity of his choreographic intelligence through his profound knowledge of dance and dancers, coupled with his seemingly limitless capacity for invention.

Cunningham, Merce, with Frances Starr. *Changes*. NY: Something Else, 1968.

Kostelanetz, Richard, ed. *Merce Cunningham: Dancing in Space and Time*. Pennington, NJ: a cappella, 1992.

Klosty, James. *Merce Cunningham* (1975). 2nd ed. NY: Limelight, 1986.

Lesschaeve, Jacqueline. *The Dancer and the Dance* (1980). NY: Marion Boyars, 1985.

CURRAN, Alvin (1938). An intelligent musician, educated at Brown and Yale universities, Curran usually works with electronic instruments in live performance, mostly in collaboration with others, initially with the ensemble Musica Elettronica Viva (MEV) (∗), which he organized while residing in Rome. He typically mixes natural sounds with improvised music. His strongest work is *Crystal Psalms* (1988), which was commissioned by several European radio stations for live broadcast on the fiftieth anniversary of *Kristallnacht*. Incorporating the lamentations of Jewish cantors along with the repeated sound of glass breaking and live choruses, the piece vividly and inventively evokes the night when Jewish synagogues were destroyed all over Nazi Europe.

Curran, Alvin. *Crystal Psalms: Live from 6 European Countries* (1988). San Francisco, CA: New Albion, 1993.

CYBERNETICS (c. 1945). This word was Norbert Wiener's coinage for self-steering mechanisms, which is to say those entities that, like human beings, respond intelligently to considerations of their own output. For example, if you step (output) on a hot coal (input), you'll probably pull back your foot and won't step on hot coals again. The idea was to make robots capable of this human trait. Necessarily incorporating the new disciplines of information theory, control systems, automatons, artificial intelligence, computer-simulated activities, and information-processing, cybernetics had great influence, particularly in the 1960s.

A good example of cybernetic art would be the responsive mechanism, such as James Seawright's *Scanner* (1966), which is a large, plastic-ribbed, ball-shaped cage some six feet in diameter that is suspended from the ceiling. From the ball's lowest point extends a thin metal arm that contains photocells. A strobe light is projected upwards out of the piece's vertical core and then reflected by mirrors at its top, both down the plastic ribs and into the field around the sculpture. The photocells respond to decided changes in the room's lighting (natural as well as artificial, depending upon the hour) by halting the arm, which then swings in either direction (depending upon whether the alternating current is positive or negative at the precise moment of contact). The turning of the arm inevitably gives the photocells a different perspective on the field, causing another decisive change in the light that prompts the system to halt again and electronically reconsider the direction of its movement. In sum, then, this self-considering activity makes *Scanner* a genuine example of a feedback machine whose output (the movement of the arm) causes it to reconsider its input (the field of light) and to continually adjust itself. Within its normal operations are the cybernetic processes of response, information-processing, selection, and self-control.

Cynthia Goodman describes Nicolas Schöffer's (∗) earlier "Cysp" series (the term being an abbreviation of cybernetics and spatiodynamics), which were Constructivist (∗) structures that performed like robots. "They were mounted on four rollers that gave them the capability to move. Photoelectric cells, microphones, and rotating blades powered by small motors were connected to their scaffold-like structures. Controlled by an electronic brain developed by Philips [the Dutch electronics business], a Cysp responded to variations in color intensity, light, and sound." Goodman, who is the principal American critic/curator of this turf, praises a robot (1984–1987) modeled after Andy Warhol (∗) that was constructed by a former Walt Disney animator to be a surrogate for Warhol on lecture tours. "An appropriate tribute to a man who so often claimed he wanted to be a machine, the computer-controlled robot is endowed with preprogrammed speech and fifty-four separate body movements

that supposedly will be barely distinguishable from Warhol's."

Seawright, James. "Phenomenal Art." In *Esthetics Contemporary*, ed. Richard Kostelanetz. 2nd ed. Buffalo, NY: Prometheus, 1989.

Goodman, Cynthia. *Digital Visions*. NY: Abrams, 1987.

DADA (c. 1916). Dada and Surrealism (∗) are popularly regarded as nearly synonymous movements, or as precursor and successor in the step-by-step history of modern art. Although their memberships overlapped and both espoused two major esthetic positions in common—the irrelevance of 19th-century forms of comprehension and the rejection of established modes of artistic rendering—they differed from each other in one crucial respect. Whereas Surrealism was the art of representing subconscious psychological terrains, Dada artists dealt primarily with the external world: the character of the commonly perceived environment; patterns of intellectual and artistic coherence; and standard definitions of meaning and significance. Therefore, while Surrealistic art presents the experience of hallucinations, Dada favors the distortion, usually ludicrous, of familiar contexts, and the portrayal of worldly absurdity. Surrealists André Breton (∗) and Salvador Dali (∗) purportedly cast their interior fantasies in objective forms and, unlike the Dadaists, acknowledged the theories of Sigmund Freud. Dada master Marcel Duchamp (∗), by contrast, drew his models from the mundane environment (often *finding* his actual material there) and thereby confronted "Art" with "non-art," implicitly questioning all absolutist esthetics and creating impersonal objects that relate not to the psychic life of his audience but to their perception of the world around them.

The masters of Dada used a variety of esthetic designs on behalf of their purposes. One consisted of infusing distortion and mundane gesture into a conventional form: painting a mustache on Leonardo's Mona Lisa, speaking gibberish at a poetry reading, fragmenting an image or narrative beyond the point of comprehension, introducing a urinal into an exhibition of sculpture, etc. At its best, this dash of nonsense revealed the ridiculous irrelevance of certain social or artistic hierarchies and conventions, as well as initiating such anti-conventions for subsequent modern art as the artistic validity of all manufactured objects. This rejection of established forms of order complemented an anarchistic political bias. Whereas Surrealism is concise and imagistic, like poetry, Dada is more diffuse, like fiction.

Dada historically began in Zurich in 1915–1916 when young people, very much disinclined to the burgeoning world war, made esthetic actions, collectively and individually, that seemed socially subversive and politically revolutionary. The origin of the name has been endlessly debated, some saying it comes from the French word for a "hobbyhorse," while others regarding it as taken from the Slavonic words for "yes, yes." Within two years, similar developments happened in New York and Berlin particularly but also in Hanover, Cologne, and Paris. Zurich Dada was predominantly literary and theatrical. Richard Huelsenbeck (∗) brought to Berlin a Dada more predisposed to art exhibitions and political satire. Hanover Dada was mostly the invention of Kurt Schwitters (∗); Cologne Dada depended upon Max Ernst (∗). Paris Dada initially consisted mostly of young writers briefly enamored with Tristan Tzara (∗); most of them eventually became, like Tzara, Surrealists. New York Dada has a more complicated history, including as it does immigrants such as Marcel Duchamp and Francis Picabia (∗) along with natives, all of whom gathered regularly at the apartment of the art patron Walter Conrad Arensberg (1878–1954). So strong were Dada ideas that they persisted even among those who publicly converted to Surrealism, who sometimes insisted that they were Dadaists at heart. So strong was the Dada esthetic that a Dada magazine appeared in the mid-1920s in the European boonies of the Soviet republic of Georgia (I remember the Slavic scholar John Bowlt [1943] sharing this information with a professional audience, all of us as ignorant of Georgian as he). So strong was Dada politics that even today we sympathize with the 1918 demand for "the introduction of progressive unemployment through comprehensive mechanization of every field of activity."

Dachy, Marc. *The Dada Movement*. NY: Rizzoli, 1990.

Kuenzli, Rudolf E., ed. *New York Dada*. NY: Willis Locker & Owens, 1986.

Rubin, William S. *Dada, Surrealism and Their Heritage*. NY: Museum of Modern Art, 1968.

———. *Dada and Surrealist Art*. NY: Abrams, n.d. (c. 1969).

DALI, Salvador (1904–1989). A painter and filmmaker, Dali is best remembered for meticulously rendered Surrealist (∗) paintings that portray a dreamlike world with images of melting watches and half-open drawers with erotic resonances. Such paintings influenced subsequent realists, sometimes called Magic Realists, who adopted the Surrealist interest in dream imagery while primarily portraying the real world. Dali also collaborated with Luis Buñuel (∗) on two classic avant-garde films, *Un Chien andalou* (1928) and *L'Age d'or* (1931), which feature Surrealist imagery and allusions to both classical mythology and Freudian symbolism. Such classic/contemporary juxtapositions of often violent images greatly influenced later filmmakers both avant-garde and mainstream.

From roughly 1940 onwards, Dali spent most of his time in ceaseless self-promotion, making his face (with its outrageously wide-open eyes

Salvador Dali, "Birth of Liquid Desires," 1931–1932. *Photo: Myles Aronowitz © The Solomon R. Guggenheim Foundation, New York.*

and pointed, pencil-thin mustache) as famous in its day as Andy Warhol's (*) or Joseph Beuys's (*) visages would become years later, in all cases the face becoming a stronger professional signature, or after-image, than any other creation. In this sense, Dali's persona was his most successful creation, a Surreal figure come to life. Among other affronts to the ideals of professional integrity, Dali produced numerous signed editions that were printed *after* he signed them. He published books whose pages as well as their titles reflect his commitment to relentless self-promotion: *The Secret Life of Salvador Dali* (1961) and *Diary of a Genius* (1966).—with Richard Carlin

Dali, Salvador. *Diary of a Genius* (1966). London, England: Hutchinson, 1990.

————. *Dali*. NY: Abrams, 1968.

DAVIS, R.G. See SAN FRANCISCO MIME TROUPE

DAVIS, Stuart (1894–1964). Beginning as a social realist, Davis created some of the earliest American pseudo-collages in the early 1920s, incorporating trompe l'oeil depictions of cigarette packs and lettering drawn from advertising art into his paintings (much as Nicolas Slonimsky [*], say, incorporated jingles into his music compositions around that time). Later in the twenties, Davis created a series of Cubist-influenced portraits of two mundane objects, the percolator and eggbeater, forecasting Pop Art (*). From the thirties to his death, Davis's work took an original, if limited, direction in emphasizing colorful shapes arrayed in flat, poster-like patterns that emulated the rhythms of jazz (*) music.—Richard Carlin

Blesh, Rudi. *Stuart Davis*. NY: Knopf, 1960.

DE ANDREA, John (1941). De Andrea, among others, has created awesomely lifelike sculptures of people, especially nudes with nothing to hide. Such sculptures reflect as they transcend the illusions typical of the traditional wax museum. Hyperrealism is more successful in sculpture than in painting or photography, in part because three-dimensionality is unavailable to the latter artforms, but mostly because of new materials, as well as new intelligence, that have become available to sculptors.

De Andrea has an unusual ability to give his sculptures humanity. It was the British poet-critic Edward Lucie-Smith who pointed out, "They somehow give away both their class and their national origin through details of posture, hair style, and expression." The cleverest de Andrea in my experience involved three figures—two nude women and a clothed man facing them. You knew the women were "fake," so to speak, but you had to look and think twice to realize that the man with his back to you was a sculpture as well.

Lucie-Smith, Edward. *Art Now*. Rev. ed. NY: Morrow, 1981.

DE KOONING, Willem (1904). Born in Holland, de Kooning emigrated to America as a young man and worked as a W.P.A. muralist. His midlife innovation came from imaginatively developing and extending a major stylistic contribution of European Cubism (*), breaking up the representational plane to portray an object or field as seen from two or more perspectives simultaneously. The initial paintings in his *Women* series, done in the early fifties, evoke in impulsive and yet well-drawn strokes (and colors identical to those in the environment portrayed) a single figure regarded from a multitude of perspectives, both vertical and horizontal, in several kinds of light and, therefore, implicitly at various moments in time. Not only are the differences between figure and setting, past and present, and background and foreground all thoroughly blurred, but nearly every major detail in this all-over and yet focused field suggests a different angle of vision or a different intensity of light. De Kooning never did as well again, even in roughly similar styles, though his admirers were forever hailing later works with the wish that he had.

Gaugh, Harry. *De Kooning*. NY: Abbeville, 1983.

DE MARIA, Walter (1935). A true eccentric, de Maria first made sculptures that posed genuine dangers to viewers, such as a bed of spikes pointed upwards, and pioneered Conceptual Art (*) with *Mile Long Drawing* (1968), for which he drew two parallel lines, twelve feet apart, in the Mojave Desert. (Because the original is inaccessible, this is commonly seen and experienced through documentary photographs.) In 1968, de Maria filled an entire Munich gallery with earth a few feet deep, which was such a good idea that he was asked to do it again, first at another gallery in Cologne, and then in a former gallery in SoHo (*), where it has been on museum-like display for over a dozen years as The New York Earth Room. Nearby in SoHo (*) is another apparently permanent de Maria installation, *The Broken Kilometer* (1979), where the entire floor of an 11,000-square-foot space has highly polished brass rods arrayed in parallel rows.

Walter de Maria: The 2000 Sculpture. Zürich, Switzerland: Kunsthaus, 1992.

DE STIJL (1917–1931). A Dutch periodical of art and esthetics edited by Theo van Doesburg (*) until his premature death, *De Stijl* was commonly considered the most influential avant-garde art magazine of its time, representing not just Dutch Constructivism (*) but a rationalist approach to art and society. Its title, meaning "the style," is pronounced (in English) as, roughly, "duh style." Among the member-contributors were Piet Mondrian (*), Georges Vantongerloo (*), El Lissitzky (*), George Antheil (*), Jean/Hans Arp (*), and lesser-known architects and industrial designers. "This periodical hopes to make a contribution to the development of a new awareness of beauty," van Doesburg wrote in the initial issue. "It wishes to make modern man receptive to what is new in the visual arts." This "new" they called the "new plasticism," which not only rejected representation (Mondrian having once specialized in flowers) but, instead, strictly limited painting to straight lines, 90-degree angles, and the three primary colors of red, yellow, and blue (along with the neutrals of black, white, and gray). Thinking their art socially redemptive, they wanted to convey its significance to a larger public. As H.L.C. Jaffé wrote in the principal history of the magazine, "The purification of the plastic means of expression should also serve to solve various actual problems of our present time." Because van Doesburg as a polyartist (*) was as much a writer as a painter, one of *De Stijl*'s issues was devoted to literature that was avant-garde at the time; and because he became involved with Dada (*), a 1922 issue had a Dada supplement titled *Mecano*.

Jaffé, H.L.C., ed. *De Stijl * 1917–1931*. Cambridge, MA: Harvard University, 1986.

DEAN, Laura (1945). As a choreographer once closely associated with Steve Reich (*), Dean made highly inventive dances that depended upon simple repeated moves. In *Jumping Dance* (1973), twelve performers, lined up in three rows of four, jump up and down, making their own noises, until everyone is exhausted, incidentally illustrating John Cage's (*) classic remark about doing something again and again until it is no longer boring but interesting. *Circle Dance* (1973) has ten performers shuffling their feet around four concentric circles in unison. However, since they move around four completely different circumferences, the performers go in and out of visible phase (the work thus resembling early Reich music). As in *Jumping Dance*, the music comes only from sounds made by the performers themselves.

McDonagh, Don. "Laura Dean." In *The Complete Guide to Modern Dance*. Garden City, NY: Doubleday, 1976.

DENCKER, Klaus Peter (1941). A German visual poet and cultural administrator, he has produced books composed entirely of newspaper headlines and clippings—*. . . grünes erlangen.* (1979)—as well as a pioneering German anthology of visual poetry (*) (*Text-Bilder Visuelle Poesie International* [1972]) and a wonderfully thick, annotated collection of *Deutsche Unsinnspoesie* (1978), or nonsense poetry. For a while in the 1970s, Dencker promoted *Poesia vivisa*, a mostly Italian art that depended upon mixing language with photographs large enough to hang in art galleries, as distinct from the primarily linguistic, smaller-scale orientations of both visual poetry and Concrete Poetry (*).

Dencker, Klaus Peter, ed. *Deutsche Unsinnspoesie*. Stuttgart, Germany: Reclam, 1978.

DEPEW, Wally (1938). An experimental poet-publisher from his professional beginnings, Depew published *Nine Essays on Concrete Poems* (1974), which are not conventional expositions but substantial visual-verbal self-reflective displays of qualities unique to Concrete Poetry (*), which he defines as I do here—dealing with the elements of language apart from syntax or semantics. In his own visual poetry (*), he tends to favor images in sequence, at times verging on visual fiction, using rubber-stamp letters in his recent books.

Depew, Wally. *Nine Essays on Concrete Poetry*. Alamo, CA: Holmgangers Press, 1974.

DERRIDA, Jacques (1930). A Frenchman from North Africa, Derrida has become in some academic literary circles the most influential critical theorist since Northrop Frye (*). His books seem designed for the classroom, which means that they are most successfully read with a guide, in concert with other seekers. Where they are comprehensible, at least in my experience, their ideas are obvious; where they are incomprehensible, Derrida's theories of deconstruction offers the cognoscenti rich opportunities for the kinds of one-upmanship endemic to such hierarchical societies as the military and most universities.

To my mind, Derrida's originality comes from his way of thinking, which I discovered not from reading his works but from hearing him speak. In Jerusalem several years ago, I witnessed a question/answer performance before a mostly academic audience, most speaking, as he, nonnative English. Whenever Derrida took a question, you could see him fumble for the beginnings of an answer, but once he got on track, an elaborate digression followed, at once elegant and idiosyncratic, until he reached a pause. Having followed him so far, you wondered whether he would then turn to the left or to the right, each direction seeming equally valid, only to admire the next verbal flight that led to another roadstop, with similarly arbitrary choices before continuing or concluding. In response to the next question, Derrida improvised structurally similar rhetorical gymnastics.

What separates Derrida from traditional literary theorists is this commitment to improvisatory thinking, with all of its possibilities and limitations. Should you have a taste for highflown intellectual gymnastics, consider Marshall McLuhan (*), whose similarly improvised perceptions were sociologically more substantial. If you think improvisation is "no way to play music," you might judge that Derrida's example is no way to think.

Derrida, Jacques. *Of Grammatology*. Trans. G.C. Spivak. Baltimore, MD: Johns Hopkins, 1976.

DER STURM. See WALDEN, Herwarth

DI SUVERO, Mark (1933). Born in Shanghai of an Italian-Jewish family, di Suvero moved with his family to California in 1941 and majored in philosophy at the University of California at Berkeley. Taking off from David Smith's (*) sense of sculpture as an outdoor art and Franz Kline's (*) taste for thick lines and odd angles, he fabricated monumental sculptures initially of wood and then of scrap steel beams gathered from demolished buildings and junkyards. Asymmetrical and to the eye precariously balanced, these sculptures sometimes contain seats inviting the spectator to have a more intimate experience of the work. Though Cubist (*) in syntax, they look like nothing found in life and could thus be considered Constructivist (*) as well. A distinguished older sculptor, Sidney Geist (1914), greeted di Suvero's first exhibition in 1960 with this generous encomium: "I myself have not been so moved by a show of sculpture since the Brancusi exhibition of 1933." In a classic of appreciative criticism, Geist continued: "History is glad to record the arrival of any new artist, the creation of a new beauty, or the presence of a singular work of art; but the real stuff of history is made of those moments at which one can say: from now on *nothing will be the same.*" Geist added, "Constructivism is Cubism with the object left out." After leaving America in protest against the Vietnam War, di Suvero returned to Long Island City, where he located his studio in an abandoned waterfront pier and later established on shorefront property an outdoor sculpture park.

Mark di Suvero. NY: Rizzoli-Guggenheim Museum, 1993.

Geist, Sidney, "A New Sculptor: Mark di Suvero" (1960). In *Mark di Suvero*. Stuttgart, Germany: Wurttembergischer Kunstverein, 1988.

DIAGHILEV, Sergei Pavlovich (1872–1929). One of the greatest organizers of innovative artistic events, he first became known as a leading figure in the Petersburg World of Art Group, as founder and editor of the journal *World of Art* (*Mir iskusstva*, 1899–1904), which introduced important new European art movements to the Russian public in an elegantly printed format, setting the standard for subsequent Russian art and literary journals. Diaghilev ceaselessly promoted native Russian achievements, as well as innovative trends in the fields of art, music, opera, and ballet. His most significant accomplishment was the creation and management of the renowned Les Ballets Russes, which, beginning in 1909, produced some of the most

The Joffrey Ballet's revival of "Parade" with costumes by Pablo Picasso. *Photo © 1993, Jack Vartoogian.*

brilliant spectacles in the history of ballet. To do this, he engaged the services of the most talented avant-garde artists, composers, choreographers, and dancers of Russia and France, including Leon Bakst (1866–1924), Aleksandr Benois (1870–1960), Natalia Goncharova (1881–1962), Mikhail Larionov (1881–1964), Pablo Picasso (*), Henri Matisse (1869–1954), Georges Braque (1882–1963), Igor Stravinsky (*), Sergei Prokofiev (1891–1953), Maurice Ravel (1875–1937), Claude Debussy (1862–1918), Mikhail Fokine (1880–1942), Vaslav Nijinsky (1890–1950), Anna Pavlova (1881–1931), and Tamara Karsavina (1885–1978). Perhaps his most artistically successful production was *Petrushka* (1912), with music by Stravinsky, stage design by Benois, choreography by Fokine, and Nijinsky dancing the title role. His most scandalous success occurred in May 1913, with the premier of Stravinsky's *The Rite of Spring.* Nijinsky's unusual choreography, evoking pagan rituals in pre-Christian Russia, plus the wild music, caused a riot during the performance. Diaghilev's role was to stimulate, in fact to demand, innovative work from his collaborators and to provide them with the resources to stage the results. His motto was "surprise me."—Gerald Janecek

Garafola, Lynn. *Diaghilev's Ballets Russes.* NY: Oxford University, 1989.

Bowlt, John E. *The Silver Age: Russian Art of the Early Twentieth Century and the "World of Art Group."* Newtonville, MA: Oriental Research Partners, 1979.

Percival, John. *The World of Diaghilev.* NY: Dutton, 1971.

Pozharskaya, M.N. *The Russian Seasons in Paris.* Moscow, Russia: Iskusstvo Art Publishers, 1988.

Spencer, Charles. *The World of Serge Diaghilev.* NY: Penguin, 1974.

DIGITAL. This term is a euphemism for any mechanism, commonly computer-assisted, that converts an input to numerical quantities, which are positive or negative impulses (commonly characterized as 0/1). The term is applicable to visual and video as well as audio machines. Digital-to-analog conversion refers to the process of taking material stored in a computer medium, such as on a tape or a floppy disc, and making it more accessible, whether on paper or on analog audiotape.

Dodge, Charles, and Thomas A. Jerse. *Computer Music: Synthesis, Composition, and Performance.* NY: Schirmer, 1985.

DISNEY, Walt. See *FANTASIA*

DODGE, Charles (1942). One of the first trained composers to work with computers in the creation of digital information that was then transferred to audiotape, Dodge produced several pieces whose claims to originality depended less upon their structures and thus acoustic experiences than upon the computer assisted means used to produce them. Exceptions to that generalization include *Earth's Magnetic Field* (1970), in which readings of the Earth's magnetic field were serendipitously translated into musical notes (a method structurally comparable to the sun-based sculptures of Charles Ross [*]); *The Days of Our Lives* (1974), which is a kind of operatic dialogue for male and female voices that are resynthesized with computer assistance; and *Any Resemblance* (1981), his masterpiece in which a computer was used to take away the accompanying instruments from a tenor resembling Enrico Caruso. Dodge then composed fresh accompaniments, each insufficient, until the theme of this eight-minute comedy becomes the singer's search for an appropriate backing. More recently, Dodge has been using the concepts of fractal geometry for fairly familiar music, creating works that are again further ahead technically than esthetically.

Dodge, Charles. *Any Resemblance*. On *Computer Music*. NY: Folkways FTS 37475, 1983.

DORIA, Charles (1938). A poet and translator, initially trained in classical languages, Doria turned his profound knowledge of contemporary avant-garde poetry toward finding precursors in ancient writing, compiling anthologies by himself and in collaboration with others, as well as writing critical articles about previously unexamined classical examples. In *The Game of Europe* (1983), his own book-length poem, each section expires as it extrapolates a different writing convention, beginning with that of the novel, passing through Greek chorus, medieval sequence, ballad, literary epistle, newspaper article, and shaped poems/text-sound, concluding with riddles, graffiti, and broken texts from the Tibetan and Egyptian books of the dead, all of which indicates that the range of its allusion includes forms as well as contents. (Another translator from the classical languages, likewise reflecting avant-garde intelligence, is Geoffrey Cook [1946].)

Doria, Charles. *The Game of Europe*. Athens, OH: Swallow-Ohio University, 1983.

————, and Harris Lenowitz, eds. and trans. *Origins*. Garden City, NY: Doubleday Anchor, 1976.

DUCHAMP, Marcel (1887–1968). The grandson of a painter, this Duchamp had three siblings who were also visual artists; but unlike his relatives, he turned his ironic skepticism about art into an extraordinary career built on the smallest amount of work. Indeed, it was his unique and improbable talent to endow, or get others to endow, even his inactivity with esthetic weight. Ostensibly, he went to Paris at sixteen to study art. From 1905 to 1910 he contributed cartoons to French papers. Early paintings, from 1910 and 1911, depict members of his family. His next paintings reflect an interest in movement, presaging the themes of Italian Futurist (∗) work; the epitome is the multi-frame *Nude Descending a Staircase No. 2* (1913), which became the single most notorious work at the New York City Armory Show (∗). Abandoning painting for three-dimensional art, Duchamp offered such everyday objects as a *Bicycle Wheel* (1913) and *Bottle Rack* (1914) as "ready-mades." Moving to New York in 1915 he spent eight years working on *Large Glass: The Bride Stripped Bare by*

Marcel Duchamp, "Bicycle Wheel," original 1913; reproduction 1951. *Photo © 1993, Fred W. McDarrah.*

Her Bachelors, Even (1915–1923), which is often regarded as his single most important piece. Built from lead wire and tinfoil affixed to a sheet of glass, it is nearly nine feet high and six feet wide. Exhibited at the Brooklyn Museum in 1926, it was later found shattered and then restored in 1936 with repaired glass for permanent installation at the Philadelphia Museum of Art. (A facsimile was made for a Duchamp exhibition in London in 1966.)

Meanwhile, Duchamp became the modern master of the provocative and resonant esthetic gesture. With courage based upon self-confidence, he submitted a urinal titled *Fountain* to the 1917 exhibition of the Society of Independent Artists, which he had cofounded and whose vice president he was. When the exhibition organizers refused to accept it, he resigned. (The implication, subsequently developed by others, was that esthetic value could be bestowed upon commonly available objects.) Similarly, to a Dada (∗) exhibition in Paris in 1920 Duchamp submitted a full-color reproduction of Leonardo's *Mona Lisa* to which he had added a beard and mustache; its official title was *L. H. O. O. Q. (Elle a chaud au cul)*. By the mid-1920s, Duchamp had publicly abandoned art in favor first of chess, his principal pastime, and then certain experiments in kineticism: *Rotary demisphere precision optics* (1925), film collaborations with Man Ray (∗), and *Rotoreliefs* (c. 1935), or discs with regular lines that create three-dimensional illusions when rotated like a phonograph record.

Returning to New York in 1942, Duchamp became a presence, even in his inactivity, especially at exhibitions including his early work. Yet so controversial was his art, and so generally unacceptable to the reigning authorities, that not until 1963, past his own seventy-fifth year, did he have an institutional retrospective, which was not in New York or Paris but in Pasadena, CA. After he died, even Duchamp aficionados were surprised to find in his studio a tableau, *Étant données*, on which he had secretly worked for many years. The viewer must peer through a crack in a door to see a diorama of a nude young woman (which must be seen firsthand at the Philadelphia Museum, because photographs of it are forbidden); this work culminates Duchamp's erotic obsessions, for which he was also famous. (As the poet Mina Loy remembered, "Marcel was slick as a prestidigitator; he could insinuate his hand under a woman's bodice and caress her with utter grace.")

Perhaps because Duchamp's works are so few in number and so inscrutable, they have generated an incomparable wealth of interpretations, offering different things to different people. In no other modern artist can commentators find such a variety, if not a wealth, of deep meanings. (By this measure, Duchamp resembles Leonardo da Vinci of all artists and James Joyce [∗] among his contemporaries.) Because new discoveries are still being made, it is appropriate to provide admittedly incomplete guidance to the Duchamp literature:

The subtitle of *Salt Seller: The Writings of Marcel Duchamp* (1973; NY: Da Capo, n.d.) suggests a completeness that is not entirely true. Besides, Duchamp (the writer) does not illuminate much about Duchamp.

The Bride Stripped Bare by Her Bachelors, Even (London: Percy Lund Humphries, 1960) is Richard Hamilton's "typographical version" of Duchamp's notes and sketches about his masterpiece.

Robert Lebel's *Marcel Duchamp* (NY: Grove, 1959) is a substantial introduction, including an early catalogue raisonné and a French-centered bibliography. A paperback edition (NY: Paragraphic, n.d. [1967]) omits the color plates but updates the catalogue and bibliography to 1967.

Pierre Cabanne's *Dialogues with Marcel Duchamp* (NY: Viking, 1971) transcribes conversations made in French just before Duchamp's death. It Includes one of those stupendous bibliographies for which the Museum of Modern Art's librarian at the time, Bernard Karpel, was famous, itemizing published texts, interview transcripts, and secondary literature to 1970.

Calvin Tomkins's *The World of Marcel Duchamp* (NY: Time-Life, 1966) is a well-illustrated introduction.

Arturo Schwarz's *The Complete Works of Marcel Duchamp* (NY: Abrams, 1969, 1970) includes a critical catalogue raisonné and an exhaustive descriptive bibliography. It is scheduled to appear in a third, elaborately revised edition (NY: Delano Grenidge, 1993).

The Mexican Nobelist Octavio Paz's *Marcel Duchamp or the Castle of Purity* (NY: Grossman, 1970) is an unpaginated chapbook written while its author was a diplomat in India. Paz also contributed one of the strongest essays to the catalog *Duchamp* edited by Anne d'Harnoncourt and Kynaston McShine for the Museum of Modern Art in 1973 (reprinted 1989), along with Lucy R. Lippard (∗), David Antin (∗), Richard Hamilton, and Bernard Karpel with a fuller bibliography.

Shigeko Kubota's *Marcel Duchamp and John Cage* (Tokyo: Takeyoshi Miyazawa, n.d) has thirty-six photos of the two subjects playing chess on an amplified board, taken only a few months before Duchamp's death. It comes in a sleeve, accompanied by a small, plastic long-playing recordlette.

New York Dada, edited by Rudolf E. Kuenzli (NY: Willis Owens & Locker, 1986), contains Craig Adcock's "Marcel Duchamp's Approach to New York: 'Find an Inscription for the Woolworth Building as a Ready-Made.'" Adcock's book about Duchamp's use of geometry is *Marcel Duchamp's Notes from the Large Glass: An N-Dimensional Analysis* (Ann Arbor, MI: UMI Research, 1983). Kuenzli collaborated with Francis M. Naumann in editing *Marcel Duchamp: Artist of the Century* (Cambridge, MA: M.I.T., 1990), which contains an introduction to William A. Camfield's spectacularly elaborate essay on "Marcel Duchamp's *Fountain*" (aka the urinal), which, as he points out, survived only in a photograph that was ignored until the conceptual assumptions of the work became relevant to esthetic issues established in the 1960s. The book concludes with a yet fuller "Selective Bibliography." The full Camfield essay appeared as *Marcel Duchamp's Fountain* (Houston: The Menil Foundation, 1989).

Ecke Bonk's *Marcel Duchamp: Box in a Valise* (NY: Rizzoli, 1989) itemizes the artist's boxed (and thus alternative) 1936 autobiography.

Joseph Maschek's *Marcel Duchamp in Perspective* (Englewood Cliffs, NJ: Prentice-Hall, 1975) reprints criticism unavailable elsewhere, including an interview with John Cage about Duchamp. Theirry de Duve's anthology *The Definitively Unfinished Marcel Duchamp* (Cambridge, MA: M.I.T., 1991) recycles many of the same scholars.

DUCKWORTH, William (1943). An untypical university composer, Duckworth composed one piece of such brilliance and originality that it has become a hard act for him to top. Especially in the Neely Bruce (∗) recording, which remains superior to other renditions, *The Time Curve Preludes* (1979) reflects modular music (∗), as well as the popular concern with generating audible overtones, without resembling any previous music conceived in those ways. Composed for a specially retuned piano, the *Preludes* are brief pieces, twenty-four in sum, based upon the Fibonacci series (in which each number is the sum of the two preceding it, in a continuous sequence), one hour in total length, rich with allusions to both contemporary and pre-Renaissance music. Very much in the great tradition of exhaustive modernist compositions for solo piano (including Dmitri Shostakovitch's [1906–1975] *Preludes and Fugues*, Paul Hindemith's [1895–1963] *Ludus Tonalis*, and John Cage's (∗) *Sonatas and Interludes*), *The Time Curved Preludes* are also lushly beautiful.

Duckworth, William. *The Time Curve Preludes* (1979). NY: Lovely Music, 1990.

DUDEK, Louis (1918). "Context is criticism" is an insight that sheds light on the life and work of Louis Dudek. The Montreal-born poet and critic, who taught at McGill University from 1951 to his retirement in 1982, advanced the causes of modern, contemporary, and Canadian literatures through teaching, writing, and publishing. In a Canadian context, Dudek is a proponent of new poets and poetries ("Is it the destiny of Montreal to show the country from time to time what poetry is?"). In a Western context, he stands as a literary modernist, a sometime correspondent of Ezra Pound (∗), and a critic of the ideology *du jour* and *de la patrie*. In the context of the avant-garde, his writings are intransigently intelligent, idiosyncratically free-flowing, and unfashionably humanistic. Book-length poetic meditations like *Atlantis* are characteristic; so are needling aphorisms that shed both light and friends: "Of all sad fates, the Avant-Garde's the worst: /They were going nowhere, and they got there first."—John Robert Colombo

Dudek, Louis. *Continuation I*. Montreal, Canada: Véhicule Press, 1981.

———. *Continuation II*. Montreal, Canada: Véhicule Press, 1990.

———. *Some Perfect Things*. Montreal, Canada: DC Books, 1991.

DUFRÊNE, François (1930–1982). Initially an associate of Lettrism (∗), he developed in the 1950s "cri-rhythmes," as he called them. Though these word-based wails initially reflect Antonin Artaud (∗), their style acoustically resembles the 1960s Expressionist (∗) jazz of Ornette Coleman (∗) and Albert Ayler (∗). They were quite spectacular, whether performed live (say, at sound poetry festivals) or on a record. At times he overdubbed his voice, creating a level of declamatory intensity that, even after his premature death, remains unsurpassed. Dufrêne also published Lettristic Concrete Poetry (∗) and poster poems.

Chopin, Henri. *Poèsie sonore internationale*. Paris, France: Jean-Michel Place, 1979.

DUGUAY, Raoul (1939). Since the middle 1960s, no other French-Canadian poet has so completely reflected international avant-garde activities. As Caroline Bayard summarizes his "writing techniques":

> The first is the breaking down of sentences and words into atomized units. The second is his use of simultaneity—words or phonemes being projected at the same time, by different voices, from different places. The third is the search for a notation system, a score—words being placed on bars with annotations which indicate measure, tonality, and length. In effect, the poem becomes a musical score, the notes being either words or phonemes. The fourth is the need for a visual presentation, one which, however, has little to do with visual concrete principles. Most of his poems present a typography similar to that of old illuminated texts. Graphic designs form the background, words the foreground.

Bayard continues, "On the whole, Duguay's contribution to international concrete theory is his exploration in the areas of sound, phonetics, and phonology."

Bayard, Caroline. *The New Poetics in Canada and Quebec*. Toronto, Canada: University of Toronto, 1989.

Duguay, Raoul Luoar Yaugud. "On the Vibrant Body." *Open Letter* III/8 (Spring 1978).

DUKE, Jas (1939–1992; b. James Heriot D.). Duke was an Australian poet I know mostly through extraordinary recordings. A note accompanying his declamation of "Nikola Tesla" says,

Duncan, Isadora. *My Life*. NY: Liveright, 1927.

"Since starting to write sound poetry in 1966, Jas Duke has produced a large and varied body of work including the publication of two books and innumerable performances. His recitals often employ simple modifications to the acoustic of his voice, achieved, for example, by filling his mouth with paper." Another "modification" clearly audible is speech unique to Australia. From sketchy information, I gather that Duke went as a young man to England, where he edited *Archduke* (1968–1974) and *Brighton Head and Freak Mag* (1969–1970) and made experimental films with Jeff Keen before returning to his native Australia. Once back home, he became the principal advocate for literary and performance art that extended the historical avant-gardes, as well as becoming a devout anarchist. (If not for Duke and Chris Mann [*], Australia would be as off the avant-garde map as, say, Saudi Arabia or Papua.)

Duke, Jas. *Tribute* (unnumbered CD), in *Going Down Swinging* 13 (P.O. Box 64, Coburg, Victoria, Australia 3058), 1993.

———. *Poems of War and Peace*. Melbourne, Australia: Collective Effort (GPO 2340v, 3001), 1987.

DUNCAN, Isadora (1877–1927). She won notoriety for her flamboyant lifestyle, memorialized in a pop movie, and genuine fame for her artistic evocation of a "natural" style of dance that contradicted the ballet conventions of her time. Though Duncan had in fact received some ballet training and performed on vaudeville stages, she questioned the validity of established modes of movement, seeking her inspiration instead in her perceptions of nature (for example, the motions of the sea) and antiquity (Greek art and architecture). Her dance vocabulary included loose, graceful, flowing gestures and childlike runs, skips, and leaps. An expressive dancer, she touched people by the deep emotion and passion of her performances. She cherished great music and chose to perform to masterpieces (at a time when some ballet dancers were frequently performing to mediocre scores). Duncan was associated with some of the great artists of her time, including the innovative stage designer Edward Gordon Craig (1872–1966, by whom she bore a child) and the Russian poet Sergei Esenin (1895–1925, whom she married).—Katy Matheson

DYLAN, Bob (1941; b. Robert Allen Zimmerman). Consider Dylan an avant-garde artist on several grounds. He broadened the subject matter of popular vocal music beyond young love and cars, incidentally extending the length of the typical pop song; he also broke down the structure of verse-chorus-bridge typical of other pop artists. His manner is everything other than that of an earlier teen idol. He demonstrated that a singer-guitarist of only modest natural abilities could be a better interpreter of his own material than a more attractive "star." Dylan also experimented with free-form poetry and prose, inspired by sources as diverse as the Bible, James Joyce (*), and Allen Ginsberg (*). *Tarantula* (1966) collects his early literary experiments.—with Richard Carlin

Dylan, Bob. *Collected Writings*. NY: Knopf, 1985.

———. *Biograph*. NY: Columbia Records C5X 38830, 1984.

DYMSHITS-TOLSTOYA, Sophie (1889–1963). According to John Bowlt, Dymshits-Tolstoya made several glass reliefs exhibited in Tatlin's Moscow exhibition *The Store* in 1916. "It was within this enterprise [of reliefs] that many of the avant-garde came together, particularly those working in three dimensions: Bromirsky, Bruni, Dymshits-Tolstoya, Rodchenko, Tatlin, et al." A New York gallery recently showed a small work of hers from the period featuring abstract shapes painted on two pieces of thick glass, securely framed. Previously married to the novelist Aleskei Tolstoy, she lived in Paris, where she worked closely with Vladimir Tatlin (*), but returned to Russia after the revolution. In a familiar photograph of Tatlin working on his projected *Monument to the Third Communist International*, she is the woman on the far left. She wrote a memoir that lies in manuscript in the Russian Museum in St. Petersburg. Toward the end of her life, I'm told, she painted flowers. Her name is so unfamiliar, even to those who should know, that in an unfortunate caption on the wall of a 1991 Kazimir Malevich (*) exhibition at New York's Metropolitan Museum she was cited as "Symshits-Tolstoya." I initially knew about her as my grandmother's sister.

Bowlt, John. "The Construction of Space." In *Von der Fläche zum Raum/From Surface to Space*. Cologne, Germany: Galerie Gmurzynska, 1974.

EAMES, Charles and Ray (1907–1978; 1912–1988, b. R. Kaiser).

In addition to being prominent industrial designers, very much for hire, the Eames, husband and wife working with equal credit, made several innovative films for their clients. *Glimpses of USA* (1959) consisted of seven films, composed from still photos projected simultaneously on seven thirty-two-foot screens that were shown continuously for twelve-minute stretches at the Moscow World's Fair. *House of Science* (1962) was a six-screen film, fifteen and one-half minutes long, created for the Seattle World's Fair. *Think* (1964–1965), made for the New York World's Fair, featured twenty-two screens of various shapes.

A Rough Sketch for a Proposed Film Dealing with the Powers of Ten and the Relative Size of Things in the Universe (1968) became the preliminary version of *Powers of Ten* (1977), both of which deal concretely with questions of

L: Eames molded plywood chair, 1946; r: Eames molded fiberglass chair, 1952. *Courtesy Henry Miller Archives.*

scale. (The later videotape produced by Charles Eames's daughter, Demetrios Eames, reverses the sequence of the films.) Though these shorts were made for instructional purposes (with funding from IBM, no less), the concept of enlargements (and then contractions) by powers of ten (at a quick and regular speed) is so original and breathtaking that the results attain esthetic quality. After pulling back continuously from the hand of a sleeping man into the galaxies (10 to the 24th power), in each ten seconds moving ten times the distance traveled in the previous ten seconds, the camera returns at a yet faster pace, entering the man's skin, revealing finally the structure of the atom (10 to the minus-13th power), in sum traversing the universe and the microcosm, all in less than eight minutes. On the left side of the screen in the earlier film are three chronometers measuring distance and time. This sort of conceptual tripping makes even *2001* (∗), say, seem as elementary as scientific exposition.

The French arts historian Frank Popper credits Charles Eames with constructing a *Do-Nothing Machine* (1955) powered by solar energy, while several histories of contemporary architecture acknowledge the residential house that the Eameses built for themselves. Charles is also credited with the inventive design of chairs and the discovery of alternative materials, particularly molded plywood, for their manufacture.

Morrison, Philip, and Phylis Morrison, and the Office of Charles and Ray Eames. *Powers of Ten*. San Francisco: Scientific American Library–W.H. Freeman, 1982.

Schrader, Paul. "The Films of Charles Eames." *Film Quarterly* XXIII/3 (Spring 1970).

EDGERTON, HAROLD (1903). See STROBE LIGHT

EGGELING, Viking (1880–1925).

Born in Sweden, Eggeling moved to Paris before the end of the 19th century and then to Switzerland, where he became an early contributor to the Dada (∗) movement. In collaboration with Hans Richter (∗), he worked initially with abstract picture strips, hoping to discover "rhythm in painting" through all the possible permutations of certain linear and spatial relationships. After making scroll paintings, the two artists put their scrolls onto animated films. Producing more than a thousand drawings by his own hand, Eggeling made the classic film *Diagonalsymphonien* (1924, *Diagonal Symphony*), in addition to two other films completed just before his premature death.

O'Konor, Louise. *Viking Eggeling: Life and Work.* Trans. Catherine G. Sundström and Anne Bibby. Stockholm, Sweden: Almqvist & Wiksell, 1971.

EINSTEIN, Carl (1885–1940). Trained in philosophical esthetics, Einstein published at the beginning of the century a pioneering book on African sculpture that influenced both Cubism (∗) and Dada (∗). His novel *Bebuquin* (1912), subtitled "The Dilettantes of Miracles," incorporated incoherence into its text. "Too few people have the courage to talk complete nonsense," he wrote. "Nonsense which is frequently repeated becomes an integrating force in our thought; at a certain level of intelligence we are not at all interested in what is correct or rational any more." *Bebuquin* became a milestone of advanced fiction. Einstein fought on the loyalist side in the Spanish Civil War (1936–1939), after which he went to Paris. When it fell to the Nazis, he escaped to southern France; but, unable to emigrate to America because of his prior service against Franco, he committed suicide.

Einstein, Carl. *Werke.* 4 vols. Berlin, Germany: Fannei & Walz (Kantstr. 152, W-1000/12), 1980–1992.

EISENSTEIN, Sergei Mikhailovich (1898–1948). His *Battleship Potemkin* (1925; aka, simply, *Potemkin*) was the first distinctly Soviet film to receive international acclaim. Exemplifying the power of montage, or the rapid cutting between scenes to portray conflict, this film showed how radically different film could be from the theatrical stage, or from the filming of staged activities. His reputation established, Eisenstein became enough of a cultural celebrity for Soviet officials to worry about and thus restrict his subsequent activities. While the original negative of *Battleship Potemkin* was mutilated, his next film, *October* (1927), had to be re-edited after Leon Trotsky's demotion, reportedly under Joseph Stalin's personal scrutiny. Invited to work in Hollywood in 1930, Eisenstein made several film proposals that were not accepted. With the help of Upton Sinclair (1878–1968), he began a feature about Mexico that was not finished until decades after Eisenstein's death, albeit in incomplete form. Returning to the Soviet Union,

Sergei Eisenstein, *The Battleship Potemkin*, 1925. *Courtesy Kultur/White Star video.*

Eisenstein was allowed to work on only a few of several possible projects, and then production was often halted before the film was complete. Before his death at fifty, of a second heart attack, Eisenstein also wrote classic essays that have been read by everyone seriously interested in film.

Eisenstein, Sergei. *Film Form/The Film Sense* (1949, 1942). Ed. and trans. Jay Leyda. NY: Meridian, 1957.

EL TEATRO CAMPESINO (1965; Farmworkers' Theater, aka ETC). Formed by Luis Valdez (1942), who had worked with the San Francisco Mime Troupe (∗) and retained the SFMT's love of signs and songs, ETC recruited untrained, instinctive performers, initially to publicize a grape strike in California and, by extension, to organize Mexican-American itinerant farm laborers into the United Farm Workers union. Addressing Chicano audiences during the working summers, ETC presented short plays, called "actos," in a mixture of Spanish and English, showing stereotypes of workers and bosses in the manner of *commedia dell'arte*. ETC staged

El Teatro Campesino, *Simply Maria*, 1992; l to r: Linda Lopez, Dena Martinez, Wilma Bonet. *Photo: Brad Shirakawa, courtesy California Artists Management.*

such highly original theater that, thanks to prompt critical recognition, it toured American universities during the off-farm seasons. A skilled scenarist-director, Valdez subsequently produced the play *Zoot Suit* (1978), which transferred from Los Angeles to Broadway, and feature-length films, including *La Bamba* (1987).

Valdez, Luis y El Teatro Campesino. *Actos.* San Juan Bautista, CA: Cucaracha, 1971.

Weisman, John. *Guerilla Theater: Scenarios for Revolution.* Garden City, NY: Doubleday, 1973.

ELECTRO-ACOUSTIC MUSIC. See MUSIQUE CONCRÈTE; HANSON, Sten

ELECTRONIC BOOKS. See HYPERTEXT

ELECTRONIC MUSIC (c. 1910). Used accurately, Electronic Music describes not one new thing but many new things that are still appearing; for music, of all the arts, has been the most constant beneficiary of recent technological developments. These inventions offer not only new instruments but technically superior versions of older ones for both composers and performers. Do not forget that modern technologies created new listening situations for music, beginning, of course, with the capacity to record musical sound to be played back at a later date (initially through a phonograph), and then with the capacity (initially provided by radio) to transmit in live time musical sound from one source to many outlets. Neither of those capabilities existed in the 19th century.

The American who co-invented night lights for outdoor sports arenas, Thaddeus Cahill (1867–1934), also built at the beginning of this century the Telharmonium, a 200-ton machine that could synthesize musical sounds for distribution over telephone lines. The machine had to be big and loud, because Cahill did not know the principle of acoustic amplification. Nowadays, even a common home-audio system can radically transform an existing instrumental sound, not only making it louder but also accentuating its treble or bass, if not redefining its timbre and extending the duration of such redefined sound to unlimited lengths.

By the 1960s, microphone pickups were incorporated into a whole range of instruments—guitar, double bass, piano, saxophone, clarinet, flute—to give each more presence than it previously had. Whereas early electronic pop musicians performed with only single speakers, groups new to the 1960s used whole banks of huge speakers to escalate their sounds to unprecedentedly high volumes, thereby also creating such technical dysfunctions as distortion, hum, buzzing, and ear-piercing feedback. Among classical musicians, Philip Glass (*) and Mauricio Kagel (*) exploited the volume controls and mixing panel of a standard recording studio to radically modify the music made by live performers, so that what the audience heard—what became available on record—would be radically different from the sounds originally made.

Electronic Music also includes wholly new instruments, beginning with the Theremin (*) in the early 1920s. In 1928, the French inventor Maurice Martenot (1898–1980) introduced the Ondes Martenot ("Martenot's Waves"), a keyboard that electronically produces one note at a time and can slide through its entire tonal range. In 1930 came Frederick Trautwein's (1888–1956) Trautonium, another electronic one-note generator that could be attached to a piano, requiring the performer to devote one hand to each instrument.

Unlike the Ondes Martenot and the Theremin, which were designed to produce radically different sounds, the Hammond organ was invented in the 1930s to imitate electronically the familiar sounds of a pipe organ, but musicians discovered the electronic organ had capabilities for sustained reverberation and tremolo that were impossible before. The original synthesizers (∗) were essentially electronic organs designed to generate a greater range of more precisely specified (and often quite innovative) musical sounds. Synthesizers became something else when they could incorporate sounds made outside of the instrument and process them into unprecedented acoustic excperiences. This tradition became the source of what is currently called live Electronic Music.

Another line of Electronic Music depended upon the development of magnetic audiotape that could be neatly edited and recomposed; audiotapes also became the preferred storage medium for electronic compositions. Sound previously recorded in the environment could be enhanced by being played at a faster speed or a slower speed, or by being passed through filters that removed certain frequencies or added echo or reverberation. Extended echoing dependent upon tape-delay was also possible. *Musique concrète* (∗) was based upon these techniques.

The next step was to work entirely with electronically generated sounds, beginning with those from elementary sound generators, such as sawtooth, triangular, and variable rectangular waves. One of the best early endeavors in this vein was Bülent Arel's *Music for a Sacred Service* (1961). The step after that involved mixing sounds that were originally live with artificial sources on a single fixed tape. Once stereophonic and then multi-track tape became available, sounds from separate sources, even recorded at separate times, could be mixed together. When played back, these sounds could be distributed to speakers that could surround the spectator with sound; they could conduct pseudo-conversations with one another.

Because wholly Electronic Music did not depend upon instruments, it eschewed conventional scoring. Indeed, if a piece were created entirely "by ear," so to speak, there would be no score at all, initially creating a problem with the American copyright office, which would accept scores but not tapes as evidence of authorship. Partly to deal with this problem, tape composers developed all kinds of inventive timeline graphings in lieu of scores.

A quarter-century ago, the composer Virgil Thomson (1896–1989) suggested, in the course of an article on John Cage (∗), that any sound emerging from loudspeakers (and thus electronic at some point in its history) was fundamentally debased. Although his opinion was dismissed and is perhaps forgotten, can I be alone in having the experience, usually in a church, of hearing music that initially sounds funny? I know why, I must remind myself—no amplification.

Since the arrival of Robert Moog's (∗) synthesizer (∗) and then the computer (∗) brought other kinds of Electronic Music, they are discussed separately in this book.

Darter, Tom. *The Art of Electronic Music*. Ed. Greg Armbruster. NY: Morrow, 1984.

Thomson, Virgil. "Cage and the Collage of Noises." In *A Virgil Thomson Reader*. NY: Dutton, 1981.

ELIOT, T.S. (1888–1965, b. Thomas Stearns E.).

Where and when was Eliot avant-garde? Not in his pseudo-juvenile *Old Possum's Book of Practical Cats* (1939), or in the solemn footnotes at the end of *The Waste Land* (1922). One could make a case for *Sweeney Agonistes* (1932) as a conceptual play, because it cannot be staged as is; but to my mind, Eliot's greatest departure was publishing, even in his initial *Collected Poems* (1930), several works that are explicitly introduced as "Unfinished." The heirs and editors of a dead poet might have made that qualifying term, but rarely has a living poet done it, especially in his or her early forties. The assumption is that even in an admittedly unfinished state a text such as "Cariolan" can be read on its own.

Advocates of poems composed from words "found" in the works of others, rather than wholly created from within, have quoted Eliot's essay on Thomas Massinger for this rationale: "Immature poets imitate; mature poets steal; bad poets deface what they take, and good poets make it into something better, or at least something different." However, by no measure was Eliot a pioneering found poet (∗).

Eliot, T.S. *The Complete Poems and Plays*. NY: Harcourt, Brace, 1962.

EMSHWILLER, Ed (1925–1990).

Emshwiller began as an illustrator, particularly of science fiction, before producing his first film, *Dance Chromatic* (1959), combining live action with animated Abstract painting. In addition to working as a cameraman on numerous television documentaries and independent films, he produced

Relativity (1966), which he called a "film poem." While continuing to work with film, he pioneered video art, particularly in *Scape-mates* (1972), which uses an animation technology partly of his own design and ranks among the earliest artistic videotapes that can still be screened without embarrassment. Independent for most of his professional life, Emshwiller became in 1979 a dean at the California Institute of the Arts. His wife, Carol E. (1921) has published several collections of scrupulously strange experimental short fiction.

Russett, Robert and Cecile Starr. *Experimental Animation*. NY: Van Nostrand, 1976.

Emshwiller, Carol. *Toy in Our Cause*. NY: Harper & Row, 1974.

ENO, Brian (1948). A prolific producer of recordings, formally untrained in music, Eno adapts avant-garde ideas for more popular purposes; only occasionally do they survive as consequential innovative art. He collaborated on Gavin Bryars's (*) recordings; Eno also recruited Bryars and Cornelius Cardew (*), among others, to make *"1, 2, 1-2-3-4"* (for Eno's Obscure label), in which several musicians, each wearing headphones, hear music that they must try to reproduce in live performance. The Eno classic is *Portsmouth Sinfonia* (1974), for which musically subamateur art-school students were recruited to perform such classical warhorses as Rossini's *William Tell Overture* and Johann Strauss's *Blue Danube Waltz*. Though the joke may be simple, the result is complex humor. The idea was not to create chaos but to establish preconditions that could only result in chaotic and highly original comic semblances of familiar originals.

Eno, Brian. *Portsmouth Sinfonia*. NY: Columbia KC 33049, 1974.

ENVIRONMENT. This term describes an enclosed space that is artistically enhanced. The materials defining the space might be visual, sculptural, kinetic, or even acoustic, or may have combinations of all these elements, but they give the space an esthetic character it would not otherwise have. To put it differently, thanks to what the artist does, the space itself becomes a surrounding work of art. Among the classic Environments are the Sistine Chapel in Rome and the Dome of the Rock in Jerusalem. In recent art, consider Stanley Landesman's multiply mirrored room, *Walk-In Infinity Chamber* (1968), in which spectators inside the Environment see themselves infinitely reflected; the kinetic galleries mounted by the artists' collective known only as USCO (*) in the late 1960s; Claes Oldenburg's (*) *The Store* (1962), which was filled with ironic renditions of seedy objects; and John Cage's (*) *HPSCHD* (*), which filled a 15,000-seat basketball arena with sounds and images for several hours (but could have gone on forever). An Environment differs, on one hand, from a mixed-means (*) theatrical piece that has a definite beginning and an end and, on the other, from an installation (*), which describes art made for a particular site, theoretically to inhabit it forever or be destroyed when the exhibition is over.

Kostelanetz, Richard. "USCO." In *On Innovative Art(ist)s*. Jefferson, NC: McFarland, 1992.

ERDMAN, Jean (1914). As a member of Martha Graham's (*) dance company in the early 1940s, Erdman collaborated with Merce Cunningham (*), who also danced with Graham at the time. On her own, Erdman wrote, directed, and choreographed *The Coach with the Six Insides* (1962), which ranks among the most extraordinary theatrical productions in my lifetime. Initially an adaptation of James Joyce's *Finnegans Wake* (*), on which her husband, Joseph Campbell (1908–1989), had incidentally coauthored the first critical book, *The Coach* faithfully portrays the technique of multiple reference that defines Joyce's classic, even if a woman, Anna Livia Plurabelle, played by Erdman herself, replaces H.C. Earwicker at the center of Joyce's five-person mythology. As Don McDonagh remembers, "At one moment she is the keening Irishwoman bemoaning the sorrows of her life and her race's difficulties. At another moment she is Belinda the hen, who scratches and reveals a letter that no one can read, and she transforms herself into a dancing rain." The piece offered a flood of puns and striking turns of phrase that, in my experience even after several visits, were never entirely assimilated. It was magnificent; I'd see it again tomorrow.

McDonagh, Don. *The Complete Guide to Modern Dance*. Garden City, NY: Doubleday, 1976.

ERNST, Max (1891–1976; b. Maximilian E.). After six years studying philosophy, Ernst fought in World War I; soon after his demobilization, he became a leader of Cologne Dada (∗), known by 1919 as "Dadamax." Quickly moving over to Parisian Surrealism (∗), Ernst is credited with introducing the techniques of collage (∗) and Photomontage (∗) to Surrealist art. Surrealist collage differed from Dada in aiming not to juxtapose dissimilars but to weave from "found" pictures a coherent subconscious image. Ernst's best collages draw upon banal engravings, some of which he incorporated into book-art narratives that I rank among his strongest works: *La Femme 100 Têtes* (1929) and *Une semaine de bonté* (1934). The latter, subtitled *A Surrealist Novel in Collage*, is actually a suite of separate stories that depend upon pasting additions onto existing illustrations. Ernst developed *frottage*, which comes from tracing patterns found in an object (e.g., the grain of a floorboard, the texture of sackcloth) as a technique for freeing the subconscious by relieving the author of direct control, becoming the visual analog for André Breton's (∗) automatic writing. During World War II, Ernst went to New York, where he

Max Ernst, image from *Une semaine de bonté*, 1934. *Collection Richard Kostelanetz.*

married successively Peggy Guggenheim (1898–1979), a major patron of the avant-garde, and Dorothea Tanning (1910), herself an important artist and writer. Ernst remained in America until 1952. While in the U.S., he collaborated with Breton and Marcel Duchamp (∗) on the periodical *VVV* (1942).

Ernst, Max. *Une Semaine de bonté* (1934). NY: Dover, 1976.

Russell, John. *Max Ernst: Life and Work.* NY: Abrams, 1967.

Tanning, Dorothea. *Birthday.* Santa Monica, CA: Lapis, 1986.

ESCHER, M.C. (1898–1972; b. Maurits Cornelis E.).

The art cognoscenti can be divided almost evenly into those who appreciate Escher and those who think his visual art slick kitsch. What is interesting about this particular dichotomy is that, unlike other opinion-splitters, this test has no ostensible relation to anything else. After establishing a style of repeated symmetrical configurations of animals, Escher made geometrical illusions, such as a stairway that appears to be constantly ascending or a water sluice that is constantly descending, using reason to portray what is, as a whole, not credible, which is to say that he made a rational art to portray what is not rational. As these images became more familiar in the late sixties, when they appeared on T-shirts, posters, and even coffee mugs, Escher's work was dismissed as decorative—a kind of contemporary Dutch equivalent of Irish illuminated manuscripts (e.g., *The Book of Kells* [c. 8th–9th century]). The simplest measure of Escher's originality is a visual intelligence that is easily identifiable as his.

Schattschneider, Doris. *M.C. Escher: Visions of Symmetry.* NY: W.H. Freeman, 1990.

Locher, J. L., ed. *M.C. Escher.* NY: Abrams, 1982.

EUROPERA (1987).

John Cage's (∗) first opera produced with the assistance of Andrew Culver (1953) is an encompassing pastiche of sounds and costumes from the repertoire of traditional (i.e., European) operas that are no longer protected by copyright. The title, a shrewd verbal invention, incorporates not only "Europe" and "opera," but it also sounds like "your opera," which is to say everyone's opera. From the score library of New York's Metropolitan Opera, Cage

John Cage, *Europera*, 1987. *Photo © Beatriz Schiller, courtesy Arts Services/Lovely Music.*

pulled music pages to be photocopied at random. Though flutists, say, each received music previously composed for their instrument, each flutist was given different scores. Thus, motifs from various operas could be heard from the same instruments simultaneously.

Noticing that operatic voices are customarily classified under nineteen categories (for sopranos alone, for instance, coloratura, lyric coloratura, lyric, lyric spinto, and dramatic), Cage requested nineteen singers, each of whom are allowed to select which public domain arias they might sing; but only in the performance itself would they find out when, where, or if they could sing them. So several arias, each from a different opera, could be sung at once, to instrumental accompaniment(s) culled from yet other operas.

The costumes were likewise drawn from disparate sources, and these clothes were assigned to individual singers without reference to what they would sing or do onstage. From a wealth of opera pictures, Cage selected various images that were then enlarged and painted, only in black and white, for the flats. These flats are mechanically brought onstage from left or right or above with an arbitrariness reminiscent of the changing backdrops in the Marx Brothers' *A Night at the Opera* (1935). Once a flat or prop is no longer needed, it is simply laid to rest beside the performing area, visibly contributing to the chaotic mise-en-scène. A computer program

ensures that the lighting of the stage will be similarly haphazard.

For the libretti offered to the audience, Cage simply extracted sentences from traditional operatic plot summaries, replacing specific names with pronouns like "he" and "she." These sentences are scrambled to produce twelve different pseudo-summaries, each two paragraphs long (to coincide with the two acts), none of which has any intentional connection to what actually occurs on stage. Each program distributed at *Europera*'s premiere had only one of the twelve synopses, which meant that people sitting next to one another had different guides, further contributing to the chaos.

What *Europera* is finally about, from its transcriptions of phrases and images to its libretti, is the culture of opera, at once a homage and a burlesque, offering a wealth of surprises with familiar material; its theme could be defined, simply, as the conventions of 19th-century European opera after a 20th-century avant-garde American has processed it. As with *HPSCHD* (∗), Cage made "chamber" versions that, if only for diminished scale, were far less successful.

Kostelanetz, Richard. "John Cage, 75, Writes First, 'Great American' Opera" (1988). In *On Innovative Music(ian)s.* NY: Limelight, 1989.

EXPRESSIONISM (c. 1895). This concept is so unsympathetic to me that I fear misrepresentation, but here goes. The central assumption is that, through the making of a work, the artist transfers his or her emotions and feelings to the viewer/reader. Such art is judged "expressive" to the degree that feelings and emotions are represented in it; therefore, the success of such communication often depends upon the use of images or subjects familiar to the audience. (The trouble is that different viewers get different messages, especially in different places and at different times. That difficulty perhaps accounts for why the concept of Expressionism is scarcely universal, being almost unknown in Eastern art.) Arising from Romanticism that tied Expression to the notion of "genius," the term became popular around the turn of the century, beginning with Edward Munch's (1863–1944) famous woodcut depicting a face proclaiming terror. Indeed, the term "Expressionistic" became an honorific, implicitly excluding whatever arts lacked such quality. Responding to the examples of Munch and Van Gogh in painting, as well as Oskar Kokoschka (1886–1980) and Egon Schiele (1890–1918) after them, critics began to confine Expressionism to art produced in Northern and/or Teutonic European countries, in contrast to French and/or Mediterranean traditions. This notion legitimized German Expressionism of the 1920s and 1930s and perhaps American Abstract Expressionism (*) afterwards. The German dancer Mary Wigman (*) appropriated Expressionist esthetics for her dance works.

Kandinsky, Wassily, and Franz Marc, eds. *The 'Blaue Reiter' Almanac* (1912). NY: Viking, 1974.

Zigrosser, C.D. *The Expressionists.* NY: Braziller, 1957.

EXTER, Alexandra (1882–1949). Exter's earliest distinguished paintings, from the time of the Russian Revolution, display geometric shapes in a larger field, somewhat more reflective of Italian Futurism (*) than other Russian Abstract Art in that period. For these planes that appear to float around one another, she favored the primary colors of red, yellow, and blue. The art historian Andrei B. Nakov, who published the first contemporary monograph on her work, speaks of a "centrifugal structure . . . based on a center of energy within the work. For this possibility is based not on the static weight of the mass but rather on its own dynamic potential whose principal role is to counteract the immobility of forms." For Yakov Protazanov's science-fiction film *Aelita* (1924), based on an Aleksei Tolstoy story about Russians transported to Mars, Exter designed costumes that emphasized geometric asymmetry, black-and-white contrasts, and the use of shiny materials. Because *Aelita* was at the time the most popular Russian film in the West, Exter emigrated to Paris, where she worked mostly as a designer for stage, fashion, and architectural interiors.

Nakov, Andrei B. *Alexandra Exter.* Paris, France: Galerie Jean Chauvelin, 1972.

———. *Russian Constructivism: "Laboratory Period."* London, England: Annely Juda, 1975.

FAHLSTRÖM, Öyvind (1928–1976). A Swede born in Brazil, Fahlström moved to Sweden in 1939 and began his artistic career with theater and Concrete Poetry (*). About the latter he wrote a manifesto about a language art that "kneaded" language apart from conventional meanings. Next came long narrative paintings that implied theatrical events. By the end of the 1950s, his use of comic-strip imagery, so different from Roy Lichtenstein's (*) subsequent exploitations, made Fahlström seem a progenitor of Pop Art (*). In the early 1960s, he made "playable" pictures whose parts the spectator could move about with magnets. Once he moved to America in 1966, where Robert Rauschenberg (*) became his principal sponsor, Fahlström's paintings became journalistic cartoons. He died too soon to capitalize on his genuine innovations.

Öyvind Fahlström. NY: Sidney Janis Gallery, 1971.

FANTASIA (1940). Aside from what you might think of Walt Disney (1901–1965), a *schlockmeister* if ever there were one, consider his most ambitious film for its virtues: luscious animation, pioneering stereo sound, and the visualizing of classical music (the last element making it a precursor of MTV's [*] "rock videos"). Even though this last idea was "stolen" from Oskar Fischinger (*), who had come to Hollywood only a few years before (and who worked on the project before resigning because his designs were compromised), Disney went far beyond previous schemes for filming classical music. Remember that *Fantasia* has sections, each produced by a different army of Hollywood technicians, and that some sections are better than others; the original soundtrack conducted by Leopold Stokowski (*) is superior to that used for the 1982 release. There has been nothing quite like *Fantasia* before or since (as it makes rock videos seem inelegant and impatient); the only films to come close, *A Corny Concerto* (1943) produced under the banner of Bugs Bunny, typically having a sharper edge, by the competing Warner Bros. studio, and Bruno Bozzetto's *Allegro Non*

Troppo (1976), an Italian feature combining rather mundane live-action with some clever animation (particularly to Maurice Ravel's *Bolero*). Rereleased every few years since its premier, *Fantasia* has recently become available, fortunately with the original Stokowski soundtrack, on both videotape and videodisc.

Finch, Christopher. *The Art of Walt Disney.* NY: Abrams, 1973.

FAULKNER, William (1897–1962). Faulkner seemed so stupid, in person and at times in print, while conservative critics were predisposed to overpraise his conventional virtues, that we tend to forget he wrote some of the greatest avant-garde fiction of the 20th century. I'm thinking initially of *The Sound and the Fury* (1929) and *As I Lay Dying* (1930), both with multiple narrators, each so radically different in intelligence (and thus style) from the others, and then of *Absalom, Absalom!* (1936), with its inimitable prose, composed of English words rushing over one another. No one wrote English like this before, and no one has quite done so since (though several have tried). A style so strong makes any plot, in this case about a Southern dynasty in the 19th century, seem secondary. Some of this extraordinary style also appears in Faulkner's short story "The Bear" (1940).

Faulkner, William. *Absalom, Absalom!* NY: Random House, 1936.

FEDERMAN, Raymond (1928). Born in France, Federman came to the U.S. after World War II, a survivor of distinctly modern disasters. After completing one of the first academic monographs about Samuel Beckett (∗), Federman published a bilingual collection of poems, some initially written in French, others initially written in English, with all translations by himself, and then *Double or Nothing* (1971), which is a highly inventive sequence of typewritten pages. Except for the bilingual prose of *Take It or Leave It* (1976), which portrays in both languages the narrator's coming to America, Federman's subsequent fiction has been less innovative. The new typeset edition (1992) of *Double or Nothing* is decidedly inferior to the original, reflecting the compromises of a university professor who is trying to be acceptable in spite of his wayward imagination.

Federman, Raymond. *Double or Nothing.* Chicago, IL: Swallow, 1971.

FELDMAN, Morton (1926–1987). Initially regarded as a composer working in the wake of John Cage (∗), Feldman eventually forged a different career, first as a tenured professor, mostly at SUNY-Buffalo, and eventually in his compositional style. His characteristic scores of the fifties and sixties are graphic notations (within fixed pagination) that merely approximate dimensions and relationships of pitches, registers, and attacks, all of which the individual performer is invited to interpret to his or her taste. Nonetheless, the sounds of Feldman's music tend to be soft and isolated, with a consistency that is audibly different from the chaos cultivated by Cage. This aural pointillism, indebted in part to Feldman's interest in contemporary painting, superficially sounds like Anton Webern's (∗) music, but the compositional choices owe more to personal intuition and thus a sense of *taste* (which is a key word in Feldman's vocabulary, unlike Cage's) than either serial (∗) systems or strictly Cagean indeterminate vocabulary. Late in his life, Feldman composed several very long pieces that are belatedly becoming available.

Feldman, Morton. *Essays.* Kerpen, Germany: Beginner, 1985.

———. *Why Patterns?/Crippled Symmetry.* Therwil, Switzerland: Hat Hut CD 2-60801-2, 1991.

FERRER, Rafael (1933). An innovation in site-specific sculpture, Ferrer's work was based upon creating preconditions for natural processes to occur. For a 1969 "Anti-Illusion" show at New York's Whitney Museum, he made *Hay Grease Steel*, which consisted of what remained after hay was tossed against a steel frame along a museum wall to which wet glue had just been applied. *Ice* (1969), an even less permanent piece, consisted of leaves piled on blocks of ice that slowly melted away. "The act of conceiving and placing the pieces takes precedence over the object quality of the works," wrote this show's co-curator James Monte. "The fact of [the unusual materials'] inclusion in the art work is much less interesting than the way in which they are used." Since the late 1970s, Ferrer has concentrated on easel paintings that mostly depict his native Puerto Rico.

Monte, James, and Marcia Tucker. *Anti-Illusion: Procedures/Materials*. NY: Whitney Museum of American Art, 1969.

FINCH, Peter (1947). Since the early 1970s, Finch has been the principal innovator in Welsh poetry, the most genuine successor to Dylan Thomas (*); but instead of florid, drunken Thomasian rhetoric, Finch has favored a variety of tight sober structures, including parodies of other poets, visual poems (*), sound poems (*), and, say, verbal imitations of Philip Glass's (*) music. The strongest work in his *Selected Poems* (1987) is "Some Blats," which is a world of interrogations, printed as individual lines without punctuation, beginning "is England green," including "is a lawnmower an object of beauty," continuing with "is really chuzz chuzz" and "is gadsass," and concluding "is sssssssss," in an implicit parody of drunken writing (and you know who). Finch also edited *Second Aeon* (1967–1974) which was the only Welsh magazine of its time to swim with the international avant-garde, not only for what it printed but for Finch's considered, small-print reviews of publications both straight and wayward. If not for him and the aforementioned Mr. Thomas, Wales wouldn't appear in this book at all; for that alone (and since no living Irish person is here), Finch deserves a Welsh knighthood.

Finch, Peter. *Selected Poems*. Mid Glamorgan, Wales: Poetry Wales, 1987.

FINLAY, Ian Hamilton (1925). I wish I liked Finlay's work more, because he is among the few contemporaries to be included in both the history of contemporary poetry and contemporary visual art. He began as a conventional Scottish poet whose first book, *The Dancers Inherit the Party* (1960), contained traditional rhymed sentiments about people in the Scottish outlands. Within a few years, he had become the principal Scottish participant in international Concrete Poetry (*), often writing poems that were just collections of nouns. His next development was visual poems (*) that transcended the limitations of the printed page, some of them created in collaboration with professional visual artists. Many of these pieces began as additions to his home garden in Lanarkshire, a remote area he rarely leaves, because he regards it (and thus the works collected there) as a refuge from the cruel modern world. Many of them have military images reminiscent of World War II. As Finlay's work assumed more political themes in the 1980s (and he came into conflict with art officials over one thing or another), his pieces have often been included in thematic exhibitions that were installed outdoors.

Abrioux, Yves. *Ian Hamilton Finlay: A Visual Primer*. Cambridge, MA: M.I.T., 1992.

FINLEY, Karen (1952). She is such a limited and thus repetitious writer that it is easy to wonder about the reasons for her current celebrity. Her subject and theme are anger, particularly in exposing what she thinks men do to women; and, though her critique is often right, she is not immune from exaggerations unfortunately devoid of irony. Her principal talent as a writer is heavy, very heavy satire. Her celebrity seems the result of a complimentary publicity campaign involving the implicit collaboration between two publicly opposed cultural groups. When the conservative columnists Evans-Novak, among others, vociferously objected to the National Endowment for the Arts' (*) funding of her work, they gave Finley the best free publicity, making her more important than she really was. On another side, the folks at the NEA, by trying to deny subsequent panel-awarded grants to Finley and comparable performers, contributed to the publicity push. (It was not for nothing that commercial publishers fifty years ago would try to have their new books banned in Boston; the publicity would guarantee increased sales everywhere else, so easily were the Boston censors manipulated, exploited, and duped.) All this notoriety prompted cultural liberals to respond by inflating Finley's importance initially with publicity and then by sponsoring her presentations (more than recompensing her for lost NEA funds), even though her art invariably disappoints those not predisposed to Finley's particular ideology. The question raised is whether tax money should pay public officials, such as Jesse Helms and the NEA chiefs, who successfully promote mediocre anti-erotica while pretending to do otherwise. The second tragedy was that the others also denied NEA grants did not receive such success, in part because their work was too profoundly shocking to be publicized.

Finley, Karen. *Shock Treatment*. San Francisco, CA: City Lights, 1990.

———. *The Truth Is Hard to Swallow*. NY: Pow Wow 069, 1990.

Bolton, Richard, ed. *Culture Wars*. NY: New Press, 1992.

Zeigler, Joseph Wesley. *Arts in Crisis: The National Endowment for the Arts vs. America*. Pennington, NJ: a cappella books, 1994.

FINNEGANS WAKE (1939). One reason why James Joyce's (∗) final book remains a monumental masterpiece is that its particular inventions have never been exceeded. The principal index of its originality is that no other major modern work, except perhaps Gertrude Stein's (∗) *Geography and Plays*, is still as widely unread and persistently misunderstood, decades after its initial publication. Unlike journalism, which tries to render complex experience in the simplest possible form, the *Wake* tells a simple story in an exceedingly complex form. Its subject is familial conflict—among two brothers, a sister, and their two parents. Exploiting the techniques of literary Symbolism, Joyce portrays numerous conflicts taking the same familial forms. The metaphors for the two brothers include competing writers, such as Pope and Swift, or competing countries, such as Britain and America, among other antagonistic pairs of roughly equal age and/or authority. This interpretation of human experience hardly ranks as "original" or "profound," but thanks to the techniques of multiple reference, incorporating innumerable examples into a single text, the theme is extended into a broad range of experience. No other literary work rivals the *Wake* in textual density; in no other piece of writing known to me are so many dimensions simultaneously articulated.

Congruent with his method, Joyce coins linguistic portmanteaus that echo various familiar words; the use of many languages serves to increase the range of multiplicity and allusion. He favors puns that serve a similar function of incorporating more than one meaning within a single unit—a verbal technique reflecting the theme of history repeating itself many times over. Thus, the book's principal theme is entwined in its method. As Samuel Beckett (∗) put it, back in 1929, "Here form *is* content, content *is* form." One implication of this method is that *Finnegans Wake* need not be read sequentially to be understood.

Whether an individual reader "accepts" or "rejects" Joyce's final masterpiece is also, in my observation, a fairly reliable symbolic test of his or her sympathy toward subsequent avant-garde writing. (Another similarly useful test can be done with the more experimental writings of Gertrude Stein.)

Joyce, James. *Finnegans Wake*. NY: Viking, 1939.

Beckett, Samuel. "Dante . . . Bruno . Vico . . Joyce." In *Our Exagmination Round His Factification for Incamination of Work in Progress* (1929). NY: New Directions, 1962.

FISCHINGER, Oskar (1900–1967). Initially a painter precociously interested in abstract interpretations of music and poetry, Fischinger produced his first animated shorts in 1920 with a wax-cutting machine of his own design. In 1926, he presented a series of shorts called "absolute film studies," individually named *Study 1*, *Study 2*, and so on, in the tradition of Abstract Art (∗). With the arrival of sound, such kinetic abstractions could accompany music. In 1933, Fischinger began working in color with a special process he helped to develop, and in 1935 he won an international prize for his *Komposition in Blau/Composition in Blue*. After emigrating to Hollywood, he made *Allegretto* to accompany jazz (∗) and later worked with Walt Disney on the J.S. Bach segment of *Fantasia* (1940) (∗). However, because his original designs were dismissed as too abstract and modified against his wishes, Fischinger acquired a deserved reputation as an animator with more artistic integrity than Disney. His *Motion Picture No. 1*, which accompanies Bach's *Brandenburg Concerto No. 3*, won the Grand Prix at the Brussels Exhibition of 1949. The last time I asked, his "absolute film studies" were not yet available on videotape.

Starr, Cecile. "Oskar Fischinger." In Russett, Robert, and Cecile Starr. *Experimental Animation*. NY: Van Nostrand, 1976.

FLAVIN, Dan (1933). Perhaps the epitome of the avant-garde minimal artist, Flavin uses the simple means of fluorescent lamps (manufactured not by himself but by others) to produce complex effects. He typically runs his lamps, sometimes various in color, along walls or locates them in corners of darkened spaces to induce a meditative atmosphere. His early works range in complexity from simple rows of vertical tubes to quite intricate arrangements of crossing tubes of green, pink, orange, and blue on the ceiling of a long corridor in his untitled piece (dedicated to Elizabeth and Richard Koshalek) shown at the Castelli Gallery in New York in 1971. Not only are the tubes in this piece set at right angles to one another and in four layers, but two of the colors are placed with their diffuser pans facing out, so that they are seen only as reflected light. One theme is visual qualities peculiar to pure fluorescent light (in contrast to the more familiar incandescent lamp). Because Flavin uses light to transform radically (and brilliantly) an architectural space, he has received many commissions. Though his preference for rectangular formats inevitably suggests the medium of painting (and the color shadings of Morris Louis [*] and Jules Olitski [1922], among others), the final experience of his exquisite art broaches qualities closer to those produced by such sacred objects as religious icons.

Smith, Brydon. *Dan Flavin, Fluorescent Light, etc.* Ottawa, Canada: National Gallery of Canada, 1969.

FLEISCHER, Dave and Max (1894–1979; 1889–1972). These two brothers were principal innovators in cinematic animation, developing films with human rather than animal characters and, in Betty Boop, the epitome of the sophisticated urban woman (who even today makes human sex symbols look reserved). In contrast to Walt Disney's crew, who were largely farm boys working in the bright light of Hollywood, the Fleischers were immigrants' children, the older born in Vienna, whose studio was located in New York City. It was their good fortune that the censors who restricted live action films were slow to discover what was happening in cartoons. Eventually forced to clean up Betty Boop's highly erotic act, the Fleischers developed several technical innovations, such as creating the illusion of depth by filming their protagonists on clear cels against a background diorama. What most impresses me, as a sometime dance critic, is the choreography of the Fleischers' people, whose continuous movements are at once evocative and delicate. My own feeling is that the Fleischers' post-censorship films, such as *Gulliver's Travels* (1939), while longer and more ambitious, are

less original and less consequential. The Fleischer studio also initiated the characters of Popeye the Sailor, whose superhuman strength depends upon spinach, and Grampie, who lives in a world of Rube Goldberg (*) inventions. Perhaps because I come from the culture of reading, I've always found conventional Hollywood films terribly slow, if not soporifically languid, in ways that cartoons by the Fleischers or Tex Avery (*) and his associates are not. The tragedy is, that while books about Disney continue to appear, appreciations of the Fleischers are scarce.

Cabarga, Leslie. *The Fleischer Story* (1976). Rev. ed. NY: Da Capo, 1988.

Maltin, Leonard. *Cartoon Madness: The Fantastic Max Fleischer Cartoons.* A retrospective feature on the A&E network, which should eventually be available on videotape.

FLUXUS (1962). A multi-art group, both formed and decimated by George Maciunas (*) roughly on the hierarchical model of Surrealism (*), though in the irreverent spirit of Dada (*). Fluxus included at various times Dick Higgins (*), Robert Watts (1923–1988), Ken Friedman (1949), Jean Dupuy (1926), Wolf Vostell (1932), Ay-O (1931), and Alison Knowles (*), among others. The myth of Fluxus has always had more success in Europe, which is more predisposed to understand the concept of an artists' group than America, even though most of its participants were Americans. Most of the best works displayed under the Fluxus banner are extremely comic, though some of the participants were scarcely so.

In the Spirit of Fluxus. Minneapolis, MN: Walker Arts Center, 1993.

FONTANA, Lucio (1899–1968). Born in Argentina of Italian parents, Fontana moved to Milan in 1905. He began as an abstract sculptor, prolific through the 1930s; but with World War II, he relocated to Buenos Aires, where he published his *Manifesto Blanco* (1946), which advocated a new art that would exploit such recent technologies as neon light and television (*). Once he returned to Italy, Fontana issued additional manifestos advocating *Spazialismo*. In 1947, he pioneered Environmental Art (*) with a room painted entirely black; two years later came his *Ambiente Spaziale*, with ultraviolet light that deliberately disoriented the viewer's perception. In the early 1950s, he made monochromic canvases to which by the late 1950s he added a clean slit that became his trademark, purportedly suggesting space behind the canvas. In the 1960s, he made massive sculptures that were slashed open like his canvases. Though one may disagree about the final value of his work, it is clear that he anticipated many ideas that others developed later.

Lucio Fontana 1899–1968: A Retrospective. NY: Guggenheim Museum, 1977.

FORD, Charles Henri (1909?, 1913?). Born in Mississippi, in a year he keeps unknown, Ford edited the first issues of the literary periodical *Blues* in Columbus, Mississippi, in 1929–1930 before moving to Paris in the early thirties, in time to be noticed favorably in Gertrude Stein's *The Autobiography of Alice B. Toklas* (1933). He subsequently collaborated with Parker Tyler on *Young and Evil* (1933, in Paris), a pioneering fictional exploration of homosexuality, more courageous in its choice of subject than its esthetic decisions. Once back in America, Ford edited *View* (1940–1947), a journal at the center of American Surrealism (*). Ford's most innovative literary art were his visual poems (*) largely made from newspaper clippings, appearing first in the self-published and extremely colorful *Spare Parts* (1966), then in *Silver Flower Coo* (1968, printed in black and white). He has also exhibited his photographs, his paintings, and his film *Johnny Minotaur* (1971).

Ford, Charles Henri. *Out of the Labyrinth: Selected Poems.* San Francisco, CA: City Lights, 1990.

———, ed. *View: 1940–47.* NY: Thunder's Mouth (54 Greene St., 4-S, 10013), 1991.

FOREMAN, Richard (1937). Since I have known Foreman since high school (and he was a few years ahead of me in college), I have followed his work sympathetically from its very beginnings and so feel obliged to say something special here. However, every time I begin to write anything, I find myself so impressed by his own statements that, remembering my vow never to do anything professionally that anyone else can do better, I reprint one of them here:

In 1968, I began to write for the theater that I wanted to see, which was radically different from any style of theater that I had seen. In brief, I imagined a theater which broke down all elements into a kind of atomic structure— and showed those elements of story, action, sound, light, composition, gesture, in terms of the smallest building-block units, the basic cells of the perceived experience of both living and art-making. The scripts themselves read like notations of my own process of imagining a theater piece. They are the evidence of a kind of effort in which the mind's leaps and inventions may be rendered as part of a process not unique to the artist in question (myself) but typical of the building-up which goes on through all modes of coming-into-being (human and non-human). I want to refocus the attention of the spectator on the intervals, gaps, relations, and rhythms which saturate the objects (acts and physical props) which are the "givens" of any particular play.

Perhaps because his work is not easily understood by others, Foreman customarily directs his texts, as well as designing both the stage and the sound.

Foreman, Richard. *Plays and Manifestos.* Ed. Kate Davey. NY: New York University, 1976.

———. *Reverberation Machines: The Later Plays and Essays.* Barrytown, NY: Station Hill, 1985.

———. *Unbalancing Acts.* NY: Pantheon, 1992.

FORTI, Simone (1935). Italian-born, American-raised, this dancer/choreographer studied with Anna Halprin (*) and collaborated with her husbands Robert Morris (*) and Robert Whitman (*) in their mixed-means (*) performances. Some of her dances reflect Minimalism (*) in their simple organizational structures and their use of everyday movements to accomplish particular tasks (thereby meriting the term "task dances"). In *Slantboard* (1961), for instance, dancers maneuver on a slanted board by holding onto ropes to prevent total slippage. *Huddle* (1961) involves dancers huddling in a mass to form a base for members to emerge from and climb over. While continuing to work with improvisational forms, Forti became increasingly interested in childlike and animal movements as a basic vocabulary for her works.—Katy Matheson

Forti, Simone. *Handbook in Motion.* Halifax, Canada, and NY: Nova Scotia College of Art & Design and New York University, 1974.

FOUND ART (c. 1910s). One of the principal innovations of avant-garde visual arts in the 1910s was the introduction of real objects into an artistic context. In America, while Charles Ives (*) incorporated hymn tunes into classical music, Marcel Duchamp (*) insisted through his "ready-mades" that a *Bicycle Wheel* (1913), a *Bottle Rack* (1914), and even a urinal he called *Fountain* (1917) be regarded as art. Back in Europe, painters introduced ticket stubs and newspaper clippings into collages that were exhibited as paintings. Not until the 1960s did visual artists become so concerned with estheticizing mundane objects that George Maciunas (*) for one coined the term "Concretism," which he defined as "the opposite of abstraction." He continued:

> The realistic painting is not realistic; it's illusionistic. You can have illusionistic music; you can have abstract music, you can have concrete music. In music, let's say if you have an orchestra play, that's abstract music, because the sounds are all done artificially by musical instruments. But if that orchestra is trying to imitate a storm, say, like Debussy or Ravel do it, that's illusionistic; it's still not realistic. But if you're going to use noises like the clapping of the audience or farting or whatever, now that's concrete. Or street car sounds, or a whole bunch of dishes falling from the shelf. That's concrete—nothing illusionistic or abstract about it.

By the 1980s, found sculptural objects became an over-publicized movement that, at least to those who knew history, seemed terribly derivative.

Rosenblum, Robert. *Cubism and Twentieth-Century Art* (1961). NY: Abrams, 1977.

Maciunas, George. "Transcript of a Videotaped Interview by Larry Miller, March 24, 1978." In *FLUXUS, etc./Addenda I*, ed. Jon Hendricks. NY: INK, 1983.

FOUND POETRY. The found poet discovers poetry in language not her or his own. The simplest strategy is to break apart prose into lines, with appropriately sensitive line breaks. William Butler Yeats took Walter Pater's prose evocation of the Mona Lisa and, turning it into free verse, made it the initial poem in his *The Oxford Book of Modern Verse* (1936). The *Times Literary Supplement* in 1965 published a serial debate over the Scottish poet Hugh MacDiarmid's authoring a poem that begins with a verse arrangement of another poet's short story. The Canadian practitioner John Robert Colombo (*) identifies the first book wholly of found poetry as John S. Barnes's *A Stone, A Leaf, A Door* (1945), which consists entirely of the novelist Thomas Wolfe's prose broken apart to look like poetry. Bern Porter (*) composed his "founds" from words found in advertising, appropriating typography as well as language, while John Cage (*) has drawn on Henry David Thoreau and James Joyce (*), among others, for his shrewdly chosen source texts. Recent developments in the visual arts have given to "appropriation" a new authority that has, curiously, not extended into literary appreciation.

Colombo, John Robert. "Found Poetry." In *The Avant-Garde Tradition in Literature*, ed. Richard Kostelanetz. Buffalo, NY: Prometheus, 1982.

THE FOUR HORSEMEN (1970–1989). They were four Canadians of independent literary reputations who came together to jam, much as freelance jazz musicians do: bp Nichol (*); Paul Dutton (1943), who has worked solo in various experimental modes; Rafael Barreto-Rivera (1944), born in Puerto Rico, who has likewise published both texts and tapes; and Steve McCaffery (1948), a London-born writer who deserves a separate entry here, if I could figure out how to summarize his difficult, perhaps excessively obscure work (and so refer curious readers to Marjorie Perloff's 1991 book, *Radical Artifice*). The Horsemen's initial text-sound (*) works were collected on a record called *CaNADAda* (1972), in which the strongest piece is a fugue ("Allegro 108") that opens, "Ben den hen ken len men pen ken fen men yet," with one voice chanting alone on a single note. Then a second voice enters, at first chanting nonsynchronously, but then in unison with the initial voice, as a third voice enters, chanting along on a single note. "Allegro 108" develops a steady emphatic rhythm typical of voices clearly accustomed to working with one another, all devoid of instrumental accompaniment. Other Horsemen collaborations incorporate sentences and fully written texts. After Nichol's sudden death, the Horsemen fulfilled prior commitments as a trio and then disbanded. Another Canadian sound poetry group with a similar multi-man makeup called itself Owen Sound.

Four Horsemen. *CaNADAda*. Toronto, Canada: Griffin House, 1972.

————. *Horse d'Ouevres*. Toronto, Canada: General Publishing, 1975.

————. *The Prose Tattoo: Selected Performance Scores*. Kenosha, WI: Membrane (P.O. Box 4190, 53141), 1983.

FRANK, Peter (1950). The James Gibbons Huneker (∗) of his generation, Frank is a polymathic critic, better at enthusiasm than discrimination, who has written about all the arts. More skilled at reviews than books, he should have become an interdepartmental newspaper critic; but, since this has not occurred, there is reason to believe that newspaper executives today are not as culturally sophisticated as they were in Huneker's times. Thus, at various times, Frank has written for innumerable art and music magazines. In the late 1980s, this native New Yorker moved to California, editing a new journal there. His books include an intelligently annotated bibliography of the Something Else Press and a less intelligent survey of visual arts in the 1980s.

Frank, Peter. *Something Else Press*. N.p.: McPherson & Co., 1983.

————, and Michael McKenzie. *New, Used & Improved*. NY: Abbeville, 1987.

FREE JAZZ (c. 1960). This type of jazz (∗) was supposed to be free of any preconceived notions of melody, harmony, or rhythm. The crucial example was the 1960 Ornette Coleman (∗) LP, *Free Jazz*, in which two four-man ensembles were invited to play simultaneously, supposedly with no preconceived score. Actually, group passages were preplanned, while the rhythm section never drops out completely. Because all eight musicians never improvise at once, usually a solo voice emerges from the crowd only to be reabsorbed into the ensemble.

What Coleman actually did is free the soloist from having to follow a set chord pattern, thus putting an even greater burden on him or her to create interesting melodies. He felt that jazz players had fallen into predictable ruts and that the only way out was to avoid (as much as possible) the established riffs and melodic lines that were associated with classic jazz compositions. He also hoped that members of the ensemble, instead of eyeballing a score, would listen more carefully to what each musician was doing, becoming more sensitive to minute variations in timbre, melody, or rhythm.—with Richard Carlin

Coleman, Ornette. *Free Jazz*. NY: Atlantic SD-1364/-2 (LP/CD), 1960.

Budds, Michael J. *Jazz in the 60s: The Expansion of Musical Resources and Techniques*. Iowa City, IA: University of Iowa, 1978.

FREYTAG-LORINGHOVEN, Elsa von (1874–1927). Born in eastern Germany, the daughter of a contractor, she married a baron whose hyphenated family name she took. Arriving in the New York art world before the beginning of World War I, she became known as the "Baroness," patronizing new art and writing in her second language, English, the most hysterical, Expressionist (∗) poetry to appear in avant-garde magazines at that time. A typical title is "Mineself-Minesoul-and-Mine-Cast-Iron Lover," which includes such lines as this: "Heia! ja-hoho! hisses mine starry-eyed soul in her own language." (She also wrote hundreds of German poems that remain untranslated.) She collaborated with the American artist Morton Schamberg (1881–1918) in his classic sculpture *God* (1916), made out of a miter box and a plumbing trap. Though she had not participated in any European Dada (∗), she became the center of its New York incarnation.

Though scarcely young when she came to America, her displays of her nude self make subsequent artist-exhibitionists seem esthetically slight. In his *Life Among the Surrealists* (1962), Matthew Josephson remembers: "She decorated her own person in a mechanistic style of her own device, shaving her head and painting it purple; wearing an inverted scuttle for a hat, a vegetable grater as a brooch, long ice-cream spoons for earrings, and metal teaballs attached to her pendulant breasts. Thus adorned and clad in an old fur coat, or simply a Mexican blanket, and very little underneath, she would saunter forth to serve as one of the truly curious sights of the 'Village' forty years ago." In *An American Artist's Story* (1939), George Biddle recalls:

> Having asked me in her high-pitched German stridency, whether I required a model, I told her I should like to see her in the nude. With a royal gesture she swept apart the folds of a

scarlet raincoat. She stood before me quite naked—or nearly so. Over the nipples of her breasts were two tin tomato cans, fastened with a green string around her back. Between the tomato cans hung a very small bird-cage and within it a crestfallen canary. One arm was covered from wrist to shoulder with celluloid curtain rings, pilfered from a furniture display in Wanamaker's. She removed her hat, trimmed with gilded carrots, beets, and other vegetables. Her hair was close cropped and dyed vermillion.

Decades later, someone not too swift coined the term "Body Art" for self-decoration of this sort.

Josephson, Matthew. *Life Among the Surrealists.* NY: Holt, 1962.

Reiss, Robert. "'My Baroness': Elsa von Freytag-Loringhoven." In *New York Dada,* ed. Rudolf E. Kuenzli. NY: Willis Locker & Owens, 1986.

FRYE, Northrop (1912–1991). A loyal Canadian, Frye spent his entire professional life in the country where he was born and mostly educated, even though he became for a time the most influential literary theorist in the English-speaking world. Perhaps because his first major book dealt with William Blake (*), Frye had a broad conception of literary possibility; and with an extraordinary memory for literary details, as well as a capacity to view the largest cultural terrain from the greatest distance, he could make generalizations appropriate to many examples. He belongs in this book less for his major theories, which remain influential, than for passing insights into avant-garde writing that remain freshly persuasive: "Literature seems to be intermediate between music and painting: its words form rhythms which approach a musical sequence of sounds at one of its boundaries, and form patterns which approach the hieroglyphic or pictorial image at the other. The attempt to get as near to these boundaries as possible form the main body of what is called experimental writing." This has the virtue of accurately placing visual poetry (*) and text-sound (*) in the largest cultural context.

Frye, Northrop. *Anatomy of Criticism.* Princeton, NJ: Princeton University, 1957.

FULLER, Buckminster (1895–1983). The architectural historian Wayne Andrews noted, in *Architecture, Ambition, and Americans* (1955), two indigenous architectural traditions, producing buildings as fundamentally different as their rationales. One, typified in American thought by William James (1842–1910), holds that a beautiful building will enhance the lives of all who dwell within and around it, as elegant architecture does elegant people make. The second tradition, from Thorstein Veblen (1857–1929), holds that, because a building's usefulness as a human habitat is primary, technical efficiency and human considerations create architectural quality and perhaps a certain kind of beauty.

The most original and profound Veblenian was Fuller, who based his architecture upon the "dymaxion" principle (the maximalization of dynamic performance), which he related to industrial ephemeralization: the achievement of increasingly more results from increasingly less materials; the practical advantages of mass production; and the universal applicability of all architectural solutions. Because Fuller came to architecture from an education in engineering and experience in the construction-materials business, his designs lack discernible stylistic antecedents.

His Dymaxion House (1927) is a circular multi-room area fifty feet in diameter, suspended by cable from a central unit, forty feet high, that can be set into the ground anywhere on earth. The living space is partitioned into several rooms, while the volume between its floor and the ground can be curtained and filled to the owner's taste, its most likely use being an indoor parking place.

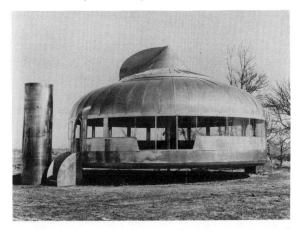

R. Buckminster Fuller, "Wichita Dymaxion House," full assembly 1945. *Photo © 1960, Estate of Buckminster Fuller; courtesy Buckminster Fuller Institute, Los Angeles.*

R. Buckminster Fuller in front of Montreal Expo '67 Dome, 1967. *Photo © 1984 Estate of Buckminster Fuller; courtesy, Buckminster Fuller Institute, Los Angeles.*

Above the living space is an open-air landing partially shaded from the sun by a suspended roof. A later version, built closer to the ground, was the Wichita House, a circular aluminum shell-plus-utility-core that Fuller tried to mass-produce after World War II. The dymaxion principle also informed the Kleenex House, a fifteen-foot surrogate tent designed for the U.S. Marine Corps. He claimed it would be "one-third the weight of a tent, cost one-fifteenth as much, use less than ten dollars' worth of materials, and be packed into a small box," in sum exemplifying his three principles.

With his bias for doing more with less, Fuller suggested that distances commonly bridged by cables or girders should instead be spanned by a network of three-dimensional triangles (actually, tetrahedrons) often built up into larger networks; for Fuller's innovative truth, strangely not recognized by earlier builders, was that the tetrahedron more effectively distributes weight and tension than the rectangular shapes traditionally favored. The best overarching form for these tetrahedrons was the geodesic dome, which could span spaces of theoretically unlimited diameters with an unprecedentedly light structure, demonstrating the dymaxion principle of high performance per pound. The first full realization of this last innovation was the 93-foot rotunda for a Ford plant in Detroit (1953); the most successful is the nearly complete sphere, over 200 feet in diameter, that Fuller built for Expo '67 in Montreal. This has a grandeur that, in my experience, was implicitly Jamesian, particularly since several interior levels made its tetrahedrons visible from various angles and the lucite skin changed color in response to the outside climate. Because other structures were as large as 384 feet in diameter, enclosing two and one-half acres, Fuller proposed constructing domes miles in diameter over whole cities or neighborhoods. One proposal for midtown Manhattan would have weighed 80,000 tons and cost 200 million dollars.

Don't forget Fuller's writings, which are in their coinages and complex sentences as stylistically original as his thinking: "Living upon the threshold between yesterday and tomorrow, which threshold we reflexively assumed in some long ago yesterday to constitute an eternal *now*, we are aware of the daily-occurring, vast multiplication of experience-generated information by which we potentially may improve our understanding of our yesterday's experiences and therefrom derive our most farsighted preparedness for successive tomorrows." It is not surprising that Petr Kotik (*), who had previously composed an extended choral piece to a difficult Gertrude Stein (*) text, *Many Many Women* (1978/80), did likewise with selected passages from Fuller's two-volume *Synergetics* (1976, 1979).

Fuller, Buckminster. *Synergetics I*. NY: Macmillan, 1976.

————. *Synergetics II*. NY: Macmillan, 1979.

Meller, James, ed. *The Buckminster Fuller Reader*. London, England: Cape, 1970.

Kenner, Hugh. *Bucky*. NY: Morrow, 1973.

Kotik, Petr. An excerpt from *Explorations in the Geometry of Thinking, S.E.M. Ensemble*. Berlin, Germany: Ear-Rational ECD 7553, 1989.

Marks, Robert W. *The Dymaxion World of Buckminster Fuller*. Carbondale, IL: Southern Illinois, 1960.

FULLER, Loïe (1862–1928). An American dancer, Fuller achieved great fame in Europe, especially in France, where she made her debut at the Folies-Bergère in 1892 and where, at the 1900 Paris World Fair, a special theater was built to house her performances. Fuller was renowned for spectacular stage effects that she accomplished through the use of colored lights, transparent cloth (such as silk), and mechanical devices (such as the use of wooden sticks to extend the lines of her arms). Although she apparently had little dance training, improvised movement became an important element in her performances. Because many leading artistic figures found her work enchanting—among them Anatole France, Auguste Rodin, and Stéphane Mallarmé (*)—her performances were remembered long after she ceased presenting them.—Katy Matheson

Harris, Margaret Haile. *Loïe Fuller: Magician of Light.* Richmond, VA: The Virginia Museum, 1989.

FURNIVAL, John (1932). Trained as a visual artist and for many years a professor at the Bath Academy in western England, in the early sixties Furnival developed a highly original and indubitably personal style of building up layers of words, usually chosen with taste and literacy, into architecturally representational structures, done not on small sheets of paper but pieces of wood (doors, actually) six feet high and a few feet wide. In the words that make the shape of *La Tour Eiffel* (1964) are the puns "eye full" and "Eve fall." The word "lift" turns into "ascenseur" where the elevator is, and among other representational markings is "échafaudage" (or "scaffolding") on the other leg. If only for its scale and scope of reference, *Tours de Babel Changées en Ponts* (1965) is Furnival's great work, if not the masterpiece of its kind. In six panels, each originally a wooden door onto which Furnival drew and stamped words in ink, all together twelve feet in length and six and one-half feet high (and usually displayed in a semicircular form), this work tells of the evolution of language. A key image is a succession of word bridges (with here and there the names of the great 19th-century bridge builders) connecting the otherwise isolated towers. The panels can be read from left to right as well as right to left, and from top to bottom and back again. As they contain more secrets than anyone can count, the words must be read as closely and completely as those of any modern poet.

Kostelanetz, Richard, ed. *Imaged Words & Worded Images.* NY: Outerbridge & Dienstfrey, 1970.

FUTURISM (ITALIAN) (1909). Italian Futurism began with the poet F.T. Marinetti (*) publishing in, of all places, the Parisian newspaper *Le Figaro* on 20 February 1909 a manifesto that, in bombastically provocative language, proclaims the birth of a new literary and social movement purportedly of the young. In what remains a masterpiece of manifesto writing (apart from its impact), Marinetti exalted movement and change, in addition to appealing to Italian pride. "Courage, audacity, and revolt will be essential elements of our poetry" is his second tenet. "A racing car" is portrayed as "more beautiful than the *Victory of Samothrace.*" What began in literature was seen to have more currency in visual art, with the *Manifesto of the Futurist Painters,* signed the following year by the painters Giacomo Balla (1871–1958), Umberto Boccioni (1882–1916), Carlo D. Carrà (1881–1966), Gino Severini (1883–1966), and Luigi Russolo (*). While his associates continued to publish manifestos with titles like *Futurist Photodynamism* (1911), *Technical Manifesto of Futurist Sculpture* (1912), *Chromophony—The Colors of Sounds* (1913), *The Painting of Sounds, Noises and Smells* (1913), and *Futurist Manifesto of Men's Clothing* (1913), Marinetti's subsequent declarations focused upon literature: *Destruction of Syntax—Imagination without Strings—Words in Freedom* (1913), *The Variety Theatre* (1913), *The Futurist Synthetic Theater* (1915), and *The Futurist Cinema* (1916, with others). Apart from what one might think of individual Futurist artists and works, it is hard to dispute the opinion that no other group published so many brilliant manifestoes, filled as they are with lines that remain no less radical today than seventy-five years ago.

It was in painting, more than any other art, that Futurist ideas generated major work. Needing devices for portraying movement within two-dimensional frames, the painters turned to Cubism (*) for overlapping planes that, since Cubism was new at the time, contributed to Futurism's avant-garde image. However, Futurism distinguished itself from Cubism by a visual agitation that was perceived to represent emotional expression. Among the masterpieces of Futurist painting are Boccioni's *The Forces of a Street* (1911), Severini's *Nord-Sud* (1912),

Carrà's *Interventional Demonstration* (1914), and Boccioni's sculpture *Unique Forms in Space* (1913). Energized by one another, these Futurist painters developed so rapidly that, by 1915, they had individual identities, united only by memories of the initial manifestos. It is commonly said that the highest phase of Italian Futurism ended in 1916 with the death of Boccioni (who fell from a horse during World War I). Nonetheless, thanks to frequent translations of those manifestos, Futurist ideas had a discernible influence especially upon artists in Russia, and also those in England, Germany, and America.

Futurism. NY: Museum of Modern Art, 1961.

Apollonio, Umbro, ed. *Futurist Manifestos*. Trans. Robert Brain, et al. NY: Viking, 1973.

FUTURISM (RUSSIAN) (1909–1917).

The premier avant-garde movement in Russian literature, Futurism was in part a reaction to Symbolism, which nonetheless shared the latter's interest in the sound texture of the word and in the work's suggestive power beyond its denotative meaning. Russian Futurism is customarily divided into two wings. Ego-Futurism, centered in St. Petersburg, focused upon romantic hyperbolization of the poet-ego. Its chief figures were Igor Severyanin (1887–1941, who gave the movement its name in 1911), Konstantin Olimpov (1889–1940), and Ivan Ignatyev (1892–1914). The last was particularly important as a publisher of a series of Futurist miscellanies. While the Ego-Futurists' imagery could be extravagant, they were verbally less experimental than the second group, the Cubo-Futurists (*), centered in Moscow. This group numbered among it three of the most important and innovative poets of the 20th century: Velimir Khlebnikov (*), Aleksei Kruchonykh (*), and Vladimir Mayakovsky (*). Vasilisk Gnedov (1890–1978), nominally associated with the Ego-Futurists, demonstrated some of the same verbal inventiveness as the Cubo-Futurists.

While both groups had been active since 1909 and were to some extent familiar with the activities of the Italian Futurists (*), they developed independently of the Italian movement and did not share its militaristic aspirations. What finally caught the attention of the Russian public was "A Slap in the Face of Public Taste" (1912), signed by Kruchonykh, Khlebnikov, and Mayakovsky, along with David Burliuk (1882–1967), if only for this oft-quoted line: "Throw Pushkin, Dostoevsky, Tolstoy, etc. etc., overboard from the Ship of Modernity." Other statements in the manifesto argued for the poet's right to create "arbitrary and derivative words (word-novelty)" and for the "self-sufficient word." This soon led to the rise of Zaum (*) (transrational language), the most radical development in 20th-century poetry. Kruchonykh's "dyr bul shchyl" (1913) and his opera *Victory Over the Sun* (1913) epitomize early Zaum. The Cubo-Futurists were also innovative in introducing visual effects into Russian literature, ranging from primitive manuscripted books to floridly typographed works.

The year 1913 was the high point of Russian Futurism, the most important events and publications occurring all in that year, which ended with a well-publicized tour of the provinces. By 1917, a new center had formed in the Georgian capital of Tiflis with Ilia Zdanevich (aka Iliazd) (*), Kruchonykh, and Igor Terentyev (1892–1937) as the core of a group called 41°. This group produced particularly radical examples of Zaum and innovative visual effects in their texts.

In 1921, Kruchonykh joined forces once again in Moscow with Mayakovsky, around whom the group Left Front of the Arts (LEF) formed and published a journal of the same name. They propagandized for the role of Futurism as the true revolutionary art most appropriate for the new socialist society. However, neither the Bolshevik government nor proletarian writers and critics were sympathetic. By the later 1920s, the movement had disappeared, its members succumbing to the demand to produce less radical and politically more acceptable writing.

Futurism is credited with having a strong impact on the development of Russian Formalism, Constructivism (*), and Oberiu, a group of writers, formed in the late 1920s, that included the prose miniaturist Danil Kharms (1905–1942). Futurism's achievements are still being discovered by a new generation of Russian avant-gardists who were ignorant of the movement until recent liberalization under glasnost.—Gerald Janecek

Compton, Susan. *The World Backwards: Futurist Books 1912–16*. London, England: The British Library, 1978.

Janecek, Gerald. *The Look of Russian Literature*. Princeton, NJ: Princeton University, 1984.

Lawton, Anna. *Russian Futurism through Its Manifestoes 1912–1928*. Ithaca, NY: Cornell University, 1988.

Livshits, Benedikt. *The One and a Half-Eyed Archer*. Newtonville, MA: Oriental Research Partners, 1977.

Markov, Vladimir. *Russian Futurism: A History*. Berkeley, CA: University of California, 1968.

G

GABO, Naum (1890–1978; b. Naum Neemia Pevsner).

Born in Russia, Gabo studied medicine and engineering in Germany before returning to his homeland in 1920. Back in Russia, he joined his brother Antoine Pevsner (1886–1962) in drafting a *Realistic Manifesto* (1920) that established the principles of what became European Constructivism (*), in contrast to the Constructivism that Vladimir Tatlin (*), among others, advocated in Russia. While in Russia, Gabo made *Virtual Kinetic Volume* (1920, also known as *Kinetic Sculpture*), a vibrating strip of steel that is customarily identified as the first artwork to incorporate a motor. Objecting to government regimentation of artistic activities, he moved west, first to Berlin, then to Paris, and then to England, until he came to the U.S. in 1946, becoming an American citizen in 1952. Once in America, Gabo specialized in monuments, which often remained proposals, and monumental sculptures for new buildings.

Nash, Steven A., et al. *Naum Gabo: Sixty Years of Constructivism*. Munich, Germany: Prestel, 1986.

GABURO, Kenneth (1926–1993).

Gaburo was a problematic composer who was rarely written about, in part because he did many good things only fairly well. My sense is that he had an avant-garde intelligence but he spent too many years around universities to do genuinely alternative work. As a composer, he produced a number of works for both instruments and electronic media, of which the most ambitious, *Lingua I–IV* (1965–1970), deals with language used in a variety of once-original ways. As a performer, he founded and directed the New Music Chorale Ensemble. As a publisher, Gaburo established Lingua Press (once in San Diego, recently in Iowa City), which issued scores by composers, mostly university-based, whose work reflected avant-garde activities without contributing to them.

Gaburo, Kenneth. *Lingua II: Maledetto* (1967–1968). NY: CRI SD 316, 1974.

———. *Music for Voices, Instruments & Electronic Sounds*. NY: Nonesuch H-71199, (c. 1969).

GALÁS, Diamanda (1955).

Drawing upon experience of both jazz (*) and opera, as well as her ease with languages other than English, Galás has created a highly aggressive vocal style that can exploit not only her wide vocal range but new technologies to create vocals of unprecedented hysteria. The result is high-tech emotive singing in the tradition of Screamin' Jay Hawkins and Johnny Ray on the one hand and Maria Callas on another. Anger is the principal emotion of her performances, such as *Plague Mass* (1990), in memory of her brother, Philip-Dimitri Galás (1954–1986), a playwright who died of AIDS. Typical Diamanda Galás titles hum with barbed wire: *Litanies of Satan* (1982) and *Wild Women with Steak Knives* (1981–1983). Inspiring controversy, her performances have been banned, which is neither easy nor frequent in our time, especially in Italy.

Galás, Diamanda. *Plague Mass* (1990). NY: Mute 961043-2, 1991.

GANCE, Abel (1889–1981).

Initially an actor, Gance made unsuccessful short silent films before returning to the stage. Resuming his film career during World War I, he experimented with close-ups and tracking shots, which were at the time thought to be confusing techniques. By 1917, according to the film lexicographer Ephraim Katz (1932), "He was considered important enough as a director for his picture to appear ahead of the stars in a film's title sequence. This was to become a personal trademark of all Gance's silent films." He made the first major film about the horrors of the Great War, *J'accuse/I Accuse* (1919), with footage he shot with real soldiers in real battles, for successful release just after Armistice Day. His technique of quickly cutting from scene to scene, from horror to horror, influenced filmmakers coming of age at that time. After the commercial failure of *La Roue* (1923), which began as thirty-two reels (over five hours) before being abridged to twelve, he made his most stupendous film, *Napoléon* (1927), which remains a monumental masterpiece. Initially an epic on the scale of D.W. Griffith's (∗) *Intolerance* (1918), it is also technically innovative. Parts were shot by three synchronized cameras to be shown simultaneously on three screens, in a technique resembling Cinerama (∗), which came thirty years later. When these appear, toward the end of the film, they produce a gasp of awe even now. Other parts were shot in two-camera 3-D and in color but not used. Unfortunately, the film failed commercially. According to Katz, only eight European cities saw the three-screen format. The version shown at the time in America was so drastically butchered it was incomprehensible. Several years later, Gance recorded stereophonic sound effects that he wanted to add to the print. Only in the 1970s, thanks to the culturally responsible Hollywood director Francis Ford Coppola (1939), was the original three-screen version made available to American audiences. Though Gance lived long enough to see his innovations exploited elsewhere, he was never again encouraged to make innovative film.

Gance, Abel. *Napoléon* (1927). Universal City, CA: MCA Home Video 80086, 1986.

GANGEMI, Kenneth (1937). An early Minimalist (∗) writer, Gangemi published a "novel" called *Olt* (1969) that was only sixty pages long. It was written not as a sequence of paragraphs but as a collection of highly resonant sentences, all about a man with minimal emotional affect. His next book, *Lydia* (1970), has even more severe fictions, some of them merely listings of elements in a narrative; some poems consist of only a single word. He has also published prose poems, a novel in the form of an unrealized film script (*The Interceptor Pilot*, 1980), and a memoir of traveling in Mexico (*Voyages from Puebla*, 1979). His books are typically published abroad before they appear in his native America.

Gangemi, Kenneth. *Lydia*. Santa Barbara, CA: Black Sparrow, 1970.

GARDNER, Martin (1914). A truly independent writer for most of his life, noted mostly for his books about science and pseudo-science, Gardner is also a primary scholar of truly eccentric literature, beginning with elaborately annotated and introduced editions of Lewis Carroll: *The Annotated Alice* (1960) and *The Annotated Snark* (1962), the latter dealing with a less intelligible text. Some of Gardner's appreciations of Oulipo (∗), among other avant-garde writers mentioned here, appeared in his regular column in *The Scientific American*, illustrating the principle that understanding advanced science might be good preparation for understanding advanced literature, and vice versa. His *Ambidextrous Universe* (1964) influenced, among others, Vladimir Nabokov (∗), who mentions the book on page 542 of his novel *Ada* (1969). In 1992, when John Robert Colombo (∗) edited an anthology of stories less than fifty words long, he sent copies to several like-minded enthusiasts, asking in part for suggestions for a future edition. The most nominations came from Martin Gardner. Don't be surprised to find that no other book about contemporary art or literature mentions his name.

Gardner, Martin. *The Annotated Alice*. NY: Potter, 1960.

————. *The Annotated Snark* (1962). Harmondsworth, England: Penguin, 1967.

GARRARD, Mimi (c. 1937). Early in Garrard's choreographic career, this former Nikolais (∗) dancer produced a brilliantly original work, *Flux* (1968), that stands above everything she has done since. To a score by Bülent Arel, one of the more accomplished tape composers of the 1960s, and a foreground film made in collaboration with her husband James Seawright (∗), several Garrard dancers move themselves and some tall panels as the quickly cut color film, composed entirely of kinetic geometric patterns (verticals, horizontals, dots, rainbows, etc.), continually rearticulates the hues of their leotards and the visual activity on the stage. The result is a theatrical field whose overwhelming intensity is more typical of serial music (∗). The elements are quite precisely integrated and yet nonsynchronous, for one theme is the qualitative differences between live and filmed movement.

Kostelanetz, Richard. *On Innovative Performance(s)*. Jefferson, NC: McFarland, forthcoming.

GAUDI, Antoni (1852–1926). By the measure of image alone, Gaudi was the most original architect of early modern times. Influenced by Catalonian philosophers who glorified earlier Spanish arts and crafts, Gaudi developed a taste for undulating lines, ornamental details, ornate additions, colorful materials, and paint, all in sharp contrast to the esthetic that resulted in the streamlined International Style (∗). For instance, Gaudi's Church of the Sagrada Familia (1883–1926, Sacred Family) has three open doorways leading to four towers intertwined at their bases, their diagonal spires rising to a height over 100 meters. At the top of each tower is an ornate echo of a flower. One Gaudi assumption, made particularly clear in his later years, was that, whereas the straight line belonged to man, the curved line was God's. Because Gaudi's style is so eccentric, it had scarce acceptance and little influence. Curiously, the later structure most resembling Gaudi is the Los Angeles *Watts Towers* of Simon Rodia (∗).

Collins, George R. *Antoni Gaudi*. NY: Braziller, 1960.

GAUDIER-BRZESKA, Henri (1891–1915). A French sculptor who added his Polish wife's name to his own (as she added his to hers), Gaudier-Brzeska went to London in 1911, befriending influential British writers and artists who supported and exhibited his work. Beginning with abstracted modeling that reflected Auguste Rodin (1840–1917), he rapidly assimilated Vorticism (∗), contributing both essays and illustrations to Wyndham Lewis's (∗) *Blast* (∗). Enlisting in the French Army in 1914, Gaudier-Brzeska was killed in battle in the following year. His late sculptures are commonly credited as influencing subsequent abstraction, particularly in England. Ezra Pound (∗) memorialized him in a classic essay.

Pound, Ezra. *Gaudier-Brzeska: A Memoir* (1916). NY: New Directions, 1970.

GENDER. Along with the general acceptance of homosexuality and bisexuality (among other behaviors previously regarded as "deviant"), the avant-garde has long stretched the notion of gender. Famous female avant-garde artists have adopted male attire (Gertrude Stein [∗], for one), while others, both male and female, have created their own unisexual image (Andy Warhol [∗]). This has degenerated in pop culture into "gender-bender" fashions—from the "moptop" long-haired rock stars of the 1960s to the shaved-head look of the popular Irish singer Sinéad O'Connor (1967). The visual assault of gender-bending is meant to make the viewer question his or her own sexual preconceptions while expanding social acceptance for alternative ways of interhuman relating. In the best sense, these artists transform themselves into living artistic statements, to shock, to amuse, or to befuddle the general public. In the worst sense, as in the case of commercial celebrities like Madonna (1958; b. M. Ciccone), sex is used as the ultimate tool to sell a bill of goods.—Richard Carlin

In contrast to my publisher, usually a smart guy, I think gender one of many current categories that really don't belong in this book, because its terms relate to *jour*nalism, which by definition lasts only a day, rather than to books, which are meant to last years. My own opinion is that understandings based on gender have become the great heresy of an emerging generation, just as intelligence based on psychotropic drugs was the great heresy of my contemporaries and alcoholic unintelligence sabotaged the best minds of a previous generation.

Too many references are applicable to make invidious distinctions.

GERZ, Jochen (1940). Though Gerz has been a friend of mine for nearly a quarter-century, I hardly understand his work and career, perhaps because we live in different cities, mostly because we have pursued drastically different directions from similar beginnings. Born in Berlin and raised in Düsseldorf, Gerz began as a visual poet (∗) whose first exhibition (1968) was in conjunction with Jean-François Bory (∗); and, like Bory, Gerz made some striking book-art. From here he moved into one-person performances, presented nearly entirely in Europe, which depend upon a striking narrative. A recurring motif involves burying something in the earth, so that only a memory of the piece survives. He has made photographs and videotapes both distinguished more for their conceptual/documentary resonance than their mediumistic artistry.

Jochen Gerz: Griechische Stücke. Ludwigshafen, Germany: Heidelberger Kunstverein, 1984.

GIBSON, Jon (1940). As an improviser before becoming a veteran flutist in the Philip Glass (∗) Ensemble, Gibson assimilated modular music (∗) before creating his own work, which typically mixes repeated elements with free improvisation, at times with environmental sounds, often in performances for his wife, the choreographer Nancy Topf (1942). Two of his strongest earlier pieces, *Cycles* (1973) and *Untitled* (1974), appeared on a single disc. He has also produced book-art books of his abstract systemic art.

Gibson, Jon. *Two Solo Pieces.* NY: Chatham Square, 1977.

———. *Melody III, Book II.* NY: Printed Matter, 1977.

GILBERT and GEORGE (G. Proesch, 1943; and G. Passmore, 1942). Meeting as sculpture students at the St. Martin's School of Art in 1967, these two men, known only by their first names, have lived and worked together ever since. Their innovation was to exhibit themselves as "living sculptures," cleanly dressed in identical gray suits, their faces and hands painted silver. In vaudeville-like, scheduled performances that had announced beginnings, they would sing "Underneath the Arches," a British music-hall tune, again and again. In the early 1970s, Gilbert and George were ubiquitous, illustrating how a truly original idea can find rapid acceptance in visual-arts venues. In 1970 alone, they had over

Gilbert and George at the Sonnabend Gallery, 25 September 1971. *Photo © 1993, Fred W. McDarrah.*

a dozen solo exhibitions in venues as various as museums in Düsseldorf, Krefeld, Oxford, Copenhagen, Stuttgart, Turin, and Oslo, and private galleries in Milan, London, Berlin, Cologne, and Amsterdam. Not unlike celebrities in other areas, they exploited their fame to produce book-art, videotapes, drawings, and, especially, large photographs arrayed in photogrids, some of which portray naked young males. (As photographers, Gilbert and George were curiously far less successful than Robert Mapplethorpe [1946–1988] at making nude bodies appear sculptural in a two-dimensional medium.)

Gilbert and George: The Complete Pictures 1971–1985. Bordeaux, France: Musée d'Art Contemporain, 1986.

GILLESPIE, Abraham Lincoln (1895–1950). Commonly regarded as the most eccentric of the literary Americans gathered in Paris in the 1920s, Gillespie produced prose so unique it must be read to be believed; excerpts are not sufficient. He made visual poetry (∗); he worked with neologisms in a piece/poem characteristically titled "A Purplexicon of Dissynthegrations (Tdevelop abut Earfluxsatisvie-thru-Heypersieving)," which tells almost everything that need be known about Gillespie in an introductory entry. It is indicative that no book of his writings appeared until thirty years after his death.

Milazzo, Richard, ed. *The Syntactic Revolution: Abraham Lincoln Gillespie.* NY: Out of London, 1980.

GILLETTE, Frank (1941). A pioneering video artist, Gillette collaborated with Ira Schneider (1938) in producing *Wipe Cycle* (1969), one of the first video installations to create the illusion of art responding to the spectator. Hidden in a bank of nine television screens (arrayed three by three) is a camera that constantly photographs in live time the area in front of the work (including, in a matter of course, the work's spectators). This image is instantly broadcast through the middle monitor. The same image is rebroadcast eight seconds later on two screens (varying between the horizontal and vertical axis) and then, after a sixteen-second delay, over the other monitors on the perpendicular axis. In the four corner monitors are two different sets of identical images from previously taped materials. To make the system more complex (and the perceptual experience more ambiguous and involving), the delayed live images switch their axes at periodic intervals, as do the corner images, and the monitors are all wiped blank one at a time in a regular cycle. The spectator feels caught in an intelligent, watchful, oblivious system whose incessant and variable observations remain compelling and mysterious even after their operation is explained. I saw *Wipe Cycle* in New York in 1969, and again twenty years later in Berlin, recreated as part of a traveling exhibition of "video sculpture" using color monitors, and it was no less compelling. After producing other acclaimed videotapes, Gillette later became the first noted video artist to give his professional renunciation of video (for painting, no less) a Duchampian (∗) significance.

Gillette, Frank. *TV as a Creative Medium*. NY: Howard Wise Gallery, 1969.

GINS, Madeline (1941). It is hard to explain how Gins's first novel *Word Rain* found a commercial publisher in 1969, because its theme is the epistemological opacity of language itself. The first sign of the book's unusual concerns is its subtitle: "(or a Discursive Introduction to the Philosophical Investigations to G,R,E,T,A, G,A,R,B,O, It Says)"; a second is the incorporation of several signs of new fiction: special languages, expressive design, extrinsically imposed form—most of these devices reiterating, in one way or another, the book's theme. What distinguishes the book are numerous inventive displays of printed material: lists of unrelated words with dots between them, entire pages filled mostly with dashes where words might otherwise be, pseudo-logical proofs, passages in which the more mundane expressions are crossed out, an appendix of "some of the words (temporary definitions) not included," even a photographed hand holding both sides of a printed page, and a concluding page of dense print-over-print that reads at its bottom: "This page contains every word in the book." I've found Gins's later books comparably obscure, though perhaps less ambitious, even when her subject is presidential politics; but because no one else risks writing about her work, let alone reading it critically, there is no one other than yourself, dear reader, with whom you can compare my impression. It may or may not be important that she has been married for at least a quarter-century to the painter

(Shusaku) Arakawa (∗), with whom Gins has collaborated on an extremely opaque, large-format visual/verbal book that has gone through three highly different editions, *The Mechanism of Meaning*.

Gins, Madeline. *Word Rain*. NY: Grossman, 1969.

———. *What the President Will Say and Do!!!* Barrytown, NY: Station Hill (Station Hill Rd., 12507), 1984.

———, and Arakawa. *The Mechanism of Meaning*. 3rd ed. NY: Abbeville, 1988.

GINSBERG, ALLEN (1926). The avant-garde Ginsberg is the author not of post-Whitmanian lines that live in the head of every literate American but of certain sound poems that he publishes without musical notation. (Remember that he has also published, as well as sung, many conventionally configured songs.) One of them, "Fie My Fum," appears in his *Collected Poems* (1984), while most do not. An example is "Put Down Yr Cigarette Rag," whose verses conclude with variations on the refrain "dont smoke dont smoke dont smoke dont smoke": "Nine billion bucks for dope/ approved by Time & Life/ America's lost hope/ The President smokes his wife/ Dont Smoke dont smoke dont smoke dont smoke dont smoke nope/ nope nope nope." Especially when I hear Ginsberg perform this, I wish there were more poems like it.

Ginsberg, Allen. *First Blues*. NY: Full Court, 1975.

GIORNO, John (1936). Giorno's principal poetic innovation extended Found Poetry (∗) by chopping apart a prose sentence so that its words are repeated in different linear arrangements, with different line breaks, and often duplicated in adjacent columns. As a strong performer of his own texts, Giorno turned to electronic technology for a single capability—echoing—so that variations other than those he was saying could be electronically reproduced as faint replicas of his initial voice, thereby increasing the potential for *after-sound* analogous to the afterimage of the visual arts. His contributions to later records in his own *Dial-A-Poem* anthologies have yet more complicated kinds of echoing. Because Giorno's poems generally have a distinct subject, as well as syntax, semantics, and narrative, they represent not text-sound (∗) but inventively amplified poetry that no doubt contrasts with the general decadence of the principal current forms of literary recital. Every time I see the much-touted Karen Finlay (∗), I'm reminded of her work's resemblances in both style and content to Giorno.

John Giorno and William S. Burroughs. NY: Giorno Poetry Systems (222 Bowery, 10012), 1975.

GLASS, Philip (1937). Traditionally trained, not only at Juilliard but with the legendary teacher Nadia Boulanger in Paris, Glass began as a conventional composer before creating music of distinction: a sequence of pieces that included *Strung Out* (1967), *Music in Similar Motion* (1969), *Music in Contrary Motion* (1969), and *Music in Fifths* (1969). Essentially monophonic, these compositions have lines of individual notes, with neither harmonies nor counterpoint; they are tonal without offering melodies, accessible without being seductive. What made this music seem radical in the 1960s was its avoidance of all the principal issues that preoccupied nearly all contemporary composers at that time—issues such as chance and control, serialism and atonality, improvisation and spontaneity. It is scarcely surprising that before his music was performed in concert halls it was heard in art galleries and in art museums. Though this music was frequently characterized as Minimal (∗), the epithet "modular" (∗) is more appropriate in that severely circumscribed bits of musical material are repeated in various ways. One minor innovation is that even in live concerts his music would always be heard through amplifiers, the

Philip Glass, "Einstein on the Beach," Brooklyn Academy of Music production, 1984. *Photo © 1993, Jack Vartoogian.*

man at the electronic mixing board (Kurt Munkasci) becoming one of the acknowledged "musicians."

Within *Music in Changing Parts* (1970), Glass moved progressively from monophony, in its opening moments, to a greater polyphonic complexity and then, toward its end, into the kinds of modulations that would inform his next major work, *Music in Twelve Parts* (1974), an exhaustive four-hour piece that epitomizes Glass's compositional ideas to that time and remains the zenith of his avant-garde art. Glass subsequently moved into operatic collaborations, beginning with *Einstein on the Beach* (1976, with Robert Wilson [∗]), and then *Satyagraha* (1980), which is based upon Mahatma Gandhi's early years, among other operas. The requirements of music theater, as he prefers to call it, made his music more accessible and more popular, as it did for Aaron Copland (1900–1990) before him. Glass's composing in the 1980s became more lyrical and more charming, which is to say devoid of those characteristics that would make it problematic to his new larger audience.

Glass, Philip. *Music by Philip Glass.* Ed. Robert T. Jones. NY: Harper & Row, 1987.

GOFF, BRUCE (1904–1982). Influenced by Frank Lloyd Wright (∗), Goff built numerous houses in the middle and far west that blend structure into the environment. His masterpiece, the Bavinger House (1950) in Norman, Oklahoma, has a ninety-six-foot wall that follows a logarithmic spiral into the living space and ultimately around a steel pole from which the entire roof, interior stairway, and living areas are suspended. Plants inside the structure duplicate those outside, so that the environment seemingly flows into the home, or vice versa. "They wanted a large open space, and liked the idea of living on different levels," Goff told an interviewer. "They wanted many interior plants, and preferred natural rather than synthetic materials." Though other Goff architecture worked with similar ideas, none of his later works were so spectacular.

Heyer, Paul. "Bruce Goff." In *Architects on Architecture.* NY: Walker, 1966.

GOLDBERG, Rube (1883–1970; b. Reuben Lucius G.). Do not dismiss Goldberg as a mere cartoonist, because his pictures tell within single

Rube Goldberg, "When You Say 'Have a Drink.'" *Collection Richard Kostelanetz.*

frames complicated stories, filled with unobvious moves that defy reality, mostly about the ironic relation between effort and result. By no measure are they "cartoons" whose point can be understood instantly, which is to say that, for all their resemblance to popular art, they approach more serious work by requiring time merely to go back and forth between the verbal and the visual. It is not for nothing that his influence can be observed in the kinetic sculpture of George Rhoads (*) and the poetic art of David Morice (*), among others.

Rube Goldberg vs. the Machine Age. NY: Hastings House, 1968.

Rube Goldberg: Inventions and Comics. NY: Truman Gallery, 1977.

GOLYSCHEFF, Jef (1897–1970; b. Jefim G.). A scarcely remembered minor polyartist (*), Golyscheff was a Russian who happened to be in Berlin at the beginnings of Dada (*) and understood its implications for music. An early Berlin Dada exhibition included a performance of his *Anti-Symphony* (1919), subtitled "Musical Circular Guillotine," which included movements emblazoned "Provocational Injections," "Chaotic Oral Cavity, or Submarine Aircraft," and "Clapping in Hyper F-sharp Major." For another Dada concert later that year, Golyscheff offered *Keuchmaneuver* (Cough Maneuver). Five years before, while still a teenager, he composed a string trio containing "Zwelftondauer-Komplexen," as he called them—passages in which the twelve tones of the chromatic scale have different durations; this work is considered protoserial (*). Golyscheff also worked as a chemist and, in 1956, moved to Brazil, where he devoted himself exclusively to paintings. It is appalling how many histories of Dada neglect music in general and Golyscheff's work in particular.

Slonimsky, Nicolas. *Music Since 1900.* 5th ed. NY: Schirmer Books, 1993.

GÓMEZ DE LA SERNA, Ramón (1888–1963). A Spanish writer whose specialty was a fictional aphorism (as distinct from a philosophical one) that he called *greguería*, Gómez de la Serna was probably the most original author of his generation in Spain (whose contemporaries included José Ortega y Gasset and Miguel de Unamuno). Though he published essays, short stories, plays, novels, biographies, memoirs, and even chronicles of the gatherings at his favorite literary café in Madrid, he is best remembered for his thousands of *greguería*, which he claimed to have invented around 1910: "The little girl wants to dance because she wants to fly"; "Moon and sand are mad for each other"; "Tigers of somnambulists and they cross rivers of sleep over bridges of leaps"; "We should take more time to forget; thus we would have a longer life." (No one would ever confuse these with philosophical aphorisms.) Miguel Gonzalez-Gerth writes, "He opposed esthetic hierarchies, advocating instead that the artist should have complete freedom and start with everything at zero level." Though Gómez thought of *greguería* as a combination of "metaphor + humor," Spanish-English dictionaries translate his key word as "irritating noise, gibberish, or hubbub," which is less nonsense than a kind of inspired ridiculousness.

Gómez de la Serna, Ramón. *Aphorisms.* Trans. Miguel Gonzalez-Gerth. Pittsburgh, PA: Latin American Literary Review Press, 1989.

GOMRINGER, Eugen (1925). A Swiss-German born in Bolivia, Gomringer pioneered the idea of Concrete Poetry (*), publishing early examples and writing the most visible early manifesto. His key idea was the "constellation," or words connected by qualities apart from syntax, freely distributed within the space of the printed page. Given his polyglot background, Gomringer was able to write his poems in Spanish, French, English, and German. For instance, down a single page are widely spaced three words: "berg land see," or "mountain," "land" (i.e., territory, ground), "sea," preceding by several years comparable Minimal poems by Clark Coolidge (*). The English poems reprinted in his 1969 retrospective include "butterfly," nine lines divided into three stanzas, which would be striking in any American poetry magazine even today: "mist/ mountain/ butterfly//mountain/butterfly/missed//butterfly/meets/mountain."   Perhaps because the initial American anthologies of Concrete Poetry were not as good as they should have been, Gomringer failed to have as much influence here as he deserved.

Gomringer, Eugen. *Worte Sind Schatten*. Hamburg, Germany: Rowhohlt, 1969.

———. *das studenbuch/the book of hours/le livre d'heures/el libro de las horas/timbok*. Stamberg, Germany: Josef Keller Verlag, 1980.

GONZÁLEZ, Julio (1876–1942). Born into a family of Barcelona metal artisans, González learned techniques that, after a decade of painting, he put to esthetic use in sculpture, beginning with masks. He first forged sculpture in iron in 1927, and, the following year, though already in his early fifties, he decided to devote himself exclusively to sculpture whose innovations depend upon the use of welding. González was a close friend of his countryman Pablo Picasso (*), to whom he introduced the possibility of metal sculpture, and González's works initially reflected the influence of Cubism (*). Later assimilating the radical example of Alexander Calder (*), the Spaniard made open works defined less by solidity than by an assembling of rods and ribbons of metal. All subsequent welded sculpture, including David Smith's (*), implicitly acknowledges González's influence.

Julio González. NY: Museum of Modern Art, 1956.

GOREY, Edward (1925). Gorey is the master of visual fiction, which is to say images, generally composed of pictures mixed with words, whose sequences suggest narrative. Superficially similar to comic books, they are more profound in theme and more serious in subject, with an adult use of language and more-detailed pictures. In a more extreme Gorey work, like "The West Wing," the images appear without words; for "The Wuggly Ump," he added color. Gorey has also produced literary ballets, which is to say scenarios for dance. His works are superficially similar as well to Frans Masereel's (*), but he is a far superior draftsman with a superior narrative imagination. Though Gorey's works are well-known, thanks to their publication in prominent magazines, it is not acknowledged in histories or encyclopedias of American fiction.

Gorey, Edward. *Amphigorey: Fifteen Books*. NY: Putnam, 1973.

GOULD, Glenn (1932–1982). While Gould's piano performances represented a departure from standard classical interpretation, especially in his recordings of J.S. Bach, they gained immediate acceptability not available to his creative works, which were audiotape compositions of speech and sound done mostly for the Canadian Broadcasting Corporation. The first three deal with isolation in Canada: *The Idea of North* (1967) focuses on individuals who live near the Arctic Circle; *The Latecomers* (1969) depicts Newfoundland; and *Quiet in the Land* (1973) portrays religious fundamentalists. A second trilogy deals with the musicians Arnold Schoenberg (*), Leopold Stokowski (*), and Richard Strauss (1864–1949), again incorporating interviews into an audio montage that gives the illusion of a live symposium with ingeniously appropriate musical backgrounds. While discs of his piano playing continue to appear, his avant-garde compositions remain unavailable, more than a decade after his death. Gould also collaborated with the French musician Bruno Monsaingeon in producing what remains, in my judgment, the most exquisite and unaffected film/video of a musical performance, *The Goldberg Variations* (1981).

Kostelanetz, Richard. "Glenn Gould." In *On Innovative Music(ian)s*. NY: Limelight, 1989.

GRAHAM, Dan (1942; b. Daniel Henry G.). Though I have known Graham most of my adult life and followed his activities as often as I could, my sense of his achievement is incomplete. As a critical writer, Graham published some of the most insightful essays about 1960s avant-grade sculpture; as the director in the mid-sixties of a New York gallery bearing his name in part (John Daniels), he also exhibited advanced work. As a creator of original language structures, he published highly unprecedented poems that were anthologized in my *Possibilities of Poetry* (1970) (and others have been critically discussed). He was early into video, with pieces in which he tapes himself taking a picture of himself. His

Video-Architecture-Television (1979) documents his individual moves without becoming as generally edifying as his best writing about others. One difference between the world of visual art and that of literature is that the former is far more receptive to genuine eccentrics such as Graham.

Graham, Dan. *Video-Architecture-Television*. Halifax, Canada and NY: The Press of the Nova Scotia College of Art and Design and New York University, 1979.

GRAHAM, John (1881–1961; b. Ivan Dabrowsky). Active among New York artists from the time of his arrival in the U.S. in 1920, Graham became influential not just because he was older but because of his direct experience of avant-garde developments in both his native Russia and elsewhere in Europe. According to the anonymous author of the *Oxford Dictionary of Twentieth-Century Art*, "He discussed the automatism of the Surrealists before this was generally understood in America, and he anticipated the doctrines of minimalism. In his *System and Dialectics of Art* (Paris, 1937), he elaborated his doctrines of the occult, his mysticism, and his aesthetics of contemporary art. He is chiefly remembered today for the great influence he had on the evolution of modernism in the U.S.A." Graham's paintings were mostly Cubist (∗) in style.

Graham, John D. *System and Dialectics of Art* (1937). Ed. Marcia Allentuck. Baltimore, MD: Johns Hopkins University, 1971.

GRAHAM, Martha (1894–1991). Initially noted for her dynamic performing presence, this American modern-dance pioneer also developed a unique technique for movement. Trained with the Denishawn company, she broke from its style, which was indebted to ballet and François Delsarte (1811–1871), to explore deep motions of the torso, especially "contraction and release." A barefoot modern to the end (despite an occasional sandal), she nonetheless increasingly encouraged performing virtuosity in her dancers.

In her long, sustained career as a choreographer, Graham created over 200 works, including such early Abstract (∗) and Expressionist (∗) pieces as *Lamentation* (1930), in which, enshrouded in fabric and poised on a bench, she enacted grief distilled through her movements and gestures. She explored American forms and themes in

Martha Graham, "Frontier," 1935. Set by Isamu Noguchi. *Photo © 1992, Barbara Morgan, courtesy the Willard and Barbara Morgan Archives.*

Primitive Mysteries (1931), inspired by Native American ritual, and in *Letter to the World* (1950), which was based on Emily Dickinson's poetry and life. Graham developed narrative dances exploring Jungian theory and Greek mythology in works such as *Cave of the Heart* (1946) and the evening-length *Clytemnestra* (1958). She explored alternative narrative devices such as flashback in *Seraphic Dialogue* (1955). Although the predominant feeling of her work was dark and serious, notable exceptions include the joyous *Diversion of Angels* (1948) and her last work, the surprising *Maple Leaf Rag* (1990) to music by Scott Joplin, which poked fun at her own stylistic conventions. She also collaborated with many notable artists, including Isamu Noguchi (∗) in set design. Due to her significance, longevity, and relative accessibility, more has been written about her than anyone else in American modern dance.— Katy Matheson

De Mille, Agnes. *Martha*. NY: Random House, 1991.

Graham, Martha. *Blood Memory*. NY: Doubleday, 1991.

────. *The Notebooks of Martha Graham*, ed. Nancy Wilson Ross. NY: Harcourt Brace Jovanovich, 1973.

Armitage, Merle, ed. *Martha Graham* (1937). NY: Da Capo, 1978.

Horosko, Marian. *Martha Graham: The Evolution of Her Dance Theory and Training, 1926–1991*. Pennington, NJ: a cappella, 1991.

GRAND UNION (1970–1976). This collaborative improvisational dance group grew out of the Judson Dance Theater (∗) of the early 1960s and Yvonne Rainer's (∗) *Continuous Project Altered Daily* (1970). Though membership varied, with nine people participating at various times, the core group included Rainer, Trisha Brown (∗), David Gordon (1936), Douglas Dunn (1942), Steve Paxton (∗), and Barbara Lloyd (1938; b. B. Dilley), most of whom would sustain independent choreographic careers. Always unpredictable, a typical Grand Union performance would have a casual tone. The performers were usually dressed in street or rehearsal clothes (although they might play with costumes or props). They talked, chatting with one another, reciting, giving one another visible cues. As performances were not planned in advance, the playful, process-oriented evening was supposedly as fun for the participants as for the audience.—Katy Matheson

Banes, Sally. "The Grand Union." In *Terpsichore in Sneakers* (1980). Middletown, CT: Wesleyan University, 1987.

Ramsey, Margaret Hupp. *The Grand Union*. NY: Peter Lang, 1991.

GRAYSON, Richard (1951). In the late 1970s, Grayson was the most prolific and interesting young fiction writer in America, working with several interesting ideas and publishing in a variety of magazines, much as Joyce Carol Oates (∗) did at the beginning of her career. Though some of Grayson's fictions were more experimental than others, two qualities distinguishing his work were weighty sentences and the appearance of names similar to those of real people, including himself. Intentionally confusing fiction with reality, he acted out the fiction of running for president, issuing press releases that were picked up by newspapers, even though he was underage. I use the past tense in talking about Grayson here, not because he has passed, but because he published less and less through the 1980s until, at last report, he was getting a law degree. Essays and perhaps books will no doubt be written accounting for the premature disappearance of such a prodigal talent from contemporary literature.

Grayson, Richard. *I Brake for Delmore Schwartz*. Somerville, MA: Zepher (13 Robinson, 02145), 1983.

GREENBERG, Clement (1908). By common consent, Greenberg was the great American art critic of the middle 20th century, the one whose essays on the Abstract Expressionist (∗) painting of the postwar decade seem as smart today as they did then (as does his 1939 classic on "Avant-Garde and Kitsch"). In subsequent decades, he advocated painterly painting, not necessarily Abstract, especially against those who preferred painting that reflected performance, philosophy, or something else. Though he stopped publishing in the mid-1970s, Greenberg remains influential, not only as an occasional lecturer but as the touchstone that his successors are continually either inflating or rejecting.

Greenberg, Clement. *Art and Culture*. Boston, MA: Beacon, 1961.

GREENFIELD, Amy (1940). Elementary actions like spinning, falling, and rising to one's feet are laden with meaning in Greenfield's cinema. Greenfield believes such physical movements can evoke primal experiences recalled by individuals and cultural memories held by generations. Her *Element* (1973) is a glistening meditation on a solitary female figure struggling through a sea of total mud, but also a metaphor for perseverance and survival. Coming to film from modern dance, Greenfield understands the latent meanings of simple gestures. Though her cinema draws energy from dance, it does not resemble theater. In *Element*, mud spatters onto the camera lens, reminding us of its presence. In *Dervish* (1974), a real-time spinning ritual-dance that was videotaped with two cameras, images of the whirling figure dissolve into each other, building a picture that is unique to video. Greenfield consistently tailors the subjects of her films, videotapes, or holograms (∗) to the special characteristics of each medium. In her 1979 *Videotape for a Woman and a Man*, a couple whirls at the end of the work, freezing into immobility and then rushing back to life in shared moments that are electronic and ecstatic. Greenfield's short film *Tides* (1980) and her feature-length *Antigone* (1989) continue the concerns of her earlier works: ordeal; human movement registered and magnified by an active camera; and a fluid treatment of narrative that retroactively upsets our sense of space and time. Quite remarkably, in a 1968 essay for *Filmmakers' Newsletter*, she outlined an artistic agenda very similar to what she would actually do, from *Encounter* (1969), which echoes Stan Brakhage (∗), to all of her other films.—Robert Haller

Greenfield, Amy. *Antigone* (1989). NY: Mystic Fire Video, 1990.

———. *Videotape for a Woman and a Man* (1979). NY: Filmmakers' Cooperative (175 Lexington Ave, 10016), 1990.

GRIFFITH, D.W. (1875–1948; b. David Llewelyn Wark G.). Initially the most prolific director of early silent films, Griffith belongs here less for his general achievement than for a single film, *Intolerance* (1916), which in crucial respects utterly transcended everything made before it. Among the film's innovations was its structure of telling four separate but interwoven stories ("The Modern Story," "The Judean Story," "The French Story," and "The Babylonian Story") that were linked by the common theme announced in its title and explained in an opening statement. The technical departure of interweaving four stories (more than a decade before William Faulkner's [∗] structurally similar *The Sound and the Fury*, 1929) gives the film a fugal form, a

D.W. Griffith, *Intolerance*, 1916. *Courtesy Kino International Corporation.*

grand scope, and a historical resonance previously unknown and subsequently rare.

As Seymour Stern pointed out, Griffith worked without a script, even editing from memory, meaning there was nothing for his superiors to approve prior to his making the film. The spectacle is a reflection of, in Stern's luminous phrases, "a creative titan's hand, moving puppet-forces, but moving them in a resplendent esthetic of coordinated masses, counterpointed rhythms, orchestrated tempos, parallel movements, structured multiple movement-forces, configurations both static and dynamic, visual confluences of timeless space, imagistic symphonies of people, objects, and light: the filmic architecture of history and tragedy beyond emotion and beyond criticism." The surviving print has subtitles, contrary to Griffith's original intention of making a purely visual film with the integrity of a Beethoven string quartet. Griffith also varied the size and shape of the screen, forecasting images of alternative projection, including circular screens and the ratios of CinemaScope (∗). Perhaps because of the commercial failure of *Intolerance*, he subsequently made only more modest films. Much of his energies were then devoted to finding better ways for serious directors to fund their films, first by cofounding the collaborative United Artists Corporation (with Charlie Chaplin, Mary Pickford, and Douglas Fairbanks), later by legally incorporating himself, all without sufficient success to permit him to control his subsequent filmmaking. He died alone and forgotten in a Hollywood hotel room.

Stern, Seymour. "D.W. Griffith's *Intolerance*" (1974). In *The Essential Cinema*, ed. P. Adams Sitney. NY: Anthology Film Archives and New York University, 1975.

Williams, Martin. *Griffith: First Artist of the Movies.* NY: Oxford, 1980.

GRÖGEROVÁ, Bohumila (1921), and Josef HIRŠAL (1920). They edited the anthology *experimentální poezie* (1967), which (even though it was published in Czechoslovakia) ranks among the best anthology of Concrete Poetry (∗). It included the strongest works not only from their contemporaries, such as Eugen Gomringer (∗), Jean-François Bory (∗), and John Furnival (∗), but from earlier writers, including Michel Suephor (∗), Raoul Hausmann (∗), and Pierre-Albert Birot (∗), only some of which they translated into Czech. Their book even has a good visual poem by Václav Havel (1938), who a quarter-century later was elected leader of their country. Grögerová has also produced poetic objects and drawings, in addition to experimental prose, radio plays, and cycles of diaries in the form of literary montages. Hiršal has published several books of poetry. Not unlike other prominent writers in minority languages, they have both translated from the major Western tongues.

Grögerová, Bohumila, and Josef Hiršal, eds. *experimentální poezie*. Prague, Czechoslovakia: Odeon, 1967.

GROSS, Milt (1895–1953). Gross was a cartoonist, famous in his time, with sufficient literary ambition to write a book-length narrative that had, as its title page boasted, "not a word in it—no music, too." In a series of finely drawn pictures, it tells of a frontier trapper going into the woods to earn enough money to marry his girlfriend who, while he is gone, succumbs to a city slicker who cons the woman into believing the trapper has died. (John Barth [*] used to quote the Latin poet Horace saying that if an experimental writer wants to use an unfamiliar

Milt Gross, image from *He Done Her Wrong*, 1930. Collection Richard Kostelanetz.

form, he or she would be wise to choose a familiar plot.) As representational images devoid of words, *He Done Her Wrong* is very much the precursor of, among other books, several marvelous, strictly visual narratives of Martin Vaughn-James (1943), whose books *Elephant* (1970) and *The Projector* (1971) were published in Canada in the early seventies; more recently, Vaughn-James's special fictions (which need not be translated) have appeared in the French literary periodical *Minuit*.

Gross, Milt. *He Done Her Wrong: The Great American Novel*. Garden City, NY: Doubleday Doran, 1930.

GROTOWSKI, Jerzy (1933). From modest professional beginnings directing a theatrical company in a small Polish city, Grotowski quickly became known for radical stagings. He put the audience for Calderón de la Barca's *The Constant Prince* on a four-sided balcony behind a high wooden fence, so that spectators had to stand and peer like voyeurs over the barrier. His production of Stanisław Wyspiański's (1869–1907) *Akropolis* (1904) has the performers build structures through the audience. "The actors can play among the spectators, directly contacting the audience and giving it a passive role in the drama," Grotowski has written. "Or the entire hall is used as a concrete place: [staging] Faustus's 'last supper' in a monastery refectory, where Faustus offers episodes from his life to the spectators, who are guests at a baroque feast served on huge tables." Grotowski has also developed an innovative program for training actors for extraordinary, almost superhuman (e.g, trance-like) performances. Sometime in the seventies, Grotowski became, no joke, a California academic.

Grotowski, Jerzy. *Towards a Poor Theatre*. NY: Simon & Schuster, 1970.

GRUMMAN, Bob (1941). With his regular contributions to the review-periodical *Factsheet Five* and his book *Of Manywhere-at-Once* (1990), Grumman has become a major critic of avant-garde American poetry. His strengths are relating new developments to the high modernist tradition and elaborate, penetrating close-readings of texts that would strike most readers as initially impenetrable. For instance, looking at George Swede's "graveyarduskilldeer," Grumman notices, "Here three words are spelled together not only to produce the richly resonant 'double-haiku,' graveyard/dusk/killdeer//graveyard/us/killdeer, but strikingly to suggest the enclosure (like letters by a word) of two or more people (a couple—or, perhaps *all* of us) by an evening—or some greater darkening." Very keen on distinctions, Grumman coins useful discriminatory categories where previous commentators saw only chaos: "intra-verbal" and "alphaconceptual" are two examples.

Grumman, Bob. *Of Manywhere-at-Once*. Port Charlotte, FL: Runaway Spoon (P.O. Box 3621, 33946-3621), 1990.

GUERILLA GIRLS (1985). The name taken by a scrupulously anonymous collective whose specialty is the provocative poster, customarily realized with considerably irony and wit. Such posters appear wherever they can be placed, beginning with the walls of SoHo (*) but including other venues, such as pages of magazines. The posters customarily have a large-type headline over a series of short assertions. My favorite is headlined "Relax Senator Helms, the Art World *Is* Your Kind of Place" (1989). Among the assertions, each preceded by a bullet in ironic reference to advertising styles, are: "Museums are separate but equal. No female black painter or sculptor has been in a Whitney Biennial since 1973. Instead, they can show at the Studio Museum in Harlem or the Women's Museum in Washington"; "The majority of exposed penises in major museums belong to the Baby Jesus." These statements are not only true, but stylishly presented; and when you're appealing to people receptive to art, that last quality helps.

For literature, write 532 La Guardia Place, Box 237, New York, NY 10012.

GUERILLA THEATER. See THE SAN FRANCISCO MIME TROUPE

GUTAI (c. 1950s). A group of Japanese visual artists, founded in Osaka by Jiro Yoshihara (1905–1972), they produced collective paintings and mixed-means (*) theater pieces, some of them quite spectacular. Among the participants were Atsuko Tanaka (1931), Sadamasa Motonaga (1922), Kazuo Shiraga (1924), and Minuro Yoshida (1935). Michael Kirby (*) describes them as expanding "the means used in

the action of painting. One artist tied a paintbrush to a toy tank and exhibited the marks it left on the canvas; others painted with their feet, with boxing gloves made of rags and dipped in paint, or by throwing bottles filled with paint at a canvas with rocks under it." He continues, "In 1957 the Gutai presented more formal theater works for an audience. A large plastic bag filled with red smoke was pushed through a hole at the back of the stage and inflated. Smoke puffed out through holes in the side. Another presentation employed a large box with three transparent plastic walls and one opaque white wall. Performers inside the box dropped balls of paper into buckets of paint and threw them against the white wall, coloring the surface. Then colored water was thrown against the plastic walls that separated the spectators from the performers." The critic Udo Kultermann writes, "The Gutai artists built huge figures after designs by Atsuko Tanaka and lighted them from the inside with strings of colored lamps. The lamps flashed rhythmically, suggesting such disparate effects as outdoor advertising and blood circulation. A moving strip covered with footprints snaked across the forest floor and up a tree. There were also spatial constructions that could be entered, traffic signs, jellyfish-shaped mounds of mud, plastic, and rope, stuffed sacks hanging from trees tied with ribbons." As far as I can tell, this major avant-garde group disbanded by the middle 1960s, the individual members pursuing separate, less consequential careers.

Kirby, Michael. *Happenings*. NY: Dutton, 1965.

Kultermann, Udo. *Art and Life*. NY: Praeger, 1971.

Falk, Ray. "Japanese Innovators." *New York Times* (8 December 1957).

GYSIN, Brion (1916–1986). An Anglo-Canadian who became an American citizen by virtue of service in the U.S. Army, where he studied Japanese, Gysin went to France on a Fulbright in 1946 and, instead of coming back, moved to Tangier. A lesser polyartist (*), he painted as well as wrote. He collaborated with William Burroughs (*) on experiments in cutting apart and recomposing texts. He wrote a great permutational poem, "I Am That I Am," in which those five words are subjected to all 120 combinations, which he then read aloud for the BBC in

1959. Fortunately reproduced on the initial *Dial-A-Poem* record (1972), this performance remains among the indisputable classics of sound poetry (∗). The Belgian-Parisian critic Marc Dachy (1952) remembers Gysin as the most generous elder supporter of the young French avant-garde.

Gysin, Brion. *Brion Gysin Let the Mice In*. W. Glover, VT: Something Else, 1973.

———. *The Process*. London, England: Cape, 1970.

———. *The Last Museum*. Boston, MA: Faber, 1986.

HAAKE, Hans (1936). Born in Germany, Haacke came to America as an art-school teacher. His principal esthetic achievement has been getting galleries to display artworks that emphasize highly pointed social exposé and commentary. Descending from conceptual art (∗), Haacke began in the early 1970s exhibiting photographs of buildings held by Manhattan slumlords he viewed as particularly unctuous. (This prompted the cancellation of an announced exhibition of his work at the Guggenheim Museum and the firing of its curator, the critic Edward Fry [1935–1992], in a scandal that decades later is not forgotten.) Subsequent work often uses the slogans from art-supporting corporations for ironic ends, such as a single horizontal aluminum plaque on which are polished letters with Alcoa's president's declaration, "Business could hold art exhibitions to tell its own story." Naming names, Haacke is skilled at satirical retitling, such as calling PBS the "Petroleum Broadcasting Service." His recurring theme is exposing the connections between art institutions and corporate bullies. Though Haacke's admirers claim he is making "unacceptable art," his work is exhibited and discussed respectfully while he remains professionally employed, perhaps because exposé exhibitions—in contrast, say, to publication especially in newspapers—epitomize the safe enterprise of preaching to the converted.

Haacke, Hans, et al. *Unfinished Business*. Cambridge, MA–NY: M.I.T.–New Museum, 1986.

HALPRIN, Anna (1920, b. Ann Shuman). After studying with Margaret H'Doubler (1889–1982), a pioneer dance educator at the University of Wisconsin, Halprin emphasized non-dance "natural" movements, improvisation, and process in both workshops and performances beginning in the late 1950s. Though she lived and worked in San Francisco, her work was first recognized in European festivals in the early 1960s. Her *Parades and Changes* (1965), a complex and ever-varying piece, caused a scandal for its total nudity. Halprin became interested in the healing aspects of dance, in how it feels to the participant more than how it looks to an audience. In 1980, she began a community workshop called *Search for Living Myths* with her husband, Lawrence (∗). She has become committed to creating modern-day rituals—in exploring collective power, archetypal forms that emerge from groups, and the possibility for concrete results from the process of creation and performance. One such ritual—a performance of *Planetary Dance* (19 April 1987)—involved seventy-five groups in thirty-five countries.—Katy Matheson

Kostelanetz, Richard. "Ann Halprin." In *The Theater of Mixed Means* (1968). NY: Archae, 1980.

Halprin, Anna. "A Life in Ritual." *The Drama Review* 122 (Summer 1989).

Schechner, Richard. "Interview with Anna Halprin." *The Drama Review* 122 (Summer 1989).

Anna Halprin, "Parades and Changes," 1965. L to r: Daria (Halprin) Rose, A.A. Leath, Anna Halprin, John Graham. *Photo courtesy Anna Halprin.*

HALPRIN, Lawrence (1916). The husband since 1940 of Anna Halprin (∗), he studied conventional architecture before taking his advanced degree in landscape architecture. Commonly credited with helping develop "the California garden concept," Halprin subsequently expanded his range to, to quote his summary, "group housing, suburban villages, shopping centers. Gradually these issues have aggregated into larger ones—how people, in regions, can live together in towns and villages without raping the land and destroying the very environment they live in. This led to concerns about transportation, both freeways for cars and mass transportation (BART), with particular concern for how these mammoth constructions could do more than just function as carriers, but go further and become forms of sculpture (as well as sociology) in the landscape." Halprin's ideas reflect, as they continually quote, such artists as Buckminster Fuller (∗) and John Cage (∗), among others featured in this *Dictionary*.

Halprin, Lawrence. *RSVP Cycles: Creative Processes in the Human Environment*. NY: Braziller, 1970.

HANSON, Sten (1936). Born in northern Sweden, Hanson was initially an experimental poet before turning to audiotape composition, in which he is largely self-taught. His earliest electroacoustic works were short collages of text and sound, usually with a political theme. ("Electroacoustic" music differs from purely Electronic Music [∗] in using pre-recorded sounds that are processed and mixed.) Subsequently Hanson realized audio art (∗) that could be comic for much the same reason that animation is, because it portrays humans performing in superhuman ways. Formerly recognized as a promising poet, he became a composer, even writing for live instrumentalists. A natural publicist, calling himself a "sonophosopher," Hanson has organized text-sound (∗) festivals, served as chairman of the Swedish Composers Society, and traveled around the world representing Swedish culture.

Hanson, Sten. *The John Carter Song Book* (1979–1985). Stockholm, Sweden: Phono Suecia PS CD 30, 1987.

HAPPENING. Coined by Allan Kaprow (∗), a gifted wordsmith as well as an innovative artist, for his particular kind of nonverbal, mixed-means (∗) theatrical piece, this term came, in the late sixties, to characterize any and every chaotic event, particularly if it wasn't immediately definable. Especially because the epithet had been vulgarized elsewhere, it became, within the community of visual performance, exclusively the property of Kaprow, who defined it thus: "An assemblage of events performed or perceived in more than one time and place. Its material environments may be constructed, taken over directly from what is available, or altered slightly, just as its activities may be invented or commonplace. A Happening, unlike a stage play, may occur at a supermarket, driving along a highway, under a pile of rags, and in a friend's kitchen, either at once or sequentially. If sequential, time may extend to more than a year. The Happening is performed according to a plan without rehearsal, audience, or repetition." Like all good definitions, this excludes more than it encompasses, including some examples that one might think belong.

Kaprow, Allan. *Assemblage, Environments & Happenings*. NY: Abrams, 1966.

Kostelanetz, Richard. *The Theatre of Mixed Means* (1968). NY: Archae Editions, 1980.

HARD-EDGE ABSTRACTION. See COLOR-FIELD PAINTING

HAUSMANN, Raoul (1886–1971). Born in Vienna, Hausmann spent his teen years in Berlin, where as a young man he met Johannes Baader (∗), who joined him and Richard Huelsenbeck (∗) in founding the Dada (∗) Club in 1918. Before long Hausmann became, in Marc Dachy's summary, "painter, draftsman, photographer, creator of photomontages, visual concrete poet, sound poet, theoretician, prose writer, technician, journalist, historian, magazine editor, dancer, and performer," which is to say a polyartist (∗). In 1919, Hausmann started the periodical *Der Dada* and organized the first Dada exhibition in Berlin. Politically radical, he allied with Baader in placing fictitious articles in Berlin daily newspapers and in proposing a Dada Republic in the Berlin suburb of Nikolassee, announcing their political activities through eye-catching posters. Hausmann invented the Optophone, which was a photo-electric machine for transmitting kaleidoscopic forms into sound, and also created the Dada "phonetic poem" before Kurt Schwitters (*) took the idea to a higher level. "The sound poem," according to Hausmann, "is an art consisting of respiratory and auditive combinations. In order to express these elements typographically, I use letters of different sizes to give them the character of musical notation," preceding Ernest Robson (*), among others. Hausmann probably invented Photomontage (*) before Moholy-Nagy (*) and John Heartfield (*). His career is best defined by an epithet more popular in Europe than America: "multiple researches."

Bory, Jean-François. *Raoul Hausmann*. Paris, France: L'Herne, 1972.

Dachy, Marc. *The Dada Movement*. NY: Rizzoli, 1990.

HAYS, Sorrel (1941; b. Doris H.). Initially a contemporary pianist, renowned for her interpretations of Henry Cowell (*) among others, Hays turned in the late 1970s to multi-media performance and audiotape composition. The epitome of her multi-media work is *M.O.M.'N P.O.P.* (1984, which means "Music Only Music, Piano Only Piano"), which is a fantasized reflection (with film, taped sounds and narration, three pianos, and mimes) on the comic difficulty of reconciling 19th-century virtuosic pianism with 20th-century cultural ideals. By contrast, the audiotape *Southern Voices* (1981) is an extraordinarily rich interweaving of speech rhythms and melodies indigenous to the American South (included in her album *Voicings*). In the early 1980s, she confused historians by changing her first name to that of "an edible stubborn wild plant" (with which she identifies). She has since composed a piece about the sounds of feminist affirmation (*A Celebration of No*, 1983) and an opera, *The Glass Woman* (1992).

Hays, Sorrel Doris. *Voicings*. NY: Folkways FTS 37476, 1983.

———. *The Piano Music of Henry Cowell*. NY: Finnadar SR 9016, 1983.

HEARTFIELD, John (1891–1968; b. Helmut Herzfelde). The son of a socialist poet, he anglicized his names as a protest against his forced military service in World War I. A founding member of Berlin Dada (*), Heartfield differed from his colleagues by actually joining the Communist party. An early adventurer in Photomontage (*), he specialized in cut-ups that ridiculed Fascist politicians. These were published as cartoons, posters, book covers, and illustrations—wherever he could, in his aspiration to be a popular political artist. Heartfield's most famous image is *Adolf, Der Ubermench: Schluckt Gold und redet Blech* (1932), depicting Hitler swallowing large coins and spewing junk. Once Hitler took power, Heartfield fled to Prague and then to London (while his brother, Wieland Herzfelde, a prominent publisher, escaped to New York). After settling in East Germany in 1950, Heartfield received all the benefits and privileges a Communist state could offer.

Heartfield, John. *Photomontages of the Nazi Period*. NY: Universe, 1977.

Siepmann, Eckhard. *Montage: John Heartfield*. Berlin, Germany: Elefanten, 1977.

HECKERT, Matt (1957). One of the advantages offered by amplification is making music loud, not only to spread its sound but also, by La Monte Young (*) among others, to reveal overtones that would not be available at lower volumes. The principal innovation of Matt Heckert's self-constructed unamplified instruments is a loudness previously unknown. In his Mechanical Sound Orchestra are "Oscillating Rings" that generate rhythmic whirring sounds whose pitch varies with speed, "Resonators" made from disemboweled water heaters whose membranes thunder when tickled at their most resonant frequencies, and the "Boxer," an inverted wok that bounces around a steel table. Scarcely a technophobe, Heckert "conducts" his instruments through a computer that sends commands to the electric motors that power his band. This obviously epitomizes what Luigi Russolo (*) had in mind for *The Art of Noise* but did not know how to do. Heckert must be seen to be heard; no recording can capture the physically overwhelming presence of his "natural" sound.

Dery, Mark. "The Art of Crash, Hum, and Hiss." *New York Times* (15 March 1992).

HEIDSIECK, Bernard (1928). A pioneering sound poet, whose spoken work has a propulsive sound instantly identifiable as his, Heidsieck has since the early 1950s pursued a singular path, devoted to French language and French history, usually with identifiable subjects, producing many tapes and records as well as books that includes seven-inch records and even films. He coined the epithets "poésie sonore" in 1955 and "poésie action" in 1962, the first an approximation of sound poetry (*), the second of performance poetry. He began to work with audiotape recorders as early as 1959. Heidsieck is one of the few writers mentioned in this book who has won a major prize from his own government (in his case, the Grand Prix National de la Poésie [1991]); the story is that the judges, divided over more conservative candidates, picked Heidsieck to take revenge on one another. Accidents like that appear to be the only way that the prize- and fellowship-givers ever reward avant-garde writers.

Heidsieck, Bernard. *Partition V*. Paris, France: Soleil Noir, 1973.

HEISSENBÜTTEL, Helmut (1921). Initially a student of architecture, art history, and "Germanistik," he is regarded as one of the foremost exponents of post–World War II German avant-garde poetry. An influence upon the new poets of the 1960s (Peter Handke [1942] and Franz Mon [*]), he approached poetry, as well as his prose, from, in his words, a linguistically "an-anarchic" point of view. His poems are calculated, experimental, and carefully crafted, occasionally including lines in English or French; he called them "texts" and thus his collections, literally, "textbooks." His writings often deal with trivia, with thoughts anyone could have in the course of a day, in a language as ungrammatical as everyday language can be; once spelled out, such thoughts get generalized and yet are alienating.

Heissenbüttel has been a renowned essayist, who worked from 1959 to 1981 as the director of "Radio-Essays" at the Stuttgart radio station. His novels, usually called "projects," are mostly parodies of historical events. In *Wenn Adolf Hitler den Kreig nicht gewonnen hätte* (If Adolf Hitler Would Not Have Won the War), Hitler and Stalin have triumphed, and Europe has become a socialist computer society whose totalitarian government lets superfluous people die for the sake of economic advantage. Triangular relationships among Friedrich Nietzsche, Paul Rée, and Lou von Salomé become the center of *1882. Eine historische Novelle* (1882, an Historical Novella). *Das Ende der Alternative,*

Fast eine einfache Geschichte (The End of the Alternative, Almost a Simple Story) tells about a beautiful tall woman, the "alternative," who commits suicide by drowning herself in the ocean after several attempts to kill her have failed.— Ulrike Michal Dorda

Heissenbüttel, Helmut. *Texts*. Trans. and ed. Michael Hamburger. London, England: Marion Boyars, 1977.

Waldrop, Rosmarie. *Against Language?* The Hague, The Netherlands: Mouton, 1971.

HELMES, Scott (1945). An architect by training and by trade, Helmes has made strong visual poems for nearly two decades, beginning with simple word-images and progressing through more complex word-based works realized in a variety of ways, some of them, for instance, suggesting motion by rubber-stamping the same letters across a page, often making the familiar strange. "Some work concentrates on letter shape and connections to other letter poems," he writes. "Others are based upon the patterns of letters/words on pages, rather than lines and paragraphs." Helmes speaks of his most recent poems as "tautological texts deconstructed from repetitive patterns in order to jar memories and force the reader into evaluating how they see and construct their language frameworks." Though his poems appear widely in exhibitions and periodicals, he has yet to collect them into a book.

HELMS, Hans G. (1932). In 1969, I met this German writer who, in the course of discussing something else, claimed to have written a polylingual novel. Skeptical, I replied, "not bilingual, like Anthony Burgess's *A Clockwork Orange* [1961]?" His response was an awesome number of languages. This book, *Fa:m' Ahniesgwow* (1959), comes in a box with a ten-inch record in which the author reads selected pages. Some pages are predominantly German, others predominantly English. My own sense is that, like James Joyce (*) before him, Helms made linguistic decisions based on sound and rhythm. The disc reveals that Helms hears white space as silence. The book concludes with extensive notes (in German only, alas) by Gottfried Michael Koenig (1928), himself a noted German composer, who sees the title, for instance, combining English, Danish, Swedish, South American Spanish, and North American slang. Around the same time, Helms produced *Golem*, a speech piece that he characterizes as "polemics for nine solo vocalists." More recently, Helms has written Marxist social criticism.

Helms, Hans G. *Fa:m' Ahniesgwow*. Köln, Germany: DuMont, 1959.

HERRIMAN, George (1880–1944). Herriman's *Krazy Kat* comic strip is the zenith of the form. Krazy Kat (sometimes male but more frequently female) loved Ignatz Mouse, and the scatterbrained Krazy always believed that a brick thrown at her head by Ignatz was a sign of his love. The newspaper-reading public did not eat this up. All of the adventures of Krazy Kat took place in the mythical Kokonino Kounty, a desert decorated with weird geological and botanical forms. Herriman's genius, however, accounted for more than the strangeness of the physical landscape he developed or the emotional landscape of his characters. His experiments with the form of the comic strip were what made his work remarkable. Panels were inserted into panels, overlaid upon panels that served as establishing shots, or laid askew of the defining grid. Colors were used not logically but brashly. The fiction of the comic strip was laid bare by visual puns that broke through the wall of the newspaper and made clear the other reality that the characters lived within. Herriman explored, as fully as anyone has, the esthetic possibilities of the comic strip through design, language, color, and characterization. The sense that no one has ever surpassed his work indicates how confining the modern strip format is—remember that Herriman had a whole newspaper page to work with, and occasionally only one panel filled that space—and how conservative the comic-strip syndicates have become.—Geof Huth

Blackbeard, Bill, and Martin Williams, eds. *The Smithsonian Collection of Newspaper Comics*. Washington, DC: Smithsonian Institution, 1977.

HERTZBERG, Hendrik. See O'ROURKE, P.J.

HESSE, Eva (1936–1970). In her brief career as a sculptor, cut short by terminal brain cancer, Hesse discovered the feasibility of using several materials previously unknown to three-dimensional visual art. The classic Hesse work, *Expanded Expansion* (1969), has vertical fiberglass poles, taller than a man is tall, with treated cheesecloth suspended horizontally across them; her rubberizing and resin treatment give the cloth a density and tension previously unavailable to it. Given the softness of her materials, this sculpture would necessarily assume a different look each time this work was exhibited. Though *Expanded Expansion* is already several feet across, there is a suggestion, which the artist acknowledged, that it could have been extended to surrounding, thus Environmental (*), length. Hesse also used latex. In part because she was, along with Lee Bontecou (1930), among the first American women sculptors to be generally acclaimed, Hesse also became, posthumously alas, a feminist heroine.

Lippard, Lucy R. *Eva Hesse*. NY: New York University, 1976.

HIGGINS, Dick (1938). Though his abundant output may be conventionally divided into such categories as writing, theater, music, film, criticism, and book publishing, it is best to regard Higgins not as a specialized practitioner of one or another of these arts, but as a true polyartist (*)—a master of several nonadjacent arts, subservient to none. In over thirty years, he has produced a wealth of work, both large and small, permanent and ephemeral, resonant and trivial—uneven, to be sure; but no two people familiar with his activities agree on which are best (other than book publishing, his Something Else Press [*] being revered almost universally as the most substantial avant-garde publisher ever in America).

All of his diversity notwithstanding, Higgins reveals five fundamental ways of dealing with the materials of each art he explores. These procedures are collage (*), representation, permutation, aleatory, and Expressionism (*). In nearly all his works, one or two of these procedures are dominant. Briefly, collage is the juxtaposition of dissimilars; representation is the accurate portrayal of extrinsic reality; permutation is the systematic manipulation of limited materials; aleatory depends upon chance; and Expressionism reflects personality or personal experience.

Among his many works are *7.7.73* (1973), a series of 899 unique prints of various visual imagery, both abstract and representational, with forms repeated from one print to the next. *Amigo* (1972) is a book-length poetic memoir of

Higgins's Five Methods

	Collage	Representation	Permutation	Aleatory	Expressionism
Visual Arts	7.7.73 (1973)	Some Poetry Intermedia (1976)	7.7.73 (1973)	Graphis (1957 to present)	A Thousand Symphonies (1967)
Writing	Foew&ombwhnw (1969)	Postface (1962)	Modular Poems (1975)	A Book about Love & War & Death (1965, 1969, 1972)	Amigo (1972)
Theater	St. Joan at Beaurevoir (1959)	Act (1969)	The Freedom Riders (1962)	Stacked Deck (1958)	Death and the Nickel Cigar (1973)
Music	In Memoriam (1961)		To Everything its Season (1958) Glasslass (a text-sound piece, 1970)	Graphic scores	"Danger Music No. 17" (May 1962)
Film	Men & Women & Bells (1969)	Flaming City (1962)	Hank and Mary Without Apologies (1969)	Men & Women & Bells (1969)	Flaming City
Publishing	Emmet William's An Anthology of Concrete Poetry (1967)	Henry Cowell's New Musical Resources (1930, 1962)	Gertrude Stein's The Making of Americans (1926, 1965)	John Cage's Notations (1968) Merce Cunningham's Changes (1969)	Geoff Hendricks's Ring Piece (1973)

Higgins's love for a young man. "Danger Music # 17 (May 1962)" reads in its entirety: "Scream! Scream! Scream! Scream! Scream! Scream!" *Postface* (1962) is a percipient and prophetic critical essay about advanced arts in the early 1960s. *Saint Joan at Beaurevoir* (1959) is a complicated long scenario that includes such incongruities as Dr. Johnson and Saint Joan appearing on the same stage. *Men & Women & Bells* (1959) is a short film that incorporates footage made by both his father and his grandfather. *Foew&ombwhnw* (1969)—pronounced F,O,E,W, for short—is a book with four vertical columns across every two-page horizontal spread. One column continuously reprints critical essays, a second column poetry, a third theatrical scenarios (including *Saint Joan at Beaurevoir*), a fourth drawings. Though the experience of reading *Foew* is that of collage, the book as a whole is an appropriate representation of a multi-faceted man. Higgins also published a historical study of *Pattern Poetry* (1987), which is by common consent the richest book on its multi-cultural subject.

Higgins, Dick. *Foew&ombwhnw*. NY: Something Else, 1969.

———. *Modular Poems*. W. Glover, VT: Unpublished Editions, 1974.

Frank, Peter, ed. *Something Else Press: An Annotated Bibliography*. N.p.: McPherson & Co, 1983.

HIJIKATA, Tatsumi (1928–1986). The leading figure and principal founder of the Japanese dance-theater form Butoh (*), Hijikata determined that established dance forms did not satisfy the concerns of his generation or survivors of the shock and horror of Hiroshima. He evolved Butoh from a wide variety of influences, including his own extensive readings and studies of European avant-garde writers, artists, and performers. His presentation of *Kinjiki* (Forbidden Colors, 1959), based on a novel by Yukio Mishima (1915–1970, at the time one of Japan's most famous authors), is considered to be the founding event in the development of Butoh. In it, a dancer appears to have sexual relations with a chicken and is subjected to sexual advances from another man. Both subject matter and tone shocked the Japanese establishment. In 1960, Hijikata applied the term "ankoku buyo" ("darkness dance") to the evolving form; in 1963 he

renamed it "Butoh" (based on a nearly obsolete term for dance that connotes something more basic than "buyo"). His *Rebellion of the Flesh* (1968) was another milestone that was also shocking in that he killed a chicken as part of the performance. He collaborated with Kazuo Ohno (*), who was his student (though more than twenty years his senior), and taught and worked with almost all the younger performers who are now continuing the Butoh movement.—Katy Matheson

Viala, Jean, and Nourit Masson-Sekine. *Butoh: Shades of Darkness*. Tokyo, Japan: Shufonotomu, 1988.

Butoh: Dance of the Dark Soul. NY: Aperture, 1987.

The Drama Review T110 (Summer 1986).

Blackwood, Michael. *Butoh: Body on the Edge of Crisis*. NY: Michael Blackwood Productions, 1990.

HIRŠAL, Josef. See, GRÖGEROVÁ, Bohumila

HIVNOR, Robert (1916). Hivnor's play *Too Many Thumbs* (1948) tells of an exceptionally bright chimpanzee with a large body and a comparatively small head. In the course of the play, this figure moves up the evolutionary ladder to become, first, an intermediate stage between man and beast, and then a normal man, and ultimately a godlike creature with an immense head and a shriveled body. The university professors who keep him also attempt to cast him as the avatar of a new religion, but unending evolution defeats their designs. The play's ironically linear structure is original (preceding by a few years Eugène Ionesco's [*] use of a similar form in *The New Tenant* [1957]). By pursuing the bias implicit in evolutionary development to its inevitable reversal, the play pointedly questions mankind's claim to a higher stage of existence.

Hivnor, Robert. *Too Many Thumbs*. Minneapolis, MN: University of Minnesota, 1949.

HOLOGRAPHY. A technology new to the 1960s, drawing upon scientific discoveries of the late 1940s, holography superficially resembles photography in capturing an image on two-dimensional photoemulsion (film), but it differs in capturing an image in different situations (and thus, at least implicitly, at different times) and then in situating that image in illusory space. That is to say that the principal feature of holography is creating the illusion that things are located where they are not. (A variant, called a multiplex or stereogram, is created by shooting an image with motion-picture film that is then compressed anamorphically into vertical slivers that, once illuminated from below, creates the illusion of an image suspended in space.)

Exploiting a laser split-beam process to register information on a photographic plate, holography is also a far more recalcitrant medium than either photography before it, or video, which arrived around the same time. Whereas there are millions of photographers and millions of video users, nearly all of them amateur, there are only a few dozen holographers, nearly all of them professionals. They make *holograms*, which are not the same as a "holograph," which at least in English refers to a document wholly written, usually by hand, by the person who is its author. Among the most distinguished hologram artists are Margaret Benyon (1940), Rudie Berkhout (1946), Arthur David Fonari (1949), Dieter Jung (1940), Sam Moree (1946), Dan Schweitzer (1946), Fred Unterseher (1945), and Doris Vila (1950).

Unterseher, Fred, et al. *The Holography Handbook*. Berkeley, CA: Ross Books, 1982.

HOLZER, Jenny (1950). Holzer is included only because some readers might expect to find information and insight into her work here; by no measure known is it avant-garde. Her use of language is prosaic, bordering on dull; there is no invention in either syntax or diction. Her departures, scarcely significant, are to make her words large (without the afterimage resonance of, say, Robert Indiana [*]) and then to use signage technologies that are scarcely unfamiliar. Her language style descends from slogans; her sentences are designed to impress not for any linguistic excellence but as counter-adages for the cognoscenti whose prejudices, for another measure of kitchiness, are assuaged rather than challenged. Invariably as dumb and unoriginal as possible, her art cons an audience predisposed to the obvious, becoming thereby the litmus test for identifying the unsophisticated, which is the inadvertent but beneficial "political" function of her work. If you see a Jenny Holzer in a gallery, in a museum, in a private collection, or illustrated in a magazine, you'll know a dummy is lurking somewhere. Do not dismiss the social value of such art, for every profession needs an idiot-identifier if it is to remain a profession.

Waldman, Diane. *Jenny Holzer*. NY: Rizzoli, 1992.

HÖRSPIEL. See RADIO ART

HOUÉDARD, Dom Sylvester (1924–1992). Born in the Channel Islands, Dom Sylvester became in 1949 a Benedictine monk, thereafter residing in Prinknash Abbey in Gloucester, England. The leading English-language theorist of Concrete Poetry (*) in the 1960s, he published and exhibited elaborate, typewriter-composed visual poems that his colleague Edwin Morgan (*) called typestracts, speaking of them as "ikons for contemplation, topological tantric forms linked to language or 'poetry' only by the lingering literary hookup anything typewritten still tends to retain." Because Dom Sylvester's poetry has been scattered through numerous chapbooks, among them *Kinkon* (1965) and *Tantric Poems Perhaps* (1966), while his religious humility undermines his innate idiosyncrasy, what is needed now is a thicker book representing his unique achievement. Houédard published a good deal of criticism, as eccentric in its typography as his learning, for instance defining his poetic tradition as:

> benedictine baroque as contrasted with the jesuit—& poetmonks in the west [who] have always cultivated what [Cardinal] newman calls "the alliance of benedict & virgil," eg: s-abbo s-adelhard agobard b-alcuin s-adlhelm (the concretist) s-angilbert s-bede s-bertharius (caedmon) s-dunstan (another concretist) florus fridoard gerbert (sylvester II) heiric hepidamn-the-newsallust herimann v-hildebert hincmar b-hrabanus-maurus (concrete).

Houédard also collaborated in the editing of the *Jerusalem Bible* (1961).

Houédard, Dom Sylvester. *(Poems)*. Ed. Charles Verey. Sunderland, England: Ceolfrith, 1972.

***HPSCHD* (1969).** One of John Cage's (*) most abundant pieces, done in collaboration with the composer Lejaren Hiller (1924), *HPSCHD* was premiered at Assembly Hall at the University of Illinois's Urbana campus, 16 May 1969, for five hours. The venue's name is appropriate, because Cage assembled an immense amount of visual and acoustic materials. On the outside walls were an endless number of slides projected by fifty-two projectors. In the middle of the circular sports arena were suspended several parallel sheets of Visquine, each 100 by 40 feet, and from both sides were projected numerous films and slides whose collaged imagery passed through several sheets. Running around a circular ceiling rim was a continuous 340-foot screen on which appeared a variety of smaller images, both representational and abstract. Beams of light spun around the upper reaches, both rearticulating the concrete supports and hitting mirrored balls that reflected dots of light in all directions. Lights shining directly down upon the asphalt floor also changed color from time to time. Complementing the abundance of images was a sea of sounds that had no distinct relation to one another—an atonal and astructural chaos so continually in flux that one could hear nothing more specific than a few seconds of repetition. Most of this came from fifty-two tape recorders, each playing a computer-generated tape composed to a different scale divided at every integer between five and fifty-six tones to an octave. Fading in and out through the mix were snatches of harpsichord music that sounded more like Mozart than anything else. These sounds came from seven harpsichordists on platforms raised above the floor in the center of Assembly Hall. Around these islands were flowing several thousand people. *HPSCHD* was an incomparably abundant visual/aural uninflected Environment (*), really the most extravagant of its kind ever done. A few years later, Cage mounted a "chamber version," with far fewer resources, at New York's Brooklyn Academy of Music. With abridged elements, this slighter *HPSCHD* did not have a comparable impact.

Kostelanetz, Richard. "Environmental Abundance." In *John Cage* (1970), ed. Richard Kostelanetz. 2nd ed. NY: Da Capo, 1991.

HUELSENBECK, Richard (1892–1974). Incidentally residing in Zurich in 1916, this young doctor participated in the beginnings of Dada (*), which he continued to support in Berlin in 1918. Huelsenbeck wrote the first history of Dada in 1920–1921 and edited the *Dada Almanach* (1920), an anthology so well selected it was reissued in the original German by Something

Else Press (*) in 1966. After years as a ship's doctor cruising the world, he landed in 1936 in New York, where he became a psychiatrist (taking the name Charles R. Hulbeck) and, after World War II, the only first-rank participant in Dada based in New York. His 1916 poem "End of the World" resembles Guillaume Apollinaire's (*) "Zone" in its disconnected lines, universal scope, and lack of punctuation. Huelsenbeck's *Memoirs of a Dada Drummer* (1969) is very candid, not only about his colleagues but about his success as a New York shrink who, as he boasts, sent his children to the best schools. Given the scant rewards for avant-garde art in New York, it is always gratifying to learn that its creators can find other vehicles of patronage.

Huelsenbeck, Richard. *Memoirs of a Dada Drummer* (1969). Berkeley, CA: University of California, 1991.

HUNEKER, James Gibbons (1860–1921). Educated in music in Paris, initially a music critic for Philadelphia and New York newspapers, Huneker became a distinguished commentator on all of the arts, the polyartistic critic who popularized European avant-gardes on these alien shores from the 1880s until his premature death. He wrote books about music, literature, and drama, in addition to short fictions and a novel. His two-volume autobiography, *Steeplejack* (1920), is about enthusiastic living with all the arts.

Schwab, Arnold T. *James Gibbons Huneker: Critic of the Seven Arts.* Stanford, CA: Stanford University, 1963.

HUTH, Geof (1960). As a poet and publisher in and around Schenectady, NY, Huth has produced an abundance of work based upon linguistic invention by himself and others. Rather than quote examples, why don't I mention that his periodicals are called *Alabama Dogshoe Moustache, A Voice Without Sides,* and, most indicatively, *The Subtle Journal of Raw Coinage.* His imprint, "dbqp," which is a pseudoacronym for "goodbooqpres" (and also is identical if inverted), specializes in "language, visual, and conceptual poetry, comics, prose, and other artistic investigations into language and meaning." For its 101st publication, Huth produced an anecdotal history that came in a plastic box slightly less than four-inches square. Huth was also a regular reviewer for *Factsheet Five* (1982–1991), the Michael Gunderloy (1959) periodical that, in its lifetime, provided the most complete review of the alternative produce in print and electronic media.

Huth, Geof. *An Introduction to the History and Data Base of dbqp*. Schenectady, NY: dbqp, 1990.

HYDE, Scott (1927). A photographer who had studied with John Cage (∗), Hyde reacted to the cult of the "autograph club," as he called it, by exploring offset/lithographic printing as a photographic medium. He gave publishers black-and-white negatives, sometimes complementary and other times contrary, to be printed with different colors over one another. "I regard the picture printed in this way as a kind of 'original' print, since no 'reproductive' steps are involved. If I am satisfied with the way the picture looks, I do not permit that picture to be published [i.e., printed] again." Needless to say perhaps, Hyde's pictures look like no one else's. "Synthetic color, variations on themes, montages created directly on the press, and a simple but effective form of stereographic imagery" are among "the technical and structural issues" that the critic A.D. Coleman (1943) finds in Hyde's work, citing especially his influence on "many younger photographers and artists who have come to see the photographic print as an intermediary step en route to an offset print or book." Hyde has also made brilliant meta-photomontages (∗) differing from traditional photo-pastiche by piecing together bits from many photographs of a single subject, thereby transforming its appearance. In the late 1960s I remember seeing elaborate redesigns of New York's Washington Square arch that have never been publicly exhibited, at first because they were thought to be too original, later because the British painter David Hockney (1937) produced photo works that are similar, albeit less distinguished.

Coleman, A.D. "Scott Hyde." In *Contemporary Photographers*, ed. George Walsh, et al. NY: St. Martin's, 1982.

HYKES, David (1953). In concert with his Harmonic Choir, Hykes produces sustained open chords that, like earlier La Monte Young (∗) music with a similar structure, generate overtones; and by favoring performance spaces where overtones can last several seconds, such as the Cathedral of St. John the Divine in New York,

they can fill a theater with sounds other than those currently produced. This is Minimal (∗) music that gains from doing more with much less. Though the initial impact is stunning, whether live or on record, Hykes's music does not become richer within itself, at least in my experience. Anyone first familiar with the recordings is invariably surprised that so few performers—five in one concert I saw—generate so many sounds.

Hykes, David, and the Haromic Choir. *Harmonic Meetings*. Wilton, CT: Celestial Harmonies, n.d. (c. 1985).

HYPERTEXT (c. 1965). Reportedly coined by Theodor H. Nelson, this term defines writing done in the nonlinear or nonsequential verbal structures made possible by the computer, for a true computer exposition, whether an essay or a story, offers multiple paths in linking segments. "With its network of alternate routes (as opposed to print's fixed unidirectional page-turning)," writes the novelist Robert Coover, "hypertext presents a radically divergent technology, interactive and polyvocal, favoring a plurality of discourses over definitive utterance and freeing the reader from domination by the author." Though multi-path fiction appeared before in *Hopscotch* (1963) by Julio Cortázar (∗) and Charles Platt's "Norman vs. America," which was reprinted in my anthology *Breakthrough Fictioneers* (1973), as well as in a new kind of juvenile adventure story available through the 1980s, it becomes more feasible with computers. (Hypertext also enables scholars to find linkages through tracing key words not just through single books but through whole bodies of scholarship.)

In his introductory survey, Coover credits Michael Joyce's *Afternoon* (1987) as the "granddaddy of full-length hypertext fictions" (though the year before, Paul Zelevansky [∗] published *Swallows*, which is a mostly visual fiction of immeasurable length). Hypertext literature frequently appears in literary periodicals that are published on computer discs, such as *Postmodern Culture* (1990) in Raleigh, North Carolina (Box 8105, 27695), and Richard Freeman's *PBW* (1990) in Yellow Springs, Ohio (130 W. Limestone, 45387). The Art Com Electronic Network (ACEN) that is connected to the WELL

(Whole Earth 'Lectronic Link) makes works by Jim Rosenberg (*), Fred Truck (*), and John Cage (*), among others, available gratis through the home modem.

Tuman, Myron D., ed. *Literary Online*. Pittsburgh, PA: University of Pittsburgh, 1992.

Coover, Robert. "The End of Books." *The New York Times Book Review*, 20 June 1992.

I

ILIAZD (1894–1975; b. Ilia Mikhailovich Zdanevich). One of the most radical of the Russian literary avant-garde of the early decades of this century, Iliazd grew up in Tiflis, Russian Georgia, and by 1911, while still a teenager, became a proponent of Italian Futurism (*). From 1911 to 1917, while studying law, he was active in the Petersburg avant-garde, closely associated with the artists Mikhail Larionov (1881–1964), Natalia Goncharova (1881–1962), and Mikhail Le-Dantiu (1891–1917). He developed the theory of "Everythingism" which declared "all forms of art past and present, here and elsewhere, are contemporary for us," and thus that an artist was free to use them as desired. Beginning in 1913, he composed a series of five one-act "dras" called "Dunkeeness" that use Zaum (*) (transrational language) as their basic medium. The action of these plays is satirical-absurdist, in the style of Aleksei Kruchonykh's (*) *Victory Over the Sun* (1913) and Alfred Jarry's (*) *Ubu Roi* (1896). They feature a donkey as a character, either explicitly or metaphorically. Themes range from political power to the role of free artistic creativity. In contrast to other Zaum (*) poets, Iliazd uses phonetic spelling of his invented words; he arranges them in quasi-musical ensembles, such as duets, trios, and choruses, concluding the fifth play, *Le-Dantiu as a Beacon* (Paris, 1923), with an ensemble of eleven separate simultaneous voice lines. Collectively, Iliazd's plays constitute the largest work of Zaum yet composed. For *Le-Dantiu* alone, he coined over 1,600 new words. As he was also an expert typographer, these works are also noteworthy for their visual elaborateness.

Instead of pursuing a career in law in Petersburg, Iliazd returned in 1917 to Tiflis, where with Kruchonykh and Igor Terentyev (1892–1937) he formed the group 41° and the Fantastic Little Inn cabaret, which became a focal point for Futurist-style evenings and lectures. The first four dras were published and performed, while Iliazd's typographical skills were applied to publishing his own works and those of his colleagues, the most compendious being his anthology dedicated to the actress Sofia Melnikova (1919).

In 1921, he moved to Paris and for several years led the Russian avant-garde there, giving lectures publicizing the achievements of the Russian Futurists (*) and allying with the Parisian Dadaists. He organized the famous "Coeur à barbe," a ball at which the split between Dada (*) and Surrealism (*) emerged. Thereafter he led a quieter life, writing several innovative novels, only one of which has been published, and cycles of poems that are formally conservative, if unusual in content and style. He devoted the later part of his life to the creation of elegantly designed limited editions of rare literary works with original illustrations by artists such as Pablo Picasso (*), Max Ernst (*), and Joan Miró (1893–1983).—Gerald Janecek

Gayraud, Régis. "Il'ja Zdanevič (1894–1975): L'Homme et l'oeuvre." *Rev. Étud. slaves* (1991).

Iliazd. Paris, France: Centre Pompidou, 1978.

Janecek, Gerald. *The Look of Russian Literature*. Princeton, NJ: Princeton University, 1984.

Markov, Vladimir. *Russian Futurism: A History*. Berkeley, CA: University of California, 1968.

IMAX (1970). This is a registered pseudo-acronym, written entirely in capitals even if it means "Maximum Image," of a new projection technology that the Canadian Graeme Ferguson developed in the wake of the brilliantly successful multi-screen films shown at Expo '67 in Montreal. Using special cameras (and thus special projectors as well), a 70-millimeter film runs sideways through the camera, so that the equivalent of three frames is shot at once. Producing a negative image nine times the size of the standard 35-millimeter frame, such footage offers far finer detail on large screens than the prior techniques of Cinerama (∗) and CinemaScope (∗). In specially installed theaters around the world, such films are customarily screened with six-channel sound. The paradox is that, in this age of ever smaller public motion picture theaters, certain developments exploit the possibilities of bigger screens. OMNIMAX is a derivative technology for smaller spaces, with a wide, deeply dished, concave, almost spherical screen. The IMAX company has also developed three-dimensional film projection more popular than the cumbersome system briefly popular in the 1950s, and IMAX HD, which doubles the speed at which its film passes through the camera.

Elmer-Dewitt, Philip. "Grab Your Goggles, 3-D Is Back!" *Time*, 16 April 1990.

IMPROVISATION. See JAZZ

INDETERMINACY (c. 1954). Incidentally, the title of John Cage's (∗) first solo record (1957), this term refers to music composed with the assistance of chance operations—such as throwing dice to make decisions, observing the imperfections in paper to discover notes on staves, or using random tables—and to the use of musical instructions likely to produce radically unpredictable results. In the latter case, the composer may provide only generalized directions; or collections of notes that may be played in any order, at any speed, in any combination, etc.; or allow for a surprise that, if observed, will necessarily redirect the performance. Indeterminate performance differs from improvisation in providing ground rules that will prevent the performers from seeking familiar solutions. Indeterminacy differs from aleatory music, which was an alternative popularized by Pierre Boulez (∗) in the 1960s, with compromises typical of him, purportedly to represent a saner avant-garde. In my experience, indeterminacy, aka "chance," functioned as a divisory issue in talking, say, about John Cage's music until the late 1970s, when everyone both pro and con realized that it wasn't as important as it once seemed.

Childs, Barney. "Indeterminacy." *Dictionary of Contemporary Music*, ed. John Vinton. NY: Dutton, 1974.

Kostelanetz, Richard. *Conversing with Cage*. NY: Limelight, 1989.

INDIANA, Robert (1928; b. R. Clarke). Initially classified among the Pop Artists (∗), Indiana is actually a word painter, which is to say that his very best paintings are mostly, if not exclusively, made of language. Using bold letters and sometimes numbers, rendered in the tradition of American commercial sign painting, Indiana exposes very short Americanisms to art, or vice versa, establishing himself as a master of color, shape, and craftsmanship (though repetitiously favoring Roman letters and numerals within circles, as well as circles within circles). His single most famous work, *Love* (1966), depends upon tilting the letter O, which in this heavy Roman style evokes the sexuality embodied in its shape, and then upon the fact that all four letters are literally touching each of their adjacent letters. One version is a painting, since reproduced on a postage stamp, with the red, blue, and green so even in value that the foreground does not protrude from the background. Four of these LOVE shapes, each five by five feet, were grouped into *Wall* (1966), ten feet by ten feet of rearrangeable panels, each deployed perpendicularly to its companions, all of which can be rotated so that

Robert Indiana, "Love" stamp, first day cover, 1966. *Collection Richard Kostelanetz.*

different common letters meet at the center of the field. My favorite numerical Indiana is the extended vertical progression from zero to nine that was displayed at Expo '67. I think Indiana's design for the basketball court at the Milwaukee Mecca (1977) is the best floor done by an American artist in recent memory.

Weinhardt, Carl J., Jr. *Robert Indiana*. NY: Abrams, 1990.

INSTALLATION (c. 1980). The term "installation" identifies art made for a particular space, which need not be a gallery. Such art theoretically exploits certain qualities of that space, which it will inhabit forever or be destroyed when the exhibition is terminated. The category arose in the 1980s as an open and yet debased term for what had previously been called "site-specific art," as exemplified by the sculptors Nancy Holt (1938) and Mary Miss (1944), among others. Examples include Walter de Maria's (*) Earth Room (1968), which, in its third incarnation (or installation), has been permanently on display in New York City since the late 1970s. Both installations and site-specific art differ from an Environment (*), which is an artistically enhanced, circumscribed space.

Land Marks. Annandale, NY: Bard College Center, 1984.

INTERMEDIA (1966). This term was coined by Dick Higgins (*) to define new varieties of art that combined the aspects of two heretofore separate types of art. (Only later did he become aware of Samuel Taylor Coleridge's earlier uses of the epithet.) Intermedia is different from "multi-media," which implies something much less dramatic: the inclusion of different art media, such as different kinds of material, within one work. A most frequently cited example of intermedia is visual poetry (*), the combination of literary and visual arts. Although there is a long (and mostly unknown) tradition of visual poetry, the combination of the two represents a distinct intermedium, something not quite literature and not fully visual art. During the 20th century, experimentation with intermedia became more common as artists searched for new modes of expression. It is possible, however, that sometime in the future such intermedia will be considered perfectly usual forms of art and that other intermedia will appear on the continuum of art forms.—Geof Huth

Higgins, Dick. *Horizons: The Poets and Theory of the Intermedia*. Carbondale, IL: Southern Illinois University, 1983.

INTERNATIONAL STYLE (c. 1920). Born in Germany, mostly at the Bauhaus (*), this architecture was popularized in America, first with the publication of Henry-Russell Hitchcock's and Philip Johnson's book *The International Style* (1932). With the immigration to the U.S. of Walter Gropius (1883–1969) and Mies van der Rohe (*), both masters of the mode, the International Style became the dominant architectural fashion, particularly in office buildings, in the 1950s. Also known as the Functional Style and the Machine Style, it stood for six general principles: the marriage of art and the latest technology; geometric Constructivist (*) forms whose "streamlining" symbolized the spirit of the machine more than intrinsic technological quality; the building as a volume rather than a mass (and thus the penchant for glass walls that visually denied a building's massive weight); a rejection of axial symmetry typical of classic cathedrals, in favor of noncentered, asymmetrical regularity, as epitomized by, say, rows of glass walls; the practice of making opposite sides, if not all four sides, resemble one another so that, formally at least, the building has no obvious "front" or "back"; and finally a scrupulous absence of surface ornament. For these reasons, buildings cast in the International Style suggest no-nonsense efficiency and economy, if not a physical environment consonant with both modern technology and bureaucratic ideals, all tempered by geometric grandeur and numerous subtle visual effects produced, for instance, by colors in the glass or intersecting lines and planes. What is called "postmodern" (*) in architecture reacted against the purported sterility of this International Style.

Hitchcock, Henry-Russell, and Philip Johnson. *The International Style* (1932). NY: Norton, 1966.

Giedion, Sigfried. *Space, Time and Architecture*. Cambridge, MA: Harvard University, 1941.

IONESCO, Eugène (1912). Born in Rumania of a French mother, Ionesco grew up in both his parents' countries before moving permanently to France in 1938. Most famous for his plays, he has also written fiction and criticism. His play *The Chairs* (1952) is the epitome of the Theatre of the Absurd (✳). He also has a keen ear for authoritarian lingo that, for all its fashionable propriety, does not make sense. This example comes from *The Lesson* (1951): "That which distinguishes them, I repeat, is their striking resemblance which makes it so hard to distinguish them from each other—I'm speaking of the neo-Spanish languages which one is able to distinguish from one another, however, only thanks to their distinctive characteristics, absolutely indisputable proofs of their extraordinary resemblance, which renders indisputable their common origin, and which, at the same time, differentiates them profoundly—through the continuation of the distinctive traits which I've just cited." And, of course, the students respond: "Oooh! Ye-e-e-e-s-s-s. Professor!" The tragedy of his career is that nothing Ionesco has written since the early 1950s, in any genre, equals those few short plays for satirical edge and originality.

Ionesco, Eugène. *Four Plays.* Trans. Donald M. Allen. NY: Grove, 1958.

IRCAM. See BOULEZ, Pierre

IRELAND, Patrick. See O'DOHERTY, Brian

IRWIN, Robert (1928). The classic Robert Irwin work, *No Title* (1967), is a white circular plate, five feet in diameter, mounted from behind to stand several feet away from the wall. When illuminated by four spotlights distributed to the corners of a rectangle in front of the disc, an illusion is formed on the background wall of four overlapping discs, creating a three-dimensional tension between the original and its shadows, as well as faint concentric bands of color on the real disc's face. The background wall, the surrounding space, and the quality of the light all become as important as the disc. More recently, Irwin made an untitled installation in New York's Pace Gallery (1992), where one initially sees a black rectangle behind several layers of rectangular gauze. As the illumination in the spaces between the gauze changes color, so does the black. Because the spectator is allowed to go between the layers, he or she can look back on

the piece in different ways. In discussing Irwin, as well as his colleague James Turrell (✳), simple descriptions scarcely convey the remarkable experience of light transformations apart from any object. For obvious reasons, photographs of Irwin's art are insufficient.

Irwin, Robert. *Being and Circumstance.* Larkspur, CA: Lapis, 1985.

IVES, Charles (1874–1954). It is perhaps typically American that an avant-garde composer so neglected in his own time should be so widely acclaimed by generations after. Though Ives's works were so rarely played during his lifetime that he never heard some of his major pieces, nearly all of his music is currently available on disc; and though he taught no pupils and founded no school, he is generally considered the progenitor of nearly everything distinctly American in American music. He was not an intentional avant-gardist, conscientiously aiming for innovation, but a modest spare-time composer (who spent most of his days as an insurance salesman and then as a long-term convalescent).

A well-trained musician, who worked as a church organist upon graduating from college, Ives was essentially a great inventor with several major musical patents to his name. While still in his teens, he developed his own system of polytonality—the technique of writing for two or more keys simultaneously. In a piece composed when he was twenty (*Song for Harvest Season*), he assigned four different keys to four instruments. Ives was the first modern composer who consistently didn't resolve his dissonances. Many contemporary composers have followed Ives's *The Unanswered Question* (1908) in strategically distributing musicians over a physical space, so that the place the music comes from affects what is heard. For the *Concord Sonata*, composed between 1909 and 1915 (and arguably his masterpiece), he invented the tone cluster, where the pianist uses either his forearm or a block of wood to sound simultaneously whole groups, if not octaves, of notes.

He originated the esthetics of Pop Art (✳), for Ives, like Claes Oldenburg (✳) and Robert Indiana (✳) after him, drew quotations from mundane culture—hymn tunes, patriotic ditties, etc.—and stitched them into his artistic fabric. Though other composers had incorporated "found" sounds prior to Ives, he was probably the first to allow a quotation to stand out dissonantly from the context, as well as the first, like the Pop Artists after him, to distort a popular quotation into a comic semblance of the original. Just as Claes Oldenburg's famous *Giant Hamburger* (1962)—seven feet in diameter, made of canvas, and stuffed with kapok—creates a comic tension with our memory of the original model, so Ives evokes a similar effect in his *Variations on a National Hymn* ["America"] (1891, composed when he was seventeen!). In juxtaposing popular tunes like "Columbia, the Gem of the Ocean" in the same musical field with allusions to Beethoven's *Fifth Symphony*, Ives employed another Pop strategy to create a distinctly American style that suggests that both classical music and popular, both formal and informal cultures, are equally immediate and perhaps equally relevant.

Other Ivesian musical innovations include polyrhythms—where various sections of the orchestra play in wholly different meters, often under the batons of separate conductors, all to create multiple cross-rhythms of great intricacy. In his rhythmic freedom, as well as his unashamed atonality, Ives clearly fathered the chaotic language of modern music, a tradition that runs through Henry Cowell (∗) and early Edgard Varèse (∗) to John Cage (∗). Indeed, Ives preceded Cage by inventing indeterminancy (∗)—where the scripts offered the musicians are so indefinite at crucial points that they could not possibly play exactly the same sounds in successive performances. In *The Unanswered Question*, he further discouraged musical unanimity by placing three separate groups of musicians in such a way that one could not necessarily see the others.

As one of the first modern composers to develop a distinctly eccentric music notation, Ives anticipated contemporary composers' practices of using graphs, charts, and abstract patterns—manuscripts that resemble everything but traditional musical scores—to make their works available to others. He also wrote notes that he knew could not be played, such as a 1/1,024 note in the *Concord Sonata*, followed by the words "Play as fast as you can." Indeed, Ives's scripts were so unusually written, as well

as misplaced and scrambled in big notebooks, that editors have labored valiantly to reconstruct definitive versions of his major pieces, some of which had their debuts long after his death.

There is a conceptual similarity between Ives and Gertrude Stein (∗), who, born in America in the same year, was as radically original in her art as Ives was in his. While we can now identify what each of them did quite precisely, given our awareness of the avant-garde traditions to which they contributed, it is not so clear to us now what either of them thought they were doing—what exactly was on their minds when they made their most radical moves—so different was their art from even innovative work that was done before or around them.

Ives, Charles. *Essays Before a Sonata & Other Writings.* Selected and ed. Howard Boatwright. NY: Norton, 1962.

Cowell, Henry, and Sidney Cowell. *Charles Ives and His Music.* NY: Oxford University, 1955.

Rossiter, Frank R. *Charles Ives and His America.* NY: Liveright, 1975.

Wooldridge, Dean. *From the Steeples and Mountains.* NY: Knopf, 1974.

Feder, Stuart. *Charles Ives: "My Father's Song."* New Haven, CT: Yale University, 1992.

Burkholder, J.P. *Charles Ives: The Ideas Behind the Music.* New Haven, CT: Yale University, 1985.

Hitchcock, H. Wiley, and Vivian Perlis, eds. *An Ives Celebration.* Urbana, IL: University of Illinois, 1977.

JANCO, Marcel (1895–1984). Born in Bucharest, Janco happened to be studying architecture and painting in Zurich in 1916, at the beginnings of the Dada (∗) movement. Joining Hugo Ball (∗), Richard Huelsenbeck (∗), and his Rumanian compatriot Tristan Tzara (∗), Janco made paintings and reliefs that are still regarded as his strongest visual art, as well as neo-African masks and woodcut illustrations to a Tzara poem. Going to Paris in 1919, Janco soon broke with Tzara over politics and returned to Rumania, where he founded *Contimporanul* (1922–1940) and worked as an architect. By 1941 he was safely in Palestine, where he remained until his death, in a country so inhospitable to avant-garde art (in contrast to avant-garde science, say) that its more pioneering creative personalities necessarily make their careers abroad, much as comparable Americans did in the 19th century.

Dachy, Marc. *The Dada Movement*. NY: Rizzoli, 1990.

JANECEK, Gerald (1945). One of the few full-time academics to write successfully on avant-garde subjects, he authored *The Look of Russian Literature* (1984), which documents the development of visual devices mostly in Futurist (*) writing of 1900–1930. In contrast to previous commentators, such as Vladimir Markov (of *Russian Futurism: A History*, 1968), who tended to favor the poetry of Velimir Khlebnikov (*), Janecek concentrates upon the most radical figure, Aleksei Kruchonykh (*), finding more sense than anyone else previously unearthed in his innovations and extravagances. What makes Janecek's avant-garde criticism special is his willingness to understand the most extreme: not only the most advanced individual in a group but his or her furthest departures. At last report he was finishing a book on Zaum (*), or "transrational language," which his predecessor Markov called "the most extreme of all Futurist achievements."

Janecek, Gerald. *The Look of Russian Literature*. Princeton, NJ: Princeton University, 1984.

JARGON. In critical writing, the function of jargon is not to illuminate but to suggest that its author is "verbally correct"; it is most likely to succeed with literate society's underling-suppliants, such as students and untenured professors. So should you come across a piece of criticism filled with imposing terms (such as "ambiguity," "tension," and "metonomy" in days gone by; "dialectical," "signifier," "disruption," "confrontation," "contradiction," "deconstruction," "differance" [sic], "logocentrism," "asymptotic," "indexical," "decentering," and the like nowadays), to all appearances used in unfathomable ways, do not worry and, most of all, don't be intimidated (unless you're a student or an untenured professor, whose function in the academic hierarchy is to be predisposed to intimidation). You're not supposed to understand anything but merely be impressed by the author's modish choice of lingo, much as, in other contexts, you might be awed by his or her choice of dress, shoes, or car.

It was the American sociologist Thorstein Veblen (1857–1929) who pointed out a century ago that inefficient expression is meant to reflect "the industrial exemption of the speaker. The advantage of the accredited locutions lies in their reputability; they are reputable because they are cumberous and out of date, and therefore argue waste of time and exemption from the use and the need of direct and forcible speech." That is to say, you must be economically comfortable to talk that way and, by doing so, are explicitly announcing that you are. The reason why leftish jargon amuses working people is that they know instantly, as a measure of their economic class, what its real purpose is.

Veblen, Thorstein. *The Theory of the Leisure Class* (1899). NY: New American Library, 1953.

JARRY, Alfred (1873–1907). An eccentric's eccentric, Jarry wrote plays and fiction so different from the late Victorian conventions that they are commonly regarded as having anticipated Surrealism (*), Dada (*), the Theatre of the Absurd (*), James Joyce (*), and much else, which is to say that Jarry was a slugger in spite of himself. His play *Ubu Roi* (King Ubu, 1896) opens with *Merdre*, which is customarily translated as "Shittr," proclaiming from the start its ridicule of bourgeois false propriety. The freewheeling movement from line to line, and scene to scene, makes it different from any plays written before. Yet more innovative, to my mind, are Jarry's novels, such as *Gestes et Opinions du Dr Faustroll, Pataphysicien* (1911) and *Le Surmâle* (*The Supermale*, 1912), in which ridiculousness is raised to a higher level. The former begins as a satire on Lawrence Sterne's *Tristram Shandy* (1759–1767), if that is possible, but it ends in the modern world with pseudo-mathematics in an extraordinary chapter "Concerning the Surface of God," which concludes: "GOD IS THE TANGENTIAL POINT BETWEEN ZERO AND INFINITY."

Though Jarry was a limited writer, the image of the man and his work had a great influence upon his avant-garde betters; in this respect, he resembles his near-contemporary compatriot, Raymond Roussel (∗), and his successor Antonin Artaud (∗). (Another useful divide within avant-garde consciousness is separating those who treasure Jarry from those who worship Artaud.) After initiating a *Collège de 'Pataphysique* (∗), Jarry died young of tubercular meningitis aggravated by alcoholism, which was in its time no more avant-garde, alas, than drug abuse is today.

Shattuck, Roger, and Simon Watson Taylor, eds. *Selected Works of Alfred Jarry*. NY: Grove, 1965.

JAZZ (c. 1885). Arising from forgotten origins in the American South, this indigenous music first became prominent in New Orleans at the beginning of the 20th century. While revealing African and African-American concepts of alternative rhythm, jazz followed gospel music in observing European harmonies. Other musical strategies seem peculiar to jazz itself: melodic improvisation within a predetermined harmonic range; continuous harmonies either within a solo instrument or a backup band; and certain kinds of instrumentation and thus timbre and intonation. Even when adopted by musicians other than African-Americans, such as Jewish Klezmer musicians, the result is called jazzy—or, in the Klezmer example, "Jewish jazz." Though many prominent jazz musicians had compositional careers, it has remained essentially a performer's music.

Avant-garde jazz is the fringe that was initially unaccepted because of formal deviations, beginning with Louis Armstrong's (c. 1900–1976) transcending the piano-based ragtime predominant between 1900 and 1920 by featuring the trumpet as a solo instrument, including the big bands of the 1930s that featured brass instruments that customarily played in harmonic unison. One alternative to this in the 1940s was the dissonance cultivated by Charlie Parker (∗) in smaller bands; next came Ornette Coleman (∗) and Albert Ayler (∗), among others, who eschewed any metronomic beat while often playing as quickly as possible.

The development of jazz is a paradigm for American avant-garde growth. Instead of moving linearly from classic to Dixieland jazz through big band jazz to Bebop (∗) and Free Jazz (∗) to jazz/rock fusion to new acoustic jazz (in emulation of a European model of development), jazz both moves forward and looks backwards. Although the heyday of New Orleans jazz was the 1920s, New Orleans jazz continues to be played today, both by musicians raised in this style and by others who emulate it. In this sense, each new style does not replace an old, but rather compliments it.

Classically trained composers could hardly resist the influence of jazz, many of them incorporating one or another jazz device (or, sometimes, a live jazz musician) into essentially avant-garde work; and though such fusions are sometimes hailed for representing a "third stream," that concept has never had much acceptance with either the jazz public or that devoted to modernist classical music. The real influence of jazz on classical avant-garde music lies in the ambition, and acceptance, of improvisation. One interesting measure of jazz's success is that, since 1950, most purportedly comprehensive histories of American music acknowledge jazz.—with Richard Carlin

Hitchcock, H. Wiley. *Music in the United States* (1969). 3rd ed. Englewood Cliffs, NJ: Prentice-Hall, 1988.

Berendt, Joachim. *The Jazz Book: From Ragtime to Fusion and Beyond*. 5th ed. Brooklyn, NY: Lawrence Hill, 1992.

Gridley, Mark C. *Jazz Styles: History and Analysis*. 3rd ed. Englewood Cliffs, NJ: Prentice-Hall, 1987.

JOHNS, Jasper (1930). Though he was initially paired with his friend Robert Rauschenberg (∗), who is five years his senior, Johns is a different sort of artist, concerned less with exploring unfamiliar materials than with creating objects that pose esthetic questions. In looking at his early and prototypical *Target with Four Faces* (1955), one cannot help but ask: Is this a replica of a target? A collection of concentric circles? Or something else? What relationship do those four sculpted bottoms of heads (noses and mouths, to be precise) have to the two-dimensional picture? Why is the target-image represented so realistically and yet the heads so surrealistically? Is there some symbolism here, or do all meanings exist within the picture? "I thought he was doing three things," John Cage (∗) once wrote, "five things he was doing escaped my notice." By painting a realistic image without a background, Johns followed Jackson Pollock (∗) in abolishing the discrepancy between image and field that is the core of traditional representational art, again raising the question of whether the target-image was a mechanical copy of the original target, or a nonrepresentational design (and what in this context would be the difference anyway?). Later Johns works develop this love of images and objects unfamiliar to painting, as well as displaying his taste for ambiguity, puzzle, and enigma. Given such a high level of exploratory richness, it is not surprising that the first major critic of his work should have been Leo Steinberg (1921), an art-history professor whose forte has been the exhaustive examination of meanings available in a single picture.

Steinberg, Leo. "Jasper Johns: The First Seven Years of His Art" (1962). In *Other Criteria*. NY: Oxford University, 1972.

JOHNSON, B.S. (1933–1973; b. Brian Stanley J.).

The most experimental British novelist of his generation, Johnson began with *Traveling People* (1963), in which narrative gives way to impressionistic stream-of-consciousness, and *Albert Angelo* (1964), which, telling of an impecunious architect working as a substitute teacher, includes a section where spoken thoughts on the right side of the page become a counterpoint to the monologue on the left-hand side. Pages 149–153 of the latter book contain a hole that is purportedly caused by the knife that killed Christopher Marlowe (how British!). "Why do the vast majority (it must be over 95 per cent at a reasonable guess) of novelists writing now still tell stories," Johnson asked in *Books and Bookmen* (1970), "still write as though *Ulysses* (let alone *The Unnameable*) had never happened?" Johnson's greatest departure was *The Unfortunates* (1967), which came in a box whose opening and closing chapters were fixed, while the remaining twenty-five were loose, to be read and reread in any order.

Johnson also published poems and stories, in addition to making a film that won several prizes, *You're Human Like the Rest of Them* (1968). Of the ten books he published before his suicide, only one, his first collection of poems, was published in America in his lifetime.

Johnson, B.S. *The Unfortunates*. London: Secker & Warburg, 1969.

JOHNSON, Bengt Emil (1936).

His *Hyllningarna* (Greetings, 1963) is said to be the first book of Concrete Poetry (∗) in Sweden, containing a "Homage to John Cage" (1962) that, as miscellaneous words typed to the edge of the page, reflects an accurate understanding of Cagean esthetics that was rare at the time. While Johnson's later poetry has moved closer to traditional lyricism that draws upon his respect for nature in rural Sweden, his music, initially composed of words for audiotape, has assumed a more radical edge. More recently, he has composed texts and music for live instrumentalists, especially his wife, the singer Kersten Ståhl.

Johnson, Bengt Emil. *Im Time Vittringar Escaping*. Stockholm, Sweden: Caprice CAP 1174, 1979.

JOHNSON, Scott (1952).

For *John Somebody* (1983), he collected spoken sounds whose ostinatos resembled those of rock and roll. Analyzing these samples for inadvertent qualities of pitch and rhythm, he used audiotape editing to evoke, as he wrote, "musical regularities that my ear imposed on these spontaneous sounds. The fragments were then looped and layered in synchronization on a multitrack tape machine, and the resultant whole was carved into by mixing processes." His unique achievement is a speech-based electro-acoustic dance music.

Johnson, Scott. *John Somebody* (1983). NY: Icon-Nonesuch 79133, 1986.

JOHNSON, Tom (1939).

Notwithstanding not one but two degrees from Yale University, Johnson has been an innovative composer working with a variety of severe constraints, or, in his words, "logical progressions and highly predictable structures." *The Four Note Opera* (1972) is what it says it is (like other Johnson work). *Music for 88* (1988) is actually nine pieces for all the keys of the standard piano. For *The Chord Catalogue* (1987) he spends two hours playing all 8,178 chords available within a single octave; the experience depends upon the audience's appreciation of his conceptual (∗) feat. Another vein of Johnson's work requires an instrumentalist to follow instructions that appear suddenly on a screen, purportedly as new to him or her as to the audience. I remember a skilled pianist, performing before a sophisticated audience, being subjected to the repeated instruction that he play a "yet more spectacular cadenza" than the one before. *Falling* (1975) requires a string bass soloist to declaim a prepared text as he or she plays. Like much of Johnson's other performance pieces, this can be profoundly comic in unfamiliar ways.

From 1972 to 1982, Johnson was, as the music reviewer for the *Village Voice*, New York's most sympathetic and knowledgeable regular critic of new music, and the best of these notices have been collected in a book published not in his native country but in Holland. Since 1983 he has lived mostly as an American in Paris.

Johnson, Tom. *The Voice of New Music*. Eindhoven, Holland: Apollohuis (Tongelrestraat 81, NL-5613 DB), 1989.

JOLAS, Eugene (1894–1952). Born in New Jersey, Jolas grew up in Lorraine, France (near Germany), before returning to the U.S. in 1911. Back in Paris in the 1920s, he edited *transition* (1927–1938), which was the most distinguished avant-garde magazine of its time. It published not only episodes from James Joyce's (*) *Finnegans Wake* (*), among other literature that was avant-garde at the time, but illustrations of advanced paintings and even writings by vanguard artists.

The most distinctive Jolas poems draw upon his multi-lingual background, some like "Mountain Words" broaching self-invented language, others combining German, French, and English, yet others reflecting the influence of Surrealism (*). All books of Jolas's poetry have long been out of print, and the only anthologists to reprint him recently are Jerome Rothenberg and myself. His daughter, Betsy J. (1926), is a distinguished American composer who has resided mostly in France.

Jolas, Eugene, ed. *transition workshop*. NY: Vanguard, 1949.

McMillan, Dougald. *transition: The History of a Literary Era, 1927–1938*. NY: Braziller, 1976.

JOPLIN, Scott (1868–1917). An itinerant Midwestern pianist, Joplin is generally credited with composing the first popular piano piece to sell a million copies of sheet music, "Maple Leaf Rag" (1899). Although the term "ragtime" was meant to be semi-derogatory, Joplin's piano pieces were as classically rigorous as Chopin's etudes, with four parts, composed AA-BB-AA-CC (trio)-DD. Joplin's music also incorporated dissonant harmonies, intuitively expanding the musical idioms of popular composition; his "Stop-Time Rag" was the first sheet music to include markings for foot-tapping.

One misfortune of his life is that, not unlike George Gershwin (1898–1937) after him, Joplin thought himself worthy of more ambitious music, composing both an opera and a ballet based on ragtime, and then a full-scale opera, *Treemonisha* (1911), which everyone wishes were better than it is. He died just short of fifty, a full fifty years before his music was revived, first in brilliant records by the conductor-pianist-musicologist-arranger Joshua Rifkin (1944), then in the popular film *The Sting* (1974).—with Richard Carlin

Rifkin, Joshua. *Piano Rags of Scott Joplin*, Vols. I–III. NY: Nonesuch H-71248, H-71264, H-71305, 1970–1974.

Joplin, Scott. *King of the Ragtime Writers* [piano roll transcriptions]. Port Chester, NY: Biograph BCD-103, c. 1988.

Blesh, Rudi, and Harriet Jans. *They All Played Ragtime*. 4th ed. NY: Oak Publications, 1971.

Gammond, Peter. *Scott Joplin and the Ragtime Era*. NY: St. Martin's, 1976.

JOSHUA LIGHT SHOW (1967–1972). Of all the late 1960s light shows, as they were called at the time, the Joshua Light Show, in residence at New York's Fillmore East, a former movie palace seating 3,000 or so spectators, was the strongest. The esthetic innovation was to expand the concept of the Lumia, or the Thomas Wilfred (*) light box, to fill, in live time, a large translucent screen hung behind performing rock musicians. These lights were projected from several sources *behind* the screen, which at the Fillmore measured thirty feet by twenty and was always filled with bright and moving imagery. In the middle, usually within a circular frame (reflecting the glass bowl necessary to make it), nonrepresentational, brilliantly colored shapes pulsated in beat to the music, changing their forms unpredictably (thanks to the fact that the colors were composed of oil, water, alcohol, glycerine, and other materials that do not mix). Around that

The Mothers of Invention performing at The Fillmore East, c. 1968, with The Joshua Light Show projection behind them; Frank Zappa in center with guitar. *Courtesy Joshua White.*

frame was a less blatant, fairly constant pattern whose composition and color mysteriously changed through variations repeated in a constant rhythm (these coming from slides fading over one another). Across the entire screen flashed rather diaphanous white shapes that irregularly fell in and out of patterns (these coming from an individual situated apart from the others, using a collection of mirrors to reflect white light onto the screen). From time to time representational images also appeared on the screen—sometimes words, other times people; sometimes stationary, other times moving. For instance, when musicians were tuning their instruments on stage, on the screen appeared a gag image of, say, Arturo Toscanini hushing his orchestra. (Those pictures came from slides and sometimes films.) For good reason, the Joshua Light Show received a billing line directly under the musicians, for what they did contributed enormously to the theatrical experience.

Kostelanetz, Richard. "Joshua Light Show" (1968). In *Twenties in the Sixties.* Brooklyn, NY, and Westport, CT: Assembling and Greenwood, 1979.

JOYCE, James (1882–1941). My job in a book like this is to distinguish the avant-garde Joyce from the more traditional writer. *Finnegans Wake* (∗) obviously belongs and, if only to measure its excellence, deserves a separate entry. For his stories, *Dubliners* (1914), the innovation was the concept of the epiphany, which is the revelatory moment, customarily appearing near the end, that would give meaning to the entire fiction. "The epiphany is, in Christian terms, the 'showing forth' of Jesus Christ's divinity to the Magi," writes Martin Seymour-Smith. "They are 'sudden revelation[s] of the whatness of a thing,' 'sudden spiritual manifestation[s]—in the vulgarity of speech or gesture or in a memorable phase of the mind itself.'" Thus the Joycean story has not the form of an arc, where events proceed to a climax before retreating to a denouement, but events that establish a flat form until the flashing epiphany.

One innovation of *Ulysses* is the elegant interior monologue, also called stream-of-consciousness. Retelling in many ways the story of an oafish Jew, who has as much resemblance to the classic Ulysses as a bulldog to a greyhound, this thick book incorporates a wealth of parodies, epiphanies, allusions, extended sentences, and contrary philosophies within a fairly conventional story.

What also distinguishes Joyce's career is the escalation of his art, as each new book was even more extraordinary than its predecessor. One's mind boggles at the notion of what he might have produced had he lived twenty years longer. Indeed, this sense of esthetic awe, if not incredulity, is intrinsic in our appreciation of Joyce's progressive achievement.

Joyce, James. *Dubliners.* London: Grant Richards, 1914.

———. *Ulysses.* NY: Random House, 1934.

JUDD, Donald (1928). A pioneer of Minimalist (∗) sculpture, Judd composed simple forms, devoid of any base, that were distributed in evenly measured ways, such as protruding three-dimensional rectangles up the side of a wall. Viewed from various angles, such definite forms suggested a variety of interrelated shapes; it was Judd's point to make one thing that could look like many things. With success, he used more expensive metals fabricated to his specifications, often with seductive monochromic coloring, and produced many variations, only slightly different from one another, on a few ideas. As a writer, Judd contributed regular reviews to the art magazines of the early sixties, urging the move away from emotional Expressionism (∗) toward intellectual structuring, and away from art, particularly sculpture, as interrelated parts toward a single "holistic" image. Quite radical and influential in the sixties, his art has neither changed nor significantly developed since then.

Judd, Donald. *Complete Writings, 1959–1975*. Halifax, Canada: Nova Scotia College of Art and Design, 1976.

Smith, Brydon. *Donald Judd*. Ottawa, Canada: National Gallery, 1975.

JUDSON DANCE THEATER (1962–1964). Out of the composition classes taught in the early 1960s by Robert Ellis Dunn (1928) at the Merce Cunningham (∗) Studio came young dancers wanting to create their own pieces. The Judson Memorial Church—a Greenwich Village landmark, which had already gained cultural fame, rare for a church at that time, by making its space available for a Poet's Theater—was receptive to the dancers. The result was, in Sally Banes's succinct summary, "the first avant-garde movement in dance theater since the modern dance of the 1930s and 1940s. The choreographers of the Judson Dance Theater radically questioned dance aesthetics, both in their dances and in their weekly discussions. They rejected the codification of both ballet and modern dance. They questioned the traditional dance concert format and explored the nature of dance performance. They also discovered a cooperative method for producing dance concerts." In addition to involving dancers who subsequently had distinguished choreographic careers, such as Yvonne Rainer (∗), Trisha Brown (∗), Lucinda Childs (∗), and Steve Paxton (∗), the Judson

Yvonne Rainer, "Terrain," 1963. L to r: Steve Paxton, William Davis (?), Trischa Brown, Yvonne Rainer, and Albert Reid. *Photo © 1990, Al Giese.*

Dance Theater hosted performances authored by such visual artists as Robert Rauschenberg (∗) and Robert Morris (∗).

Banes, Sally. *Democracy's Body: Judson Dance Theater 1962–1964* (1983). Durham, NC: Duke University, 1993.

McDonagh, Don. *The Rise & Fall & Rise of Modern Dance* (1970). Rev. ed. Pennington, NJ: a cappella, 1990.

KAC, Eduardo (1962). A Brazilian experimental poet since his teens, Kac was among the first writers to realize that holography (∗), a visual technology new to our times, could be a medium for language. In the 1980s, he created holograms in which, among other clever constructions, words from two languages meld into one another, the same letters are reorganized to create different words, a cylinder reveals a series of words, seen only in parts, that reads differently clockwise from counterclockwise ("Quando?" ["When?" 1987]). For art such as this Kac coined the epithet "holopoetry," whose significance he has explained in several manifestos: "The perception of a holopoem takes place neither linearly nor simultaneously, but rather through fragments seen at random by the observer, depending upon his or her [physical] position relative to the poem." Originally from Rio de Janeiro, Kac moved to Chicago in 1989.

Kac, Eduardo. *Holopoetry-2/Holopoesia-2*. Rio de Janeiro, Brazil: Privately published, 1986.

———, and Ormeo Botelho. *Holofractal*. Rio de Janeiro, Brazil: Galeria de Fotografia da Funarte, 1988.

KAGEL, Mauricio (1931). A theatrical composer far better known in Europe than in his native country, Kagel, born in Buenos Aires, has lived in Cologne since 1957. Possessed of a fecund imagination, he has composed instrumental music as well as Electronic Music (∗), produced films as well as new scores to classic silent films, and authored books and produced gallery exhibitions. One of his specialties is music in which his own performance is key, such as a "Requiem" where he is a conductor who collapses on stage while the musicians play on. Another specialty is to draw upon classical texts, as often of literature as music. Thus, *Aus Deutschland* (1977–1980) is a "Leider-Oper" about 19th-century Germany; *Sankt-Bach-Passion* (1983–1985) portrays the life of J.S. Bach as resembling that of Jesus Christ; *Ensemble* (1967–1970), an opera without words (or orchestra) is described as "a satirical look at the previous history of opera"; and *Ludwig van* (1970) is "a Kagelian montage of Beethoven motifs." A principal esthetic idea is metacollage in which disparate materials are all drawn from a single source.

Schnebel, Dieter. *Mauricio Kagel: Musik Theater Film.* Köln, Germany: DuMont, 1970.

Kostelanetz, Richard. "Mauricio Kagel (1988)." In *On Innovative Art(ist)s.* NY: Limelight, 1989.

KANDINSKY, Wassily (1866–1944). Born in Moscow, Kandinsky studied law and social science at the local university, where he later taught law. Excited by the first Russian exhibition of French Impressionists in 1895, he traveled in 1897 to Munich to study painting. Older than the other students, Kandinsky progressed quickly, organizing exhibitions throughout Europe. By 1909, he became a founding member of *Neue*

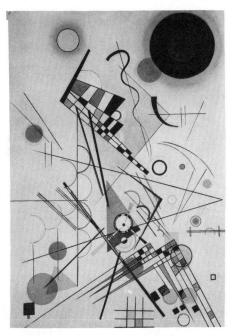

Wassily Kandinsky, "Composition 8," 1923. *Photo: Robert E. Mates © The Solomon R. Guggenheim Foundation, New York.*

Künstlervereinigung (NKV), which initially represented the style of the Fauves against the German version of Art Nouveau called *Jugendstil.* By the following year, the NKV exhibition included a broader range of advanced European painting. By 1912, Kandinsky belonged to a dissident group that published the *Blaue Reiter Almanach*, which he co-edited; in the same year, he authored *Über das Geistige in der Kunst* (*Concerning the Spiritual in Art*), which still ranks among the major essays in the development of nonrepresentational painting for insisting upon the primacy of expressive and compositional elements in art. During World War I, Kandinsky returned to Russia, where he worked in arts administration, until he was invited in 1921 to teach at the Bauhaus (*), remaining there until it was closed by the Nazis. He then moved to Paris, where he lived until his death.

Kandinsky's own mature paintings emphasized bright color, an intentionally flat field, and irregular abstract forms whose unfettered exuberance seems reminiscent of the art of his sometime colleague at the Bauhaus, Paul Klee (1879–1940). Perhaps because of the softness of their abstraction, both Klee and Kandinsky are now less influential than they used to be.

Kandinsky, Wassily. *Concerning the Spiritual in Art* (1912). NY: Wittenborn, 1947.

KAPROW, Allan (1927). To the claim that American universities are inhospitable to avant-garde art and artists, Kaprow will always be cited as a principal counter-example, as well he should be, having taught at universities (albeit four of the more sophisticated—Rutgers, SUNY–Stony Brook, Cal Arts, UCSD) for forty years while inventing the Happening (*) as a form of alternative performance. Beginning around 1956 with assemblages (*) incorporating materials found in public places, he progressed to Environments (*), or artistically defined enclosures, and mixed-means (*) performance pieces he called Happenings. The last typically involved people following instructions to unexpected results, initially in gallery spaces, later in public places. By the late 1960s, Kaprow's elegantly written and masterfully designed book, *Assembling, Environments & Happenings*, had appeared; and his term "Happening" was being used indiscriminately by the media to define anything chaotic.

Relocating in California (which can be hazardous to the artistic output of New Yorkers), Kaprow turned to more intimate situations he called successively "Work Pieces" and "Activities," which are reportedly more psychological than spectacular in effect. Few artists are as effective in talking about their own work and esthetic purposes. Kaprow combines rigorous thinking with a broad vision, in well-turned sentences stylistically indebted to his graduate school mentor, the art historian Meyer Schapiro (1904).

Kaprow, Allan. *Assemblage, Environments & Happenings.* NY: Abrams, 1966.

Allan Kaprow: Collagen, Environments, Videos, Broschüren, Geschichten, Happening-and Activity-Dokumente 1956–1986. Dortmond, Germany: Museum am Ostwall, 1986.

KASPER, Michael (1947). While working as a reference librarian at Amherst College, Kasper has produced a series of tart chapbook-length visual/verbal fictions, mostly self-published, that his colleagues commonly rank among the best. The third "expanded" edition of his *All Cotton Briefs* (1992), his biggest collection yet, contains his strongest work. A brief interview with Kasper, along with an illustration, appears in George Myers Jr.'s (∗) *Alphabets Sublime* (1986).

Kasper, Michael. *All Cotton Briefs* (1981, 1985). Florence, MA: Benzene–Left Lane (106 High St., 01060), 1992.

KAWARA, On (1933). An austere conceptual artist (∗), Kawara has spent his professional life doing (or redoing) only a few works: painting in sans-serif letters the words for the day's date (in the language of wherever he is currently staying), sending local picture postcards on whose backsides he stamps "I got up at [at whatever time]," recording separate sheets with the names of the individuals he met that day, and posting telegrams that read "I am still alive/ On Kawara" (Editions René Block in Berlin published a book of that quoted title, consisting wholly of reproductions of telegrams). I have in the course of my life saved works from many artists, some by purchase and others as gifts, but you can imagine my surprise when the first works from my collection to tour in an international show were unsolicited picture postcards that Kawara had sent me for several weeks, several years before.

On Kawara: Continuity/Discontinuity 1963–79. Stockholm, Sweden: Moderna Musset, 1980.

KEATON, Buster (1895–1966; b. Joseph Francis K.). Among the most innovative of all silent-film directors, Keaton created a character with so little external affect that much of his comedy depends upon his deadpan reaction to the catastrophes occurring around him. Nicknamed "Stoneface," the Keaton persona remained unchanged whether he was in the midst of a hurricane (as at the end of his classic *Steamboat Bill, Jr.* [1928]) or fleeing from Union troops in the Civil War (*The General* [1927]). Keaton's comic conceptions often bordered on Dada (∗), as in the famous short (*One Week* [1920]) in which a newly married couple struggle to build their dream house. A villain has so scrambled the directions that the house comes out resembling a wild Cubist (∗) construction. (Because the main entry is on the second floor, one continuing gag in the film is Keaton's pratfalls when he exits the house.)

Keaton was among the first to experiment with the nature of reality and illusion in film. His 1922 short *The Playhouse* features some of the earliest trick photography, in which Keaton, through multiple exposures, portrays an entire

Buster Keaton, *Steamboat Bill Jr*, 1928. *Courtesy Kino video.*

orchestra, performing troupe, and audience. In *Sherlock, Jr.* (1924), his first feature-length film, Keaton portrays a film projectionist who, in his dreams, leaps into the film that he is showing, becoming unwittingly involved with the action on screen. As his own director, Keaton was also a masterful film editor, often working with striking juxtapositions. In *Cops* (1922), he created a classic chase sequence in which gangs of police appear and disappear (almost magically) as they pursue the unwitting hero through a busy city landscape. Much of the comedy depends upon the cuts between scenes where the lone Keaton is shown running down a street and then, moments later, a sea of policemen run through the same space.

With the advent of sound (and thus more expensive productions), Keaton unfortunately lost creative control of his films, appearing in a series of lame MGM features, often paired with the hopelessly overbearing Jimmy Durante. Late in his life, when his silent masterpieces were rediscovered, Keaton starred again in some wonderful short films, including a dialogue-less film portraying him traveling across Canada on a small handcar (*The Railroader* [1965]) and the Samuel Beckett (*)-scripted short, entitled simply *Film* (1965), that was left incomplete at the time of his death.—Richard Carlin

Dardis, Tom. *Keaton: The Man Who Wouldn't Lie Down* (1979). NY: Limelight, 1988.

Blesh, Rudi. *Keaton*. NY: Macmillan, 1966.

KEITH, Bill (1929). Initially a painter, long a photographer as well as a poet, Keith has recently produced visual poetry (*) discernibly different from what others are doing and have done. (Can the same be said for the latest practitioners of free verse?) Drawing upon African and African-American traditions, he has "written" a highly original alphabet and "Harlequinade," which I would gladly anthologize if I still did poetry anthologies. Keith has also organized exhibitions of visual poetry.

Keith, Bill. *Sphinx*. Lafarge, WI: Xerolage (Rt. 1, Box 131, 54639), 1992.

KELLY, Ellsworth (1923). A veteran of U.S. Army camouflage units, who studied in France under the G.I. Bill, Kelly began in the early 1950s to make paintings divided into rectangular panels that were identical in size but different in color. Because these colors were usually bright and unmodulated, they produced a shimmer along the straight edge where they touched each other. Such work customarily requires the painter to apply the paint thickly and evenly and the viewer to find an optimal viewing distance. Because Kelly uses two or more colors, this is customarily called color-field (*) or hard-edge painting. (Were there only one color, the epithet "monochromic" would be more appropriate.)

Goosen, E.C. *Ellsworth Kelly*. NY: Museum of Modern Art, 1972.

KENNER, Hugh (1923). From his beginnings an audacious, independent, and prolific literary critic-scholar, Kenner has produced two kinds of books—eccentric and often oblique studies of the accepted literary modernists and less oblique books about such avant-garde figures as Ezra Pound (*) (back in 1951, when his subject was still imprisoned and academically unacceptable), Wyndham Lewis (*), and Buckminster Fuller (*). This means that Kenner is as courageous in his choice of subjects as his interpretations; among the more unfashionable of the latter is his demolition of Sigmund Freud, a modern icon if ever there were one, in "Tales of the Vienna Woods," collected in Kenner's *Gnomon* (1958). It is indicative that this sometime student of Marshall McLuhan (*), likewise born Canadian and likewise Catholic, should write sensitively in *The Mechanic Muse* (1987) about the computer as a successor to the typewriter, and that he should be among the first of his cultural generation to become familiar enough with computers to produce programs that are widely used. Though common opinion regards *The Pound Era* (1972) as Kenner's best book, my own sense is that his essays and books on more avant-garde subjects represent his greater achievement.

Kenner, Hugh. *The Mechanic Muse*. NY: Oxford University, 1987.

KERN, W. Bliem (1943). A sometime student of Norman Henry Pritchard II (*), Kern adapted the idea of the rapidly repeating phrase in his sound poetry to his own purposes, reiterating, for example, "belief in the illusion of" until it sounds like something else. His printed texts range from "straight" poetry to visual texts of words and letters to poems that mix familiar words with unfamiliar, some of which come from an entirely fictitious language that Kern calls "Ooloo." Whereas most sound poetry is static, Kern's pieces often suggest a narrative direction, as in "Dream to Live," a long poem that tells in words, phrases, and phonemes of the end of a love affair. His principal collection (1973) appeared as a box with both a book and an audiotape, one element no less important than the other. Rarely publishing any more, Kern works as an astrologer and an ordained interfaith minister.

Kern, W. Bliem. *Meditationsmeditationsmeditationsmeditations*. NY: New Rivers, 1973.

KEROUAC, Jack (1922–1969). The avant-garde Kerouac is not the chronicler of hitchhiking through America in *On the Road* (1957) or the embarrassing drunk of his later years, but the author of certain abstract prose in which words are strung together not about a subject but for qualities indigenous to language. *Visions of Cody* (1972, though written many years before) and, especially, "Old Angel Midnight" are thought to be examples of "automatic writing," Kerouac purportedly transcribing words at the forefront of his consciousness. Whether that is true or not, the result is extraordinary prose, as in the following from the latter:

> Stump—all on a stump the stump—accord yourself with a sweet declining woman one night—I mean by declining that she lays back & declines to say no—accuerdo ud. con una merveillosa—accorde tue, Ti Pousse, avec une belle femme folle pi vas' t'councer—if ya don't understand s t t and tish, that language, it's because the langue just bubbles & in the babbling void I Lowsy Me I's tihed.

Like other Kerouac writing, this is about the possibilities of memory and language but differs from most other Kerouac in being about the limitless *intensities* of each. His major experimental poems are "Sea," which initially appeared as an appendix to *Big Sur* (1962), and *Mexico City Blues (242 Choruses)* (1959), which displayed linguistic leaps similar to those quoted from "Old Angel Midnight."

Kerouac, Jack. *Visions of Cody*. NY: McGraw-Hill, 1972

———. "Old Angel Midnight [Part II]" and "Sea." In *Text-Sound Texts* (1980), ed. Richard Kostelanetz. NY: Archae, 1984.

KHLEBNIKOV, Velimir (1885–1922; b. Viktor Vladimirovich K.). The brilliant pathfinder of Russian Futurism (∗) and one of the greatest Russian poets of the 20th century, Khlebnikov was a quiet, reclusive man who led a nomadic existence, in contrast to the brash behavior of the other Cubo-Futurists (∗). They nonetheless recognized him as the genius of the movement, one whose ceaseless innovation and great poetic achievement served as a creative stimulus in the areas of both practice and theory.

His earliest poems (1906–1908) already show the marks of originality and innovation that made him a leader of Futurism when the movement began to organize itself in 1910. One of his most famous early poems is "Incantation on Laughter," a series of neologisms based on the root *smekh* ("laughter") and published in 1910. His major poetic quest was to uncover the true creative roots of language that existed in primitive times, when presumably there was a close iconic link between linguistic signs and their meaning. Many of Khlebnikov's theoretical works are devoted to uncovering these links in the Slavic language, and many of his poems are partly illustrations of his theories. He was a Slavophile in his attitude toward language, and he avoided borrowings from European languages (especially from French and German, which are heard frequently in spoken and literate Russian). The goal of many of his coinages was to demonstrate the capacity of Slavic to generate all the words necessary for present and future needs, not only to replace foreign borrowings in current use but also to name new phenomena. While the term "Zaum" (∗) was used by him and others to describe these linguistic inventions, Khlebnikov, in contrast to Aleksei Kruchonykh (∗), intended his coinages to be clearly understood and not to be indeterminate in meaning, at least in the long run. Often he provided keys to their interpretation either explicitly by giving definitions or implicitly by providing analogies to known words within the same context.

His innovations were not limited to word-creation, but covered the full linguistic range, from attempting to define universal meanings of individual sounds and letters to new ways to create metaphors, to rhythmic and syntactic experiments, and to new syntheses of all of these elements in larger forms called "supersages," one of the most noted of which is *Zangezi* (1922). Khlebnikov was also a significant writer of prose fiction and theater texts. His "The Radio of the Future" (1921) is filled with suggestions that still seem radical today.

He preferred to depict the primitive state of man in close contact with nature, a state analogous to primitive man's close contact with the roots of language. Slavic mythology is a notable element. Khlebnikov was not as enamored of modern technology and urban life as other Futurists. However, in addition to his principal concern for creating a perfect language for the future, he penned a number of Utopian descriptions of futuristic life. As a trained mathematician, his favorite project was attempting to discover the mathematical laws governing human destiny according to which the pattern of historical events could be understood and future events predicted.

Because of his nomadic existence and personal eccentricity, publications of his works during his lifetime were often to some degree faulty, filled with typographical errors, misreadings, and variant or fragmentary versions, the author's final wishes being to varying degrees uncertain. These problems continued in posthumous editions until very recently, when rigorously edited volumes have begun to appear. Khlebnikov was fortunate, however, to have had champions throughout the Soviet period when his work appeared with some regularity, though not abundantly. As the difficulty of his poetry still challenges even the most sophisticated reader, he has never been and is unlikely ever to become broadly popular; he will remain a "poet's poet" whose work continues to inspire new generations of Russian writers.—Gerald Janecek

Cooke, Raymond. *Velimir Khlebnikov: A Critical Study.* NY: Cambridge University, 1987.

Khlebnikov, Velimir. *Collected Works.* Trans. Paul Schmidt. Vol. 1. Cambridge, MA: Harvard University, 1987.

————. *Tvoreniia.* Ed. M. Poliakov. Moscow, Russia: Sovetskii pisatel', 1989.

Markov, Vladimir. *The Longer Poems of Velimir Khlebnikov.* Berkeley, CA: University of California, 1962.

Vroon, Ronald. *Velimir Khlebnikov's KRYSA.* Stanford, CA: Stanford University Slavic Studies, 1989.

KIENHOLZ, Edward (1927). An American original, Kienholz makes tableaus, usually with decrepit detritus, of people living at the margins of society—in a homely bar, in a state hospital, etc. He typically places life-sized maimed figures in such real settings as a double bunk bed in *State Hospital* (1966), a chopped-apart 1930s automobile in *Back Seat Dodge '38* (1964), and a bar counter in the mammoth *Beanery* (1965), where almost all the figures have clocks for heads. Because he incorporates various sub-art materials into three-dimensional constructions, Kienholz was initially classified as a master of assemblage (∗); but what he is really doing is designing static theatrical sets. The suggestion is that the spectator could enter them, even if they are customarily blocked off, perhaps because Kienholz's "human" figures are customarily less lifelike than their surroundings. In *State Hospital* (1966), recently installed at the Nationalmuseum in Stockholm, the viewer peers through a small barred window into a room containing a double-decker bed with two naked, emaciated men facing the window. Their hands are tied to the bed. In place of their faces are fishbowls. For its original installation, Kienholz infused a hospital smell into the scene. Often living in Berlin since the middle 1970s, he once mounted an installation of old radios that, when activated, played raucous Wagnerian music reminiscent of a discredited era. In 1981, he decided that the name of his wife, Nancy Reddin K. (1943), should retroactively accompany his own on all works produced after 1972.

Pincus, Robert L. *On a Scale That Competes with the World: The Art of Edward and Nancy Reddin Kienholz.* Berkeley, CA: University of California, 1990.

KIESLER, Frederick (1896–1965). An Austrian who came to the U.S. in 1926, Kiesler was a visionary architect whose proposals were mostly unrealized. His few projects that were built were commonly judged to be "ahead of their time": peripatetic scenery and a theater in the round in 1924; a long cylindrical space for Peggy Guggenheim's "Art of This Century" gallery in 1942; and an egg-shaped white grotto made of fabric over curved stretchers for the last major Surrealist (∗) exhibition. His art seemed to hypothesize an intermedium incorporating architecture and theater along with painting and sculpture. One great architectural proposal was endlessness, or infinite continuity, first conceived for a theater in 1923 and then exhibited as the "Endless House" at New York's Museum of Modern Art in 1960—a series of concrete shells with no structural members. Others remember *Galaxies* (1952), also at MoMA, which Irving Sandler describes as "environmental 'clusters' of painting and sculpture." Kiesler coined the term "Corealism" to acknowledge continuity of time and space, as well as the idea that artwork depends upon its environmental context. From 1933 to 1957 he worked as Scenic Director at the Juilliard School of Music.

Frederick Kiesler: Environmental Sculpture. NY: Guggenheim Museum, 1964.

Phillips, Lisa. *Frederick Kiesler.* NY: Whitney Museum/ Norton, 1989.

KINETIC ART (c. 1920). Several artists between 1910–1920—among them, Naum Gabo (*), Alexander Archipenko (1887–1964), Marcel Duchamp (*), and Giocomo Balla (1871–1958)—came up with the idea to make art move, utilizing motors to propel their sculptural works. In a famous 1920 manifesto, Gabo joined his brother Antoine Pevsner in suggesting, "In place of static rhythm in the plastic arts, we announce the existence of a new element, kinetic rhythm which is to be the basis of a new perception of real time." In his book *The Origins and Development of Kinetic Art* (1969), the French critic Frank Popper distinguishes among several genres of kinetic art. One depends upon some kind of machinery (e.g., the artists already cited, Pol Bury [*] and Moholy-Nagy [*]). A second, called mobiles, realizes movement without motors (e.g., Alexander Calder [*] and George Rickey [*]). A third depends upon moving light (e.g., Thomas Wilfred [*] and Clyde Lynds [*]). A fourth, such as that made by Julio Le Parc (*) and Yacov Agam (*), depends upon spectators' movement for the illusion of movement to occur in the work of art. A fifth is a kind of Optical Art that, if stared at fixedly, will generate the illusion of movement; the examplars here are Bridget Riley (*) and Victor Vasarely (*). To Popper's list I would add one genre of machines that respond to outside influences (such as works by James Seawright [*] and Robert Rauschenberg [*]) and a second of kinetic sculptures that function autonomously. One contemporary master in the last category is George Rhoads (*), who uses a motor to lift a small ball to the top of a multi-route contraption that then depends upon pre-technological forces of gravity to make the artwork move. The sculptures of Wen-Ying Tsai (*) transcend Popper's categories by incorporating both motors and changing light. Some contemporary kinetic art depends upon computers, at times to make the activity more various than was possible in the mechanical age, or to make it respond to viewers' presence.

Malina, Frank, ed. *Kinetic Art: Theory and Practice.* NY: Dover, 1974.

Popper, Frank. *The Origins and Development of Kinetic Art.* Greenwich, CT: New York Graphic Society, 1969.

KING, Kenneth (1943). A profoundly original mind from the beginnings of his professional career, King has worked inventively in both dance and writing. For *Camouflage* (1966), he jumped in place for several minutes, and the most spectacular passages of *Blow-Out* (1966) had him dressed in dark glasses, his hands in gloves attached by elastic strings to the side walls, his feet firmly planted, his body contorting within the severely constraining frame. In *M-o-o-n-b-r-a-i-n with SuperLecture* (1966), King emerges in the costume of an old man, which he proceeds to remove piece by piece, later putting back on a few items. Midway through this work begins an audiotape of prose written and spoken by King in a style that imitates and parodies both James Joyce (*) and Marshall McLuhan (*), lamenting the impossibility of choreography in the electronic age. At one point King takes a single familiar dance step, only to return to plodding around the stage, concluding his danceless dance about the difficulties, if not the death, of modern dancing. That last theme informed *Print-Out* (1967) in which King, dressed in black from head to toe, supervised the playing of a tape on which he reads a prose essay whose Joycean words are simultaneously projected on a screen. While the *SuperLecture* was reprinted in my anthology *The Young American Writers* (1967), the text of *Print-Out* appears in my selection of *Future's Fictions* (1971).

As an innovative dancer, King developed an extremely light flutter step; he has also performed solos entirely to his live spoken accompaniment. Perhaps because he initially publishes in contexts far from literary magazines and even conventional theater, his brilliant writings are scarcely noticed. When I was directing a small press (*), we applied regularly for grants to publish a book of his prose, without success.

King, Kenneth. *Dancing W-o-r-d-s*. NY: Privately published (106 Forsyth St., New York, NY 10002), 1990.

———. *Five Appreciations/Concretics X*. NY: Privately published, 1992.

KIRBY, Michael (1931). Kirby's early critical writings include an introduction to *Happenings* (1965), and essays, such as his classic "The Aesthetics of the Avant-Garde," which became *The Art of Time* (1969). As a sculptor, Kirby took six sets of photographs from four sides of six subjects and then printed them on cubes that, if turned in complimentary ways, would show different sides of six different subjects. As a theater artist, he made mixed-means (*) pieces that depended upon the appearance of a double for himself (his identical twin brother, E.T. Kirby [1931–1985], who also published books about alternative theater), and scripted plays whose principal subject is their structure, which is "played out," as he puts it, in ways unusually rigorous for live theater. These were so original, in both writing and staging, that it is scarcely surprising that even the latest *Contemporary Dramatists* (1993) lacks an entry on Michael Kirby's work.

Kirby, Michael. *The Art of Time*. NY: Dutton, 1969.

Kirby, E.T., ed. *Total Theatre*. NY: Dutton, 1969.

KIRSTEIN, Lincoln (1907). A writer and effective arts activist, Kirstein made many contributions that benefit American culture, beginning with the founding and editing of the literary magazine *Hound and Horn* (1927–1934). In 1928, while an undergraduate at Harvard, he also cofounded a Society of Contemporary Art that leased a two-room suite above the Harvard Co-op Bookstore and mounted the first American exhibitions of Constantin Brancusi (*), Buckminster Fuller (*), and Alexander Calder (*), among others. Also the founder of the School of American Ballet, Kirstein helped bring George Balanchine (1903–1983) to America and supported his reign as choreographer for the New York City Ballet. Kirstein was also one of the first American dance critics (as distinct from newspaper reviewer), a writer on the visual arts, and a poet.

Kirstein, Lincoln. *Ballet: Bias and Belief*. Brooklyn, NY: Dance Horizons, 1982.

Hamovitch, Mitzi Berger, ed. *The Hound and Horn Letters*. Athens, GA: University of Georgia, 1982.

KLEIN, Yves (1928–1962). A sometime jazz musician who also wrote a book about judo (at which he earned a black belt), this French artist purportedly made in 1946 monochromic canvases, painted edge to edge in a single color. Though he claimed to have exhibited them privately as early as 1950, they were not publicly shown until 1956. Succès de scandale prompted him to devote his activities to "International Klein Blue," as he called it, which was applied not only to canvas but sculpted figures and even nude models who then imprinted it onto canvas. Though his blue was lush, he claimed a disinterest in color in favor of metaphysical resonances. In 1958, he enhanced his reputation with a pre-Conceptual Art (*) "exhibition" in an empty gallery painted white. He also claimed (but typically could not document) that in 1957 he mounted in Milan an exhibition entirely of identical, blue, monochrome canvases with different prices purportedly reflecting different qualities in surface texture. Klein is commonly identified among the first artists to exploit publicity to make himself, as well as the photograph of himself (especially flying through the air), more important than any of his works.

Yves Klein. NY: Jewish Museum, 1967.

Restany, Pierre. *Yves Klein: Le feu au coeur du vide*. Paris, France: La Différence, 1990.

KLINE, Franz (1910–1962). Initially a painter of urban silhouettes as shadowless forms, Kline in the 1950s developed an extremely original style of abstraction with broad brushstrokes assuming the quality of ideograms. It is said that he projected an image of one of his drawings onto a wall and in the contrast between large black and white fields saw his mature painting. Precisely because so much of his paintings were black, the white areas attained the status of independent images. In their avoidance of colors typical of nature, these canvases could be regarded as an epitome of a New York City sensibility. As a native New Yorker, I once suggested that only two colors are worthy of art—black and white; all other colors are appropriate for illustrations.

Gaugh, Harry. *The Vital Gesture: Franz Kline.* NY: Abbeville, 1985.

KLINKOWITZ, Jerome (1943). In addition to many conventionally written expositions mostly about contemporary American fiction, Klinkowitz has produced one extraordinary book that is so different neither he nor anyone else has done anything like it since. The chapters of *The Life of Fiction* (1973) introduce a new form for literary criticism, mixing fragments of textual quotation from both primary and secondary sources, transcribed interviews, personal letters, biography both formal and informal, and Klinkowitz's own comments, all presented at a speed roughly comparable to film montage, in an attempt to provide a "more complete picture" than that available by drawing from only one of those materials. The book's square pages are imaginatively designed by Roy H. Behrens, who often mixes type more than six inches wide with double columns half as wide, adding oblique illustrations. The book's problem is less its method, which is avant-garde, than Klinkowitz's choice of subjects, including, as it does, several writers who are not (among them Russell Banks, Jonathan Baumbach, Ishmael Reed, and Kurt Vonnegut, Jr.).

Klinkowitz, Jerome. *The Life of Fiction.* Urbana, IL: University of Illinois, 1973.

KLUCIS, Gustav (1895–1944). A Latvian who arrived in Moscow in 1918 as a part of a Latvian regiment assigned to guard the Kremlin, Klucis became active in art, producing, in collaboration with his wife Kulagina, a lithograph called *Dynamic City* (1919), in which, over the background of a filled-in circle, planes appear to extend forward and backward. He produced photomontages (*) for Vladimir Mayakovsky's (*) *V.I. Lenin* (1925); he co-designed Aleksei Kruchonykh's (*) book *Chetrye foneticheskikh romana* (Four Phonetic Novels, 1924). Klucis produced model "Radio Announcers" designed to serve, within one structure, as both a newspaper stand and a platform for public speakers

(which would still look innovative if displayed today). In 1928 he became a founding member of the group October, which had a major show in 1930. Though always a loyal Communist, Klucis was arrested in 1938 as a Latvian and sentenced to a labor camp, where he died several years later.

Art into Life: Russian Constructivism 1914–1932. NY: Rizzoli, 1990.

KNOWLES, Alison (1933). One of the founders of Fluxus (*), Knowles has been mainly concerned with re-creating and conceptualizing the act of reading. In her *Big Book* (1966), she gestalts the book as a gigantic stage construct, through, around, and into which the performers crawl, slide, slip, hop, and bend, thus realizing as activity the many stages, psychic and emotional, that we as readers undergo when encountering a book. In her later *Finger Book* (1986), the book is imaged as a small tactile assemblage (*), composed of representative elements from all over the planet—shells, mirrors, tablets, coins, etc.—all uniting to form a book object that is covered with a crystallized Braille text. Knowles has also produced radio plays for Westdeutscher Rundfunk.—Charles Doria

Knowles, Alison. *Spoken Texts.* Barrytown, NY: Left Hand (P.O. Box 27, 12507), 1992.

KOCH, Kenneth (1925). Not unlike that of his Harvard College buddy John Ashbery (*), Koch's early poetry was more experimental than what he later produced. His classic avant-garde text is *When the Sun Tries to Go On*, which was written in 1953, first published in a one-shot magazine, *The Hasty Papers* (1960), and later reprinted as a book. Many pages long, it offers interminable unintelligibility in a regularly irregular meter, evenly measured lines, and consistent diction. The critic Jonathan Cott (1942) wrote long ago that it "defies explication or even persistent reading." Koch has also written plays, some considerably more experimental (and substantial) than others. At their best, such as *Pericles* (1960) and *Bertha* (1959), they include inspired parodies and nonsensical writing. In *George Washington Crossing the Delaware* (1962, which originated as a response to a Larry Rivers painting of the same title), Koch swiftly ridicules the myths of

American history, the language of politicians, war films, military strategies, patriotism, and much else, the theme of his burlesques being that accepted familiar versions are no more credible than his comic rewritings. Also a Professor of English at Columbia University, Koch has written popular treatises on the teaching of poetry. Though Stephen Koch (1941) is likewise a writer and a Columbia professor who pronounces his surname "Coke" (in contrast to former NYC mayor "Kotch"), they are not related.

Koch, Kenneth. *When the Sun Tries to Go On*. Santa Barbara, CA: Black Sparrow, 1969.

———. *Bertha and Other Plays*. NY: Grove Press, 1966.

KOLÁŘ, Jiří (1914).

If one's name is one's fate, then it was inevitable that this Czech, whose family name is pronounced like "ko-large," should produce the most original collage (*) of the past two decades. Initially a poet, who had published books as early as 1941, Kolář was progressing toward Lettrism (*) and Concrete Poetry (*) when, during the post–World War II Soviet occupation of his country, he incorporated other materials into his works. "Screws and razor blades, nuts and bolts took the place of words, thereby creating a poetry of things," recalls Thomas Messer, himself a Czech who for many years headed the Guggenheim Museum in New York. "By controlled crumpling of reproduced images borrowed mostly from art history he created the *crumplage*; by introducing into the collage composition movable parts that could be lifted, the *ventilage*; and through the fragmentation and reconstitution of written and printed texts (which often used occult and arcane alphabets) he created his plastic style through the Greek-lettered *chiasmage*." In *rollage*, thin strips from one image are interspersed with thin strips taken from another image so that, especially if both images are familiar, one comments on the other. Eventually a fully conscious visual artist, Kolář has extended his compositional principles into reliefs and even three-dimensional objects. Some Kolář work is funny; all of it is indubitably clever and identifiable as his. Perhaps because Kolář is self-taught in visual art, he works exclusively with texts and images that have already been printed. In 1975, the Guggenheim Museum mounted a retrospective so filled with surprises that I rank it among the strongest one-artist exhibitions I have ever seen.

Jiří Kolář. NY: Guggenheim Museum, 1975.

Kotik, Charlotta. *Jiří Kolář*. Buffalo, NY: Albright-Knox, 1978.

KOSTELANETZ, Richard (1940).

"The taken name of a collective composed of twelve industrious elves," he has produced countless books of poetry, fiction, experimental prose, criticism, cultural history, and book-art, in addition to audiotapes, videotapes, holograms (*), and films. By his own admission less a polyartist (*) than a *writer* influenced by the ideal of polyartistry, he thinks of all his creative work, in every medium, as "essentially writing." *Wordsand* was the title of a traveling retrospective exhibition of his art (1978–1981); "Wordship" is the name of the urban castle in which he lives. His poetry in particular is a record of formal inventions, beginning with visual poems (*), subsequently including permutational poems, recompositions of familiar words, found poems (*), video poems, poetic holograms, and other alternatives not yet classifiable. Even his set of documentary films

J. Nebraska Gifford, "The Thirteen Studios of Richard Kostelanetz," 1982. *Collection Richard Kostelanetz.*

about the great Jewish Cemetery of Berlin (with soundtracks in six different languages, made in collaboration with Martin Koerber [1956], 1984–1988) are in part about the visual poetry of gravestones.

His fiction favors such departures as several narratives interwoven into a single text, stories in which each sentence contains one word more or one word less than its predecessor, single-sentence stories, three-word, two-word, and one-word stories, permutational prose, and sequences of Abstract (*) drawings, among other inventions. Appearing in scores of literary magazines, his fictions have barely become available in books. They also exemplify his taste for comedy. Some of his productions are more successful than others, but detractors as well as admirers disagree about which is which.

Not unlike his heroes Moholy-Nagy (*), John Cage (*), and Ad Reinhardt (*), Kostelanetz writes frequently, and accessibly, about his esthetic ambitions. Numerous anthologies, many of and about new art/literature, bear his name. One recurring concern is alternative historiography, both in forms and in content (e.g., several autobiographies, this *Dictionary*). He is no less radical in his professional politics than his art, his single most famous critical book being an elaborate examination of "Literary Politics in America," *The End of Intelligent Writing* (1974). A libertarian anarchist in both word and deed, he has spurned positions and power, even founding an annual of "otherwise unpublishable" graphic work, *Assembling*, whose implicit purpose was the abolition of editorial power. His devotion to the idea and subject of the avant-garde, as well as critical standards, has survived changing fashions. His uncle André K. (1901–1980) was a pioneering conductor/arranger of classical music for recording media, beginning with radio in the early 1930s.

Kostelanetz, Richard. *Wordsand*. Burnaby, Canada: The Gallery at Simon Fraser University, 1978.

———. *Autobiographies*. Brooklyn, NY: Future, 1981.

———. "André Kostelanetz." In *On Innovative Music(ian)s*. NY: Limelight, 1989.

KOSUGI, Takehisa (1938). Born in Tokyo, Kosugi came to America in 1962 to do mixed-means (*) theatrical pieces, often in collaboration with Fluxus (*) artists. In 1969, he founded the Taj Mahal Travelers to perform group improvisations in various venues, and toured with them during 1971–1972. He also belonged to the group Transition, founded in Brussels in the early seventies by Jacques Bekaert with Marc Dachy (1952), Rio Koike, and Michael Herr. In 1977, he joined David Tudor (*) among the musicians producing "live electronic music" in concerts with the Merce Cunningham (*) Dance Company. Kosugi's sound installations have been exhibited around the world.

Kosugi, Takehisa. *Violin Improvisations*. NY: Lovely Music, 1992.

KOTIK, Petr (1942). Born in Prague, Kotik came to America in 1969, where his composing flourished. The principal signature of his best work is a quasi-polyphonic structure of overlapping solos, sometimes proceeding in parallel perfect intervals (i.e., fourths, fifths, and octaves). One departure was adapting his compositional style to the setting not of poetry but of prose and then not classic prose, like the Bible, say, but high modernist prose. By this departure Kotik produced a sound wholly different from that established for the contemporary singing of words. The texts he chooses are not simple, easily understood writing but more difficult texts, sometimes prompting him to write to epic lengths. His masterpiece is *Many Many Women* (1976–1978), to Gertrude Stein's prose of the same title, which in Kotik's hands becomes polyphonic and antiphonal. His second major work in this genre is *Explorations in the Geometry of Thinking* (1978–1980), to Buckminster Fuller's (*) two-volume *Synergetics* (1976, 1979). Kotik's instrumental music, performed mostly under the elastic umbrella of the S.E.M. Ensemble (its initials meaning, he says, nothing), confronts the post-Cagean problem of writing nonclimactic, uninflected music that nonetheless moves forward.

Kotik, Petr. *Many Many Women*. NY: Labor LAB-6/10 (c/o S.E.M., 25 Columbia Place, Brooklyn, NY 11201), 1981.

KOVACS, Ernie. See TELEVISION

KRIWET, Ferdinand (1942). A precocious visual poet (*), Kriwet made typewriter poems in 1960 and a few years later "Rundscheibe," which are brilliantly composed lines of overlapping words put into roughly concentric circles. His book about his own early work, *Leserattenfaenge* (1964), includes impressively detailed analyses of those complex early word-image texts. He also produced "poem-paintings" entirely of words drawn in dramatically different letters, usually to fracture familiar and recognizable words ("Beat Us"); constructed columns imprinted with words and letters in various typefaces; made films animated with words; and created audiotape collages that are still rebroadcast over German radio. *Textroom* (1969) extends his way with words into an entire room whose walls, ceiling, and floor are filled with rows of metal plates, each embossed with two eleven-letter combinatory words.

Kriwet 69. Köln, Germany: Kölnischer Kunstverein, 1969.

KRONOS QUARTET. See ARDITTI QUARTET

KRUCHONYKH, Aleksei Eliseevich (1886–1968).
The wild man of Russian Futurism (∗), notorious for his Zaum (∗) poetry, Kruchonykh began his career as an art teacher but became associated with the Hylaea branch of the Russian Futurists and, in 1912, began publishing a series of lithographed primitivist booklets with his own and other Futurists' poetry, with illustrations by Mikhail Larionov (1881–1964), Natalia Goncharova (1881–1962), Kazimir Malevich (∗), and others. Kruchonykh's most famous poem, "Dyr bul shchyl," is the first Russian poem written explicitly in an "indefinite" personal language.

Although the idea of writing poetry in "unknown words" was suggested to him by David Burliuk (1882–1967), it was Kruchonykh who developed this form of poetry in all its ramifications. His most elaborate creation was the opera *Victory Over the Sun*, performed in St. Petersburg in December 1913, with music by Mikhail Matiushin (∗) and sets and costumes by Kazimir Malevich. A scandalous success, the performances were sold out. Kruchonykh continued to experiment in various ways to create indeterminacy in language on all levels from the phonetic to the narrative, until the early 1920s. Throughout this period, he was often the critical whipping boy of Russian Futurism; his works were treated as examples of the most ridiculous extremes of the movement. While Vladimir Mayakovsky (∗) and Velimir Khlebnikov (∗)

were sometimes granted reluctant respect, Kruchonykh was always treated as beneath serious consideration. His anti-esthetic imagery, crude eroticism, and deliberately clumsy language contributed to an impression of a lack of talent and culture. His most famous poem, when acknowledged, was (and still is) almost always misquoted.

During World War I, Kruchonykh was drafted to work on the southern railroad, which brought him into contact with Iliazd (∗) and Igor Terentev (1892–1937) in Tiflis, and he formed with them the avant-garde group 41°. At this time his works consisted of a long series of handmade ("autographic") booklets duplicated by carbon copy or hectograph; others were elegantly typographed by Iliazd. In the former, his Zaum (∗) poetry reached a Minimalist level in sparse compositions of individual letters and lines and even blank pages. For Kruchonykh, the visual appearance of poetry was always important, as was its sound texture.

In 1921, he moved permanently to Moscow, where he attempted to enter literary life by arguing for the usefulness of his literary experiments for the new socialist culture and producing a series of valuable theoretical texts. However, his poetry was already less adventurous. Because of his reputation and a certain residual thickness of texture, his efforts to write works that would appeal to the common reader or theatergoer were unsuccessful. Though shunned by Soviet publishers after 1930, Kruchonykh continued to write significant poetry afterward; he survived into the 1960s by collecting and trading in avant-garde and mainstream poetic materials.

Kruchonykh remained the most consistent publicist for Futurist views. His works are still largely unknown to the Russian reader, in part because the sole edition of his work has appeared in Germany (1973); only in the past decade have his works begun to receive serious scholarly attention, initially in the West but now in Russia as well.—Gerald Janecek

Kruchonykh, A.E. *Izbrannoe.* Ed. Vladimir Markov. Munich, Germany: Funk, 1973.

Janecek, Gerald. *The Look of Russian Literature.* Princeton, NJ: Princeton University, 1984.

Markov, Vladimir. *Russian Futurism: A History.* Berkeley, CA: University of California, 1968.

KRUGER, Barbara (1945). Kruger has made a large-scale visual art of advertising imagery, customarily enlarged to monstrous proportions, coupled with commercial slogans in billboard type. The pretense is saying something significant about consumer culture; yet art-world viewers have no difficulty deciphering her accessible, if not familiar, messages. (And it is highly unlikely that such paintings ever affected anyone who was not already converted.) The critic Paul Mann comments, "Neocritical gestures frame recuperation so as to preserve some fiction of critical distance that the work's various representations are already in the process of erasing." Imagine a work, he continues, "not to resist recuperation in any form, by either the myth of autonomy or the myth of internal resistance, but to embrace it completely, to represent the fullest and most uncompromising portrait of the way in which the critique of recuperation produces and reproduces its own recuperation in discourse, in order to expose the critical poverty of one's own work and of criticism at large. That is what Barbara Kruger finally accomplishes."

Mann, Paul. *The Theory-Death of the Avant-Garde.* Bloomington, IN: Indiana University, 1991.

KUBRICK, Stanley. See *2001*

KUENSTLER, Frank (1928). In 1964, from the imprint of Film Culture, a New York publisher noted for its film magazine of the same title, appeared *Lens*, a book so extraordinary that it was completely unnoticed at the time. It opens with a single-page "Emblem," a sort of preface that establishes in six sections that anything might happen in the following pages, including the destruction of both sense and syntax. The last section of "Emblem" reads: "aura.Dictionary. aura.Crossword Puzzle. aura.Skeleton. aura.Poem./Once upon a time." What follows are eighty long paragraphs so devoid of connection, from line to line, from word to word, that you realize only a human being could have made them; even the most aleatory computer program would have put together, even inadvertently, two words that made sense. The book concludes with the tag "New York, N.Y., 1952–64," suggesting that *Lens* took a full dozen years to write; I can believe it, because anyone who thinks such writing easy to do should try it sometime

(and send me the results). Kuenstler's later publications include *13 1/2 Poems* (1984), which is a progression of increasingly experimental poems (though none as radical as *Lens*). He has for many years been selling antiquarian books on the street in New York, usually on Broadway north of 86th Street.

Kuenstler, Frank. *Lens*. NY: Film Culture, 1964.

LA BARBARA, Joan (1947; b. J. Linda Lotz). Initially a vocalist adept at "extended" vocal techniques, including "circular breathing" while producing sound, La Barbara became a composer, mostly of pieces for herself, sometimes as continuous sound installations. She has also written articles and reviews of avant-garde music. Her second husband is the composer Morton Subotnick (1933), whose career includes synthesizer (*) music excessively reliant upon repetition and mixed-media (*) installations, roughly as moderately innovative as his wife's. It is one of the mysteries of artists' marriages that two people who have pursued independent careers, once together in mid-lives, come to resemble each other.

Zimmermann, Walter. "Joan La Barbara." In *Desert Plants*. Cologne, Germany: Berginner, 1981.

LA GRAN SCENA OPERA CO. (1981). The idea of men playing female operatic roles is not new, but never before has it been so elaborate and sustained. The effect is initially that of parody and thus of camp, which comes from being so awful it is good. (By the late 20th century, all 19th-century opera seems campy, while many noticed that Maria Callas, for one, often seemed to be a man playing a woman, or perhaps a woman playing a man playing a woman.) However, the Gran Scena performance transcends those effects, being lovingly done, with strong falsetto voices that take pride in their resonance. The typical program consists of excerpts from classic operas, usually just scenes, sometimes

Les Ballets Trockadero de Monte Carlo, "Le Corsaire," 1990. *Photo © 1993, Jack Vartoogian.*

whole acts. The sections are framed by "Miss Sylvia Bills," who has the verbal jokes. Precisely because it must be seen that men are playing women, their productions succeed on videotape but not on audio discs. The work of two all-male ballet companies, *The Trockadero Gloxinia Ballet* (1972) and its descendent and rival, the sumptuously named *Les Ballets Trockadero de Monte Carlo* (1974), is esthetically similar.

La Gran Scena Opera Co. NY: Video Artists' International 69031, 1986.

LA MAMA EXPERIMENTAL THEATRE CLUB (E.T.C.) (1961). Founded in 1961 by Ellen Stewart (1919), a born impresario, and the playwright Paul Foster (1931), it became the exemplar of off-off-Broadway, producing plays that, not only for reasons of avant-garde difference, were not acceptable to producers on Broadway and an increasingly commercialized off-Broadway. Though most of its productions belong to the tradition of staged plays, La Mama became a receptive venue for many touring productions of more performance-oriented theater. As Ellen Stewart wrote, "The plays that we're doing are the plays I want to do. I don't interfere in how they get to be that way."

Stewart, Ellen. "La Mama Experimental Theatre Club." In *Eight Plays from Off-Off-Broadway*, eds. Nick Orzel and Michael Smith. Indianapolis, IN: Bobbs Merrill, 1966.

LAFFOLEY, Paul (c. 1936). Trained in classics and architecture before turning to painting, Laffoley makes work so eccentric it is innovative by virtue of its waywardness. He is essentially a visionary painter, in the great American tradition, whose paintings represent unseen forces, mostly cosmological. Some of his paintings have a density of words and symbols that reflect as they transcend charting. *The Levogyre* (1976), which he describes as "nested shells connected by gimbels," is, he says, "an attempt to model a photon creating light, and in turn an atom of consciousness. The structure of the Levogyre derives from the structure of the Universe proposed by Eudoxus (the astronomer pupil of Plato). Eudoxus stated that the Universe is a series of nested crystalline spheres which contained the stars as fixed, the planets which moved, down to the central non-rotating Earth. Each sphere is connected to the next by gimbel-like axes which are randomly distributed." Other thoughtful and thought-filled paintings portray *The Orgone Motor* (1981), *The Astrakakiteraboat* (1983), *De Rerum Natura* (1985), *The Aetheiapolis* (1987), and *Thanaton III* (1989). To say that Laffoley's work looks like no one else's is an indisputable compliment. Some of his activities are conducted under the name of The Boston Visionary Cell, Inc. His illustrated book about his own work—more precisely, his own imagination—ranks among the greatest artist's self-expositions.

Laffoley, Paul. *The Phenomenology of Revelation.* Ed. Jeanne Marie Wasilik. NY: Kent, 1989.

LANGUAGE-CENTERED POETRY (aka "Language" poetry, c. 1975). Whether this constitutes a genuine artistic category or simply an opportunistic banner is a good question. Excessive mutual backslapping, very much in imitation of the earlier "New York Poets," raises suspicions, especially because the work of those paraded under this newer rubric is quite various (while the work of others working in esthetically similar veins, but not included, is often superior). The interior mental states of Hannah Weiner's (1929) poetry, for instance, scarcely resemble the dry experimentalism of Bruce Andrews (1948), whose poetry has little in common with the fragmented, elliptical narratives of Michael Palmer (1943) or Barrett Watten's (1948) extracting phrases from ulterior texts. (If any artists' group lacks esthetic principle, it is really functioning as an exclusive club more worthy of acknowledgment in a history of false snobbery;

because willfully excluding individuals who might by esthetic right belong smacks too much of elitism for common comfort.)

Andrews, Bruce, and Charles Bernstein, eds. *The L-A-N-G-U-A-G-E Book*. Carbondale, IL: Southern Illinois, 1984.

Messerli, Douglas, ed. *"Language" Poetries: An Anthology*. NY: New Directions, 1987.

Silliman, Ron, ed. *In the American Tree*. Orono, ME: National Poetry Foundation, 1986.

LANSKY, Paul (1944). Lansky's strongest work uses the computer to create a pseudo-speech reminiscent of the best acoustic poetry of Charles Amirkhanian (∗) while also exemplifying the principle that with a sophisticated computer the composer can realize speech-music that is beyond the capabilities of live human beings and even earlier electronic techniques. Lansky's *Idle Chatter* (1985) creates the illusion of thousands of people speaking, each at roughly equal volume. The notes accompanying its CD release speak of "an eloquent attempt to say nothing without taking a breath for 565.9 seconds, 9.43 minutes, 31,690,400 samples, or 63,380,800 bytes—take your pick." Knowing a good idea when he invents one, Lansky has produced *Justmore-I.C.* (1987) and *Notjustmore-I.C.* (1988), as well as *Small Talk* (1988). Formerly a French hornist, currently a Professor of Music at Princeton University, he has composed in other ways with speech and with instruments.

Lansky, Paul. *Idle Chatter* (1985). On *New Computer Music*. Mainz, Germany: Wergo 2020-50, 1987.

LARDNER, Ring (1885–1933). Lardner is remembered mostly as a light writer whose baseball stories were recently collected into a book, *Ring Around the Bases* (1992). However, it was Martin Esslin (1916), in *The Theatre of the Absurd* (1959), who discovered a more experimental writer in his very short plays. "Some of their funniest lines occur in the stage directions, so that the little plays become more effective when read than when seen," Esslin writes. "How, for example, is a stage direction like the following, in *Clemo Uti (The Water Lilies)*, to be acted? '(Mama enters from an exclusive waffle parlor. She exits as if she had had waffles.)'" Another play is credited as "translated from the Squinch,"

while a third compresses five acts into a few minutes. Precisely in broaching the unperformable, these resemble Gertrude Stein (∗) plays written about the same time. Until Lardner's publisher collects these theatrical texts into a single book, they remain hard to find.

Lardner, Ring. "The Tridget of Greva"; "Abend di Anni Nouveau." In *Theatre Experiment*, ed. Michael Benedikt. Garden City, NY: Doubleday Anchor, 1967.

LAUTRÉAMONT, Comte de (1846–1870; b. Isidore Ducasse). Born in Uruguay of French parents, Lautrémont came to Paris to prepare for the polytechnic high school. Failing in this mission, and plagued by poverty, he began a prose poem, *Les Chants de Maldoror* (posthumously published in 1890), which, while reflecting classical literature, became a precursor of Surrealism (∗). As his protagonist, Maldoror, suffers gruesome misfortunes, Lautrémont's language becomes extremely hallucinatory: "Who could have realized that whenever he embraced a young child with rosy cheeks he longed to slice off those cheeks with a razor, and he would have done it many times had he not been restrained by the thought of Justice with her long funereal procession of punishments."

Lautrémont, Comte de. *Maldoror*. Trans. Guy Wernham. NY: New Directions, 1946.

LAX, Robert (1915). A Columbia College chum of both Ad Reinhardt (∗) and Thomas Merton (∗), Lax has sought linguistic purity comparable to the visual purity of the former and the spiritual purity of the latter. It is fair to say that Lax writes the poetry that Merton should have written, were he a true Trappist artist. Lax's poetry is extremely spare, sometimes with only a few words arrayed in various ways. In his great long poem *Black and White* (1966), the total vocabulary consists of only three different words and an ampersand. Because Lax resides on a Greek island and does not actively submit his poems to publishers, it is not surprising that they have appeared sparingly, first in chapbooks from Emil Antonucci's Journeyman Press in Brooklyn and then in larger bilingual books from Pendo Verlag in Zürich, Switzerland. The principal available collection of his work unfortunately omits many of his best poems.

Lax, Robert. *33 Poems*. NY: New Directions, 1987.

LE CORBUSIER (1887–1965; b. Charles-Édouard Jeanneret).

A prime mover behind the International Style (∗), Le Corbusier made one construction so different from prevailing ideas, as well as so original, that it expands any earlier sense of his architecture: the Chapel of Notre-Dame-du-Haut in Ronchamp, France. Built between 1950 and 1955, it has a tower reminiscent of a grain silo, along with a sweeping roof that resembles a floppy hat, covering curved walls with rectangular apertures of various sizes and shapes, in sum reflecting his taste for articulated light and reinforced concrete, as well as qualities sparse and ascetic. Because one wall is set several feet inside the edge of the roof, it is possible to be under the roof and yet open to the elements. About the interior of this chapel, Russell Walden has written: "He used the east wall as a cyclorama against which the public and more private altars were set, incorporating a swiveling virgin in the reredos wall." The forms of this building remind us that Le Corbusier began as a Cubist (∗) painter who initially signed his works "Jeanneret" and that he continued to produce two-dimensional visual art throughout his career.

Le Corbusier in front of the Seagram building (under construction), 1946. *Photo © 1990, Barbara Morgan, courtesy the Willard and Barbara Morgan Archives.*

Walden, Russell. "Le Corbusier." In *Contemporary Masterworks*, ed. Colin Naylor. London, England: St. James, 1991.

Le Corbusier. *Towards a New Architecture* (1927). NY: Praeger, 1960.

LE PARC, Julio (1928).

An Argentine who held off going to Paris until 1958, Le Parc joined several groups working with optical abstraction and kineticism, including Groupe de Recherche d'Art Visuel, commonly known as GRAV. His art developed static surface patterns that generated radically different appearances if viewed from different angles, which is to say that it includes not one principal "look" but several, all of them equally legitimate. Le Parc also made reliefs of different materials that rotated at various speeds. He used other materials to vary the reflection of light and made objects with adjustable parts that respond to spectators' manipulations. Because I have not seen any of these latter pieces at first hand, I quote Edward Lucie-Smith's testimony in *Late Modern* (1969): "Le Parc creates devices which belong partly to the laboratory, partly to the funfair. They are experiments with mechanisms and also experiments upon the psychology of the spectator. Mirrors, distorting spectacles, balls which run through complicated labyrinths—he has made use of all these things."

Lucie-Smith, Edward. *Late Modern*. NY: Praeger, 1969.

LEAR, Edward (1812–1888).

When you consider how wary contemporary editors are of any writing faintly unclear, it is amazing that this Victorian writer had such encouraging publishers, prompting him to produce several editions of *A Book of Nonsense* (1845), *A Book of Nonsense and More Nonsense* (1862), *Nonsense Songs, Stories, Botany and Alphabets* (1871), *More Nonsense, Pictures, Rhymes, Botany, Etc.* (1872), and *Laughing Lyrics, a Fresh Book of Nonsense Poems* (1877), which, all would agree, is a ridiculous bibliography for an adult writer. The mark of his verse is a limerick that turns back on itself, the last line echoing, if not repeating, the first: "There was an Old Person of Rhodes,/Who strongly objected to toads;/He paid several cousins/To catch them by dozens,/That futile Old Person of Rhodes." (This gains from its "politically correct" (∗) gender-usage, a century in advance.) Lear was also a travel writer and a landscape painter.

Jackson, Holbrook, ed. *The Complete Nonsense of Edward Lear* (1947). NY: Dover, 1951.

LEGER, Ferdinand (1881–1955). A Cubist (∗) painter of the second generation and second rank, Leger belongs to avant-garde history first as a stage designer whose work is remembered mostly through insufficient photographs, and then as a filmmaker whose *Ballet mécanique* (1924), exploring rhythm and motion, survives as classic avant-garde cinema. Technically, it is commonly credited as the first film made without a scenario. During World War II, Leger lived in America, collaborating with Hans Richter (∗) on part of the latter's *Dreams That Money Can Buy* (1944–1946), at various times teaching at American universities along with such distinguished French refugees as the art historian Henri Focillon, the essayist André Maurois, and the composer Darius Milhaud.

Lawder, Standish D. *The Cubist Cinema*. NY: New York University, 1975.

LEHRER, Warren (1955). One of the most imaginative book-artists of our time, Lehrer has produced several large-format, elegantly printed, self-published volumes filled with a wealth of images and words. The latter sometimes come from himself, at other times from collaborators such as the poet Dennis Bernstein (1950). Technically scripts, they address major cultural issues, typically in a style more intimidating than communicative. One of the technical innovations of *French Fries* (1984), perhaps Lehrer's most sumptuous work, is that a summary of its obscure pages appears continuously in the upper outside corners. Lehrer also works in audio, co-composing with Harvey Goldman the song cycle *The Search for It & Other Pronouns* (1991), a full-length compact disc that has the most intelligently and imaginatively designed (not to mention legible) accompanying CD booklet to come my way, reminding us that the secondary elements of any artifact deserve as much attention as the primary ones. His wife, Judith Sloan (1958) is a feminist Performance Artist (∗).

Lehrer, Warren, and Dennis Bernstein. *French Fries*. Purchase, NY: Ear/Say (Main P.O. Box 299, 10577), 1984.

LENNON, John (1940–1980). At the height of the success of the Beatles (1962–1969), for which he played rhythm guitar, Lennon published two self-illustrated books of free-form prose, *In His Own Write* (1965) and *A Spaniard in the Works* (1966), that reflect the influence of Edward Lear (∗), Lewis Carroll (∗), and James Joyce (∗) but did not sell enough copies to persuade publishers to hound the celebrated singer for more. Lennon reportedly initiated the Beatles' experiments with feedback (in "I Feel Fine"), backwards tape (in "Rain" and "Tomorrow Never Knows"), and aural collage (∗) ("Strawberry Fields Forever" and "A Day in the Life"). In collaboration with his second wife, Yoko Ono (∗), he created less successful self-consciously experimental music beginning with the tape montage "Revolution No. 9" featured on *The Beatles* (1969; commonly known as "The White Album") and the Lennon-Ono albums *Two Virgins* (1968) and *Life with the Lions* (1969).—with Richard Carlin

Lennon, John. *In His Own Write and A Spaniard in the Works* (1966). NY: New American Library, 1967.

LETTRISM. Founded in the mid-1940s in Paris by Isidore Isou (1925; b. Jean-Isidore Goldstein), himself a young refugee recently arrived from Rumania, Lettrism is perhaps the epitome of a circumscribed European literary group, with its untitled head, its insiders, and its hangers-on. Lettrist work seems based on calligraphy, initially for books, but also for visual art, and thus in the age of print seems quite innovative (though it might not have fared as well in pre-print times). One recurring device is letters that resemble verses, even though they are devoid of words. Jean-Louis Brau (1930), Gil J. Wolman (1929), Maurice Lemaître (1926), Roberto Altmann (1942), Roland Sabatier (1942), and Jean-Paul Curtay (1951) were among the other prominent writer/artists based in France who were associated with the group at various times. Not unlike other self-conscious agglomerations, Lettrism has been particularly skilled at the production of manifestos, which can be read with varying degrees of sense. By discounting semantic and syntactical coherence for language art, their works can be seen as precursors of Concrete Poetry (∗). Among the alumni are Guy-Ernest Debord (1931), who, under the name Guy Debord, is commonly credited with initiating the Situationalist International, which can be seen as representing artists' most profound, courageous, and, it follows, most successful involvement in radical politics.

Foster, Stephen C. *Lettrisme: Into the Present.* Iowa City, IA: University of Iowa Museum of Art, 1983.

Knabb, Ken, ed. and trans. *The Situationist International.* Berkeley, CA: Bureau of Public Secrets, 1981.

LEVENDOSKY, Charles (1936). His *perimeters* (1970) ranks among the very best long poems of recent times, achieving what Walt Whitman suggested, what Michel Butor (∗) attempted (in *Mobile*), and what Allen Ginsberg (∗) projected (in "These States")—a comprehensive panoramic portrait of the forty-eight continental states. Its success stems not only from Levendosky's attention to suggestive details, but also from its distinctive visual and verbal rhythms, the excellence of particular passages, and the sustained coherence of the encompassing whole. At the time, I heard that he was planning a comparably long poem about Middle America. A collection, *Hands & Other Poems* (1986), appeared instead. Levendosky subsequently became a prominent editorial writer and columnist in Wyoming.

Levendosky, Charles. *perimeters.* Middletown, CT: Wesleyan University, 1970.

LEVY, D.A. (1942–1968). In a life so short he seems to have been the American Arthur Rimbaud (∗), Levy published all sorts of poetry, including visual poems (∗), obliterated texts, collages (∗), and Blakean (∗) mixtures of pictures with calligraphy, in addition to more conventional lyrics and visionary prose. Some of his Blakean visual poems are particularly marvelous; along with Kenneth Patchen (∗) he ranks among the few who have worked that vein without seeming too derivative of the master. Levy made poems from advertising print ("found art" [∗]) similar to Bern Porter's (∗), just as his cover for the thirteenth issue of *The Buddhist Oracle* resembles Ad Reinhardt's (∗) comics. Living in relative isolation in Cleveland, Levy was not included in any of the late 1960s anthologies of visual poetry, even though, on its intrinsic merits, his work deserved being there. Harassed by the police, arrested for publishing poetry purportedly obscene, Levy took his own life. A recent collection of his poetry, lovingly edited, thankfully features his more experimental work.

Levy, D.A. *Zen Concrete & Etc.* Ed. Ingrid Swanberg. Madison, WI: Ghost Pony Press (2518 Gregory St., 53711), 1991.

LEWIS, Wyndham (1882–1957). Born off the Canadian coast on his British father's yacht, Lewis studied at the Slade School of Art in London before becoming an Abstract (∗) painter and the founder of Vorticism (∗), a British sort of Italian Futurism (∗) favoring geometrical recompositions and aggressive colors. He founded and edited *Blast* (∗), one of the great avant-garde magazines not only for its contents but for its typography (which still looks avant-garde, eighty years later).

Initially the author of plays and short stories, collected in various volumes, Lewis eventually wrote novels, beginning with *Tarr* (1918), which some think had an influence on James Joyce (∗), and continuing with a tetralogy, *The Human Age*, which Martin Seymour-Smith for one ranks as "the greatest single imaginative prose work in English of this century." (It includes *The Childermass* [1928; rev. ed. 1956], *Malign Fiesta, Monstre Gai* [1955], and the incomplete *Trial of Man*.) Lewis also wrote criticism and polemics, and painted highly evocative portraits of his contemporaries, including T.S. Eliot (∗) and Ezra Pound (∗).

He spent World War II under-recognized in Canada and five postwar years as an art critic for the weekly *Listener* in London. Not unlike other avant-garde writers of his generation, he is continually being rediscovered. He is not to be confused with D.B. Wyndham Lewis, who wrote polite biographies.

Kenner, Hugh. *Wyndham Lewis.* NY: New Directions, 1954.

Michel, Walter. *Wyndham Lewis: Paintings and Drawings.* Berkeley, CA: University of California, n.d. (c. 1977).

LeWITT, Sol (1928). An Abstract (∗) artist from his beginnings, a geometric artist interested in systems, and a prolific artist with a generous collection of assistants, LeWitt is best known for his sculptures, his wall drawings, and his writings on conceptual art (∗). The theme of the former, especially in sum, is variations on the cube, which over the years have been arrayed, stacked, and left partially incomplete, among other unprecedented moves. His wall-drawings, which are customarily executed in his absence, affix a geometric scheme—say different sets of curved lines a few inches apart—to a space from which it will be removed at an exhibition's end. It is a rigorously nonreferential art that is concerned with purity of both concept and execution, precisely by suggesting nothing that is not obviously perceptible. LeWitt's much-reprinted "Paragraphs on Conceptual Art" rationalizes work where "all of the planning and decisions are made beforehand and the execution is a perfunctory affair. The idea becomes a machine that makes the art. This kind of art is not theoretical or illustrative of theories; it is intuitive; it is involved with all types of mental processes and it is purposeless."

My own alternative opinion holds that, good as his other work has been, LeWitt's masterpieces are book-art books that he has been producing since the early 1970s. The first masterpiece is *Arcs, Circles & Grids* (1972), which has 195 progressively denser combinations of the linear geometric images announced in its title. Though LeWitt may have had something else in mind, I see this book as an elegantly simple narrative about increasing linear density. *Autobiography* (1980) has a large number of square black-and-white photographs, each two and five-eighths inches square, of every object in LeWitt's living and working space, none of them featured over any others; and although no photograph of the author or any of his works appears, the book does indeed portray not only a life but the roots of his particular imaginative sensibility. Among LeWitt's many books and booklets are *Incomplete Open Cubes* (1974), *The Location of Lines* (1974), *Lines & Color* (1975), *Squares with Sides and Corners Torn Off* (n.d.), *Red, Blue and Yellow Lines from Sides, Corners and the Center of the Page to Points on a Grid* (1975), *Photogrids* (1977), and *Sunrise & Sunset at Praiano* (1980), all of which accurately reflect their titles, for throughout the 1970s he cleverly made it his custom to do fresh book-art in lieu of catalogs for his exhibitions.

LeWitt, Sol. *Arcs, Circles & Grids*. Bern, Switzerland: Kunsthalle & Paul Biancini, 1972.

———. *Autobiography*. NY & Boston, MA: Multiples, Inc., and Lois and Michael K. Torf, 1980.

Legg, Alicia, ed. *Sol LeWitt*. NY: Museum of Modern Art, 1978.

LICHTENSTEIN, Roy (1923). His name is most familiar from his Pop Art (*) canvases of the early sixties, often consisting of blowups of single frames from comic strips, bubble-gum wrappers, and advertising-art images. His use of exaggerated dot screens (imitating newspaper printing), bold colors, and even comic-strip bubbles to portray his characters' "thoughts" all contribute to an essentially ironic vision of his subject matter. Later Lichtenstein paintings parodied 20th-century masters, including Picasso (*), Mondrian (*), and Abstract Expressionist (*) painters in deadpan canvases that reproduce their typical themes and techniques.—Richard Carlin

Alloway, Lawrence. *Roy Lichtenstein*. NY: Abbeville, 1983.

LIGETI, György (1923). Born in Transylvania, educated at the Budapest Music Academy, Ligeti left Hungary in 1956, reportedly walking to Cologne, where he found employment at Westdeutscher Rundfunk's Electronic Music (*) academy; within fifteen years, he was a professor at the Hamburg music school. His most successful pieces incorporate clusters of closely related sounds, more closely resembling acoustic bands than traditional separate notes, articulated with a strong sense of instrumental texture, he says to produce "acoustic motionlessness." The most familiar is the "Kyrie" from *Requiem*, which incidentally appeared in the soundtrack to the Stanley Kubrick film *2001* (*). Among Ligeti's more eccentric pieces is *Poème symphonique*, its title alluding to Varèse (*), except that Ligeti's is for 100 metronomes, all running at different speeds.

Ligeti, György. *Aventures (1962)/Nouvelles Aventures (1962–65)*. NY: Polydor 2549 003, 1970.

LIGHT ART (c. 1900). It seems odd, in retrospect, that visual artists were slow to realize the esthetic possibilities of electric light—that light had been around for many years before artists recognized that it could become the principal material of their work. The principal innovator of light art is commonly considered to be Thomas Wilfred (*), whose specialty was projections from behind a translucent screen; among subsequent projection-light artists were the Joshua Light Show

(*), Gyorgy Kepes (1905), and Earl Reiback (1943), who purchased Wilfred's studio after the latter's death.

Subsequent light artists have used fluorescent lamps, such as Dan Flavin (*); neon lamps, such as Chryssa (*) and Stephen Antonakis (1926); or small bulbs so transparent their flickering filaments are visible, such as Otto Piene (1930); lamps of various colors, programmed to change constantly, such as Boyd Mefferd (1941); or lasers, as in Rockne Krebs's (1938) *Aleph [squared]* (1969), where intense, narrow beams, either red or green, projected over one's head, bounce off mirrored walls in a dark room. Some light art depends upon reflecting or refracting materials, such as Moholy-Nagy's (*) *Light-Space Modulator* (1930), which is a kinetic sculpture designed to redirect projected light in various ways, and Clyde Lynds's (*) use of fiber optics to make light turn corners. Though individual light artists have had major exhibitions over the past few years, I'm not aware of any recent comprehensive overview, either in books or a museum.

Doty, Robert. *Light: Object and Image.* NY: Whitney Museum, 1968.

Kostelanetz, Richard. "Artistic Machines." In *Metamorphosis in the Arts.* Brooklyn, NY: Assembling, 1980.

LINDSAY, Vachel (1879–1931). More than any American before him, more than any of his contemporaries (except perhaps Gertrude Stein [*], five years his senior), Lindsay discovered what we now call text-sound (*) in poetic onomatopoeia. You can hear it on reading the following aloud to yourself (aside from the unfortunate racist implications): "Walk with care, walk with care, /Or Mumbo-Jumbo, god of the Congo, / And all of the other gods of the Congo, /Mumbo-Jumbo will hoo-doo you. /Beware, beware, walk with care, /Boomlay, boomlay, boomlay, boom. [repeated two additional times] /Boomlay, boomlay, boomlay, BOOM." For a fuller experience of Lindsay's acoustic poetry, listen to the recording that he made shortly before his suicide.

Educated mostly in fine art, Lindsay also published in 1915 the first intelligent book on the esthetics of film, as distinct from stage and photography, declaring prophetically that, "The motion picture art is a great high art, not a process of commercial manufacture," and then noting that, "The key-words of the stage are *passion* and *character*; of the photoplay, *splendor* and *speed*."

Lindsay, Vachel. *Reads the Congo and Other Poems* (1931). NY: Caedmon, n.d.

———. *The Art of the Moving Picture* (1915). NY: Liveright, 1970.

LIPPARD, Lucy R. (1937). Lippard was for many years the first major independent female art critic in America (as distinct from newspaper-based female art reviewer), and her early books, beginning with *Changing* (1968) and continuing perhaps through *Overlay* (1983), rank among the best at understanding new art. Her brilliant monograph on *Ad Reinhardt* (*) (published in 1981, but written a decade before) makes all subsequent writing on this avant-garde American seem amateur. I use the past tense, even though Lippard is still alive, because around 1975 she "got religion," as we would say, which in her case was a leftist feminism that generated articles and books that, in my considered opinion, won't survive the times. *Mixed Blessings* (1989), perhaps the most absurd, advocates artists of privileged birth, in this case females "of color," who are introduced with their appropriate racial/ethnic/tribal tags (much like individuals in the old *Social Registers* were), as though these tags should compensate, in Lippard's mind as well as the reader's, for any persuasive appreciation of their individual art. It is unfortunate that some of these recent books have sold more copies than her better ones (and probably gotten her more ancillary jobs as well), because in America that sort of success can make a writer think nothing has been lost.

Lippard, Lucy R. *Changing.* NY: Dutton, 1968.

LISSITZKY, El (1890–1941; b. Eliezer Markowich L.). Born in Smolensk, Russia, Lissitzky studied engineering in Germany before returning to Russia during World War I. After collaborating with Marc Chagall (1887–1985) on the illustration of Jewish books and with Kazimir Malevich (*) in establishing Russian Constructivism (*), he moved to Berlin where he published *The Story of Two Squares* (1922), which, as its title says, is a pioneering abstract visual fiction, as well as a modest masterpiece of modern typography. He then finished a series of Constructivist paintings that he called *Proun*. In 1928, for a museum in Hanover, he designed an "abstract gallery" that Alexander Dorner described in *The Way Beyond "Art"* (1958):

> The walls of that room were sheathed with narrow tin strips set at right angles to the wall plane. Since these strips were painted black on one side, gray on the other, and white on the edge, the wall changed its character with every move of the spectator. The sequence of tones varied in different parts of the room. This construction thus established a supraspatial milieu of the frameless compositions [i.e., suspended paintings].

Dorner continues, "This room contained many more sensory images than could have been accommodated by a rigid room." By current categories, this was a proto-Environment (*). Lissitzky also made innovative photomontages (*) and wrote about architectural possibilities (*An Architecture for World Revolution*, 1930) before returning in the 1930s to Russia, where he confined himself mainly to typography and industrial design (e.g., the Soviet Pavilion at the New York World's Fair in 1939) until his premature death.

Lissitzky-Küppers, Sophie. *El Lissitzky: Life, Letters, Texts* (1967). Intro. Herbert Read. Greenwich, CT: New York Graphic Society, 1968.

Lissitzky, El. *Russia: An Architecture for World Revolution* (1930). Trans. Eric Dluhosh. Cambridge, MA: M.I.T., 1970.

LIVING THEATRE (1947). Founded by Judith Malina (1923) and Julian Beck (1925–1985), long wife and husband, the Living Theatre has forever epitomized whatever might be radical in American theater. At their beginnings, at a time when naturalistic theater predominated, their specialty was poet's plays (e.g., Gertrude Stein [*], Kenneth Rexroth [*], W.B. Yeats, Paul Goodman, et al.); that perhaps accounts for why they spell "theater" to this day in the British way. By the 1960s, they had assimilated *The Theatre and Its Double* by Antonin Artaud (*), creating in their productions of Jack Gelber's *The Connection* (1961) and especially Kenneth Brown's *The Brig* (1963) theater that moved audiences, in Artaud's words, "with the force of the plague." In 1963, after their home theater was seized by the Internal Revenue Service for the nonpayment of withholding taxes, they moved to Europe where, in Eric Mottram's words, "they developed the idea of a theater company as creative political critics and emotional gurus." They returned to the U.S. in 1968 with *Paradise Now*, which was a series of scripted provocations that succeeded in involving theatrical audiences like nothing before or since.

Though Beck died in 1985, the company persists at last report in a storefront in New York's East Village, on the rougher side of Avenue A. Though new productions invariably disappoint those who remember previous masterpieces, it has after forty-five years survived longer than any other theater company of its avant-garde and politically radical kind, incidentally outliving nearly all of its imitators; for this alone, the Living Theatre deserves national honors.

Silvestro, Carlo, ed. *The Living Book of the Living Theatre*. Greenwich, CT: New York Graphic Society, 1971.

The Living Theatre. *Paradise Now*. NY: Random House, 1971.

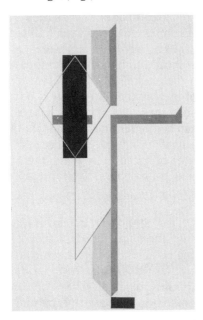

El Lissitzky, "Proun Composition," c. 1922. *Photo courtesy The Museum of Modern Art, New York; Gift of Curt Valentin.*

LOUIS, Morris (1912–1962; b. M.L. Bernstein).
His innovation was self-referring paintings that emphasized not the forms of gestural abstraction but the textures of variously applied paints, the relationships of colors within the field, and, in some cases, the possible subtle shadings of a single hue. Adapting Jackson Pollock's (∗) alternative way of applying paint to his own ends, Louis in the mid-1950s poured thinned-out acrylic paint directly on unprimed cotton-duck canvas. For a series called *Veils* (1954, again in 1957–1960), the thinned paint was poured onto canvas in overlapping patterns that are patently beautiful. The curator-critic John Elderfield finds that, "With Louis . . . fully autonomous abstract painting came into its own for really the first time, and did so in paintings of a quality that matches the level of their innovation." One appropriate epithet was "color-field painting" (∗), whose later advocates included Kenneth Noland (1924) and Jules Olitski (1922).

Elderfield, John. *Morris Louis.* NY: Museum of Modern Art, 1974.

Upright, Diane. *Morris Louis: The Complete Paintings.* NY: Abrams, 1985.

LOUIS, Murray (1926). For many years the principal male dancer in the Alwin Nikolais (∗) company, Louis became the only prominent modern dancer influenced by Charlie Chaplin, which is to say that his choreography tends to stylized movements and parody, making as much fun of their ostensible subjects as of numerous styles of dance. In his classic *Junk Dances* (1964), the set

Murray Louis, "Ten Legs," 1989. *Photo: Tom Caravaglia, courtesy Nikolais and Murray Louis Dance Company.*

is a mockery of Pop Art (∗); one sequence parodies the courtship mannerisms evident in 1930s movies; another sequence, as brilliantly performed by Phyllis Lamhut, satirizes the standard theatrical rendition of the busy secretary; another episode mocks Nikolais's prop-heavy choreography. The piece closes with Louis himself draped in Christmas tinsel and a network of lights that actually illuminate as the collage (∗) tape sounds the opera star Galli-Curci hitting her final high note. I saw *Junk Dances* perhaps a dozen times, never with decreasing pleasure.

Louis, Murray. *On Dance.* Pennington, NJ: a cappella, 1992.

———. *Inside Dance.* NY: St. Martin's, 1981.

LUCIER, Alvin (1931). Interested in the musical resonances of ambient sounds, particularly in live electronic performance, Lucier composed *I Am Sitting in a Room* (1970), which begins with him reading a 100-word prose statement that is recorded on tape. This recorded version is then played in the same place in which the original statement was made and rerecorded on new tape one generation away from the initial live statement. This procedure of broadcasting and rerecording is continued through several generations, as feedback progressively obliterates the text with the increasingly amplified sounds of the space. I remember his *Chambers* (1968), in which four musicians played conch shells through the auditorium, down the stairs, and out into New York's 57th Street, where Lucier himself stood on the double white line in the middle of the street. As cars whizzed by in both directions, a taxicab honked a horn that was louder and perhaps more musical than the sounds Lucier was producing. Then out of a building came a uniformed doorman—a "found player," so to speak—to tell Lucier to move on. Lucier has also worked creatively with devices to amplify brain waves in live musical performance, as an example of live Electronic Music (∗). He also worked with sound vibrations to generate visual imagery, and with instrumentalists accompanying electronically generated sound.

Lucier, Alvin, with Doulgas Simon. *Chambers.* Middletown, CT: Wesleyan University, 1980.

———. *I Am Sitting in a Room.* NY: Lovely Music/Vital Records, 1981.

LUDLAM, Charles (1943–1987). Ludlam gladly accepted the epithet "Theatre of the Ridiculous," which represented an extension of the Theatre of the Absurd (∗); for if the former used absurd means to portray worldly absurdity, Ludlam took the satirical impulse a step further, using ridiculous means to portray worldly ridiculousness. "We have passed beyond the Absurd," wrote his colleague and sometime collaborator Ronald Travel (1941), "Our position is absolutely preposterous." Ludlam's manifesto typically emphasizes "axioms to a theater for ridicule," including "the things one takes seriously are one's weaknesses." Even though most of his plays drew upon classical models, they were filled with bad taste, sexual confusion, phallic worship, and operatic extravagance. With success, his imagination inflated these aberrations. Of the plays familiar to me, the most inspired is *Der Ring Gott Farblonjet* (1977), subtitled "A Masterwork," which it truly is. Initially a take-off of Richard Wagner's *Ring* cycle of operas, it deflates their pomposity initially with a Yiddish euphemism for getting hopelessly lost (*Farblonjet*, which is pronounced "far-BLAWN-jit"). The characters all have atrociously Teutonic names (the Valkyries being "Brunnhilda," "Helmvige," "Schwertheita," "Valtrauta," etc.); and, as is typical in Ludlam plays, female roles are often assumed by men. Ludlam makes language work in ways ironically reminiscent of *Finnegans Wake* (∗), opening his *Ring* with: "Weia! Water! Waga! Waves of wasser! Waves of wasser! Wagalawei! Wallalla weiala weia!" True to his means, Ludlam also wrote ridiculous stage directions: "(The weaves giftoff to scrimmist sheerest parting until all is clear, clearing on a mountain's height. Lustering glistering tamples pinnacles of casteln hinterground.)" He died prematurely of complications from AIDS, which is not avant-garde—just a deadly disease.

Ludlam, Charles. *The Complete Plays*. NY: Harper & Row, 1989.

———. *Ridiculous Theater: Scourge of Human Folly.* NY: TCG, 1992.

LUENING, Otto (1900). Born in Milwaukee, the son of a German-American musician, Luening was educated in the U.S., Germany, and Switzerland. One among many American avant-garde composers in the 1930s and 1940s, better known

as a flutist and for his administrative skills, Luening established a unique reputation in the 1950s as a pioneer of Electronic Music (∗). On 28 October 1952, he played the flute in *Fantasy in Space* to an audiotape accompaniment; two other premieres on that program, *Low Speed* and *Invention in 12 Tones*, were audiotapes wholly of electronically manipulated instrumental sounds. Luening later collaborated with his Columbia University colleague Vladimir Ussachevsky (1911–1990) in producing tapes that would function as soloists in orchestral concerts, their *Rhapsodic Variations* (1954) preceding by months an Edgard Varèse (∗) piece that worked similarly. Compared to what followed, he remains a traditional electronic composer. (Ussachevsky, curiously, spent his last years in Utah, composing music reflective of Russian Romanticism.)

Luening, Otto. *The Odyssey of an American Composer.* NY: Scribner's, 1980.

LYE, Len (1901–1980). Born in New Zealand, Lye lived in the South Sea Islands in the 1920s, assimilating Polynesian art, before moving to London. Working with John Grierson's documentary film unit at the General Post Office, he invented around 1934 a technique for painting directly on film, producing the short *Color Box* (1935). In later films, Lye developed this technique, which consequently influenced the Canadian Norman McLaren (1914–1987), among others. Rarely profiting from filmmaking, he abandoned that art for equally innovative, if esthetically different, work in kinetic sculpture.

Russett, Robert, and Cecile Starr. *Experimental Animation*. NY: Van Nostrand, 1976.

LYNDS, Clyde (1936). After training in classical painting, Lynds seized upon a new technology called "fiber optics" to open new esthetic territory. Fiber optics uses translucent cable as thin as a strand of hair to transmit light or data. More important for Lynds's purposes is its capacity to carry light around corners, which is to say that light entering at one end or tip of this thin cable will emerge at the other tip, no matter how the cable is twisted and turned. What Lynds does is distribute these ends to strategic points in a concrete surface, so that they become visible only when illuminated from within. The hidden element responsible for the continuous variations in surface light—for the appearance of endlessly changing "painting"—is color wheels, which are plastic discs whose sections have various colored gels, including black. Situated between the strong light source and the interior ends of the fiber optic strands, the gels determine not only whether light is propelled to the exterior ends, black of course preventing it, but also what color the light will be. By introducing two discs, each rotating at different speeds, Lynds further varies the communication, literally, of light to the fiber optic ends. The visible result is slowly metamorphosing combinations of dots of light, in continuously varying patterns, with minimal repetition, so that the principal afterimage for Lynds's kinetic paintings becomes not one or another stilled pose but flow itself.

The David Bermant Collection: Color, Light, Motion. Hartford, CT: Wadsworth Athenaeum, 1984.

MAC LOW, Jackson (1922). As a poet, composer, and dramatist, Mac Low has used indeterminacy (∗) in the creation of his works. In his own words, "My work, especially that of 1954–80, is closely related to that of such composers as John Cage [∗], Morton Feldman [∗], Earle Brown [∗], Christian Wolff [∗], and La Monte Young [∗]." He describes his work from 1954 as "incorporat[ing] methods, processes, and devices from modern music, including the use of chance operations in composition and/or performance, silences ranging in duration from breath pauses to several minutes, and various degrees of improvisation by performers. Many of the works are 'simultaneities'—works performed by several speakers and/or producers of musical sounds and noises at once." Some of these texts are based on grids whose words (both horizontally and vertically arrayed) are spoken in an order determined by chance operations. Avowedly eclectic, Mac Low also writes fairly conventional free verse and even Expressionistic (∗) lyrics.

Mac Low stated in *Talisman* 8 (Spring 1992), "Open to all poetries, I'm shipwrecked amid terms such as 'avant-garde' and 'experimental'—words largely abandoned by many who share my universe of discourse. On the superficial—that is, the most serious—level, I hate the military provenance of 'avant-garde.' And to this noxious connotation the authoritarian split off from democratic Marxism added the concept of the 'vanguard party.'" As a veteran anarchist who uses those epithets generously (as in this book) and has written whole books about opening the professional field, I find it odd that anyone purportedly advocating openness would want to push some positions (and thus people) off the map. It's unfortunate to see Mac Low take this abnegating position, because he has for some fifty years been producing genuinely experimental, avant-garde poetry and theater.—with Richard Carlin

Mac Low, Jackson. *Stanzas for Iris Lezak.* Barton, VT: Something Else, 1971.

———. *Representative Works 1938–85.* NY: Roof, 1986.

MACIUNAS, George (1931–1978). A legendary character to all who knew him, Maciunas, a Lithuanian-born American who forever seemed an immigrant here, was at once the founder and sometime generalissimo of Fluxus (∗) and the developer/renovator of artists' cooperatives in SoHo (∗). His own art consisted of ingenious architectural proposals, small boxes accumulating debris similar in some way (such as excrement), and audacious graphic designs. His artistic masterpiece is the *Expanded Arts Diagram* (1966), which is a complex graphic history portraying the relationships of the new arts to the old arts (aka Intermedia [∗]). Using lists turned at various angles and flow-chutes, Maciunas identified the roles of Dada (∗), Vaudeville, Marcel Duchamp (∗), church processions ("Baroque Multi-Media Spectacle"), circuses, fairs, and the Bauhaus (∗) as precursors to such activities as "acoustic theater," "kinesthetic theater," "expanded cinema," "events—neo-haiku theater," "verbal theater," "Happenings" (∗), etc., all positioned in the sans-serif type that always marked his graphic work. To quote Ken Friedman on Maciunas, "He saw the artists fulfilling in their work a long evolution of ideas, fluid rather than rigid, part of a millennia-long human dialogue. The . chart reveals a designer with an eye for broad historical scope and a visual humor." I own a larger, later chart, some six feet by two, that Friedman says is an incomplete draft "published in Sweden after Maciunas's death," even though my recollection is that Maciunas gave it to me a few years before.

Friedman, Ken, "George Maciunas." In *Contemporary Masterpieces*, ed. Colin Naylor. London, England: St. James Press, 1991.

MAIL ART. Out of the reasonable assumption that the commercial gallery system is limited and perhaps corrupt, many artists emerging in the 1970s and 1980s around the world decided it would be more feasible to exhibit their work not through galleries and ancillary museums but through the postal system, especially if they lived in areas where galleries and other artists were scarce. For the production of imagery, they drew often upon xerography (*) and the earlier technology of rubber stamps. They would also announce exhibitions in venues previously devoid of art, such as city halls in remote parts of the world, ideally accepting everything submitted and issuing a catalog with names, usually accompanied by addresses and selected reproductions. While such work had little impact upon commercial galleries (and the "art magazines" dependent upon galleries' ads), one result was a thriving alternative culture, calling itself "The Eternal Network," as intensely interested in itself as serious artists have always been.

Crane, Mike. *Correspondence Art.* San Francisco, CA: Contemporary Arts, 1984.

Welsh, Chuck. *Networking Currents.* Brookline, MA: Sandbar Willow (P.O. Box 883, 02146), 1986.

MALEVICH, Kazimir (1878–1935). Malevich came to Moscow in his late twenties, initially working as an Impressionist painter. Befriending political radicals in the pre–World War I decade, Malevich produced paintings depicting rural peasants in a deliberately primitive style. Working with flat planes of unmodulated color, Malevich called his art Cubo-Futurism (*). Changing his style again, he made collages (*) and juxtapositions of realistically rendered details in the manner of Pablo Picasso (*) and Georges Braque (1882–1963). In 1913, he designed stage sets and costumes for Mikhail Matiushin's (*) and Aleksei Kruchonykh's (*) Futurist (*) opera *Victory Over the Sun*, by common consent a monument of avant-garde theater. By 1915–1916, Malevich reached his most radical style of nonobjective painting which he called Suprematism, which is best seen as a radical development within Constructivism (*). Not unlike his near contemporary Piet Mondrian (*), Malevich, in writing about his art, made claims that are hard to verify: for example, "Suprematism is pure feeling." In their fields of unmodulated color, these works resemble monochromic paintings that became more familiar after 1960.

In the 1920s, Malevich extended Suprematist principles to sculpture. A supporter of the Soviet Revolution, he became head of the Viebsk art school; but sensing trouble, he traveled in 1927 to Germany, leaving some of his more radical paintings there, to remain undiscovered until the 1970s. Back in Leningrad, he returned to figurative painting, concluding his career with portraits of friends and family. Given all the rapid changes (through, in Valentine Marcadé's sweeping summary, "Impressionism, Neo-Primitivism, Fauvism, Futurist, Cubism, Alogism, Suprematism, the *arkhitekton* constructions and then, in the 1930s, back to figurative art"), the critical question posed by his career was whether he was mercurial or opportunistic.

Marcadé, Valentine. "The Peasant Theme in the Work of Kazimir Severinovich Malevich." In *Kasimir Malewitsch.* Köln, Germany: Galerie Gmurzynska, 1978.

Kazimir Malevich. Amsterdam: Stedelijk Museum, 1989.

MALLARMÉ, Stéphane (1842–1898). His avant-garde masterpiece is the long poem *Un Coup de Dés* (1897). The radical idea for this work was making the page a field receptive to various typographies and verbal relationships both syntactical and spatial, and in this respect, Mallarmé preceded Guillaume Apollinaire (*) and Charles Olson (*), among many other poets, who developed that idea. "The word image-complex," Charles Mauron wrote, "is the fundamental quality of poetry, and melody is ancillary to that." Because the theme of *Un Coup* seems to be that everything perishes unless it is remembered in print, the form complements the content. Mallarmé's short poems are so precious and obscure that they are still treasured by those who regard preciosity and obscurity as the essence of poetic art. (Not I.) As Mauron puts it, "This cumulative effect of the auras of words is the essential quality of the poetic act." The fact that the standard French edition of Mallarmé's complete works contains less than 100 poems abets this image of preciosity. A teacher of English by trade, he is frequently credited with revolutionizing French narrative and with an Olympian detachment so contrary to the Expressionists (*) who followed him. The Anthony Hartley translations are prose footnotes to the French, while Roger Fry's follow the structure of verse. Jean-Paul Sartre (1905–1980), frequently obsessed with writers profoundly unlike himself, produced an inspired monograph that was translated only recently.

Mallarmé, Stéphane. *Poems.* Trans. Roger Fry, with commentaries by Charles Mauron. NY: New Directions, 1951.

———. *Mallarmé.* Ed., intro., prose trans. Anthony Hartley. Harmondsworth, England: Penguin, 1965.

———. *Selected Poetry and Prose.* Ed. Mary Ann Caws. NY: New Directions, 1982.

Sartre, Jean-Paul. *Mallarmé or the Poet of Nothingness* (1980). Trans. Ernest Strum. University Park, PA: Penn State University, 1988.

MAN RAY (1890–1976; b. Emmanuel Rudnitsky).

A sort of minor polyartist (*), Man Ray was considerably more skilled at some of his arts than others. Largely self-taught, he made collages (*) and Cubist (*) paintings before World War I. In 1915, he published out of a New Jersey artists' colony a proto-Dada (*) magazine, *The Ridgefield Gazook*, and after meeting Marcel Duchamp (*) later that year, Ray became a principal participant in New York Dada. Moving to Paris in 1921, he joined organized Surrealism (*) and moved from photography into film, producing in *Emak Bakia* (1927) his closest claim to a classic. "Man Ray was adamant that there be no script for *Emak Bakia*, no discernible narrative progression," his biographer Neil Baldwin writes, "in keeping with his belief that there generally was no progress in art. Nevertheless, there *are* motifs in the film, repetitions of patterns of light as Man Ray paints with light, exploring more deeply dazzling contrasts engineered to stir the viewer's emotions, . . . dark objects upon light backgrounds, light faces against dark backdrops, dark words against light paper." Man Ray challenged Moholy-Nagy's (*) claim to have invented the photogram, where a photograph is made by placing objects directly on photographic paper and then exposing it to light; he called these works "rayographs." He also worked, with considerable commercial success, as a fashion photographer. *Self Portrait* (1963) is Man Ray's immodest, incomplete autobiography.

Baldwin, Neil. *Man Ray: American Artist.* NY: Clarkson Potter, 1988.

MANN, Chris (1949).

Perhaps the only Australian poet to have an international avant-garde reputation, Mann has produced highly inventive prose; unusual books, such as *On Having Words* (1978), which is actually a single sheet of paper approximately sixty inches by forty-two inches, printed on both sides, folded to fit between a pseudo-book cover; and *Quadraphonic Cocktail* (1987), multi-track radio programs that were broadcast over different Australian channels simultaneously; among other audacious inventions. He is not the South African poet of the same name whose name appears in the 1991 edition of the otherwise encyclopedic *Contemporary Poets* (St. James Press).

Mann, Chris. *On Having Words.* Australia: Outback Press, 1978.

———. *Chris Mann and Grammar.* N.p.: Lingua, 1990.

MANZONI, Piero (1933–1963).

A student of Lucio Fontana (*), Manzoni extended his mentor's taste for radical challenges within the art context, signing his name on the lower backside of a nude model (1961) purportedly to guarantee the natural beauty of the woman's skin, producing balloons inflated with "artist's breath" and tins containing "artist's shit," exhibiting "Achromes," as he called them, made of polystyrene soaked in cobalt chloride, and making "tubes containing kilometers of lines designed to mock the idea of space." According to Giulio Carlo Argan, Manzoni was "the first to see that Duchamp was one of the most important protagonists of the century, the first artist for whom there was no work of art that wasn't also an idea about the essence and historical condition of art." That is a lot of philosophical weight to attribute to Manzoni's second-generation gestures, and that observation may account for why remarkably few Anglo-American critics, to different degrees predisposed to the ethics of verification, have written about Manzoni's work.

Argan, Giulio Carlo. "Reconstruction: Art in Postwar Italy." In *Breakthroughs*. NY: Rizzoli, 1991.

MARINETTI, Filippo Tommaso (1876–1944). The founder of Italian Futurism (*), Marinetti wanted to be known as a poet and playwright; he is remembered mostly as a reportedly personable publicist who authored some of the strongest sentences advocating alternative art: "Literature having up to now glorified thoughtful immobility, ecstasy, and slumber, we wish to exalt the aggressive moment, the feverish insomnia, running, the perilous leap, the cuff, and the blow." The principal effect of Marinetti's rhetoric was making a few good artists famous— Giacomo Balla (1871–1958), Fortunato Depero (*), etc.—at least for a while. His reputation suffered from his early support of Benito Mussolini and Fascism.

Marinetti, F. P. *Selected Writings*. Ed. R.W. Flint. NY: Farrar, Straus, 1972.

———. *La Cucina Futurista/Futurist Cookbook* (1932). Ed. Lesley Chamberlain. San Francisco, CA: Bedford Arts, 1989.

MARSHALL, Ingram (1943). Not unlike Elliott Carter (*) before him, Marshall passed through undistinguished beginnings to bloom in his forties, mostly with pieces that mix taped accompaniments with live instrumentalists in harmonious ways different from and more elegant than earlier tape-live mixes. One reason is Marshall's use of unfamiliar sounds, such as the slamming of a huge steel door at Alcatraz prison, a funeral procession in Yugoslavia, and exotic church bells. *Hidden Voices* (1989) draws upon tapes made in Mordovian Russia, Rumania, and Hungary; *Three Penitential Visions* (1986), upon a colleague's saxophone playing in a large church at Eberbach in Germany's Rheingau province.

Marshall, Ingram. *Three Penitential Visions/Hidden Voices*. NY: Nonesuch 9 79227-2, 1990.

MARTIN, Agnes (1912). In the early 1960s, a few years after relocating from New York to New Mexico, Martin began producing paintings of grids composed of horizontal bricks, so

to speak, that run from edge to edge, both vertically and horizontally. Perhaps sensing that she had reached an ultimate image, much as her near-contemporary Ad Reinhardt (*) had, she stopped painting for several years before returning to grids that were even more subtle in making thin straight parallel lines that shimmer and thus evoke a spiritual experience outside of themselves. Not unlike Reinhardt again, Martin is also an assertive writer: "Art work is a representation of our devotion to life. Everyone is devoted to life with an intensity far beyond our comprehension. The slightest hint of devotion to life in art work is received by all with gratitude." Especially in group exhibitions, in my experience, her work shines through the strength of subtlety.

Haskell, Barbara. *Agnes Martin*. NY: Whitney Museum of American Art–Abrams, 1992.

Gruen, John. "Agnes Martin." In *The Artist Observed*. Pennington, NJ: a cappella, 1991.

MASEREEL, Frans (1889–1972). Born in Flemish Belgium, Masereel began as an illustrator of books written by others; but because his drawings were strong enough to stand apart from any texts, he made them in sequences that suggested narratives, such as *Mein Stundenbuch* (subtitled variously "a novel without words" or "a novel told in 165 pictures"), thus becoming the precursor of such later visual fictioneers as the Americans Lynd Ward (*), Milt Gross (*), Edward Gorey (*), and Giacomo Patri (1898), and the Canadian Martin Vaughn-James (*). Masereel was a leftist and a pacifist.

Masereel, Frans. *Passionate Journey* [*Mein Studenbuch*] (1920). Intro. Thomas Mann. San Francisco, CA: City Lights, 1988.

Patri, Giacomo. *White Collar* (1940). Millbrae, CA: Celestial Arts, 1975.

MATHEWS, Harry (1930). Educated in music at Harvard and then at the École Normale de Musique in Paris, Mathews has, not unlike other experimental American writers before and since, lived most of his adult life abroad. At the service of prosaic plots, Mathews uses highly original and playful language as would be expected of the only American member of Oulipo (*); and like other experimental writers, he works in more than one genre. Linguistic possibilities appear to be his principal theme. Commercially published novels include *The Conversions* (1962), *Tlooth* (1966), *The Sinking of the Odradek Stadium* (1975, bound into a single volume with its two predecessors), and *Cigarettes* (1987). From smaller presses have come *Selected Declarations of Independence* (1977) and *20 Lines a Day* (1988).

Mathews, Harry. *The Sinking of the Odradek Stadium and Other Novels*. NY: Harper & Row, 1975.

MATHIEU, Georges (1921). Among the originators of post–World War II Parisian Expressive Abstraction (∗), Mathieu worked rapidly, purportedly without sketches or other plans, often on large canvases whose imagery sometimes reflected calligraphy. "The only true creation," he once wrote, "is one which invents its means on the spot, calling everything into question." Even though Mathieu organized as early as 1950 an exhibition joining Parisian and New York Expressionists (∗), his work remains less familiar than, say, Jackson Pollock's (∗) or Franz Kline's (∗), so that the comparative neglect of his art can serve as a measure of recent American dominance in this area. Mathieu preceded Harold Rosenberg (∗) in formulating the image of painting as the result of physical action. Educated in law and philosophy, Mathieu has also published books about contemporary art.

Mathieu. Paris: Musée des Beaux-Arts de la Ville de Paris, 1963.

MATIUSHIN, Mikhail (1861–1934). He was the third collaborator, along with Aleksei Kruchonykh (∗) and Kazimir Malevich (∗), in the path-breaking opera *Victory Over the Sun* (1913). Though Matiushin was at the time a violinist in the Court Orchestra, where he had worked for the previous twenty years, his music includes dissonances and sounds evocative of cannon shots and airplanes. Turning to writing and publishing, Matiushin in 1914 established a press, The Crane, printing vanguard texts by Velimir Khlebnikov (∗) and Kazimir Malevich, among others, in addition to his own translations of French theoretical writings. Because less is known about him, at least in English, I quote from Andrei B. Nakov's history of 1915–1921 Russian avant-garde art: "Taking off from certain

presuppositions of the famous 'fourth dimension,' he situated man at the center of a new cosmic image. While taking into account the interaction of the visible and the audible, in his plastic system a very special place was reserved for psycho-sensorial sensation. The superseding of the synthesist theories of the symbolists led him to the conception of synthetic images, the formulation of which was carried out with the intermediary of abstract-geometrical images." Some of these findings appeared in Matiushin's 1932 book whose title translates as "The Rules and Variability in Color Combinations," which he thought would be applicable to various applied arts.

Nakov, Andrei B. *Avant-Garde Russe*. NY: Universal, 1986.

MAVO. See MURAYAMA, Tomoyoshi

MAXIMAL ART (c. 1970). This was my coinage, which I'd be the first to admit has scarcely taken, for works that, in contrast to Minimal art (∗), have more of the stuff of art than previous art. A principal example is James Joyce's *Finnegans Wake* (∗), which, though it relates a simple story, has a wealth of words and, by extension, a wealth of references. Another is Milton Babbitt's (∗) multiple serialization (∗), where each note contributes to several musical developments. (I remember telling Babbitt that another composer claimed his work had several hundred "musical events" within a few minutes; as true to his esthetic as ever, Babbitt thought that number was not particularly high.) Influenced by James Joyce, the playwright Charles Ludlam (∗) used "Maximal" to measure his own ambitions. The term "Maximal art" is also applicable to my favorite John Cage (∗) pieces: *Williams Mix*, which likewise has several hundred acoustic events in only a few minutes; *Europera* (∗), which draws upon dozens of classic operas; and *HPSCHD* (∗), which comes from a large number of independent sound sources. Maximality in visual art might be harder to measure. It is certainly implied in the multiple references of Jasper Johns (∗); it is explicit in the several Plexiglas levels of John Cage's *Not Wanting To Say Anything About Marcel* (1969) and in the kinetic sculptures of George Rhoads (∗). I find Maximality in Ad

Reinhardt's (*) cartoons about the art world (in sharp contrast to his Minimal paintings) and in Merce Cunningham's (*) choreography, though others may disagree.

Hess, Thomas B. *The Art Comics and Satires of Ad Reinhardt.* Düsseldorf, Germany: Kunsthalle, 1975.

MAYAKOVSKY, Vladimir (1893–1930). Born in Russian Georgia, Mayakovsky studied art before turning to poetry, which made him famous, initially among the Futurist (*) painters and poets before the Revolution, then as one of the first avant-gardists to support the Revolution actively, and later as a favored beneficiary of the new state. He visited New York in the mid-1920s and wrote a poem about it. Mayakovsky collaborated with major avant-garde artists in poster designs and, in his own poetry, broached enough visual devices to warrant an extended analysis by Gerald Janecek (*) in his classic book *The Look of Russian Literature.* Though Mayakovsky's poetry was never as experimental as that of Velimir Klebnikov (*) and, especially, Aleksei Kruchonykh (*), the other principals in Futurist poetry, it was popular (for reasons that remain mysterious to the reader of English translations). Precisely because he was a state-favored poet, much as Dmitri Shostakovich (1906–1975) became a state-favored composer, every new work of his was subjected to excessive critical scrutiny, as often by ignorant commissars as by knowledgeable critics. Perhaps because his last two plays, *The Bedbug* (1929) and *The Bath House* (1930) were negatively received, Mayakovsky committed suicide in 1930. His name, long spelled in America as I have it, is now sometimes spelled Maiakovskii.

Janecek, Gerald. *The Look of Russian Literature.* Princeton, NJ: Princeton University, 1984.

Mayakovsky, Vlaidmir. *The Bedbug and Selected Poetry.* Ed. Patricia Blake. NY: Meridian, 1960.

MAYER, Peter (1935). Born in Berlin, Mayer was taken at a very young age to England, where he became the principal scholar of avant-garde poetries both visual and aural. His taxonomies and bibliographies, the latter sometimes produced in collaboration with others, are particularly brilliant and incomparable. He has also made three-dimensional poems and film poems. Among his publications are 'Yin Yang' Cube (1968), *Gamme de gamma* (1970), and *Earmouth* (1972). Along with Dom Sylvester Houédard (*) and Bob Cobbing (*), Mayer coedited the periodical *Kroklok* (1971). He was the sole editor of *Alphabetical and Letter Poems* (1978), a pioneering anthology. He is not related to someone with the same name, born around the same time, who heads the corporation owning Penguin-Viking, or to Peter R. Meyer, a younger language-artist who works at Swedish radio.

Mayer, Peter, and Bob Cobbing, eds. *Concerning Concrete Poetry.* London, England: Writers Forum, 1978 (and continually updated).

Mayer, Peter, ed. *Alphabetical and Letter Poems: A Christomathy.* London, England: Menard, 1978.

McCAFFERY, Steve. See FOUR HORSEMEN, THE

McCAY, Windsor (1869–1934). McCay was one of the comic's most skillful draftsmen, producing Sunday strips so visually dazzling that they would be inconceivable in today's newspapers. They were filled with colorful details and experiments with visual distortion, all of which were simply the dreams of Little Nemo. McCay's strip (variously called "Little Nemo in Slumberland" or "In the Land of Wonderful Dreams," depending upon whom he was working for at the time) had serious weaknesses, including bland storylines, boring writing, and predictable conclusions (as each strip ended with Nemo awaking from his dream in a little square at the bottom corner of the page). Despite these shortcomings, McCay expanded the visual repertoire of the comic strip as no one else had (as his talents as a draftsman far outshone those of his contemporary George Herriman [*]). One of the first people to experiment with film animation in the first decade of this century, McCay did not have the advantage of background cells, so he had to redraw the background for each frame of his black-and-white cartoon *Gertie the Trained Dinosaur* (1909). Though lacking much of a story, the cartoon has a stunning visual reality, even as the entire background (and Gertie herself) shimmers with each slight misstep of his pen.—Geof Huth

Blackbeard, Bill, and Martin Williams, eds. *The Smithsonian Collection of Newspaper Comics*. Washington, DC: Smithsonian Institution, 1977.

McFERRIN, Bobby (1950). Initially a virtuoso vocalist, McFerrin is the first human singer to resemble the electronic sampler (∗), a technology new to the 1980s that "stores sounds," as they say, remembering them to be instantly evoked at a later time. What is most remarkable is the sheer number and variety of sounds in McFerrin's acoustic library. With the assistance of audio overdubbing, he can vocally accompany himself, in addition to producing with his voice alone the sounds of percussion and other instruments. I've seen a videotape where McFerrin pulls classic pop albums off the shelf and evokes sounds characteristic of each, and heard a live performance in which he renders, both accurately and ironically, all the sounds at the end of *The Wizard of Oz*. You would think that no sound was beyond McFerrin's instant vocal recall until you realize that he must have spent a good deal of time learning how to make his mouth reproduce each of them.

McFerrin, Bobby. *Simple Pleasures*. NY: EMI-Musician E11H-48059, 1988.

Kostelanetz, Richard. "Bobby McFerrin." In *More on Innovative Music(ian)s*. Forthcoming.

McLUHAN, Marshall (1911–1980). Beginning with *The Mechanical Bride* (1951), McLuhan examined mass-cultural artifacts and then mass culture itself with a critical sensibility honed on the close rhetorical analysis of English literature. This approach generated a wealth of original insights, such as the perception that the representational discontinuity distinguishing modernist painting and literature resembled the newspaper's front page with its discontinuous field of unrelated articles, oversized headlines, and occasional captioned pictures. One theme of *Understanding Media* (1964) holds that this discontinuity reflects the impact of electronic information technology and that, differences in quality notwithstanding, "the great work of a period has much in common with the poorest work." All this insight into mass culture did not prevent McLuhan from proposing a necessary and persuasive measure for distinguishing esthetic quality from kitsch: "How heavy a demand does it make on the intelligence? How inclusive a consciousness does it focus?" Few commentators have written more insightfully about the general structure and operation of *Finnegans Wake* (∗).

McLuhan, Marshall. *Understanding Media*. NY: McGraw-Hill, 1964.

———. *The Interior Landscape*. NY: McGraw-Hill, 1969.

McPHEE, Colin (1901–1964). A Canadian composer who lived mostly in the U.S. and spent several years in Bali, McPhee, more than anyone else, introduced the intelligence of Indonesian music to Western composers, initially with his own music, but also with such publications as the memoir *A House in Bali* (1946) and *Music in Bali* (1966), which appeared after his death. In this respect, his implicit influence upon subsequent avant-garde music is immeasurable. None of McPhee's own compositions, not even *Tabuh-Tabuhan* (1936), have survived as well as his books. Carol Oja's (1953) biography is a model of its scholarly kind.

Oja, Carol. *Colin McPhee*. Washington, DC: Smithsonian, 1990.

MEDICINE SHOW THEATRE ENSEMBLE (1970). Founded by Barbara Vann (1938) and James Barbosa (1932), previously founding members of the Open Theatre (∗), it remains among the strongest off-off-Broadway theater companies, staging the best modernist work—including texts by Gertrude Stein (∗), Paul Goodman (1911–1972), William Carlos Williams (∗), E.E. Cummings's (∗) *him* (1927)—and indicatively resisting postmodernist fashions. Their name comes from a uniquely American form of entertainment, popular around the turn of the century, that was particularly successful at involving its audience. In the tradition of the Open Theatre, their performances favor physical presence, the juxtaposition of styles and forms, and rapid shifts of focus.

MERTON, Thomas (1915–1968). A Frenchman who became an American, a Protestant who became a Roman Catholic and then a Trappist monk, Merton was also an extremely various and prolific writer whose work falls into many categories. There is a classic young man's autobiography, *The Seven Storey Mountain* (1948);

there are pacifist polemics; there are sympathetic explanations of the monastic life and Catholic faith. After his death, his principal American literary publisher issued not only a thick book of *Literary Essays* (1981) but a yet thicker book of poems (1977). Merton's avant-garde masterpiece is a novel written in 1941, inspired by his friendship with two Columbia College classmates, Robert Lax (*) and Edward Rice, not to mention the publication of *Finnegans Wake* (*). Likewise published after his death as *My Argument with the Gestapo* (1969), this novel has the subtitle *A Macaronic Journal*, that adjective referring to the mixing of languages in the text: "Descendumi, piccolo ceri, mon vero, descendimo, escape mientras el si fuo, pendant que is in the stairs nullo, nip: no pod." Merton never did anything like it again.

Merton, Thomas. *My Argument with the Gestapo.* NY: New Directions, 1969.

————, and Robert Lax. *A Catch of Anti-Letters.* Kansas City, KS: Sheed, Andrews & McMeel, 1978.

MERZ. See SCHWITTERS, Kurt

MEV—MUSICA ELETTRONICA VIVA (1966, "live Electronic Music").
Formed in Rome by expatriate American composers Alvin Curran (*), Allan Bryant (*), Jon Phetteplace (1940), and Frederic Rzewski (1938), this group specialized in using electronic instruments, beginning with keyboards and amplifying processors, later including early synthesizers (*) in live concerts. Descending from John Cage (*), they were predisposed to perform in public spaces, allowing outside noises to infiltrate their concert space, and to incorporate into their collective improvisations musics both highbrow and lowbrow, formal and informal. At various times, other musicians were included, such as the American Richard Teitelbaum (1939) and the Hungarian Ivan Vandor (1932), MEV describing itself as "a performing group, a way station, and a school where older and younger learn from one another and play together on the same stage." MEV resembled AMM, which was formed by Cornelius Cardew (*) with British musicians in London, also in the late 1960s.

MEV and AMM. *Live Electronic Music Improvised.* NY: Mainstream MS 5002, 1970.

MICHALS, Duane (1932).
Michals has produced sequences of photographic images not to document stages in an event but to evoke a story. Two qualities that make these stories appropriate for photography, rather than film or print, are that the distance between images approximates the time it takes the reader to turn the page, and that the mystery of the plot depends upon actions that must have happened between the images. As Martin Vaughn-James (*) said of his own visual fiction, "Between one frame and the next something has happened—an unknowable event." In Michals's book of wordless photographic *Sequences* (1970) is a set of six photographs entitled "The Lost Shoe." The first image shows a deserted urban street with the fuzzy backside of a man walking away from the camera and up the street. In the second frame he drops on the pavement a blurred object that in the third frame is seen to be a lady's shoe; and this frame, as well as the next two, suggests that he departs up the street in a great hurry. In the sixth frame, the man is nowhere to be seen, while the shoe is mysteriously burning. The realism of all the photographs starkly contrasts with the mysteriousness of the plot, while the large changes between the frames reveal the absolute immobility of the camera. For this last reason, the authorial perspective is as Chekhovian as both the work's title and its passive acceptance of something inexplicably forbidding.

Michals, Duane. *Sequences.* NY: Doubleday, 1970.

MICROPRESS (c. 1965).
This flourished in the 1980s, although such publishing had begun earlier. Smaller than the literary-cultural small press (*), the micropress also depends upon cheaper methods of reproduction: mimeography, spirit-duplicating, and especially xerography (*). These cheap, and sometimes homegrown, varieties of printing permitted the almost instantaneous reproduction of text and image. Since the 1980s, literally thousands of publications have been produced, both chapbooks and periodicals (customarily called "zines"), in print runs rarely exceeding 100, across the U.S. and the rest of the world. True, much of the output from these publishers is (like most art everywhere) ill-formed, but in the U.S., some of these micropresses

have become the major avenue for the publication of advanced writing, now that all the major publishers and nearly all the small presses have no contact with the literary avant-garde.— Geof Huth

Gunderloy, Mike, and Cari Goldberg Janice. *The World of Zines*. NY: Penguin, 1992.

MICROTONALITY (c. 1920). In the first half of the 20th century, composers around the world separately began to explore intervals smaller than the halftone, which is traditionally the smallest interval in Western music, including quarter tones (or more precisely, half of a halftone) and even slighter fractions. Though musicologists were aware of such microtones, especially in Asian music, it is only in the 20th century that self-conscious composers systematically investigated the possibilities of using them in their works. Among the pioneers were the Czech Alois Hába (1893–1973), the Mexican Julián Carrillo (1875–1965), the American Harry Partch (∗), and Ivan Wyschnegradsky (1893–1980), a Russian long resident in Paris. Charles Ives (∗) briefly explored quarter tones in certain late pieces. All these composers either made their own instruments or had instruments specially made to play microtones. Carrillo had a "harpzither" built that reportedly had ninety-seven tones within an octave. Among older living composers, Easley Blackwood (1933) is perhaps the most prominent microtonalist. Though microtonal music is infrequently performed, in part because it sounds strange to Western ears (and is not conveniently available to instruments with fixed pitches), it remains one of those secondary innovative ideas that have had more influence than is commonly acknowledged. Johnny Reinhard (1956), a young American bassoonist, has been sponsoring festivals of microtonal music since 1981.

Read, Gardner. *Twentieth-Century Microtonal Notations*. Westport, CT: Greenwood, 1990.

MIES VAN DER ROHE, Ludwig (1886–1969). Unlike Le Corbusier (∗), Mies van der Rohe did not deviate from the International Style (∗) in any consequential way. *Contemporary Masterworks* (1991) makes a case for the Farnsworth House (1945–1950), designed early in Mies's stay in America, as an example of his break, even though it epitomizes the International Style in its unadorned geometries and glass walls. The book's contributor makes a claim for "the placement of furniture": "Functional and aesthetic requirements were carefully balanced. With sophistication and subtlety, beds, chairs, and tables served as counterpoints to the fixed elements, animating the total composition and enhancing the total spatial experience." Mies also coined one of modernism's most popular aphorisms, "Less is more," which is only sometimes true.

Arsenault, Andrea Kalish. "Ludwig Mies van der Rohe." In *Contemporary Masterworks*, ed. Colin Naylor. London, England: St. James, 1991.

Mies van der Rohe. Chicago, IL: Art Institute, 1986.

MINIMAL MUSIC. See MODULAR MUSIC; YOUNG, La Monte

MINIMALISM (c. 1965). The idea of doing more with less was so persuasive that, once Minimalism was articulated in the late 1960s (first by whom remains a question of dispute), it conquered not only the arts but arts writing. The term particularly refers to work with a usually low degree of differentiation, which is to say a monochromic (or nearly monochromic) canvas or a piece of music composed with only a few notes, ideally to suggest, at times by critical inference, meanings that would otherwise be unavailable. (Processes of inference could be used to locate a work's ultimate meanings outside of itself, say in the contexts of art history.) Once the idea of Minimalism won adherents, many earlier artists could be identified as proto-Minimalists— among others, Kazimir Malevich (∗) in painting, or Tony Smith (∗) in sculpture. Back in his *System and Dialectics of Art* (1937), the Russian-born American painter John Graham (∗) mentioned the "reducing of painting to the minimum ingredients for the sake of discovering the ultimate, logical destination of painting in the process of abstracting." At first the term also referred to work that revealed a meager amount of artist's work, such as Marcel Duchamp's (∗) exhibition of a urinal, but most art reflecting that strategy has since assumed other names. I have used it to characterize poems, such as certain texts by Yvor Winters (∗) and Robert Lax

(∗), among others, with drastically few words. Used sometimes to refer to fiction that by most measures is scarcely Minimal, containing as it does full pages of conventional sentences, the term fell (much like "Happenings" [∗] just before it) into the mouths of opportunistic publicists who, for their success, necessarily depended upon ignorance of what the term really meant and honored.

Baker, Kenneth. *Minimalism*. NY: Abbeville, 1989.

MIXED-MEANS THEATER (c. 1960). This was my epithet, in a book of that title, for performances that de-emphasize speech in the course of using a variety of means, including human bodies, lights, film, objects, and stagecraft. Even though the term did not become common parlance, I find it useful for encompassing pure Happenings (∗), which was only a certain kind of piece done by Allan Kaprow (∗), along with the film-based staged performances of Robert Whitman (∗) and kinetic environments of, say, USCO (∗) or La Monte Young (∗). To distinguish among various genres, my book proposed this typology.

"Closed" space was my euphemism for a theater, which could also be any kind of enclosed performance space; "variable" time could range from a few seconds to infinity, depending upon the performance. The assumption of a "Happening" was that generalized instructions could generate unforeseen results. The chapters of my book are extended interviews with practitioners who seemed major at the time: Robert Rauschenberg (∗), Ann(a) Halprin (∗), Claes Oldenburg (∗), John Cage (∗), Ken Dewey (1934–1972), and the artists mentioned before. Not unlike the classic old fogey, I think this mixed-means theater superior to that performer-centered Performance Art (∗) that became more prominent in the 1980s; and, as a contrarian resistant to fads, I think I'm right.

Kostelanetz, Richard. *The Theatre of Mixed Means* (1968). NY: Archae Editions, 1980.

MODERNISM. What this book is about: art reflecting modern times, which includes the development of new technologies, the spread of alternative ideas, the influence of new arts upon one another, the transcendence of transient content and transience-based media (aka journalism), unprecedented appreciation of innovation, among other processes that continue, indicating that modernism has not ended any more than "modern times" have ended. Any theory that advocates the end of modernism in art, usually for the purpose of justifying retrograde and probably inferior work, should not be called "postmodernist" (∗) but "anti-modernist." The most authentic history of modernism today will be the one that ignores "postmodernism" for the opportunism that it is. Accept no substitutes. One reason for writing this *Dictionary* has been to defend modernism and modernist standards not only from traditionalists, who have scarcely disappeared, but from their de facto allies, the Philistines disguised as sophisticates. To define my position, consider this from Paul Mann: "Studies that focus on the similarity or partnership between modernism and the avant-garde tend to emphasize aesthetic issues, whereas studies that argue for the distinction between them tend to emphasize ideology." With this thought in mind, consider how many prominent "critics" proclaiming the death of the avant-garde vulgarize their polemic with one or another ideological bias.

Bradbury, Malcolm, and James McFarlane, eds. *Modernism*. NY: Penguin, 1976.

Mann, Paul. *The Theory-Death of the Avant-Garde*. Bloomington, IN: Indiana University, 1991.

Types of Mixed-Means Theater

GENRE	SPACE	TIME	ACTIONS
Pure Happenings	Open	Variable	Variable
Staged Happenings	Closed	Variable	Variable
Staged performance	Closed	Fixed	Fixed
Kinetic environments	Closed	Variable	Fixed

MODULAR MUSIC. In the middle seventies, most of this work was first called Minimal (*) music, in acknowledgment of self-imposed severe limitations on the use of musical materials (and perhaps to capitalize upon the growing reputation of Minimal visual art); but since all of its practitioners (other than La Monte Young [*]) produced work far more various in surface texture than monochromic paintings or simple geometrical shapes, another epithet would be more appropriate. I prefer "modular" in that composers/performers such as Philip Glass (*), Steve Reich (*), Terry Riley (*), Meredith Monk (*), Jon Gibson (*), John Adams (1947), and the Canadian composer Lubomyr Melnyck (1948), among others, tend to use circumscribed musical materials, such as a limited number of phrases (e.g., Terry Riley's *In C*), as modules that are repeated either in different ways or in different combinations with other instruments.

Dreier, Ruth. "Minimal Music." In *The New Grove Dictionary of American Music*, eds. H. Wiley Hitchcock and Stanley Sadie. NY: Macmillan, 1986.

Melnyck, Lubomyr. *KMH: Piano Music in the Continuous Mode.* Toronto, Canada: Music Gallery 18, 1978.

MOHOLY-NAGY, László (1895–1946). Born in Hungary, Moholy, as he was commonly called, produced masterful paintings as well as writing first-rate books. In Berlin, he made innovative and influential book designs, photographs that are sometimes exhibited and reprinted, films that are still screened, sculptures that are in MoMA and other major museums, all while developing a revolutionary program of artistic education. He worked across the constraints of professional training and the disciplinary conventions still associated with artists' standard careers. He made arts he was not expected to make and produced work in domains where he had neither specialized schooling nor apprenticeship.

The key ideas of Moholy's sensibility had their origins in the Bauhaus (*)/Constructivist (*) synthesis. Nearly everything he did favored rectangular and circular forms. As the designer of the first great series of modern art books, the Bauhaus editions, he repudiated both "gray inarticulate machine typesetting" on the one hand and highly ornamental beaux-arts affectations in typography on the other. His alternative was the now familiar hyperrectangular "modern" style, in which illustrations and occasional epigraphs mix with paragraphs sometimes prefaced by boldface subheadings in two-page spreads of rectangular blocks of uniform, justified, sans-serif type that are always much narrower than the width of the page. Visually the design of a typical Moholy page could be characterized as rectangles within rectangles, with no disruptive ornaments. One virtue of his style is placing illustrations in close proximity to commentary about them. The epitome is Moholy's overlooked masterpiece, *Vision in Motion* (1946), a book he designed and wrote in American English while living in Chicago.

In his paintings are rectangles, straight lines, and the regular curves of circles, parabolas, and spirals, sometimes overlapping. Even in his artistic inventions—such as the Space Modulator, made by putting a sheet of Plexiglas a few inches above a background canvas so that shapes painted on or cut out of the Plexiglas make shadows on the canvas—Moholy favored his idiosyncratic iconography. It can be found as well in his photography: not only in the representational pictures he took in various cities but in his photograms and photomontages (*). Even in commissioned assignments, such as the photographs for *John Betjeman's Oxford* (1938), Moholy put a geometric image in the center of every picture. These Moholyan forms also appear in his stage designs; in his poster art for all sorts of commercial products, including conveniently geometric automobile tires; and in his 1946 extraordinarily brilliant charting of multiple referents in James Joyce's (*) *Finnegans Wake* (*), which had been published only a few years before.

This last artifact appeared in *Vision in Motion*, which I take to be Moholy's single greatest creation, representing the sum of his imagination and intelligence. Not only is it the single most insightful survey I know of avant-garde modernism in the arts (including literature, in a chapter often ignored), *Vision in Motion* is also an "artist's book" of the very highest order, demonstrating that few practitioners of any art ever wrote as well or as truly about their own esthetic aspirations. Appearing posthumously, it concludes an artist's life as only a book can do.

Moholy-Nagy, L. *Vision in Motion*. Chicago, IL: Paul Theobald, 1947.

Kostelanetz, Richard, ed. *Moholy-Nagy* (1970). 2nd ed. NY: Da Capo, 1991.

——. *On Innovative Art(ist)s*. Jefferson, NC: McFarland, 1992.

Passuth, Krisztina. *Moholy-Nagy*. NY: Thames & Hudson, 1985.

MOHR, Manfred (1938). A pioneering computer artist, Mohr owned his own PDP-11 computer well before most writers had their word processors. Trained in fine art, married to a mathematician, he began as a concrete (rather than mystical) Constructivist (∗) committed to rational structures in black-and-white art. His book-art book (∗), *Artificiata I* (1968), contains a succession of geometric shapes on a continuous field of horizontal lines, broaching narrative in the transitions from page to page. Soon afterwards, he began to use the computer not to execute drawings (which has become its predominant use) but to find possible shapes through inventing algorithms, or a logical set of rules, to generate results that he could then realize initially on a computer-assisted plotter. "Generative art" was an appropriate term he used for such work. One of his principal subjects has been the hypercube, a geometric figure incorporating many dimensions, which he typically subjects to exhaustive alternatives. A principal paradox of Mohr's work is that it can be rationally understood, with generally verifiable perceptions, even though at first glance it may appear inscrutable. He is an extremely intelligent artist in the sense that he knows how to optimally realize his purposes and his works represent what he says they should. In Mohr's work, the critic Richard Gassen finds a search "for the 'integrated art work,' as he calls it, a structure from which all works can be derived, a 'hyper-structure' that one day will encompass all his works."

Mohr, Manfred. "Programmed Esthetics." In *Esthetics Contemporary*, ed. Richard Kostelanetz. 2nd ed. Buffalo, NY: Prometheus, 1989.

Gassen, Richard, et al. *Fractured Symmetry: Algorithmic Works 1967–1987*. Ludwigshafen, Germany: Wilhelm-Haack-Museum, 1988.

MON, Franz (1926; b. F. Lofferholz). One of the most persistent and consistent German avant-garde writers, Mon has produced collections and selections of his poems, in addition to radio plays, that for one measure of their excellence are frequently rebroadcast. He also collaborated with two others in editing *Movens* (1960), one of those rare landmark anthologies that announced accurately the more experimental directions to come. Mon's typographic texts have been exhibited around the world.

Mon, Franz, et al., eds. *Movens*. Wiesbaden, Germany: Limes, 1960.

MONDRIAN, Piet (1872–1944; b. P. Mondriaan). Though the best geometric paintings resemble one another more than anything else, any sense of a single family is an illusion. Whereas one line reflects a rational Constructivism (∗) that includes Moholy-Nagy (∗), Sol LeWitt (∗), François Morellet (∗), and Manfred Mohr (∗), another strain, epitomized by traditional Islamic art and among the moderns Mondrian, regards geometries as a key to ultimate truths. It should first be said that Mondrian came to his mature, familiar style after many years of doing something else. His first known paintings are landscapes; he painted flowers; he passed through Cubism (∗) to a style that abstracted lines and rectangles from naturalistic scenes. Joining those artists, mostly Dutch, gathered around *De Stijl* (∗) in 1917, he developed a compositional style, limited to horizontals and verticals, that he called Neo-Plasticism. Making precision an ideal, he eliminated from these paintings all signs of brushstrokes and individual technique. A purist, Mondrian objected to van Doesburg's (∗) use of diagonals and over that issue, incredible though it seems, broke with *De Stijl*. Should you think Mondrian a dogged rationalist, consider his writings, which include his "opposition to art which is purely abstract. In removing completely from the work all objects, 'the world is not separated from the spirit,' but is on the contrary, *put into a balanced opposition* with the spirit, since the one and the other are purified. This creates a perfect unity between the two opposites." He continues, "Precisely by its existence non-figurative art shows that 'art' *continues always on its true road*. It shows that 'art' is *not the expression of the appearance of reality such as we see it, nor of the life which we live*, but that *it is the expression of true reality and true life. . . indefinable but realizable in plastics*." Surprised, aren't you?

Mondrian, Piet. *The New Art—The New Life* (1986). Ed. and trans. Harry Holtzman and Martin S. James. NY: Da Capo, 1993.

————. "Plastic Art and Pure Plastic Art." In *Circle*, eds. J. L. Martin, et al. London, England: Faber, 1937.

MONK, Meredith (1942). A major mixed-means (*) performance artist, Monk has, since her breakthrough *16 Millimetre Earrings* (1966), created a rich series of performance pieces incorporating choreography, music, language, and film customarily produced mostly, if not entirely, by herself. She has explored alternative theatrical spaces, performing the three parts of *Juice* (1969) weeks apart in a museum, a university theater, and a downtown loft. Much of Monk's work is autobiographical to differing degrees; much, epitomized by *Education of the Girlchild* (1974), has content congruent with feminism. Working separately in various arts, she is most successful as a composer, especially when she sings by herself her own compositions in an eerily unique voice. She has also produced discrete films and, with less success, an opera, *Atlas* (1991).

Monk, Meredith. *Key*. Los Angeles, CA: Increase 2008, 1971.

————. *Dolmen Music*. Munich, Germany: ECM 1197 2301 197, 1981.

MOOG, Robert (1934). Moog invented the first generally available Electronic Music (*) synthesizer (*). Whereas the previous comprehensive music-making machines were unique behemoths that filled whole rooms, Moog combined his experience as a builder of Theremins (*) (a touch-sensitive continuous sound generator) with the new transistor technology. As a synthesizer in the purest sense of the word, Moog's machine worked by combining discrete parts into an aural whole, producing sounds that represented, literally, syntheses of different specifications of elements. By no means a composing (i.e., decision-making) machine, in that it makes no musical choices, a synthesizer merely executes musical designs that, like the traditional score, customarily precede the composer's contact with the instrument. The initial Moogs of the late 1960s were monophonic, which is to say capable of producing only one note at a time; later Moogs were polyphonic. Among the most expert Moogists is Wendy Carlos (*). By the 1980s, there were so

many synthesizers, most of them technically more advanced, that Moogs became antiques, while Moog himself became an advisor to some of the successor manufacturers.

Kostelanetz, Richard. "Robert Moog (1970)." In *On Innovative Music(ian)s*. NY: Limelight, 1989.

MORELLET, François (1926). Though for most of his adult life the manager of a family factory, Morellet has been a prolific and consistent artist specializing in rationally derived, superficially simple, and yet awesomely clever geometric works that generate complex structures. Implicitly rejecting Mondrian's (*) reliance upon intuition, Morellet has worked with systems, which are customarily announced in the title of his pieces (e.g., "6 Canvases with a 5m Perimeter and a Horizontal Diagonal," 1973), and it follows that Morellet denies Mondrian's obsession with hidden meanings. He speaks of families of systems: juxtaposition; superimposition; random; interference; fragmentation; and destabilization. As a painter and book-artist, Morellet has worked almost exclusively in black and white.

Morellet has also made light objects and kinetic sculptures. Edward Lucie-Smith (1933) describes "*sphère-trames* (sphere-webs)—a sphere made up of rods laid at right angles to one another to form a cellular structure which, through its multiple perspectives, has strange effects on light. A related work is a lattice of fluorescent tubes, which seems to dissolve the wall behind it." In significant respects, Morellet's art predates similar developments in the work of Frank Stella (*), Donald Judd (*), and Sol LeWitt (*), among others. Morellet has written about wanting to "reduce my arbitrary decisions to a minimum. To put limits on my 'artist's' sensibility, I among others have made use of simple and obvious systems, of pure chance, and of spectator participation."

François Morellet. Berlin, Germany: Nationalgalerie, 1977.

Kotik, Charlotta, et al. *François Morellet: Systems*. Buffalo and Brooklyn, NY: Albright-Knox and Brooklyn Museum, 1984.

MORGAN, Edwin (1920). A Glasgow academic, Morgan has produced, along with scholarship, several poems that rank among the best of the era. "Opening the Cage" is a sonnet based upon fourteen variations of the fourteen words in John Cage's (∗) "I have nothing to say and I am saying it and that is poetry." "The Chaffinch Map of Scotland" uses a few typically Scottish words to represent the shape of his native land. "Pomander" uses words that sound like the title word to make that fruit's shape, the visual prosody (such as the repeated *p*s) complementing the aural. (This updating of the George Herbert shape poem is superior to the American poet John Hollander's [1929] forays in the same direction in *Types of Shape* [1969, 1991], which suffer, curiously, from prosaic language.) "Seven Headlines" finds English words embedded in the French phrase "il faut être absolument moderne." "Space Poem 1" mixes English words with Russian, the latter apparently chosen for their sounds. One virtue of Morgan's experimental poems is that each invention is unique to one poem; none of his alternative devices are repeated.

Morgan, Edwin. *The Second Life: Selected Poems*. Edinburgh, Scotland: Edinburgh University, 1967.

MORGENSTERN, Christian (1871–1914). Though he might have intended otherwise, Morgenstern is best remembered for his nonsense poems and a certain wordless poem composed entirely of typographical marks (dashes and parentheses tilted 90 degrees and thus arrayed horizontally, like inverted umbrellas) and customarily translated as "Fish's Nightsong." Martin Seymour-Smith credits Morgenstern with anticipating "most of the modern tendencies that came after his early death from tuberculosis [among them] the realization that bourgeois 'values' are mechanisms for self-evasion, experiments with words as things-in-themselves as well as (arbitrary?) symbols of things they denote." The American translation mentioned below curiously omits the classic Morgenstern sound/nonsense poem "Das grosse Lalula," which begins: "Kroklowafzl? Semememl!/ Selokrontro—prafriplo:/ Bifzl, bafzl: hulalemi:/ quastl bastl bo. . ./ Lalu lalu lalu lalu la!" perhaps because no translation is necessary.

Morgenstern, Christian. *Gallows Songs*. Trans. W.D. Snodgrass and Lore Segal. Ann Arbor, MI: University of Michigan, 1967.

MORICE, Dave (1947). One of Morice's original ideas was a poetry marathon in which he would write as many poems as possible within an extended period of time, usually in a public place. Morice claims to have written "a thousand poems in twelve hours, a mile-long poem, and a poem across the Delaware River." His feats belong in the *Guinness Book of World Records*, among other competitors to this *Dictionary*. Remembering two principles—that a special mentality can produce special work and that if you write a lot you increase the likelihood that something might be good—I would wager that somewhere in this produce is some remarkable poetry. A second Morice idea was to cast the words of poems, both classic and contemporary (Allen Ginsberg [∗], W.C. Williams [∗], John Cage [∗]), into comic strips of various styles, at once introducing the poems and, largely through images, making his own ironic commentary on the texts. Under the heading "abuse the muse," these poetry comics first appeared as a photocopied periodical and then in an oversize book that, since it came from a hypercommercial publisher, quickly disappeared from public view. A third idea was the creation of a female pseudonym, Joyce Holland (1969–1978), whose specialty was Minimal (∗) poems, in contrast to Morice's garrulous predisposition. The classic, in collaboration with the late Darrell Gray (1945–1980), is "Days of the Week": "mungday . twosday . weedsday . thirty . fryday . sat her day .

Dave Morice, "Poetry Comicard #13," © 1982. *Courtesy the artist.*

someday." An actress claiming to be Holland often appeared, usually with Morice in tow, at art festivals and at conferences. Holland was also the editor-in-name of *Matchbook* (1973–1974), in which one-word poems by many authors were stapled into a matchbook cover. He is one of the few writers mentioned in this book to have an M.F.A. from the mass-production lines of the Writer's Workshop at the University of Iowa.

Holland, Joyce. *The Final E: Selected Poems 1969–73.* Iowa City, IA: X Press, 1978.

Morice, Dave. *Poetry Comics.* NY: Simon & Schuster, 1982.

———. *A Visit from St. Alphabet.* Pennington, NJ: a cappella, 1993.

———. *More Poetry Comics.* Pennington, NJ: a cappella, forthcoming.

MORRIS, Robert (1931). A radical sculptor and sculptural theorist, working with a variety of alternative ideas, Morris produced in the late 1960s a series of works, accompanied by several essays, that challenge previous ideas in several ways. Morris favored sculptors working outside of the studio, with materials offered by nature, such as earth; the use of previously neglected materials, such as felt, whose shapes necessarily depend upon gravity; and the creation of easily comprehended structures, which he called "unitary" forms, in contrast to the Cubist (*) complexity of, say, David Smith (*). The result is work that presented a single image, rather than interrelated parts. "Such are the simpler forms that create strong gestalt sensations," Morris wrote at the time. "Their parts are bound together in such a way that they offer the maximum resistance to perceptual separation. In terms of solids, or forms applicable to sculpture, these gestalts are the simpler polyhedrons." Unlike Donald Judd (*), who has similar biases, Morris eschewed modular formats. He also collaborated in mixed-means (*) performance.

Michelson, Annette. *Robert Morris.* Washington, DC: Corcoran Gallery, 1969.

MOSOLOV, Alexander (1900–1973). His contribution to the avant-garde tradition was the use of shaking sheet metal to suggest the sound of a working factory in his composition *Zavod* (Iron Foundry, 1927). Like the composer Nicolas Slonimsky (*), Mosolov wrote songs to the texts of newspaper advertisements. Slonimsky the lexicographer reports that such explicitly proletarian music "elicited a sharp rebuke from the official arbiters of Soviet music. On Feb. 4, 1936, he was expelled from the Union of Soviet Composers for staging drunken brawls and behaving rudely to waiters in restaurants. He was sent to Turkestan to collect folk songs as a move toward his rehabilitation." (If not for the historic Soviet Union, we could regard the U.S.A. as incomparably inhospitable to the avant-garde.) Mosolov does not rate an entry in John Vinton's *Dictionary of Contemporary Music* (1974), perhaps because, unlike many of the lesser composers included, Mosolov was not connected to an American university that purchases books.

Mosolov, Alexander. *Four Newspaper Advertisements, Op. 21; Three Children's Sketches, Op. 18.* Moscow, Russia: Melodiya MCD 170, 1990.

MOSS, David (1949). A large man, trained in percussion, Moss has been concerned with alternatives in the placement of his drums and thus with different physical strategies in using available soundmakers. Meanwhile, he developed a unique kind of propulsive scat singing, reflecting a variety of declamatory styles but commonly identifiable as uniquely his. Usually in conjunction with amplifiers that he controls while he sings (sometimes playing percussion as well), he succeeds at what many other composers have tried to do far less effectively—making music that suggests the end of the world. Not unlike others active on the current "performance scene," Moss tours widely and collaborates generously, reportedly having given over a thousand discrete concerts.

Moss, David. "Language Linkage" (1988). In *The Aerial #1.* Santa Fe, NM: Nonsequitur Foundation (P.O. Box 15118, 87506), 1990.

MOSTEL, Rafael (1948). Mostel's innovation comes from using ancient Eastern artifacts, Tibetan Singing Bowls, to play distinctly contemporary music. Actually made to receive sounds rather than make them, the small bowls respond to wooden mallets run around their rims. Realizing that the different acoustics of various venues can affect the humming sound of these bowls, Mostel has performed in New York's Central Park, which has little echo amid an abundance of natural sounds, and in the humongous Cathedral of St. John the Divine, which has a rich extended echo. In these performances, Mostel adds such Eastern instruments as wooden and clay flutes, thigh-bone trumpets, a ram's horn, and various kinds of non-Western percussion.

Mostel, Rafael. *Night Songs*. NY: Digital Fossils #1008 (P.O. Box 1066, Cooper Station, 10276), 1992.

MOTHER MALLARD'S PORTABLE MASTER-PIECE COMPANY (c. 1969). Founded by David Bordon (1938), they were among the first to play Moog (∗) synthesizers live, performing mostly modular music (∗), successfully demonstrating that an instrument thought to belong exclusively to the recording studio (thanks to Wendy Carlos [∗]) could also be used on a concert stage. In their first New York City concert, three musicians played several Moogs, incorporating a variety of riffs that overlapped one another, each musician beginning his or her bit before the other was finished. Not unlike other early compositions for the Moog, their music relied heavily upon the "sequencer," as it was called, which could easily generate the repetition characteristic of modular music. The group survived in spite of unjustified neglect, caused in part by residing in Ithaca, rather than New York City, and by changing personnel. MMPMC set a precedent not only for other live synthesists but for later groups like *The Hub*, which is composed of Chris Brown, John Bishoff, Mark Trayle, Tim Perkins, Scott Gresham-Lancaster, and Phill Stone sitting before cathode-ray tubes, not only generating computer music in live time but also silently sending one another word-messages that appear on their screens, supposedly altering their collaborative performance.

Mother Mallard's Portable Masterpiece Co. Ithaca, NY: Earthquack EQ0001 (1191 East Shore Drive, 14850), 1973.

MTV (1982). Its technical innovation, to stretch that noun, is presenting music-based video art in which no scene is more than a few seconds long, purportedly because its viewers have the attention span of young children. Although the songs behind the video might have a few *minutes* of unbroken sound, the picture hops from image to image, from singer(s) to accompanying scene, with a rapidity more typical of commercials (making it hard for the MTV viewer to distinguish between the official commercials and the programming). The epitome of this MTV style in my experience is *Decade: MTV's Review of the 1980s* (1989), billed as "a sight and sound explosion"—a two-hour "documentary" that must be seen to be believed, as history is compressed, or chopped apart, into scenes as short as those in commercials. Nothing, not even interviews with distinguished informants, is given sufficient time (or space) to be more important than anything else. Those of us accustomed to exposition, even expositions as short as those in this book, question the efficacy of this lightning-fast style in conveying understanding. It is unfortunate that the MTV intelligence has infiltrated video art (∗), where any extended, continuous shot has come, merely by contrast, to be a measure of mature intelligence.

Available from your local cable television company.

MULTI-TRACKING (c. 1960). This is one of the great technical innovations in the development of recorded music, comparable to the development of the typewriter in the production of writing. The original recording technologies—first the wax cylinder, then discs, then wire, and finally audiotape—were monophonic in the sense that they could record only one line of sound. Two-track tape recorders arrived in the 1950s, to record simultaneously live sound through two separate microphones, each of which purportedly had a different perspective (comparable to that of two eyes). It later became possible to record or modify each track separately without affecting the other.

In the 1960s came four-track tape, with the possibility of four-line recording, which was what the Beatles used to create their *Sgt. Pepper's Lonely Hearts Club Band* album, and thus the opportunity to produce in the late 1960s "quadraphonic" records for those listeners with four loudspeakers.

In the 1970s came tape with sixteen, twenty-four, thirty-two, and even sixty-four tracks, each of which could be recorded independently of the others; so that sound producers were offered the possibility of adding sounds well after the original tapings were made. Sounds from each of these tracks could then be modified in the "mixing down" process to the stereophonic (two-track) tape required for standard distribution. Each of these technological developments generated alternative musical possibilities.

With the advent in the late 1980s of digital (∗) editing consoles, such as the Lexicon Opus, a simulation of multi-tracking could appear on a computer screen; so that instead of going through the cumbersome process of rerecording a sound on, say, track two to have it begin a few seconds earlier, the audio engineer/computer operator needed only to punch a few instructions into his machine, greatly accelerating the re-editing process.

Holmes, Thomas B. *Electronic and Experimental Music.* NY: Scribner's, 1985.

MUNRO, Thomas (1897–1974). An encyclopedic art historian, Munro championed as early as 1928 "Scientific Method in Esthetics," which he defined as "broadly experimental and empirical, but not limited to quantitative measurement; utilizing the insights of art criticism and philosophy as hypotheses, but deriving objective data from two main sources—the analysis and history of form in the arts, and psychological studies of the production, appreciation, and teaching of the arts." However, to establish the preconditions for such an esthetics, Munro, very much a positivist, wrote several prodigiously exhaustive, valuable, needlessly forgotten studies of the categories of artistic endeavor, *The Arts and Their Interrelations* (1949), and then historiographical theory in *Evolution and Art* (1963). His interest in "scientific" esthetics parallels that of the Harvard mathematician George Birkhoff (∗).

Munro, Thomas. *The Arts and Their Interrelations* (1949). Rev. ed. Cleveland, OH: Case Western Reserve University, 1967.

———. *Form and Style in the Arts.* Cleveland, OH: Case Western Reserve University, 1970.

MURAYAMA, Tomoyoshi (1901–1977). Murayama introduced Dada (∗) to Japan. After spending several months of 1922 in Berlin, he returned with an esthetic platform he called "Conscious Construction," even though it resembled Dada more than Constructivism (∗). Once home, he quickly mounted several exhibitions, mostly of small works, because, as Tsutomu Mizusawa writes, "He could not wait for larger pieces to arrive by sea freight. He called the show 'Exhibition of Small Conscious Constructivist Works by Tomoyoshi Murayama Dedicated to the "Overbearing Beauty" of Niddy Impekoven.'" She was a teenage dancer in Berlin. Mizusawa continues, "Looking at the catalog made of art paper, which was unusual for the time, we see four photographs. The three photographs of the works are a valuable record since most of them were destroyed during the war, but the photograph of the artist himself is even more interesting. We see Murayama here as a dancer. He appears with long hair cut in the *Buben-kopf* style (a kind of Dutch-boy), which was to become the trademark of the Mavo group, bare feet, and wearing a dark-colored tunic, posing self-consciously for the camera." Mizusawa concludes, "There was probably no other artist who had made his debut in the Japanese art world quite this way before."

Murayama's ideas spawned a group called Mavo, which, according to Mizusawa, "broke down the boundaries of the art system, and carried out activities on the stage of Tokyo quite different in character from anything done by the established art societies." One associate made a "sound constructor" of oil cans, logs, and wire, while Murayama designed modernist stage sets, especially for productions in translation of German avant-garde plays. After publishing several issues of a monthly magazine, Mavo fell apart. By the late 1920s, Murayama had assimilated Marxism and moved into making political theater that was esthetically less significant.

Mizusawa, Tsutomu. "Japanese Dada and Constructivism: Aspects of the Early 1920s"; and Toshiharu Omuka, "To Make All of Myself Boil Over." In Andrei B. Nakov, Marc Dachy, et al. *Dada Constructivism.* Tokyo, Japan: Seibu Museum of Art, 1988.

MUSIQUE CONCRÈTE (c. 1947). This epithet arose after World War II, in the wake of the development of magnetic audiotape. Sound had previously been recorded on wax cylinder, shellac disc, or magnetic wire, none of which offered the opportunity for neat editing. Tape, by contrast, could be cut with a razor blade, much like film, its loose ends spliced together with a minimum of audible signs. Musique concrète differs from subsequent Electronic Music (∗) in drawing only upon the sounds of the world, rather than artificial sound generators. These natural sounds could then be played at faster or slower speeds, modifying not only pitch and rhythm but timbre, while parts separately recorded could be spliced together. Once stereo and then multi-track (∗) tape were developed, the composer could play separately produced sounds simultaneously. One practical advantage was that the tape composer did not need to know how to read music.

As the epithet suggests, the prime movers of musique concrète were based in Paris, often working at European radio stations: Pierre Henry (1927) and Pierre Schaeffer (1910). The masterpiece in this mode is John Cage's (∗) *Williams Mix* (1953), which consists of six tapes, each made from the tiniest feasible fragments, that are designed to emerge from six transducers/speakers simultaneously (but not synchronously) as a kind of prerecorded chorus. One familiar example of musique concrète is John Lennon's (∗) "Revolution No. 9" (1968), which is as close to contemporary avant-garde music as any Beatle ever came; it purportedly has a different sound if played backwards (a feat possible only with reel-to-reel audiotape). A later term for audiotape produced mostly from live sources is "electroacoustic" (∗), as distinct from Electronic Music.

Cage, John. *Williams Mix* (1953). In *The 25-Year Retrospective Concert of the Music of John Cage*. Riverdale, NY: George Avakian (795 W. 254th St., 10471), 1958.

Electronic Music/Musique Concrète [with twelve composers]. N.p.: Mercury SR-2-9123, n.d.

MUYBRIDGE, Eadweard (1830–1904; b. Edward Muggeride). Born in England, he came to America in 1852 and settled in San Francisco in 1855. As a pioneering photographer, Muybridge took early pictures of Yosemite Valley and, in 1867, became Director of Photographic Surveys for the U.S. Government. Influenced by American landscape painting, he became interested in representing photographically unusual atmospheric effects. Beginning in 1878, Muybridge used several still cameras to portray movement, initially of a galloping horse, later of nude men and women. This led to his development of a "zoopraxiscope," as he called it, in which motion could be reproduced through a sequence of photographs mounted on the inside of a rotating cylinder. The books collecting his motion studies, at once accurate and evocative, remain in print.

Muybridge, Eadweard. *Muybridge's Complete Human and Animal Locomotion* (1887). NY: Dover, n.d. (c. 1975).

MYERS, George, Jr. (1953). Myers began as a small-press (∗) publisher who worked nights at a local newspaper in Harrisburg, Pennsylvania. On the side Myers wrote the essays that became *An Introduction to Modern Times* (1982), which was then and still remains a good and true guide to emerging esthetic alternatives. He also produced the abstract visual poems (∗) that became *The News* (1985) and *Sub-Text* (1987). *Alphabets Sublime* (1986) is a book of interviews with Bern Porter (∗), Paul Zelevansky (∗), John M. Bennett (∗), Kenneth Gangemi (∗), and Carolee Schneemann (∗), among others. In 1984 Myers became a book editor and occasional columnist at the Columbus (Ohio) *Post-Dispatch* and subsequently the winner of a state award for "criticism," but neither his poetry nor his criticism of the avant-garde has been the same since. The only other American newspaperperson known to be doing advanced writing and publishing is Jerry Madson in Bemidji, Minnesota. Perhaps there are others.

Myers, George, Jr. *An Introduction to Modern Times*. N.p. (Grosse Point Farms, MI): Lunchroom (P.O. Box 36027, 48236), 1982.

NABOKOV, Vladimir (1899–1977). An aristocratic Russian emigré of profoundly conservative prejudices, Nabokov nonetheless wrote one truly avant-garde novel, a book so original and subtle that it is easily misunderstood, even by his academic biographers. Written in the wake of *Lolita*'s success and Nabokov's retirement from university teaching, *Pale Fire* (1962) consists of a long poem, attributed to an American poet named John Shade, followed by an elaborate commentary by Kinbote, an African-born scholar teaching in America. Though some commentators, including a recent Nabokov biographer, have praised the poem as masterful, it strikes me to be a subtle parody of Robert Frost in particular and American poetics in general. Kinbote's commentary is the work of a megalomaniac whose typical stunt is to see himself and his experience as a deposed African prince writ large in lines that don't ostensibly refer to him at all. This misreading becomes a sustained joke that only gets bigger with each Kinbote abuse of Shade's text, all abetted by the reader's suspicion that if Kinbote were a sufficiently titled academic, his juniors would no doubt kowtow to his delusions. My own hunch is that, in the course of writing his elaborate commentary to Pushkin's *Eugene Onegin*, Nabokov, as a profound ironist, decided to write a fiction about a madman (with an aristocratic emigré background superficially similar to his own) writing a skewed commentary.

Nabokov, Vladimir. *Pale Fire*. NY: Putnam, 1962.

NAGY, Paul. See PAPP, Tibor

NANCARROW, Conlon (1912). Born in Arkansas, initially a trumpeter in jazz (∗) orchestras, Nancarrow studied composition with Nicolas Slonimsky (∗) and Roger Sessions (1896–1985). Having fought with the Abraham Lincoln Brigade on the Loyalist side in Spain, he emigrated to Mexico City, where he still lives, and became a Mexican citizen. After producing undistinguished music for conventional instruments, he began in the late 1940s to compose directly on player-piano rolls, perforating the paper to mark notes and rhythms, incidentally rescuing an instrument commonly scorned. Thanks to such painstaking procedure, Nancarrow produced a kind of proto-electronic composition in the sense that he was using machines to make piano sounds whose rapid articulations and multiple voicings were beyond human capabilities. In his notes to recent Nancarrow CDs issued in Germany, James Tenney (∗) writes: "The two most distinctive characteristics of Nancarrow's work as a whole are his *rhythmic procedures* and his exploration of manifold types of *polyphonic texture*—and thereby, *polyphonic perception*. The most prominent of Nancarrow's explicit compositional concerns has always been rhythm. But an exploration of polyphonic texture, which follows almost of necessity from the fullest development of rhythm, may one day be seen as the area of his greatest achievement." Though Nancarrow has begun to receive greater recognition in the country of his birth, his music remains more available in Europe than America.

Nancarrow, Conlon. *Studies for Player Piano*. NY: Columbia MS 7222, 1970.

———. *Studies for Player Piano*. Vols. I–V. Mainz, Germany: Wergo 6168-2, 60166/67, 60165-50, 1988–1991.

NASH, Ogden (1902–1971). Surprise. Nash's prosaic subjects and corny sentiments notwithstanding, he was an inventive poet, beginning with couplets uniquely identifiable as his: "I think it very nice for ladies to be lithe and lissome,/ But not so much so that you cut yourself if you happen to embrace and kissome." Writing out of conventional forms, Nash played not only with fulfillment and violation but with symmetry and asymmetry, as in couplets such as: "I know another man who is an expert on everything from witchcraft and demonology to the Elizabethan drama,/ And he has spent a weekend with the Dalai Lama." This, like all good wit (as well as avant-garde art), depends upon unexpected shifts. As an alternative poet, Nash avoided what his contemporaries were doing—there is no myth, no symbolism, no enjambment, no obscurity, no deep mysteries or anything else that academic critics influential at the time would have thought particularly important. Nonetheless, the best Nash epitomizes Robert Frost's definition of poetry as that which cannot be translated. Just as limericks are unique to English, so is the best Nash, who made qualities indigenous to our language a favorite subject: "English is a language than which none is sublimer/ But it presents certain difficulties for the rhymer/ There are no rhymes for orange or silver/ Unless liberties you pilfer."

So strong is Nash's poetry that few remember that he also wrote stories, a kind of avant-garde skeletal fiction that depended not upon linguistic play but narrative ellipses (and incidentally makes subsequent so-called Minimal

(*) fictions seem verbose). This is the opening of "The Strange Case of Mr. Donnybrook's Boredoms":

> Once upon a time there was a man named Mr. Donnybrook.
> * * *
> He was married to a woman named Mrs. Donnybrook.
> * * *
> Mr. and Mrs. Donnybrook dearly loved to be bored.
> * * *
> Sometimes they were bored at the ballet, other times at the cinema.

This passage introduces a wild story about fantasies incurred during insomnia. Needless to say perhaps, this more extreme Nash has been less acceptable to anthologists than the pap-master.

Nash, Ogden. *The Pocket Book*. NY: Pocket, 1962.

THE NATIONAL ENDOWMENT FOR THE ARTS (1965; aka NEA). Founded as a minor contribution to Lyndon Johnson's Great Society, as a means of supporting the development of all the arts in America, the NEA has been uneven in its support of the American avant-garde, mostly because of different levels of sophistication in its various departments. On this issue, Media Arts and Visual Arts, say, have better records than Literature and Music, both of which in twenty-five years have rarely supported the writers and composers mentioned in this book, almost taking pride in their dogged Philistinism. Thus, the problem becomes that nobody at the higher NEA levels seems to care about persistent deviance in particular departments. Secondly, in contrast to more sophisticated European governmental cultural agencies, which often support avant-garde Americans (particularly in Germany), the NEA rarely supports comparable Europeans, to the detriment of our cultural reputation abroad. (You get the impression of administrators working overtime to look Bush league.)

The NEA's companion, the National Endowment for the Humanities (aka NEH), has an even sorrier record when presented with opportunities to support criticism/scholarship about avant-garde art and literature. I've written elsewhere that the NEH's outlook and politics—its devotion to hierarchy and a circumscribed collection of approved authorities, its enthusiasm for embarrassing America—are essentially Stalinist. The fact that Senator Jesse Helms, Patrick Buchanan, and their ilk have missed this last ripoff of the American taxpayer tells everyone all that need be known about their unfortunate ignorance and innocence. (My suspicion, which I've put into print before, is that these "conservatives'" attack on the NEA looks like a classic example of a KGB diversionary tactic.) The surest way to find out what the NEA and the NEH have actually done, rather than what people say they have done, is to get their *Annual Reports*, which are public documents.

Kostelanetz, Richard. *The Grants-Fix*. NY: Archae Editions (P.O. Box 73, Canal St., 10013), 1987.

NEA and NEH. *Annual Reports*. Washington, DC (1100 Pennsylvania Ave., N.W., 20506), 1967 to the present.

Zeigler, Joseph Wesley. *Arts in Crisis: The National Endowment for the Arts vs. America*. Pennington, NJ: a cappella, 1994.

NEVELSON, Louise (1899–1988). Nevelson's innovation was a sculptural image—more precisely, a rectangular relief, best viewed perpendicularly from the front—that is divided into smaller rectangular compartments containing miscellaneous scraps of wood, ranging from newel posts to pegs, sometimes including chair legs and other discarded wooden pieces and then painted entirely in a single color, usually black, sometimes white or gold. Though Nevelson did not change her compositional style after 1955, it did become more complex in internal relationships, culminating perhaps in the grandiose *Homage to the World* (1966). In the late sixties, she favored Plexiglas for open rectangles within a larger frame or smaller assemblages of geometric wooden parts within a Plexiglas case. Nevelson also did outdoor sculptures in aluminum and steel.

Nevelson, Louise. *Dawns and Dusks*. Ed. Diana MacKown. NY: Scribner's, 1976.

Glimcher, Arnold. *Louise Nevelson*. NY: Dutton, 1976.

NEW YORK SCHOOL, SCHOOL OF PARIS, BLACK MOUNTAIN POETS, etc. Any purportedly categorical classifications based upon geography, biography, sex, race, or academic background do not belong in art criticism, as they say nothing significant about the style of an artist's work.

Such epithets customarily function as sales slogans, capitalizing upon the favorable auras of key words (e.g., New York, Paris, feminism, etc.) in the marketing both of works and of opinions (and even "critical" books), mostly to establish significance for art or artists about which and whom nothing more substantial can be said. Whereas some consumers of art lap up these sorts of deceptions, others avoid them like a plague. *Caveat emptor.*

Too many examples, many of them book-length, to cite.

NEWMAN, Barnett (1905–1970). Though a painting contemporary of de Kooning (*) and Pollock (*), Newman created a different sort of work, proceeding from different assumptions, which was thus not acknowledged until the 1960s. Typical works consist of a predominantly monochromic canvas interrupted by only a few contrasting marks that often take the form of vertical stripes. *The Wild* (1950), for instance, was nearly eight feet high and only one and five-eighths inches wide. Because Newman's first one-person exhibitions in 1950 and 1951 aroused hostile responses, he did not show again in New York until 1959, when he was in his mid-fifties.

Only with a 1966 exhibition at the Guggenheim Museum, featuring his *Stations of the Cross*, was his genius fully acknowledged. In the fourteen paintings comprising that work, each six and one-half feet by five feet, the traditional Biblical narrative is "told" through vertical stripes of various widths and shapes, against a background field of raw canvas, so that the absence of familiar iconography becomes a commentary on the classic myth as well as an echo of the simple cosmological forms of primitive art. His most notable sculpture, *Broken Obelisk* (1963–1967), is similarly vertical, with a ground-based pyramid on whose pointed top is balanced a rectangular volume whose bottom comes to a point. In retrospect, Newman can be regarded as a primary precursor of color-field painting (*), monochromic painting, the conundrum art of Jasper Johns (*), and much else. He was also a strong writer and talker whose prose was posthumously collected into a book.

Newman, Barnett. *Selected Writings and Interviews*. Ed. John P. O'Neill. NY: Knopf, 1990.

Rosenberg, Harold. *Barnett Newman*. NY: Abrams, 1978.

NICHOL, bp (1944–1988; b. Barrie Phillip N.). Perhaps the most prolific notable Canadian poet of his generation, Nichol worked in several veins, only some of which were avant-garde. *Konfessions of an Elizabethan Fan Dancer* (1967) contains typewriter poems. Later visual writing incorporates press-on type. *Still Water* (1970) is a box of poems. Of the last, his fellow Canadian Michael Andre (1946) writes, "Many are funny, like this rap at high coo: '2 leaves touch/bad poems are written.' Others are one-liners using onomatopoetic permutations: 'beyond a bee yawned abbey on debby honda beyond.'"

Though Nichol's poetry won a Canadian Governor General's Literary Award in 1970, by international avant-garde standards he ranked among neither the best nor the worst. Even in his strivings for profundity, he tended toward the superficial. Nichol also participated in the Four Horsemen (*), the most prominent sound-poetry (*) quartet of its time, and in the collective compositions of the Toronto Research Group. Among his less experimental masterworks is *The Martyrology* (1972, 1976, 1977, 1982), five volumes about imaginary saints. In his success—with one bibliography listing over seventy titles, nearly all of them published in his native country—he demonstrated that no English-speaking country can be as supportive of experimental poetry as Canada.

Nichol, bp. *Zygal: A Book of Mysteries and Translations*. Toronto, Canada: Coach House, 1984.

Scobie, Stephen. *bp Nichol: What History Teaches*. Vancouver, Canada: Talonbooks, 1984.

NIDITCH, B.Z. (1943, b. Ben Zion N.). He is one of those frequent contributors to American literary magazines whose work is invariably more advanced and distinctive than the common run; and rather than confining himself to coterie publications (as would writers with little confidence in their work's presence in any larger world), Niditch publishes widely, working out of classic avant-garde traditions. Given that his favorite subject is the recurring disasters of European history, typical titles of his very best poems, some of them adopting numerative forms, are "Thoughts Before Dachau," "1944," "Vienna's Last Waltz," and "1944: Mid Europa." Niditch has also written plays that have mostly been produced in and around Boston. He writes me,

"I am active in the Boston Avant-Garde Society—BAGS."

Niditch, B.Z. *Unholy Empire*. Browns Mills, NJ: Ptol-
emy, 1982.

———. *Milton*. Miami, FL: Earthwise, 1992.

NIKOLAIS, Alwin (1912–1993). Though initially trained in dance, Nikolais developed a
theater in which the movements of individuals
are subordinated to larger theatrical patterns
established by scenery, costumes, and lights. His
major works use all kinds of props, most of
which function as dramatic extensions of the
dancers' limbs, and brightly colored costumes
that puff out from the natural lines of the body,

Alwin Nikolais, "Imago," 1963; 1992 revival. *Photo
courtesy Nikolais and Murray Louis Dance Company.*

to generate what he called a "direct kinetic statement." Technologically more advanced than
other choreographers, Nikolais composed his
own electronic scores (and was historically the
first customer for a Moog [*] synthesizer) and
developed original theatrical illuminations, including portable lights carried by performers. Perhaps because his choreography was not as innovative as his spectacular stage images, Nikolais's
pieces tend to be experienced as a series of episodes that establish breathtaking new scenes for
less engaging movements.

Siegel, Marcia B., ed. "Nik: A Documentary Study of
Alwin Nikolais." *Dance Perspectives* 48 (Winter 1971).

Nikolais, Alwin. "Growth of a Theme." In *The Dance
Has Many Faces*, 3rd ed., ed. Walter Sorrell. Pennington,
NJ: a cappella, 1992.

NOGUCHI, Isamu (1904–1988). Born in Los
Angeles, Noguchi grew up in Japan and later
studied art in both New York and Paris, where
he befriended Constantin Brancusi (*), and then

Isamu Noguchi, "Fishface," 1945. Black slate, six
elements, 30 X 14 1/2 X 8 3/4". *Courtesy The Pace
Gallery.*

studied further in both China and Japan. It is
often said that his art synthesized Eastern and
Western influences more profoundly than anyone else's. His early stone and metal sculptures
favored a post-Brancusi reduction of forms to
simple smooth surfaces that assumed organic
qualities. Beginning in the 1940s, he sometimes
placed electric lamps inside his works. He experimented with various base supports; he designed
gardens, furniture, and lamps. His decors for
ballets by George Balanchine (1904–1983) and
Martha Graham (*) are remembered as among
the best of their kind. Perhaps because Noguchi
was moderately famous for so long, little was
written about his later exhibitions. In Long Island
City, just over the East River from Manhattan,
he made his studio-home into a museum that
survived his death.

Noguchi, Isamu. *The Isamu Noguchi Garden Museum.*
NY: Abrams, 1987.

Hunter, Sam. *Isamu Noguchi*. NY: Abbeville, 1978.

"NONSENSE" (forever). Actually there is no
such thing, for any human creation that can be
defined in one way, rather than another way, has
a certain amount of esthetic sense. Indeed, some
of the most inspired avant-garde writing, from
Edward Lear (*) through *Finnegans Wake* (*) to
the present, has struck many who should have
known better, if only as a measure of esthetic

intelligence, as "nonsense." That means that the use of that word as derogatory criticism indicates that the writer/speaker is none too smart about contemporary art. The anthology of criticism noted below has essays on Edward Lear, Lewis Carroll (∗), the Marx Brothers, Flann O'Brien (∗), and Stefen Themerson (∗), as well as a useful bibliography.

Tigges, Wim, ed. *Explorations in the Field of Nonsense.* Amsterdam, Holland: Rodopi, 1987.

NOUVEAU ROMAN (c. 1958; "New French Novel").

European critics and cultural audiences are more predisposed than Americans to identify groups, whether they be composed of artists who consciously band together (e.g., Surrealists [∗], Fluxus [∗]) or of artists whose works are perceived to be similar, perhaps because they arrived at roughly the same time (e.g., "Generation of '98"). "New French Novel" identifies several French fictioneers who first became prominent in the late 1950s, differences among them notwithstanding. Nathalie Sarraute (1900) portrays the subtleties of consciousness, very much in the tradition of Henry James. Claude Simon's (1913) specialty was capturing the mind's awareness of the dynamic relationship between memory and present experience, much like William Faulkner (∗) attempted to do. Michel Butor (∗) turned out to be the most innovative, exploring various formal alternatives for narrative. Alain Robbe-Grillet (1922) initially seemed the most original, his narrator assimilating a scene very much as a movie camera does, catching lots of details, regardless of their relevance; in contrast to Simon and Sarraute, both psychological novelists, Robbe-Grillet believes that surfaces reveal as much human truth as we are likely to know. His style is both original and haunting, although limited; and *La Jalousie* (1957; *Jealousy*, 1959), as the most accessible of his novels, is the best introduction to his peculiar sensibility. Though Robbe-Grillet also wrote *Pour un nouveau roman* (1963), which is filled with healthy, quotable, audacious prejudices, this group as a whole is far less avant-garde and thus more acceptable than those gathered around Oulipo (∗).

Mercier, Vivian. *A Reader's Guide to the New Novel.* NY: Farrar, Straus, 1971.

Sturrock, John. *The French New Novel.* NY: Oxford University, 1969.

OATES, Joyce Carol (1938). Buried in Oates's bottomless bibliography are several genuinely experimental stories, most of them ironic take-offs on conventional forms, such as the contributors' notes in the back of a literary magazine. Quite wonderful, such fictions suggested a direction for Oates's work far more avant-garde and fundamentally distinguished than those she has since pursued. As far as I can tell, these stories haven't been collected in any of her books, perhaps because they represent the kind of departures that an upwardly mobile, self-consciously "acceptable" novelist would find it opportune to discard.

Oates, Joyce Carol. "Notes on Contributors." *Tri-Quarterly* 20 (Winter 1971).

O'BRIEN, Flann (1911–1966; b. Brian O'Nolan; aka Myles na gCopaleen). As a civil servant who wrote a newspaper column under the name Myles na gCopaleen, Brian O'Nolan needed yet another pseudonym for his fiction and so chose Flann O'Brien. His clever masterpiece is *At Swim-Two-Birds* (1939), a novel about an author whose characters turn against him by writing a novel about him. Because the initial narrator is a student writing a book, *At Swim-Two-Birds* has three beginnings and three endings. The extremely witty writing includes this interrogation of a cow: "State your name. . . . /That is a thing I have never attained, replied the cow. Her voice was low and guttural and of a quality not normally associated with the female mammalia." As this novel initially failed in the marketplace, it became a genuine underground classic that is reissued from time to time. Its sequel, written around the same time, was posthumously published as *The Third Policeman* (1967). About a later novel, *The Dalkey Archive* (1964), Hugh Kenner (∗) writes: "Neither [James] Joyce nor he ever surpassed the nested ingenuity of its contrivances, the insidious taut language to make everything at all seem plausible, or the unforced beauty of such episodes as our man's dialogue with his soul, when, not knowing he's already dead, he supposes he's about to be hanged." O'Brien also published another novel entirely in Gaelic. Some would nominate him to be the final wing of the trinity of James Joyce (∗) and Samuel Beckett (∗). It is said that Myles na gCopaleen's newspaper column had a stylistic distinction similar to, though greater than, Art Buchwald's.

O'Brien, Flann. *At Swim-Two-Birds* (1939). NY: Viking, 1967.

Jones, Stephen, ed. *A Flann O'Brien Reader.* NY: Viking, 1973.

OCKERSE, Tom (1940). Born Dutch, Ockerse came to America in the late 1950s and was initially active among those producing visual poetry (∗) at Indiana University in the middle 1960s. Trained in visual art, he differed from other early visual poets in using colors, at the same time respecting the literary convention of eight and one-half inch by eleven-inch sheets of paper. One distinguishing mark of his first major collection, the self-published *T. O. P.* (or Tom Ockerse Project; 1970), is design solutions so various that the book as a whole lacks character. However, in his works that are most frequently reproduced elsewhere, there is a distinct signature reflecting elegance and Constructivist (∗) simplicity. Around this time, Ockerse also produced *The A-Z Book* (1970), an awesomely inventive alphabet in which he used die-cutting to produce a sequence of pages in which the portion cut away from the front page belongs to the letter behind it.

Ockerse, Tom. *The A-Z Book.* NY: Colorcraft-Brussel, 1970.

———. *T. O. P.* Bloomington, IN: Self-published (now 37 Woodbury, Providence, RI 02906), 1970.

Tom Ockerse, image from *T.O.P.*, 1970. *Collection Richard Kostelanetz.*

O'DOHERTY, Brian (1934). Born in Ireland, educated in England, O'Doherty began as an art critic and has worked mostly as an administrator, most recently for the federal government as the director of the esthetically most progressive department at the National Endowment for the Arts (∗). As elaborate investigations of the new circumstances of art galleries and museums, the essays he collected as *Inside the White Cube* are true avant-garde criticism. As an artist customatrily exhibiting under the name Patrick Ireland, he has realized a highly original, rigorously relational Constructivism (∗), at times in drawings on paper, at other times with installations of taut strings stretched to the edges of a space, interacting in geometric ways.

O'Doherty, Brian. *Inside the White Cube.* San Francisco, CA: Lapis, 1986.

OHNO, Kazuo (1906). Considered to be the soul and cofounder of Butoh (∗), Ohno began dance studies with Baku Ishii (1886–1962) in 1933 and later studied with Takaya Eguchi (1900–1977), who had been a pupil of the German Expressionist (∗) dancer Mary Wigman (∗). In

Kazuo Ohno, "Admiring La Argentina," 1985. *Photo © 1993, Jack Vartoogian.*

1977, Ohno created and performed *Admiring La Argentina*, in which, dressed in a flowing gown, he impersonated and honored the Spanish dancer Antonia Mercé (1888–1936), whose performances had inspired Ohno early in his career. Ohno's son, Yoshita, is also a Butoh performer.—Katy Matheson

Sempel, Peter. *Just Visiting This Planet* (film). Hamburg, Germany: Peter Sempel, 1991.

O'KEEFFE, Georgia (1887–1986). Apparently learning from photography about the esthetic advantages of enlargement, she discovered formal qualities and radiant colors in the extremely close observations of biomorphic objects, such as flowers, plants, and pelvic bones. O'Keeffe often painted similar objects many times over, in series. Moving to rural New Mexico in the late 1940s, she again echoed photography by using the contrary strategy of painting broad expanses in a compressed scale. These paintings in turn echo her remarkably stark and lyrical 1920s horizontal views of New York. The thin paint of her early watercolors presages the innovations of Morris Louis (*), among others. She lived long enough to become a feminist exemplar whose celebrity could support a commercial publisher releasing a strong collection of images accompanied by her writings.

Georgia O'Keeffe. NY: Studio-Viking, 1976.

OLDENBURG, Claes (1929). Born in Sweden, raised in Chicago as the son of a Swedish diplomat, educated in English literature at Yale, Oldenburg mounted a 1959 exhibition of sculpture made from urban junk and soon afterward created his first truly memorable works: semblances of such common objects as ice-cream cones, hamburgers both with and without an accompanying pickle, cigarette ends, pastries, clothespins, toasters, telephones, plumbing pipes, and so forth. Compared to their models, his fabrications are usually exaggerated in size, distorted in detail, and/or dog-eared in texture. By such transformations, these pedestal-less sculptures usually gained, or accentuated, several other, less obvious resonances, most of them archetypal or sexual in theme, in the latter respect echoing Francis Picabia (*). Epitomizing Pop Art (*), his *Ice Cream Cone* (1962) is indubitably phallic; *Soft Wall Switches* (1964) looks like a pair of nipples; the soft *Giant Hamburger* (1963), several feet across, is distinctly vaginal; and so forth. "Appearances are not what counts," he once wrote, "It is the forms that count."

After 1962, Oldenburg's strategy of ironic displacement took another elaborate form in his "soft" sculpture, in which semblances of originally hard objects are fabricated in slick-surfaced, nonrigid materials different from the traditional sculptural staples. These representations of a toilet, a bathtub, a typewriter, and a drum set are so flabby that they behave contrary to the original object's nature and thus customarily need some external support for effective display. They also create a perversely ironic if not ghostly relation between the sculpture and its original model.

Possessing an adventurous imagination, Oldenburg has worked in various media. *The Store* (1962) was a real Lower East Side storefront filled with artistically fabricated but faintly representational (storelike) objects. Because regular hours were kept, people could browse through the place and even purchase objects, so that *The Store* was indeed an authentic store, but it was also an artistically defined space, an Environment (*), wholly in Oldenburg's early sixties style of colorful but ironic renditions of seedy objects. As an ingenious writer, Oldenburg authored *Store Days* (1967), a large-format, glossy book that contains a disconnected collection of prose and pictures as miscellaneous in form as the stuff of his store: historical data, replicas of important printed materials (such as a business card), sketches, price lists for the objects, photographs, scripts for his staged performances, various recipes, esthetic statements, parodies, declarations, and even an occasional aphorism (which may not be entirely serious). The result is an original open-ended potpourri of bookish materials that, unlike a conventional artist's manifesto, "explains" Oldenburg's Environmental art less by declarative statements than by implied resemblances. He has also published books of his theatrical scripts, some of which were staged as mixed-means (*) performance, and of comparably ironic *Proposals for Monuments and Buildings* (1969).

Oldenburg, Claes. *Store Days*. NY: Something Else, 1967.

Rose, Barbara. *Claes Oldenburg*. NY: Museum of Modern Art, 1969.

OLIVEROS, Pauline (1932). Long an academic, Oliveros threw up, as the British would say, a full professorship at the University of California to become an itinerant musician, working with a wealth of superficially divergent ideas, including feminist consciousness, improvisation, meditative experience, and possibilities for playing the accordion (which is her instrument of virtuosity). She writes that "All of my work emphasizes attentional strategies, musicianship, and improvisational skills." Through the Oliveros Foundation (156 Hunter Street, Kingston, NY 12401), she has organized the independent distribution of avant-garde music.

Gunden, Heidi von. *The Music of Pauline Oliveros.* Metuchen, NJ: Scarecrow, 1983.

OLSON, Charles (1910–1970). He was an American poet whose lifework was his *Maximus* poems, its title reflecting his goal of creating a Maximal (∗) literary art. Like Ezra Pound (∗) in his *Cantos* or Louis Zukofsky (∗) in his *A*, Olson attempted to incorporate his entire life experience and a fair amount of literary history into the framework of this one, ever-expanding megapoem. Like these other poets, Olson was doomed to failure, creating an open-ended work that could never be satisfactorily completed. He differed from other writers of his generation in viewing the page as a field, onto which he could spread his words. This notion, as well as his experimental typography, influenced later poets. He also wrote criticism distinguished for luminous sentences.—with Richard Carlin

Olson, Charles. *The Maximus Poems.* Berkeley, CA: University of California, 1986.

———. *Reads from the Maximus Poems.* NY: Folkways 9738, c. 1958.

———. *The Human Universe and Other Essays.* NY: Grove, 1967.

ONO, Yoko (1934). Born in Japan, she came of age in upper-middle-class America; and though she has returned to Japan for visits and speaks English with a Japanese accent, she was an American Conceptual (∗) artist who gained unintentional celebrity from her 1969 marriage to the pop singer-songwriter John Lennon (∗). Ono's strongest avant-garde works are the performance texts collected in her book *Grapefruit* (1964). For "Beat Piece" (1965), the entire instruction is "Listen to a heartbeat." Her "Cut Piece" requires the performer, usually herself, to come on the stage and sit down, "placing a pair of scissors in front of her and asking the audience to come up on the stage, one by one, and cut a portion of her clothing (anywhere they like) and take it." (One charm of this piece is that the

Yoko Ono, "Cut Piece," 9 September 1966. *Photo © 1993, Fred W. McDarrah.*

spectator courts as much embarrassment as the performer-author.) Ono's films customarily have the same audacious image repeated to excess (e.g., human butts). She also collaborated with Lennon on musical works where her Expressionist (∗) singing, part chanting and part screaming, continues to excessive durations (and for that reason influenced punk [∗] musicians in the mid-1970s). It is unfortunate that, for too many, Ono will never be more than a famous pop singer's widow.

Ono, Yoko. *Grapefruit* (1964). NY: Simon & Schuster, 1970.

———. *Onobox.* Lee's Wharf, MA: Rykodisc, 1992.

THE OPEN THEATRE (1963–1973). Founded by Joseph Chaikin (1935), a charismatic anti-leader who had previously worked with the Living Theatre (∗), the Open Theatre began with plays, such as Jean-Claude van Itallie's *America Hurrah* (1966), before focusing upon predominantly physical performances that were collectively developed. (As Robert Pasolli explained, "The writer is defined not by the fact that he has written a script on which the work is based . . . but on the fact that he *will* write a script related to the work which the troupe is improvising.")

The most memorable was *Terminal* (1969), which opens with a verbal fugue that repeats the word "dead" over and over until it becomes percussive sound; its subject (strange for a company so young) is attitudes about death. A horrifying portrayal of embalming is repeated, as visual fugues complement verbal fugues. The principal props are rolling platforms of various heights and large pieces of plywood, both props serving as beds, embalming tables, and graves. The play is divided into sections, each with its own title, which are announced by the performers: "The Calling Up of the Dead"; "The Last Biological Rites"; and "The Dying Imagine Their Judgment." *Terminal* ends in just over an hour with all the performers crawling along the floor, their voices becoming progressively more incoherent. The group's final production, *Nightwalk* (1973), investigated sleep.

Pasolli, Robert. *A Book on the Open Theatre.* Indianapolis, IN: Bobbs Merrill, 1970.

Shank, Theodore. *American Alternative Theatre.* NY: Grove, 1982.

OPTICAL ART (aka Op Art). See KINETIC ART; RILEY, Bridget; VASARELY, Victor

O'ROURKE, P.J. (1947). What is *he* doing here, I can hear you say. Well, in 1975 he published (perhaps self-published under an otherwise unfamiliar imprint) a loose-leaf collection of typewriter poems (*) printed on legal-size (eight and one-half inch by fourteen inch) pages, and dedicated to the actress Shelly Plimpton. They are carefully wrought, witty, and at times delicate, especially in the opening dedication piece, which is as good as any typewriter poem done anywhere. O'Rourke subsequently worked as a columnist for *The National Lampoon* and *Rolling Stone*, among other mass magazines, contributing witty, anti-liberal, political criticism that, while esthetically less distinguished and certainly less avant-garde, has been more remunerative, America being America. In this respect, his career resembles that of Hendrik Hertzberg (1940), who coauthored *One Million* (1970), an imaginatively designed book-art (*) essay on size and number, before he became a speech-writer for Jimmy Carter and the editor of *The New Republic*.

O'Rourke, P.J. *Our Friend the Vowel.* Aspers, PA: Stone House, 1975.

Hertzberg, Hendrik. *One Million.* NY: Simon & Schuster—Gemini, Smith, 1970.

OULIPO. Founded in 1961 by Raymond Queneau (*) and François Le Lionnais (1901–1984), this Parisian-based group began with the intention of basing experimental writing on mathematics. Its name is an acronym for Ouvroir de Littérature Potentielle (Workshop for Potential Literature). Once others came aboard, the group's theme became the use, at times the invention, of highly restrictive literary structures. According to Harry Mathews (*), its principal American participant, "The difference between constrictive and ordinary forms (such as rhyme and meter) is essentially one of degree." Jean Lescure (1912) took texts written by someone else and by rigorous methods substituted, say, each noun with the seventh noun to appear after it in a common dictionary. Others wrote "recurrent literature," as they called it, which was defined as "any text that contains, explicitly or implicitly, generative rules that invite the reader (or the teller, or the singer) to pursue the production of the text to infinity (or until the exhaustion of interest or attention)." One associate, by trade a professor of mathematics, wrote a sober analysis of "Mathematics in the Method of Raymond Queneau."

No other literary group, in any language known to me, has produced quite so many extreme innovations; and perhaps because Oulipo does not distinguish among members living and dead, its influence continues to grow. Among the writers contributing to its first major self-anthology, *Oulipo, la littérature potentielle* (1973), were Queneau, Georges Perec (*), Jean Queval (1913), Marcel Bénabou, Jacques Roubaud (1932), and Noël Arnaud (1919), all of whom are, by any measure, consequential experimental authors. In the American translation of much of this anthology are two new names: Mathews and Italo Calvino (1923–1985). I wanted to spell it OuLiPo, acknowledging the component words, but Mathews himself insisted that I do otherwise.

Mathews, Harry. "Vanishing Point [G. Perec and the Oulipo]." In *The Avant-Garde Tradition in Literature*, ed. Richard Kostelanetz. Buffalo, NY: Prometheus, 1982.

Oulipo. *La littérature potentielle.* Paris, France: Gallimard, 1973.

Motte, Warren F., Jr., ed. *Oulipo: A Primer of Potential Literature*. Lincoln, NE: University of Nebraska, 1986.

Rouband, Jacques. *The Great Fire of London* (1989). Normal, IL: Dalkey Archives, 1991.

P

PAIK, Nam June (1932). Born in Korea, educated in music in Japan and then Germany, where his work earned support from both John Cage (*) and Karlheinz Stockhausen (*), Paik came to America in 1964 as a celebrated young international artist. His initial forte was Electronic Music (*), thanks to three years of work at a Cologne studio. He was among the first to realize a lesson since lost—that training in high-tech music might be a better preparation for video than education in film and visual art, and thus that video programs belong in music schools rather than art schools. (Reynold Weidenaar [*] is another major video artist [*] who began in Electronic Music, initially depending upon a competence required there—the ability to decipher complicated technical manuals.) After several outrageous performance pieces in Europe,

Nam June Paik in his studio, 20 November 1965. *Photo © 1993, Fred W. McDarrah.*

many of them in Fluxus (*) festivals, some of them involving genuine danger (e.g., leaving a stage on which a motorcycle engine was left revving, thus filling a small space with increasing amounts of carbon monoxide), Paik installed the first exhibition of his video work in a gallery in Wuppertal, Germany—thirteen used television sets whose imagery he altered by manipulating the signal through the use of magnets, among other techniques.

Though he continued producing audacious live Performance Art (*), it was his video activities that had greater impact. Late in 1965, he showed a videotape made with a portable video camera he had purchased earlier that day and soon afterward had an exhibition that depended upon a videotape recorder. He was among the first artists-in-residence at the Boston Public Television station WGBH, where he also developed a video synthesizer (*) that, extending his original video-art principle, could radically transform an image fed into it. Another oft-repeated move involved incorporating television monitors into unexpected places, such as on a bra worn by the cellist Charlotte Moorman (1938–1992), amid live plants, or in a robot. Into the 1970s, if any exhibition included some video art, the token representative was usually Paik.

Precisely because the most sophisticated American television stations and private foundations concentrated so much of their resources on Paik's career, there has been reason for both jealousy and disappointment. From the beginning, his art had remarkably few strategies, most of them used repeatedly: performances that are audacious and yet fundamentally silly; tapes that depend upon juxtapositions of initially unrelated images, which is to say collage (*), which has become old-fashioned in other arts; installations depending upon accumulations of monitors that show either the same image or related images; expected placements of monitors. Nonetheless, Paik was the first video artist to have a full-scale retrospective at the Whitney Museum of American Art.

Hanhardt, John G., et al. *Nam June Paik*. NY: W.W. Norton and Whitney Museum of American Art, 1982.

PALESTINE, Charlemagne (1945). A polyartist (*) of sorts, Palestine was particularly distinguished at realizing elegant modular music (*)

on the carillon and on a Boisendorfer grand piano, on which he pounded away frenetically, realizing rapidly transforming clouds of overtones. Because concerts of his music were invariably stunning, it is unfortunate that few recordings survive. He has recently been working more on visual art.

Zimmerman, Walter. "Charlemagne Palestine." In *Desert Plants*. Cologne, Germany: Beginner, 1981.

PAPP, Tibor (1936), and Paul NAGY (1935). These two Hungarians, long residents of Paris, are, as far as I can tell, the most interesting visual poets (∗) currently working in France. Beginning their collaboration as part of a group called L'Atelier, which was also the title of their magazine, they have produced a series of highly inventive books and poster-books (drawing in part upon their common experience as working typographers) in addition to the richest edition known to me of Stéphane Mallarmé's (∗) avant-garde classic *Un coup de des*, which includes commentaries both visual and verbal. They also publish in Hungarian not only a French-sponsored magazine but books of their own poems that Hungarians tell me are quite marvelous, both visually and verbally. Papp has also written a pioneering book on computer literature (whose title translates as "With or Without Muse?") that is currently available only in Hungarian, alas.

Papp, Tibor. *Vendègszövegek 2, 3*. Paris, France: Magyar Mühely, 1984.

————. *Múzsával Vagy Múzsa Nélkül?* Budapest, Hungary: Balassi Kiado, 1992.

————, et al. *Un coup de des*. Paris, France: Change errant/d'atelier, 1980.

Nagy, Paul. *Sadisfactions*. Paris, France: D'Atelier—NY: Future, 1977.

————. *Journal in Time, 1974–1984*. Paris, France: Magyar Mühely, 1984.

PARKER, Charlie (1920–1955; b. Charles Christopher P.; aka Yardbird, Bird). Essentially self-taught on the alto saxophone, Parker became the premier jazzman of his generation, beginning his professional life at fifteen, coming to New York in 1939 and recording when he was twenty-one, in an initially precocious career. As one of the progenitors of the new style of the 1940s called Bebop (∗), he excelled, in Nicolas Slonimsky's (∗) summary, at "virtuosic speed, intense tone, complex harmonies, and florid melodies having irregular rhythmic patterns and asymmetric phrase lengths."

Instead of big bands characteristic of the preceding generation, Parker and his closest colleagues favored smaller "combos," as they are called, in a kind of chamber art that was precious to some and pathbreaking to others. He made jazz (∗) a modernist art of a quality distinctly different from its slicker predecessor; and knowing where he had gone, he once asked Edgard Varèse (∗) for lessons in composing. It is hard to imagine Ornette Coleman's (∗) subsequent departures without Parker's foundation. He had recurring trouble with everyday life and died young, essentially of self-abuse. One of the more interesting appreciations of him appears in William Austin's scholarly history of modern music.

Giddins, Gary. *Celebrating Bird*. NY: Morrow, 1986.

Austin, William W. *Music in the Twentieth Century*. NY: Norton, 1966.

PÄRT, Arvo (1935). Initially a tonal composer and then one of Estonia's few serial (∗) composers, Pärt developed in the mid-1970s his "tintinnabuli style," derived from tintinnabulation, or the sound of ringing bells. These pieces are tonal, with gradual scalar shifts and resounding rhythms in the tradition of plainsong and Russian liturgical music; they also incorporate repetition and extended structures that are totally absent from serial music. Like ringing bells, they are filled with overtones and undertones. Pärt's best works are profoundly religious: *Cantus in Memory of Benjamin Britten* (1976), where the repeated sound of bells comes to epitomize his tintinnabuli style; and *Stabat Mater* (1985), which echoes his earlier *Passio* (1982). Fully entitled *Passio Domini nostri Jesu Christi secundum Joannem*, the latter opens with a choral chord reminiscent of Bach. With gorgeous writing for voices alone, especially in the highest and lowest registers, this seventy-minute oratorio fully intends to stand beside Bach's work. Because *Passio* has a single movement that runs without pause, the CD has no sections; perversely or not, it can be heard only from the beginning.

Pärt, Arvo. *Passio*. Munich, Germany: ECM 1970, 1989.

PARTCH, Harry (1901–1974). An eccentric western American, Partch was a self-taught musician who repudiated his earlier compositions and then, in the 1930s, developed a forty-four tone scale. Patiently building his own instruments, mostly percussive, on which to play his microtones, he christened his inventions with such appropriately outlandish names as zymoxyl, chromolodeon, kathara, and cloud-chamber bowls, as well as eventually training musicians to play them. His microtonal (*) scales produced interesting relationships, and his instruments fresh timbres; yet the forms of Partch's music seem archaic, and his rhythms are too regular, while his arrangements are perhaps too reminiscent of the Indonesian gamelan. In short, innovations in tonality did not induce comparable revolutions in other musical dimensions. Partch customarily wrote the texts for his spoken works. His forceful expository writings have perhaps had more influence than his music; that befits any aphorist who can write: "Originality cannot be a goal. It is simply inevitable."

Partch, Harry. *Genesis of a New Music* (1949). NY: Da Capo, 1974.

———. *Bitter Music*. Ed. by Thomas McGeary. Urbana, IL: University of Illinois, 1991.

'PATAPHYSICS (c. 1900; 1948). In May 1960, *Evergreen Review*—in some respects the most distinguished American avant-garde magazine of its time—published an issue headlined "What Is 'Pataphysics?" Co-edited and introduced by Roger Shattuck (1923), it included contributions from Alfred Jarry (*) (purportedly 'Pataphysics's founder); Raymond Queneau (*); and Eugène Ionesco (*), among other less familiar but comparably wayward writers, all of them identified as "Satraps" of the Collège de 'Pataphysique. In his introduction, Shattuck defines 'Pataphysics as "the science of imaginary solutions. 'Pataphysics is the science of the realm beyond metaphysics; or, 'Pataphysics lies as far beyond metaphysics as metaphysics lies beyond physics—in one direction or another." From this assertion follow these corollaries, which Shattuck states without reservation: "Life is, of course, absurd, and it is ludicrous to take it

seriously. Only the comic is serious." As an extension of Dada (*), officially inaugurated at the end of 1948, 'Pataphysics suggested the kind of ludicrous paradox-loving intelligence informing absurd literature. 'Pataphysics did not die so much as move underground, way underground, until it recently surfaced in Australia, in a magazine of that title, indicating that Australia is perhaps becoming the Western world's cultural frontier, much as America was through most of the 20th century.

Shattuck, Roger, and Simon Watson Taylor, eds. "What Is 'Pataphysics?" *Evergreen Review* IV/13 (May–June 1960).

'Pataphysics. (G.P.O. 1718P, Melbourne, Victoria, Australia 3001)

PATCHEN, Kenneth (1911–1972). Patchen was an inspired Expressionist (*) writer with attractive sympathies, as well as a more original visual poet (*) who, in the tradition of William Blake (*), combined pictures with his own handwritten words in works that are as much idiosyncratic as innovative. There are reasons to regard as his greatest achievement two books of extended prose, *The Journal of Albion Moonlight* (1941) and *Sleepers Awake* (1946), which, though they

Kenneth Patchen. *Photo courtesy New Directions Publishing Corp.*

have always been in print, are, shame of shame, rarely mentioned in histories of American literature. (Indeed, any purportedly comprehensive survey of American literature that omits Patchen's name should be discarded unread; the latest offender to come my way is Richard Ruland and Malcolm Bradbury's *From Puritanism to Postmodernism* [1991].) Patchen was also among the first poets to read publicly along with jazz (*) accompaniments, making several recordings combining poetry and jazz, and inspiring other poets to perform in nightclubs to musicians' accompaniment.

Patchen, Kenneth. *The Journal of Albion Moonlight*. NY: New Directions, 1941.

———. *Sleepers Awake*. NY: New Directions, 1946.

———. *Reads with Jazz*. NY: Folkways 9718, 1960.

Veres, Peter, ed. *The Argument of Innocence: A Selection from the Arts of Kenneth Patchen*. San Francisco, CA: Scrimshaw, 1976.

Smith, Larry. *Kenneth Patchen*. Boston, MA: Twayne, 1978.

PATTERN POETRY (c. 325 B.C.). This term is most appropriate in defining poems, usually conventional in syntax, whose typography represents a shape that may be figurative or abstract. The term thus defines lines of poems whose ends suggest the shape of a horse; it defines as well the classic geometric shape poems of the 17th-century British poet George Herbert (1593–1633). It differs from visual poetry (*), which is generally nonsyntactical, and Poesia Vivisa (*), which customarily incorporates photographs along with words. Thanks to Dick Higgins's (*) prodigious research, we know that the tradition goes back to classical times in the West, it recurs in all Western literatures from time to time, and that similar works were produced in China, India, and the Middle East, all of which is to say that it remains a recurring alternative stream in the history of literary writing.

Higgins, Dick. *Pattern Poetry*. Albany, NY: State University of NY, 1987.

PATTERSON, Clayton (1948). With his videotape *Tompkins Square Park Police Riot* (1988), Patterson revealed how video as a documentary medium can differ from film. On a hot summer Saturday night, after five weeks of 90-degree days, the City of New York decided to close Tompkins Square Park in the East Village at one o'clock in the morning. The implicit purpose was to evacuate the squatters who had been sleeping in the park, after parks elsewhere in the city were closed to them. Well before the 1 a.m. curfew, protesters opposed to the park's closing began to gather on Avenue A, and plenty of police came as well, as did Patterson, a Canadian who lives nearby, carrying the battery-powered lightweight video camera he makes an extension of his body. When walking among people, he carries his camera on his hip, which means that the camera (and thus the spectator) participates in the events to the same degree that Patterson participates (for example, when others ran from the rampaging police, his camera ran as well); and since his camera has no light and makes slight noise, people are generally not aware that they are being intimately recorded. Patterson has learned from experience how to refocus distance without actually looking through the lens, capturing as well the peculiar light of New York at night. Patterson's tape, more than anything else I've seen, shows how video is far more effective than film at realizing the informal "cinema verité" ideal of a quarter-century ago.

Patterson, Clayton. *Tompkins Square Park Police Riot* (1988). NY: Privately published (P.O. Box 103, Prince St. Station, 10012-0002), 1991.

PAXTON, Steve (1939). Though a member of the Merce Cunningham (*) Dance Company from 1961 to 1964, Paxton also participated in the Judson Dance Theater (*) and, later, in the Grand Union (*) improvisational ensemble. A skilled performer, improviser, and polemicist, Paxton developed a form of dance that by 1972 he called "contact improvisation." Drawing on a movement vocabulary that evolved from martial arts, social dances, sports, and child's play, Paxton's contact improvisation has a relaxed, easygoing quality. Although some training in this form is necessary for safety (when, say, one dancer's body becomes the "floor" or support for another's in a free-flowing exchange), participation has been open to people of all backgrounds. Because it has become both a theatrical and social dance form, there is now an international network of contact improvisers.—Katy Matheson

Novack, Cynthia. *Sharing the Dance: Contact Improvisation and American Culture*. Madison, WI: University of Wisconsin, 1990.

Banes, Sally. "Steve Paxton: Physical Things." In *Terpsichore in Sneakers* (1980). 2nd ed. Middletown, CT: Wesleyan University, 1987.

PENDERECKI, Krzysztof (1933). An idiosyncratic Polish composer, Penderecki has appropriated a variety of avant-garde ideas in ways that may or may not be original. His *String Quartet* (1960) had old instruments resonating in new ways, while his genuinely moving *Threnody for the Victims of Hiroshima* (1960) had fifty-two strings realizing smoothly modulated frequency bands, mostly at their highest possible pitches, superficially resembling György Ligeti's (*) stunning *Atmospheres* (1961) and *Lux Aeterna* (1966). As Penderecki gained recognition, his music became slickly pretentious, if not simplistic and derivative; his *Passion According to St. Luke* (1965) is highly congenial to listeners who don't much like modern music (much as Carl Orff's [1895–1982] *Carmina Burana* was a few decades before). Nicolas Slonimsky (*) credits Penderecki with inventing "an optical notation, with symbolic ideograms indicating the desired sound; thus a black isosceles triangle denotes the highest possible pitch; an inverted isosceles triangle, the lowest possible pitch; a black rectangle for a sonic complex of white noise within a given interval;" etc. It is unfortunate that such innovative intentions do not produce comparably innovative results.

Penderecki, Krzysztof. *The Passion According to St. Luke/ Threnody for the Victims of Hiroshima*. N.p.: Philips PHS2-901, n.d.

PEREC, Georges (1936–1982). The most ambitious experimental French writer of his generation, Perec began as an author of crossword puzzles; and few writers, ever, could match his dexterity with innovative linguistic structures. A member of Oulipo (*), he wrote many other books, including *La Disparition* (1969), a novel totally devoid of the most popular letter in both English and French—the *E* (only to discover that the stunt had been done years before, with less literary distinction, by the American Ernest Vincent Wright in *Gadsby*, 1939). "By the end of *La Disparition*," writes Harry Mathews (*),

"*e* has become whatever is unspoken or cannot be spoken—the unconscious, the reality outside the written work that determines it and that it can neither escape nor master. *E* becomes whatever animates the writing of fiction; it is the fiction of fiction."

Perec, Georges. *W or the Memory of Childhood*. Boston, MA: Godine, 1988.

PEREIRA, I. Rice (1907–1971; b. Irene R. P.). Pereira's work was perhaps too avant-garde to be incorporated into the recent feminist revival. After beginning with paintings of machines, Pereira favored abstract shapes on transparent materials that were customarily hung without a frame. In the 1940s, she used layers of glass to explore resonating light sources, which she regarded as extending painting. A geometric mystic in the tradition of Mondrian (*), she thought her trapezoidal shapes subsumed spiritual presences. During the 1950s, her textures got thicker, featuring floating rectilinear forms. This work was so different from what others were doing that it remains memorable. She also wrote books whose titles tell all: *Light and the New Reality* (1951), *The Transformation of "Nothing" and the Paradox of Space* (1955), *The Nature of Space* (1956), *The Lapis* (1957), and *The Crystal of the Rose* (1959).

Baur, John I. H. *I. Rice Pereira*. NY: Whitney Museum of American Art, 1976.

PERELMAN, S.J. (1904–1979; b. Sidney Joseph P.). Not unlike other original American writers who appeared largely in slick media (e.g., Ogden Nash [*], and Robert Benchley [*]), Perelman had an avant-garde streak that is insufficiently appreciated. It depended upon destroying clichés with inspired non sequiturs: "Six months of revelry and an overzealous make-up man have left their stamp on the Fool when we again see him; the poor chap is shipping water fast. He reels around the mansion squirting seltzer at the help and boxing with double-exposure phantoms, and Theda, whose interest in her admirers wanes at the drop of a security, is already stalking a new meatball. Apprised of the situation, Kate goes to her husband bearing an olive branch, but their reunion is thwarted by his mistress, who unexpectedly checks in and kisses him back into submission." By any measure, few other writers have incorporated so many imaginative leaps into so few sentences.

Perelman, S. J. *The Most of*. NY: Fireside, 1980.

PERFORMANCE ART (c. 1975–). This is a 1970s epithet for what had previously been called Happenings (∗) or mixed-means theater (∗), which is to say a performance in which the author is customarily her or his own director, if not a principal performer as well. Much turns on the paradoxical treatment of language. If the performer was trained in theater, words, if used at all, play a secondary role to the articulation of image and movement. If, however, the performer was trained in dance, language might predominate over movement. Performance Art differs esthetically from the masterpieces of 1960s mixed-means theater in reflecting the influence of Minimalism (∗) and Conceptual Art (∗).

Goldberg, Roselee. *Performance Art* (1979). Rev. and enlarged ed. NY: Abrams, 1988.

PERFORMANCE GROUP (1967–1980). Organized by Richard Schechner (1934), a drama professor at New York University, this began as the resident company for a downtown New York alternative space called the Performance Garage

Performance Group, *Dionysius in '69*, 1968. Photo © 1993, Fred W. McDarrah.

(because it was previously a garage housing large trucks) that was renovated with wooden platforms and rafters that allowed everyone to sit where he or she wished. The group's best production, *Dionysus in '69* (1968), followed the academic tradition of adapting classic texts, in this case Euripides's *The Bacchae*, rather than creating theater wholecloth. It begins with company members performing various exercises in the middle of a carpeted floor. After an exchange of words between one performer and the woman tending the door, the actors begin to "perform," moving in and out of the Euripides lines and characters. Now and then they shift into contemporary speech and use their real names. They move at times among the audience, occasionally challenging individual spectators. Early in the play, a Dionysian dance is performed, which members of the audience are invited to join, and also a stunning birth ritual in which Dionysus's body, clad in a minimum of clothing (and sometimes none), is passed through five pairs of female legs and over a carpet of similarly semiclothed male bodies. In a concluding Dionysian frenzy, the audience is again invited into a melee of stroking figures. The title refers to a line in the election-year play—a vote for the lead male actor would "bring Dionysus in '69." Out of the Performance Group came the Wooster Group (1976), cofounded by Elizabeth Le Compte (1944) and Spalding Gray (1941), who later became a distinguished monologist. Initially utilizing many of the same performers, the Wooster Group took over the Performance Garage.

Schechner, Richard, ed. *Dionysus in '69*. NY: Farrar, Straus, 1970.

PESSOA, Fernando. See PSEUDONYMNS

PHILLIPS, Michael Joseph (1937). Though a Ph.D., Phillips writes monumentally simple poems that, if only for their audacious simplicity, are instantly recognizable as his. His intentionally limited vocabulary and his penchant for exact repetition represent radical repudiations of two traditional values of English poetry; for whereas even Gertrude Stein (∗) claimed that nothing she wrote was ever repeated precisely, Phillips often repeats exactly. The most successful of his poems in this mode is "On Claudia Cardinale," in which the phrase "I have never seen so much so well put-together" is repeated in a staggered visual form that generates an erotic complement. In contrast to Aram Saroyan (*), who gave up poetic Minimalism (*) to write commercial prose, Phillips continues mining his personal vein.

Phillips, Michael Joseph. *Selected Love Poems*. Indianapolis, IN: Hackett, 1980.

PHILLIPS, Tom (1937). Educated in English literature, trained as a composer, Phillips became a visual artist, not only as a gallery painter but as the author of one of the great book-art books of our time, *A Humument* (1980). What he did was take a Victorian novel, W. H. Mallock's *A Human Document*, and paint or draw over most of its pages so that only certain words from the original text were visible, in effect composing his own visual-verbal poems using another man's text. (Phillips's title comes from *removing* the middle letters from Mallock's original.) Over the missing words Phillips put an endless wealth of designs, made in a wide variety of ways. The results appeared in several forms, beginning with publication of sample pages in literary magazines in the late 1960s, then as suites from a graphics publisher, later in a book of black-and-white reproductions (*Trailer*, 1971), and finally as a full-color book (1981) that seven years later reappeared in a revised form. Phillips has meanwhile recorded a musical version of pages from *A Humument* and made another visual-verbal creation with Blakean echoes, an illustrated edition of his own translation of Dante's *Inferno*.

Phillips, Tom. *A Humument*. London, England, and NY: Thames & Hudson, 1980.

PHOTOMONTAGE. Literally, a photomontage is made by using montage techniques to assemble photographic images. Technically, photomontage would really be called photocollage, as montage implies sequence, as in film. (True photomontage would thus be two images in time, as in superimpositions; collage means glueing in French.) For me at least, the epitome of this genre is Paul Citroën's (1896–1983) *Metropolis*, which is the name not for one image but several that he composed around 1923. Taking bits of distinctly metropolitan images, particularly buildings whose height exceeds their width, he filled a vertical rectangle, from top to bottom, from side to side, making a persuasive image of an all-encompassing urban world (that had no relation to primary nature). Though the image itself is frequently reprinted, there is no book in English about Citroën. To others, the great photomontagist is John Heartfield (*), a German who took an English name for publishing photomontages that resembled political cartoons, really, by customarily mixing the faces of politicians, particularly Adolf Hitler, with critical imagery, such as coins replacing Hitler's spinal structure. As Richard Huelsenbeck (*) writes of Heartfield's photomontage: "It has an everyday character, it wants to teach and instruct, its rearrangement of parts indicates ideological and practical principles."

Heartfield, John. *Photomontages of the Nazi Period*. NY: Universe, 1977.

PICABIA, Francis (1879–1953). Born in Paris of a Cuban father and French mother, Picabia grew up a French artist, beginning as an Impressionist, becoming a Cubist (*), and by 1912 following Robert Delaunay's (1885–1941) Orphism. Traveling to New York in 1913, he collaborated with his compatriot Marcel Duchamp (*), who was by 1915 also in New York, in establishing American Dada (*). Having contributed to Alfred Stieglitz's (*) periodical *291* in 1916, Picabia published the first number of his Dada review *391* in Barcelona. Returning to Paris in the 1920s, he joined the Surrealists (*), collaborating with Erik Satie (*) on the ballet *Relâche* (1924) and with René Clair (1898–1981) on the film *Entr'acte* (1925). During the 1920s and 1930s he produced his most substantial visual art, which he called Transparencies because they were lyrical collages (*) made from cellophane.

Camfield, William. *Francis Picabia*. Princeton, NJ: Princeton University, 1979.

PICASSO, Pablo (1881–1971). Picasso began his career as an exceptionally talented realistic Spanish painter. His first genuine breakthrough came after he settled in France. He is generally credited with initiating Cubism (*) in the first decade of this century. Over the years, until World War II, he passed through a succession of artistic styles, mirroring the rapidly changing art

Pablo Picasso, "Man with Violin," c. 1910–1912. *Courtesy Philadelphia Museum of Art: The Louise and Walter Arensberg Collection.*

world with its many "isms" (Analyistic Cubism, Synthetic Cubism, Neo-Classicism, Surrealism [*], and so forth). Some of Picasso's many contributions to world art include the assimilation of African art into Western painting, incorporating several vantage points into a single portrait, and introducing into his still lifes such found objects as newspaper headlines, wallpaper fragments, and ticket stubs. His constant changing is considered avant-garde, because it reflected a restlessness and dissatisfaction with the status quo, even when that status quo was largely his own creation.

Historians also identify Picasso as initiating Cubist sculpture, and his subsequent three-dimensional art took a variety of forms. A whimsical sculpture of a gorilla whose face was sculpted around one of his children's toy cars predicted later Pop Art (*). His many Cubist constructions of guitars brought the intersecting planes of Cubist painting into three dimensions; they also utilized scrap metal, wire, and scrap wood, among other materials not often found in fine-art sculpture at the time. Picasso also worked for a brief period as a stage designer for Sergei Diaghilev's (*) Ballets Russes, contributing Cubist backdrops and costumes to innovative productions, most notably *Parade* (1917). As an aspiring

polyartist (*), Picasso spent two years mostly writing poetry and plays that, though experimental, are now forgotten.—with Richard Carlin

Rubin, William S. *Picasso: A Retrospective*. NY: Museum of Modern Art, 1980.

Ashton, Dore, ed. *Picasso on Art*. NY: Grove, 1972.

PIETRI, Pedro (1944). To the pioneering anthology of *The Puerto Rican Poets/Los Poetas Puertorriqueños* (1972) Pietri contributed "The Broken English Dream," which consists entirely of punctuation marks (that are different in Spanish *en face*, of course). *Invisible Poetry* (n.d.) is twenty-eight blank pages; in my copy he inscribed on the opening page, "Read this and pass on the message to others . . . and others." He once sent me *I Never Promised You a Cheeseburger*, which is a box with unbound but numbered pages, all cut into the shape of an ellipse, each with discrete writing in various styles. Pietri's stand-up poetry readings rank among the more inspired, incorporating theatrics that, while they have little to do with poetry, reflect his unfettered imagination. Pietri has also written plays that, while eccentric in parts, are comparatively more conventional.

Pietri, Pedro. *Puerto Rican Obituary*. NY: Monthly Review, 1973.

PISCATOR, Erwin (1893–1966). An actor and director in pre-Nazi Berlin, Piscator is credited with introducing photomontage (*) and film into his stagecraft. As he was Bertolt Brecht's collaborator in Epic Theater, his work had a proletarian-communist political thrust. Among Epic characteristics his widow identified "a theatre for vast audiences, a theatre of action, whose objective is to bring out the stirring questions of our time and to bring about a total re-education of both men of the theatre and the audience." Emigrating to America in 1938, Piscator became an influential teacher, counting among his prominent pupils the founders of the Living Theatre (*). He returned to (West) Germany in 1951.

Ley-Piscator, Maria. *The Piscator Experiment* (1967). Carbondale, IL: Southern Illinois University, 1970.

PLURALISM. One assumption behind the individual selections in this book, not to mention its title, holds that there is not one and only one avant-garde in any art but several; and, because monopoly is impossible in an open, plural society, where culture develops mostly apart from state influence, these avant-gardes move in different, if comparably original, directions. For instance, the field of painting has in the past thirty years witnessed Pop Art (∗), Op Art (∗), shaped canvases, monochromic fields, nonhierarchical pastiche, conundrum art (associated with Jasper Johns [∗]), conceptual art (∗), as well as assemblage (∗), space-encasing Environments (∗), and works that resemble paintings but are not, such as the light pieces of James Turrell (∗). Whereas only followers of Arnold Schoenberg (∗) on one side and John Cage (∗) on the other were identified with avant-garde music three decades ago, now we can speak of aleatory, modular (∗), microtonal (∗), and multi-track (∗) tape developments as each generating new art. Indeed, it seems that a period of pluralism in all the arts has succeeded an era of dichotomies. Although avant-garde is a useful general measure for distinguishing the new from the old, and thus one work can be more avant-garde than another (even if created by the same artist), beware of anyone who says that one or another decidedly innovative direction is necessarily "more" avant-garde than others.

One fundamental difference in the current avant-gardes is that some would isolate the processes, capabilities, and materials of the established medium—say, the application of paint to a plane of canvas—while the other direction would mix painting with concerns and procedures from the other arts, such as working in three dimensions or using light. Similarly, the new music descending from Schoenberg would isolate phenomena particular to music—pitch, amplitude, timbre, dynamics, and duration—and then subject each of these musical dimensions to an articulate ordering, creating pieces of exceptionally rich musical activity. The other new music, traditionally blamed on John Cage (∗), would combine sound with theatrical materials in an original way, creating an experience not just for the ear but for the eye too. In dance, one avant-garde would explore the possibilities of movement alone—Yvonne Rainer (∗) and Molissa Fenley (1954), for two—while the other favors theatrical conceptions, mixing in unusual ways such means as music, props, lights, setting,

and costumes: Alwin Nikolais (∗), Anna Halprin (∗), or Meredith Monk (∗). Paradoxically, Merce Cunningham (∗), who was at his beginnings avant-garde in the first sense, switched his emphasis in the early sixties to become an innovating figure in mixed-means (∗) dance, only to return after 1967 to pieces predominantly about movement. The avant-garde is thus not a single step built upon an old house but a diversity of radical and discontinuous alternatives to previously established paradigms. The result is not worldwide stylistic uniformity but numerous pockets of exponents of one or another particular style. It has been the bias of art historians to portray one style as succeeding another (and thus fresh artists gain reputations by climbing over their predecessors' backs), whereas the contemporary truth holds that several new styles can develop and thrive simultaneously and that there is not "progress" in art but an expansion of the possibilities.

Kostelanetz, Richard. *Metamorphosis in the Arts* (1970). NY: Archae, 1980.

Kubler, George. *The Shape of Time.* New Haven, CT: Yale University, 1962.

Kuhn, Thomas S. *The Structure of Scientific Revolutions.* Chicago, IL: University of Chicago, 1962.

Munro, Thomas. *The Arts and Their Interrelations.* Cleveland, OH: Case Western Reserve University, 1969.

Peckham, Morse. *Man's Rage for Chaos.* Philadelphia, PA: Chilton, 1965.

POLITICAL CORRECTNESS (PC, c. 1985). Beginning as a reaction against the ethnocentricism and male-dominated language of the West, PC has spawned a noisy debate about what should be taught in American colleges. On one level, this is purely an argument over linguistic propriety, especially on isolated college campuses—it is not "PC" to call a young woman a "babe," for example. On another level, there is a cultural argument, with dunderheads such as the late University of Chicago professor Allan Bloom dismissing current popular culture as trash and manic list-makers such as University of Virginia professor E.D. Hirsch, Jr., itemizing "What Every American Needs to Know," to cite the subtitle of his best-selling book. On the other side are "radical," "feminist," and "third-world" critics insisting that anyone who reads Charles Dickens must be hopelessly retrograde. The PC controversy has inspired collegiate humor, such as numerous "PC dictionaries" that attack cultural awareness by mocking it. Sadly, PC issues have become a sledgehammer for both sides, with conservative academics bashing more liberal ones, and vice versa, with neither group showing greater sensitivity from the process.—with Richard Carlin

Hirsch, E.D., Jr., et al. *The Dictionary of Cultural Literacy*. Boston, MA: Houghton Mifflin, 1988.

Bloom, Allan. *The Closing of the American Mind*. NY: Basic, 1988.

POLKINHORN, Harry (1945). Among the strongest of the new visual poets (*) to emerge in the 1980s, Polkinhorn also writes traditional verse, including a highly original anti-war epic, *Anaesthesia* (1985), which is composed of phrases, rather than poetic "lines," and is filled with unobvious turns. *Bridges of Skin Money* (1986) collects his early visual poetry. He has exhibited paintings, drawings, and photographs. Formerly a professor at the Imperial Valley campus of San Diego State University (and currently the director of its press), he translated an invaluable anthology of statements by Spanish- and Portuguese-language experimental poets, *Corrosive Signs* (1990). His critical essays on avant-garde literature rank among the best.

Polkinhorn, Harry. *Anaesthesia*. Clarence Center, NY: Textile Bridge, 1985.

———, trans. *Corrosive Signs*. Ed. by César Espinosa. Washington, DC: Maisonneuve (P.O. Box 2980, 20013), 1990.

POLLOCK, Jackson (1912–1956). Born in Wyoming, Pollock studied art with Thomas Hart Benton (1889–1975), among others, who taught him realisms that he quickly outgrew. Whereas de Kooning (*) radically extended Cubism (*), Pollock developed the other major innovation of early 20th-century European art—Expressionism (*). His art depended upon innovative methods of applying paint to canvas. He laid it on the floor and then in a series of rapid movements literally poured and splattered paint all over the surface. Though he rejected many of the canvases produced by these impulsive and purposeful actions, certain pictures made in this way

realized an overwhelming density of visual activity. One radical innovation is that such Expressionist intensity is visible *all over* the nonhierarchical, nonfocused canvas, thereby creating the sense that the imagery could have extended itself well beyond the painting's actual edges, if not forever. Pollock's best paintings, like de Kooning's, suggest different levels of illusionistic space, but Pollock's differed from de Kooning's by eschewing any reference to things outside of painting. Such a complete meshing of image and field, content and canvas, even stasis and movement, creates a completely integrated, autonomous, and self-referring work that differs radically from the fragmented, allusive, and structured field of post-Cubist painting. Once Pollock's innovation earned international acclaim, the self-destructive painter stopped doing it; his premature death in an auto accident seems, in retrospect, almost an esthetic convenience.

Greenberg, Clement. *Art and Culture*. Boston, MA: Beacon, 1961.

POLYARTIST. This is my honorific, coined back in 1969 and occasionally used by others, for the individual who excels at more than one nonadjacent art or, more precisely, is a master of several unrelated arts. The principal qualifier in my definition is "nonadjacent." In my understanding, painting and sculpture are adjacent, as are both film and photography, and both poetry and fiction (as many individuals excel at each pair). However, poetry and music are not adjacent. Nor are painting and fiction. Thus, John Cage (*) was a polyartist for excelling at poetry and music. So in different ways were Wyndham Lewis (*), Moholy-Nagy (*), Theo van Doesburg (*), Kurt Schwitters (*), Jean (Hans) Arp (*), Jean Cocteau (*), and William Blake (*). Among contemporaries other than Cage I would rank Yvonne Rainer (*), Dick Higgins (*), and Kenneth King (*). I distinguish the polyartist from the individual who excels at one art but not in another, such as Pablo Picasso (*), who quit painting for eighteen months in order to write modest poetry and plays; from the artist who incorporates several media into a single performance, in the tradition of the Wagnerian *Gesamtkunstwerk* (literally, "total artwork"); and from the dilettante who, as I understand that epithet, excels at nothing. "No one capable of genuine polyartistry," I once wrote, "should want to be merely an 'artist' anymore." One critical advantage of the term is forbidding the interpretation of work in one art with the terms of another (such as "poet's paintings"). Consider too that the great movements of classic modernism—Dada (∗), Surrealism (∗), Futurism (∗), the Bauhaus (∗)—were all essentially polyartistic enterprises. True polyartistic criticism attempts to identify the esthetic ideas that are reflected in the polyartist's various works.

Kostelanetz, Richard. "Two Ways of Polyartistry." In *On Innovative Art(ist)s*. Jefferson, NC: McFarland, 1992.

POP ART (c. 1960). It was quite stunning at the beginning—the first post-World War II representational reaction to Abstract Art (∗) that was not primarily conservative (or anti-modernist) in spirit. As the creation of painters conscious of art history, who had assimilated and revealed the influence of Abstraction, these paintings and sculptures of popular icons are primarily about "Art" (in contrast to commercial art, which is thoroughly worldly). One Pop style, exemplified by James Rosenquist (1933), uses both the scale and flat color, as well as the sentimentally realistic style and visible panel-separating lines, of billboard art to create large, glossy paintings that, like his classic ten-foot by eighty-eight-foot *F-111* (1965), are full of incongruous images. As the critic Harold Rosenberg (∗) once cracked, "This was advertising art advertising itself as art that hates advertising." Another Pop artist, Roy Lichtenstein (∗), painted enlarged comic-strip images, which are so refined in their realism that they even reproduce the dots characteristic of comic-book coloring. This theme of ironic displacement—the incongruous relation between the identifiable image and its model—informs not only Lichtenstein's highly comic paintings but also the pop sculpture of Claes Oldenburg (∗) and the paintings of Andy Warhol (∗). To Barbara Rose, at that time as sharp a critic as any, "These artists are linked only through subject matter, not through stylistic similarities."

Lippard, Lucy R., et al. *Pop Art*. NY: Praeger, 1966.

Rose, Barbara. *Autocritique*. NY: Weidenfeld & Nicholson, 1988.

PORTER, Bern (1911). Think of Porter as a 20th-century Walt Whitman, a sometime printer and courageous publisher, a long-time servant of both U.S. letters and his own very American muse. He began as a physicist, only to become disillusioned with science during World War II. By its end, he published the first critical anthology on Henry Miller (1891–1980). *The Waste Maker* (1972) represents Porter's assiduous discovery of America writ large in the smallest "found" details, which he exposes in the guise of visual poetry (∗) that is formally similar to that of his contemporary Charles Henri Ford (∗). Collecting native waste into artlessly designed pages, Porter reflects not only his love and bitterness, but exposes cultural insights and perspectives. *The Waste Maker* ranks with Michel Butor's (∗) *Mobile* (1963) as an encompassing pastiche of modern America. A yet bigger book, *Found Poems* (1972), measuring (in its original hardback edition) eight-and-a-half by eleven inches, with several hundred pages, collects all sorts of witty and incisive word-based poetic images. Though recognitions of Porter's greatness surface now and then, customarily in independent literary journals based in New England, his name does not appear in *Contemporary Poets* or, shamefully, in the standard histories of American literature.

Porter, Bern. *Found Poems*. Millerton, NY: Something Else, 1972.

———. *The Book of Do's*. Hulls Cove, ME: Dog Ear (04644), 1982.

PORTER, Donald (1939). Educated in classics at the University of the South and in English literature at King's College, Cambridge, Porter wrote in the early seventies several highly original and complicated stories. The most visible, *As If a Footnote* (1974), is a fiction in which elaborate footnotes, beginning with numbers, continuing as letters (and then numbers doubled), become a comic counterpoint to the principal text. Porter remains one of the few to do what John Barth (∗) could not—elaborate on the advanced, highly literary position established in the latter's *Lost in the Funhouse* (1968). Finding familiar resistances to experimental fiction, Porter subsequently wrote several pop paperbacks and less innovative fictions, which is unfortunate, because *As If a Footnote* remains a classic, by any standards.

Porter, Donald. *As If a Footnote*. NY: Assembling (P.O. Box 444, 10012-0008), 1974.

POSTMODERN (c. 1949). This term is included here not because it belongs but because too many people think it might belong. It is commonly used to characterize work that is not avant-garde at all but still purportedly contemporary, usually because of its journalistic subject matter (the assumption being that modernism [*] has died, to be replaced by something else). My personal opinion holds that anything characterized as postmodern, whether by its author or its advocates, is beneath critical consideration, no matter how immediately popular or acceptable it might be. The assumption of this book is that the revolutions implicit in modernism continue and thus that current avant-garde art simply extends modernism, which is dead only to dodos. Charles Jencks proposes the term "late modern" as separate from early modern and postmodern; and while I accept Jencks's term as a useful antidote, I wish it were not necessary.

Jencks, Charles. *What Is Postmodernism?* NY: St. Martin's, 1986.

POTAMKIN, Harry Alan (1900–1933). One of the first film critics in America, Potamkin had only a brief life in the field. From 1927 to his sudden death (from a botched operation), a period that witnessed the end of silent film and the birth of sound movies, Potamkin wrote extended, literate, thoughtful essays on American cinema, more frequently on French and Soviet films, on Chaplin, on the earliest American avant-garde filmmakers, and on the creative use of the moviecamera. A posthumous collection of Potamkin's texts is *The Compound Cinema* (1977), edited by Lewis Jacobs (1906) (who would in turn fulfill Potamkin's unfulfilled objective of writing the first important history of American film). Potamkin stressed the internal analysis of films, not their social or historical context—a position that set him apart from his peers, Marxist and otherwise. And he had a vision of cinema evolving: "Years hence, a Joyce will not think of attempting his compounds with words. He will go into cinema which unifies the verbal and aural with the visual and ultimately the spatial. . . ." Potamkin's nephew Milton Babbitt (*) is a distinguished American composer.—Robert Haller

Potamkin, Harry Alan. *The Compound Cinema.* Ed. Lewis Jacobs. NY: Teachers College, 1977.

Jacobs, Lewis. *The Rise of the American Film* (1939). Rev. ed. NY: Teachers College, 1968.

POUND, Ezra (1885–1973). Pound's innovation was poetic collage (*), in which an abundance and variety of both experiential and linguistic materials are pulled together into a poetically integral mosaic—so that even where striking images are evoked, the effect of their structural principle is unfamiliar, perhaps telling juxtapositions. The achievement of the final edition of *The Cantos* (1970), which were begun over fifty years before, is the wealth of reference and language, both historic and contemporary, incorporated into a single sustained pastiche. The paradox of the poem's long history is that the collage form that seemed so innovative when the poem was begun had become familiar, if not old-fashioned, by the time it was complete. Back in 1970, I was compelled to moan, "More bad poetry in America today is indebted to Pound than anyone else." Pound's translations of Chinese and classic Latin and Greek poetry were innovative in that he did not attempt literally to translate these works. Though he often "translated" poems from languages he could not read,

Ezra Pound, c. 1970. *Photo: Boris De Rachewitz, courtesy New Directions Publishing Corp.*

his nonliteral versions were often thought better at capturing the essence of the originals than more "accurate" translations. Pound was also a strong literary publicist who identified the best literary minds of his generation, such as T.S. Eliot (*) and James Joyce (*), and even visual artists such as Henri Gaudier-Brzeska (*). Pound's classic literary essay, *ABC of Reading* (1935), is no less provocative today.

Pound, Ezra. *The Cantos*. NY: New Directions, 1970.

Kostelanetz, Richard. "Impounding Pound's Milestone" (1970). *The Old Poetries and the New*. Ann Arbor, MI: University of Michigan, 1981.

PREPARED PIANO (c. 1938).

John Cage (*) coined this term to describe his internal modifications to the standard piano in order to change the sounds it produces. Typically, he inserted pieces of metal, paper clips, erasers, rubber bands, wooden spoons, and other objects between the strings. He played both the keys and the strings, sometimes depressing the keyboard in order to free the strings from the dampers. These modifications transformed the piano from primarily a melodic instrument into a percussive one. Among the other American composers to use variations on this contemporary instrument are Lou Harrison (1917), August M. Wegner (1941), Samuel Pellman (1953), Alan Stout (1932), and Richard Bunger (1942), who recorded an album wholly of compositions for prepared piano before his departure from the music profession.

Bunger, Richard. *Prepared Piano: The First Four Decades*. Tinton Falls, NJ: Musical Heritage 4187L, 1983.

PRITCHARD, Norman Henry II (1939).

A New Yorker of West Indian descent, Pritchard published in 1970 and 1971 two books of innovative poetry. The first, *The Matrix Poems: 1960–70* (1970), includes visual poems (*) along with Minimal (*) poems and text-sound texts (*). His style in the last vein depends upon repeating the same phrase until something other than the original phrase results. In the only conveniently recorded example, "Gyre's Galax," the phrase "above beneath" is rapidly repeated with varying pauses between each line. (The reader repeating these two words rapidly aloud to himself or herself will get a faint sense of the effect.) Pritchard stopped publishing in the early 1970s, and was at last report residing in rural eastern Pennsylvania.

Pritchard, Norman. "Gyre's Galax." On *New Jazz Poets*, ed. Walter Lowenfels. NY: Folkways/Broadside 9751, 1967.

PROJECTION TELEVISION (c. 1967).

It was at a Janis Joplin concert in the late 1960s that I first saw a face projected live onto a large television screen, and this has since become a common sight at rock concerts. In the mid-1970s, a two-piece projection TV was common particularly in educational institutions, on airplanes, and in bars featuring sporting events. A three-lens, three-color system situated several feet away from a screen was used to project the image. The next development came in the early 1990s from Sharp, which offered a projection system that differs from the earlier versions in several respects. Whereas the heavy old two-piece systems had to be kept permanently in place, SharpVision (at thirty-one pounds) could be moved about easily; whereas the old system required the installation of a fixed screen especially designed for it, SharpVision could be projected onto any flat surface, such as a clean wall. Thanks to liquid crystal display (LCD) panels (similar to those in digital watches), the picture emerges from a single source.

All of these projection systems differ from the single-piece rear-projection boxes with screens measuring from forty inches, diagonally, to seventy; because they weigh upwards of 200 pounds, rear-projection systems are nearly always mounted on the floor. In my own experience of the separate screen, which I placed directly above a normal monitor, I found my eye preferring the monitor for most television programs but the screen for movies, especially if made before 1960, and for sports, where the television directors have less control over the scale of the images on the screen. Once projection systems outnumber monitors, as I expect they will, you can assume that directors will shoot live images to a scale more familiar to motion pictures.

The first book on this subject has yet to be written.

PROUST, Marcel (1871–1922).

In his multi-volume fiction, *A la Recherche du temps perdu* (*Remembrance of Things Past*, 1913–1927), this French author transcended earlier conventions of novel-writing. Drawing upon Henri Bergson's theories of time—chiefly the difference between historical or chronological time and interior or psychological time—Proust weaves a story that is as much about the processes of memory (voluntary, involuntary, rational, and especially sensate) as it is about its main characters (Charles Swann and the wealthy Guermantes family). The novel amplifies late 19th-century realism with rich and abundant detail, for example using many pages to describe lying in bed or taking a piece of cake with a cup of tea. At the same time, "real" objects and events assume "symbolic" and mythic import in Proust's poetic evocation. Although dealing with issues of morality and decadence in its depiction of French culture at the turn of the century, Proust's work consciously displays the power of art to fix permanently what in life, time, and memory are always in flux. Originally published in sixteen French volumes, Proust's masterpiece was available in English first in C.K. Scott Moncrieff's translation (1927–1932) and now in Terence Kilmartin's revision of Scott Moncrieff's text. Proust's influence on subsequent writers such as William Faulkner (∗) and Jack Kerouac (∗) is immeasurable.—Katy Matheson

Proust, Marcel. *Remembrance of Things Past.* Trans. C. K. Scott Moncrieff and Terence Kilmartin. NY: Random House, 1981.

Fowlie, Wallace. *A Reading of Proust.* Garden City, NY: Anchor, 1964.

Kilmartin, Terence. *A Guide to Proust.* London, England: Chatto & Windus, 1983.

Brée, Germaine. *Marcel Proust and Deliverance of Time* (1960). 2nd ed. Westport, CT: Greenwood, 1982.

PSEUDONYMS (forever). Though human beings have forever been taking other names for professional purposes, the most familiar being women who have assumed male names to make their writing acceptable (e.g., George Eliot, George Sand), only in modern times, as far as I can tell, have pseudonyms functioned to identify alternative artistic identities. If the name Vernon Duke identified the light music of Vladimir Dukelsky (1903–1969), so the names Patrick Ireland and Flann O'Brien (∗) grace works by civil servants Brian O'Doherty (∗) and Brian O'Nolan, respectively. At their most effective, pseudonyms enable their authors to do something considerably different from their normal activity, P.D.Q. Bach (∗) becoming not only a container for Peter

Schickele's comedy but a more interesting composer. (Pseudonyms have also functioned to hide the identities of writers who were politically blacklisted, as during the McCarthyite 1950s in Hollywood, when an Academy Award was offered to someone who, in a Dada [∗] mockery, could not show up to receive it.)

Marc Dachy reminds us that Arthur Cravan (1887–1918), a true free spirit, wrote the entire issue of a proto-Dada magazine, *Maintenant* (1915), by himself: "W. Cooper for articles on Oscar Wilde, Eduard Archinard (almost a phonetic anagram of *anarchie*) for a poem in classical alexandrines, Marie Lowitska for aphorisms, Robert Miradique for literary criticism. The boxer-poet signed his own name to his apocryphal encounters with André Gide and to his detailed, mordant comments upon the artists exhibiting at the Salon des Indépendants."

The most distinguished user of multiple pseudonyms—"heteronyms" was his name for them—was the Portuguese poet Fernando Pessoa (1888–1935), who used, in addition to his own name, Alberto Caeiro, Ricardo Reis, and Álvaro de Campos, each for a different sort of poetry. (Raised in South Africa as a Portuguese diplomat's stepson, he also wrote poems in 17th-century English.) As Pessoa explained, "I put into Caeiro all my power of dramatic depersonalization, into Ricardo Ries all my intellectual discipline, dressed in the music that is proper to him, into Álvaro de Campos, all the emotion that I do not allow myself in my living."

Pessoa, Fernando. *Selected Poems.* Trans. Edwin Honig. Chicago, IL: Swallow, 1971.

PUNK ROCK (c. 1975). Punk developed in England as a reaction of those born in the 1950s and 1960s to the increasingly slick, commercial popular music associated with the first generation of rock stars born in the 1940s. (It is awesome to recall that the Rolling Stones, so raucously offensive in 1965, especially to older people, could be perceived a decade later as slick.) One assumption of punk was that anybody could play or write music—indeed, that musical talent might even be a liability. Punk clubs made little distinction between performer and audience. While the performers often held their audiences in contempt, the audience responded by ignoring the performance on stage, all in reaction to the mutual seductiveness of earlier popular music. British punk also had a political dimension as a reaction to increasingly conservative British politics. When punk came to lower Manhattan in the mid-1970s, it had more impact on fashion than music, as new kinds of hair styles, clothing, makeup, and demeanor seemed stronger than any musical message. Griel Marcus (1945), perhaps the most literate of the American rock critics, wrote a fat, unpersuasive book that regarded punk as the legitimate heir of avant-garde radicalism.—with Richard Carlin

Marcus, Griel. *Lipstick Traces*. Cambridge, MA: Harvard University, 1988.

PYNCHON, Thomas (1937). I would love to write an entry that portrays Pynchon's spectacular development from precociously sophisticated short stories about scientific concepts, such as "Entropy" (1960), through the absurdist vision of history portrayed in his first novel *V.* (1963), to *Gravity's Rainbow* (1973), which parades many signs of an avant-garde masterpiece. The problem is that I have never been able to finish that last 600-plus-page book (having taken it on airplanes, to the beach, even to Europe!) and would not on my own authority begin to introduce it. I am told its subject is conspiracies, which is certainly unfashionable intellectually. I do know that *Vineland* (1990) represents a falling away from its predecessor, much as Pynchon's second novel, *The Crying of Lot 49* (1966), is a much slighter book than *V.*

Pynchon, Thomas. "Entropy" (1960). In *Slow Learner*. Boston, MA: Little, Brown, 1984.

———. *V.* Philadelphia, PA: Lippincott, 1963.

———. *Gravity's Rainbow*. NY: Viking, 1973.

QUANT, Mary (1934). Credit her with inventing the miniskirt and the companion minidress, which, by bringing hemlines above the knee, gave woman more genuine freedom of movement than previous fashions. The miniskirt depended, like so much else new in art, upon a technological development, in this case low-cost tights (aka panty hose) as a replacement for cumbersome stockings that required a garter belt. As tights became more visible, designers gave them patterns and colors bolder than those previously associated with stockings. Minis also forced the elimination of girdles and looked better in low-heeled, "sensible" shoes. Sociologically, miniskirts permitted young women to become the trendsetters in fashion. Though some of Mary Quant's sketches from 1958–1961 reportedly included short-length dresses, she did not manufacture for a mass market until 1962. Negative reaction was vociferous, if short-lived; by the end of 1966, Quant herself wore a miniskirt to receive her OBE from the Queen. Though fashion publicists are forever predicting repudiation of the mini styles, they have survived.

Quant, Mary. *Quant by Quant*. NY: Putnam's, 1966.

QUENEAU, Raymond (1903–1976). Very much a smart writer's smart writer, Queneau was brilliant beyond measure, working in a variety of mostly original ways. After Surrealist (*) beginnings, he became involved with 'Pataphysics (*), an avant-garde parody-philosophy calling itself the "science of imaginary solutions." Later, along with the mathematician François Le Lionnais, Queneau cofounded *Ouvroir de Littérature Potentielle*, commonly known as Oulipo (*). In addition to working as a publisher, a translator into French (of books such as *The Palm Wine Drinkard* by Amos Tutuola [*]), and the principal editor of the Pleiade encyclopedia, Queneau published comic pop novels, such as *Zazie dans le métro* (1959; *Zazie*, 1960), along with such experimental works as *Exercises de style* (1947; *Exercises in Style*, 1958), a tour de force, or farce, in which the same scene is described in ninety-nine different ways.

His avant-garde masterpiece, so audaciously extraordinary it will never be transcended or even repeated, is *Cent mille milliards de poèmes* (100,000 billion poems, 1961), in which he writes ten sonnets whose lines (in place) are interchangeable, because they are die-cut into strips bound to the book's spine, creating sonnet possibilities numbering 10 to the 14th power. The result is the creation of preconditions for the reader to discover a multitude of relationships not intended.

Queneau, Raymond. *Cent mille milliards de poèmes.* Afterword by François Le Lionnnais. Paris, France: Gallimard, 1961.

Esslin, Martin. "Raymond Queneau." In *The Novelist as Philosopher*, ed. John Cruickshank. NY: Oxford, 1962.

R

RADIO ART. Radio art exploits the capabilities unique to audio broadcast. Mark E. Cory tells of Richard Hughes's 1924 radio play set in a mine after a cave-in had extinguished all light. As Cory writes, "Listeners and characters work out the consequences of being trapped in darkness in a bond no other dramatic medium could forge as well. NBC would later exploit the principle in its *Lights Out* series of ghost stories." Orson Welles's (∗) celebrated *War of the Worlds* broadcast depended upon the convention, used even in 1938, of interrupting a program with on-the-scene news bulletins. More recently, the Australian Chris Mann (∗) simultaneously broadcast his *Quadraphonic Cocktail* over two mono AM stations and one stereo FM station, depending upon the fact that even in Australia listeners are likely to have three radios in fairly close proximity to one another.

Within broadcasting institutions in the past three decades, radio art matured mostly in Germany, usually in departments called *Hörspiel*, or "hear-play." The principal development is away from reproducing the illusion of live theater or poetic monologues, with their literary base, toward audio experience based in sound. In *Der Monolog der Terry Jo* (Saarländischen Rundfunks, 1968), by Ludwig Harig and Max Bense, the voice of an unconscious accident victim is rendered by an electro-acoustic vocoder, which is able to create approximations of human speech until recognizable words appear. One theme is the kind of message communicated by incomprehensible speech. Other radio works, such as my own *Invocations* (Sender Freies Berlin, 1981), bring into the same acoustic space sounds that would normally be heard separately—in my case, prayers spoken by ministers of various (even antagonistic) faiths. The principal sponsor of this *Akustische Kunst* ("acoustic art") has been Klaus Schöning (1936), who has also edited anthologies of scripts and criticism. More recently, German stations have broadcast radio art designed to be heard through earphones, *kunstkopf* (literally, "art-head") stereo, surrounding the listener with stereophonic effects. Though such special audio experience might be made available in the U.S. on discs or cassettes, in Germany at least it is more likely to be heard over the radio.

Cory, Mark E. *The Emergence of an Acoustic Art Form.* Lincoln, NE: University of Nebraksa Studies, 1974.

———. "New Radio Drama as Acoustic Art." In *Esthetics Contemporary*, ed. Richard Kostelanetz. Buffalo, NY: Prometheus, 1989.

Schöning, Klaus, ed. *Neues Hörspiel*. Frankfurt, Germany: Suhrkamp, 1969.

RAINER, Yvonne (1934). Originally a dancer, she choreographed pieces that incorporated movements previously unknown to dance, such as running, climbing, tumbling, and other elementary athletic activities. In one sequence of *The Mind Is a Muscle* (1966), perhaps her greatest single dance, a professional juggler commands the left side of the stage while the company of six mill disinterestedly on the right side of the stage. In another part, behind a movie

Yvonne Rainer, "Terrain," 1963. *Photo © 1990, Al Giese.*

screen filled with the image of someone's legs, the dancers execute mundane movements and at one point dribble a basketball. Another section, known as "Trio A," includes her choreographic innovation of circular swinging of both arms and a concomitant shifting of the body's weight in an intrinsically endless phrase. In the 1970s, Rainer became a filmmaker whose reels, never too experimental to begin with, have turned increasingly slick.

Rainer, Yvonne. *Work 1961/73*. Halifax, Canada: Nova Scotia College of Art and Design, 1974.

McDonagh, Don. "Why Does It Have to Be That Way?" In *The Rise and Fall and Rise of Modern Dance*. Rev. ed. Pennington, NJ: a cappella, 1990.

RANDALL, J.K. (1927). After taking his M.F.A. at Princeton, Randall became a pioneering computer composer, whose *Mudgett: Monologues of a Mass Murderer* (1965) ranked among the best work produced for "converted digital tape" at the time. However, by the 1980s he gave it up in favor of eccentric improvisations that are self-published on cassettes that he and his esthetic compatriot Benjamin Boretz (1934) distributed to an interested few. Even more eccentric are his highly visual essays "Compose Yourself: A Manual for the Young," which are published from time to time in the university-based periodical *Perspectives of New Music* and will someday appear as the book they are meant to be.

Randall, J.K., Benjamin Boretz, et al. Numerous cassettes and CDs. Red Hook, NY: Open Space (R.D. 2, Box 45e, 12571), 1983–ongoing.

RAUSCH, Mechthild (1940). A German critic, Rausch is one of the few who have a sure sense of the difference between genuinely avant-garde work and its pretenders, for instance distinguishing in an elaborate essay between the highly avant-garde Vienna Poets (*) and the more derivative writers associated with the Austrian city of Graz, epitomized by Peter Handke (1942). Not unlike other independent German writers, Rausch has produced films and radio features as well as essays, most notably about the art critic–novelist Carl Einstein (*) and Paul Scheerbart (*), in addition to producing several volumes of and about the latter. Her criticism remains as untranslated as the writing of her principal enthusiasms, so backward is the English-speaking world.

Rausch, Mechthild. *70 Trillionen Westgrüsse*. Berlin, Germany: Argon-Verlag, 1991.

RAUSCHENBERG, Robert (1925). His innovations were based upon two principles: that literally everything could be appropriate in painterly art and that one part of a picture need not dominate, or even relate to, the others. In the first respect, he painted his own bed, transforming a sub-esthetic object into something that was purchased and displayed by the Museum of Modern Art (*Bed*, 1955); he put a whole stuffed Angora goat into a painted field (*Monogram*, 1959); added a live radio to another (*Broadcast*, 1959); and even added a clock to another (*Third Time Painting*, 1961). His earlier *White Painting* (1951) has reflective surfaces designed to incorporate lights and images from the surrounding environment (in contrast to Ad Reinhardt [*], say, whose monotonal canvases were intentionally nonreflective). For painted assemblages (*) that had three dimensions and yet were not quite sculpture, Rauschenberg coined the term "combine." In the late sixties, he worked with technology and theatrical pieces.

Otherwise, the typical Rauschenberg painting (or graphic) is a disparate collection of images, some of them painted, others applied in other ways (such as silkscreen or glue), in which no image is more important than any other, though they may comment upon one another. By the 1970s, he had become the Leonard Bernstein (1918–1990) of visual art, a sort of elder statesman whose public activities were exemplary, even though his art ceased being interesting or influential.

Klotz, Mary Lynn. *Robert Rauschenberg*. NY: Abrams, 1990.

REICH, Steve (1936). Not unlike his sometime classmate and colleague Philip Glass (*), Reich began as a difficult avant-garde composer and has become more accessible and popular over the years. What *Music in Twelve Parts* is for Glass, *Drumming* (1971) is for Reich, which is to say the apex of his radical style—a composition that benefits from being longer and thus more ambitious than his other works. Reich's original radical idea was a strain of modular music (*), in which bits of material would be repeated, customarily in slightly different forms, until through repetition alone it generated a pulsing sound. The clearest example was *It's Gonna Rain* (1965), where that phrase becomes a chorus of itself, as Reich realizes an incantatory intensity unequalled in audio language art. Another, similarly composed work, *Come Out* (1966), depends upon more violent language, as initially spoken by a black teenager who had suffered a police beating. Whereas Glass is a melodist, the best Reich, as in *Drumming*, marks him as a rhythmicist. Of the later Reich, I like *Tehillim* (1981) for its imaginative setting of a Hebrew text.

Reich, Steve. *Writings about Music.* NY: New York University, 1974.

————. *Early Works* (*It's Gonna Rain* [1965], *Come Out* [1966], *Piano Phase* [1967], *Clapping Music* [1972]). NY: Nonesuch 79169, 1987.

————. *Drumming* (1971), *Six Pianos* (1973), *Music for Mallet Instruments, Voices and Organ* (1973). Hamburg, Germany: DGG 427428-Z-GC2, 1974.

REINHARDT, Ad (1913–1967; b. Adolf R.). A college chum of both Robert Lax (*) and Thomas Merton (*), Reinhardt was, from his professional beginnings, a severe Abstractionist (*), perhaps the only major American Abstract artist of his generation never to have exhibited representational paintings. His most distinctive early paintings had geometric shapes on a multicolored field, while works of the late forties favored less definite abstract shapes. By 1953, he offered canvases painted entirely in different shades of the same color—all red, all blue, all black, in one case all white—usually divided into geometric shapes whose slight differences in hue became more visible with the spectator's increased attention. His *Black Paintings* of the early sixties, each five feet square, contain not a sole black color evenly painted from edge to edge, but many rectilinear forms, each painted a slightly different black hue. Viewing Reinhardt's work from the perspective of subsequent art history (which generally makes earlier innovations clear), the critic Lucy R. Lippard judges that his "innovations consist largely of the establishment of a valid function for nonrelational, monotonal concepts, progressive elimination of texture, color contrast, value contrast and eventually of color itself, which was replaced by a uniquely nonillusionistic painted light." In addition to being a masterful cartoonist of ideas and

life in the New York art world, Reinhardt was also a witty and aphoristic writer, saying, for instance, "An avant-garde in art advances art-as-art or it isn't an avant-garde."

Reinhardt, Ad. *Art-as-Art.* Ed. Barbara Rose. NY: Viking, 1975.

Lippard, Lucy R. *Ad Reinhardt.* NY: Abrams, 1981.

REXROTH, Kenneth (1906–1982). I'd like to think Rexroth belongs here, because anyone who is radical in both his literary and social politics serves as an avant-garde model. However, Rexroth's poems at their best were simple and accessible, usually in appreciation of nature, with scarcely any interest in the possibilities of poetry. I have scoured them, hoping to find avant-garde aberrations comparable to those existing in, say, Cummings (*) and Ogden Nash (*), but have uncovered one and only one, "Fundamental Disagreement with Two Contemporaries," which is indicatively dedicated "for Tristan Tzara & André Breton" and opens with fragmented language ("gonaV/ ; /ing evlT / dras pRoG") before lapsing into the underpunctuated declarative phrases more typical of Rexroth's poetry.

Rexroth, Kenneth. *The Collected Shorter Poems.* NY: New Directions, n.d. (c. 1966).

Mottram, Eric, ed. *The Rexroth Reader.* London, England: Jonathan Cape, 1972.

RHOADS, George (1926). As a painter skilled at fixing watches, Rhoads began in the 1970s to create kinetic sculptures that use a minimum of technology by mostly depending upon gravity for their effects. Rhoads typically uses a motor to bring a single kind of ball (billiard balls, golf balls, etc.) to the top of a structure. The balls flow at random down one of several available paths, customarily hitting noisemakers and moving parts until they reach a bottom level, from which they are, by machine, carried back to the top. These audiokinetic sculptures, as he calls them, are customarily placed in shopping centers (two in West Edmonton, Canada; one in Plattsburg, NY), popular institutions (Boston's Science Museum), bus stations (New York's Port Authority), and airport terminals (Logan C in Boston), which is to say places where people congregate. It is not unusual to see individuals fixated for minutes at a time, intent on discovering

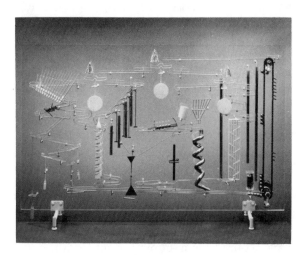

George Rhoads, "Wallpiece IV," 1984. *Courtesy Rock Stream Studios.*

a sculpture's many possible movements. No other public art succeeds as well with the general public, perhaps explaining why, in contrast to unpopular public art, they are rarely, if ever, defaced. My own favorite is an untitled piece installed at the Allendale Shopping Center in Pittsfield, MA, where golf balls are propelled into the air. As they fall into different channels, they activate different switches that open different organ pipes, producing a variety of sounds. I consider Rhoads's machines to be a kind of mechanical theater in the tradition of Oskar Schlemmer (*) and thus note that, because the only technology they require is a simple motor, they would have been technically feasible long ago.

Kostelanetz, Richard. "George Rhoads." In *On Innovative Performance(s)*. Jefferson, NC: McFarland, forthcoming.

RIBEMONT-DESSAIGNES, Georges (1884–1974). Initially a painter, Ribemont-Dessaignes focused primarily on writing without ever abandoning visual art. Active in Dada (*), he wrote innovative plays, an early book about Man Ray (*), and several novels. From 1929 to 1931 he edited the magazine *Bifur* which, in its short life, made a remarkable synthesis in publishing Tristan Tzara (*), James Joyce (*), Ramón Gómez de la Serna (*), and William Carlos Williams (*), along with statements by Buster Keaton (*) and the Russian Formalist Victor Shlovsky (1893–1983). Ribemont-Dessaignes's history of Dada, initially

written in 1931 for a Parisian magazine, became a 1958 book.

Dachy, Marc. *The Dada Movement.* NY: Rizzoli, 1990.

RICHTER, Hans (1888–1976). A polyartist (*) of sorts, Richter is now remembered for his films and his books, beginning with his 1921 abstract film *Rhythmus 21*, which focuses upon a single formal element, the rectangle. In Germany, he worked with Viking Eggeling (*) and with Sergei Eisenstein (*). Once settled in America, where he became director of the Institute of Film Techniques at New York's City College (1942–1952), Richter organized *Dreams That Money Can Buy* (1946), a feature-length color film that drew upon scenarios by Alexander Calder (*), Marcel Duchamp (*), Max Ernst (*), and Man Ray (*), among others. Another longer film, *8 X 8* (1957), made after his return to Switzerland, involved Jean Cocteau (*), among others. Richter compiled a two-part self-retrospective, *Forty Years of Experiment* (1951, 1961), in addition to writing histories featuring his own involvements in the arts. In the concluding two decades of his life, he worked principally as a painter.

Richter, Hans. *Dada: Art and Anti-Art.* NY: McGraw-Hill, n.d. (c. 1966).

————. *Hans Richter.* Ed. Cleve Gray. NY: Holt, Rinehart, and Winston, 1971.

RICKEY, George (1907). Alexander Calder's (*) innovation (of a nonmechanical kinetic three-dimensional art) was so different from traditional sculpture that his sort of work, apparently requiring competences different from those learned in art school, had remarkably few successors. The most important, as well as original, has been George Rickey, a Scotsman who has spent most of his life in the U.S. (and learned mechanics in the U.S. Army Air Corps). His delicately poised pieces move, like Calder's, in response to the gentlest shifts of air (even drafts within museums). Whereas Calder usually suspends his floating and spatially intersecting parts from a central point (itself usually suspended from the ceiling), providing a pivotal axis, Rickey either suspends his metal pieces individually from several axes or pitches them up from an axial point close to the ground, as in his classic *Two Lines* (1964), where intersecting blades, like scissors, run thirty-five feet high into the open air. Though

Rickey's *oeuvre* may not be as rich as Calder's, it suggests that the medium of nonmechanical kinetic art is scarcely exhausted. Rickey has also published one of the strongest critical histories of Constructivism (*).

Rickey, George. *Constructivism: Origins and Evolution.* NY: Braziller, 1967.

RIEFENSTAHL, Leni (1902). Riefenstahl was the Eadweard Muybridge (*) of film, which is to say that she mastered, as no one before her, the art of capturing human motion. Her masterpiece is *Olympia* (1938), ostensibly about the 1936 Berlin Olympics but stylistically a glorification of human performance at its highest. (Ironically, this female follower of Hitler made African-American athlete Jesse Owens famous through her portrayal of his achievements at the Olympics.) Nearly every major sports film since seems in some way or another indebted to Riefenstahl. Because of her Nazi involvements, most notoriously as the producer of *Triumph of the Will* (1936) about the 1934 Nuremberg Nazi Party Convention, she was interned in various prison camps. Though she worked for European magazines as a photographer, she never again produced film.

Infield, Glenn B. *Leni Riefenstahl: The Fallen Film Goddess.* NY: Crowell, 1976.

RILEY, Bridget (1931). It is fair to say that Riley and Victor Vasarely (*) initiated modern Optical (aka Op) Art; and whereas Vasarely popularized it, with an increasing number of colorful prints, Riley has maintained a near monopoly on its masterpieces. These are typically visual fields of such an ingenious regularity that they generate the illusion of shimmering movement. What seems at first scrupulously Constructivist (*) is really involved with nonrational retinal-perceptual processes, exposing, as Cyril Barrett put it, "certain physiological processes in the eye and brain which we are not normally aware of either in ordinary vision or in looking at other works of art." Beginning with only black and white, Riley introduced color around 1965, with middling success.

Barrett, Cyril, S.J. *An Introduction to Optical Art.* London, England: Studio Vista, 1971.

Seitz, William C. *The Responsive Eye.* NY: Museum of Modern Art, 1965.

RILEY, Terry (1935). A sometime ragtime pianist, Riley developed in the mid-sixties a radical alternative to the predominant schools of music composition. Sometimes called Minimal (*), its operation is actually modular (*). For *In C* (1964), some two dozen musicians are given fifty-three separate phrases (or modules) to play in sequence, moving from one to the next whenever they wish, ideally in sensitive response to one another. Meanwhile the pianist plays a continuous beat on the top two C's of the keyboard for the entire duration. The performance ends when all performers have arrived at the final module. As the composer/record producer David Behrman wrote about its first recording, "A good performance reveals a teeming world of groups and subgroups forming, dissolving, and forming within a modal panorama which shifts, over a period of about forty-five to ninety minutes, from C to E to C to G." Later in the 1960s, Riley worked with audiotape delay, where a live sound is recorded on one machine that feeds tape to a second machine that plays back the sound that is recorded by the first machine, generally at a lower level (a process that is repeated until the sound decays away). Meanwhile, the live performer can add new sounds that are likewise recycled until they become inaudible. By this process, Riley, also a virtuoso on the soprano saxophone, created *Poppy Nogood and the Phantom Band* (1966). Later Riley recordings reveal his taste for highly sensuous music, especially when played by himself.

Riley, Terry. *In C.* NY: Columbia Records MS 7178, c. 1968.

———. *Poppy Nogood and the Phantom Band/A Rainbow in Curved Air.* NY: Columbia Records MS 7315, c. 1971.

RIMBAUD, Arthur (1854–1891). Running away from home, the teenage Rimbaud befriended Paul Verlaine (1844–1896), who left his wife to live and travel with Rimbaud, until the older man shot the younger. That prompted Rimbaud to write *Une Saison en enfer* (1873, *A Season in Hell*), which consists mostly of prose poems filled with extreme imagery. Rimbaud's other important prose poem, *Illuminations*, also composed before 1874, introduces his theory of the poet as seer, thereby influencing poetic practice well into the 20th century. The legend is that he abandoned poetry at age nineteen. Without roots, in constant rebellion against his family and social conventions, he explored both mental and social derangements, producing an art of hallucination and irrationality through symbolism that is often obscure. For generations thereafter, the acceptance or rejection of Rimbaud's example became an important decision for aspiring poets.

Rimbaud, Arthur. *The Complete Works*. Trans. Paul Schmidt. NY: Harper & Row, 1978.

ROBSON, Ernest (1902–?). An industrial chemist who returned to poetry in his retirement, Robson developed a sophisticated, pre-computer technique for visually notating his radical articulations, similar to those of sound poetry but in his case of conventionally syntactical texts. He called it "An Orthographic Way of Writing English Poetry," or "prosodynic print." Robson also published theoretical treatises with titles such as *Transwhichics* (1970), *Prosodynic Print* (1975), *Vowel and Diphthong Tones* (1977), and *Poetry as a Performance Art On and Off the Page* (1976), all of which are filled with shrewd perceptions and good ideas, in addition to reviving conventional fiction written in his youth (*Thomas Onetwo*, 1971, billed as "the roaring twenties refracted through a jar of pickles"). His single strongest book is the large-format 1974 retrospective created with his wife, Marion.

Robson, Ernest and Marion. *I Only Work Here*. Chester Springs, PA: Dufour, 1974.

RODCHENKO, Aleksandr Mikhailovich (1891–1956). An early champion of Abstract Art (∗), who was also a photographer, theoretician, and designer, Rodchenko emphasized a rational approach over the intuitive and mystical one favored by Wassily Kandinsky (∗) and Kazimir Malevich (∗). Therefore, beginning with compositions of 1915, he drew with a ruler and compass in an attempt to eliminate the emotional and psychological influence of the artist's personality. This orientation made Rodchenko a leader in Constructivism (∗) and Productivism, which applied the principles of Abstraction to furniture design, book design, and advertising for the new collectivist proletarian society. He pioneered photomontage (∗), his most noted work being illustrations for Vladimir Mayakovsky's (∗) *About This* (1923). In 1924, he turned more

to the "real" world of photography, but his photographs retain Abstract compositional elements, most notably strong diagonal lines resulting from unusual viewpoints. He designed Futurist (∗) sets and costumes for Mayakovsky's play *The Bedbug* (1929), among other theatrical works. In the 1920s, Rodchenko held influential administrative and teaching positions, only to retire in the 1930s and 1940s to a quiet life working in photography, book design, and easel painting of a more biomorphic sort.—Gerald Janecek

Khan-Magomedov, Selim O. *Rodchenko: The Complete Work*. Cambridge, MA: M.I.T., 1987.

RODIA, Simon (b. Sabbatino R.; c. 1879–1965). One of the most awesome works of American art is several brightly colored skeletal towers, one of them nearly a hundred feet high, at the end of a dead-end street, next to a railroad siding, in the notorious Watts section of Los Angeles. They were constructed between 1921 and 1954 by an Italian immigrant tile setter/laborer working alone in his spare time. In their skeletal structure they resemble the Eiffel Tower, constructed only two decades before Rodia began,

Simon Rodia, "Watts Towers," segment. *Photo: Thomas K. Meyer, courtesy the City of Los Angeles.*

which was a powerful popular image in the early 20th century. In their multi-colored brightness they resemble the architecture of Antoni Gaudi (*), the Catalonian Spaniard whose work Rodia might have seen (at least in photographic reproductions). Otherwise, the towers have no esthetic antecedents.

Literally rooted in the fireplace of Rodia's own house, the Watts Towers, as they are now commonly called, are constructed out of steel rods covered with cement that is reinforced with wire. Into the cement Rodia put tile chips, broken bottles (especially if their glass was tinted), sea shells, and anything else that might reflect the Los Angeles sun. As Calvin Trillin revealed, in a 1965 *New Yorker* profile, Rodia had no plan and no building permit. "To judge by pictures taken at various times over the thirty-three years he was working on his towers, he actually tore down sections of them and started over when he felt that they did not match his image or when his image changed." Sometime before his death, Rodia abandoned them to live elsewhere in California. More than one commentator has identified the Watts Towers as Los Angeles's (or America's) equivalent of Athens's Parthenon.

Trillin, Calvin. "Simon Rodia: Watts Towers." In *Naives and Visionaries*. NY: Dutton, 1974.

ROSENBERG, Harold (1906–1978).

When I first began writing about the arts, three decades ago, Rosenberg's writings about avant-garde art, in general and in particular, shaped ideas that I continue to hold. It was easy to be seduced by his humanistic image of Action Painting (which was his less successful coinage for Abstract Expressionism [*]): "At a certain moment the canvas began to appear to one American painter after another as an arena in which to act—rather than as a space in which to produce, re-design, analyze or 'express' an object, actual or imagined." However, before the 1960s were over, it was clear that Rosenberg no longer believed in his idea of the avant-garde—at least not in his critical practice. He was invited to become the art critic for *The New Yorker*, a forum quite different from the literary quarterlies and art journals in which Rosenberg's strongest work previously appeared. Instead of pursuing his enthusiasms, he felt obliged to write about whatever was currently "hot" or newsy in the art world, most of which he didn't like (and wouldn't have bothered with before, at least in print).

Rosenberg, Harold. *The Tradition of the New*. NY: Horizon, 1959.

ROSENBERG, Jim (1947).

As a poet with degrees in mathematical logic, Rosenberg has worked since the late sixties with "nonlinear poetic forms." I remember a 1975 "reading," *Permanent and Temporary Poetry*, in which he placed a disparate collection of words on the walls and floor of a performance space. In the middle of the floor was a pile of unattached words that he began spreading around the room. Meanwhile he played tapes that repeated these words, both with and without standard syntax. He also read aloud passages of conventional prose, mostly drawn from newspapers. For all of its verbal diffusion, the piece was coherent stylistically and thus poetically. In Roger Johnson's anthology *Scores* (1981), Rosenberg speaks of this piece as part of "an ongoing project in which words and word constructions are accumulated in reservoirs as elements kept autonomously for free combination with other elements, in either temporary or permanent works." Rosenberg subsequently contributed computer programs to John Cage's (*) mesostic rewritings of traditional texts.

Rosenberg, Jim. "Intermittence." In *Scores: An Anthology of New Music*, ed. Roger Johnson. NY: Schirmer, 1981.

ROSENTHAL, Rachel (1926).

Rosenthal is a French-born American Performance Artist (*) about whom I have heard much but could find out little, so negligent were some of her sponsors in caring about her work. The book mentioned below describes a 1979 piece, *The Arousing (Shock, Thunder)*, subtitled "A Hexagram in Five Parts," in which she played a videotape of her face while she read a monologue and part of the *I Ching*. When the video ends, Rosenthal, masked, began jogging in place. When the mask is torn off, the audience sees her face wrapped in bandages. As she unwinds them, photographs and personal letters fall to the floor; she is revealed wearing a beard and mustache that she strokes in a self-satisfied way. In a later section, she appears as a woman who points to an old trunk stuffed with her bandages. It explodes as the piece ends. Another piece from 1979, *My Brazil*, incorporates Brazilian songs, visions of Nazi rallies, and the entire audience waving sparklers. A publicity flier claims she "has written and performed twenty-eight full-length pieces."

"Rachel Rosenthal." In *The Amazing Decade: Women and Performance Art in America 1970–1980*, ed. Moira Roth. Los Angeles, CA: Astro Artz, 1983.

ROSS, Charles (1937).

A visual artist educated in science, Ross specializes in the refraction of light. *Prism Wall/Muybridge Window* (1969–1970) has mineral oil enclosed in acrylic casings that create a wall of slanted trapezoids and triangles. These casings rhythmically reflect and slightly refract and magnify their background (because the weight of the oil bulges their sides). Refraction causes startling spatial displacements and sequences of motion—seen through the prism, two people may appear to be standing in exactly the same spot at the same instant—and creates multiple, constantly changing spectra. In Ross's subsequent series, *Sunlight Convergence/Solar Burn: The Equinoctial Year 1971–1972*, sunlight is focused through a large lens into energy that burns the arc of the sun into a different wooden plank for each day. The size and severity of the burn—a deep gouge on a clear day, a blank one on a rainy day—reflect atmospheric conditions; the shape and direction of the burned arc changes with the seasons, making the physical energy of light tangible. Ross has recently been constructing in New Mexico a 200-foot-long *Star Tunnel* that he hopes to open to the public before the century's end.

Star Axis. Albuquerque, NM: Jonson Gallery of the University of New Mexico, 1992.

ROT, Dieter (1930; b. Karl-Dietrich Roth, perhaps).

The most original and fecund Swiss artist of his generation, Rot began as a graphic designer, and so it is scarcely surprising that he has published over a hundred books, many of which rank as extraordinary book-art. He has also exhibited organic materials, particularly feces, that change color, not to mention odor, over the course of an exhibition. He once collected two years of personal trash into transparent plastic bags that were stacked into two pyramids in Zurich's Helmhaus. In addition to giving concerts with instruments he was not trained to play (and frequently concocting new versions of his

name), Rot has published highly innovative prose in more than one language.

Rot, Dieter. *Books and Graphics (part 1): from 1947 to 1971*. Stuttgart, Germany: Editions Hansjörg Mayer, 1971.

ROTHKO, Mark (1903–1970).

Born in Russia, raised in Portland, Oregon, Rothko came to New York in 1925 and was for decades one among many serious painters struggling in New York. Finally, in the 1950s, he realized his original, mature style of large hand-shaped rectangles, usually stacked one above the other, together filling nearly the entire field of a canvas. The rectangles have only slightly different hues, while the background color differs only a little more from that of the rectangles. Each area has not a uniform color but ever-changing hues, whose gradations become more apparent if the work's visibly hand-painted strokes are looked at fixedly. What Rothko wanted to realize was unprecedented sublimity. His paintings became the foundation for subsequent artists' exploration of surface tensions, color relationships, and ways of negating suggestions of "depth." To my mind, the most visible sign of Rothko's influence has been the proliferation of nearly monochromic paintings in the past three decades.

Waldman, Diane. *Mark Rothko*. NY: Guggenheim Museum, 1978.

Le Colour Seule. Lyon, France: Musée d'Art Contemporain, 1988.

ROUSSEL, Raymond (1877–1933).

One of the great eccentrics of early modern French literature, Roussel was born rich and, shall we say, touched. A maniac in the true sense of the word, he wrote at nineteen a novel entirely in alexandrines (nearly 6,000 of them); he later used parentheses with an abandon that others find inspiring. An admirer of Jules Verne above all others, Roussel wrote about largely imaginary travels in Africa, first in prose and then (decades later) in verse, publishing both books under the same title, *Impressions d'Afrique* (1910, 1932; only the first has been translated as *Impressions of Africa*, 1967). For the self-publication of the verse novel, he used only the right-hand pages, alternating his text with crude illustrations commissioned from a nobody selected by a private detective agency (but if the whole text is read without cutting the pages, as required of books printed in

Europe at that time, the illustrations aren't seen at all!). Roussel's plays are disjunctive, their titles coming from concluding lines that, as Rayner Heppenstall points out, "are equally unrelated to all that has gone before." Because of his wealth, Roussel did not need to be popular, which he wasn't anyway. The posthumously published *Comment j'ai écrit certains de mes livres* (*How I Wrote Some of My Books*, 1935) accounts for the liberties of extreme imagination, even in recalling one's professional life and purposes. Perhaps because of his influence on Alain Robbe-Grillet (*), Eugène Ionesco (*), and John Ashbery (*), among others, Roussel is continually revived.

Roussel, Raymond. *Impressions of Africa* (1910). Trans. Lindy Frood and Rayner Heppenstall. Berkeley, CA: University of California, 1967.

Heppenstall, Rayner. *Raymond Roussel: A Critical Study*. Berkeley, CA: University of California, 1967.

RUSCHA, Edward (1937). Though Ruscha's meticulous paintings of words, usually in a modestly expressive shape, echo Robert Indiana's (*) without transcending them, his true innovations are book-art (*) books. The single most successful contains standard black-and-white aerial photographs of Los Angeles parking lots, most of them empty; the only words beyond the title page identify each lot's location. Though one theme might be the peculiar beauty of such magnificent non-artistic edifices, *Thirty-Four Parking Lots* (1967) is a reiterated, scathing critique of Los Angeles urban design and its bondage to the automobile. Ruscha's formally most remarkable volume, likewise self-published, is a strip of heavy paper that folds into the shape of a book, becoming a ladderbook, which can be "read" in either direction. Along the entire length of each edge run amateurish photographs of buildings on both sides of *The Sunset Strip* (1966), arranged bottom to bottom, separated only by a white space down the middle of the paper.

Ruscha, Edward. *Sunset Strip*. Los Angeles, CA: Edward Ruscha, 1966.

———. *Thirty-Four Parking Lots*. Los Angeles, CA: Edward Ruscha, 1967.

RUSSOLO, Luigi (1885–1947). The notoriety of Russolo's book *L'arte dei rumori* (*The Art of Noise*, 1913) obscures the fact that he was mostly a painter (and one of five cosigners of "Futurist Painting: Technical Manifesto," 1910). His *Treno in velocita* (*Speeding Train*, 1911) is said to be the first Futurist (*) painting to use a speeding machine as both its subject and theme. His major canvases of the next few years explored motion in both machines and people—crowds, thunderbolts, automobiles, political protesters, etc. In his famous manifesto on noise, he used capital letters to "take greater pleasure in ideally combining the noises of trams, explosions of motors, trains, and shouting crowds than in listening again, for example, to the 'Eroica' or the 'Pastorale.'" Russolo's appreciation of noises made by nonpitched machines, many of them new to his time, incidentally forecast the musics of George Anthiel (*), Edgard Varèse (*), and John Cage (*), among others. As a proto-polyartist, Russolo invented several *intonarumori*, or noisemaking instruments, even writing music for them.

Russolo, Luigi. *The Art of Noise* (1913). Trans. Robert Filliou. NY: Something Else, 1967.

RUTTMANN, Walter (1887–1941). Originally an architect and painter, Ruttmann turned to film after serving in the German army in World War I, initially producing in the early 1920s handpainted kinetic geometric films, which he gave such abstract titles as *Lightplay Opus One* (1921). His reputation is based upon an innovative 1927 documentary that captures a day in the life of a metropolis—*Berlin—Symphonie einer Großstadt* (*Symphony of a Big City*). In addition to proceeding to a silent rhythmic beat, this film portrays scene after scene uniquely identifiable, even decades later, as Berlin; precisely by being always about its announced subject, Ruttmann's film remains a model for subsequent urban portraits throughout the world. A few years later, Ruttmann realized that the magnetic soundtrack of a film could be edited for its audio possibilities alone and so, a generation before the availability of editable audiotape, made an audio composition of sounds unique to a *Week-End*, which remains a classic of avant-garde radio art (still scarcely known, alas). He advised Leni Riefenstahl (*) on the editing of *Olympia*, and in 1940 filmed the German invasion of France.

Russett, Robert, and Cecile Starr. *Experimental Animation*. NY: Van Nostrand, 1976.

RUUTSALO, Eino (1921). A Finnish polyartist (∗) who attended New York's Parsons School of Design in the early 1950s, Ruutsalo has made kinetic art (∗) considerably different from the common run, in part because he often uses language as his principal material. In his *oeuvre* are over forty short films (many of them made without a camera by painting directly on celluloid), numerous sculptures, paintings, and prints. He sometimes takes the same title through various media. Ruutsalo speaks of wanting "to move freely among the different areas of art, depending upon which mode of expression is required at the time. My aim is to avoid becoming confined to a particular mode of art." By most measures, he ranks among the most neglected older avant-garde artists of the Western world.

Eino Ruutsalo: Kinetic Poems, Pictures and Paintings. Helsinki, Finland: Aquarian, 1990.

RYMAN, Robert (1930). While art of one color no doubt remains a good avant-garde idea, it is hard to discern who in the second generation of monochromists is better and/or more original than the rest. There are general discriminations to be made between pure monochromists and those who would dilute their fields with alternative colors, and between those who use colors with varying degrees of seductive appeal, such as Marcia Hafif's (1929) *pink*, and those who work only with the noncolors of black and white. Ryman has favored the second side in both of these dichotomies, preferring a white painting adulterated with various degrees of gray shadings, often created in series of approximately similar appearance, generally in a square format. He experimented with different kinds of white paint and with a variety of surfaces, including plywood, fiberglass, and linen. While such works are individually impressive, a gathering of them makes clear, at least to me, that the better Ryman paintings are those with the weakest or most subtle shadings, especially if the monochromic fields are framed with edges painted a different color. However, at a 1992 exhibition, his second solo show at the Guggenheim Museum, the room in which they were displayed had at its ends tall clean white curtains whose presence made the paintings look messy, if not uncharacteristically *schmutzik*.

Waldman, Diane. *Robert Ryman*. NY: Guggenheim Museum, 1972.

SAFDIE, Moshe (1938). The architectural star of the 1967 Montreal World's Fair was Safdie's *Habitat '67* (1967), which was composed of prefabricated modular apartments stacked twelve high in various, apparently chaotic overlappings. As steel-reinforced modules whose exterior dimensions are seventeen and one-half feet by thirty-eight and one-half feet, with prefabricated bathrooms and kitchens, the apartments were nearly completely constructed before being lifted into place by cranes. Precisely because the modules were not placed directly atop one another, but literally strewn over land, most of the apartments have at least three exterior views. *Habitat '67* was so clever that I have never ceased to wonder why it has not been replicated a thousand times; but perhaps like his mentor Buckminster Fuller (∗), Safdie made architecture too practical, too Veblenian, to succeed.

Safdie, Moshe. *Beyond Habitat*. Cambridge, MA: M.I.T., 1970.

SALZMAN, Eric (1933). One of the clearest and most accurate writers of notes and reviews of avant-garde music, including a twice-revised introductory book on the subject, Salzman is also a composer devoted to his own idea of an innovative musical theater. He has collaborated with choreographers, as well as formed a performance company called Quog; he has codirected an annual music-theater festival. The stylistic pastiche of his *The Nude Paper Sermon* (1969) successfully eschews obvious juxtapositions (the primary fault of simplistic collages [∗]) to mix a huge variety of both historical styles and musical articulations, as well as a spoken narration (which provides, or parodies, a basso continuo) and electronic sounds, all around the unifying theme of "the end of the Renaissance—the end of an era and the beginning of another." Although sometimes performed live, as a kind of "opera," *The Nude Paper Sermon* was originally written for stereophonic tape to exploit opportunities peculiar to recording, which, if you think about it, is really a far more feasible medium for musical theater than live performance.

Salzman, Eric. *Twentieth-Century Music: An Introduction* (1967, 1974). 3rd ed. Englewood Cliffs, NJ: Prentice-Hall, 1988.

SAMARAS, Lucas (1936). Born in Greece, Samaras came to America in 1948 and studied art and art history at Rutgers and then Columbia. Participating in early mixed-means theater (*), he recognized the artistic value of his own body, which he later photographed promiscuously, mostly with a Polaroid camera, sometimes altering the image through pressure during developing or by the addition of ink. Narcissistic beyond belief, Samaras used extended exposures to make images of himself nude hugging his nude self and even making love to himself. Many of these photographs were collected in *Samaras Album* (1971), which ranks among the finest artist's books (*). As a sculptor, he began with boxed tableaus reminiscent of Joseph Cornell (*), giving the form a new identity through knives, pins, and tacks, which become erotic imagery also evocative of terror. In 1964, Samaras exhibited a replica of the small room in which he spent his teenage years; the following year he created a

Lucas Samaras, "Box #124," 1988. *Photo: Bill Jacobson, courtesy The Pace Gallery.*

completely mirrored room that reflects everything inside it, including mirror-surface furniture, to infinity in all directions. Even if one dislikes Surrealism (*) or Expressionism (*) as much as the author of this book, it is hard not to be impressed with Samaras's art.

Levin, Kim. *Lucas Samaras*. NY: Abrams, 1975.

Samaras, Lucas. *Samaras Album*. NY: Whitney Museum, 1971.

SAMPLING (c. 1985). The technique of taking short melodic or rhythmic fragments of limited durations and incorporating these "samples" into a new composition. This was made possible by the invention of electronic equipment that can record or "sample" external sounds, store them digitally, and then, in the course of recalling them, enable the composer to re-create and/or change their pitch, duration, or other musical qualities. (That is why I characterized Bobby McFerrin [*] as the "human sampler.") Commonly used by "rap" artists, who prompt controversy by drawing upon copyrighted recordings, sampling has raised delicate questions of the value of cultural property on one hand and freedom of the artist on the other. For example, if a rap artist extracts the basic riff from a James Brown recording, should he or she be forced to pay a royalty to Brown (or at least acknowledge the source of the riff)? What's the difference between an artist playing a Chuck Berry riff on the guitar in a new composition and sampling the actual riff from a Chuck Berry recording? Didn't Marcel Duchamp (*) "sample" Da Vinci's *Mona Lisa*, not to mention a J.L. Mott Iron Works urinal? Such questions of authenticity versus artistic licence recur in the history of avant-garde creation.—with Richard Carlin

THE SAN FRANCISCO MIME TROUPE (1962; aka SFMT). Formed by R.G. Davis, who directed the company until 1970, it has specialized in political plays, sometimes called Guerilla Theater because these plays were often performed outdoors on portable stages, supposedly attracting people who would not normally attend an enclosed performance space. SFMT performed pantomime in the American tradition of Buster Keaton (*) and Charlie Chaplin (1889–1977), rather than the more precious performance of, say, Marcel Marceau (1923). One mark of the

SFMT performance style was the clever use of both large signs and songs. After Davis's departure, SFMT became a commune, supporting its activities largely by asking spectators for money, in the great tradition of street theater. *Telephone* (1969) demonstrates how to cheat the telephone company by forging a credit-card number. Their longest and most complex work, a critical memorial to the American Bicentennial, *False Promises/Nos Engañaron* (1976, the Spanish meaning "we've been had"), takes place in 1898–1899, portraying racism at the time of the Spanish-American War as it incorporates, as its title suggests, both Spanish and English throughout. A book collecting several texts from 1970–1976 gives individual credits that did not appear in the company's programs.

Davis, R.G. *The San Francisco Mime Troupe: The First Ten Years.* Palo Alto, CA: Ramparts, 1975.

The San Francisco Mime Troupe. *By Popular Demand: Plays and Other Works by.* San Francisco, CA: Privately published, 1980.

SANDERS, Ed (1939). Initially a poet, he became both a novelist and then the lead voice in the counter-culture band known as The Fugs (c. 1965–1970; 1984–1989), whose typical songs had titles such as "Kill for Peace" and "Slum Goddess of the Lower East Side." Sanders also edited and published the broadside periodical, *Fuck You: A Magazine of the Arts* while operating The Peace Eye Book Store on New York's Lower East Side. As a poet, he favors energized, outrageous language that sometimes works better in his prose, such as in *Shards of God* (1971): "He prayed over the sexual lubricant in the alabaster jar and swirled his cock directly into it, signaling to one of the air corps volunteers to grab her ankles as he oiled himself up like a hustler chalking a pool cue." The author of a commercially published investigative report on the notorious Charles Manson, *The Family* (1971), Sanders has also made cultural exposé a recurring purpose of his poetry and even his librettos.

Sanders, Ed. *Shards of God.* NY: Grove, 1971.

SAPORTA, Marc (1923). In 1963, a hyperslick American publisher released an English translation of *Composition No. 1,* "a novel" apparently published the year before in Paris. It came as a box of loose pages that the reader is invited to shuffle "like a deck of cards," because "the pages of this book may be read in any order." More than once I've laid them out on the floor, picking up pages as one might colored sticks, reading scenes in the life of a Frenchman during World War II. Its pseudo-musical title acknowledges a debt to certain musical ideas new in the late 1950s. This combinatory book is so original it is not mentioned in Vivian Mercier's 1971 *Reader's Guide to the New [French] Novel.* Because *Composition No. 1* must have failed in the bookstores, no American commercial publisher has done anything similar since. Other shuffle books, all but one self-published, are Peter H. Beaman's *Deck of Cards* (1989), Henry James Korn's (1945) *The Pontoon Manifesto* (1970), Elton Anglada's untitled box (1973), Pedro Pietri's (∗) *I Never Promised You a Cheeseburger* (n.d.), Richard Hefter and Martin Stephen Moskof's juvenile *A Shuffle Book* (1970), and my own long poem, *Rain Rains Rain* (1975). My suspicion is that as long as publishers ignore this form, its esthetic potential is scarcely exhausted.

Saporta, Marc. *Composition No. 1.* Trans. Richard Howard. NY: Simon & Schuster, 1963.

SAROYAN, Aram (1943). Before he became a pop memoirist, Saroyan was briefly an avant-garde poet whose specialty was running words together to create something else that must be seen, because it could not be read aloud: "lighght," "eyeye," for two instances, the ideographic effect of the latter additionally benefiting from the suggestion of eyeglasses. A pioneering Conceptual (∗) poet, Saroyan also "published" in the mid-1960s a book that was simply a box of blank paper.

Saroyan, Aram. *Aram Saroyan.* NY: Random House, 1968.

SATIE, Erik (1866–1925). A slow starter, whose early adult years were devoted more to radical religion and politics than music (and his music mostly to tickling the ivories in Paris cabarets), Satie returned to music school in 1905 for three years of intensive study. Not until 1915 did his more serious music begin to receive recognition, and his reputation has grown since his death. The last decade of his life was consumed with such commissions as *Parade* (1917) for Serge Diaghilev's (∗) Ballets Russes; *Socrate* (1919), which is a symphonic drama for four sopranos and a small orchestra; and music for the René Clair (1898–1981) film of the ballet *Relâche* (1924), whose original form was a comic masterpiece that Satie produced in collaboration with Francis Picabia (∗) and Jean Borlin of the Swedish Ballet. Satie's most popular compositions were short pieces for piano collectively known as *Gymnopédies* (1888). Others have programmatic titles (e.g., in the shape of a pear). His music frequently depends upon unresolved chords; some works encourage unconventional distribution of musicians in a performance space. John Cage (∗) uncovered certain radical experiments ignored by most Satie scholars, such as *Vexations* (1892–1893), which is a page of piano music meant to be repeated 840 times, and furniture music that, because it is not meant to be heard, presages not only Muzak but Brian Eno's (∗) ambient music. Satie was also a master of ironic aphorisms: "Although our information is incorrect, we do not vouch for it"; "I want to compose a piece for dogs, and I already have my decor. The curtain rises on a bone."

Shattuck, Roger. *The Banquet Years* (1958). Garden City, NY: Doubleday Anchor, 1961.

Templier, Pierre-Daniel. *Erik Satie*. Trans. Elena L. and David S. French. Cambridge, MA: M.I.T., 1969.

Perloff, Nancy. *Art and the Everyday: Popular Entertainment and the Circle of Erik Satie*. Oxford, England: Oxford University, 1991.

Satie, Erik. *Trois Gymnopédies*. NY: RCA Gold Seal 7989-2-RG, 1991.

SCELSI, Giacinto (1905–1988).
Trained in pre–World War II Vienna in twelve-tone technique, Scelsi also studied Eastern musical philosophy, in which scales and rhythms are regarded not as independent structures but as reflections of psychology. In addition to essays on music, he wrote poetry in French; one of his best-known and most ambitious works, *La Naissance du verbe* (The birth of the verb, 1950), is a setting of one of his poems. After his death, another Italian composer claimed to have "ghosted" Scelsi's compositions from twelve-tone sketches.

Scelsi, Giancinto. *Bot-Ba (1952) and Other Works*. Therwil, Switzerland: Hat Hud CD 6092, 1992.

SCHAFER, R. Murray (1933).
A Canadian composer who shared a prominent teacher with his near-contemporary Glenn Gould (∗), Schafer was initially known for tape-recording "soundscapes" in various places around the world. This research informed a brilliant book about varieties of acoustic experience, *The Tuning of the World* (1977), which has an additional virtue of quoting past novels and plays to reveal acoustic experience at earlier times. As a true musician of letters, Schafer has produced other expository books, including *Creative Music Education* (1976), and several chapbooks of genuinely experimental poetry and prose, some of it very good, in addition to editing and elaborately annotating *Ezra Pound and Music: The Complete Criticism* (New Directions, 1977). As a composer, Schafer is best known for operas, such as *Patria II* (1966–1974) and *Patria I* (1966–1972), for which he wrote the libretto and produced picture-filled scores that, because of superlative visual qualities, can be read apart from any musical experience.

Schafer, R. Murray. *The Tuning of the World* (1977). Philadelphia, PA: University of Pennsylvania, 1980.

———. *Patria II: Requiems for the Party Girl*. Toronto, Canada: Berandol Music (11 St. Joseph St., Toronto, Ontario M4Y 1J8), n.d.

SCHÄUFFELEN, Konrad Balder (1929).
One of the more inventive European writers, he specializes in unusual containers for words. *Erdglobus* (1978) is a clay globe about sixteen inches in diameter onto which words have been stamped. *Schäuffelens lotterie romane* (1964, 1975) is a wooden box, six by four and one-quarter by two inches high, in which are tightly squeezed 365 pieces of light blue paper, each about six by two inches, tightly rolled, their ends up, which can be extracted with tweezers from the box in any order. On each sheet of paper are unpunctuated words. The principal problem of this *"entwicklungsroman"* (or novel-in-progess), as Schäuffelen calls it, is that the configuration of rolled up, light blue papers in the box is so elegant that one is reluctant to remove them from the box. Trained in medicine, Schäuffelen works as a psychiatrist in Munich.

Schäuffelen, Konrad Balder. *Gegen Stände Sätze*. Erlangen and Munich, Germany: Klaus G. Renner, 1979.

SCHECHNER, Richard. See PERFORMANCE GROUP

SCHEERBART, Paul (1863–1915). A prolific German writer, active in Berlin, Scheerbart published stories, novels, poems, and plays. He also illustrated some of his own works with stylized, imaginary scenes, theorized about perpetual motion, and envisioned a new architecture. His artistic philosophy, explained in *Das Paradies, die Heimat der Kunst* (Paradise, the Home of Art, 1893), was based on fantasy, imagination, and a search for newness. Scheerbart's writings employ a wit and humor that sometimes becomes grotesque and nonsensical. He often wrote about the cosmos—his "Asteroid Novel," *Lesabéndio* (1913), presaging German science fiction. Other works were meant as social satire—*Revolutionäre Theater-Bibliothek* (1904) is a collection of twenty-two "revolutionary" theater pieces. In his plays he advocated extreme reduction and simplification of stage setting, plot, and dialogue. Some works eschew language altogether, favoring pantomime, as in *Kometentanz* (Dance of the Comets, 1903), for which Scheerbart also created an accompanying score that would now be considered "noise music." He favored experiment in poetry as well, creating, in addition to other works, three sound poems (*); one, for example, begins, "Kikakokú! / Ekoraláps!" Scheerbart attempted to create a perpetual motion machine. His plan and sketches for this project comprise the book *Das Perpetuum Mobile* (1910). Subtitled "The Story of an Invention," this book could be considered an early example of conceptual art (*). Though unschooled in architecture, Scheerbart worked closely with the architect Bruno Taut (1880–1938) on the highly influential Glass Pavilion displayed at the German Werkbund exhibition in Cologne in 1914. His manifesto *Glasarchitektur* (1914)—an important, prophetic work, if only for its influence on the International Style (*)—remains the only book of his to be translated into English.—H.R. Brittain

Scheerbart, Paul. *Glass Architecture* (1914). Ed. and intro. Dennis Sharp. NY: Praeger, 1972.

SCHILLINGER, Joseph (1895–1943). After studies at the St. Petersburg Conservatory, Schillinger taught in post-Revolutionary Russia before emigrating to the U.S. in 1928. Beginning with classes at New York's New School for Social Research, he established a reputation for teaching music composition based upon strict mathematical principles. George Gershwin (1898–1932) was one of his personal students; among those influenced by him are Earle Brown (*), the ragtime pianist/composer Eubie Blake (1883–1983), and the blues singer B.B. King (1926). As a composer, Schillinger is credited with the *First Airphonic Suite* (1929) for Theremin (*) and orchestra.

Dowling, Lyle, and Arnold Shaw, eds. *The Schillinger System of Musical Composition* (1946). 2 vols. NY: Da Capo, 1978.

Schillinger, Joseph. *The Mathematical Basis of the Arts* (1948). NY: Da Capo, 1976.

SCHLEMMER, Oskar (1888–1943). After undistinguished beginnings, Schlemmer made reliefs of concave and convex shapes and in 1921 exhibited abstract free-standing sculpture. On the faculty of the Bauhaus (*) from 1920 to 1929, he initially taught stone-carving and then theatrical design. Beginning with the *Triadic Ballet* (1922), he made costumes that resembled figurines more than traditional ballet garb, giving props and lighting as much presence as performers (presaging Alwin Nikolais [*], among others). The result was a Constructivist (*) theater more attuned to Bauhaus ideals (and contrary to Expressionism [*]). "Theater is the concentrated orchestration," he wrote, "of sound, light (color), space, form, and motion. The Theatre of Totality with its multifarious complexities of light, space, plane, form, motion, sound, man—and with all the possibilities for varying and combining these elements—must be an organism." Any traditional "dramatic" script was thus a "literary encumbrance" lacking "the creative forms peculiar only to the stage." Schlemmer's 1926 plans for a "total theater," which would incorporate a deep stage and a center stage, in addition to a conventional proscenium and a fourth stage suspended above the others, still look radical today.

Schlemmer, Oskar, et al. *The Theater of the Bauhaus*. Ed. and intro. Walter Gropius, trans. Arthur S. Wensinger. Middletown, CT: Wesleyan University, 1961.

SCHMIDT, Arno (1914–1979). A prolific, innovative writer, Schmidt produced twenty-five novels or compilations of short stories that all deal with the author's life, feelings, and opinions, in addition to numerous radio features, essays on literature, and translations of a wide range of European and American authors. Often called the *German* James Joyce (∗), Schmidt produced typescripts (camera-ready copies of elaborate texts that he typed himself): *Zettels Traum* (Bottom's Dream, 1970), which particularly reflects Joyce's *Finnegans Wake* (∗); *Schule der Atheisten* (School for Atheists, 1972); and *Abend mit Goldrand* (*Evening Edged in Gold*, 1975, 1979), all of which have at least two simultaneously continuous dialogues, adjacent to one another on a page, in a form reminiscent more of film scripts, drama, or even painting than a novel. Interspersed throughout these typographical feasts are quotations mostly from 19th-century literature, which was the German writing he felt closest to, probably because he found it filled with sexual overtones.

Like Joyce, Schmidt incorporated several languages (German, English, French, Latin) and German dialects (Silesian, Franconian, Alsatian, Low German, etc.) and then developed his "eytm"-theory (the art of misspelling), so that visual representation changed the meaning of certain words. To give an English example, to write "son" but mean "sin," Schmidt would have them appear as:

i
s-n
o

While his early work was quite Expressionistic (∗), his language became increasingly visual, his spelling phonetic, and his metaphors bolder.

A misanthrope and a cultural pessimist who (like his characters) could survive only amidst books and archives, he became a recluse at an early age, serving as a cartographer in the German occupation of Norway. He never overcame his proletarian upbringing, his sister's marriage to a Jewish merchant, his aborted study of mathematics and astronomy, the decade he lost at menial jobs and at war, the loss of his library and his early writings as a World War II refugee from Silesia (now Poland), and his sense of having become a writer "too late."

Though most of Schmidt's work has been translated into English by John E. Woods, thanks to a generous grant from Jan Philip Reemtsma, who owns the rights to Schmidt's work, many of these translations remain unpublished.—Ulrike Michal Dorda

Schmidt, Arno. *Evening Edged in Gold.* Trans. John E. Woods. NY: HBJ, 1979.

———. *Scenes from the Life of a Faun: A Short Novel.* Trans. John E. Woods. NY: Marion Boyars, 1983.

Ott, F.P., ed. "Arno Schmidt Number." *The Review of Contemporary Fiction* VIII/1 (Spring 1988).

SCHNEEMANN, Carolee (1939). An exponent of messy Expressionism (∗) in several media, Schneemann introduced its esthetic to mixed-means theater (∗) in her *Meat Joy* (1964), which was commonly ranked among the best of its kind and was thus frequently reproduced, not only on stage but as a script. After the stage lights go out, colored spotlights flash through the darkness, revealing the performers slowly undressing one another down to feathered bikinis. The couples engage one another slowly, their bodies clustering on the floor, their legs sticking out. The performers are given flashlights that they suddenly shine on one another. Apart from this group, a woman dressed as a serving maid tosses dead fish and chickens and other food onto the scene, which assumes the image of chaos until the lights are turned on. Schneemann has written: "*Meat Joy* has the character of an erotic rite: excessive, indulgent, a celebration of flesh as material: raw fish, chickens, sausages, wet paint, transparent plastic, ropes, brushes, paper scrap. Its propulsion is towards the ecstatic." Perhaps because nothing she has done since has commanded as much respect, Schneemann titled a book-length retrospective of her work *More than Meat Joy* (1979).

Carolee Schneemann, *Meat Joy*, 1964. *Photo © 1993, Al Giese.*

Schneemann, Carolee. *More than Meat Joy.* New Paltz, NY: Documentext, 1979.

McDonagh, Don. *The Rise and Fall and Rise of Modern Dance* (1970). Rev. ed. Pennington, NJ: a cappella, 1990.

SCHNEIDER, Ira. See GILLETTE, Frank; VIDEO ART

SCHOENBERG, Arnold. See SERIAL MUSIC

SCHÖFFER, Nicolas (1912). Though Schöffer is commonly regarded among the most distinguished European kinetic (∗) sculptors, his work is hardly seen in the U.S. and, worse, rarely written about in English. Schöffer belonged to a group of Parisian artists, gathered around the Denise René Gallery in the late 1950s, who appropriated industrial methods as a prerequisite to eliminating the purported conflict between science and art. Alastair Mackintosh speaks of his pieces having "two parts: a solid sculptural core and its reflection cast upon a suitable surface. The sculptural half usually moves and is made of many small pieces of reflective steel, put together in a Constructivist (∗) manner. The whole edifice turns, and within this principal movement there is often other movement, creating a positive waterfall of light. Aimed at this are spotlights, often of different colors, which cast a huge shadow onto a screen." Mackintosh continues, "Frequently these pieces are equipped with cybernetic [∗] systems that react to environmental influences. The largest outdoor pieces are often huge weathervanes reacting to wind speed, atmospheric pressure, sunlight, and so on." Born in Hungary, Schöffer has lived in France since the mid-1930s; the Hungarian government named a museum after him in his hometown of Kalocsa. He is also the prolific author of books that remain untranslated, some of which propose leisure cities constructed on pylons raised above the earth in large enclosed spaces similar to those envisioned by Buckminster Fuller (∗).

Mackintosh, Alastair. "Nicolas Schöffer." In *Contemporary Artists*, ed. Colin Naylor. 3rd ed. Chicago, IL: St. James, 1989.

SCHOOL OF PARIS. See NEW YORK SCHOOL

SCHÖNING, Klaus. See RADIO ART

SCHWARTZ, Francis (1940). A Texan long resident in Puerto Rico, he has initiated and sponsored many avant-garde activities there, beginning in the late 1960s with his involvement with the Grupo Fluxus (which operated independently, if barely aware, of the principal Fluxus [∗] activities), continuing with Performance Art (∗) that incorporates odors as well as sounds, and speech compositions that typically exploit his polylinguistic competence. Extending the Wagnerian idea of the *Gesamtkunstwerk* ("total artwork"), Schwartz added audience participation (customarily conducted from the stage, with the performers functioning like cheerleaders). His mammoth *Cosmos* (1980), based on the University of Puerto Rico campus, incorporated several music performance groups with gymnasts and aquatic ballerinas, in addition to telephone contact with collaborating artists around the world. His *Mon Oeuf* (1979) was a construction seven feet high, three and one-half feet wide, and four inches deep that, he writes, "was at once a sculpture, a mini-theater, and an instrument that had electronic music, aromas, video, temperature manipulation, and tactile stimuli."

Schwartz, Francis. *Caligula.* San Juan, PR: Institute of Puerto Rican Culture ICP-C 17, 1987.

SCHWARTZ, Tony (1923). A veteran American audio artist, in the 1950s Schwartz pioneered the use of the recently developed portable tape recorder to capture, literally on the street, sounds that previously could not be brought into a radio studio (and thus common acoustic experience). *Sound of My City* (1956), his audiotape portrait of New York people, won the Prix Italia for radio art (∗). Realizing that American radio would be a less receptive medium for extended audio art than records, Schwartz produced several records, mostly about the sounds of his own neighborhood on New York's midtown West Side, that represent a unique achievement. For radio, he has produced thousands of audio-based commercials and acoustic features. He also wrote two provocative books on the media, extending Marshall McLuhan's (∗) general ideas in specific ways.

Schwartz, Tony. *Media: The Second God.* NY: Random House, 1981.

———. *The Responsive Chord.* Garden City, NY: Doubleday, 1973.

———. *New York 19*. NY: Folkways FD 5558, 1955.

SCHWITTERS, Kurt (1887–1948). Born and raised in Hanover, a modest city roughly halfway between Berlin and Cologne, Schwitters was denied membership in the Berlin Dada (∗) Club and so took the word "Merz," which he made the title of his Hanover magazine (1923–1927). (Marc Dachy characterizes it as "a verbal and semantic clone of Dada.") His initial masterpieces were brilliantly colored collages (∗) composed of printed ephemera, such as ticket stubs, used toward abstract ends (that is, an appreciation of the composition as a composition, rather than, say, a political commentary). What most impressed me about his visual art, in an exhibition at MoMA in the mid-1980s, was the small size of most of his works, few of them being larger than a foot square.

Schwitters also built within his home the *Merzbau*, which was a Constructivist (∗) assemblage (∗) of discarded junk that eventually pierced the ceiling. Once the Nazis took hold, even the avowedly apolitical Schwitters fled to Norway, where he began a second *Merzbau* that was destroyed by fire after he left it, and then to England, where he began a third in a countryside barn, with funds from New York's Museum of Modern Art; it was incomplete at his death. His first major poem, *Anna Blume* (1919), is a Dada classic in which the conventions of love poetry are rendered nonsensical. His literary masterpiece is *Ursonate* (1922–1932), in which the musical form is filled with nonsemantic vocables for thirty-five minutes. His previously uncollected writings, which appeared in Germany in five rich volumes—over 1,700 pages in total length (1973–1981)—established him as a polyartist (∗).

Schwitters, Kurt. *Poems Performance Pieces Proses Plays Poetics*. Ed. and trans. Jerome Rothenberg and Pierre Joris. Philadelphia, PA: Temple University, 1993.

Schmalenbach, Werner. *Kurt Schwitters*. NY: Abrams, n.d. (c. 1967).

SCRIABIN, Alexander (1872–1915). Nicolas Slonimsky (∗) summarizes Scriabin's achievements in this way: "Scriabin was a genuine innovator in harmony. . . . He gradually evolved in his own melodic and harmonic style, marked by extreme chromaticism; in his piano piece, *Désir*, op. 57 (1908), the threshold of polytonality and atonality is reached; the key signature is dispensed with in his subsequent works; chromatic alternations and compound appoggiaturas [grace notes] create a harmonic web of such complexity that all distinction between consonance and dissonance vanishes. Building chords by fourths rather than by thirds, Scriabin constructed his 'mystic chord' of 6 notes (C, F-sharp, B-flat, E, A, and D), which is the harmonic foundation of *Promethée* (1911)." Also titled *Poème du feu*, the latter included a score for a color keyboard designed to project changing colors programmed to individual notes (C major as red, F-sharp major as bright blue, etc.), because, to quote Slonimsky again, "at that time he was deeply immersed in the speculation about parallelism of all the arts in their visual and auditory aspects." Just before his early death from blood poisoning, Scriabin was working on a "Mysterium" to be performed in the Himalayas. The American author and translator Faubion Bowers (1917) has produced several indispensable volumes about Scriabin.

Bowers, Faubion. *Scriabin: A Biography of the Russian Composer*. 2 vols. Palo Alto, CA: Kodansha, 1969.

SEAWRIGHT, James. See CYBERNETIC ART

SERIAL MUSIC. It was an extraordinary invention, really, even if serial music is now widely criticized as esthetically impractical. As a radically different way of cohering musical notes, this was, literally, a new musical language that had to discover its own rules for organizing musical sounds (its own "grammar," so to speak), its own patterns of procedures (syntax), and its own kinds of structures (sentences). In brief, Arnold Schoenberg (1874–1951) postulated that the composer, working within the open range of twelve tones to an octave, could structure any number of tones (up to twelve), without repeating a tone, into a certain order of intervals that are called, variously, the "row," "series," or "set."

Once the composer chooses a row, it becomes his or her basic pattern for the piece. This pattern of intervals can be used in one of four ways: (1) in its original form; (2) in a reversed or retrograde order; (3) in an inverse order (so that if the second note in the original was three steps up, now it is three steps down, etc.); (4) in an inverted, reversed order. This row, we should remember, is less a series of specific musical notes than a pattern of intervallic relations. Suggesting that traditional musical notation is insufficient, the composer Milton Babbitt (∗), perhaps the foremost contemporary theorist of serial procedure, proposes instead that a row be represented in the following terms:

0,0; 1,1; 2,7; 3,5; 4,6; 5,4; 6,10; 7,8; 8,9; 9,11; 10,2; 11,3

with the first number of each pair marking the individual note's position in the entire set. Therefore, as the left-hand numbers in each pair escalate from 0 to 11, the second number in each pair refers to that particular note's intervallic relation to the first or base note of the row. (Because they must have different distances, no number in the second part of each pair is duplicated.)

If we transpose this row up two intervals, we would then mark it as follows:

0,2; 1,3; 2,9; 3,7; 4,8; 5,6; 6,0; 7,10; 8,11; 9,1; 10,4; 11,5

This kind of notation illustrates the nature of the row, as well as how the elements relate to one another, more clearly than musical notes do; but these numbers, don't forget, are like notes on a staff, which is to say instructions for producing musical sounds.

Whereas note number 6 in the original numerical notation had the interval designation of 10, now it becomes 0, for what adds up to 12 becomes 0 (as 11 + 2 in note number 9 becomes 1). Once the row's pattern is imposed upon musical notes, the numbers refer not just to specific notes but to what Babbitt calls "pitch classes." That is, if note number 6 in this row produces C-sharp, then serial composers can designate any of the C-sharps available to their instruments. Second, just as the notes of a row can be strung out in a line, so they can be bunched into a single chord. The row used in this illustration comes from Arnold Schoenberg's opera *Moses und Aron* (1932). The fact that Schoenberg could successfully transform this basic material into continuously various structures for an evening-length opera demonstrates, quite conclusively, that the serial language is not as constricting as all the rules superficially suggest—tonal music, one

remembers, has its rules too. Instead, just as twelve-tone procedure discourages the kind of repetition endemic in tonal music, so it creates its own kind of syntactical and grammatical possibilities.

The history of the twelve-tone language has been rather checkered and its development uneven. Soon after Schoenberg invented it, the idea quickly spread through Europe; by the late 1920s, Schoenberg was invited to succeed Ferrucio Busoni (1886–1924) as professor of composition at the Berlin Academy of Art. However, once the Nazis assumed power, Schoenberg, born a Jew but raised a Christian, resigned his post, emigrating first to England and then to America, where he eventually taught at UCLA. After Fascist cultural authorities classified twelve-tone music as "degenerate," other musicians devoted to the new technique either left German territories or moved culturally underground: the Spanish-born Roberto Gerhard (1896–1970) moved to England; Nikos Skalkottas (1904–1949) returned to his native Greece; while Anton Webern (∗), deprived of his conducting jobs, nonetheless remained in Austria, where he eventually became a copy editor and proofreader for the same firm that earlier published his music.

After Schoenberg arrived in America, several important composers who were previously counted among its opponents adopted the serial language: Igor Stravinsky (∗) and Ernst Krenek (1900–1992), among the immigrants; and among the American-born, Babbitt, Roger Sessions (1896–1985), Arthur Berger (1912), and even Aaron Copland (1900–1990) toward the end of his compositional career. Meanwhile, in post-World War II Europe, temporary converts to serialism included such prominent young composers as Karlheinz Stockhausen (∗) and Pierre Boulez (∗), who differed from the Americans in declaring particular allegiance to Webern as purportedly the more consistent and rigorous serial composer (and thus more advanced than Schoenberg).

Babbitt, Milton. Numerous uncollected essays, but particularly "*Moses und Aron*: An Introduction to the Music." In *Perspectives on Schoenberg and Stravinsky*, eds. Benjamin Boretz and Edward Cone. NY: Norton, 1972.

Perle, George. *Serial Composition and Atonality* (1963). 6th ed. Berkeley, CA: University of California, 1991.

SERNER, Walter (1889–1928? 1942?). A poet, art critic, and the author of erotic detective stories that have been recently revived in Germany, Serner published the magazine *Sirius* (1915–1916). He joined Zurich Dada (∗), to which he was already predisposed, and copublished *Zeltweg* (1919) in collaboration with Tristan Tzara (∗). Described by Hans Richter (∗) as "the incarnation of revolt, . . . the cynic of the movement, the declared anarchist," Serner could effectively climax an evening of short Dada performances. Manuel E. Grossman speaks of his making an entrance before an audience of a thousand carrying a headless dummy: "Placing the dummy down, he went back behind the curtain and returned bearing a bunch of artificial flowers which he motioned for the dummy to smell. Laying the flowers at the dummy's feet, he then proceeded to sit in a chair in the middle of the stage with his back to the audience and to recite from his nihilistic tract 'Final Dissolution.'" Richter remembers, "The tension in the hall became unbearable. At first it was so quiet that you could have heard a pin drop. Then the catcalls began, scornful at first, then furious. 'Rat, bastard, you've got nerve!' until the noise almost entirely drowned Serner's voice."

Most historians say Serner disappeared without a trace around 1928 (his Dada example thereby preceding the American composer Dante Fiorello [1905–?], who vanished around 1952, even though he had received an unsurpassed four Guggenheim fellowships two decades before). Both Marc Dachy and the catalog of a 1989 Berlin exhibition assert that, in August 1942, Serner "was shipped with other deportees from Prague to Theresienstadt." Dachy also reprints from the magazine *391* "Carnet [Notebook] du Docteur Serner," which has opinionated thumbnail sketches of his colleagues (e.g., "Tristan TZARA, très intelligent, pas assez DADA").

Dr. Walter Serner. Berlin, Germany: Literaturhaus, 1989.

Dachy, Marc. *The Dada Movement*. NY: Rizzoli, 1990.

Grossman, Manuel L. *Dada*. NY: Bobbs-Merrill, 1971.

SERRA, Richard (1939). Serra's innovation was to make three-dimensional visual art—sculpture—that emphasized presence over appearance and thus weight over even the illusion of lightness. He began by hanging a row of loops of

Richard Serra, "Tilted Arc," 1981. Installed Federal Plaza, New York; destroyed by the U.S. government, 15 March 1989. *Photo courtesy The Pace Gallery.*

rubber from nails in a wall (that even in their stillness resembled some of Len Lye's [∗] motorized sculptures exhibited around the same time) and by pouring molten lead into the corners of an exhibition space before pulling away a lead island whose jagged edge corresponded to the part remaining against the wall, in both cases revealing process. Later Serra took large sheets of lead and propped them precariously against each other or against a wall, at times injuring people when they were moved. As an example of art with an aggressive presence, the curving wall of his mammoth *Tilted Arc* (1981) bisected a public piazza in lower Manhattan. As the steel began to rust, assuming a color associated with decay, it became an affront to the people working there (and, incidentally, a blackboard for graffiti). People employed in the vicinity of the sculpture agitated for its removal and, after controversial hearings, in 1989 succeeded, illustrating the possibility of a distinguished artist making public sculpture that the public, alas, finds unacceptable.

Guse, Ernst-Gerhard. *Richard Serra*. NY: Rizzoli, 1987.

SEUPHOR, Michel (1901; b. Fernand-Louis Berckelaers). Born in Antwerp of Flemish parents, he published in Belgium from 1921 to 1925 the journal *Het Overzicht*, which featured both art and writing. Moving to Paris, he took a French name that scrambles the letters in Orpheus and founded a group, that included Piet Mondrian (∗), and published a magazine, *Cercle et carré*. In April 1930, he co-organized with Joaquín Torres-García (∗) the first international exhibition of modernist Abstract Art (∗). Seuphor wrote *L'Art abstrait—ses origines, ses premiers maîtres* (1949), which became a standard guide to Abstract Art in the French-speaking world, as well as *Dictionnaire de la Peinture Abstraite* (1957), which contains his "History of Abstract Painting." It is not surprising that in 1956 he wrote a major monograph on Piet Mondrian, who influenced Seuphor's paintings and graphic art. Seuphor also published poetry.

Seuphor, Michel. *Piet Mondrian*. NY: Abrams, 1956.

SHERMAN, Stuart (1945). In the 1970s, Sherman developed a sort of chamber theater, or miniature theater, in which he presents for only a few minutes, through mime and the manipulation of objects, his responses to specific subjects, such as people or places he has known. A typical Sherman evening thus consists of several pieces in sequence. As such theater can be set up quickly, he has worked in a variety of nonstandard venues, including street corners and public plazas. Especially in mixing props not normally seen together (e.g., taking a telephone receiver from a flower pot, unscrewing the receiver's cap to release rose petals, etc.), his works suggest Surrealism (∗). Sherman has also made films and done extraordinary visual fictions that I have seen, even though they have not yet been published. In 1992, he founded *The Quotidian Review*, a "monthly magazine" to be wholly devoted to "new and recent artwork (verbal and visual) and articles by Stuart Sherman." Such a personal periodical is not something every artist can expect to produce monthly.

Sherman, Stuart. *The Quotidian Review*. NY: Privately published (P.O. Box 209, Old Chelsea Station, New York, NY 10011), 1992–ongoing.

SIMPSON, N.F. (1919; b. Norman Frederick S.). The most innovative playwright of his English-speaking generation, Simpson has released remarkably few works, beginning in 1957 with *A Resounding Tinkle*. The play opens with Mr. and Mrs. Paradock purchasing for their suburban house an elephant that, since it is too large, they exchange for a snake, very much as suburbanites purchase and exchange new furniture. They invite to their home two comedians who learnedly discuss Henri Bergson's theory of laughter. The Paradocks seem unperturbed that their son has returned home as a woman. The author himself appears to apologize for the play, which he says came to him in Portuguese, which is alien to him, while I apologize for a summary that hardly equals the wild fundamental absurdity of *Tinkle*.

In another Simpson play, *The Hole* (1957), literally about a hole in the street, a crowd gathers around a "visionary" whose specialty is double-talk: "I make a practice of eating far more than I need. And for that reason food is of no interest to me. I eat merely to put food out of my mind. I eat all the time so that I shall not be preoccupied with supplying my bodily needs so far as food is concerned. It leaves my mind free." As more people arrive, projecting their preoccupations upon the hole, their talk becomes a survey of suburban fantasies, beginning with sports, continuing through nature to crime and then political fantasies. All the metaphysical aura collapses when a laborer emerges to say the hole contains a junction box serving the electrical supply. This prompts incredible pseudo-philosophical discussion. After everyone else departs, the self-styled visionary is still waiting for a revelation.

One Way Pendulum, subtitled *An evening of high drung and slarrit*, portrays a family, the Groomkirbys, whose individuals are so self-preoccupied they barely make contact with one another. The climax of absurd events is their son's confession that he has murdered forty-three people simply because he enjoys mourning for them. In addition to satirizing the idealized family and the legal system, the play mocks conventional playwrighting in its ridiculous twists and turns.

Simpson, N.F. *The Hole and Other Plays and Sketches*. London, England: Faber, 1964.

———. *One Way Pendulum*. NY: Grove, 1961.

Esslin, Martin. *The Theatre of the Absurd* (1958). Rev. ed. Garden City, NY: Doubleday, 1969.

SITE (1969). The taken name of an architectural collaborative formed by the sometime sculptor James Wines (1932), who remains its principal contributor, SITE became noted in the early 1970s for spectacular contextual humor. In the parking lot of a Connecticut shopping center, they buried automobiles to various depths, their upper parts encased in cement that visually echoes their original shapes, creating the image of a car cemetery. For the front wall of a Houston discount showroom, they created the image of falling bricks, suggesting the striking image of a collapsing building. In another showroom, the corner wall cuts away from the building to provide an entranceway, only to close up at night. Not only are the images different, they are strong, giving SITE's buildings a definition far more memorable than that offered not only by familiar post-Bauhaus (*) boxes but also the modish, modest "postmodern" alternatives to rigorous geometry.

Wines, James. "De-Architecturization." In *Esthetics Contemporary* (1978), ed. Richard Kostelanetz. 2nd ed. Buffalo, NY: Prometheus, 1989.

SITE-SPECIFIC ART. See INSTALLATION

SITUATIONIST INTERNATIONAL. See LETTRISM

SLONIMSKY, Nicolas (1894). More famous as a pioneering conductor of American avant-garde music (whose 1931 premieres included Edgard Varèse's [*] *Ionisation* and Charles Ives's [*] *Three Places in New England*) and as the most

prodigious musical lexicographer—not only the author of such celebrated, stylish reference books as *Music Since 1900* (1938; 5th ed., 1993) and *Lectionary of Music* (1989), but since 1958 the sole editor of *Baker's Biographical Dictionary of Musicians* (8th ed., 1992)—Slonimsky is also a composer of works that are innovative and yet modest in ways that his books are not. His compositions are short, none being more than seven minutes in length, and all scored for limited instrumentation (for not unlike other avant-garde composers he tends to write for himself and his immediate friends). They fall into three groups: songs, piano miniatures, and others. *Five Advertising Songs* (1924) is a suite composed to jingles he found in the slick magazines of the time. The opening phrases become their subtitles: "Make this a day of Pepsodent!"; "And then her doctor told her. . ."; "Snowy-white"; "No more shiny nose!"; and "Children cry for Castoria!" The wit comes from setting distinctly American words to post-Rimsky-Korsakov harmonies that make such doggerel sound even more ridiculous. To my mind, these songs resemble Dada (*), especially in putting together elements not normally found together, and by that technique deflating all sides.

For "Bach Dislocated," the music of J.S. Bach's C-minor fugue starts in the correct key only to shift down a semitone, and then continues similar shifting for the remainder of the piece. For "Czerny, Schmerny," exercises from the most famous piano pedagogue of Beethoven's time are played with one hand while the other hand pounds chords in a deviant key. Other instrumental pieces begin with a radical structural premise. For "Studies in Black and White" (1927), Slonimsky posited a complex experiment in mutually exclusive counterpoint. Essentially, the right hand plays the white keys one note at a time in consonant intervals, and the left hand plays only on the black keys. Though pieces with two hands playing in different keys should sound dissonant, the structure of alternate monodies permits the illusion of aural consonance. Just as *Five Advertising Songs* resembles Dada, "Studies" extends into music the esthetics of another European visual art development—Constructivism (*), which de-emphasized emotion and representation in favor of

Nicolas Slonimsky, "Palindromic Canons." *Collection Richard Kostelanetz.*

both pure abstraction and the fairly rigorous deployment of structural ideas.

In the meantime, Slonimsky developed a theoretical interest in musical scales other than major, minor, or chromatic. More than two thousand of them were published as a book, *Thesaurus of Scales and Melodic Patterns* (1947), which is a collection of "every possible succession of notes arranged by intervals as counted in semitones." In his preface to this book, he compares it to language "phrase books and dictionaries of idiomatic expressions. But while phrase books are limited to locutions consecrated to usage, this *Thesaurus* includes a great number of melodically plausible patterns that are new," which is to say hypothetical structures. My own opinion is that such a gathering represents, so to speak, Slonimsky's most extraordinary conceptual composition—a "big piece" of scales (or materials for extended composition) that epitomize his systematic intelligence and radical musical interests. It is not surprising that this *Thesaurus* is his most perfect book, the only one that has never been revised in forty years, notwithstanding numerous reprintings.

Slonimsky, Nicolas. *Thesaurus of Scales and Melodic Patterns* (1947). NY: Macmillan, 1975.

———. *Music Since 1900.* 5th ed. NY: Scribner's, 1993.

———. *The First 100 Years.* Ed. Richard Kostelanetz. NY: Schirmer Books, forthcoming.

SMALL PRESS (c. 1970). This has become the accepted term for modestly financed book publishers that issue the sorts of titles that commercial publishers will not do. Customarily printing less than 1,000 copies of any title (in contrast to the commercial minimum of 10,000), they tend to base their editorial selections not upon financial prospects but love, which may be literary love, political love, esthetic love, personal love, or even self-love. Thus, compared to commercial publishers, Small Presses have been particularly open to those who are generally excluded—political or sexual radicals, avant-garde writers, black writers, or religious writers, to name a few. In contrast to "general publishers," Small Presses tend to specialize in one kind of book. Many Small Presses are one-person operations where the "publisher" functions as editor, designer, secretary, and delivery boy, if not the

printer as well. As loans for this kind of venture are not easy to come by, most alternative publishers are self-financed, their founders scarcely compensating themselves for their working time. Too many are excessively dependent upon a single individual's health and energy. Only a scant few, unlike little magazines, are currently subsidized by universities or other cultural institutions. As I wrote two decades ago, "The best of them print serious writing that would otherwise be lost."

Kostelanetz, Richard. "Alternative Book Publishers." In *The End of Intelligent Writing.* NY: Sheed & Ward, 1974.

SMITH, David (1912–1965). On one hand drawing upon his training as a painter who had assimilated Cubist (∗) lessons of diverse planes and Abstract (∗) imagery and, on the other, upon his experience on the assembly line of an automobile plant, Smith produced sculpture that measured its distance from the past by rejecting the traditions of modeling (carving the semblance of an extrinsic image out of a block of material) and representational space and proportion. The innovative equal of Alexander Calder (∗), Smith assembled sculpture (which was generally welded) from contemporary industrial materials that were displayed for their own properties and identities—steel looked like steel, etc. As early as the middle 1930s, he established his signatures that he sustained for the remainder of his career: first, skeletal images in iron that he forged himself and, then, large metal abstractions with faintly representational semblances, such as *Hudson River Landscape* (1951). So inappropriate as a setting for his tall pieces was the enclosed space of traditional galleries that Smith himself would "house" his largest works on his own front lawn, exposed to the elements; and museums would tend to display them in their gardens. He spoke frequently of his disdain for architects and the limits their buildings imposed upon sculptors. By the 1950s, Smith had progressed beyond the Cubistic form of overlapping planes into favoring a flat and spineless sculptural field, usually circular in overall shape, populated with sparsely constructed images. This lifetime consistency distinguished him from other major artists of his generation, most of whom were metaphorically rehatched into their most successful styles.

McCoy, Garnett, ed. *David Smith*. NY: Praeger, 1973.

Krauss, Rosalind E. *The Terminal Iron Works of David Smith*. Cambridge, MA: M.I.T., 1971.

SMITH, Jack (1932–1989). A film so shocking in its content that it was legally proscribed soon after its birth, Smith's *Flaming Creatures* (1963) has become the mythic avant-garde American film, known by all film students who think themselves sophisticated, in part because of its portrayal of a sustained polymorphous orgy with a few females and several males, some of whom are dressed as women. Yet precisely because of its stylistic character, with sharp visual contrasts (such as quick shifts between close-ups and long-range shots), dizzying spins of a hand-held camera, and passages of overexposed footage, the effect is finally less pornographic than hallucinatory to an extraordinary degree. This impression depends as well upon a soundtrack full of harsh juxtapositions, ranging from non-sequitur Chinese music to a mixture of rock music with church bells. Smith also had a truly underground reputation for theatrical performances that depended upon his own strong presence for their success. Ephemeral at their beginnings, witnessed only by a few, some of them are described by Stefan Brecht (∗).

Brecht, Stefan. *Queer Theatre*. Munich, Germany: Suhrkamp, 1978.

SMITH, Tony (1912–1980). After apprenticing himself to Frank Lloyd Wright and practicing architecture for twenty years, this Smith emerged in the 1960s as an extremely Minimal (∗) sculptor, making large cubes, as tall as a man is tall, sometimes in steel, usually in wood, which were sometimes painted black to give them the illusion of density and weight. Some sculptures were composed of modular cubes that could be tastefully distributed, much as rocks in Japanese gardens. Smith's rise in status from a friend of artists to an influential sculptor was meteoric; he was even featured on the cover of *Time* magazine. As a teacher, he could devote a sculpture course to the close reading of *Finnegans Wake* (∗).

Lippard, Lucy R. *Tony Smith*. London, England: Thames & Hudson, 1971.

SMITHSON, Robert (1938–1973). A brilliant theoretician at a time receptive to radical esthetic theories, Smithson gained considerable influence in his short life, mostly for advocating earth

Tony Smith, "Smug," 1973. Installation St. John's Rotary, NY, October 1988–October 1989. *Photo: James Dee, courtesy The Paula Cooper Gallery.*

as a material valid for sculpture; but because many of Smithson's major sculptures no longer exist, perhaps the principal achievement of his career was making works that successfully survive in secondary literature, beginning with his own writings. To my mind, the paradigmatic Smithson achievement is "Incidents of Mirror-Travel in the Yucatan" (1968), which tells in elaborate prose of him placing mirrors in a sequence of Mexican places. Even though the placements were temporary, the essay becomes so rich with insight and reference, with esthetic observations and stylistic flourishes, that a reader comes away believing that the activities may not have happened at all—that even the accompanying photographs (in color in the original periodical publication) may have been faked. Indeed, given that the ironic essay survives as a brilliant work of literary art, the placements could have been purely fictitious. The *Spiral Jetty*, the principal open-air project of his short life, now exists only in a film. Smithson's essay "A Tour of the Monuments of Passaic" is a classic of alternative American autobiography. Precisely because his writings reflect both advanced literature and advanced art, they come to epitomize what I have elsewhere called the literature of SoHo (∗).

Holt, Nancy, ed. *The Writings of Robert Smithson*. NY: New York University, 1979.

Kostelanetz, Richard, ed. *The Literature of SoHo*. NY: Shantih, 1983.

SNELSON, Kenneth (1927). If some visual art students at Black Mountain College (∗) took from Albers, and others learned from de Kooning

(∗), Snelson followed Buckminster Fuller (∗), who gave him the concept of "tensegrity." Snelson's most familiar sculptures are aluminum tubes suspended in space by taut steel cables; so that if the viewer moves sufficiently far away, the cable disappears from the unaided eye, leaving the illusion of shiny objects suspended in space, in defiance of gravity. (They are one of the few examples of sculpture designed to be seen from a great distance, and thus represent a position contrary to that of Carl Andre [∗] and George Rhoads [∗], among others, whose sculptures depend upon the principle of revealing gravity.) Also a photographer, Snelson has made highly detailed 360-degree photographs of cityscapes around the world: Paris, Venice, Rome, Siena, and Kyoto. More recently, he has been using a sophisticated computer to make pictures of otherwise invisible atoms.

Snelson, Kenneth. *Full Circle*. NY: Aperture, 1990.

SNOW, Michael (1929). A pre-eminent Canadian polyartist (∗), Snow has produced major films, exhibited memorable paintings and sculpture, played jazz (∗) (with less distinction), and authored book-art. Though I admire individual works of his, I find it hard to discern what principles, other than cool cleverness, animate Snow's entire *oeuvre*. Of his films, I was especially awed by *Le Region Centrale* (1970–1971) for which he mounted a camera on a supple revolving tripod in a barren but beautiful area of northern Quebec. As the camera spins around in various ways for three full hours, we witness the changing colors of a terribly barren and starkly beautiful landscape. *Wavelength* (1966–1967) is a single, slow, forty-five minute long zoom shot down the length of Snow's loft. For the new baseball stadium in Toronto, he made a collection of striking gargoyles. *Cover to Cover* (1975) is a two-front book, composed entirely of photographs that bleed to the edges of 360 pages, that can be read in either direction, requiring the reader to flip the book over somewhere in the middle. Some find significance in his cutout paintings, done throughout the 1960s, collectively titled *Walking Woman* because they portray a striding female. Though honored as a Canadian genius (in a country very respectful of its geniuses), Snow has not had a comprehensive retrospective in his home country since 1970; and, though he lived for several years in New York, his work is rarely exhibited in the U.S.

Snow, Michael. *Cover to Cover*. Halifax, Canada: Nova Scotia College of Art & Design, 1975.

Fulford, Robert, et al. *Michael Snow/A Survey*. Toronto, Canada: Art Gallery of Ontario, 1970.

SOHO (c. 1967). Called SoHo because it lies *so*uth of *Ho*uston Street in lower Manhattan, it became, especially in the 1970s, a center for avant-garde activities in American visual art, Performance Art (∗), music, theater, and literature. Though previously an industrial slum with empty lofts, SoHo—bounded by West Broadway to the west, Broadway to the east, and Canal Street to the south—in the 1960s attracted artists looking for working space in empty industrial spaces, at first renting from landlords, later purchasing whole buildings that would then be divided among "co-op" owners, most of whom lived in their studios. Because this area was zoned for industrial activities, New York City required that resident artists who need a lot of space to do their work (e.g., painters, sculptors, musicians, dancers, playwrights, but *not* writers) obtain a city-certified "variance" to live there. Precisely because no one had resided there before and nonartists could not do so legally, SoHo became a one-industry town, so to speak, within a larger city, perhaps the first exclusively artists' enclave in the history of U.S. culture. The art galleries came in the 1970s, followed by the boutiques that exploited the neighborhood's growing reputation for advanced taste. By 1979 or so, the real estate prices suddenly escalated, forbidding entrance to newcomers unless they were considerably wealthier than the previous inhabitants. It is said that 25 percent of all the applicants for individual grants from the Visual Arts Program at the National Endowment for the Arts reside in zip codes 10012 (which is SoHo proper) and 10013 (the contiguous, architecturally similar neighborhood of Tribeca), both of which are considerably different from Greenwich Village to the north, the Lower East Side to the east, and the financial district to the south.

SoHo. West Berlin, Germany: Akademie der Kunst, 1976.

Simpson, Charles R. *SoHo: The Artist in the City*. Chicago, IL: University of Chicago, 1981.

SOLT, Mary Ellen (1920). Solt was, for a moment in the mid-1960s, the most impressive visual poet (*) in America, the author of a portfolio of prints, *Flowers in Concrete* (1966), whose images were widely reproduced at the time. Ostensibly poems about flowers, realized in collaboration with professional designers, they used large typeset letters and incorporated various visual devices to enhance their subjects, such as circles of letters within circles of letters for "Zinnia" and both letters for the flowers and Morse code symbols for the stems of "Forsythia." Solt also compiled the first compendious anthology of Concrete Poetry (*), with almost as many pages devoted to critical introductions, notes, and manifestos as poems, initially as a special issue of *Artes Hispanics/Hispanic Arts* (I/3–4, Winter-Spring 1968) and then as a book (1969).

Solt, Mary Ellen, ed. *Concrete Poetry: A World View*. Bloomington, IN: Indiana University, 1969.

SOMETHING ELSE PRESS (1964–1974). Though its efforts were taken for granted during its short lifetime, it is now clear that this Small Press (*) was not only the most distinguished of its kind ever in America, it was the publishing equivalent of Black Mountain College (*) in the education of avant-garde intelligence. Quite simply, SEP issued, in well-produced editions, the more experimental works of Gertrude Stein (*), which were not available before in the U.S. and have not been available since; book-art (*) books by Claes Oldenburg (*), Emmett Williams (*), John Giorno (*), Bern Porter (*), Merce Cunningham (*), Jackson Mac Low (*), Brion Gysin (*), Eugen Gomringer (*), Ruth Krauss (1910), Geoff Hendricks (1931), and Daniel Spoerri (1930), among others, including its founder and principal editor, Dick Higgins (*); and anthologies of Concrete Poetry (*) and radically alternative fiction. In its initial years, SEP also published major pamphlets, really among the best of their kind, by George Brecht (*), David Antin (*), John Cage (*), and Allan Kaprow (*), among others.

It would be disingenuous for me not to acknowledge SEP's impact on my own education. Perhaps the simplest measure of the void caused by SEP's demise is that most of what it did, even by individuals of the first rank, is no longer in print anywhere. Peter Frank (*) produced an annotated bibliography whose intelligence reflects that of his subject.

Frank, Peter. *Something Else Press*. N.p.: McPherson & Co., 1983.

SOUND POETRY. See TEXT-SOUND

SPIEGEL, Laurie (1945). Drawing upon her various experience as a string musician, Spiegel began in 1973 to compose with computers (*) at Bell Laboratories, the source of the GRØØVE program that was prominent at the time. In contrast to those composers who employed the computer to realize a serial (*) complexity impossible with live musicians, she initially favored modal and dramatic pieces. Using the computer to control synthesizers (*), she was able to perform with them live (in "real time") well before the development of the computer as a live performing instrument. She also designed and wrote the computer program *Music Mouse* (1986), a floppy disc "intelligent instrument," which, because it "requires no previous musical training" is conducive to improvisation and thus popular with users of Amiga, Atari, and Macintosh computers.

Spiegel, Laurie. *Music Mouse*. NY: Aesthetic Engineering (175 Duane St., New York, NY 10013), 1986.

STERN, Gerd. See USCO

STEIN, Gertrude (1874–1946). She was, simply, the Great American Person-of-Letters in that she produced distinguished work in poetry as well as prose, theater as well as criticism, nearly all of it unconventional, if not decidedly avant-garde. She could not write an ordinary sentence if she tried; for though her diction is mundane and her vocabulary nearly always accessible, her sentence structures are not. One early development, evident in *Three Lives* (drafted around 1904), was the shifting of syntax, so that parts of a sentence appear in unusual places. These shifts not only repudiate the conventions of syntactical causality, but they also introduce dimensions of subtlety and accuracy. Instead of saying "someone is alive," Stein writes, "Anyone can be a living one," the present participle indicating the *process* of living.

It is clear that there are two Gertrude Steins in American literature. Those who prefer *Three Lives* and the *Autobiography of Alice B. Toklas* tend to dismiss as "incomprehensible junk" an *oeuvre* that I find the richest experimental writing ever done by an American. More than a half-century after her death, even eighty years after it was written, much of this writing is not understood, is not taught in the universities, and, for the most part, is not even in print. In the unabridged, 925-page *The Making of Americans* (1926; first drafted around 1906–1908, well before the innovative novels of James Joyce [*] and William Faulkner [*]), she developed what subsequently became her most notorious device—linguistic repetition. To be precise, she repeats certain key words or phrases within otherwise different clauses and sentences; so that even though the repetitions are never exact, this repeated material comes to dominate the entire paragraph or section, often becoming the primary cohering force within an otherwise diffuse passage. As Stein neglected subject, setting, anecdote, conflict, analysis, and many other conventional elements, *style* became the dominant factor in her writing, more important than "theme" or "character."

Freed from conventional syntax (and the Aristotelian logic informing it), Stein was able to explore the possibilities of not just one but several kinds of alternative English. Having worked with accretion and explicitness, as well as syntactical transpositions, she then experimented with ellipses and economy; having written about experience with many more words than usual, she tried to write with far, far fewer. In *Tender Buttons* (1914), for instance, her aim was the creation of texts that described a thing without mentioning it by name. Other prose pieces have as their real theme, their major concern, kinds of coherence established within language itself: "Able there to ball bawl able to call and seat a tin a tin whip with a collar"; or, "Appeal, a peal, laugh, hurry merry, good in night, rest stole." The unifying forces in such sentences are stressed sounds, rhythms, alliterations, rhymes, textures, and consistencies in diction—linguistic qualities other than subject and syntax; and even when divorced from semantics, these dimensions of prose can affect readers.

Having abandoned prolix paragraphs, she then made fictions out of abbreviated notations, such as these from "The King of Something" in *Geography and Plays* (1922):

PAGE XVI.
Did you say it did.
PAGE XVIII.
Very likely I missed it.
PAGE XIX
Turn turn.

Not only does such compression (along with the omission of page XVII) represent a radical revision of fictional scale, but writings like these also realize the French Symbolist theoretical ideal of a completely autonomous language—creating a verbal reality apart from extrinsic reality. However, whereas the Symbolists regarded language as the top of the iceberg, revealing only part of the underlying meaning, Stein was primarily concerned with literature's surfaces, asking her readers to pay particular attention to words, rather than to the content and the motives that might lie behind them. What you read is most of what there is.

Her plays consist primarily of prose passages that are sometimes connected to characters (and other times not). Only occasionally are characters identified at the beginning of the text, while the customarily concise texts rarely include stage directions of any kind. Stein was not adverse to having "Act II" follow "Act III," which had followed a previous "Act II." There is typically nothing in her theatrical scenarios about tone, pace, costumes, decor, or any other specifics, all of which are thus left to the interpretation of the plays' directors. Because scripts like these are simply not conducive to conventional realistic staging, most directors have favored highly spectacular, sensorily abundant productions that incorporate music and dance, in sum exemplifying Stein's idea of theater as an art of sight and sound.

Her essays were also unlike anything written before in that vein. In discussing a particular subject, she avoided the conventions of exposition, such as example and elaboration, in favor of accumulated disconnected details and miscellaneous insights. Stein's reputation for distinguished prose has obscured her poetry, which was likewise concerned with alternative forms, beginning with acoherence, especially in her monumental "Stanzas in Meditation," and including the horizontal Minimalism (*) of one-word lines:

There
Why
There
Why
There
Able
Idle

Stein frequently boasted that in writing she was "telling what she knew," but most of her knowledge concerned alternative writing. It is indicative that the principal theme of her essays, reiterated as much by example as by explanation, is the autonomy of language.

Stein, Gertrude. *Geography and Plays* (1922). NY: Something Else, 1968.

———. *The Making of Americans* (1925). NY: Something Else, 1966.

Bowers, Jane Palatini. *"They Watch Me As They Watch Me."* Philadelphia, PA: University of Pennsylvania, 1991.

Kostelanetz, Richard, ed. *The Yale Gertrude Stein.* New Haven, CT: Yale University, 1980.

———. *Gertrude Stein Advanced.* Jefferson, NC: McFarland, 1990.

Sutherland, Donald. *Gertrude Stein.* New Haven, CT: Yale University, 1951.

STELLA, Frank (1936). Hailed before he turned twenty-five, Stella's early canvases consist of regularly patterned geometric shapes painted with evenly applied strokes out to the canvas's edge, so that the viewer cannot distinguish any one figure from the background, or form from content, or one image from any larger shape. These faintly mechanical paintings depend upon the appreciation of such strictly visual virtues as the relation of one color to another, the solidity of the geometric shapes, and the potential complexity of elemental simplicity, as well as Stella's decidedly cerebral deductive solution to certain problems in painting's recent history. In 1960, the twenty-four-year-old artist told an undergraduate audience: "I had to do something about

relational painting, *i.e.*, the balancing of the various parts of the painting with and against one another. The obvious answer was symmetry—make it the same all over." Even though his initial innovation succeeded rather quickly, nothing he has done since is comparably pioneering.

Rubin, William. *Frank Stella.* NY: Museum of Modern Art, 1970.

STETSER, Carol (1948). Because visual poetry (*), like other avant-gardes, is forever being pronounced "dead" by those opposed to or ignorant of it, one is always gratified to see the emergence of new talents, even in the 1990s. The principal virtue of Carol Stetser's *Currents* (1992) is demonstrating other ways to do it, in her case by mixing black-and-white images with words, which are handwritten as well as typeset, which may be drawn from newsprint or originate in her own head, all with a unique signature style that is always the measure of a mature artist. In the afterword to that book she writes, "The role of today's visual poetry is to carry on in the tradition of the Indian vedic poets, the Zen Buddhists, poets Chuang Tzu and William Blake, and the philosopher Ludwig Wittgenstein who each attempted to explode our familiar language patterns so we can see clearly and directly. . . . Visual poetry can provide the jolt necessary for us to cut through the conceptualizations of language and to experience the transcendence of The Word." True.

Stetser, Carol. *Currents.* Village of Oak Creek, AZ: Padma, 1992.

STEWART, Ellen. See LA MAMA EXPERIMENTAL THEATER CLUB

STIEGLITZ, Alfred (1864–1946). Had Stieglitz not existed, the development of more than one American art would have been retarded. As an art dealer at 291 Fifth Avenue in New York during the first two decades of this century, he exhibited first photographs and then other avant-garde visual art, initially European, eventually American. His gallery presented the first American exhibitions of Henri Matisse (1869–1954), Francis Picabia (*), and Constantin Brancusi (*), in addition to introducing Georgia O'Keeffe (*) and Marsden Hartley (1887–1943), among many others. From his gallery he published the periodical *Camera Work* (1903–1917), which

Alfred Stieglitz, n.d. *Photo: Dorothy Norman, courtesy The Philadelphia Museum of Art; collection of Dorothy Norman.*

included not only photography and reviews of the visual arts but advanced American writings, such as one of the first appearances of Gertrude Stein (∗) in print. Stieglitz also edited *291* (1915–1916), which represented New York Dada (∗). After the building at 291 Fifth was torn down in 1917, his work as cultural impresario continued in other galleries to his death. As a practicing photographer, Stieglitz imitated various painterly styles, including Hudson River Impressionism (in a famous photograph of lower Manhattan behind the East River) and several kinds of abstraction.

Norman, Dorothy. *Alfred Stieglitz.* NY: Random House, 1973.

STOCKHAUSEN, Karlheinz (1928). Stockhausen is at once the most successful and thus powerful of contemporary composers and, to no surprise, the most problematic. His success is easy to measure—decades of support from the strongest European music publisher and the strongest German record label, not to mention the incomparable German radio stations. He has received commissions from orchestras and opera houses all over the world; he has been a Visiting Professor in America and, as Nicolas Slonimsky (∗) put it, "a lecturer and master of ceremonies at avantgarde meetings all over the world." No composer since Igor Stravinsky (∗) has been as successful at getting the world's major music institutions to invest in him. If only to keep his patrons happy, Stockhausen has produced a huge amount of work, often accompanied by willful declarations of embarrassing pretension. The history of Stockhausen-envy and Stockhausen-mockery is nearly as long as his career. I remember hearing as early as 1962 the joke that "When Karlheinz gets up in the morning, he thinks he invented the light bulb."

The problems are harder to define: The works are uneven, they often fall short of Stockhausen's announced intentions, and, it follows, they are not as inventive or pioneering as he claims. Indeed, they are often patently derivative, of old ideas as well as new. He has composed in various distinctive ways, with a succession of governing ideas. He was initially a serial (∗) composer concerned with extending Schoenberg's compositional innovation beyond pitch to duration, timbre, and dynamics, to which Stockhausen added directions, serially distributing his performers over different parts of the concert hall. *Gruppen* (1959), for instance, requires three chamber orchestras and three conductors beating different tempi.

Stockhausen meanwhile became involved with Electronic Music (∗), producing in *Der Gesang der Jünglinge* (1956) an early classic of vocal processing that succeeded on disc, even though two-track stereo recording compromised its initial form of having five synchronized monophonic tapes resound through five loudspeakers surrounding the audience. By the 1960s, he was incorporating various radical live human sounds (including screaming, stamping, whispering, whistling) that perhaps reflected new electronic possibilities. Later, with *Stimmung* (1967), Stockhausen appropriated aleatory esthetics by having dancers activate eggshells placed on the floor or piano wires strung across the stage. *Kurzwellen* (1969) depends upon sounds inadvertently discovered on shortwave radios at the time of the performance; in the current age of digital radio tuners, which avoid fuzz from unfocused reception and the static between stations, *Kurzwellen* must necessarily be performed "on original instruments."

With *Hymnen* (1967–1969), Stockhausen appropriated collage (∗), producing a spectacular pastiche of national anthems that is, depending upon one's taste and experience, either the last great musical collage ever or an example of how collage, the great early 20th-century innovation, has become an expired form. (I used to hold the second position on *Hymnen* until moving closer to the first.) By the late 1970s, he had appropriated Wagnerian operatic conceptions with *Light: The 7 Days of the Week* (1977), which is a cycle of seven operas, one for each day of the week (with no sabbatical). I could go on; he goes on. Though several books of his miscellaneous writings have appeared in German, only one has been translated into English, curiously demonstrating that even in lives of great success are episodes of minor failure.

Cott, Jonathan. *Stockhausen: Conversations with the Composer*. NY: Simon & Schuster, 1973.

Wörner, Karl H. *Stockhausen: Life and Work*. London, England: Faber & Faber, 1973.

STOKOWSKI, Leopold (1882–1977). Of all the famous 20th-century orchestral conductors, Stokowski, more than any other, was predisposed not only to new music but new technologies for both the production and reproduction of music. From his earliest years, initially with the Philadelphia Orchestra, he presented avant-garde music, often addressing the audience about it in advance, including Arnold Schoenberg's (*) *Gurrelieder* (1911) in 1932 and Alban Berg's *Wozzeck* (1917–1921) in 1931. Stokowski premiered Edgard Varèse's (*) *Amériques* in 1926 and Alan Hovhaness's (1911) *Mysterious Mountain* in 1955, among many others. When audience noises disturbed his performance of Anton von Webern's (*) sole symphony, Stokowski stopped conducting, walked off the stage, and then returned to repeat the work from its beginning. He was the first to use a Theremin (*) to boost the orchestra's bass section. The only current American conductor to do as well by contemporary music is Dennis Russell Davis (1944), who works mostly, to no surprise, in Germany.

Daniel, Oliver. *Stokowski: A Counterpoint of View*. NY: Dodd, Mead, 1982.

STRAMM, August (1874–1915). A civil servant with a family, Stramm wrote short plays and poems that formally surpass what self-conscious bohemians were doing at his time. The story is that in November 1913 he heard F.T. Marinetti

(*) lecture in Berlin. Prompted to destroy all his earlier work, he began anew, initially by befriending Herwarth Walden (*), who edited *Der Sturm*. Stramm's literary esthetic had three principles: use the fewest words, say as concisely as possible, and avoid all clichés. Thus, "In the Fire" (1915) puts eight words into six lines: "Death drags/Dying rattles/Lonely/Immures/World-deep/Loneliness." Many years later we can recognize such poetry as proto-Minimalism (*). Stramm died on 1 September 1915 fighting on the Eastern front in World War I.

Stramm, August. *Twenty-Two Poems*. Trans. Patrick Bridgewater. Wymandham, England: Brewhouse, 1969.

STRAVINSKY, Igor (1882–1971). Like the New York Armory Show (*) of 1913, the Paris premiere of *Le Sacre du Printemps* (*The Rite of Spring*) in the same year, with music by Igor Stravinsky and choreography by Vaslav Nijinsky (c. 1889–1950), became a turning point in the development of the modernist arts. Outraged public reaction—including catcalls, hissing, and a near riot in the audience—helped rally the avant-garde, the occasion becoming, for critics sympathetic to the new, a standard against which subsequent avant-garde art could be measured.

Fortunate to be part of Serge Diaghilev's (*) Ballets Russes, newly established in Paris in 1910, Stravinsky scored three of the dance company's first important works: *L'Oiseau de Feu* (*The Firebird*, 1910), *Petrouchka* (1911), and, of course, *Sacre*. Two hallmarks of Stravinsky's ballet scores were a reliance on folk melodies and harmonies, sounding remarkably dissonant and strange to Western ears unfamiliar with Slavic traditions, and heavy, shifting rhythmic patterns.

After working sporadically with Diaghilev through the early twenties, Stravinsky turned his back on innovation, composing in a "neo-classical" style that paralleled the return of balletic choreography in the works of George Balanchine (1904–1983) and classical literary ideals in the poetry of T.S. Eliot (*). Making another radical shift in the 1950s, after the death of his arch-competitor Arnold Schoenberg (*), Stravinsky flirted with serial music (*), although never accepted its rigorous theoretical basis. Late in life, Stravinsky, like his near-contemporary

Picasso, lived off his reputation as an innovator, rather than continuing to represent the avant-garde in any meaningful way in his work.—with Richard Carlin

Read, George, and Selma Jeanne Cohen. *Stravinsky and the Dance*. NY: New York Public Library, 1962.

Rivière, Jacques. "Le Sacre du Printemps." In *What Is Dance?* ed. Roger Copeland and Marshall Cohen. NY: Oxford University, 1983.

Libman, Lillian. *And Music at the Close: Stravinsky's Last Years*. NY: Norton, 1972.

STROBE LIGHT. The strobe, as it is commonly called, is an intensely bright, rapidly flashing light that, when directed at a moving object, appears to freeze its movement, often in a succession of postures. Invented by Harold Edgerton (1903), originally for the industrial purpose of examining the movement of machine parts, the strobe has since the 1930s enabled photographers to represent within a single image a movement as a sequence of moments. A classic Edgerton photograph, *Golf Drive by Denmore Shute* (1938), portrays within one photograph over four dozen different positions of a single golf swing. The strobe also became popular in the 1960s in some mixed-means (*) theatrical performances and even social dance palaces (aka discos). The first strobes featured a revolving disc that passed in front of the light source; one advance in strobe design came from the development of electronic switching, which enabled the strobe user to adjust the flicker to speeds as quick as one-millionth of a second. While artists as various as USCO (*) and Wen-ying Tsai (*) incorporated strobes into their work, Edgerton himself, though nominally an electrical-engineering professor at M.I.T., from time to time exhibited and published his extraordinary photographs.

Edgerton, Harold. *Stoping Time*. NY: Abrams, 1987.

STRZEMINSKI, Władysław (1893–1952). Influenced by Kasimir Malevich (*), in 1924 Strzeminski formed a group of several Abstract (*) Polish artists who published the periodical *Blok*. Other members included Henryk Stazewski (1894–1988) and Henryk Berlewi (1884–1967), both of whom had experienced Western European Abstraction (*) at first hand, and Strzeminski's Russian-born wife the sculptor Katarzyna Kobro (1898–1950). Strzeminski preceded later geometric artists in making the canvas a nonhierarchical field in which imagery was continuously present, from end to end. The esthetic behind seeing paintings as a single entity he called Unism. He recognized that this forced the painter to renounce divisions within a painting and thus compositional rhythms and contrasts. Strzeminski claimed he transcended Malevich by abolishing any image as distinct as the latter's squares.

Constructivism in Poland. NY: Museum of Modern Art, 1976.

STURTEVANT, Elaine (1930). From the beginning of her remarkable career, Sturtevant has made replicas (and only replicas) of works by famous, mostly living artists. Among the modern masters whose work she has duplicated are Marcel Duchamp (*), Roy Lichtenstein (*), Frank Stella (*), Robert Morris (*), Jasper Johns (*), and James Rosenquist (1933), sometimes with their cooperation (which is to say that they lent her work to be copied). She customarily signs her replicas and insists they differ from the originals, although in ways not immediately discernible. In a New York City exhibition in the mid-1980s, she showed one and only one of several contemporaries—one Stella, one Duchampian urinal—as though she was a collector proud of her masterpieces. While each was technically a forgery, a room full of such replicas represented an esthetic vision. Few exhibitions ever raised so many substantial questions about esthetic/financial value, authorship, professional integrity, and, yes, originality. (The obvious paradox is that such a meticulous duplicator can be so innovative.) Not unlike other work so strong, Sturtevant's has had its imitators, such as Sherrie Levine (1947), who works mostly with photographs (a medium in which imitation is easier to do), and Mike Bidlo (1953), of whom Peter Frank (*) writes, "Bidlo's work transforms the fetish of originality into the fetish of replication—the oxymoronic 'original copy' made flesh. He has refabricated Warhols, Pollocks, Brancusis, Légers, Matisses, Kleins, Cezannes, and numerous other modern museum pieces and auction-house goodies," with less technical accuracy than Sturtevant.

Frank, Peter. *New, Used & Improved.* NY: Abbeville, 1987.

SUBOTNICK, Morton. See LA BARBARA, Joan

SURREALISM (c. 1920). I would be remiss if I did not confess my reluctance to write this entry, from a lack of sympathy for the esthetics, the art politics, and even the practitioners of organized Surrealism. As for the latter, consider the authoritarian structure that placed André Breton (∗) as a kind of pope who was forever excommunicating those with whom he disagreed or those who disputed his authority. (Would such "grotesque parodies of Stalinist purges," in Paul Mann's phrase, have been as feasible in a Protestant culture?)

The epithet "Surrealism" comes from Guillaume Apollinaire (∗), who used it in passing in the preface to *Les Mamelles de Tiresias* (implicitly raising the question, whose answer is not obvious, of whether someone of his anti-authoritarian temper would have survived as a Surrealist had he lived into the 1920s). Surrealist art and writing purportedly depended upon the unconscious as the source of images not otherwise available—and by extension upon deranged mentality—on the assumption that surreality offered more truth and insight than social reality.

Within Surrealist art can be found the revelation of unconscious imagery analogous to automatic writing, extending from the amoeba forms of Joan Miró (1893–1983) to the Expressionistic (∗) calligraphy of Mark Tobey (∗) and Jackson Pollock (∗); neatly rendered representations of hallucinations, in Giorgio de Chirico (1888–1978) and René Magritte (1898–1967); and collages (∗) and assemblages (∗) of unrelated objects supposedly making a surreality apart from the quotidian norm. Perhaps the principal index of Surrealism's general deficiencies as a polyartistic (∗) movement is the absence of Surrealist music.

After 1925, the Parisian Surrealists were forever arguing over politics, and it is perhaps an index of their general stupidity that from 1927 through the mid-1930s they officially supported the French Communist Party. Another problem is that artists not affiliated with the group accomplished its esthetic aims better, the American Theodore Roethke (1908–1962), for instance, writing dream poems far superior to those by any Surrealist, and the Greek-American Lucas Samaras (∗) epitomizing Surrealist sculpture. Though some current artists and writers profess an allegiance to Surrealism, they are rarely, if ever, of the first rank. Enough already?

Jean, Marcel. *The Autobiography of Surrealism.* NY: Viking, 1987.

Nadeau, Maurice. *The History of Surrealism.* Trans. Richard Howard. NY: Macmillan, 1965.

SUVERO, Mark di. See DI SUVERO, Mark

SVOBODA, Josef (1920). At the 1967 Montreal World's Fair, I saw Svoboda's Diapolyscreen, which was a wall of 112 adjacent screens, each roughly two feet square, distributed evenly in rows 8 screens high and 14 screens across (making the grand image roughly thirty feet across and twenty feet high). Each of these screens could be moved slightly forward and back from its moorings in the wall, and each received its own image from projectors behind it. That meant that the entire field could cohere into a larger image or that the field could be split up into several different images, if not 112 disconnected fragments. Though the fifteen-minute show in Montreal, which depended upon 15,000 slides, was disappointingly linear and obvious, I'd wager dollars to donuts that Svoboda's medium was used more imaginatively elsewhere.

Siskind, Jacob. *Expo 67: Films.* Montreal, Canada: Tundra Books, 1967.

SWIFT CURRENT (1984). Founded by the Canadian poet-critic-editor Frank Davey (1940), this is a national kind of computer-assisted literary database that has texts, including works in progress and otherwise unavailable materials, that can be retrieved on members' desktop computers via modems. Peter and Meredith Quartermain write, "Any variety of selections can be printed for discussion in literature classes. By making works and literary dialogue in progress available almost instantaneously and in an extremely flexible format, Davey has both opened the way for new expression and challenged the authority of established publishers, editors, and methods." I am not aware of any comparable repository in other literary cultures, perhaps because the nationalistic solidarity of Canadian writers is rare elsewhere in the world.

Quartermain, Peter and Meredith. "Frank Davey." In *Canadian Writers Since 1960*, ed. W.H. New. 1st series. Detroit: Gale Research, 1985.

Jirgins, Karl. "Swift Current: Interview with Frank Davey." *Rampike* III/3-4 (1984–1985).

SYNTHESIZER (c. 1955). This has become the standard name for pre-computer (∗) electronic machines that produce musical sound by assembling specifications of its elements into a synthesis that, thanks to analog conversion (∗), can be heard as sound. The first synthesizers were, like the first computers, mammoth machines that cost hundreds of thousands of dollars and could fill a room. However, once transistors replaced vacuum tubes, multiple production become feasible; once integrated circuits superseded transistors, portability became possible. Robert Moog (∗) was a pioneering entrepreneur. Synthesizers can create sounds wholecloth or process sounds fed into them. Video synthesizers also exist, if less popularly, and have been used by Stephen Beck (∗) and Nam June Paik (∗), among others. The book listed below, originally an exhibition catalog, includes detailed histories of both audio and video synthesizers.

Dunn, David, ed. *Eigenwelt der Apparatewelt/Pioneers of Electronic Art*. Linz, Austria, and Santa Fe, NM: Ars Electronica and the Vasulkas (Rt. 6, Box 100, 87501), 1992.

TARNMAN, Ian (1949). This is the taken name of a rather conventional Nevada writer and arts executive who, as sometimes happens, discovered that the use of a pseudonym (∗) gave him the *freedom* to create extraordinary visual poetry (∗). Some of his poems integrate language with astral projections in a variety of ways; others are composed of just words or just numbers in evocative arrays. Many of them appear as white images on deep black paper, reminding us of a printing option that is still rarely used. Unfortunately, soon after his book *First Principles* (1978)

appeared, Tarnman disappeared, though the owner of his name reportedly survives.

Tarnman, Ian. *First Principles*. NY: Future (P.O. Box 73, 10013-0073), 1978.

TATLIN, Vladimir (1885–1953). Commonly regarded as a founder and principal figure in Soviet Constructivism (∗), Tatlin returned from a 1913 visit to Pablo Picasso's (∗) studio to make abstract reliefs composed of sub-art materials such as tin, glass, and wood. Always rivaling Kazimir Malevich (∗), Tatlin called his art Productivist (and later Constructivist), in contrast to Malevich's Suprematism. Nonetheless, their purposes were complimentary. As Andrei B. Nakov put it, "Tatlin's sculpture is really free of any connection to extra-artistic reality in the same way as Malevich's suprematist forms are purely non-illusionistic."

Once the Soviet Revolution succeeded, the government's Department of Fine Arts commissioned Tatlin to design a *Monument to the Third International*, which he exhibited as a model. With a continuous sloping line resembling that of a roller coaster, this was intended to be 2,000 feet high and to contain a central lucite cylinder that would revolve. Though the proposal was never executed, the architectural historian Kenneth Frampton for one has testified, "Few projects in the history of contemporary architecture can compare in impact or influence to Vladimir Tatlin's 1920 design." After the Communist crackdown on vanguard art, Tatlin worked mostly on applied projects, such as furniture design, workers' clothing, and the like. Beginning in the late 1920s, he spent several years designing a landlocked glider plane which he called *Latatlin*. He died of food poisoning, in relative obscurity.

Frampton, Kenneth, et al. *Art in Revolution*. London, England: Arts Council of Great Britain, 1971.

Milner, John. *Vladimir Tatlin and the Russian Avant-Garde*. New Haven, CT: Yale University, 1983.

TAYLOR, Cecil (1933). A reclusive figure who rarely performs and whose few available recordings are reportedly not authoritative, Taylor is one of those rare artists whose reputation gains from personal absence. Active as a jazz (∗) pianist, poet, composer, and bandleader since the late fifties and early sixties, he derived compositional ideas from European Impressionism, relying more on tone and texture than rhythm and melody. His group improvisations often featured highly energetic articulations, jagged starts and stops, abrupt changes in mood, and ever-shifting structures often devoid of melody or beat. Eschewing harmonic landmarks, he refused to use a bassist; and when he played piano behind a soloist, Taylor's improvisations were less complementary than independent. When I heard his *Black Goat* performed at New York's Metropolitan Museum in 1972, I found his favorite structure to be a succession of sounds, quickly articulated and followed by a pause, so that individual instrumentalists played vertical clusters at varying speeds.

Taylor, Cecil. *Conquistador*. NY: Blue Note B11E-84260, n.d. (c. 1960).

———. *Silent Tongues*. London: Freedom FLP 41005, 1975.

———. *One Too Many Salty Swift and Not Goodbye* (1978). Therwil, Switzerland: Hat Hut CD2 6090, 1991.

TELEVISION (c. 1930s). As an alternative to radio, television should have been hospitable to an avant-garde art; but precisely because it became a medium of universal dissemination, that opportunity rapidly passed beneath the

Ernie Kovacs, c. 1959. *Still courtesy Kultur/White Star video.*

American genius for mass-merchandising a new technology that Europeans thought would belong exclusively to the elite (whether it be automobiles, motion pictures, or portable computers).

However, some early performers used television in ways radically different from the common run, exploiting capabilities unavailable in film and live performance. Before the age of videotape and so in live time, the comedian Ernie Kovacs (1919–1962) tilted the camera to create the illusion that coffee was being poured at a diagonal impossible in life; he used two cameras to situate himself inside of a milk bottle; he used smoke from a Sterno can to blur focus; he put two separate images in a split screen (echoing collage [*]); he composed live video accompaniments to the warhorses of classical music; and he used an electronic switch to make half the screen mirror the other, enabling him to stage interviews and even sword fights with himself, etc. Because of the small scale of the TV monitor (compared to the much larger movie screen), Kovacs was able to stage close-up sight gags: His femme fatale would, in David G. Walley's words, "slowly turn her head to an admiring camera and then catch a pie in the face," in an image that would not work as well on a big screen (and not at all on radio).

Once videotape was invented, producers could use such devices as instant replay for essentially modernist (*) techniques such as scrambling continuous time; most innovations in broadcast television in the past quarter-century have come less from the tinkering with the medium itself than from ingenuity with videotape. A further implication of the dissemination of the portable video camera and the home VCR was the possibility of circumventing the television stations in the creation and distribution of video art (*).

Walley, David G. *The Ernie Kovacs Phile*. NY: Drake, 1975.

TENNEY, James (1934). An American now teaching in Toronto, Tenney as a musician (pianist and conductor) was part of the Tone Roads ensemble that performed post-Cagean avant-garde music in the early 1960s. As a composer, he worked with industrial engineers at Bell (AT&T) Laboratories in the development of computer-synthesized music and, in 1961–1963, produced the first examples. His other compositions have employed a variety of instruments and tape-instrumental configurations. *Ergodos I* (1963) consists of two computer-generated tapes that may be played separately or together, backwards as well as forwards, to be performed with or without certain other Tenney instrumental compositions. As a writer, he authored *Meta (+) Hodos: A Phenomenology of 20th Century Music and an Approach to the Study of Form* (1964), as well as highly thoughtful essays on John Cage (∗) and Conlon Nancarrow (∗), among others.

Tenney, James. "John Cage and the Theory of Harmony (1983)." In *Writings about John Cage*, ed. Richard Kostelanetz. Ann Arbor, MI: University of Michigan, 1993.

TER BRAAK, Menno (1902–1940). Ter Braak and Edgar Du Perron (1899–1940) were the principal Dutch literary critics of their era, very much predisposed to the avant-garde developments introduced by Paul van Ostaijen (∗). They collaborated in starting the periodical *Forum* (1932–1935), which made the radical move of renouncing the division between Dutch and Flemish (Belgian) literature, and thus acknowledged the importance of the Belgian van Ostaijen to Holland. They also introduced polemics into a smug cultural scene, beginning with a critique of pretentious and verbose language. The more artistic Du Perron influenced the more intellectual Ter Braak. "What *Forum* stood for, and what its creators practiced," writes E.M. Beekman, "left a lasting impression on Dutch literary and intellectual life. It prepared the Dutch artist for the rapid changes of the contemporary world and dispelled from Holland's intellectual life a smothering nationalism." When the Nazis conquered Holland on 14 May 1940, Ter Braak committed suicide and Du Perron coincidentally died of a heart attack.

Beekman, E.M. "Menno Ter Braak." In *Criticism*, ed. L.S. Dembo. Madison, WI: University of Wisconsin, 1968.

TEXT-SOUND (forever). As distinct from text-print and text-seen, text-sound refers to texts that must be sounded and thus heard to be "read," in contrast to those that must be printed and thus seen. The term "text-sound" is preferable to "sound-text," if only to acknowledge the initial presence of a text, which is subject to aural enhancements more typical of music. To be precise, it is by nonmelodic auditory structures that language or verbal sounds are poetically charged with meanings or resonances they would not otherwise have. An elementary example is the tongue twister, which is literally about variations on a particular consonant. This term is also preferable to "sound poetry" because several writers working in this area, including Gertrude Stein (∗) and W. Bliem Kern (∗), produced works that, even in their emphasis on sound, are closer to prose than poetry. Only in recent times have we become aware of text-sound as an intermedium (∗) between language arts on the one side and musical arts on the other, drawing upon each but lying between both and thus, as a measure of its newness, often unacceptable to purists based in each.

Kostelanetz, Richard, ed. *Text-Sound Texts*. NY: Morrow, 1970.

THARP, Twyla (1941). Those familiar with Tharp's current choreography, so popular in larger theaters, can hardly believe, or remember, that her dance was once avant-garde. At the beginning of her choreographic career, in the late 1960s, she created a series of rigorously Constructivist (∗) pieces that, in their constrained style, were never exceeded. Using a company composed entirely of female dancers (and thus excluding any of the customary themes dependent upon sexual difference), she choreographed pieces such as *Group Activities* (1968) in which ten dancers, including herself, perform individualized instructions, themselves derived from a numerical system, on two sets of checkerboard-like floor spaces, creating an asymmetrical field of animate patterns, all to the accompaniment of only a ticking metronome. Performed totally without sound accompaniment on an unadorned stage, *Disperse* (1967) depends upon the ratio of 2:3, which requires the stage lighting to turn progressively darker as the dancers move into the right rear corner.

Tharp also choreographed dances for previously unexploited spaces, such as a playing field in New York's Central Park in the late afternoon. (I remember a rugby game beginning on an adjacent field.) "Dance in the Streets of London and Paris, Continued in Stockholm and

Sometimes Madrid" had its premier on two floors of the Wadsworth Athenaeum in Hartford, Connecticut. As Don McDonagh remembers it, "The audience flowed in and around the performers at all levels and at times trailed them from one floor to another. There was no set position from which to view the dance . . . the nine dancers kept in touch with one another by means of verbal time checks called up the stairwell and by the use of video monitors connected to a closed-circuit television hookup between the various galleries." Composed in sections, this Tharp dance could be re-created to suit different venues.

McDonagh, Don. "Twyla Tharp." In *The Rise & Fall & Rise of Modern Dance* (1970). Pennington, NJ: a cappella, 1990.

Tharp, Twyla. *Push Comes to Shove*. NY: Bantam, 1992.

THEATRE OF CRUELTY. See ARTAUD, Antonin

THEATRE OF THE ABSURD. See ABSURD, THEATRE OF THE

THEMERSON, Stefan (1910–1988). Born in

Poland, Themerson was initially a Warsaw painter who also made an avant-garde film, *Europa* (1931), that subsequently disappeared. Serving in the Polish army in France during World War II, he escaped to England, where he resided until his death, publishing poetry, fiction, and unclassifiable experimental writings almost exclusively in English, mostly with the marvelously titled Gaberbocchus Press: among them, the novels *Bayamus* (1949, which includes typographic poetry), *The Adventures of Peddy Bottom* (1951), *Cardinal Pölätüo* (1961), and *Tom Harris* (1967); philosophical essays with titles such as *factor T* (1972); and *St. Francis and the Wolf of Gubbio or Brother Francis' Lamb Chops* (1972), "an opera in two acts," complete with a musical score, handwritten plot summaries, and sketches for stage designs (which is, of course, how operas should be published). Respectful of avant-garde traditions, Themerson also published a memoir of *Kurt Schwitters in England* (1958) and, in a large-page format, the richest edition of *Apollinaire's Lyrical Ideograms* (1968). It is unfortunate that Themerson's work isn't mentioned in histories of contemporary British literature, perhaps because like most authors of avant-garde English literature written in Britain, he was born outside of the British Isles.

Themerson, Stefan. *Apollinaire's Lyrical Ideograms*. London, England: Gaberbocchus, 1968.

THEREMIN (c. 1920). One of the earliest Elec-

tronic (*) instruments, named after its creator Leon Theremin (1896, b. Lev Sergeyevich Termen), who invented it just after the First World War, this consists of two poles that come out perpendicularly from a metal cabinet. Both poles respond not to touch, like traditional instruments, but to hand movements in the air immediately around them. (Roberta Reeder and Claas Cordes write, "He created his instrument while working on an alarm system to protect the diamond collection at the Kremlin," which seems obvious in retrospect.) One pole controls the instrument's pitch, the other its volume, together producing sustained, tremulous sounds that, needless to say perhaps, were particularly popular in horror films in the 1930s and 1940s. The principal Thereminist in America, if not the world, has been Clara Rockmore (1911). One of her records was produced by Robert Moog (*), who, before he made the synthesizer (*) bearing his name, manufactured Theremins.

During his eleven years in America (1927–1938), Theremin, according to Nicolas Slomnisky (*), "on April 29, 1930, presented a concert with an ensemble of ten of his instruments, also introducing a space-controlled synthesis of color and music. On April 1, 1932, in the same hall, he introduced the first electrical symph. orch., conducted by Stoessel, including Theremin fingerboard and keyboard instruments. He also invented the Rhythmicon [with Henry Cowell (*)], for playing different rhythms simultaneously." Recent information indicates that Theremin worked for the KGB on his return to Russia, perfecting electronics for eavesdropping. In the 1990s, in his own nineties, after more than five decades back in Russia, Theremin returned to New York for a visit.

Rockmore, Clara. *Theremin*. N.p.: Delos 25437, 1975.

Reeder, Roberta, and Claas Cordes. "Light Music in the Soviet Union." In *Eigenwelt der Apparatewelt/Pioneers of Electronic Art*, ed. David Dunn. Linz, Austria, and Santa Fe, NM: Ars Electronica and the Vasulkas, 1992.

THOMAS, Dylan (1914–1953). He was the first modern poet whose work was best "published," best made public, not on the printed page or in the public auditorium but through electronic media, beginning with live radio, eventually including records and audiotape. So strongly did Thomas establish how his words should sound that it is hard not to hear his voice as you read his poetry; his interpretations put at a disadvantage anyone else who has tried to declaim his words since. It is not surprising that he also became the first prominent English-speaking poet to earn much of his income not from writing or teaching but from radio recitals, mostly for the British Broadcasting Corporation. (Given the American media's disinterest in poetry, it is indicative that Thomas's sole peer as a reader of his own verse, Carl Sandberg, a quarter-century older, made his living mostly as a traveling performer.) In 1946, Edward Sackville-West wrote: "A verbal steeplejack, Mr. Thomas scales the dizziest heights of romantic eloquence. Joycean portmanteau words, toppling castles of alliteration, a virtuoso delivery which shirked no risk—this was radio at its purest and a superb justification of its right to be considered as an art in itself." Indeed, it could be said that the principal recurring deficiency of Thomas's prose is the pointless garrulousness we associate with broadcasting at its least consequential.

Maud, Ralph, ed. *On the Air with Dylan Thomas.* NY: New Directions, 1991.

THOMPSON, Francis (1908). Initially a painter, Thompson made several masterpieces of experimental short film that are generally omitted from histories and encyclopedias of the medium. The first short, *New York, New York* (1951), views the city through distorting prisms that function to exaggerate through visual abstraction its distance from nature. The second, *To Be Alive,* made with Alexander Hammid (1907) for the Johnson Wax pavilion at the 1964 New York World's Fair, has three screens, of standard ratios, but with fifteen inches between each one to distinguish them from the *continuous* horizontal screens of CinemaScope (∗) and Cinerama (∗), which had been developed in the decade before. It opens with high-speed shots of New York City simultaneously on three screens and

subsequently depicts the maturation of people around the world. In one sequence, a prepubescent American boy is learning to ride a bicycle on one screen, a young Italian is learning to paddle a boat, and a similarly young African is learning to ride a mule. Disaster hits each simultaneously, prompting them to cry in unison. For many years after, *To Be Alive* was screened continuously at the Johnson Wax Factory in Racine, WI. For Hemisfair (San Antonio, 1968), Thompson and Hammid made *US,* which begins with the audience divided into three parts of a circle. When the walls between them go up, they are watching a circle surrounded by three screens, each 145-feet wide.

For the Canadian Pacific pavilion at Expo '67 in Montreal, Thompson and Hammid made *We Are Young* for six separate screens. The three screens in the lower row were roughly thirty feet square; the three in the upper row were a little wider, much lower, and pushed forward about a foot in front of those below. As in *To Be Alive,* each screen is clearly separated from the others. Sometimes all six screens present the same image synchronously; at other times only one screen is used (while the others are blank). One particularly stunning sequence has the audience moving down six railway tracks simultaneously, each one turned to be perpendicular to the top of the bottom middle screen, the sound of six trains emerging from the amplification system. It seems inappropriate to write about this film as though it may still be available, because once the original venue was dismantled it was never seen again and, according to the filmmaker, may not even exist any longer.

Krantz, Stewart. *Science and Technology in the Arts.* NY: Van Nostrand, 1974.

Youngblood, Gene. *Expanded Cinema.* NY: Dutton, 1970.

TIERNEY, Hanne (1940). German-born, American-educated, Tierney initially developed the traditional idea of the puppet theater to include modernist texts, such as those by Gertrude Stein (∗). While always manipulating strings, she has used such substitutes for traditional puppets as strikingly colored cloths that, hung from the ceiling, are made to swirl through the air in her imaginative adaptation of Oscar Wilde's *Salomé* (1986). In *Drama for Strings* (1988), she used geometric formations of suspended plumbing pipes that make their own sounds in a spectacular abstract theater. Even in pieces fifty minutes long, as hers customarily are, she reclaims the ideal of a "theater without actors" made by one person working mostly alone.

Marinelli, Donald. "*Drama for Strings* in Three Movements." *High Performance* XI/3 (4, 1988).

TIFFANY, Louis Comfort (1848–1933). Tiffany belongs here, no joke, because he repudiated ornate complexity fashionable in the mid-19th century to design glass lamp fixtures and window screens with uncommon geometries. Commonly classified as Art Nouveau, Tiffany's designs resemble Islamic art in their scrupulous avoidance of representation and thus suggest geometric Abstract Art (∗) done decades later. Beginning as an Impressionist painter, Tiffany studied glassmaking in the 1870s and, at the end of that decade, opened a business devoted to interior decoration. Quickly recognized for excellence, his firm was invited to redecorate the White House in 1883–1884. He persuaded churchmen to accept stained-glass windows with secular subjects. One of the most exquisite permanent exhibitions in Manhattan is that devoted to Tiffany's art in, of all places, the New York Historical Society. He was the son of Charles L. Tiffany, who founded a New York jewelry firm whose name is synonymous with luxury, which was a misfortune for the son, whose art realized elegant purity.

Duncan, Alastair. *Louis C. Tiffany*. NY: Abrams, 1992.

TINGUELY, Jean (1925–1991). Born in Germany, educated in Switzerland, Tinguely became the epitome of the inefficient kinetic artist (∗), which is to say that his flimsily constructed machines were meant to run down. Instead of being a technological artist, he was anti-technological, albeit with a sense of humor. His drawing machines of the late 1950s have moving, jointed arms attached to crayons that draw jerky, artistically trivial lines on rolls of paper mechanically fed across them, satirizing the theoretical automatism of Expressionist (∗) painting fashionable at the time. *Metamatic 17* (1959) could reportedly produce a thousand drawings in an hour, before the age of photocopying and laser

printers. Perhaps the climax of his career, certainly from a journalistic viewpoint, was his *Hommage à New York* (1960), a sculptural agglomeration that self-destructed in the garden of the Museum of Modern Art, before a distinguished group of invitees, of course.

Tomkins, Calvin. "Jean Tinguely." In *The Bride and the Bachelors*. NY: Viking, 1965.

TOBEY, Mark (1890–1976). Before becoming a profoundly original American painter, Tobey joined the Bahai religious movement and then studied calligraphy both in Seattle and in Shanghai. He was well into his forties before discovering his innovative calligraphic "white writing," in which an unmodulated collection of lines, roughly equal in width, run to the edges of the canvas, at times creating a shimmering surface. Not unlike Kazimir Malevich (∗) and Piet Mondrian (∗) before him, his turn to Abstraction (∗) reflected his religious faith, the Bahai believing in a common humanity and accessibility to all, notwithstanding cultural differences. Such painting presaged the all-over paintings of a later generation and both the Optical Art (∗) and monochromic painting of subsequent periods. In the late 1950s, Tobey began to use broader strokes, as well as other colors, including black. Not unlike other spiritual Abstractionists, Tobey had a taste for strong statements: "At a time when experimentation expresses itself in all forms of life, search becomes the only valid expression of the spirit."

Cummings, Paul. "Lines, Memories, Celebrations." In *Mark Tobey: Works on Paper*. Stanford, CA: Stanford University Museum of Art, 1990.

TOLSON, Melvin (1898–1967). A professor who spent his entire adult life teaching at black colleges and coaching consistently successful varsity debate teams, Tolson was also a poet who raised nonsensical parody to high literary levels. He was the great American Dada (∗) poet, though scarcely recognized as such, who could ridicule the allusive techniques of the great moderns in the same breath as certain African-American myths about Africa and much, much else:

> The *Höhere* of God's stepchildren
> is beyond the sabotaged world, is beyond
> *das Diktat der Menschenverachtung,*

la muertesobre el esqueleto de la nada,
the pelican's breast rent red to feed the young,
summer's third-class ticket, the *Revue des morts,*
the skulls trepanned to hold ideas plucked
from dung,
Dives' crumbs in the church of the unchurched,
absurd life shaking its ass's ears among
the colors of vowels and Harrar blacks
with Nessus shirts from Europe on their backs.

Perhaps because such lines offended as they honored (and were easily misunderstood as well), they were not easily published. Though his books appeared from general publishers, it is unfortunate that most recognition of Tolson's innovative work has appeared in special situations reserved for African-American writers.

Tolson, Melvin. *Harlem Gallery.* NY: Twayne, 1965.

TONE ROADS. See TENNEY, James

TORRES-GARCÍA, Joaquín (1874–1949). Born in Montevideo of a Catalan father and a Uruguayan mother, Torres-García studied and worked in Spain before coming in 1920 to New York, where he shared a studio with the painter Stuart Davis (*) at the Whitney Studio Club, making wooden toys that presaged his later Constructivist (*) painting. Returning to Europe in 1922, he lived in Paris, where he befriended Theo van Doesburg (*), Piet Mondrian (*), and Michel Seuphor (*), among others. Then in his forties, Torres-García collaborated with Seuphor in founding the periodical *Cercle et Carré* and in organizing the first major Abstract Art (*) exhibition, including over eighty artists. Mindful of his origins, he also organized the first exhibition in Paris of such Latin American artists as the Mexican muralists José Clemente Orozco (1883–1949) and Diego Maria Rivera (1886–1957). Returning to his native Uruguay in 1933, Torres-García published manifestos, organized the *Asociación Arte Constructivo,* founded both an art school and two magazines, in addition to writing a thousand-page book, *Constructive Universalism* (1944). His idiosyncratic paintings favored ideographic images within a grid. Though his name may be forgotten in Europe and North America, he was one of those modernists who redirected the course of Latin American culture.

Fletcher, Valerie. *Crosscurrents of Modernism: Four Latin American Pioneers.* Washington, DC: Hirshhorn-Smithsonian, 1992.

Robbins, Daniel. *Joaquín Torres-García.* NY: Guggenheim Museum, 1970.

TRANSITION. See JOLAS, Eugene

TRUCK, Fred (1946). Born in Iowa, where he still lives, Truck first published a chapbook of hieroglyphic visual poetry (*), *Tangerine Universe in 3 Refrains* (1975), and *Loops!!* (1978), an edition of fifteen jars, each containing a Möbius strip. An early user of desktop computers, he began publishing his *Catalog of the Des Moines Festival of the Avant-Garde Invites You to Show (without really being there)* (1979, 1982, 1984) out of his house. *George Maciunas, Fluxus and the Face of Time* (1984) he describes as "a graphically indexed study of Maciunas's work," which he printed on two long continuous sheets of computer paper. In 1985 Truck cofounded the *Art Com Electronic Network,* an online conference for computer-modem-assisted artists hooked into the WELL, a national arts network that incidentally puts him into continual contact with other artists similarly advanced. From 1986 through 1991, he worked on "an artificially intelligent art work, *ArtEngine,* which applies heuristics to graphics and text analysis." His book *Archaeopteryx* (1992) has "designs for an artist's flight simulator based on Leonardo da Vinci's flying machine, which flies in visual reality." Truck has become, in short, the epitome of the literary-computer artist.

Truck, Fred. *Archaeopteryx.* Des Moines, IA: Privately published (4225 University, 50311), 1992.

TSAI, Wen-Ying (1928). Tsai calls his innovative work Tsaibernetic Sculptures (a play on "cybernetic" [*]), which is his generic term for nearly 100 unique objects that are similar in their operations but different in measurements and details. Born in China, trained at American colleges in engineering, which qualified him for years of work as a project manager in the construction industry, Tsai deduced in the 1960s that he could combine engineering with his painterly interests, producing sterling examples of avant-garde technological art. At an USCO (*) exhibition in the mid-1960s, he used a flickering strobe light (*) that was aimed at shiny

Wen-ying Tsai, "Square Tops," 1969. *Courtesy the artist.*

flexible rods with tops the size of bottle caps. Thanks to a motorized base, these rods could shake at variable speeds. The strobe light, flickering at a slightly different frequency, caught these vibrating rods in a succession of striking postures. Because the result was the anthropomorphic illusion of dancing, a firm material, steel, was transformed to look as though it had lost its rigidity.

One improvement in the evolution of this genre was the ability to change the flickering speed of the strobe in response to either sounds in the surrounding space or the spectator's proximity to a sensing device in the sculptures themselves, making them a pioneering example of responsive or cybernetic art (which I take to be technically more advanced than artistic machines that move autonomously). Another later development was making the upright rods out of fiberglass, rather than stainless steel. Though no two of these Tsai sculptures are identical, they resemble one another much like siblings in a family that, at last count, is still growing.

Of his other kinetic (∗) sculptures, *Upwards-Falling Fountain* (1979) is the most impressive, creating an illusion that must be seen to be believed. As the water falling from a vibrating shower head is illuminated by a strobe, the droplets are caught dancing in response to sound; at certain strobe speeds, the droplets appear to be moving upwards, violating all rules of gravity.

Living Fountain (1980–1988) is a yet larger water sculpture, incorporating a shower head three feet in diameter plus three concentric circles of water jets all installed above a basin twelve by sixteen feet. Here the strobe is designed to respond to combinations of changes in audible music, random sensors, audio-feedback controls, and a computer program.

Cybernetic Art of Tsai Wen-Ying. Taipei, Republic of China: National Museum of History, n.d. [1990].

Kostelanetz, Richard. "Artistic Machines." In *Metamorphosis in the Arts.* NY: Assembling, 1981.

———. "Tsaibernetics." In *On Innovative Art(ist)s.* Jefferson, NC: McFarland, 1991.

TUDOR, David (1926). Trained in piano and organ, as well as music composition, Tudor established himself in the 1950s as the premier pianist for avant-garde music by giving first performances of major pieces by Pierre Boulez (∗), Earle Brown (∗), John Cage (∗), Karlheinz Stockhausen (∗), and Christian Wolff (∗), among others. Indeed, before long, pieces were written especially for him. By the 1960s, however, he gave up piano performing to become a composer, with less distinction, specializing in "live Electronic Music [∗]," in contrast to that composed in a tape studio. In live Electronic Music, the composer has at his or her disposal a variety of sound-generators and processors, some of his or her own invention, customarily performing in collaboration with others. Tudor has for many years been one of the few musicians performing regularly with the Merce Cunningham (∗) Dance Company.

Tudor, David. *Plays Cage and Tudor.* NY: Mode, forthcoming.

———. *RainForest; Pulsers/Untitled.* NY: Lovely LML 1601, n.d.

TURRELL, James (1943). The most remarkable thing about James Turrell's career, when you look back on a quarter-century of it, was that he knew from the beginning that his medium would be light. He didn't discover light after a career of exhibiting objects or a period of theorizing. His first exhibition, in 1967, just two years after his graduation from college, consisted entirely of projections within a museum space. He then created, in his own Southern California studio, a series of light-based installations by cutting slits into the walls and ceiling to let sunlight sweep through his space in various experimental ways; he used lenses to refract it strategically.

The first Turrell work I saw was *Laar* (1980). On the other side of a darkened room appeared to be a large gray monochromic painting. As you moved closer, it retained that identity, its surface shimmering, much as good monochromic painting sometimes does. Only when you were literally on top of the work, close enough to bump your head into it, did you discover that, surprise, the monochromic rectangle is really a hole in the wall—or, to be more precise, an open window into a three-dimensional space painted gray. If only to accentuate the illusion of entering a palpably different world, you could feel that the air behind the aperture had a perceptually different weight—heavier to my extended hand. In a later variation, *Daygo* (1990), shown at the SteinGladstone Gallery in New York in 1990, I stuck my head through the rectangle and noticed purplish light fixtures. In either case, the effect was magical.

For over a decade now, Turrell has been working in remote Arizona on transforming a volcanic crater into a celestial observatory. The "Roden Crater Project," as he calls it, should be a masterpiece; but until it is complete, as well as more popularly accessible, my Turrell nomination for the contemporary canon would be *Meeting*, as installed in 1986 at P.S. 1 in Long Island City. You are asked to come no earlier than an hour before sunset and to stay no later than an hour after sunset. You're ushered into a former classroom, perhaps twenty feet square; most of the ceiling has been cut away into a smaller rectangle, leaving the sky exposed. (It looked like clear glass to me until I felt the temperature change.) Benches are carved out of the walls, but it is perhaps more comfortable to lie on the floor rug, looking skyward. Along the top of the benches runs a track behind which is a low level of orange light, emerging from tungsten filaments of thin, clear, meter-long, 150 watt Osram bulbs. (Having no visible function before sunset, these lamps make a crucial contribution to an illusion.)

What Turrell has done is frame the sunsetting sky, making its slow metamorphosis visible, in an unprecedented kind of theater that proceeds apart from human intervention. The sky looks familiar until it begins to turn dark. Lying in the middle of the floor, I saw the sky pass through a blue reminiscent of Yves Klein (∗). Above me developed, literally out of nowhere, the shape of a pyramid, extending into the sky; and as the sky got darker, the apex of the navy blue pyramid slowly descended down into the space. Eventually it disappeared, as the square became a flat dark gray expanse, looking like nothing else as much as a James Turrell wall "painting," before turning a deep uninflected black that looked less like the open sky than a solid ceiling. Now, I know as well as the next New Yorker that the sky here is never black; there is too much ambient light. What made it appear black was the low level of internal illumination mentioned before. (You can see the same illusion at an open-air baseball night game where, because of all the lights shining down onto the field, the sky likewise looks black.) I returned on another day that was cloudier than before, to see textures different from those I remembered. On the simplest level, what Turrell does is manipulate the natural changing colors of the sky, first through the frame that requires you to look only upwards and then with the internal illumination that redefines its hues.

What is also remarkable is how much intellectual resonance the work carries to a wealth of contemporary esthetic issues, such as illusion/anti-illusion, painting/theater, unprecedentedly subtle perception, the use of "found objects" (in this case, natural light), and conceptualism (bestowing meaning on apparent nothing), all while transcending all of them. I personally thought of John Cage's (∗) *4'33"*, his notorious silent piece, in which he puts a frame around all the miscellaneous inadvertent sounds that happen to be in the concert hall for that duration, much as Turrell frames unintentional developments in the sky. *Meeting* is *theatrical* in that it must be experienced over a requisite amount of time; no passing glance, as well as no single photograph, would be appropriate. Indeed, though *Meeting* could have been realized technically prior to the 1950s, there was no esthetic foundation for it prior to then.

Turrell, James. *Occluded Front*. Ed. Julia Brown. Los Angeles, CA: Museum of Contemporary Art—Lapis, 1985.

Adcock, Craig. *James Turrell: The Art of Light and Space*. Berekley, CA: University of California, 1990.

———. *James Turrell*. Tallahasee, FL: Florida State University Gallery and Museum, 1979.

TUTUOLA, Amos (1920). Tutuola is Nigeria's most original novelist, a thinly educated war veteran who wrote English as only a Nigerian could. "I was a palm-wine drinkard since I was a boy of ten years of age," Tutuola's first book begins. "I had no other work more than to drink palm-wine in my life. In those days we did not know other money, except COWRIES, so that everything was very cheap, and my father was the richest man in our town." And it gets only more original. Because Tutuola reportedly grew up speaking Yoruba, he makes authentic errors of English grammar and spelling on every page; yet his several novels have clear plots, usually about a protagonist with (or with access to) supernatural powers who suffers awesome hardships before accomplishing his mission. One scholar reports that educated Nigerians "were extremely angry that such an unschooled author should receive so much praise and publicity abroad, for they recognized his borrowings, disapproved of his bad grammar, and suspected he was being lionized by condescending racists who had a clear political motive for choosing to continue to regard Africans as backward and childlike primitives." Even with modest success, authentically original artists will always be attacked for some purported deficiency or another.

Tutuola, Amos. *The Palm-Wine Drinkard and His Dead Palm-Wine Tapster in the Dead's Town*. London, England: Faber, 1952.

———. *My Life in the Bush of Ghosts*. London, England: Faber, 1954.

TWELVE-TONE MUSIC. See SERIAL MUSIC

2001 (1968). Stanley Kubrick (1927) has been a good, intelligent, morally sensitive filmmaker who, in the heady wake of success of his second-best film, *Dr. Strangelove* (1964), made this classic for CinemaScope (∗) projection. Because *2001* has not been publicly available in that form for many years, we tend to forget how it filled wide, encompassing screens with memorable moving images, all of which had an otherworldly quality: the wholly abstract, richly textured, and incomparably spectacular eight-minute "Jupiter and Beyond the Infinite" (as the clumsy subtitle announces the sequence); the stewardess performing her routine duties in the gravityless spaceship; and the opening scenes in the space vehicle (which are filled with more arresting details than the eye can comfortably assimilate). Rather than focusing our attention, the movie consistently drives our eyes to the very edges of the screen (much like another masterpiece for a large movie screen, David Lean's *Lawrence of Arabia*, 1962) in the course of emphasizing the visual over the aural.

Over two hours long, *2001* has only forty-six minutes of dialogue, making it in large part, paradoxically, a mostly silent film for the age of wide-screen color in the great avant-garde tradition of mixing the archaic with the new as a way of eschewing expected conventions. Indicatively, *2001* ends with several minutes of images-without-words, rather than, say, an exchange of lines. The central image of the monolith, whose initial mysteriousness is reminiscent of the whale in Melville's *Moby-Dick*, becomes a symbol whose final meaning is revealed as literally the sum of the movie itself, putting a seal of accumulated perception upon the preceding action.

One is surprised to recall how many intelligent people, including prominent reviewers, disliked *2001* at the beginning, and how many parents were less enthusiastic than their children. "I ought not to have found this surprising," wrote the physicist Freeman Dyson (1923), "for I am myself of the generation that was bowled over by Disney's *Fantasia* [∗] thirty years ago, while our sophisticated elders complained in vain about our shocking bad taste." Even though *2001* alludes to Georges Méliès's *Trip to the Moon* (1902), there has not been anything like it since, whether for small screens or large; it's too bad that the big-screen motion-picture theaters capable of showing it best are by now nearly extinct.

Agel, Jerome, ed. *The Making of Kubrick's 2001*. NY: New American Library, 1970.

TYPEWRITER LITERATURE. Composing literature directly on the typewriter enables authors to exploit its capacity for regularizing inscriptions and, better yet, for giving publishers camera-ready pages to print, rather than allowing typesetters to falsify the spacing and other design dimensions. Though certain typewriters presaged computers in permitting closer spacing of lines and/or letters, the creation of expressive shapes was possible on all typewriters. Among those making poems in this way were two older poets of conservative tastes, William Jay Smith (1914) and May Swenson (1919–1989), in both cases briefly, and then younger poets, among them Dom Sylvester Houédard (∗) and Karl Kempton (1943). Robert Caldwell (1946) founded his periodical *Typewriter* (1971) on the reasonable assumption that such writing deserved an outlet of its own. More interesting, to my mind, were the novels composed on the typewriter and printed directly from a typescript: the original edition of Raymond Federman's (∗) *Double or Nothing* (1971), Willard Bain's *Informed Sources* (1969), and especially Guy Gravenson's brilliant *The Sweetmeat Saga* (1971), in which fragments are splayed rectilinearly across the manuscript page.

Gravenson, Guy. *The Sweetmeat Saga*. NY: Outerbridge & Dienstfrey, 1971.

Riddell, Alan. *Typewriter Poems*. London, England: London Magazine, 1975.

TZARA, Tristan (1896–1963; b. Sami Rosenstock). A Rumanian Jew who left his native country at nineteen, Tzara almost always wrote in French, initially as a cofounder of Zurich Dada (∗) in 1917 and then as a Surrealist (∗) in Paris from 1920–1934, when André Breton ousted him from the club for his deviant radicalism. Marc Dachy credits Tzara with giving "French poetry a new impetus, a sudden acceleration. He took unpunctuated free verse, inherited in part from Guillaume Apollinaire [∗] and Blaise Cendrars [∗], and transformed it into an extraordinarily powerful instrument. By exciting the latent energies in language he created an extreme poetry filled with vertiginously polysemic meanings and the novel rhythms of substantives flashing by like telephone poles seen from a speeding car." Apart from this achievement, Tzara wrote a great long poem, *L'Homme approximatif* (1931, *The Approximate Man*), and a classic proto-conceptual (∗) manifesto in the form of a poem: "To make a Dadaist poem/ Take a newspaper./ Take a pair of scissors./ Choose an article as long as you are planning to make your poem./ Cut out the article./ Then cut out each of the words that make up this article & put them in a bag./ Shake it gently./ Then take out the scraps one after the other in the order in which they left the bag./ Copy conscientiously./ The poem will be like you." The image of the Jewish emigré working as an avant-garde literary activist in a country and language not his own has inspired later poets.

Tzara, Tristan. *Selected Poems*. Trans. Lee Harwood. Toronto, Canada: Coach House-Underwhich, 1987.

Dachy, Marc. *Tristan Tzara Dompteur des Acrobates*. Paris, France: L'Echoppe, 1992.

UKELES, Mierle Laderman (1939). A courageously unfashionable artist who has pursued the implications of her chosen subject, Ukeles has focused on the business of garbage in New York City since publishing her 1969 *Manifesto for Maintenance Art*. For one of her pieces, *Touch Sanitation Performance* (1978), she endeavored to shake hands individually with all of the city's sanitation workers; for the multi-part *Sanitation Celebrations* (1983), she made *The Social Mirror*, "a mobile public sculpture" that was actually a sanitation truck "clad in hand-fitted tempered glass mirror with Plexiglas trim," and instructed six other three-wheeled sweepers to perform a five-part "Futurist Ballet" on Madison Avenue. For the World Financial Center, she made *Ceremonial Arch Honoring Service Workers in the New Service Economy* (1988). Though Reagan's head of the NEA (∗) once ridiculed awarding her work a government grant, he lacked sufficient religious sophistication to notice that, as an observant orthodox Jew, Ukeles was drawing upon rituals of cleansing (so often nowadays does anti-Semitism come disguised as ignorance). It is not for nothing that she has also proposed *MIKVA* (1986), or a ritual bath of female purification. "Her vision unfolds in her artistic decisions," the Jewish Museum's exhibition catalog tells us, "which derive from a personal interpretation of rabbinical injunctions relating to the specifications for constructing a *mikveh*." She has been artist-in-residence at New York City's Sanitation Department for the last 13 years.

"Mierle Laderman Ukeles." In *Jewish Themes/Contemporary American Artists II*. NY: The Jewish Museum, 1986.

ULRICHS, Timm (1940). A distinguished German polyartist (∗), Ulrichs has worked with various ideas in visual poetry (∗), Performance Art (∗), graphics, and sculpture, in a bewildering variety of formats. For himself, he has taken the banners of *total kunst* and *totalkünstler* ("total artist"). His work is very popular with German *Künsthallen*, which are city-sponsored exhibition spaces more predisposed to avant-garde shows than, say, the comparable American venue of university galleries. Even though Ulrichs speaks English and has even exhibited English-language visual poetry, his work is rarely seen in the U.S.

Timm Ulrichs. Lüdenscheid, Germany: Städtische Galeries, 1980.

UNITED STATES (1776). America has historically been a country conducive to avant-garde art, in spite of an oppressively commercial civilization and an uneven history of patronage by individuals and the state. The United States was founded on the ideals of freedom and independence, no less for art than for enterprise, and so artistic opportunity becomes entwined in financial opportunity. The archetypal American creative artist has been the "pathfinder" who leaves, often with naive motives, the confines of "civilization," a metaphor for conventional, historically European notions of artistic possibility, to explore the uncharted frontier, sometimes achieving a "breakthrough" into esthetic territory unknown before. What particularly characterizes American explorations is a willingness to pursue esthetic ideas literally, wholeheartedly, and unself-consciously to ultimate and unprecedented ends. In a culture where politics and, alas, arts patronage even at its best have been the art of the possible, art exemplifies the politics of the impossible. America became the Western world's artistic virgin land, as many of the compositional ideas that have strongly influenced the organized European avant-gardes—from

Edgar Allan Poe's symbolist poetic theory through Henry James's and William Faulkner's (∗) fictional techniques to John Cage's (∗) notions of aleatory music—have been American in origin. This tradition accounts for why America's greatest representational arts, fiction as well as painting, tend, in contrast to European, to be more visionary and mythic (penetrating to the hidden essences of life), rather than concrete and realistic (encompassing a wealth of verifiable experience).

Kostelanetz, Richard, ed. *The New American Arts* (1965). NY: Collier, 1967.

UNITED STATES OF AMERICA (1967–1970). A sort of rock band formed in 1967 by Joseph Byrd (1937), an avant-garde composer who had worked with La Monte Young (∗) and Terry Riley (∗), this group featured Byrd on pre-synthesizer (∗) electronic sound generators, Dorothy Moskowitz on vocals, and others playing electronic percussion, an electric violin, and a fretless guitar-like bass. Not unlike Frank Zappa (∗), they tried to incorporate avant-garde ideas into rock music, such as using a ring modulator to alter singers' voices in live time. In spite of support from a strong record company, they lacked the popular appeal of Zappa's Mothers of Invention. They performed with a three-foot by four-foot neon American flag whose red and white stripes flashed alternately, and sometimes performed dressed as businessmen in suits, priests with Roman collars, or Japanese World War II soldiers with rifles and bayonets. "We were a Left Wing band (for ex: 'Love Song for the Dead Che')," Byrd wrote me recently, "but one which had no constituency among the political Left." Once the group disbanded, Byrd produced under his own name *The American Metaphysical Circus* (1969). Many other pop musicians have nonetheless followed the group's precedent of using electronic instruments in live time.

United States of America. NY: Columbia CS-9614, 1968.

Byrd, Joe, and the Field Hippies. *The American Metaphysical Circus*. NY: Columbia MS 7317, 1969.

USCO (c. 1965–1970). In the era of "hippie" collaboration, USCO was the epitome of a polyartistic (∗) commune—literally meaning Us Company, or Company of Us. The three principals were Michael Callahan (1944, initially a technician), Steve Durkee (1938, originally a painter), and Gerd Stern (1928, historically a poet). Collectively USCO produced posters, kinetic (*) sculptures, a mixed-media discotheque, kinetic information displays, and mixed-means (*) theatrical events. Their masterworks were kinetic Environments (*) filled with paintings, objects, audio, slides, films (sometimes looped), colored lights, and a pulsing strobe light (*). The one I remember best, and which also influenced many artists who saw it, was at the Riverside Museum in Manhattan in May 1966. It was filled with elemental symbols and materials: male and female, heartbeats, and seven spheres representing seven planets. "We also had five elements," Durkee told me. "We had sand in the box in the middle; fire in the candles; we had air; we had water in the fountain around the periphery of the column, which was also the lingam inside the yoni—a psychosexual situation. There was an 'om' tape playing on a stereo tape recorder. 'Om' was the original sound of the universe. What we had in that room, in short, was everything that is."

Kostelanetz, Richard. "USCO." In *The Theatre of Mixed Means* (1968). NY: Archae, 1980.

VALDEZ, Luis. See EL TEATRO CAMPENSINO

VAN DOESBURG, Theo (1883–1931). Van Doesburg was, like his near-contemporary Moholy-Nagy (*), essentially a polyartist (*), excelling at two or more nonadjacent arts—painting, architectural design, criticism, and creative literature. In the first respect, he was famous for rigorously geometric, Constructivist (*) paintings, such as *Composition XI* (1918) and *Counter-Composition XIII* (1924), and then for deviating from his fellow Dutchman Piet Mondrian (*) by introducing diagonals into his art. For the second art, consider particularly his spectacular designs for a cinema and dance hall in the Aubette

in Strasbourg, France. Van Doesburg's critical essays are filled with incisive distinctions and stunning prophecies, for he had mastered the manifesto writer's art of stunning, resonant sentences: "We are painters who think and measure"; "in the name of humanism one has tried to justify quite a lot of nonsense in art"; and "the best handicraft is the one which displays no human touch." Van Doesburg's contributions to creative literature began with his second *De Stijl* (*) manifesto (1920), which was devoted to "literature." However, if only to distinguish the Dada (*) side of his activity from the Constructivist, he coined not one but two pseudonyms, I.K. Bonset and Aldo Camini (the former echoing a Dutch phrase for "I am crazy"), and then labored to preserve their secrecy. Whereas Bonset published poetry (reproduced in facsimile in *Nieuwe Woordbeeldingen* [1975]), Camini wrote essays. My favorite Bonset text is "Voorbijtrekkende Troep" (Marching Infantry, 1916), a sound poem that I found in Carola Giedion-Welcker's extraordinary *Anthologie der Abseitigen/Poètes à l'Écart* (1965), which has never been translated, alas. In part because Van Doesburg's work was so various, his achievement remains incompletely understood.

Van Doesburg, Theo. *Principles of Neo-Plastic Art.* London, England: Lund, Humphries, 1968.

Baljeu, Joost. *Theo van Doesburg.* NY: Macmillan, 1974.

VAN MEEGEREN, Han (1889–1947). He was the pre-eminent forger in modern times, specializing in fake Vermeers that initially survived detection. Van Meegeren used canvases from Jan Vermeer's time (1632–1675), removing the previous paint before duplicating style and signature down to the finest details. A disappointed classical painter, van Meegeren initially fantasized that if his paintings could pass for a master's he would be regarded as Vermeer's equal. Once successful with one semblance of Vermeer, he made more, incidentally amassing a small fortune for himself. His downfall came when the Nazi Herman Goering purchased a Vermeer that originated with van Meegeren, making the living Dutchman appear to be a collaborator with the enemy. Forced to stand trial, van Meegeren had, in an unexpected twist, to prove himself a forger, which, given his own ambitions and pride, he did to an excessive degree.

His fraud incidentally has undermined the business of art certification to this day, while his career makes subsequent "appropriation" artists look like superficial beginners. Van Meegeren subsequently became, to philosophers like Nelson Goodman (1906), the most useful example in any discussion of whether esthetic value wholly depends upon authentic authorship. Though not what the artist intended, that sort of immortality constitutes an avant-garde kind of inadvertent surprise; don't dismiss it.

Goodman, Nelson. "Art and Authenticity." In *Problems and Projects*. Indianapolis, IN: Hackett, 1972.

Kilbracken, Lord. *Van Meegeren: Master Forger*. NY: Scribner's, 1967.

VAN OSTAIJEN, Paul (1896–1928). Though born in Belgium, he was by common consent the most advanced Dutch-language writer of his time. In Berlin in the early twenties, van Ostaijen assimilated Dada (*) and wrote satires he called "grotesques" that often depended upon ironically contrasting the present with the past and the sublime with the disgusting. Back in Belgium, he started an art gallery that failed and worked as a journalist before succumbing to tuberculosis before turning thirty-two. The single English-language collection of his work contains a richly envisioned film script that survives brilliantly, even though the film was never made. Van Ostaijen also wrote visual poems (*) that are mostly unavailable in English.

Van Ostaijen, Paul. *Patriotism, Inc.* Trans. and ed. E. M. Beekman. Amherst, MA: University of Massachusetts, 1971.

———. *Feasts of Fear and Agony* (1918–1920). NY: New Directions, 1976.

VANDERBEEK, Stan (1927–1984). His earliest distinguished work was animation that depended upon collaging images found in popular magazines, sometimes abetted by his own drawings, all reminiscent of outrageous Surrealism (*). VanDerBeek also made ink drawings directly on an animation stand, documenting their progress on film. Possessed of a restless, forward-looking

imagination, he was using television imagery in film as early as *One* (1958–1959) and computer graphics in the mid-1960s, collaborating with Ken Knowlton at Bell Labs in producing nine computer-generated films between 1964 and 1970, some of which he called *Poem Fields* because they combine words with rapidly moving abstractions. In the late 1960s, next to his own house in Stony Point, NY, VanDerBeek erected a small hemispheric (dome-shaped) building that he envisioned as a prototype for multiprojection spaces. Audiences were instructed to lie down at the outer edge, with their feet toward the center of the dome, looking up at an abundance of moving images. Unfortunately, VanDerBeek was more adept at envisioning than finishing; and once he became a full-time college professor, beginning in the 1960s, his propensity for procrastination increased. Another tragedy was that, not unlike other forward-looking artists, he died too soon to exploit subsequent technologies.

Russett, Robert, and Cecile Starr. *Experimental Animation*. NY: Van Nostrand, 1976.

VANTONGERLOO, Georges (1886–1965). One of the youngest members of the group founding *De Stijl* (*), this Belgian rejected Mondrian's (*) strict insistence upon only horizontal and vertical lines. In addition to introducing diagonals and then curves, Vantongerloo favored mathematics, thinking that his works would thus reveal universal truths unavailable to artists unfamiliar with math. To him the measure of beauty is $\infty + 1$. What resulted was, first, geometric constructions in the early 1930s—paintings and sculptures with curves and spirals set against straight lines; wire constructions in the 1940s; and colored Plexiglas objects in the 1950s. About his *Composition Green-Blue-Violet-Black* (1937), in the Guggenheim Museum's permanent collection, the curator Vivian Endicott Barnett writes, "The artist has arranged the five rectangles of decreasing width in a counterclockwise spiral beginning at the lower right and ending at the center. This spiral progression is, in turn, a variation of the Golden Section." Vantongerloo's principal protegé was the Swiss Max Bill (*), who organized several Vantongerloo exhibitions. Though his paintings pale beside Mondrian's, Vantongerloo remains a hero to those who value a rational art.

Vantongerloo, Georges. *Paintings, Sculptures, Reflections.* NY: Wittenborn, 1948.

Barnett, V.E. *Handbook: The Guggenheim Museum Collection.* NY: Guggenheim Museum, 1980.

VARÈSE, Edgard (1883–1965; aka Edgar V.). A Frenchman who studied in Italy and lived in Berlin before emigrating to America in 1915, Varèse developed the concept of "organized sound" that eschewed precise pitch and other traditional musical structures for alternative kinds of musical coherence. His monumental departure *Ionisation* (1931) is a wholly percussive piece that employs such nonmusical sound generators as sirens, sleigh bells, and brake drums that, incidentally, have indefinite pitch. To say that this short work, only several minutes in length, sounded like nothing done before would be an understatement. Writing in 1967, only a few years after I first heard *Ionisation* and was still awed by it, I said "The interaction of such large blocks of unusual percussive material produced a chaotic sound so distinctly unlike any previous musical experience that laymen and critics condemned the piece as merely noise (that was 'not music') and even professional composers feared that the apocalypse—the end of music—had come." What happened, however, was that the acceptance of *Ionisation*, along with Varèse's idea of "organized sound," created a precedent for further music with imprecise pitch and alternative acoustic structuring. One measure of this change in thinking is that *Ionisation*, a work requiring many rehearsals for its premiere, is by now frequently performed by amateurs.

Varèse was neglected for most of his professional life; not until 1955, for instance, was he elected to the National Institute of Arts and Letters. He frequently made his home in the American southwest, where Henry Miller (1891–1980) found him in the early 1940s and wrote a forgotten appreciation, "With Edgar Varèse in the Gobi Desert." Indeed, because his innovations were initially unacceptable, they remain so incompletely understood that debate over them continues among a curious diversity of admirers. John Cage (*) always honored Varèse as a precursor of the chaotic tradition of modernist music; the sophisticated rock musician Frank Zappa (*) staged in New York at his own expense an evening-length concert of Varèse's music in 1981; and Milton Babbitt (*), as a serial theorist, has found complex structures in Varèse's work more typical of his own kind of music. Nicolas Slonimsky (*) reports: "On the centennial of his birth, in 1983, festivals of his music were staged in Strasbourg, Paris, Rome, Washington, DC, NY, and Los Angeles."

Not unlike his near-contemporary Anton Webern (*), Varèse finished few pieces, each remarkably different from the others, each of which can be admired for different reasons. My own choice for his second innovative monument would be *Poème électronique* (1958), which ranks among the early masterpieces of music wholly for the medium new to the post–Second World War period, magnetic tape. Commissioned for Philips Radio's three-peaked pavilion designed by Le Corbusier (*) for a Brussels World Exposition, this eight-minute example of organized sound was densely composed, from source sounds both human and mechanical, to emerge through four hundred separate loudspeakers, sweeping through the space as "continuous arcs of sound," to quote from the liner notes to the first recording:

> The sound itself was accompanied by a series of projected images chosen by Le Corbusier, some of them photographs, others montages, paintings, printed or written script. No synchronization between sight and sound was attempted by the two artists; part of the effect achieved was the result of a discordance between aural and visual impressions. . . . The audience, some fifteen or sixteen thousand people daily for six months, evinced reactions almost as kaleidoscopic as the sounds and images they encountered.

Were this complete *Poème* redone today, as it should be, I sense it would still be awesome and innovative; and I'd like to experience it. Until then I know only a stereophonic audiotape once available on a long-playing record (remember them?).

Varèse, Edgard. *Music of: Ionisation, Density 21.5, Intègrales, Octandre, Hyperprism, Poème électronique.* NY: Columbia 6146, n.d.

Kostelanetz, Richard. "Contemporary Music (1967)." In *On Innovative Music(ian)s.* NY: Limelight, 1989.

Miller, Henry. "With Edgar Varèse in the Gobi Desert." In *The Air-Conditioned Nightmare.* NY: New Directions, 1945.

Babbitt, Milton. "Edgard Varèse: A Few Observations of His Music." In *Perspectives of New Music* IV/2 (Spring-Summer 1966).

VASARELY, Victor (1908). Vasarely has so popularized his work, mostly through the medium of prints, that it is hard to remember that he was once a genuinely innovative Optical (*) artist. Born in Hungary, Vasarely moved to France as a young man. His central idea was to use an array of simple geometric forms to create, on a two-dimensional static canvas, the illusion of movement. At times the illusory movements are so contrary and intense that the painting cannot be stared at without inducing dizziness. Vasarely customarily fills a good structural idea with a wide variety of unmodulated colors. His son Jean-Pierre Vasarely (1934), professionally known as Yvaral, is also a distinguished geometric artist who was a founding member of GRAV (*Groupe de recherche d'art visuel*).

Spies, Werner. *Victor Vasarely.* NY: Abrams, 1971.

VAUGHN-JAMES, Martin. See GROSS, Milt; VISUAL POETRY

VAUTIER, Ben (1935). Born in Naples of a Swiss-French father and an Irish mother, in the mid-1950s Vautier gravitated to Nice, France, where he has worked ever since. One mark of his art is ironic audacity, which begins with his signing his works only "Ben," with large open letters whose calligraphy reeks of egotism. Vautier's essential move is to give esthetic value to common things, such as lying face down on a busy sidewalk or by entitling and signing familiar objects. His Nice store, initially called *Laboratoie* and then renamed *Galeries Ben Doute de Tour,* is now owned by the National Museum of Modern Art at the Centre Pompidou. Vautier also

likes to write in large letters conundrums that are considerably wittier than similar, later pseudo-aphorisms by Jenny Holzer (*). Among other clever Vautiers is "Postman's Choice" (1965), which is classic mail art (*) because it must travel through the public post. Because each side of the standard card bears a stamp and address, it is up to the postman to decide who its recipient will be.

Vautier, Ben. *Réédition des bag'arts de Ben, 1978–1988.* 2 vols. Milan, Italy: Mudima, 1991.

VELVET UNDERGROUND (c. 1966–1972). As one of the first downtown Manhattan rock bands, initially championed by Andy Warhol (*), the Velvet Underground participated in the Exploding Plastic Inevitable, Warhol's multi-media discotheque on St. Marks Place in 1966. Their leaders were the singer/songwriter Lou Reed (1942) and the string player John Cale (1940), who had previously performed with La Monte Young (*). Their choice of subject matter (drug addiction, street life, tortured sexuality) and their contemptuous attitude toward their audience placed them squarely against the more listener-friendly groups like the Beatles. Their songs were longer than standard pop/rock fare, and they made no attempt to polish the rough edges off of their performances. Not unlike many other avant-garde combines, the Velvets had a greater impact after they dissolved, influencing the punk-rock (*) movement of the 1970s.— Richard Carlin

The Velvet Underground performing at The Filmmakers Cinematheque, 8 February 1966. L to r: Maureen Tucker, Nico, Lou Reed, Sterling Morrison, John Cale. *Photo © 1993, Fred W. McDarrah.*

Velvet Underground. *With Nico.* NY: Verve 5008, 1967.

———. *White Light/White Heat.* NY: Verve 5046, 1967.

VERCOE, Barry (1937). Born in New Zealand, Vercoe came to M.I.T. in the 1960s and created the MUSIC 360 program for synthesizing sound on IBM/360 computers. About his composition *Synthesism* (1976) he writes, "Much of its material is either derived from or modified by the totally patternless output of a random-number generator. The structural base of the work is an ordered set of sixteen numbers that comprise a geometric series from 1 to 2. This set is projected into various domains as a compositional determinant—for example, onto the octave to form an equal-tempered sixteen-note series and into the time domain to determine durations or to control successions of varying attack rates." He has recently been working in questions of perception. His wife, Elizabeth Vercoe (1940), is also a notable composer, especially noted for three song cycles, *Herstory I-III* (1975, 1979, 1986), to texts written by women, for voice and instrumental accompaniment.

Vercoe, Barry. *Synthesism* (1976). NY: Nonesuch H-71245, n.d.

Vercoe, Elizabeth. *Herstory II.* Boston, MA: Northeastern Records NR 221, 1985.

VIDEO ART (c. 1960). The pioneer here is Nam June Paik (*), who realized early in the 1960s that magnets applied to points outside a live TV screen could distort its kinetic image. Paik later placed an electrified wire across a reel of recorded videotape, thereby causing erasure every few seconds; he was among the first to assemble several monitors into unified objects called video sculptures. Once the portable video camera became commercially available, artists were among the first to purchase it. I remember Robert Whitman (*) using one to tape his outdoor mixed-means (*) piece in 1967, no doubt discovering on the small screen an image considerably different from that available on black-and-white film. Two years later, I saw Frank Gillette (*) and Ira Schneider's (*) *Wipe Cycle*, which exploited the new medium's capability to produce a picture of the scene before it, making

video different from film, which needs to be developed before being shown. Technically, video depended upon advances in the technology of magnetic tape that was previously used for sound recording (in contrast, say, to holography [*], which depended upon film technology). Though video producers could use switchers and other devices to combine images in live time (such as splitting the screen image into discrete parts or setting foreground images against a different background), one audio technique that at last count could not be reproduced was multi-tracking (*), which is the layering at equal strength of separately generated video material.

Once the cost of portable cameras decreased, video became a popular art medium, much like photography before it, so that one measure of artistry became the creation of work different from the common run. Some use video to document live performances; others, such as Amy Greenfield (*), exploited its different scale to "film" performances that were never meant to be seen live. Stephen Beck (*) eschewed the camera completely for synthesizers that could create images never seen before; Bill Viola (1951) and Buky Schwartz (1932), among others, feasted upon perceptual incongruities unique to the new medium, while Davidson Gigliotti (1939) and Mary Lucier (1944) used several monitors to portray a continuous image that ran from screen to screen.

It was perhaps unfortunate that video art developed in the 1970s and 1980s, when content-based fads became more acceptable in critical discourse than before. By the 1990s, many of the prominent video artists have done work that will date not for technical reasons (the best early photography is still exhibited) but for transiently fashionable attitudes. It is indicative that the esthetics of collage (*), long passé in all other arts, should have currency in video art, along with literal representationalism, journalistic commentary disguised as leftish agitprop, and a limited sense of what the new medium can do.

Kostelanetz, Richard. "Waiting for Revisionism" (1991). In *On Innovative Art(ist)s*. Jefferson, NC: McFarland, 1992.

Schneider, Ira, and Beryl Korot. *Video Art: An Anthology*. NY: Harcourt, 1975.

VIENNA GROUP. Several of the most experimental German-language poets gathered in Vienna in the late 1950s, and, in the manner of ambitious Europeans (but not comparably ambitious Americans), declared themselves a group: Friedrich Achleitner (1930), H.C. (Hans Carl) Artmann (1921), Konrad Bayer (1932–1964), Gerhard Rühm (1930), and Oswald Wiener (1935). They worked with visual poetry (*), language games, and alternative structures, among other innovations; nonetheless, few English translations of their work exist, none of them particularly complete. Many German-speaking colleagues of mine consider Wiener's *Die verbesserung von mitteleuropa* (The Improvement of Middle Europe, 1969) the most substantial experimental novel after Arno Schmidt's (*) works. The standard German anthology of the Vienna Group suffers from the omission of another Viennese poet, Ernst Jandl (1925), who in many ways seems more interesting (if only for his poems originally in English).

Rühm, Gerhard, ed. *Die Wiener Gruppe*. Hamburg, Germany: Rowhohlt, 1967.

Jandl, Ernst. *Der künstliche Baum*. Neuwied, Germany: Luchterhand, 1970.

VILLA, José Garcia (1908). Born in the Philippines, educated at the University of New Mexico and Columbia, Villa became an English poet in the tradition of E.E. Cummings (*), focusing upon expression through typographic inventions. His "Sonnet in Polka Dots," for instance, consists of fourteen lines of just the letter *O*, distributed horizontally as though the letters stand for words. Another poem has syntactically normal sequences of words, punctuated however with commas that give them a different rhythm and meaning: "Moonlight's, melody, alone, has, secrecy,/ To, make, watermelons, sweet, and, juicy." Whereas most experimental poets in America suffer neglect at their professional beginnings, Villa was once far more prominent, with commercial publishers issuing his work, than he is now.

Villa, José Garcia. *Selected Poems and New*. NY: McDowell, 1958.

VIOLA, Bill. See VIDEO ART

VIRTUAL REALITY. See BECK, Stephen

VISUAL FICTION. See VISUAL POETRY

VISUAL POETRY (c. 325 B.C.). This is my preferred term for Minimal (*), customarily non-syntactical language that is visually enhanced to a significant degree. It differs from Pattern Poetry (*), where the ends of conventionally syntactical lines define a perceptible shape; from Concrete Poetry (*), which at its purest identifies a materialist attitude toward language, wholly apart from syntax and semantics; and from whatever it was that William Blake (*) did (consider, word + image). Thus, the term "visual poetry" is applicable to the word-signs of Robert Indiana (*), "eyeye" of Aram Saroyan (*) (with its hint of eyeglasses), "Forsythia" of Mary Ellen Solt (*), Paul Van Ostaijen's (*) "Zeppelin," and the door-high towers of John Furnival (*), among many others. It differs as well from Poesia Vivisa, which was an Italian term, popular in the 1970s, for visual art that incorporates words, usually handwritten, along with pictures, usually photographs, largely for political content, and thus formally updates the genre of William Blake.

An extension is Visual Fiction, which is the preferred term for narrative that depends upon changes in roughly continuous pictures; among its major practitioners are Duane Michals (*), Milt Gross (*), Martin Vaughn-James (1943), and Lynd Ward (*).

Kostelanetz, Richard, ed. *Imaged Words & Worded Images*. NY: Outerbridge, 1970.

———, ed. *Visual Literature Criticism*. Carbondale, IL: Southern Illinois University, 1981.

VKHUTEMAS (1920). The Soviet term for Higher Technical-Artistic Studios, established first in Moscow in 1920 and then in both Petrograd and Vetebsk the following year. Independent of one another, they nonetheless became important for teaching and theoretical discussions, especially of Constructivism (*). Among the artists on the faculties were Kazimir Malevich (*), Wassily Kandinsky (*), and Vladimir Tatlin (*). A sort of visiting lecturer, Naum Gabo (*) remembered "seven departments: Painting, Sculpture, Architecture, Ceramics, Metalwork and Woodwork,

Textile, and Typography, but general discussions were held and seminars conducted among the students on diverse problems where the public could participate, and artists not officially on the faculty could speak and give lessons." Gabo continues, "During these seminars, as well as during the general meetings, many ideological questions between opposing artists in our abstract group were thrashed out. These gatherings had a much greater influence on the later development of constructive art than all the teaching." Qualitatively, the Vkhutemas academies represent the Soviet equivalent of the Bauhaus (∗), though, like so many other independent movements in Russia at the time, by the 1930s they fell under central Party control.

Gray, Camilla. *The Russian Experiment in Art 1863–1922*. London, England: Thames & Hudson, 1962.

VORTICISM (1913–1918). Perhaps the most avant-garde movement in the history of British visual art, Vorticism began over a quarrel between the London critic Roger Fry (1866–1934) and the writer-painter Wyndham Lewis (∗). The latter declared an allegiance to Italian Futurism (∗), which had just emerged on the continent; the Vorticists produced visual art filled with angular lines and poetry filled with hysterical declamations, some of which appeared in Lewis's two-shot magazine *Blast* (∗). Vorticism is sometimes characterized as the most avant-garde version of British Abstract Art (∗). Among those joining Lewis were younger artists such as David Bomberg (1890–1957) and Henri Gaudier-Brzeska (∗), and emerging writers, such as Ezra Pound (∗), who coined the term "Vorticism," and T.E. Hulme (1883–1917). The last writer's 1914 lecture on "Modern Art and Its Philosophy" is said to be the best introduction to Vorticist esthetics. Perhaps for the same reasons that British culture ignored Dada (∗) and hardly acknowledged Surrealism (∗), Vorticism did not survive the end of World War I.

Hulme, T.E. *Speculations*. Ed. Herbert Read. NY: Harcourt, Brace, 1936.

Cork, Richard. *Vorticism and Abstract Art in the First Machine Age*. Two vols. London, England: Gordon Fraser, 1976.

Wees, William C. *Vorticism and the English Avant-Garde*. Toronto, Canada: University of Toronto, 1972.

WALDEN, Herwarth (1878–c. 1941; b. Georg Levine). After writing music reminiscent of Claude Debussy (1862–1918) and poetry reflecting the influence of his first wife, Else Lasker-Schüler (1869–1945), Walden founded the important Berlin-based periodical *Der Sturm* (1910–1932, The Storm), publishing Futurists (∗) along with Expressionists (∗) in addition to poets such as August Stramm (∗) and painters. In 1912, Walden opened an art gallery named after his magazine and was the first to exhibit several artists who later taught at the Bauhaus (∗); his gallery survived for a dozen years. Reacting to the rise of Fascism in Germany, Walden allied with the Communist Party in 1929, emigrating to the Soviet Union in 1932. He disappeared around 1941, probably in a Russian prison camp. Perhaps because he was so much more than just an art dealer, he is among the few members of his trade to be honored, let alone remembered, decades later.

Roters, Eberhard, et al. *Berlin 1910–1933*. Trans. Marguerite Mounier. NY: Rizzoli, 1982.

WARD, Lynd (1905–1985). An American visual fictioneer, needlessly forgotten, Ward credited Frans Masereel (∗) as the "first to go beyond the idea of a short sequence of pictures" in making extended visual narratives that differ from the comic strip, say, but resemble certain silent films in completely eschewing words. Ward's medium, the woodcut, ideally suited his taste for heavy shading, which in turn reflected a penchant for melodramatic moralizing. His first visual narrative, *God's Man* (1929), starkly portrays a young artist in a hostile world, while a later work, *Wild Pilgrimage* (1932), turns upon the clever device of changing color when the narrative portrays the protagonist's inner thoughts. Ward's career as a book-artist ended late in the 1930s, which is unfortunate, because he had a sure sense for making pictures that gather meanings as the reader turns the page, becoming a precursor to Edward Gorey (∗) and Duane Michals (∗), among other first-rank visual storytellers, as well as Eric Drooker (1957), whose *Flood! A Novel in*

Pictures (1992) likewise opens with portraying a young artist in a hostile city.

Ward, Lynd. *Storyteller Without Words*. NY: Abrams, 1974.

Drooker, Eric. *Flood! A Novel in Pictures*. NY: 4 Walls 8 Windows, 1992.

WARHOL, Andy (1928–1987). Surely the most audacious of those artists initially classified as Pop (∗), Warhol created in the early 1960s representational paintings that, in retrospect, seem systematically designed to violate several earlier rules for "high art." Originally a commercial artist with a reputation for drawing shoes, Warhol used silkscreening processes to transfer photographs and advertising imagery to fine-art canvas. (The other Pop artists created their images from scratch.) In these Warhol paintings, "found" images, mostly familiar, are transformed—enlarged, recolored, reshaded—to emphasize pictorial qualities partly reflective of the silkscreening process, in other parts reflective of Warhol's tasteless, campy use of flat coloring. For images to repeat interminably in a grid previously unknown in representational art, he drew upon popular iconography, as in *210 Coca-Cola Bottles* (1962); horrifying public events, as in *Atomic Bomb* (1963), *Car Crash* (1963), and

Andy Warhol at work in his studio preparing the helium balloons for Merce Cunningham's "RainForest," 1968. *Photo © 1993, Fred W. McDarrah.*

Race Riot (1964); and the faces of either celebrities (Jacqueline Kennedy, Elizabeth Taylor) or art collectors who were flattered by being subjected to the same style of portraiture as that accorded celebrities.

Around this time Warhol also made radically under-edited films that depended upon being projected at speeds slower than the customary twenty-four frames per second and the casual performances of unusual, moderately compelling people. Of the latter, none rivaled *Chelsea Girls* (1967), which avoids becoming boring by projecting two images simultaneously. Though *Andy Warhol's Index (Book)* (1967) remains a model of inventive book-art, his other books, mostly of transcribed prose, did not survive as well as his most famous aphorism: "In the future everyone will be famous for fifteen minutes." He was also one of several celebrities, the poet Allen Ginsberg (∗) being another, who made unashamed homosexuality more acceptable, at least to the mass media, if not to society in general.

No other major modern painter learned to capitalize so well upon what was once called "selling out" (his only rival for this superlative being Salvador Dali [∗]), and none ever earned so much money, selling nearly all of the thousands of images he made. Though the subversive point of Warhol's esthetic strategy was obliterating the distinction between high art and graphics, the distinction survived, while many patrons-come-lately who thought they were commissioning or purchasing high art are stuck with decoration. Indeed, his subversive achievement, whose full measure is not yet apparent, is getting a large number of rich people to overpay, not only for his art and the bric-a-brac of his estate but for the publication of books by and even about him, making him, without doubt, the most successful "ripoff artist" of all time.

Why Warhol gave up experimental art remains a mystery; perhaps he thought he could do nothing else new and so feared becoming, say, another Willem de Kooning (∗), who would spend half of his adult life haunted by an inability to produce work equal to his acclaimed earlier masterpieces. Perhaps he lost heart after being seriously wounded in 1968. Because Warhol was no longer making consequential art, it was no small achievement for him to remain a pseudo-cultural celebrity for over a quarter-century in this fickle country, surviving the predictions of those who thought him strictly a fifteen-minute man, but also becoming an unfortunate model for aspiring artists who con themselves into believing that publicity, any publicity, can be more important than peer or critical respect, let alone esthetic achievement.

Bourdon, David. *Andy Warhol*. NY: Abrams, 1989.

Warhol, Andy. *Andy Warhol's Index (Book)*. NY: Random House, 1967.

WATSON, James Silbey, Jr. (1893–1982).

One of the neglected figures in the history of American culture, Watson was, in the 1920s, the publisher of the monthly *Dial*, the most prestigious literary magazine of its time. He earned a medical degree in his spare time. In the 1930s, he collaborated with others in making experimental films that are still shown (and available on videotape): *The Fall of the House of Usher* (1933, made with Melville Webber) and *Lot in Sodom* (1935, with Webber, Ransom Wood, and Alec Wilder). While the former, which Watson photographed, uses prisms, mirrors, and distorting lenses to Surrealistic (*) ends, the latter, with the addition of sound, has a richer plot. Telling of sensual corruption, this film depends less upon plot than the rhythmical presentation of symbolic scenes. The film historian Lewis Jacobs (1906) writes: "Its brilliant array of diaphanous shots and scenes—smoking plains, undulating curtains, waving candle flames, glistening flowers, voluptuous faces, sensual bodies, frenzied orgies—were so smoothly synthesized on the screen that the elements of each composition seemed to melt and flow into one another with extraordinary iridescence." Watson was among the first to call himself "an independent film producer," the term declaring proudly that he worked apart from the commercial studios, much as avant-garde writers ignored commercial publishing.

As a doctor, on the faculty of the medical school at the University of Rochester from the 1940s to the 1960s, he did pioneering research in cineradiography, following the gastrointestinal track with X-ray motion picture film (as a rare example of an avant-garde artist becoming an advanced scientist similar to the Russian composer Alexander Borodin [1833–1887], who was also a distinguished chemist).

Jacobs, Lewis. *The Rise of the American Film* (1939). Expanded ed. NY: Teachers College, 1968.

Wasserstrom, William. *A Dial Miscellany*. Syracuse, NY: Syracuse University, 1963.

WEBERN, Anton (1883–1945; b. A. von W.).

It was Webern, more than any other composer born in the 19th century, who explored the possibility of less becoming more, which is to say the esthetics of Minimalism (*). Indicatively, the Columbia Masterworks edition of his *The Complete Music* fits on only four long-playing discs, with eight sides, containing less than three dozen works. Born in Vienna, taking a doctorate in musicology (and thus perhaps becoming the first trained musicologist to become a distinguished composer), Webern became Arnold Schoenberg's (*) first pupil. Webern wrote the first critical study on his master's music; and along with Alban Berg (1875–1935), a less inventive composer, Webern was in almost daily contact with Schoenberg from 1906 to 1912. Meanwhile Webern earned his living as a conductor, mostly of provincial and radio orchestras (before the latter become more prestigious). Though subsequent composers admire Webern's strict observance of serial (*) rules, the layperson tends to hear his works as spare, intricate, and nonrepresentational. Such compositions are typically for small ensembles; several of them incorporate highly poetic (German) texts. At the premiere of his *Six Pieces for Orchestra*, Opus 6, 31 March 1913, "Hissing, laughter, and applause vie[d] for prominence during and immediately after the new Webern pieces [were] performed," according to Richard Burbank. "A group of composers and musicians, mostly unknown and conservative, attend[ed] this concert intent on causing a disturbance. Webern shout[ed] from his seat that the human baggage must be removed from the concert hall. The police arrive[ed] and [were] ineffective in securing order."

Not until Opus 17 (1924) does Webern fully adopt the Schoenberg invention of the twelve-tone row. Of Opus 21 (1928) and Opus 22 (1930) the conductor Robert Craft (1923) writes, "Here is Webern writing small sonata-breadth pieces with expositions, developments, recapitulations, codas, and with his only material the purest of contrapuntal forms, the canon." Opus 21, in particular, broaches subsequent multiple serialization by allowing the tone-row to influence other musical dimensions. Though his music was proscribed by the Nazis, Webern continued to live in Austria, working as a music publisher's proofreader. While taking a pre-bedtime smoke at his son-in-law's rural house, he was shot dead by an American soldier. To younger European composers immediately after World War II, Webern was a greater figure than his teacher Schoenberg.

Webern, Anton. *The Complete Works* (1956). NY: Columbia CK4L-232, n.d.

WEEGEE (1898–1969; b. Usher/Arthur H. Felig).
As a photographer employed mostly by newspapers, Weegee made distinctive realistic photographs, customarily of shocking nighttime urban scenes. Depending upon a Speed Graphic camera and a strong flashbulb, his pictures emphasize the black and the white, to the neglect of gray, which was traditionally thought to be the most subtle color in black-and-white photography. For a 1948 film usually screened as *Weegee's New York*, he drew upon primitive color film to shoot Manhattan at a very slow speed early in the morning, so that moving lights become a blur, the colors of flashing signs superimpose, and the sunrise becomes a momentous event. The background music is Leonard Bernstein's *Fancy Free* (1944), which never sounded so good. In the film's second half, depicting a crowded Coney Island on a sunny summer day, Weegee's camera is insultingly nosy, watching people dress and undress, fat girls sunbathing, and so forth. Because of his weak color stock, the sand often looks like snow and the eroticism of the beach is washed out.

Weegee. *Naked City* (1945). NY: Da Capo, n.d.

WEIDENAAR, Reynold (1945).
A trained Electronic (*) composer who became a major video artist, Weidenaar brings to the new medium a technical sophistication rare among his colleagues. His video, more than most, depends upon kinetic (*) visual synthesis and optimal picture processing to realize imagery unique to

the medium and yet painterly (as he is the son of a noted Michigan painter of the same name). He also composes his soundtracks, producing *audio* videotapes that are best seen on projection televisions and heard through hi-fi stereo audio systems. It is not for nothing that Weidenaar's very best work, *Love of Line, of Light and Shadow* (1982), which won an international prize, scarcely resembles the video art (*) most prominently exhibited in the 1980s.

Weidenaar, Reynold. *Concert Videos*. Minneapolis, MN: Intermedia Arts, n.d. (c. 1989).

WELLES, Orson (1915–1985).
By most measures, Welles was the most inspired and courageous creator of live theater ever in America; incidentally, he directed at least two great movies and was a masterful radio artist (*). Running away from Kenosha, Wisconsin, his birthplace, he made his way to Dublin, Ireland where, at the precocious age of sixteen, he joined the famed Abbey Theatre; within five years, he was back in the states directing audacious adaptations of Shakespeare in addition to new plays, initially for the Federal Theatre Project and then for his own Mercury Theatre. Invited to work in radio, he made it a medium for the adaptation of classic literary narratives, including Victor Hugo's *Les Miserables*, Joseph Conrad's *Heart of Darkness*, and both *Seventeen* and *The Magnificent Ambersons* by Booth Tarkington. His 1938 production of H.G. Wells's novel *Invasion from Mars* (popularly known as "The War of the Worlds") was so realistic that it created a panic across the nation.

Welles's first feature-length film, *Citizen Kane* (1941), weaves a complex story through the memories of several narrators, using wide-angle photography that enabled him to shoot continuous scenes by moving his camera and his actors, instead of by using conventional cutting. Drawing upon his radio experience, in only the second decade of sound films, Welles made feature films based on sound, not only of speech but of silence, as in the great scene where Kane surveys his collections. (It was not for nothing that the complete soundtrack of *Kane* was once available on two long-playing records.) My own opinion is that *The Magnificent Ambersons* (1942) is the greater film, if only for its soundtrack, drawing as it did upon his radio production of the Booth Tarkington text made only a few years before. Using such radio conventions as a spoken introduction and spoken closing credits (including Welles's identifying himself under the image of a fat microphone), the film incorporates sensitive acoustic shifts between foreground and background and overlapping conversations. As Charles Higham (1931) put it, "Just as we constantly see people framed in uprights, half-glimpsed through doorways, or reflected in mirrors and windows, so we hear their muffled voices through doorways or in the far distance of rooms, floating down a stairway or mingled with the measures of a dance or the hiss and clang of a factory."

The tragedy of Welles's life was that he wanted most to make films and that, for various reasons, not entirely his fault, his later films never equaled the first two. It is easy to say in retrospect that his last forty years could have been better spent working in those two media whose production costs are generally lower, in which his genius was already established: live theater and radio. Incidentally, though most colorized versions of black-and-white classics are embarrassingly bad, the brown-tinged *Amberson*, most frequently seen on Turner Network Television, is not.

Higham, Charles. *Orson Welles.* NY: St. Martin's, 1985.

Kostelanetz, Richard. "Orson Welles as a Wunderkindhörspielmacher." In *On Alternative Film and Video.* Forthcoming.

WHITMAN, Robert (1935). It looks as though, more than a quarter-century after the fact, Whitman's reputation remains based upon a single innovative work of 1965 visual theater, *Prune. Flat.* (sometimes spelled without the periods), which will always be, for those who have seen it during infrequent revivals, a masterpiece of alternative performance. It opens with the image of a movie projector, implicitly announcing that one theme is cinematic images, and then shows a grapefruit (that nearly fills the screen) being cut by a knife. After other images, a tomato appears, which is also cut, black egg-like objects pouring out of it; and, when the tomato sequence is repeated, two young women dressed in white

Robert Whitman, *Prune. Flat.*, 21 August 1966. *Photo © 1993, Fred W. McDarrah.*

smocks and white kerchiefs walk in front of the screen, the film blade cutting through them as well. As the film shows the two women walking down the street, one slightly behind the other, the same two women walk across the stage, at an angle perpendicular to their images on the screen, but in a similar formation. Later in the piece, the image of a woman undressing and showering is projected directly on a full-length body of one of the women performers; but once the film shuts off, the woman who appears to be undressed is suddenly revealed to be clothed. The subject of *Prune. Flat.* is the perceptual discrepancies between filmed image and theatrical presence, and it differs from other mixed-means theater (*) not only in its precise control but in its visual beauty.

Kostelanetz, Richard. "Robert Whitman." In *The Theatre of Mixed Means.* NY: Dial, 1968.

WICKHAM-SMITH, Simon (1968). In the mail, early in 1992, as I was drafting this book, came two chapbooks of visual literature that were so original that their author deserves mention here. The shorter, *indic plaid poem* (1992), sixteen pages long, has on each page several lines of a hieroglyphic language that changes beneath a continuous horizontal line that unites all the signs. The other, *The Rotations* (1992), subtitled "a novel," has hundreds of small squares, set twenty-five to a page, each square divided by a jagged channel, some of them having parts that are fully shaded in. The author, born in England, tells me that he is also a musician. Stay tuned.

Wickham-Smith, Simon. *The Rotations*. Davis, CA: Fuzzyblue Books (P.O. Box 73463, Davis, CA), 1992.

WIGMAN, Mary (1886–1973). A pioneer of German Expressionist (∗) dance, Wigman began her training with the music theoretician Emile Jaques-Dalcroze (1865–1950), who created "Eurhythmics," in Hellarau near Dresden. She later collaborated with the movement analyst Rudolf von Laban (1879–1958), who developed a movement notation system called Labanotation. Dancing barefoot, exploring primitive rhythms and motifs, experimenting with costumes, props, and masks, Wigman created numerous distinguished solos and group works. Largely abstract, frequently dark or angst-ridden, these pieces focused on fundamental forms and essential emotions. Wigman also incorporated improvisation into her training system. Many important German modern dancers attended her school, as did Hanya Holm (1898–1992), who was her assistant and later came to America sponsored by the impresario Sol Hurok (1888–1974) to open a Wigman school. Holm became a modern American dance pioneer and influential choreographer, and she taught Alwin Nikolais (∗), influencing his technique along with that of his associate, Murray Louis (∗).—Katy Matheson

Wigman, Mary. *The Language of Dance*. Middletown, CT: Wesleyan University, 1966.

Sorell, Walter, ed. *The Mary Wigman Book: Her Writings*. Middletown, CT: Wesleyan University, 1975.

WILFRED, Thomas (1889–1968; b. Richard Edgar Løvstrøm). Wilfred is commonly credited as the first modern artist to use electric light not for illumination but as an autonomous artistic medium. He called this art "Lumia," which might have become more important than his own name had other artists been able to do it as well. He began in 1905, he wrote, "with a cigar box, a small incandescent lamp, and some pieces of colored glass." By the 1920s he had developed the *clavilux*, a keyboard controller for light projectors and optical amplifiers, such as lenses and filters, which could endlessly vary the forms and colors of projected light. As the critic Donna M. Stein writes, "The simplest clavilux consists of at least four projection units, each regulating a

different function. Registers permit the coupling of one or more of the projection units to any of the manuals." While several Wilfred claviluxes were permanently installed, he made portable models for recital tours. He also accompanied classical music concerts on his clavilux and designed stage backdrops. Wilfred had his own theater, Grand Central Palace, until it became an induction center during World War II. His last successful innovation was the free-standing light box whose screen would present, thanks to cleverly complementary color wheels, a continuously original visual stream whose afterimage would be not one or another picture but a constant, ingratiating flow. I remember one that was exhibited through the 1960s in the basement of the Museum of Modern Art, *Lumia Suite (Opus 158)*. Six feet high and eight feet across, it kept the queues occupied while they waited to enter the adjacent movie theater. It seemed at the time an image-model for the rear-projected "light show" that began to appear behind rock-music performances.

Stein, Donna M. *Thomas Wilfred: Lumia*. Washington, DC: Corcoran Gallery, 1971.

Krantz, Stewart. *Science and Technology in the Arts*. NY: Reinhold, 1974.

WILLIAMS, Emmett (1925). Unlike all other American writers of his generation, Williams became intimately involved, in the 1950s, with the European intermedia avant-garde. By the 1960s, he was an initiator of Fluxus (∗). As an American who has found more acceptance for his work abroad, Williams has produced straight poetry, visual poetry (∗), visual fiction, prints, artist's books (∗), paintings, text-sound (∗), and performance, working with a variety of radical ideas that he tends to use sparingly. As a poet, he has favored such severe constraints as repetition, permutation, and linguistic Minimalism (∗). In *Sweethearts* (1967), his book-art (∗) masterpiece, the eleven letters of the title word are visually distributed over 150 or so sequentially expressive pages. The work as a whole, when read from right to left (much like a Hebrew book), wittily relates, solely by typographical rearrangement, the evolution of a man-woman relationship. His wife, Ann Noel (1944; b. Ann

Stevenson) became in the 1980s the author/artist of exquisite book-art.

Williams, Emmett. *Selected Shorter Poems*. NY: New Directions, 1974.

WILLIAMS, Jonathan (1929). This Williams calls himself "a poet" above all, but he is really an old-fashioned person-of-letters moving Literature along in a variety of ways. He is a Small Press (∗) person, whose Jargon Society (1951) probably stands second to Something Else Press (∗) in publishing the people mentioned in this book (e.g, Kenneth Patchen [∗], Bob Brown [∗], and Buckminster Fuller [∗], among others). Second, Williams is a critic whose speciality is the affectionate portrait of an undervalued artist and writer, including some of those mentioned in this book. Third, he is a poet working in a wide variety of modes, only some of them avant-garde, who has issued books and chapbooks with a greater number of alternative publishers than anyone else in America. (In this respect, he is the American equivalent of Bob Cobbing [∗], likewise an uncalculating nonacademic.)

Williams, Jonathan. *The Magpie's Bagpipe*. San Francisco: North Point, 1982.

WILLIAMS, William Carlos (1883–1963). The avant-garde W.C. Williams was less the poet-playwright-fictioneer than the essayist who, out of his broad and generous sympathies, was able to appreciate many of the most radical developments of his time. (This stands in contrast to T.S. Eliot [∗], who ignored them, for instance keeping Williams unpublished in England during their almost common lifetimes.) In this respect, consider not only Williams's early appreciation of Gertrude Stein (∗) and James Joyce's (∗) *Work in Progress* (aka *Finnegans Wake* [∗]), but the essays and notes posthumously published as *The Embodiment of Knowledge* (1974). "Pure writing is represented by all whose interest is primarily in writing as an art, of far more interest to them than what it conveys," Williams states there. "Writing as an art is of course completely inundated by journalism, which is meant to 'put something over.' But all other writing is more or less in the same class with journalism."

Vehemently opposed to Eliot's high-literary bent, deriding his *The Waste Land* at a time when it was almost universally regarded as the

William Carlos Williams, 1926. *Photo: Charles Sheeler, courtesy New Directions Publishing Corp.*

great achievement of American literature, Williams emphasized the search for American language and imagery. In his rewriting of American history (in *In the American Grain* [1925]), Williams was perhaps the first to question the white/European bias of most other accounts.

The avant-garde W.C. Williams was largely forgotten in his lifetime. In the early 1920s, he published a series of books, including *Kora in Hell: Improvisations* (1920) and *Spring and All* (1923), which were inspired by his friendship with the Dada (∗) artists in New York. *Kora in Hell* has examples of automatic writing, followed by brief explications (the doctor in Williams could not let these little pieces of Surrealism [∗] go unexplained). *Spring and All* features a mock critical introduction, upside-down chapter heads, and other typographical abnormalities. The unnamed poems often comment ironically on the texts that precede or follow them. (Predictably, when these poems were reprinted during Williams's lifetime, the experimental prose sections were removed and the poems given conventional titles.) At this time, Williams also wrote his first extended work of prose, *The Great American Novel* (1923), which makes fun of sentimental fiction by portraying a romance between a little Ford roadster and a truck. His later long poem, *Paterson* (1946–1962), incorporates historical found texts (∗), overheard conversations, short lyric fragments, letters from friends, including young Allen Ginsberg (∗) asking for advice and Williams's college buddy Ezra Pound (∗) giving it, all on the theme of one American's search for his roots.—with Richard Carlin

Williams, William Carlos. *The Embodiment of Knowledge.* Ed. Ron Loewinsohn. NY: New Directions, 1974.

———. *Imaginations: Kora in Hell, Spring and All, The Great American Novel, The Descent of Winter, A Novelette and Other Prose* (1920–1932). Ed. Webster Schott. NY: New Directions, 1970.

———. *Paterson* (1946–1962). Rev. ed. Ed. Christopher MacGowan. NY: New Directions, 1992.

WILOCH, Thomas (1953). Wiloch writes short prose pieces, poems to some and stories to others, that reflect the influence of both Surrealism (∗) and science fiction, which is a combination so complimentary that you wonder why it is not more popular. Speaking of "revelatory moments of cynical gnosis or divine terror, drawing upon Zen, Sufi, and Christian mystical sources for inspiration but rendering the insights through the dark filter of twentieth-century realities," Wiloch has published many chapbooks with small publishers, those of collages (∗) being less original than those mostly of prose. For both *Decoded Factories of the Heart* (1991) and *Narcotic Signature* (1992), short syntactical statements, like that of the first title, customarily divided into three lines (to resemble haiku), are followed by a counter-statement typeset underneath in parentheses, in the case of the title poem "(tiny sculptures)."

Wiloch, Thomas. *Decoded Factories of the Heart* (1991). 2nd ed. Port Charlotte, FL: Runaway Spoon (P.O. Box 3621, 33952), 1992.

WILSON, Robert (1941). An American theatrical artist trained in visual art, Wilson knew from the beginning that his theater would emphasize image and movement over scripts. His early works also revealed a predisposition toward thinking big—to using larger theaters, more performers, and larger props (to attract greater funding) than his predecessors in nonliterary theater did. Much more abundant in some respects, his theater also broached unprecedented

slowness in the movements of the principal performers. Wilson used amateurs who were clearly amateur, as well as freaks who had never before appeared on stage, let alone much in public; some of his images, such as a chorus of "black mammies," could be audacious beyond belief. He would tuck portions of earlier pieces into new ones that had completely different names. His masterpiece, of those I have seen, was *The Life and Times of Joseph Stalin* (1973), which ran for some twelve hours, filling the stage of the Brooklyn Academy of Music with several score performers and many props. Its first three acts incorporated much of an earlier Wilson piece, *The Life and Times of Sigmund Freud* (1969), while the fourth act included much of *Deafman Glance* (1971). In the first act, as dancers move about the stage, one performer obliquely refers to Stalin by giving an effectively concise summary of dialectical materialism, itself spoken against background music drawn from various sections of Gabriel Faure's *Messe de Requiem* (1886–1887). In the last act, a chorus of ostriches dances in unison. What did not make sense as intellectual exposition or as a theatrical script seemed reasonably coherent as a mixed-means (∗) performance experience. I'd see it again any time.

Wilson's more recent theatrical work, mostly operas in collaboration with composers as various as Richard Wagner (1813–1883) and Philip Glass (∗), is not as original as his earlier work was, though because he works primarily in Europe few of us have seen enough of it to make any definitive generalizations. He seems to be particularly receptive to accepting European commissions to produce "interpretations" of historical personages or events (much as the American playwright Paul Green [1893–1981], who made commissioned pageants for some southern states a few decades ago). Wilson also has exhibited videotapes, drawings, furniture, costumes, and theater drops. Stefan Brecht's 1978 monograph on Wilson gives elaborately detailed summaries, really a model of their kind, of theatrical events in Wilson's early productions.

Brecht, Stefan. *The Theatre of Visions: Robert Wilson.* Frankfurt, Germany: Suhrkamp, 1978.

Fairbrother, Trevor. *Robert Wilson's Vision.* NY: Abrams, 1991.

WINES, James (1932). See SITE

WINTERS, Yvor (1901–1968). It was Kenneth Rexroth (∗) who was often reminding readers that before Yvor Winters became an apostle of classicism (and a Stanford professor) he was an experimental poet whose forte was Minimalism (∗), especially in the appreciation of nature. Thus his poem "The Magpie's Shadow" (1922) has sections such as "The Aspen's Song," which reads in its entirety: "The summer holds me here." Or "Sleep," which reads: "Like winds my eyelids close." Or "A Deer": "The trees rose in the dawn." These sentences are, to my senses, poetic, rather than fictional or expository, if only for their conciseness and lyricism. Other examples of early Winters can be found, along with his later, far more traditional work, in the latest edition of his complete poetry.

Winters, Yvor. *The Poetry of Yvor Winters*. Intro. Donald Davie. Chicago, IL: Swallow, 1978.

WOLFF, Christian (1934). As a teenager in the early 1950s, Wolff joined the circle that included John Cage (∗), Earle Brown (∗), and Morton Feldman (∗), with whom he continued to be associated while pursuing academic degrees in the classics, which he has taught at Harvard and teaches currently at Dartmouth. The mark of Wolff's early music was a limited number of pitches—three for his *Duo for Violin and Piano*, four for *Trio for Flute, Cello, and Trumpet* (1951)—tending, in David Revill's words, "to encourage concentration on individual sounds and their combinations rather than progressions." Wolff pioneered in the use of "scores" whose instructions were entirely verbal and in offering variable directions on how one performer could respond to the moves of another, as though the musicians were playing a game. In the 1970s, Wolff incorporated leftist political criticism into his work, at times drawing upon traditional radical texts and songs.

Nyman, Michael. *Experimental Music*. NY: Schirmer, 1974.

DeLio, Thomas. *Circumscribing the Open Universe*. Lanham, MD: University Press of America, 1984.

WOOSTER GROUP. See PERFORMANCE GROUP

WRIGHT, Frank Lloyd (1869–1959). The ideal of Wright's architectural philosophy was organicism, which he defined as successfully relating a building to both its intrinsic purposes and surrounding environment, so that "inside" and "outside" blend into each other. "Thus environment and building are one," he wrote in *A Testament* (1957). "Planning the grounds around the building on the site as well as adorning the building take on a new importance as they become features harmonious with the space-within-to-be-lived-in. Site, structure, furnishing—decoration too, planting as well—all these become one in organic architecture." That accounts for why, in his private homes, such as the legendary *Falling Water* (1936), his architecture melts into its landscape and looks as though it belongs precisely where it is set. On the other hand, like other megalomaniacs, Wright didn't always follow his own rules, creating in the original Guggenheim Museum in New York City (1959) an awkward showcase for both works of painting and sculpture that nonetheless conquered ventilation problems, which typically plague other museums, constantly impressed its peculiarities upon everyone within it, and attained sculptural qualities by climaxing earlier Wright penchants for spirals and inverted ziggurats.

Wright, Frank Lloyd. *A Testament*. NY: Horizon, 1957.

WRITERS FORUM (England). See COBBING, Bob

XENAKIS, Iannis (1922). Born Greek in Rumania, Xenakis was trained in architecture in Athens; between 1947 and 1959, he worked with Le Corbusier (∗), reportedly contributing to the spatial installation of Edgard Varèse's (∗) *Poème électronique* at the 1958 Brussels World's Fair. While working in architecture, he studied music with Olivier Messiaen (1908–1992) and Darius Milhaud (1892–1974). Using various kinds of mathematics, Xenakis has advocated what Nicolas Slonimsky (∗) calls "the stochastic method which is teleologically directed and deterministic, as distinct from a purely aleatory [i.e., John Cagean (∗)] handling of data." Xenakis also founded and directed the Centre d'Études

Mathématiques et Automatiques Musicales in Paris (and for a while a comparable Center for Mathematical and Automated Music in the U.S.), purportedly in competition with Pierre Boulez's (∗) IRCAM. All the theory notwithstanding, I have heard thickly atonal textures, which sound like bands of frequencies in the tradition of tone clusters, often distributed among many loudspeakers. For the French pavilion at Montreal's Expo '67, Xenakis also created, as an accompaniment to his audiotape, a spatially extended flickering light show.

Xenakis, Iannis. *Arts/Sciences: Alloys*. NY: Pergamon, 1985.

XEROGRAPHIC ART (c. 1970). This mode of art began to flourish in the 1980s with the improvement and the nascent omnipresence of the effective photocopier. (It is hard for us to remember now the poor quality of photocopies in the 1960s.) Although xerographic art can take many shapes (including simple image degradation and serial imagery), its major form is the method of collaging sometimes called xerage or xerolage. While some xerages are merely photocopied collages (∗), constrained by the somewhat limited reproductive capabilities of available photocopy machines, the most expressive examples bring together elements in new and interesting ways: by actually copying (rather than pasting) one image over another; by combining different colors of monochromic xerography; by degrading individual images; and by distorting images after computer scanning. While xerage has become an important genre of avant-garde art, some of its tendencies (including overprinting and image degradation) have been appropriated by Madison Avenue in recent years, illustrating how the avant-garde in the visual arts always becomes more acceptable than its counterpart in literature.—Geof Huth

Y

YOUNG, Karl (1947). One of the great eccentric recluses of contemporary American literature, Young has produced, out of his homes in Milwaukee and Kenosha, Wisconsin, a series of remarkable books, as distinguished for their formal inventions as for his literary intelligence. A printer as well as a poet, he has used a variety of alternative formats, including poems printed on both sides of a sheet of paper folded in the shape of a folding screen (and thus requiring considerable turning to be read). His masterpiece is a perfect-bound book of used colored blotting papers, nearly three inches thick, otherwise devoid of markings, whose multiple title establishes a variety of inferential contexts: *A Book of Hours/ A Day Book/ A Log Book/ A Thesaurus/ A Wordbook/ A Book of Etiquette/ A Cumulative Record/ A Hymnal/ A Dictionary/ An Album/ A Missal/ An Illuminated Book/ A Crib/ A Testament*, none of which characterize its blotted pages, unless you take those titles, as I do, to be ironically true. The publisher of Membrane Press and Open Meeting Books, Young has also written some of the most penetrating extended critical essays on avant-garde literature.

Young, Karl. *Only as Painted Images in Your Books Have We Come to Be Alive in this Place*. Tucson, AZ: Chax, 1993.

YOUNG, La Monte (1935). The truest Minimal (∗) composer, this Young has devoted most of his professional life to exploring the possibilities of a severely limited palette. After beginning as an audacious post-Cagean composer who, among other stunts, released butterflies into a performance space as a piece of "music," he hit upon *The Tortoise, His Dreams and Journeys*,

LaMonte Young in performance, 12 December 1965. L to r: Tony Conrad, LaMonte Young, Marion Zazeela, John Cale. *Photo © 1993, Fred W. McDarrah.*

in which Young along with a few colleagues produces a continuous, barely changing, harmonic (consonant) sound that is amplified through a prodigious system to the threshold of aural pain. Designed to last several hours, filled with dancing overtones, the piece is usually performed in a darkened enclosed space that contains the odor of incense and projected wistful, abstract images made by his wife Marian Zazeela. (Sometimes called The Theater of Eternal Music, the resulting concert could be accurately classified as an Environment [*], which is to say an artistically defined space.) Though audiotape recordings of this work exist, in my experience *The Tortoise* works best as a theatrical experience that depends upon multi-sensory overload to move its listeners. Young's other major composition is *The Well-Tuned Piano* (1964), a five-hour piano work (in the great tradition of comparably exhaustive keyboard pieces by J.S. Bach, Dmitri Shostakovich [1906–1975], Paul Hindemith [1895–1963], John Cage [*], and William Duckworth [*]), in which Young plays a Boisendorfer piano that has been retuned to just intonation. To the charge, heard often, that Young's music represents a "dead end," consider *From Ancient World* (1992), a composition by his sometime piano tuner Michael Harrison (1958), who developed a harmonic piano that realizes a different form of just intonation with twenty-four different notes within an octave.

Young, La Monte/Marian Zazeela. *Selected Writings*. Munich, Germany: Heiner Friedrich, 1969.

Harrison, Michael. *From Ancient World*. San Francisco, CA: New Albion 22551-0042-2, 1992.

Z

ZAPPA, Frank (1940; b. Francis Vincent Z., Jr.). Familiar from his youth with avant-garde music and thus musically more sophisticated than others involved with 1960s rock, Zappa tried at various times, and in various ways, to introduce avant-garde elements into the formally expansive popular-music market in the late 1960s. Because successful pop musicians were allowed to transcend the short time limits of the 45 rpm disc to create long-playing 33 rpm records, Zappa's group, the Mothers of Invention, could produce music in twenty-five-minute stretches; the result were "concept albums" that he released on a label appropriately named Bizarre. Some of the stronger works mocked California fads and popular music itself. *Freak Out* (1966) includes "Return of the Son of Monster Magnet," subtitled "An Unfinished Ballet in Two Tableaux," which appropriates the techniques of musique concrète (*). I saw Zappa do a performance where he instructed various sections of the Fillmore East audience to perform pre-assigned sounds in response to his hand-signals from the front of the stage. Once we got going, he said to himself, audibly and with proud irony, "Wouldn't Pierre Boulez (*) like that?" Here and elsewhere, Zappa's conceited sense of humor is refreshing to some and tedious to others. He has produced, with less success, orchestral scores and eccentric motion pictures such as *200 Motels* (1971) and *Baby Snakes* (1980). He is perhaps the only alumnus of 1960s rock still capable of generating an esthetic surprise. Zappa also released synthesizer arrangements of an 18th-century composer authentically named Francesco Zappa.

Zappa, Frank, and the Mothers of Invention. *Freak Out* (1966). Pickering Wharf, MA: Rykodisc RCD-40062, 1988.

———. *Absolutely Free* (1967). Hollywood, CA: Barking Pumpkin/Capitol D41G-74214, 1988.

———. *We're Only in It for the Money/Lumpy Gravy* (1967). Pickering Wharf, MA: Rykodisc RCD-40024, 1986.

ZAUM (1912). Coined by a Russian Futurist (*), probably Aleksei Kruchonykh (*), to indicate language that was indefinite or indeterminate in meaning (and phonetically translated as *zaum'*, to indicate the palatalized *m'*), this term literally means something "beyond or outside of reason or intelligibility"; common English translations are "transrational," "trans-sense," or "beyond-sense" language. The idea of writing poetry in invented words was suggested to Kruchonykh by David Burliuk (1882–1967) in December 1912. By March 1913, the former published his notorious poem "Dyr bul shchyl," which is generally considered to be the first work of Zaum, though Velimir Khlebnikov (*) had for several years before this been producing poetry with obscure coinages. The principal difference is that

Khlebnikov apparently intended that his experiments be eventually understood, and thus that they be conceptual demonstrations of language's creative potential to renew itself with ancient Slavic linguistic resources, whereas Kruchonykh intended, at least in the initial stages, that his Zaum be indeterminate in meaning, though not meaningless. Such indeterminate meaning was based on the suggestiveness of sound articulations and roots.

By dislocating language units ranging from phonemes to syntactic structures, Kruchonykh created a whole range of types of Zaum, often combined within a single work. One measure of true Zaum is that it should not be able to be decoded or motivated by such factors as onomatopoeia or psychopathological states. In 1917–1919, he created a series of "autographic" works in which the verbal elements were sometimes reduced to a minimum of letters and lines. Thereafter, however, as he moved closer to the mainstream, Zaum appeared only as spice in otherwise non-Zaum works, sometimes arguing for the psychological motivation of such effects. By 1923, Kruchonykh had ceased experimenting with the use of Zaum, though he continued to theorize about its importance.

Other major Zaumniks were Iliazd (*), Igor Terentev (1892–1937), and Aleksandr Tufanov (1887–1942). Some avant-garde painters, such as Kazimir Malevich (*), Olga Rozanova (1886–1918), and Varvara Stepanova (1894–1958), also experimented with Zaum as an analog to abstraction.

Because Zaum is usually considered the most radical product of Russian Futurism, its value is still, decades later, the subject of fierce dispute.—Gerald Janecek

Beaujour, Elizabeth Klosty. "Zaum," *Dada/Surrealism* 2 (1972).

Janecek, Gerald. "A Zaum' Classification." *Canadian-American Slavic Studies* XXX/1–2 (1986).

Mickiewicz, Denis. "Semantic Functions in Zaum'." *Russian Literature* XV (1984).

ZEKOWSKI, Arlene. See BERNE, Stanley

ZELEVANSKY, Paul (1946).
Trained in painting, Zelevansky developed in his twenties a unique and precociously mature style of visual poetry (*) that mixed texts of his own authorship, set with various typefaces (including rubber-stamped), with graphic drawings. He makes each medium of communication as important as the others, so that his works take their rightful place in a tradition that includes both William Blake (*) and Hebrew illuminated manuscripts. This style informs not only the modest *Sweep* (1979), but a highly ambitious epic about a historical culture, the Hegemonians, filled with both literary and visual references. Issued as a trilogy, *The Case for the Burial of Ancestors* (1981, 1986, 1991), for depth and scope, ranks among the strongest book-art. Zelevansky has exhibited pages from it along with sculptures and other artifacts relating to the project. After working briefly with theater music, he authored one of the first narratives exclusively for computer interaction, *Swallows* (1986), only to encounter the principal difficulty in distributing literature on computer disc—the systems that can read *Swallows* (Apple IIe, II+) aren't universally popular. More recently, he has created computer-assisted response displays for the Queens Museum in New York.

Zelevansky, Paul. *The Case for the Burial of Ancestors*. 3 vols. NY: Zartscorp (333 West End Ave., 10023), 1981, 1986, 1991.

ZEND, Robert (1929–1985).
"I lost everything but my accent," noted Robert Zend, with reference to escaping from his native Hungary during the 1956 Revolution and arriving in Toronto. What he gained in the process was a fresh start in life, art, outlook, and language. In Budapest, he had worked as a humorist and columnist; in Toronto, employed as an arts producer for CBC Radio's "Ideas," he wrote reams of imaginative and fanciful poems—some in English (mostly in print) and some in Hungarian (currently being collected). He incessantly doodled and drew in pen and ink on all surfaces, from scraps of paper to toilet rolls, often incorporating found objects (like automobile gaskets) into his compositions. Three features of Zend's fanciful poems and surreal prose are noteworthy: individuality, language, and humor. Independent of prior work of Eugen Gomringer (*) and others, he "invented" Concrete Poetry (*); ignorant of the stories and poems of Jorge Luis Borges (*), he intuitively produced Borgesian "fictions"—and continued to do so in his own inimitable fashion long after his encounter with the "originals." Regarding

the use of language, he wrote with the simplicity and clarity of a non-native English speaker. So there is an odd "translated" quality about his poems and stories; they were written in the international, unidiomatic style of a George Steiner rather than in the idiosyncratic manner of a Vladimir Nabokov (*). *Oab* (1983, 1985) is an extended visual fiction.—John Robert Colombo

Zend, Robert. *From Zero to One*. Victoria, Canada: Sono Nis, 1973.

———. *Beyond Labels*. Toronto, Canada: Hounslow, 1982.

———. *Oab*. 2 vols. Toronto, Canada: Exile, 1983, 1985.

ZINES. See MICROPRESS

ZORN, John (1953). Born and bred in New York, where he lives most of the year, trained in classical music, self-educated in jazz (*), avowedly fond of motion-picture composers, Zorn has developed highly idiosyncratic, modestly original improvisations that tend to be very dissonant and disjunctive and thus aggressive, if not abrasively hideous, in acoustic quality. It is not for nothing that he speaks of himself as descending from a tradition that includes Ives (*), Varèse (*), and Ornette Coleman (*). In the course of an interview with Zorn, the writer Edward Strickland compares his music to the experience of "being in a New York subway station: the same diversity of different influences you suggested, but also there's a lot of mechanical sound in your music, as if the train pulls in once in a while. In the station you've got all these different types of musicians playing jazz sax or classical violins or Peruvian flutes. Part of the mix there is that you're blending a lot of 'high art' and 'low art.'" Zorn has collaborated with many other musicians, most less prominent than he, who are likewise active in "downtown" Manhattan.

Strickland, Edward. *American Composers: Dialogues on Contemporary Music*. Bloomington, IN: Indiana University, 1991.

ZUKOFSKY, Louis (1904–1978). There is no doubt that Zukofsky did something unprecedented in literature, particularly in poetry, but exactly what is hard to say, even a decade after his death. To point out that he was obscure or that his work remains incomprehensible is merely to avoid the issue of whether greater understanding is possible. He worked with unusual forms, including a numerical counterpoint in his early classic "Poem Beginning 'The'"; he produced a musical *Autobiography* in collaboration with his wife, Celia. He began in 1927 a "poem of a life," *A*, that is distinctive for the various ways in which not much is revealed about its author. Hugh Kenner called it "the most hermetic poem in English, which they will still be elucidating in the 22nd century." His son Paul Z. (1943) has been for many years a distinguished interpreter of avant-garde American music, initially as a violinist, more recently as a conductor.

Zukofsky, Louis. *A*. Berkeley, CA: University of California, 1978.

———. *Collected Fiction* (1961, 1970). Elmwood Park, IL: Dalkey Archive, 1990.

POSTFACE

I mentioned in the preface my love of cultural dictionaries/encyclopedias and so would be remiss if I did not mention several that I consulted more than once, initially for facts such as dates, sometimes to discover an interpretative idea (usually acknowledged), other times to knock them for failing to include individuals featured here.

Baigell, Matthew. *Dictionary of American Art*. NY: Harper & Row, 1979.

Burbank, Richard. *Twentieth Century Music*. NY: Facts on File, 1984.

Bureaud, Annick. *Guide International des Arts Électroniques/International Directory of Electronic Arts*. Paris, France: Chaos, 1992.

Hatje, Gerd, ed. *Encyclopedia of Modern Architecture*. London: Thames & Hudson, 1963.

Katz, Ephraim. *The Film Encyclopedia*. NY: Crowell, 1979.

Morgan, Ann Lee, and Colin Naylor, eds. *Contemporary Architects*. Chicago & London: St. James, 1977.

Morton, Brian, and Pamela Collins, eds. *Contemporary Composers*. Chicago & London: St. James, 1992.

Naylor, Colin, ed. *Contemporary Artists*. Chicago & London: St. James, 1977, 1989.

———. *Contemporary Masterworks*. Chicago & London: St. James, 1991.

Osborne, Harold, ed. *The Oxford Companion to Twentieth-Century Art*. NY: Oxford, 1984.

Read, Herbert, consulting ed. *Encyclopedia of the Arts*. NY: Meredith, 1966.

Richard, Lionel. *Phaidon Encyclopedia of Expressionism*. London: Phaidon, 1978.

Runes, Dagobest D., and Harry G. Schrickel, eds. *Encyclopedia of the Arts*. NY: Philosophical Library, 1946.

Seymour-Smith, Martin. *Who's Who in Twentieth Century Literature*. London: Weidenfeld & Nicolson, 1976.

Slonimsky, Nicolas. *Bakers' Biographical Dictionary of Musicians*. 8th ed. NY: Schirmer, 1992.

Vinson, James, ed. *Contemporary Dramatists*. Chicago & London: St. James, 1973, 1977, 1982, (ed. D. L. Kirkpatrick) 1987.

———. *Contemporary Novelists*. London-NY: St. James-St. Martin's, 1972, 1976, 1981, 1986, (ed. Lesley Henderson) 1991.

———. *Contemporary Poets*. London-NY: St. James-St. Martin's, 1970, 1975, 1980, 1985, (ed. Tracy Chevalier) 1990.

Vinton, John, ed. *Dictionary of Contemporary Music*. NY: Dutton, 1974.

ABOUT THE
PRINCIPAL AUTHOR

RICHARD KOSTELANETZ was born in 1940 in New York City, where he still lives. After taking his B.A. with honors from Brown University, he did graduate work in cultural history at Columbia University under Woodrow Wilson, N.Y. State Regents, and International Fellowships and at King's College, University of London, under a Fulbright Scholarship. An unaffiliated writer and artist for the past thirty years, he has published numerous books of fiction, poetry, experimental prose, criticism, and cultural history, as well as editing over two dozen anthologies of literature, esthetics, and social thought. He has received grants from many private foundations, including Guggenheim, Pulitzer, Vogelstein, CCLM, ASCAP, and the DAAD Berliner Kunstlerprogramm, in addition to several individual fellowships from the National Endowment for the Arts. He has covered the artistic avant-garde since *The New American Arts* (1965), which he edited and co-authored, and has at one time or another published criticism of all the arts.

Wordsand, a retrospective of his art with words, numbers, and lines, in several media, toured several universities between 1978 and 1981, while his texts for theater and music have been performed both live and on tape. A film he co-produced and co-directed, *A Berlin Lost* (1984), received an award from the Ann Arbor Film Festival and subsequently toured with other award-winners. Portions of another film of his, the four-hour *Epiphanies* (in progress since 1981), were broadcast over the North German Television Network. His language-based videotapes have been exhibited in both one-person and group shows since 1975. German radio has broadcast his extended critical features about the art of radio in North America. He lives in lower Manhattan among thousands of books, hundreds of discs and audiotapes, and dozens of videotapes, as well as book-length projects in various stages of realization.

OTHER CONTRIBUTORS

H.R. BRITTAIN recently completed an undergraduate degree at the University of Wisconsin at Madison.

RICHARD CARLIN is the founding publisher of a cappella books. He is the author of *Classical Music* (1992), among other books and articles on music.

JOHN ROBERT COLOMBO is a Canadian poet, writer, and editor.

ULRIKE MICHAL DORDA is a German-born historian who works as two-way translator in New York.

CHARLES DORIA is a poet and translator who specializes in the classical and romance languages.

ROBERT HALLER administers the Anthology Film Archives in New York.

GEOF HUTH is a poet and publisher whose primary interest is linguistic invention.

GERALD JANECEK is a scholar specializing in the most avant-garde Russian Futurist artists and authors.

KATY MATHESON is an independent dance critic and former editor of *Dance Magazine* living in New York.